Theory and Problems
of Adolescent Development
Second Edition

Also by Dr. Ausubel:

* Ego Development and the Personality Disorders (1952)

The Fern and the Tiki: An American View of New Zealand National Character, Social Attitudes, and Race Relations (1960)

Maori Youth: A Psychoethnological Study of Cultural Deprivation (1961)

* The Psychology of Meaningful Verbal Learning: An Introduction to School Learning (1963)

School Learning (with F. G. Robinson) (1969)

* Ego Psychology and Mental Disorder: A Developmental Approach to Psychopathology (with Daniel Kirk) (1977)

Drug Addiction: Physiological, Psychological, and Sociological Aspects, 2nd ed. (1978; in press)

Educational Psychology: A Cognitive View, 2nd ed. (with J. D. Novak and Helen Hanesian) (February 1978; in press)

* Theory and Problems of Child Development, 3rd ed. (with Edmund V. Sullivan and S. W. Ives) (1979; in press)

* Published by Grune & Stratton.

Theory and Problems
of Adolescent Development

Second Edition

DAVID P. AUSUBEL, M.D., PH.D.
Graduate School
City University of New York
New York, New York
and
Mental Health Department
Lutheran Medical Center
Brooklyn, New York

RAYMOND MONTEMAYOR, PH.D.
Family and Consumer Studies
University of Utah
Salt Lake City, Utah

PERGROUHI (NAJARIAN) SVAJIAN, PH.D.
School of Education
Brooklyn College
City University of New York
Brooklyn, New York

87

GRUNE & STRATTON

A Subsidiary of Harcourt Brace Jovanovich, Publishers
New York / San Francisco / London

Library of Congress Cataloging in Publication Data

Ausubel, David Paul.
      Theory and problems of adolescent development.

      Includes bibliographies and index.
          1. Adolescent psychology. I. Montemayor,
Raymond, joint author. II. Svajian, Pergrouhi, N.,
joint author. III. Title.
BF724.A8   1977   155.5   77-11098
ISBN 0-8089-1031-0

Grune & Stratton, Inc.
111 Fifth Avenue
New York, New York 10003

Distributed in the United Kingdom by
Academic Press, Inc. (London) Ltd.
24/28 Oval Road, London NW 1

Library of Congress Catalog Number 77-11098

International Standard Book Number 0-8089-1031-0

Printed in the United States of America

Dedicated to Carl Leff, Mr. & Mrs. Haroutan Najarian, Dr. Stephen G. Svajian, and Mario & Mary Montemayor

Contents

Preface to
the First Edition

The aim of this book is to organize around a comprehensive and integrated theory of adolescent development the vast quantity of research data that has accumulated over the past fifty years in the field of adolescent psychology. Underlying this effort is a conviction that in relation to a systematic theoretic frame of reference such data become more meaningful than a compilation of discrete findings subsumed under topical chapter headings.

Historically, the precedents for such an undertaking are not too encouraging. Partly as a consequence of the virtual collapse of G. Stanley Hall's elaborate biogenetic theory of psychological recapitulation during the past three decades, theoretic approaches to problems of developmental psychology have fallen into disrepute. This has been especially true in the field of adolescent psychology. Some attempts have been made in a theoretic direction by psychoanalytically oriented psychologists; but these efforts have neither been comprehensive in scope nor systematically related to research data.

Two unfortunate and not unrelated developments followed upon Hall's epochal failure to provide a tenable theoretic substructure for adolescent psychology. The most immediate reaction was the placing of undue emphasis upon the collection of objective data as an end in itself. Every conceivable measurable aspect of adolescence was literally measured to death. And although it is undeniable that any scientific discipline must necessarily be grounded upon empirical data, it is generally accepted today that the mere collection of facts undirected by organizing hypotheses is an unsystematic and uneconomical process leading inevitably to conceptual chaos and unintelligibility.

The other unfortunate development was largely an outgrowth of findings in the area of cultural anthropology which helped demolish Hall's theory by demonstrating the existence of cultural variability in the stressfulness and kinds of problems faced by adolescents. These findings, however, were overgeneralized to support the equally untenable position that no general principles of adolescent development exist, that adolescence is not a distinct stage in personality development but a constellation of problems common to teen-agers growing up under repressive social conditions. This point of view, which, in a sense, is a denial of the possibility of ever formulating a general theory of adolescent development, is the theoretic position most widely held today in conjunction with the empiric approach discussed above.* Most textbooks in the field implicitly accept the notion that adolescent psychology embraces no distinctive developmental principles of its own, but is merely general psychology, i.e., perception, learning, motivation, etc., in which special attention is given to variability in these latter phenomena as a function of adolescent age.

The central idea permeating every chapter of this book is that adolescence is a distinctive stage in personality development precipitated by significant changes in the biosocial status of the child. As a result of these changes, which are discontinuous with preceding biosocial conditions of growth, extensive reorganization of personality structure is required. Our thesis is that this process of reorganization shows certain basic uniformities from one culture to another— despite many specific differences in content and degree of stress— because of various common elements inherent in the general psychology of transition and in the psychological implications of sexual maturity, biological sex role, and the new personality traits associated with adult roles and status in the community. The core principle of this point of view is essentially the position adopted by Sherif and Cantril in their *Psychology of Ego-Involvements*. Starting from this basic premise, a systematic theory of adolescent development has been evolved and related to empirical evidence in the field.

Part One, the *Introduction* is devoted to an historical overview of different approaches to adolescent development and to problems of evidence and classification. A distinction is made between (1) *psychobiological* problems of adolescence, which are reflective of general developmental trends and hence universal in distribution (despite specific cultural differences in form and content), and (2) *psychoso-*

---

* To Sherif and Cantril belongs the credit for first seriously challenging this theoretical orientation (see p. 22 and reference *34* on p. 38).

cial problems of adolescence, which are *wholly* conditioned by specific socio-economic factors and modes of regulation peculiar to our own social order.

Part Two deals with *psychobiological problems,* i.e., the psychology of transition; physiologic and physical growth; personality maturation and parent–child relationships; and intellectual and moral development. In the discussion of these problems, general principles of adolescent development are illustrated by references to the specific forms they assume in our own culture.

Part Three discusses *psychosocial problems,* i.e., problems faced by adolescents in our culture because of the unique norms, traditions, and regulatory phenomena confronting them (e.g., prolongation of sub-adulthood, peer group socialization, extended schooling and vocational apprenticeship, rapid social change, war, economic depression, etc.). Hence, there are chapters dealing with social stratification, the peer culture, sexual behavior, vocational choice, and the school.

Part Four considers problems of behavior disorder, delinquency, mental hygiene, and guidance.

A word about the chapters on physiologic and physical growth is in order. Strictly speaking, much of the detail given in these chapters is not relevant to adolescent psychology as such, but in a broader sense is part of adolescent development. Much effort has been expended in reinterpreting the endocrinologic phenomena of adolescence to make them more intelligible to students who have not been primarily trained in physiology. Special attention is given to the distinction between phylogenetic and familial aspects of genetic regulation, to the genetic and physiologic bases of the chronology and sequence of pubescent changes, to the distinction between genetic and hormonal sources of variability in physiologic and sexual maturation, and to psychological correlates of pubescent phenomena. Such topics, with the possible exception of the last mentioned, have hitherto not received systematic treatment in textbooks on adolescent psychology. A special feature of Chapter 4 is a discussion of the role of the adrenal cortex with respect to various normal and pathological conditions of pubescence. In Chapter 5 concepts of hormonal regulation of skeletal growth are reinterpreted in the light of more recent data.

Although organized under separate chapter headings, the book is more of a continuous essay than a series of discrete chapters. All of the specific problems of adolescence are related to the general theoretic orientation, and old materials are constantly reintroduced in new contexts. Extensive cross-referencing is made use of to add unity to related materials separated in the text, but repetition has not been shunned if thought necessary for purposes of clarity.

This approach to the organization of subject matter is based on the premise that learning is primarily a process of progressive differentiation of an uncharted cognitive field. Hence, following a general overview, more specific materials are gradually introduced and related to the original argument. Although this method of presentation undoubtedly does violence to traditional notions of textbook organization, the writer submits that the learning process and the logic of ideas do not necessarily conform to the same principles of organization and development.

The reader might be surprised at the relative absence of tables, figures, and graphs in this book. The criterion followed in this matter was that graphic and tabular material would be included only if the concepts to be communicated could *not* be more succinctly and precisely conveyed by words. Only three illustrations and three tables were able to meet this criterion. The resulting space that was saved was used for integrative and interpretative purposes. Case histories were eliminated for similar reasons, and because they are all too frequently accepted as evidence rather than as examples. A genuine effort was also made to avoid including materials that apply to human beings in general rather than specifically to adolescents.

To save space, the characteristics of the populations on which most cited research findings are based are not described in any detail. Interested readers can refer to the original sources which are identified by numbers corresponding to the order in which they are listed in the bibliography following each chapter. In very few of these cases, however, are we dealing with representative samples of adolescents. Hence, it should be borne in mind that unless specifically stated otherwise, findings about adolescents apply only to the populations from which they were derived and not to adolescents in general.* Interpretative comments about adolescent problems are made from the standpoint of the writer's background of experience in medical and psychiatric practice, and research in child and adolescent development.

---

*This does not mean, of course, that such data are valueless. They provide the kind of preliminary empirical support for hypotheses that is necessary before large-scale, definitive research on more representative populations can be justified. Also, as pointed out on page 36, many research problems in developmental psychology do not require the use of representative populations. The reader is merely cautioned at this point not to generalize findings uncritically from unrepresentative samples of adolescents.

This book is primarily intended as a textbook in adolescent psychology for undergraduate and graduate students in psychology and education. It is also intended as a reference work for professional workers in child development, clinical psychology, social work, nursing, pediatrics, psychiatry, guidance, and education.

My conceptual debt to Sherif and Cantril has already been acknowledged. The inspiration for the title and organization of the book came from Krech and Crutchfield's *Theory and Problems of Social Psychology,** which similarly attempted to provide a theoretical foundation for the interpretation of typical problems in that area of psychology. I am indebted to the National Association of Secondary School Principals for permission to use materials originally presented in an extended article on problems of adolescent adjustment in the January, 1950 issue of *The Bulletin,* and to Grune & Stratton for materials taken from my *Ego Development and the Personality Disorders* (1952). Mrs. Shirley S. Deusch, Miss N. Catherine Hamrick, and Mrs. Irene M. Smith were of invaluable assistance in the preparation of the manuscript.

David P. Ausubel

Urbana, Illinois
October, 1953

---

*D. Kretch and R. S. Crutchfield, Theory and Problems of Social Psychology, New York: McGraw-Hill, 1948.

Preface to
the Second Edition

In the approximately 25 years since the first edition of this book
(written by the senior author) appeared, there have been many
changes in adolescent development in the United States. Some of
these changes (i.e., the generally more permissive sex attitudes and
behavior; the higher rate of juvenile delinquency; the more widespread and earlier occurrence of narcotic addiction and use of marijuana, alcohol and other drugs; the more informal standards of dress;
the growth of the feminist movement and its influence on the social
sex roles and on the marital and vocational attitudes of girls; and the
more militant stance of blacks and other minority groups) have
seemed to become relatively permanent characteristics of the current
adolescent scene in America. Other changes that occurred in the
1960's and early 1970's (i.e., the increased politicization and radicaliza-
tion of youth as shown by student demonstrations against the Vietnam War; active participation in the Civil Rights and ecology movements; undergraduate demands for greater "relevance" in the curriculum, for greater participation in University governance, and for the
elimination of examinations and grades; and the "hippie" and commune movements) were largely transitory phenomena that are now,
for the most part, chiefly of historical interest.

In many ways, therefore, the picture of adolescent development
described in the 1954 edition is closer to the present-day characteristics of American adolescent development than the picture drawn by
textbooks published in the Sixties and early Seventies. Even in the
area of sex mores, the current trend is toward less casual and less
promiscuous adolescent sexual relationships.

For these reasons, much of the earlier edition still applies to
adolescent development today, since it purported to describe and

explain the *universal* features of adolescence (as a period of personality maturation, associated with causal, related changes in the physiological, motor, cognitive, emotional, motivational, social, vocational, sexual, etc. areas) as exemplified by *current* adolescent developments in the United States. Thus, in bringing this book up to date, it was necessary only to make such changes that reflect the actual developmental differences between American adolescence in 1975–1976 and in 1951–1953. Apart from purposes of illustration and contrast, we did not consider it relevant to examine in any detail the more transitory changes of adolescent development occurring in the prior decade.

Our principal objective is still to consider adolescence as a transitional period of personality development—its description, determinants, consequences and explanation—that applies to teenagers in *all* cultures. We use the American culture as our exemplar of these pan-cultural trends only because it is more familiar and useful to most of our readers, and, in addition, because there are many *psychosocial* features of adolescence in the United States that are either not encountered at all in other cultures (e.g., many primitive cultures), or are found only to a greater or lesser degree in other industrial cultures (e.g., England, France, the Soviet Union, etc.).

It is necessary at the outset to explain why we have retained many of the older findings and references used in the first edition. First, research in adolescent development is much less active than in child development. The ratio of research or theoretical papers published in the field of child development, as compared to adolescent development, is anywhere from 25: to 100:1. Thus many of the basic longitudinal and cross-sectional studies conducted in the 1930's and 1940's have *never* been truly replicated; and, thus, are still the only valid available sources today in certain areas of adolescent development. Second, the more recent studies are generally more superficial and topical in nature, and, except in the area of cognitive development, are, generally speaking, of a much lower order of methodological and theoretical quality and sophistication. Thus it did not make sense to us to discard many of these older and more valid research findings in favor of less valid or non-existent new ones, just to create an *appearance* of being more current in our coverage.

The literature in adolescent development over the past 25 years has been exhaustively reviewed, and all noteworthy new materials relevant to our objectives have been included in this edition. Topics that we consider overemphasized in other texts (such as drug use and addiction, juvenile delinquency, etc.) are not discussed exhaustively as *ends in themselves*, but only as illustrative of certain universal features of adolescent development or maldevelopment (even though the senior author has pubiished several books and many research and theoretical papers in this field). The same consideration applies to delinquency and *particular* behavior disorders (although the senior author is a practicing psychiatrist as well as a developmental and educational psychologist). These topics, as ends in themselves, are more indigenous to textbooks of adolescent psychiatry or abnormal psychology, rather than to a textbook that is primarily concerned with the *pancultural* characteristics and causes of adolescence, as a stage in personality development (and is only secondarily concerned with its manifestations in American culture). This is not to say that the latter phenomena are not described in sufficient detail as to preclude its use as a textbook for students in psychology, psychiatry, pediatrics nursing, and social work, and for prospective junior- and senior-high school teachers in courses on adolescent development. It is also addressed to parents, nurses, clinical psychologists, psychiatrists, social workers, etc., who work with adolescents on a day-to-day basis. As a matter of fact this book is addressed to such persons, as much as it is to students in the above-mentioned fields, since it discusses behavior disorders in developmental and cross-cultural perspective. Its usefulness as a reference work for developmental psychologists and psychologists in other areas (e.g., clinical, counseling, and school psychologists) is self-evident.

We wish to thank Therese Stewart for invaluable assistance in tracking down references; Pearl Ausubel, for critical reading of the manuscript and for many helpful suggestions in expressing and organizing our ideas; and Ruth Birnbaum for her patience and accuracy in preparing the manuscript.

David P. Ausubel
Raymond J. Montemayor
Pergrouhi N. Svajian

New York, N.Y.; Salt Lake City, Utah
June 30, 1977

1

Adolescence: A Stage in Personality Development

THE FIELD OF ADOLESCENT PSYCHOLOGY

By what criteria should the various subdivisions of a given science be organized into recognized fields of specialization? This question is no longer regarded improper, except by those who hold that the arrangements defining the present structure of knowledge are inevitable, axiomatically true, and immutable orders rather than functional contrivances designed to serve social needs. Neither is this question any longer merely academic. Today new fields of knowledge are emerging at an ever accelerating rate, countless interdisciplinary ventures are being launched, and research foundations are scrapping long-established boundaries between traditional areas of specialization in an effort to stimulate the formulation of more significant and basic research problems.

Yet an answer framed in terms of abstract logic would be meaningless and unrealistic. Neither a logician nor a research administrator can abolish an existing field that is flourishing, merely on the grounds that the material it encompasses could be more logically considered under different rubrics. The growth and organization of human knowledge have their own logic, as does any developmental or historical process. The pie can be sliced in innumerable ways, more or less rationally, more or less arbitrarily, with greater or lesser precision—but never according to a preconceived plan following the rules of abstract logic.

This does not mean that the development of new areas of knowledge is arbitrary and capricious, that prevailing boundaries cannot be revised, that the direction of growth cannot be given the benefit of deliberate evaluation and planning. It means rather that to the criterion of logic must be added the criteria of availability, convenience, and the satisfaction of practical social needs. Before a new area of specialization can come into being, some accumulation of facts, principles, and techniques of investigation is necessary. Once this precondition is met, the future viability of the field is determined by whether or not the new organization of material is convenient, promotes the understanding and investigation of significant problems in the area it has staked out for itself, and facilitates the solution of problems of practical importance in human affairs. Hence, it is to these general criteria that we shall turn in answering our next question: What justification exists for the field of adolescent psychology?

Justification for a psychology of adolescence

The chief justification for a separate psychology of adolescence is that adolescence is a distinct stage of development during which important and unique changes take place in the biosocial status of the adolescent. Although it is true that change occurs throughout the life span (Baltes & Schaie, 1973; Goulet & Baltes, 1970; Nesselroade & Reese, 1973), and that much of what occurs during adolescence has its roots in earlier periods, the adolescent years can be grouped together because they possess a certain homogeneity of developmental content. Throughout the entire period the adolescent is subjected to new and powerful sexual and maturational forces, he is in a transitional stage of personality organization, his cognitive and intellectual abilities undergo a dramatic change, and he occupies a marginal social status (Lewin, 1948), neither child nor adult. In terms of social expectations, privileges, perogatives, and parent-child relationships, the 13-year-old and the 17-year-old have much more in common than the former has with the 9-year-old or the latter with the 21-year-old; yet an identical 4-year interval separates each pair of ages.

There is disagreement about whether or not adolescence should be thought of as a "stage" of development. To the extent that one views development throughout the life span as continuous and constant, the adolescent period would be no more important than any other period of development. Leta Hollingworth (1928) expresses a view of development and of adolescence which would be compatible with that of most current-day social learning theorists: "A child grows by imperceptible degrees into an adolescent, and the adolescent turns by gradual degrees into the adult. . . . (The) widespread myth that every child is a changling, who at puberty comes forth as a different personality, is doubtless a survival in folklore of the ceremonial rebirth, which constituted the formal initiation of our savage ancestors into manhood and womanhood."

Although adolescence is certainly not a metamorphosis, the occurrence of biological changes is probably the soundest basis for postulating a stage of psychological development (Kagan, 1971), particularly when this change occupies great social importance.

Another criterion for setting apart certain developmental periods for separate study—besides the criterion of homogeneity of biosocial status—is the rate at which psychological changes occur. The rate of change during adolescence, for example, is immeasurably greater than in the preadolescent years or in the third, fourth, and fifth decades of life. As a result of this accelerated rate of change, many marked and distinctive alterations of behavior and psychological functioning occur (e.g., long-term planning, need for earned status) and many unique problems of adjustment are generated (e.g., emotional instability, "transitional anxiety"). Hence, many developmental generalizations that held true a short while ago in the preadolescent era have little relevance and applicability to the adolescent period.

Some have also questioned whether developmental psychology (and more particularly adolescent psychology) constitutes a legitimate field of specialization. The objection runs something like this: The adolescent after all is a human being and is, therefore, subject to the same general laws of behavior governing all human beings regardless of age. Hence, knowledge of the broad functional areas in psychology—the psychology of perception, emotion, motivation, learning, adjustment, group behavior, mental measurement—can be applied directly to the understanding of any psychological phenomenon occurring in adolescence. As Gewirtz (1969) has stated: "There may be no fundamental difference between the laws characterizing behavior changes during other, later, time spans. All involve the determination of sequential, functional relations between stimulus input and behavior output in the individual's experience. The term 'development' in a molar psychological analysis is an abstraction for systematic changes in specific S-R patterns."

There is some truth in this argument, but only in a very limited sense. The laws of behavior that apply with equal validity at all age levels apply at such a high degree of abstraction that they are woefully inadequate in illuminating behavior at any particular age level. To know, for example, that imitation is an important technique for acquiring novel responses does not tell us anything about the importance of imitation for adolescent learning. In addition, certain concepts such as sexual drive or abstract thought may be uniquely important for understanding certain kinds of behaviors after adolescence but not before. Berlyne (1966) maintains that knowledge of age is a necessary part of any behavioral law. He feels that it is "often impossible to predict what kinds of responses will be evoked by particular stimuli unless we also know the subject's age" (p. 72).

Besides being a time of changes within the adolescent as a result of changes in his biosocial status, adolescence is a cultural and sociological time period. All societies recognize a division of labor and an assignment of roles based on age (Linton, 1936). All cultures distinguish between three broad periods of development: childhood, youth, and adulthood. Although the specific behaviors expected of individuals of different ages may differ across cultures, the division is universal. To that extent, then, adolescence is a unique transitional stage of development.

A final justification for a psychology of adolescence concerns the great social demand to understand youth and youth's problems. Young people between the ages of 13 and 19 years account for a significant percentage of the population of the United States. The problems associated with this age group—premarital sexuality, drug addiction, delinquency, alienation—have broad social consequences. Not only those who come into direct contact with adolescents—teachers, counselors, parents—need to understand their problems, but we as a society need to understand a group whose influence on our collective lives is so extensive.

We cannot, therefore, concur with Dennis' (1946) conclusion that the only proper subject matter for the psychology of adolescence is a consideration of "the effects of biological adolescence upon the behavior of the individual; (that) its aim is to examine a certain set of mental-physical correlations not to treat those aspects of behavior which, although present in adolescents, are also present to the same degree in all other biologically defined classes of subjects."

For us the psychology of adolescence shall embrace the changes in personality organization that are generated by the sudden and violent shifts in the adolescent's biosocial status. We shall be concerned with the biological, psychological, and social factors that precipitate this new period of personality development, and with the mechanisms through which basic changes in personality structure are effected. We shall focus especially on the unique problems of adjustment posed by the developmental tasks of adolescence and on some of the distinctive adjustive techniques used by adolescents.

THE PLACE OF ADOLESCENT PSYCHOLOGY IN
UNDERSTANDING HUMAN BEHAVIOR

If adolescents as a group tend to feel, learn, think, or act in certain characteristic ways, if they present certain common problems of adjustment simply because they are all passing through the same developmental period, it behooves all persons who have dealings with them to acquire some understanding of the psychology of adolescence.

By this we do not wish to imply that individual differences are no longer important or that an understanding of adolescence automatically confers insight into the problems of any particular adolescent. We simply wish to reiterate the rather widely accepted psychological principle that in order adequately to understand any behavioral sequence, four types of psychological data are necessary: (1) the characteristics of the immediate situation to which the individual is responding; (2) the cultural setting in which his behavior is taking place; (3) the significant features of his personality structure, which are the result of continuous interaction between inherited predispositions and unique patterns of individual experience; and (4) the particular developmental period through which he is passing.

Knowledge of the psychology of adolescence provides us with only the last-mentioned category of data required for understanding a given adolescent's behavior. But this in no way detracts from its significance, since behavior at any age level cannot be made intelligible until it is placed in its proper developmental setting. Before it can be meaningfully evaluated we need to know something about the characteristic goals and methods of achieving goals, the self-concepts, the ways in which new values are assimilated, the sources and the level of status and emotional instability that relate to a given stage of personality development. Without such specialized knowledge parents and teachers, for example, cannot understand such perplexing adolescent phenomena as adult-youth conflict, negativism, exaggerated conformity to peer-group standards, and resistance to accepting adult-approved values. Similarly, unless counselors, psychiatrists, and clinical psychologists are able to relate the behavior disorders of adolescents to a revised norm of emotional instability that is consonant with the unusual developmental tensions characteristic of the adolescent period, they will be apt to exaggerate the seriousness of such behavior far out of proportion to its actual significance.

It is quite evident, therefore, that no person whose effectiveness in interpersonal relationships depends in part on his ability to understand the behavior of others can afford to ignore the developmental factors that shape its form and give it special meaning. And because of the abrupt and important developmental changes that take place during adolescence, as well as the protracted length of the adolescent period, this consideration is never more crucial than at this particular stage of growth.

APPROACHES TO THE STUDY OF ADOLESCENCE

Since adolescent psychology is largely a natural (ecological) rather than an experimental science, it is hardly surprising that much of the material conventionally included in the psychology of adolescence is based on observational data. From the time of Aristotle until relatively recently, the method of observation has for the most part been applied to the study of adolescent behavior. Although pre-twentieth-century observers of children and adolescents contributed much to our understanding of development, a science of development cannot be built on a foundation of impression and intuition. Observers often neglect to distinguish precise descriptions of actual behavior from preconceived notions, unsupported opinions, and popularly held prejudices.

Partly as a reaction to this unsatisfactory state of affairs and partly as a consequence of the phenomenal growth and rapidly increasing prestige of the testing movement in psychology, developmental psychologists began to measure every conceivable aspect of the adolescent—height, weight, bone ossification, pubic hair, strength of grip, manual dexterity, intelligence, vocational interests, and social maturity. This provided a large body of empirical data for a more objective psychology of adolescence. Although this greater objectivity was a valuable corrective to the previous situation, as an end in itself it was equally unsatisfactory. Unrelated to a comprehensive and tenable theoretical frame of reference, this mass of discrete measurements proved unintelligible and chaotic.

The conventional solution to this problem was to impose some order on the empirical data by organizing it into formal categories—physical growth, intellectual growth, emotional growth, social growth—which served also as chapter headings for textbooks on adolescent psychology. But categorizing discrete measurements obliterated the central significance of adolescence as a stage in personality development. The adolescent was viewed less as a person than as a summation of functions undergoing compartmentalized change. And since integrative hypotheses about the nature of adolescent development were not available for interpretive purposes, many of the loose, generalized observations were retained and supplemented by theoretical considerations specifically applicable not to adolescents only but to human beings in general. The final result was a curious mixture of questionable platitudes and a bewildering array of anatomical, physiological, and behavioral growth curves, of which the relevance and significance for the understanding of adolescent behavior were often difficult to perceive.

Organized in this way, the subject matter of adolescent psychology could hardly provide much practical assistance to parents, teachers, and clinicians. In their everyday interpersonal relations with teenage boys and girls these persons require some general appreciation of the personality changes and adjustment problems confronting adolescents rather than an encyclopedia of facts related to various discrete aspects of adolescent growth.

Largely because of these shortcomings in its historical development—insufficient rigorousness in observational method leading to platitudinous generalizations, and lack of an adequate theory of personality development around which to organize the search for empirical data—adolescent psychology failed to fulfill the promise it showed at the turn of the century. These shortcomings, rather than want of any intrinsic justification, have subjected adolescent psychology as a legitimate field of specialization to critical and unfavorable scrutiny.

Attempts were made to devise a theoretical framework comprehensive enough to embrace the numerous and scattered data relating to adolescent development. G. Stanley Hall, who is generally credited with establishing the field of adolescent psychology in the closing years of the nineteenth century, promulgated a biogenetic theory of psychological recapitulation which among systems of psychology has few rivals in scope and internal consistency (Hall, 1904). But it was precisely with this theory that the seeds of the subsequent unfortunate series of events were sown. For when Hall's elaborate theory collapsed under the weight of its own logical untenability and the findings of cultural anthropologists, the biological approach to adolescent psychology was largely discredited. With its theoretical scaffolding undermined, the multitude of data organized in relation to the theory of recapitulation fell into hopeless confusion. An equally serious concomitant of this situation, which also discouraged the formulation of new organizing hypotheses on the nature of adolescent development, was the widespread acceptance of certain implications of the "social approach" to adolescence; this held that adolescence was not a distinct period of personality development but an abortive product of restrictive cultural conditions.

Because of their crucial influence on the subsequent development of adolescent psychology, we shall examine each of these approaches in greater detail.

Biological approaches to adolescent psychology

In its simplest and most extreme form, the biological approach to adolescence maintains that the behavioral changes that occur during this period of growth are completely conditioned by a series of physiological events depending on the function of the glands of internal secretion. Although these endocrine changes are latent for many years, they are predetermined by the genetic constitution of the individual, and their psychological effects, it was argued, are inevitable, universal in distribution, and independent of cultural influences. Moreover, to the extent that pubescence represents a period of rapid physiological, sexual, and anatomical maturation common to the life cycle of all mammalian species, proponents of this view steadfastly insisted on regarding this time as a phylogenetic phenomenon.

Implicit in the biological approach, therefore, were these assumptions: (1) Physiological factors are wholly responsible for the psychological phenomena of adolescence. (2) The genetic determination of these physiological changes necessarily guarantees that their psychological consequences will be uniform. (3) Physiological events operate directly to produce behavioral change rather than indirectly by contributing to the reorganization of personality structure. (4) The similarity between pubescent phenomena in human and infrahuman species points to a type of phylogenetic inheritance. The first three assumptions, as will be shown, were completely untenable. The fourth assumption, although tenable in itself, was unwarrantably extended by Hall to include a fanciful conception of psychological recapitulation of the history of the race in the life history of the individual. (The essential elements of this theory had been promulgated more than a century earlier by Rousseau.)

Hall's theoretical orientation to adolescent psychology, although not coextensive with the biological approach, soon became closely identified with it. First, he stressed the importance of physiological changes at puberty and their relationship to psychological events during adolescence. Second, his theory of recapitulation was biological in form. It assumed that the experiential history of the race is written into the genetic constitution of the individual, whose development, therefore, is predetermined to unfold in parallel sequence. The unique characteristics of psychological development in adolescence, then, depend on the fact that the adolescent recapitulates a turbulent transitional period in human evolution.

This theory had fascinating implications and a certain amount of superficial plausibility, partly because of its resemblance to Haeckel's famous proposition that the embryological development of the individual recapitulates the biological history of the race (Haeckel, 1879). Haeckel, however, confined his analogy to the prenatal period, in which empirical evidence is available, and did not project the parallelism beyond the realm of gross anatomical structure. By extending the analogy to include the postnatal behavior of the individual, on the one hand, and the cultural history of the race on the other, Hall was forced to go far beyond the evidence and to rely on the discredited doctrine of the inheritance of acquired characteristics (Ausubel, 1958; Grinder, 1969).

The widespread rejection of this theory tended to create a climate unfavorable to any new general theoretical position on the nature of adolescent development. Adolescence thereafter was typically viewed eclectically, as a constellation of discrete categories of growth and of adjustment problems characteristic of the second decade of life. In most instances both biological and social aspects of adolescence were considered relevant, and although they were not related to a theoretical frame of reference, the possibility of so doing was not expressly denied (but in some cases this possibility was explicitly denied). In other instances biological factors were swept aside as inconsequential, and adolescence was regarded as a social phenomenon rather than as a universal stage of personality development with a core of common psychological principles regardless of the culture in which it occurred. Dennis (1946) adopted still another position. He confined the field of adolescent psychology to the behavioral consequences of physiological pubescence. This position did not deny the contribution of the social environment to the adolescent's behavior but insisted that this aspect of the problem was outside the proper field of adolescent psychology, belonging instead to the "social psychology of youth."

Unfortunately, Hall's chief theoretical contribution was lost in the heated controversy over the specific merits of his theory of recapitulation. For unlike the advocates of the biological, the social, or the eclectic approaches he was practically alone in maintaining that adolescence is a distinct period of psychological development that can be explained by reference to a set of general theoretical propositions. Although his particular propositions failed to stand the test of time, they were directed toward a unified and integrated conception of adolescence that later investigators unfortunately chose to ignore.

Social approaches to adolescent psychology

G. Stanley Hall and all other early investigators associated with the biological point of view were naturally limited in their cultural perspective and blinded by ethnocentric bias. They worked in an era in which there was little knowledge of the psychology of adolescence in other ethnic and social settings. It is understandable, therefore, that they should have believed that adolescence the world over is characterized by "storm and stress." Having no examples to the contrary, they naturally inferred that if the behavior of adolescents is a product of their biological endowment, this behavior would have to be universal in distribution since all ethnic groups share essentially the same physiological make-up.

Underlying this inference, of course, was an assumption basic to the psychological thinking of the period: if behavior is conditioned by a physiological factor which, in turn, is genetically determined, it must inevitably take the same specific form in every social environment. It was not yet appreciated that visceral stimuli of genetic origin lead only to the universal occurrence of very general drives and propensities for behavior and that the specific patterning and content of such behavior can vary enormously depending on the social environment in which it occurs.

The importance of culture in patterning biologically determined drives was nowhere more forcefully illustrated than in the psychology of adolescence. Beginning in 1925 with Margaret Mead's investigation of adolescent behavior in Samoa, a large body of ethnological data dealing with the comparative psychology of adolescence became available.*

A survey of this material indicates that the problems facing the adolescent vary from culture to culture, rendering the transition to adulthood more or less complicated, more or less conflicting, more or less prolonged. Such studies indicate the necessity of using comparative material from different cultures and times, and the necessity of first placing adolescent ego problems in their social settings. For significant variations and factors of social change necessarily reflect themselves in the status problems of

---

* The contrast in specific detail between various aspects of adolescence in different cultures or in different subcultures within our own culture will be made in later sections when we will deal more explicitly with specific features of adolescent development. For persons who are especially interested in the problem of adolescence in different cultural settings the following works are recommended: Ausubel, 1961; Benedict, 1934; Cohen, 1964; Knepler, 1969; Mead, 1928, 1939; Opler, 1971; Whiting, 1941.

adolescents, who are themselves in a critical and unstable stage
of transition. (Sherif & Cantril, 1947)

In the face of overwhelming evidence presented by cultural anthropologists, the naive view that biological factors completely or
inevitably determine the nature of adolescent development had to be
abandoned. It became apparent that certain special features of adolescence in modern Western civilization were not necessarily inevitable; that the degree of conflict, stress, and difficulty experienced by
adolescents could be related in part to cultural differences in the
norms and restrictions regulating their behavior and aspirations for
mature status.

The proponents of the new social approach (Dollard et al., 1939;
Mead, 1939) were no better able to avoid overgeneralizing from their
findings than were their colleagues of the biological school. They
were soon proclaiming that the biological changes of adolescence
were unrelated to its psychological characteristics; that there is no
distinct transitional stage of personality development that can be
localized during the adolescent period; that no universal psychological principles of adolescent development can be formulated; and
that adolescence is a purely social phenomenon in certain cultures in
which restrictive practices prevail.

They also went far beyond their evidence in the conclusions
they drew. Because they were able to relate degrees of adolescent conflict to cultural conditions, they jumped illogically to the conclusion
that the entirety of adolescent psychology could be regarded largely
as the product of social norms and cultural characteristics. Because
they were successful in demonstrating that biological factors could not
account for the specific content of adolescent behavior, they erroneously concluded that these factors had no general influence on
behavior or development independent of the cultural setting. They
failed to recognize that the early and mistaken claims for the specific
patterning of behavior by physiological variables were in no sense
necessary or crucial for the validity of the proposition that biological
factors make important contributions to the development of human
behavior.

Hence, it is important to appreciate that the same sex hormones
may give rise to markedly different patterns of sex behavior in different cultures, and that in different ethnic and social groups tremendous variability in the accepted economic and social roles of adolescents may prevail. But more important than specific cultural
differences in the patterning of biological sex drives, or in the social
expectations of appropriate status roles for adolescents, is the com-

mon fact that in all cultures adolescence is marked by important shifts in the biosocial status of the child, shifts which are sufficiently crucial to precipitate a thoroughgoing reorganization of personality structure. It is in the causes for and the nature of these shifts and in their consequences for personality and behavior that we can expect to find our relevant subject matter for the psychology of adolescence.

The sex repression theory of adolescent emotional instability

The gross oversimplification of the problem of adolescent development by adherents to the social approach is nowhere more vividly illustrated than in the theory that adolescent emotional instability in our culture is chiefly attributable to culturally determined frustration of physiological sex drives. This theory is advanced by Dollard et al. (1939) among others, and is, of course, in line with his frustration-aggression hypothesis. It has also undoubtedly been influenced by psychoanalytic thinking, since Freud (1936) taught for many years that anxiety is an inevitable consequence of sex repression. Although this theory is (as will be shown presently) untenable for many reasons, its advocates ironically committed the very same error for which they so severely berated the champions of the biological approach—the error of minimizing the degree to which even basic drives can be altered by cultural influences, as well as the ability of human beings to adapt successfully to such extreme variations.

Data on psychosexual development in our own and other cultures support the view that there is no simple relationship between degree of overt freedom in sexual expression and the development of stress in adolescence. This material demonstrates unequivocally that the suppression of physiological sex urges need not be followed inevitably by psychological conflict. It is true that when social sanctions exist allowing for the uninhibited gratification of these urges little mental conflict about sex develops. But the same outcome holds true for many other types of cultural patterning of sex behavior.

From the Arapesh, for example, we learn that all sexuality can be successfully placed on an affectional basis, and that physiological sex urges can be so completely subordinated to affectional needs that they have no independent existence (Mead, 1939). The possibility of a spontaneous sex drive in response to a hormonal stimulus is not recognized, and both men and women find in monogamous marriage the consummation of the ideal sex life. This transformation of hormonally inspired sex impulses into a type of affection which does not differ qualitatively from the feeling one has for a daughter or sister obviates the possibility of simple physiological gratification. Yet no signs of psychological conflict about sex have been found among Arapesh adolescents.

What shall we say about the more usual type of cultural situation in which sexual needs do not rest exclusively on an affectional basis, and which when expressed seem to be, at least in part, a response to internal physiological stimuli? Ethnological and clinical evidence indicates that for those persons who practice repression no conflict results as long as the repression is so complete that at the conscious level the existence of sex feelings is not even acknowledged. At least this would appear to be true of the Manus girl, according to Mead, who manifests no signs of acute or chronic emotional conflict over sexuality despite complete suppression of sex cravings. In this respect she does not differ from many puritanically reared girls in our own culture who are able to stifle sex urgings so completely that none ever reaches the threshold of consciousness. Such girls do not suffer from prolonged abstinence, and like their Manus sisters are often incapable of enjoying sex even on an affectional basis. Hence, complete repression (just like the complete "transformation" of the Arapesh) seems to be one of the many cultural alternatives in the patterning of the hormonal sex drive that is entirely compatible with freedom from psychological conflict about sex; and, paradoxically, both possibilities were completely overlooked by socially oriented students of adolescence.

When physiological sex urges are not completely repressed and do find representation in consciousness, mental conflict will not develop as long as the adolescent does not attempt to maintain an inconsistent and unrealistic moral position on the legitimacy of their gratification. It seems to matter little whether no restrictions at all are placed on premarital sexual intercourse as in Samoa, or whether strict and serious prohibitions are applied as among the Mundugumors. As long as these prohibitions are not internalized by the adolescent and as long as clandestine opportunities for gratification are available, neither moral conflict nor emotional tension from unsatisfied psychophysiological needs will develop.

Even though we have been unable to find any simple relationship between the repression of physiological sex impulses and the degree of psychological conflict about sex, the sex repression theory of adolescent emotional instability is untenable for many other reasons. In the first place, it is quite unlikely that even for Samoan boys and girls, whose adolescent sexual activity is completely unrestricted, the transition between childhood and adult life can be accomplished painlessly. With adolescence they face a change in responsibilities, privileges, social status, and relationships with parents and age mates. Even in the sexual domain all is not without difficulty. Girls have to overcome a preadolescent attitude of hostility toward boys and customarily do not commence sexual relationships with them for the first 2 years after the onset of pubescence. Boys are vexed by having to court a girl through an intermediary, with the ever-present possibility of losing the coveted prize to that intermediary.

Second, in those primitive societies in which the degree of stress in adolescence is adversely contrasted to the idyllic situation in Samoa, other more compelling reasons for the disparity can be found besides the usually emphasized differences in social restrictions on adolescent sexual activity. The Manus child, for example, who lives in a happy and carefree world of play and easy comradeship, at adolescence is suddenly catapulted into a ruthlessly aggressive and competitive adult society in which only material values are honored. Marriage is a pure business proposition, devoid of any affectional elements, that involves the assumption of onerous financial burdens. The Manus adolescent can expect no genuine assistance from family, friends, or society in getting started in adult life; nor can he join in any communal economic enterprise. He has no choice but to become an independent entrepreneur and to surrender his self-respect by borrowing from "big men" in the village the wherewithal to do so. Release from this humiliating dependence can be accomplished only by emulating the culturally valued traits of unrelenting industry, acquisitiveness, and ruthless unconcern for human values. In this way he may himself become a successful and prosperous man of property on whom others in turn become dependent.

In sexual matters the Manus boy is faced with a two-edged dilemma: his culture acknowledges the potency and naturalness of the male physiological sex drive while it applies strict taboos that aim seriously at outlawing the extramarital expression of this drive. He is able to find some compensation in peer group and homosexual activities since his social life is not as restricted and supervised as the adolescent girl's. Petting, however, is unknown, and we have no information about masturbation. In all probability, therefore, he experiences a good deal of emotional stress about sex. The Manus girl, on the other hand, does not experience any sexual frustration despite the apparent deprivation; in her case, sex desires have never been allowed to develop. Nevertheless, once she is married, her lot is more difficult because she regards intercourse as loathesome, shameful, and repugnant.

It is apparent that although sexual problems undoubtedly add to the difficulty of adolescence for Manus boys and girls, other causes of emotional stress mentioned cannot be ignored—the severe contrast of adolescence to the carefree existence during childhood, the circumscription of the girl's social life and her isolation from her peer group, the ruthless competitiveness of the economic system and the adolescent's marginal, dependent position in it.

The same conclusion holds true also for the Kwoma (Whiting, 1941) and Mundugumor (Mead, 1939) cultures, both of which place severe restrictions on premarital sex activity. These restrictions, however, are not internalized by adolescents. Transgressions of the social standard are followed by feelings of insecurity (by the girl lest her marriageability suffer in consequence, and by the boy lest her relatives harm him) rather than by feelings of guilt or self-reproach. But here too other nonsexual sources of tension are readily apparent. The highly individualistic Mundumgumor society places a premium on the same personality traits that the Manus people value so highly. Status is not something that the culture graciously confers on the adolescent as a matter of course when he is mature enough to deserve it; it is a prize to be snatched by means of continuous aggression from elders who yield nothing unless they have to. The Kwoma adolescent, similarly, does not attain full adult status at once. As a way of emphasizing his marginal status, he is obliged to postpone for some time certain activities and to show childish deference to certain elders.

If the contrast in the stress of adolescence between primitive societies that are relatively casual, permissive, cooperative, and unconcerned about status differences (Samoan, Arapesh) and those that are relatively aggressive, individualistic, competitive, and worshipful of prestige and material success (Manus, Mundugumor) is so great, what can we expect in comparing adolescence in the former group to adolescence in our own culture? We have seen that these factors (the implications of which reach far beyond the sphere of sexual adjustment) play a crucial role in enhancing the difficulty of adolescent development in the primitive cultures in which maximal social restrictions are also imposed on adolescent sexual activity. How much more important, then, must these nonsexual factors be in our own heterogeneous culture, in which matters of status and socioeconomic organization are infinitely more complicated!

In some primitive societies adolescence occupies a relatively short time span. Its onset is clearly demarcated by ritual, and its precise nature is not shrouded in ambiguity. Conflicts among an infinite number of vaguely defined occupational choices do not plague the adolescent. He has little cultural confusion about moral values since alternative value systems are not available. Life is ordered and prearranged. There are no trying decisions to make. The social order is relatively static and does not require a series of periodic individual readjustments. The acceptable attributes of masculinity and femininity, although differing widely among cultures, are explicitly defined within a single culture. Emancipation from the home is not indefinitely prolonged; and although marital and vocational status may be hedged in by certain limiting conditions, they are attained shortly after the acquisition of physical maturity. For these reasons our four primitive cultures, despite their considerable differences, probably have more in common with each other than any one of them has in common with our culture; hence, the unique degree of difficulty during adolescence in our society.

Adolescence as a stage of personality development

From our brief ethnological survey of adolescence we have gained social perspective. We have seen that there is wide cultural variability in the form, content, length, difficulty, and stressfulness of adolescence and that no single factor, such as sex repression, can account for as complex a phenomenon as adolescent emotional instability. But the main purpose for gaining perspective from a comparative approach is not merely negative—avoiding generalizations about the basic nature of adolescence that hold true only for a single culture. The more important, positive purpose, which unfortunately has been largely neglected in the fascination over dramatic differences between cultures, is to abstract the common factors that exist in these differences—to formulate general principles of adolescent development that can be validly applied to any cultural environment. Sherif and Cantril (1947) state this very well:

> After learning. . . from the ethnologist we can return to our own work as psychologists carrying with us the implications of the lesson learned. We should start our work by reiterating a methodological consideration appropriate in this connection. With variations in the social setting, the transitional period of adolescence may be more or less prolonged, fraught with more or less intense problems. However, the basic psychological principles which operate in all of these social settings should be the same.

Adolescence in all cultures can be described as a time of transition in the biosocial status of the individual. It is a period during which marked changes occur in duties, responsibilities, privileges, social and economic roles, and relationships with others. It marks the beginning assumption of adult biological and social sex roles and of a cluster of personality traits that the culture deems appropriate for the mature adult of each sex. It includes the individual's reactions to being swept into a transitional period of development and to being confronted with a new set of social demands and expectations. Under such conditions changed attitudes toward self, parents, peers, and elders become inevitable. New aspirations are generated, new standards of behavior are incorporated, and new ways of learning are adopted.

In short, adolescence everywhere is a time of extensive personality reorganization. It could hardly be otherwise, for how could such significant shifts in status transpire without some profound impact on an individual's organization of attitudes, traits, and propensities for behavior, whatever these may be? Certainly there will be differences in the intensity and kinds of responses made to these shifts, depending on previous personality structure. But in no way can the necessity for some type of basic restructuring be avoided.

In this context a biosocial approach to adolescent development means more than an attempt to relate directly certain biological and social conditions of adolescence to their separate psychological outcomes. It implies a more explicit assessment of the component contributions that various biological and social factors make in effecting a transition from childhood to adult personality status. To avoid a mere cataloging of the psychological events incident to adolescence requires considerable selectivity in the choice of material, since personality is an inclusive term embracing the trivial and peripheral as well as the more central aspects of an individual's psychological organization. To achieve this measure of selectivity we shall be obliged to use some criterion or gradient in relation to which the contents of personality can be ordered in a hierarchy. Any such criterion to be valid would have to operate so that the more stable, recurrent, and critical aspects of personality, which give it continuity and make possible the prediction of significant behavior, would occupy a central position in the hierarchical arrangement.

The only possible criterion that meets this requirement is a gradient of self-reference or ego involvement. According to this conception most significant and crucial are those aspects of personality (attitudes, values, motives, characteristic modes of adjustment) that are endowed with the greatest amount of self-implication. We may expect to find ego-related characteristics such as these constituting the core of personality structure: an individual's conception of his own importance; his aspirations for self-enhancement; the sources from which he desires status; the degree of independence characterizing his decisions; the notions he has about his ability to control his environment; the degree of dependence-independence characterizing his relations with others; his methods of assimilating new values; his concept of his own capacity for doing things for himself; his self-esteem and feelings of security; his ability to withstand frustration; his ability to judge himself realistically; his need for pleasurable and immediate gratification; his sense of moral obligation and responsibility; the types of defenses he uses when his security or self-esteem is threatened.

These are the core aspects of personality structure that have been developed during childhood. If significant personality changes will result from the shifts in biosocial status induced by adolescence, we can confidently expect that they will occur in these areas. "From the point of view of ego development, a period during which status changes in so many important aspects of life should be of crucial significance. For shifts in objective status are reflected as ego-shifts in the psychology of the individual. Psychologically speaking, it is especially in the ego of the individual that any status problem finds its echo" (Sherif & Cantril, 1947).

PSYCHOANALYTIC APPROACH TO ADOLESCENCE

Psychoanalytic theorists have not devoted a great deal of systematic attention to the problem of adolescent development. But because they have stood virtually alone in attempting to fit the adolescent period into a general theory of personality development, a consideration of some of their scattered formulations will probably prove rewarding.

The psychoanalytic theory of adolescence (A. Freud, 1946; S. Freud, 1952, 1953) is similar in many respects to Hall's biogenetic theory of recapitulation. It, too, conceives of adolescence as a phylogenetically determined period of personality development. But here the two approaches part ways. According to the psychoanalytic view, the adolescent does not repeat in his individual development the cultural history of the race; he does retrace previous racial experience in psychosexual development. Both theories, however, are obliged to rely on the discredited doctrine of the inheritance of acquired characteristics (cultural or psychological experience). In addition, the psychoanalytic approach postulates the existence of inherited ideational material in the racial unconscious and of highly specific drives and patterns of interpersonal behavior that are transmitted through the genes and unfold in predetermined sequence.

The readiness with which the first proposition has gained acceptance is somewhat surprising when we consider that the doctrine of innate ideas hitherto had not been seriously advanced since the buffeting it received at the hands of Locke. And the second proposition on the instinctual origins of complex behavior patterns harks back to the highly elaborate "instinct" theories of behavior, theories that apparently had been successfully demolished within the past three decades by numerous widely accepted discoveries in cultural anthropology and primate development. These findings had conclusively demonstrated that the specific form and content of any human drive tend to be culturally determined.

According to Freudian doctrine, the distinguishing feature of adolescence is the reestablishment of sexual interest and activity in the pubescent individual after a prolonged latency period, during which infantile sexual drives have been successfully repressed and "sublimated" into other areas. The infant and child supposedly pass through oral, anal, and genital stages of sexuality in that order, directing their erotic attentions variously toward themselves, the parent of the same sex, and the parent of the opposite sex. In their most advanced infantile form, when the boy is between the ages of 3 and 6, his sexual urges are said to be genital and directed toward the mother. This precipitates the famous oedipal situation: an unconscious desire for sexual union with the mother and an unconscious recognition of the father as a rival with a concurrent wish for his death. Consciously the boy is unduly desirous of maternal caresses and exhibits hostility and irritability to the father. As a means both of disowning this hostility (which is dangerous because it invites retaliation) and of justifying it, he projects it onto the father whom he now perceives as threatening him with castration because of his incestuous designs on the mother.

The threat of castration aided by a phylogenetic identification with the father brings the oedipal period to a close. The father's restrictions and taboos on the child's sexual expression are internalized and result in the formation of conscience (superego); sexual feelings toward the mother are sublimated into simple affection and interest in motor, intellectual, social, and imaginative activities. Thus begins the so-called latency period in psychosexual development, which is terminated by the onset of pubescence. At this time, sexual and aggressive (id) drives are so greatly enhanced by endocrine influences that repression is no longer possible. Previous stages of infantile sexuality, including oedipal wishes and homosexual urges, are briefly reactivated; but reinforced by hormonal stimulation in the appropriate direction, heterosexual impulses of a nonincestuous nature soon become dominant and insistently seek gratification.

Freudian literature has been concerned chiefly with three main problems of personality during the adolescent period of psychosexual development: (1) the relationship between sex repression and anxiety and emotional stability; (2) the achievement of a desirable balance between the expression of sex urges and the demands of conscience; and (3) the establishment of heterosexuality. At first, widespread acceptance of Freud's earlier theory of anxiety as a psychophysiological product of sexual repression stimulated concern about the consequences for adolescent emotional stability of culturally induced repression. Freud's (1936) later modification of this theory, however, led to a marked change in emphasis: the very existence of these newly intensified sex drives rather than any attempt to repress them was regarded as the main threat and the source of anxiety. The ego was pictured as overwhelmed by their demands and in constant peril of disregarding the ethical considerations of the superego (conscience). Anxiety was evoked not by repression, but because the individual was confronted both by guilt feelings and by social reprisals as the penalties for yielding to his insistent drives. Repression was reinterpreted as a defensive consequence rather than as a cause of anxiety—as a way in which the adolescent protected himself against the dangerous implications of uninhibited sexual expression, as well as against the anxiety that contemplation of such expression induced. Some writers, therefore, have advocated the imposition of unambiguous environmental limits as a means of helping the adolescent effect the necessary degree of repression of id drives (Hacker & Geleerd, 1945) and of sublimating them into artistic, social, and athletic channels. However, the dangers of overrepression (as represented by asceticism, excessive intellectualization, and rigidity of personality structure) were also recognized, and the desirability of striking a happy balance between the respective demands of the id and the superego was advocated (A. Freud, 1958, 1968).

Finally, psychoanalytic theorists have regarded adolescence as a crucial period for the establishment of appropriate patterns of masculinity and femininity and for the achievement of normal heterosexuality in the choice of love objects. Fixation at any of the infantile levels of psychosexual development and the lack of suitable adult models of the same sex with whom an adolescent can identify have been postulated as two primary reasons for failure in this critical developmental task of adolescence (A. Freud, 1968).

A definitive critique of the psychoanalytic theory of psychosexual development would be decidedly out of place in a textbook on adolescence. We shall comment only on those aspects that are especially relevant to the theory of adolescent personality development. First, the notion of a "latency" period is not in accord with empirical findings on sex behavior during childhood. There is, on the contrary, evidence of considerable interest in and experimentation with sexual matters throughout the entire elementary school period (Kinsey et al., 1948). In lower-class families, especially, sexually immature boys and girls not infrequently make attempts at sexual intercourse. Also, there is every reason to believe that adolescent sexuality does not merely begin at the point at which infantile "sexual" activity terminates; it represents, rather, a definite break in the quality and meaning of such activity. Before adolescence it is sporadic and casual, a form of imitative or exploratory play motivated by curiosity or simple sensuality. Afterwards it becomes regular, insistent, and "an end in itself," acquiring new emotional overtones and new status implications. When the individual then for the first time experiences himself in the biological sex role of the mature adult of his species, an entirely new behavioral component must be incorporated into his changing self-portrait.

Second, we cannot concur with the psychoanalytic view that the problems of psychosexual maturation and adjustment during adolescence are coextensive with the general problem of adolescent development. The acquisition of a biological sex role and the need for regulating hormonally reinforced sex drives certainly constitute highly significant factors in the shifting biosocial status and personality configuration of the adolescent. But as already pointed out, many other status problems emerge at adolescence and many other aspects of personality structure require reorganization as a result of changing status relationships.

Third, the Freudian concept that most adolescent interests and activities are sublimated products of repressed sex drives is neither theoretically nor empirically tenable. "Human motives are constantly emerging under the impact of new experiences, new social pressures and expectations, new ways of perceiving the same experience. These motives are also outcomes of positive impulses to manipulate and explore the environment as well as adjustive reactions to frustration" (Ausubel, 1952a).

If only in establishing a new social status for himself, the adolescent certainly has sufficient provocation for initiating a host of characteristic peer group activities and relationships. Although these new functions might conceivably compensate in part for the frustration induced by the repression of sex needs, it is illogical to think of them as energized by the latter needs when a more plausible autonomous source of motivation is so apparent.

Furthermore, except in cases of complete repression of physiological sex needs, there is little evidence that repression is even possible once sex desires become consciously insistent. Among unmarried middle-class males in our culture, the existence of an absent or very low sexual outlet is a rarity indeed (e.g., Kinsey, et al., 1948). When nonmarital intercourse is shunned, compensation is found in other sexual outlets (masturbation, petting) rather than in nonsexual activities. Moreover, in cultural and subcultural groups in which no sex repression of any kind is seriously practiced (lower-class youths in our culture), sublimation does not constitute even a relevant possibility of providing the motivation for adolescent behavior.

The literary and artistic activities of adolescents—because they so often contain material illustrative of adolescent personality conflict—are sometimes offered as evidence of sublimation. Since they are so peculiarly well adapted to serve as vehicles of symbolic emotional expression, these activities would seem to be the most likely to qualify for a sublimative role. However, in the light of the evidence above, the more plausible explanation is that increased emotionality per se rather than sex repression helps to instigate the artistic creations of adolescents. If these efforts portray sexual conflicts, it does not mean necessarily that they provide a substitutive outlet for frustrated sex urges. It requires fewer untenable assumptions to postulate that the subject matter of artistic productions expresses merely amorphous and vaguely defined emotional overtones relating to current areas of significant psychological conflict in the life of the artist.

Hence, it is one thing to articulate emotional tensions through artistic expression and to find in such activity an independent satisfaction, and quite another thing to gratify vicariously in this way the frustrated needs that produce the particular emotional tensions. We know now that middle-class adolescent males generally satisfy their psychophysiological sex needs through various forms of sexual activity. Therefore, it would not be unreasonable to conclude that artistic productions expressive of sexual tension merely portray emotional reactions to the moral conflict generated by sexual problems.

ERIK ERIKSON AND THE PROBLEM OF ADOLESCENT IDENTITY

Perhaps more than any other psychologist Erik Erikson has identified an issue in adolescent development that has captured the attention and interest not only of adolescents but of our culture as a whole. Adolescents readily admit to "having an identity crisis" while parents and teachers express concern that their adolescent children and students will "find their identity." Social commentators speak of "America's identity crisis" or of the "identity crisis of the automobile industry." Indeed, many believe that the notion of "identity crisis" aptly characterizes a whole host of problems that beset modern man and his society. However, this expansion of the term is more the result of political rhetoric than of Erikson's own doing. A concept so broad and inclusive would have little scientific utility.

Before the concept of identity and its importance to adolescence are discussed, a few remarks are in order concerning Erikson's psychosocial theory of development.*

Erikson describes a sequence of eight stages or "crises" of psychosocial development. The earlier stages parallel Freud's stages of psychosexual development, but one of Erikson's more important contributions to psychology is that he has extended psychoanalytic thinking beyond adolescence, and his theory describes development from infancy to senescence. Each stage of the life cycle represents a unique developmental task for the individual, a task that must be successfully solved before the individual can move on to the next task.

The crucial characteristic of Erikson's psychosocial theory is the attempt to integrate the psychosexual development of the individual with the cultural and historical circumstances in which individual development unfolds. According to Erikson, an individual not only lives in a culture with certain norms and customs, but the culture and its norms also live within the individual. The infant is not a social creature on whom socialization "acts" to form a member of a society; rather, the infant is essentially social, biologically predisposed to seek out and interact with other individuals and by so doing to naturally become a member of the society into which he is born. Socialization, in other words, is a two way street. The manner by which an individual solves each developmental task and the potential outcomes of each solution are partly determined by the particular historical moment in which the individual is present. For example, whether an identity crisis shall be suffered violently or quietly, and whether the outcome shall be doctor or nurse will be partly dependent on the cultural models and expectations available to youth and on the allowable roles for men and women at any particular time.

According to Erikson (1968), the term "identity crisis" was first used by him to characterize the behavior of returning World War II veterans who had experienced a peculiar sense of loss of self. A delicate sense of personal consistency runs throughout our lives. We recognize ourselves in the memories of our past actions and we accept those past actions, that ontogenetic history, as our own, as our identity. We are what we have done. Some men had been so traumatized by the war, however—by what they had to do or by what was done to

---

*The reader interested in Erikson's work should consult Erikson himself (Erikson, 1950, 1968) or some of the few available secondary sources (Coles, 1970; Muuss, 1975).

them—that the sense of being the same person both before and after the war had vanished. In these soldiers the trauma of the war was so shattering, the behavior of the self so alienated from the conception of the self, that the self-image was fractured. There was a loss of "ego identity."

Although this clinical episode describes a psychiatric disorder, the feeling of a loss of personal sameness, of an alienation from one's personal past may be a normal adolescent developmental crisis. Consider the adolescent experiencing for the first time the demands of sexual release, possessing a body whose physical features are undergoing such rapid and fundamental changes that one may speak of a biological revolution occurring within. Coupled with these biological changes, the growing adolescent is subjected to new social expectations and obligations. In a very real sense the adolescent is forced to break with what is familiar—biologically, psychologically, and socially—and to enter into a new relationship with his body, his self, and his social world. In Erikson's (1968) words: "The young person, in order to experience wholeness, must feel a progressive continuity between that which he has come to be during the long years of childhood and that which he promises to become in the anticipated future."

In addition to a sense of consistency with one's past, a vertical consistency, the possession of a sense of identity also implies another kind of consistency, a horizontal consistency, a feeling that one remains the same person in all social interactions. At a time when adolescents often desire nothing more than "to be like everybody else," to be average, to fit in, the risk of the loss of the sense of "who I really am" is great. Conformity remains one of the distinguishing characteristics of the adolescent period. It is a felt need of powerful forcefulness. And its satisfaction demands a degree of adaptability that presses to the limits the adolescent's ego capacities. Many adolescents develop an almost chameleon-like personality, attempting to be all things to all people. During this time the adolescent must acquire confidence in his own personality and beliefs that he may behave genuinely with all people. The adolescent must learn to be true to himself and thereby acquire a sense of trust in his own self and in the adequacy of that self. In addition, a strong sense of identity implies the ability to play the necessarily different roles that different social situations demand, while continuing to recognize the sameness of the self. Although one's behavior changes from situation to situation, one continues to recognize a sameness of self that is independent of the self's behavior.

A third aspect of identity concerns how the adolescent views himself and how he believes other people view him. The adolescent period is often the period when the experience of loneliness is felt for the first time. Adolescents often report that they feel cut off and isolated from other people, feeling that "nobody knows me" or "nobody understands me." Adolescents often state that "nobody knows who I am" or "no one knows how I feel." The adolescent seems to be saying that people do not perceive him in the same way that he perceives himself. Presumably his actions do not convey the same meaning for others that they do for himself. Under these circumstances, one might begin to question one's ability to adequately express one's feelings and inner life. As long as this sense of disconnectedness remains, one must feel cut off not only from others but also from one's own self. A true sense of identity, according to Erikson, implies the ability to present oneself as one truly feels one is and to have that presentation correctly interpreted by others. A sense of identity in this respect is indicated by a belief that "I am who you think I am."

Finally, a resolution of the identity crisis also implies the formation of an ideology, a personal philosophy of life. Such a philosophy is a necessity for understanding one's place in the larger realm of things. No identity could be complete without some sense of the relationship between self and universe, or self and nation. Such a philosophy, although rarely articulable, brings a coherence and consistency to one's social and political choices.

The adolescent with a strong sense of ego views himself as a distinct and unique individual, apart from others yet capable of knowing others and of being known by others. A sense of identity implies a feeling of consistency and a sense of wholeness within one's self. Finally, a sense of identity includes a world view, a view by which the adolescent is able to integrate himself into his larger social milieu.

Erikson has identified an aspect of adolescent development that lies at the root of the adolescent's relationship with others and with his society. We shall return to this theory later to discuss the empirical results pertaining to the concept of "identity" and to evaluate the adequacy of Erikson's theory for explaining various aspects of adolescent development. In the meantime we should point out that Erikson identifies, but oversimplifies in terms of single causality, many of the same changes in and reactions to altered biosocial status that we do, and it is to these issues that we would now like to turn.

2

Problems of Adolescent Development

If we are to accept the proposition that the chief significance of adolescence lies in the fact that it constitutes a distinct and crucial stage of personality development, it is essential that we evolve some orderly scheme for categorizing the types of problems it encompasses. To be useful, such classification must be more than a convenient tool for organizing a multiplicity of data in a systematic fashion. It must go beyond a mere arbitrary listing of phenomena which could be ordered just as defensibly in many other equally arbitrary ways. Classification must serve the purpose of abstracting and identifying the most fundamental thread of common factors running through a variety of diverse problems. To serve this function it cannot operate on a *descriptive* level, for to do so would be to give undue weight to superficial resemblances and differences. Only by differentiating between problems in terms of their *origins* and structural features is it possible to achieve a grouping that adequately expresses underlying relationships as they actually exist rather than as they appear in their overt manifestations.

The values inherent in adequate classification are of considerable importance here. First, such classification enhances the possibility of gaining meaningful insights into the interrelationships among various aspects of adolescent development. This leads to more fruitful research hypotheses. Second, when intervention is feasible, a more realistic and potentially successful search for facilitative measures can be undertaken if the source from which distressing developmental problems arise can be identified.

Acceptance of adolescence as a distinct stage in personality development also predetermines and limits the types of problems appropriate for our classification. For by definition we can be concerned only with developmental issues that are uniquely relevant to this period of personality growth. This approach contradicts in no way the well-established generalization that developmental continuity must necessarily prevail between adolescence and the age periods that precede and follow it (Baltes & Schaie, 1973; Goulet & Baltes, 1970; Nesselroade & Reese, 1973). It simply means that in delimiting our field we shall consider only those aspects of childhood that impinge directly on the unique developmental tasks of adolescence or those aspects of adult development that are crucially affected by the outcome of the latter.

ADOLESCENCE AS A TRANSITIONAL PERIOD

In the present era of psychological sophistication, no more than a casual acquaintance with the facts of adolescence is required to realize that this stage of human development is a *biosocial* phenomenon. Biologically, it is a period of accelerated physical and sexual maturation that humans experience *in common* with each other and with all other mammalian species. Its social foundations, however, are manifested in the *contrast* it presents between human societies and in comparison to pubescence in other species. Everywhere human adolescence is an institutionalized phenomenon, a socially recognized period of transitional status, although the specific form that it takes varies with differences in culturally held values. For example, even among the Samoans, who, according to Mead (1928; p. 65) experience their adolescence in a carefree and nonconflictual manner, the period of adolescence is socially recognized and set apart.

The community [of Samoa] ignores both boys and girls from birth until they are fifteen or sixteen years of age. Children under this age have no social standing, no recognized group activities, no part in the social life except when they are conscripted for the informal dance floor. But at a year or two beyond puberty. . . both boys and girls are grouped into a rough approximation of the adult groupings, given a name for their organization and are invested with definite obligations and privileges in the community life.

The transition from child to adult among infrahumans is a little investigated area. There is some evidence to indicate that in many species there is, indeed, a transitional period from child to adult, and an examination of these periods reveals both important differences and striking similarities between human adolescence and its counterpart among infrahumans (see McKinney, 1977, for a brief discussion of "animal adolescence"). In contrast to human adolescents, juvenile or subadult animals seem to be more under the control of biological and physiological factors, although the behavior of many species of higher animals is not simply the result of hormonal action but is also learned and modified through experience. For example, most species of monkeys engage in a great deal of infantile sexual play, although the frequency and character of that behavior undergo a dramatic change from play to adult sexuality after puberty (Ford & Beach, 1951). Developmentally, the learning that takes place in the adolescence of many primates seems to be less a learning of new skills or a practicing of old ones than a transformation of child-like behavior into adult-like behavior (Poirier, 1972). At the very least we should be prepared to admit that adolescence as a period of development may not be a uniquely human phenomenon, although only in the human species has this period become an institutionalized and socially recognized time of waiting and preparation.

PSYCHOBIOLOGICAL PROBLEMS

The terms *psychobiological* and *psychosocial* usually imply concern with the psychological and behavioral consequences of the biological or social factors influencing the individual. Although this distinction is a perfectly justifiable attempt to consider separately the biological and social causes of behavior, we think that most behavior is the result of an interaction between both biological and social factors. [A theoretical attempt to untangle this interaction has been presented elsewhere (Ausubel & Sullivan, 1970).] Because the human species is unique in undergoing development within environmental conditions that differ greatly from culture to culture, it is not meaningful to talk about species uniformities and differences as such. A more productive approach is to inquire why and in what ways development (1) is similar in all cultures, (2) differs from one culture to another, (3) is very similar for most individuals within a culture, and (4) varies for individuals within a culture.

In order to deal with these different types of developmental uniformities and differences, we will use the following classification. The term *psychobiological* will refer to intercultural uniformities in development. In general, psychobiological traits are determined by the interaction between (1) certain genic predispositions and potentialities that all human beings share, and (2) certain universal features of their physical, interpersonal, and cultural environments. The term *psychosocial* will pertain to intercultural differences and intracultural uniformities in development. Psychosocial traits are those traits that reflect the influence of the particular or unique customs, values, institutions, and social conditions prevailing within a given culture (Ausubel & Sullivan, 1970).

That adolescence should be characterized by a common core of psychobiological problems in a wide diversity of cultural settings is hardly surprising. There are a number of reasons for this. First, almost without exception the period of adolescence is recognized as the appropriate time for initiating the changes in personality status that will transform the child into an adult member of his community. Although the particular constellation of personality traits characteristic of adults may differ from society to society, there is a general increase during adolescence of maturity and independence and a granting to the individual of greater social and economic status. In general the adolescent acquires new rights, privileges, and prerogatives and becomes more of an economic asset. This change in status (which is equivalent to the eventual acquisition of full rather than limited membership in the adult community) is everywhere made necessary by the need of parents to be relieved of permanent responsibility for their offspring, and by the need of the culture to equip a new generation to maintain the continuity of the social order. These shifts in status are bound to constitute a set of developmental common denominators regardless of differences in degree conditioned by cultural factors. Hence, we can anticipate that this general tendency toward enhancement of the adolescent's socioeconomic status will give rise to common inflationary changes in his self-estimate and status aspirations. It will also motivate both parents and social agencies to institute the types of training procedures best calculated to develop the personality traits commensurate with the increased responsibilities of his new status roles.

Central among these traits that home and culture strive to instill in the individual is a desire for status based on his own merit, performance, ability, and competence as a person in his own right, rather than for reflected status derived from a mere dependent relationship to parents. Internalization of this need by the adolescent motivates him to acquire those supportive attributes of personality structure that will help him realize his newly acquired aspirations.

A second source of psychobiological uniformity in the problems of adolescent development is to be found in the common group of physiological and anatomical changes that are everywhere associated with the occurrence of pubescence. These changes give rise to new types of drives, emotions, and states of awareness. Granted that these psychological phenomena will assume different forms and be differently regulated in different cultures, the fact remains that there is a universal need for adolescents to adapt to the very presence of these bodily changes and urges, to overcome feelings of bewilderment and uneasiness at their strangeness, and to subject them to control and direction in ways that are compatible with social expectations. For the first time since early childhood, potent, emergent drives of organic origin require initial handling and socialization; and like all other drives, the direction of their regulation proceeds from the relatively diffuse, experimental, and nonspecific mode of gratification to the more highly differentiated condition where, to be adequate, the form of need satisfaction must meet increasingly more stringent requirements of specificity.

Finally, a cross-cultural survey of adolescent development reveals that even when marked differences in social environment prevail, there is an unmistakable trend for personality development to proceed along roughly parallel lines. The basis for this developmental change is an interaction among developing cognitive abilities which allows the individual to more ably understand himself and his social world, in addition to the experience of participating in his social group. This interaction results in the development of certain personality traits that are more appropriate than others for promoting the physical survival of the individual and the group, and for perpetuating the ideals and way of life of a particular culture. Since the maintenance of any society requires certain social obligations from its members, it is not surprising that in these respects the social ideal of adult maturity will be similar for most cultures, and that social pressure will be exerted on the individual to make him conform to this ideal. For example, most cultures have a vested interest in developing an individual who can manifest independence and responsibility in making decisions and meeting his needs, who can postpone the desire for immediate pleasurable gratification in favor of striving for long-range objectives valued by the group, and who is capable of deferring to the moral authority of the society.

Thus far, we have presented only general reasons for believing that there must be psychobiological problems of adolescent development. Detailed discussion of these problems will be found in later sections and chapters dealing with psychological transition, physiological changes, physical growth, and personality maturation.

PSYCHOSOCIAL PROBLEMS

In the realm of psychosocial problems belong those more specific aspects of adolescent development that are especially conditioned by the special nature of the cultural environment. Here we are concerned with factors accounting for differences rather than for uniformities in the developmental process among cultures. Following the procedure adopted above, we shall examine here only the general sources of such differences, leaving for later chapters detailed treatment of particular psychosocial problems of adolescence with special reference to their manifestations in our own society.

In the first place, although the period of adolescence receives social recognition in every culture, there are marked differences in the degree of this recognition in the types of rituals, training measures, and initiation rites (Muuss, 1970); differences in the content, complexity, length, and rigorousness of the latter; and differences in the relative degrees of emphasis placed on maturation of boys as against girls. For example, among the Trukese when a boy reaches puberty he merely dons a red loincloth and goes to live in the men's house (Goodenough, 1951). Among the Apache Indians, a change of status is not so simple. "The adult men force him [an adolescent boy] to make holes in the ice and bathe, run with water in his mouth, humiliate him on his trial war parties and generally bully him" (Benedict, 1934, p. 94).

Second, these differences are closely related to the specific ideals of adult maturity in different social settings. The Trukese place a great deal of emphasis on status and rank and on acting according to one's class. The Apaches were a warrior society emphasizing courage and physical aggression particularly for males. It stands to reason that the form and content of indoctrination procedures will vary necessarily depending on which adult roles are especially valued (aggressive and competitive, mercantile, spiritual, altruistic, etc.). Every society undertakes in its own way to control and direct the period of adolescence by confronting the pubescent individual with a unique set of social demands and expectations reinforced by appropriate training procedures and institutions. And in every instance it is confidently expected that the graduating adult will embody the particular constellation of traits and virtues that the culture has selected as most befitting the mature members of its community.

Third, as already indicated, cultural differences inevitably arise because of the different ways in which newly emerging drives and emotions of physiological origin are handled and regulated by various ethnic and social groups. Such differences are exemplified in the adequacy of the opportunities afforded for gratification of these needs, the specific kinds of feelings, goal objects, and purposeful behavior with which they may legitimately be identified, the types and stringency of restrictions and taboos that are imposed, and the degree of repression required. For example, among the Kowoma of New Guinea, young boys are constantly warned not to play with their genitals. If a woman sees a boy with an erection she will beat his penis with a stick, and boys soon learn not to touch their genitals even while urinating (Ford & Beach, 1951). In contrast, the parents of Chewa children of Africa believe that unless their children begin to exercise themselves sexually early in life they will never beget offspring. Preadolescents build little huts away from their village, and there, with the complete approval of their parents, boys and girls play at being husband and wife, presumably engaging in sex play (Ford & Beach, 1951). Although the sexual attitudes and behavior of Kowoma and Chewa children are polar opposites, the appearance of the adult sexual drive in pubescence must so alter the experience of sexuality for Chewa adolescents, and for all adolescents, as to make all previous encounters mere dry runs. Chewa adolescents may find the transition into adult sexuality easier and less traumatic than Kowoma adolescents; however, both groups are faced with the common task of understanding and controlling this powerful new drive.

Fourth, it is apparent that although adolescence manifests many general structural properties of psychological transition that can be found in any culture, marked individual differences in content will nevertheless prevail among cultures. This is the result of the fact that the distinguishing features of developmental transition are crucially affected in their quantitative aspects by numerous social factors. Hence, the *degree* of abruptness, prolongation, difficulty, and stress of adolescence will vary in accordance with the particular ideals of adult maturity and the particular kinds of training procedures, institutions, and drive-regulating norms that are in force in a given social environment.

Finally, as Ausubel (1950b) has pointed out, certain transitory historical phenomena bearing no particular relation to adolescence may nevertheless profoundly affect the development of adolescents. Temporary occurrences such as war, economic depression, or a change in the social structure may alter and distort the typical experience of a generation of adolescents, and may result in significant and lasting changes in personality. The Vietnam war affected most adolescents growing up in the United States in the late 1960s. The occurrence of political protest, the development of antiestablishment values, and the appearance of a "counter culture" lead some social commentators to conclude that the period of youth itself had been permanently altered and that protest and alienation had become normative aspects of the adolescent experience (Keniston, 1971). Hindsight indicates that this conclusion was premature and that the tension between youth and society was a direct outgrowth of the Vietnam war and was not a typical characteristic of the adolescent period. Although research is currently in progress investigating the long-term effects of growing up in the 1960s, it is clearly true that many individuals growing up during that period experienced an unusually conflictual and violent adolescence.

PSYCHOBIOLOGICAL VERSUS PSYCHOSOCIAL PROBLEMS

Distinguishing between the underlying structural psychobiological problems of adolescence on the one hand and the form, content, or psychosocial expression of those problems on the other may shed some light on some long-standing controversies within the field of adolescent psychology and may aid in our understanding of adolescent development. There is much disagreement concerning whether or not "storm and stress" is an inevitable part of adolescence within our own culture and universal in all cultures. Some writers discuss the "shock of puberty" (Nixon, 1966) or the trauma of adolescence (Gustin, 1961). These authors suggest that heightened emotionality, conflict, and self-absorption are intrinsic and inevitable aspects of the adolescent experience. This traditional view has been challenged by many, in particular by Albert Bandura (1964). Bandura could find little evidence of trauma among a sample of middle-class adolescent boys. He suggests that our cultural stereotypes of adolescents in general as rebels against parental authority and as antiestablishment nonconformists are not supported by the facts. Instead, Bandura found that most of the boys he studied had internalized their parents' goals and values, had selected friends whom their parents approve of, and in general had experienced little conflict.

More recently, Offer and Offer (1975) have studied the personality development of a group of males from their entrance into high school until their middle twenties. The Offers describe three patterns of personality development with varying degrees of conflict associated with each pattern. *Continuous growth:* The subjects with a continuous growth pattern progressed throughout their adolescence with a sense of purpose and self-assurance. These individuals were usually happy and contented and were able to cope well with internal and external problems. *Surgent growth:* These subjects exerted more energy toward mastering developmental tasks than did the continuous growth group. At times these students seemed to be adjusting very well to internal and external pressures. However, at other times they seemed to be overwhelmed by events and unable to progress. *Tumultuous growth:* These individuals experienced a good deal of conflict and turmoil. They were poorly adjusted with poor defenses. These subjects coped poorly with frustration and manifested a great many behavioral problems in school and at home.

It seems clear that the experience and overt expression of conflict and stress during adolescence is not indigenous to the period itself but varies with the adolescent's adjustive capacity to cope with change and with the external social supports available to the adolescent. Adolescence is universally a transitional period, requiring of all adolescents an adjustment to their changing biosocial status. Certain psychobiological problems such as growth, sexuality, and a changing social status force the adolescent to examine and redefine himself. Whether this examination and redefinition shall be painful or pleasant, active or passive, loud or quiet, will depend on those unique personal and social factors that produce differences between individuals and societies.

THE CHIEF DEVELOPMENTAL TASKS
OF ADOLESCENCE

Thus far we have tried to show that adolescence is a distinctive period of personality development that includes certain unique and universal developmental changes requiring extensive reorganization of personality structure. This reorganization is made necessary by the adolescent's changing biosocial status, i.e., changes in biological and physiological makeup, and the acquisition of adult status. It will be useful to examine this reorganization more specifically by considering the problems, difficulties, or developmental tasks that the adolescent must successfully solve before adult status can be realized. There is a surprising degree of unanimity on what the primary developmental tasks of adolescence are.

Havighurst defines developmental tasks as the skills, knowledge, functions, and attitudes that an individual must acquire at a certain time during development in order to continue to advance to higher levels of development. Failure to master a set of tasks appropriate for a specific developmental level will result in poor adjustment and the inability to solve later tasks. Tasks appropriate for individuals at different age periods are based on the general maturational level of individuals within that age period and the societal expectations for those individuals. According to Havighurst (1951, pp. 30–55) the developmental tasks for the period of adolescence include the following:

1. accepting one's physique and accepting a masculine or feminine role;
2. developing new relations with age mates of both sexes;
3. establishing emotional independence of parents and other adults;
4. achieving assurance of economic independence;
5. selecting and preparing for an occupation;
6. developing intellectual skills and concepts necessary for civic competence;
7. desiring and achieving socially responsible behavior;
8. preparing for marriage and family life;
9. building conscious values in harmony with an adequate scientific world picture.

We would not attempt to deny that the developmental tasks of Havighurst are the essential and unavoidable tasks that adolescents are required to complete in the course of their transition to adult maturity. We would prefer, however, to relate these developmental tasks to more general developmental changes that are taking place in personality structure, such as the greater need for volitional independence and a self-determined status, the devaluation of hedonistic motivation, and the increased capacity for sustained striving in relation to long-term goals. Looked at in this way, developmental tasks are the areas of life adjustment in which the gains of adolescent personality development must be applied before the various component requirements of adult status can be met. For example, Havighurst's tasks can be thought of as different and mutually complementary ways in which the enhanced need for self-assertion can be satisfied. So regarded, they acquire greater generality of meaning in relation to the underlying personality changes of adolescence than when considered merely as separate objectives of adjustment that development during this period should be expected to accomplish.

METHODS OF OBTAINING DEVELOPMENTAL DATA
IN ADOLESCENCE

Case study

The case study method involves a careful description of the behavior of one person and achieves a depth of information not usually available with other methods of data collection. From the intimate knowledge thus gained of the interrelationships among significant aspects of an individual's developmental history, personality structure, and overt behavior, it is often possible to acquire valuable insights into the nature of personality development and behavioral adjustment. Kenneth Keniston's classic studies (1965b, 1968) of adolescent alienation and political activism provide fine examples of the depth and richness of information that can be obtained by an experienced clinician who interviews and tests individual subjects. However, we must be careful about drawing conclusions from particular adolescents to adolescents in general. Case studies may be used as illustrations, or examples, or as material from which we might derive hypotheses. However, the data of a case study cannot be used as a test of a hypothesis or of a theory, nor can the conclusions derived from a case study legitimately be applied to human behavior in gneral. The data from case studies are oftentimes based on individuals who were systematically selected by an experimenter precisely because they illustrate some theoretical proposition. Thus, case studies are not only small samples ($N = 1$) but also often biased samples. In addition, comparisons with other individuals are rarely made. Therefore, it is impossible to know if the particular interrelationship of characteristics in one individual is typical of all individuals, or if it is unique and idiosyncratic.

Cross-sectional designs

Most developmental studies in adolescent psychology have employed a cross-sectional approach in measuring the growth of psychological characteristics and behavioral capacities. This method, in brief, seeks to chart the growth of a particular characteristic by comparing mean observations or measurements of different groups varying in age. In studies of adolescent development, such growth curves are most frequently based on data obtained from a number of different grade levels ranging from junior high school to college. The attractiveness of this method lies in its relative ease, availability, and inexpensiveness. Unfortunately, serious errors may be made when attempting to derive developmental conclusions from cross-sectional data.

According to Nunnally (1973) there are two major reasons for collecting data cross-sectionally. First, the investigator may be interested in estimating age differences in certain attitudes or characteristics for a population at one particular point in time. For example, the results of surveys of political, social, and economic attitudes of Americans taken by pollsters such as Harris and Gallup are often reported by age. Assuming that the different age groups are comparable (e.g., 20-year-old college students are not compared with 40-year-old blue collar workers), and that the questions are phrased in such a way that they mean the same thing to all individuals (e.g., "Have you ever used dope?" may be interpreted as referring to marijuana by a college student or to heroin by a 40-year-old), we may legitimately conclude that whatever differences are found reflect true age differences for a particular population at a particular time. Since measures are not taken on the same individuals at many points in time, it would be erroneous to speak of developmental changes from data gathered cross-sectionally.

A second reason investigators use cross-sectional designs is to attempt to map out developmental changes, recognizing that final conclusions regarding ontogenetic changes may be obtained only from longitudinal studies. For example, the data reported in Figure 2-1 are based on a cross-sectional study of intellectual ability. This graph has been interpreted to indicate that intelligence increases until late adolescence and then begins to decline from that time onward.

There are two possible problems with this interpretation. First, the sample of individuals comprising each age group may not be representative of the population from which they were drawn. A systematic sampling error of the type that individuals with low intellectual ability were more likely to be included in samples of older people than younger people would account for an apparent decline in intelligence with age when no real decline in intellectual ability may exist. Although this problem of unrepresentative samples may be partly alleviated by careful sampling procedures, a researcher can never be certain that his population estimates for different populations are equally accurate. For this reason, one should be extremely cautious in attempting to draw developmental conclusions from cross-sectional data.

A second, and more subtle, type of problem concerning cross-sectional data involves the possible effects of the interaction of age at time of testing and generation of subjects. The individuals from whom the curve in Fig. 2-1 was obtained differ not only in age but

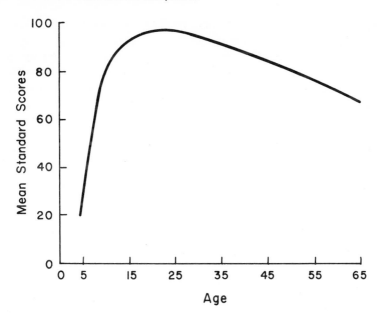

Fig. 2-1. Age differences on the Wechsler Bellevue Intelligence Scale (Adapted from Wechsler, 1944).

also in generation, or common developmental history. For example, if the hypothetical data in Fig. 2-1 were collected in 1945, then those individuals who were 25 years old would have been born in 1920, whereas those people who were 35 years old would have been born in 1910. The 35-year-olds would have spent their childhood growing up during World War I, but the 25-year-olds would have grown up during the relative calm of the early 1920s. These different cultural conditions might partly account for differences in the development of the trait, e.g., intellectual ability. If this were true then we would not conclude that 35-year-olds are not as bright as 25-year-olds, but rather that the 35-year-olds who grew up during World War I are not as smart as the 25-years-olds who did not grow up during that war. We shall return to this general type of problem when we discuss another developmental design.

Longitudinal designs

Longitudinal studies have two advantages over cross-sectional studies for investigating age changes. First, they permit a direct analysis of age changes of a particular characteristic for individuals. Since the *same* characteristic is measured in the same individuals at two or more points in time, it is possible to make more valid statements about ontogenetic changes. Second, longitudinal studies do not have the sampling problem that cross-sectional studies have. The major problem in cross-sectional studies is obtaining representative samples for each age studied. In a longitudinal study one sample of individuals is studied at many different ages, completely eliminating the sampling problem. It is of course true that developmental changes obtained from longitudinal studies are representative only of the population from which the original sample was drawn. Thus, steps should be taken to ensure that the sample to be studied longitudinally is not atypical or deviant.

Two major criticisms can be leveled against longitudinal studies. First, "practice effects" may partly contribute to apparent developmental changes. For example, individuals may obtain higher scores on some tests simply because they are taking the test over again and have become "test wise," and not because of any real change in their ability. Thus, individuals who are measured many times on the same test may show some improvement even though their actual ability remains the same. Practice effects are usually not a problem when the interval between testing is long. A second class of problems concerns the practical difficulties of maintaining a long-term longitudinal study. It is virtually impossible to obtain a 100 percent participation rate in a study that continues for many years. As time goes by, more and more subjects drop out of the study either because they lose interest in the project and no longer want to participate or because they move away and cannot be located. If there is a systematic loss of certain kinds of subjects or if the dropout rate is excessive, then the results of a longitudinal study can be called into question.

Another kind of problem involves the difficulty of obtaining financial support for a project that may be very expensive and may take many years to complete. This along with the fact that few investigators are motivated to undertake research that may not even be completed in their own lifetime makes large-scale, elaborate, long-term longitudinal studies somewhat unfeasible.

In order to overcome some of these practical problems, investigators have employed a mixed design which combines the power of the longitudinal design with the economy of the cross-sectional design. In this kind of design two or more groups of individuals are studied longitudinally with the age of the second group beginning where the age of the first group ends. For example, we might study the change in some characteristic in a group of students as they progress from their freshman year in high school to their senior year in high school, and, at the same time, study another group of students for the same characteristic as they progress from their freshman year in college to their senior year in college. The data that we obtain from these students may tell us something about the course of development for this characteristic from the freshman year in high school to the senior year in college. The primary advantage with a mixed design is time. For the example cited here, an 8-year developmental sequence can be studied in only 4 years. Although conclusions about ontogenetic changes may be drawn from studies with a mixed design, it is important to recognize that such conclusions may properly be applied only to subjects in a given historical era. We might ask if these same changes occurred for students in the 1950s or 1940s. To generalize from one historical era to another requires a cross-sequential design, which we shall now discuss.

Cross-sequential designs

Longitudinal studies share one common shortcoming—they are concerned with measuring individual change and they neglect the possible effects of cultural change. Since individuals live in a changing world, some degree of individual change may be the result of cultural change. For example, it is often said that our country is becoming more violent and that people today are more aggressive than people 10 years ago. If an investigator were interested in examining the development of aggressiveness in individuals, and if the investigator had some reason to think that our society as a whole was becoming more aggressive, then it would be necessary to employ a technique of investigation which allowed for the effects of both individual and cultural change to be separately measured and evaluated. This kind of developmental technique is known as a *sequential strategy* (Baltes, 1968; Schaie, 1965, 1970). Although there are three sequential strategies, the most important for our purposes in the cross-sequential design.

A cross-sequential design is a series of longitudinal measurements taken on individuals who comprise different birth cohorts. A cohort is a group of people born at the same time or between an arbitrary period of time. This kind of design allows the investigator to observe changes due to ontogenetic factors apart from changes due to cohort or generation differences. A recent investigation of adolescent personality development may illustrate the elegance and power of the cross-sequential design.

Nesselroad and Baltes (1974) were interested in examing the relative contributions of ontogenetic and cohort (generation) related

Table 2-1

Time of Testing for Different Cohorts of
Subjects at Different Ages

		Age of Subjects					
		13	14	15	16	17	18
	1957	1970	1971	1972			
Cohort	1956		1970	1971	1972		
	1955			1970	1971	1972	
	1954				1970	1971	1972

Adapted from Nesselroade & Baltes, 1974.

components to adolescent personality development during the period 1970–1972. Four cohorts (adolescents born in 1954, 1955, 1956, or 1957) were longitudinally tested at three different times (1970, 1971, and 1972). Table 2-1 illustrates the design of this study.

A battery of personality tests were administered to the adolescents in this study during the years shown in Table 2-1. The design of this study allowed for the effects of two types of developmental changes to be observed. First, what ontogenetic changes in personality development occurred between the ages of 13 and 18 years? Second, what changes in the personality of adolescents as a group occurred between the years 1970 and 1972? The results indicated that chronological age was a less important factor in adolescent personality development than was historical change, during the time period under investigation. It was found that regardless of age, adolescents showed a significant decrement in superego strength, social-emotional anxiety, and achievement from 1970 to 1972 and an increase in independence during this same time interval. These results indicate the utility of the cross-sequential design, and point to the necessity of considering individual change in the context of cultural change.

CONCLUSION

Logically, before obtaining definitive evidence in the field of adolescent psychology, it is necessary to relate research efforts to integrative hypotheses derived from a comprehensive theoretical orientation to the nature of adolescent development. Only in this way can we hope to find meaningful answers to crucial questions in this area with a reasonable economy of effort. One of the major purposes of this book, therefore, is an attempt to formulate a systematic theory of adolescence, which lays claim to some logical plausibility, which is consistent with general principles of developmental psychology, and which is in accord with and capable of being tested by empirical findings on adolescents.

Only after a high level of theoretical sophistication is reached will it be possible to test strong hypotheses concerning adolescent development. This will require the use of more representative experimental populations and the more extensive use of cross-sequential and longitudinal designs than has characterized most studies in this field to date. The cross-sectional approach can also provide valid data in many problem areas, provided experimental or statistical controls can be introduced to ensure comparability of age groups. Individual case studies are chiefly valuable as a source of fruitful hypotheses; but if the data from a sufficient number of case studies are consolidated and kept free of retrospective error, they can be treated in much the same way as longitudinal data for special subgroups.

3

Problems of Psychological Transition

THE MEANING OF PSYCHOLOGICAL TRANSITION

Since all natural phenomena are in a state of continual flux, we could with justice characterize the whole of development as transitional. However, this absolute use of the term would serve no useful purpose in elucidating the nature of change. But inasmuch as there is always marked variability in the rate and type of development, it is worthwhile and meaningful to distinguish between periods of relative stability and periods of rapid change, between states of being and states of becoming. Change does occur in the former condition but within a framework of qualitative constancy—in quantitative increments or decrements that do not upset the prevailing structure. However, when the rate of change accelerates markedly because of a sudden shift in the direction of development or when the old personality structures no longer appear adequate, disequilibrium sets in until the newly evolving form becomes sufficiently synthesized and consolidated to constitute a relatively stable and permanent state of being. Customarily, then, the latter situation is referred to when the term *transition* is used.

In personality development, periods of transition occur when significant changes take place in the biosocial status of the individual. Such changes generally occur in the interval between infancy and childhood, between childhood and adult life, and between the adult period and sensecence. During these transitional periods, the individual is in the marginal position of having lost an established and accustomed status and of not yet having acquired the new status toward which the factors impelling developmental change are driving him. The adolescent, for example, enjoys the status of neither child nor adult. To be sure, he is not entirely without any status whatsoever, for that, too, would be impossible; but the status that he does enjoy is vague, ambiguous, and rapidly changing. It is hardly comparable to the relatively permanent and stable type of relationship that prevails between him and his environment in the preceding and succeeding stages of his development; it is primarily a state of becoming rather than a state of being.

Theoretically, there is every reason to believe that transitional periods must necessarily be difficult and productive of stress. If the biosocial status of an individual determines his overall relationship to his environment, it must by definition provide a comprehensive and stable frame of reference for the organization of his attitudes, values, goals, and behavior. In this framework, which lasts long enough to become both familiar and highly differentiated, he feels oriented and secure in interpreting and reacting to the events that go on around him. He knows what he expects of others and what others expect of him, and he has learned values and roles that are compatible with these expectations. He develops a set of attitudes toward himself as well as a characteristic constellation of motivational traits designed to implement these attitudes. It is hardly conceivable that the impending loss of this status could fail to be anything but disorganizing and traumatic in its effects. Can he reasonably expect to find the same degree of security and experience similar feelings of confidence and orientation in a new and uncharted psychological field, the landmarks and limits of which are obscure and hazy? On what defensible basis can he learn appropriate new attitudes, goals, values, and roles when he enjoys no clear status against which to measure their suitability? And even if unambiguous criteria were available, would not a tremendous burden of new learning still fall to his lot?

The transitional difficulties of insecurity and disorientation, of having to learn a whole new set of adaptive cues and habits, give rise to a new cause for stress, namely, a growing disinclination for change. This resistance from within to surrendering the security of an established status comes into conflict with potent pressures for change that are both internal and external in origin. Hence arises a conflictful sphere of overlapping needs and loyalties, a psychological marginality of disposition to match the environmental marginality of status, As Lewin (1946) puts it:

Many conflicts in childhood are due to forces corresponding to the various groups to which the child belongs. Such conflicts are particularly important for children in marginal positions, that is, for children who are standing on the boundary between two groups. One example is the adolescent who no longer wants to belong to the children's group but who is not yet fully accepted by the adults. Uncertainty of the ground on which the child stands leads to an alternation between the values of the other group, to a state of emotional tension, and to a frequent fluctuation between overaggressiveness and overtimidity. The degree to which such adolescent behavior is shown depends upon the degree to which children and adolescents are treated as separate groups in that culture.

TRANSITIONAL ANXIETY

In addition to feelings of insecurity and disorientation and the sudden need for new adaptive learnings that inevitably accompany the onset of a transitional period in development, still another reason for stress is inherent in psychological transition. The source of this stress is to be found in the relationships that prevail among status, self-esteem, and anxiety.

According to William James, the *self-esteem* of an individual is largely a reflection of his aspirations for status and of the discrepancy existing between these aspirations and his actual or potential possession of status. His level of self-esteem tends to be high when the status he enjoys is commensurate with his aspirations, and tends to be low when the opposite condition prevails. Hence, self-esteem is threatened by situations that either endanger present and potential status or create aspirations for new status which are disproportionately high in relation to realistic possibilities for successful attainment.* When the threat to self-esteem becomes sufficiently great to be reacted to emotionally, it evokes a variety of fear response that can be best characterized as a state of anxiety. Transitional anxiety, therefore, refers to the fear reactions produced by factors inhering in periods of psychological transition that significantly threaten an individual's self-esteem.

During adolescence, for example, there are at least two good reasons for the generation of transitional anxiety. First, the adolescent

---

*An example of this latter situation occurs in some cultures such as our own where the adolescent fails to appreciate at the outset that the attainment of adult status will not only be delayed for many years but also will probably not be achieved at the level of social prestige to which he has been encouraged to aspire. However, since this is not a universal consequence of psychological transition, it will be discussed in relation to psychosocial problems of adolescence.

is required to repudiate the major source of socially acceptable status that was available to him as a child, the derived status that vicariously accrued to him because of his dependent relationship to his parents. He becomes obliged instead to seek status as a person in his own right, a status based on his own competence in adjusting to the demands of his environment. As a result of this shift there is an immediate loss in current status that threatens his self-esteem and is reacted to with fear.

Second, the culture almost universally created transitional anxiety for the adolescent by generating an aura of uncertainty about his ultimate attainment of adult status. He is coerced by the relentless pressure of social expectations into internalizing a new set of ego aspirations that are compatible with the status characteristics of adult maturity in his particular social milieu. But the eventual outcome of his strivings is always in doubt until success is finally achieved. The culture is extremely careful always to guarantee nothing from the start, to hold the benefits of future status in abeyance until final discretionary judgment is rendered. In view of the crucial issue at stake—the absolute necessity for achieving adult status and the catastrophic consequences of failure to do so—the adolescent finds even the slightest uncertainty threatening to his self-esteem and hence productive of anxiety.* He can reduce this anxiety (but never completely eliminate it) by maintaining a high level of striving in relation to the developmental tasks confronting him. Hence, although anxiety in this context is disagreeable for the individual, it undoubtedly serves a "socially-adaptive" function (Davis, 1944). Regardless of whether it is deliberately used as a training device, and quite apart from its implications for mental hygiene, it would be difficult to deny its effectiveness in keeping the course of adolescent maturation moving in the appropriate direction and at the expected rate of progress, whatever these may be in a particular cultural environment.

TEMPORAL FACTORS INFLUENCING THE DIFFICULTY OF PSYCHOLOGICAL TRANSITION

Three other important characteristics of psychological transition that affect the difficulty of adjusting to it are (1) the abruptness of its onset, (2) discrepancies in the rate of growth of various component

---

*Part of the fear response evoked in this situation is precipitated by the individual's anticipation of a threat to his physical safety and biological well-being rather than to his self-esteem. This type of fear can be referred to more appropriately as insecurity rather than anxiety.

functions, and (3) the total length of time it occupies. All three factors define crucial temporal dimensions of transitional periods. In addition, the first two factors, although extremely variable from culture to culture, may be said to be inherent in the very nature of transition. That is, almost by definition, transitional phases of development begin abruptly because of a sudden change in the rate or direction of growth, which is discontinuous with the preceding stage; and when the developmental process is sufficiently complex to encompass several constituent aspects, discrepancies in rate of growth are practically inevitable. The duration of the transitional period, on the other hand, is a completely variable dimension. To be characteristic of psychological transition the period need not be either relatively long or relatively short, since either is equally compatible with the essential properties of transitional states. However, the actual length of time involved, as will be shown below, is one of the important variables affecting both the stressfulness of transition and some of its subsidiary properties.

Abruptness of onset

Abruptness of onset is a characteristic feature of adolescent development in all cultures. This is true even though many aspects of maturation are inaugurated in the middle years of childhood and undergo preparatory completion during the preadolescent period. Although much variability prevails in this respect, children everywhere follow the general pattern of acquiring with age greater responsibility and self-sufficiency, more responsiveness to social norms, and increased capacity for postponing the gratification of hedonistic needs. In most cultures, also, children have the opportunity of gaining some degree of status in relation to the objective level of their abilities and accomplishments, and sometimes in relation to the actual contributions they are able to make to the economic life of the family or community.

Hence, since the beginnings of most adolescent changes in personality maturation can be traced to earlier periods of development, it is not possible to attribute the abrupt onset of adolescence to a sudden need for incorporating into personality structure a completely alien set of norms for the appropriate characteristics of mature behavior. The abruptness inheres, rather, in the accelerated rate of maturational change and in the sudden shift in context and importance which these developments assume for the total economy of personality organization. Imbedded in a new framework of social expectations for the appropriate content and balance of adult personality structure, the same components of maturation abruptly acquire new meaning and significance. It makes a great deal of difference, for example, whether the earned* status one achieves through one's own efforts and competence plays a relatively subsidiary role vis-à-vis the derived status one receives by virtue of a dependent relationship to parents, or becomes the major variety of status which one can legitimately possess; whether the quest for this earned status is undertaken by a sexually immature child volitionally dependent on his parents and enjoying no recognized position in the adult community, or by a biologically mature individual who is intended eventually to assume full responsibility for his own decisions and to enjoy complete recognition as a responsible member of the adult social group; whether childish irresponsibility, hedonism, and helplessness are relinquished as a means of placating parents and gaining their approval, or are given up as a necessary adjunctive step in the acquisition of the appurtenances of adult status.

Adolescence, in other words, begins abruptly because adult and childhood personality structures are qualitatively discontinuous in terms of total gestalt rather than in terms of their component constituents. A break with the past is therefore inevitable. It is true, of course, that this break could be made more gradual if the necessary changes in emphasis were introduced less drastically and over a longer period of time. However, the almost invariable relationship between pubescence and the termination of childhood personality status makes this impossible. The dramatic physical and sexual changes of pubescence give impetus to powerful individual and social pressures directed toward the reorganization of personality structure. Moreover, since these biological changes are accomplished within a relatively short space of time, the correlative pressures they generate for personality change are set in motion just as abruptly; for example, parents suddenly withdraw unconditional emotional succor and make vastly increased demands for mature behavior. Thus, although the period of adolescent development may, depending on cultural circumstances, be prolonged for a decade or more, its initiation tends to be characteristically abrupt.

Degree of abruptness obviously affects the difficulty of psychological transition by giving rise to more or less disorientation, insecurity, and anxiety, and by providing more or less time and opportunity for the learning of appropriate adaptive responses. It differs not only

---

*From this point on, the terms *earned* and *derived status* will be used, respectively, to distinguish between the actual status that an individual earns through his own competencies and efforts as an independent adult and the status that accrues to him vicariously merely because of a dependent relationship to parents.

from culture to culture but also from one transitional period to the next, and accounts in large measure for differences experienced in stressful qualities between both cultures and age periods. The transition between adulthood and sensecence (the period of involution) is generally less abrupt than the transition between either infancy and childhood or childhood and adulthood; hence, it is not surprising that for most individuals, the involutional period is less turbulent than the two earlier transitional phases of development. We shall also point out later that the almost complete discontinuity between the value systems of children and adults that prevails in our own culture (as well as in certain more primitive cultures such as the Manus) is partly responsible for the unique degree of stress characteristic of adolescent development under such social conditions.

Duration of adolescence

The duration of adolescence is not to be confused with the abruptness of its onset. The latter merely refers to the sharpness of the break that is made from childhood status, to the suddenness with which the transitional period is first inaugurated, to the degree of discontinuity that is experienced when the individual is initially confronted with the task of personality reorganization. How long before the developmental tasks of adolescent are completed, that is, before adult status is finally attained, is an entirely different matter. The difference between the two variables may be made clearer perhaps by reference to a medical analogy. The onset of a disease such as pneumonia, for example, is extremely abrupt in comparison with that of diseases such as cancer or tuberculosis; even a single day before he first reports such violent symptoms as high fever, labored breathing, and severe pain in his chest, the pneumonia patient may experience no noticeable signs of illness. This is in marked contrast to tuberculosis or cancer, which appears so gradually that several weeks or months may elapse before the patient can definitely report a decided change for the worse in his health. The duration of the disease, on the other hand, refers to the interval between initial establishment of the pathological process and eventual recovery or death. This too is highly variable and fluctuates widely for different diseases.

The duration of adolescence is a highly important dimension of ongoing transitional changes, since it not only influences the degree of adjustive difficulty experienced, but also helps determine significant aspects of the status modifications involved. We have characterized adolescence as a state of becoming rather than as a state of being, as an age period without any definite status features of its own, in which the individual is in the marginal position of having to relinquish his childhood status while still acquiring adult status. It is now necessary to qualify this generalization. The indefinite and ambiguous no-man's-land of status is tolerable as described only if self-limited in duration, that is, over a period of weeks or months, as in some primitive cultures in which the total length of adolescence is coextensive with the duration of the initiation rites that mark its occurrence. Under these conditions, "no elaborate interim arrangements need be made" (Ausubel, 1950b).

But if the transitional period is to cover an interval of several years or a decade, such marginal status is no longer psychologically tenable in terms of the prolonged disorientation, insecurity, and anxiety involved. When society is so organized as to require an extended period of adolescent transition, it becomes necessary to formalize a definite interim status. This status occupies a position intermediate between that of childhood and adult life, but it embodies nevertheless certain distinctive characteristics which in a limited sense can be considered as ends in themselves. This provides the adolescent with some recognized social standing, an opportunity for acquiring some current self-esteem, and a tangible frame of reference for selectively accepting certain attitudes, values, and goals and rejecting others.

However, no matter how elaborate and seemingly adequate this interim status may become, it still does not suffice to take from adolescence its transitional and marginal character. For concurrently the individual is still striving to attain the coveted status of an adult, the prerogatives of which society just as carefully keeps beyond his reach. The interim status he enjoys can be no more than a makeshift way station, a temporary stop to make present deprivation more bearable until the real status he seeks becomes available. Thus, the developmental tasks of adolescence are predicated on the attainment of the characteristic features of adult personality status rather than on the accomplishment of those transitory intermediate goals that are designed merely to serve a compensatory adjustive function during the bleak, frustration-laden years of transition. In other words, the adolescent individual strives primarily to become an adult and only incidentally to become an adolescent.

Hence, the prolongation of adolescence cannot do otherwise than add to its stress. Despite the compensations provided by interim status, the major status aspirations of the individual remain unfulfilled; and prolonged status deprivation can lead only to a state of chronic frustration and to a semipermanent condition of transitional anxiety. Thus, even more than to the exaggeratedly abrupt onset of adolescence, its acute emotional instability in modern Western civilization can be attributed to the unparalleled prolongation of its duration.

Discrepancies in growth rate

Although various component aspects of development are undoubtedly interrelated and frequently exhibit a certain amount of parallelism for a given individual in their relative degrees of maturity, it is apparent that even under optimal conditions, discrepancies in rate of growth are inevitable (Ausubel & Sullivan, 1970). "The reasons for this are self-evident. In nature, the characteristics of any growth process are uniquely determined by the special conditions relevant to its development" (Ausubel, 1950). Hence, it is extremely unlikely that the particular constellation of genetic and environmental factors regulating the development of any given trait or capacity would completely overlap the set of regulatory factors involved in the development of any other trait or capacity.

During transitional periods of development, there are further reasons that serious discrepancies in rate of growth will probably arise. As the tempo of development (or decline) accelerates and as discontinuities in the growth patterns of particular functions occur, greater opportunities prevail for wider disparities to develop between the relative levels of maturity attained by these different functions. It is true that the general tendency toward interdependence in the growth processes of component aspects of development tends to diminish this unevenness as developmental equilibrium is gradually restored. Growth spurts also tend to taper off with age, thereby narrowing the maturational gap between two functions. In the meantime, however, at least initially, glaring discrepancies in rate of growth constitute a characteristic and invariable feature of transitional phases of development.

In adolescence such discrepancies are particularly evident because of the important role of biological factors in precipitating the total complex of changes that arise. To begin with, the determinants of physiological and physical growth are much more constant and invariable than the determinants of intellectual, social, or emotional maturity. The physiological (hormonal) changes of adolescence are chiefly regulated by genetic factors, which by and large follow a phylogenetic timetable that is (as far as we know) independent of cultural conditions. All of the other growth functions, however, are largely influenced in their rate of development by the highly variable patterns of stimulation, repression, and expectation that prevail in particular cultural environments. Second, the very fact that the hormonal events of pubescence have important implications for emotional and personality development—both directly by giving rise to new drives, feelings, and states of awareness in the individual and indirectly by arousing new patterns of expectations in others who customarily influence his behavior—guarantees that a substantial portion of the physiological changes of adolescence, as well as of their more immediate physical and psychological consequences, will precede growth in these other aspects of development. Hence, the very interrelatedness of the growth process (in the sense that the maturation of one component may serve as the precipitating stimulus for the maturation of another component) ensures the existence of an initial discrepancy, although it makes for greater parallelism in the total pattern of growth.

There are innumerable examples of unevenness in adolescent development. When growth in one area is a necessary precondition for or stimulant of growth in another area, a certain amount of lag is inevitable. Thus, development of muscle strength lags behind the increase in muscle mass (Stolz & Stolz, 1944), but it precedes the gain in neuromuscular coordination. The growth spurts in social and emotional development necessarily begin after the physiological and physical growth spurts which play so important a role in their evolution. In some cases unevenness in the total growth pattern is caused by the lack of a growth spurt in certain areas. An illustration of this is intellectual development, which is singularly unresponsive to the stimulus of physiological maturation (Jones & Conrad, 1944) but may be adversely affected by emotional instability and the sudden influx of competing interests powered by emerging new drives. Body tissues, such as the genital, which have hardly grown since infancy for lack of adequate physiological stimulation, suddenly "outstrip [all] other body parts in velocity of growth" (Stolz & Stolz, 1944) as hormonal (gonadal) support is provided; other tissues, such as the lymphoid, decline in growth (Harris et al., 1930) as their hormonal support (the thymus gland?) is either reduced or more vigorously counteracted (by the adrenal cortex). Another type of "asynchrony of development as between leg length and stem length, hip width and shoulder width. . . is in all probability idiomatic for each individual throughout the whole span of physical growth" but becomes more noticeable when the rate of growth is accelerated (Stolz & Stolz, 1944).

Discrepancies in rate of growth also occur when biological factors are not involved. In personality development, differences in social attitudes and expectations, in the availability of certain types of status-giving activities, and in the relative flexibility of various social institutions result in marked differences in the maturity levels characterizing the several indices of adult personality status. In our own culture, for example, considerable emancipation from parents' influence on goals, values, and behavior is achieved long before a comparable measure of social and economic recognition is conferred by society at large. Yet even within the home numerous inconsistencies prevail in various aspects of the adolescent's status and independence. Generally speaking, parents are quicker to withdraw emotional support than they are to relinquish the exercise of their traditional authority. They are more intent on demanding from their children the acquisition of adult responsibility, motivations, and values than they are willing to grant commensurate rewards in increased privileges and prerogatives for appropriate accomplishment.

These growth discrepancies are not without their developmental repercussions. Just as maturation in one area may precipitate or facilitate maturation in another area, the converse holds equally true; relative retardation in a slowly growing function inevitably limits the full expression and complete development of a more rapidly growing function.

> Since in any particular segment of behavior, the adolescent can only function as a total personality, the attainment of adult status must be postponed until all of the major lines of growth are completed. Thus, the first consequence of any growth discrepancy is that earlier-maturing functions, which if considered solely in terms of their own degree of maturity would be ready for earlier use, must still await the maturation of other functions before they can be effectively or fully employed. (Ausubel, 1950b).

Thus, whenever growth in a given function greatly outstrips development in related, supporting functions, only two possibilities of expression exist: (1) the relatively precocious function will be used immediately, before the supporting areas are adequately developed, and, therefore, prematurely; or (2) its use will be deferred until related maturational tasks are completed. But regardless of the alternative, the results will prove unsatisfactory. Premature utilization can never be wholly effective or satisfying and often leads to serious dysfunction. For example, *complete* sexual gratification in our culture cannot be experienced before the attainment of some emotional maturity and socioeconomic independence, even though the physiological apparatus for sexual expression is fully mature in the earliest phase of adolescence; and in addition to its incompleteness, early sexual experience is frequently characterized by varying degrees of conflict, guilt, and other undesirable emotional consequences associated with promiscuity or various compensatory outlets.

On the other hand, postponement of functional expression until related maturational readiness would lead to emotional tension because of the frustration of current needs, and to developmental retardation resulting from disuse and insufficient role-playing experience. Were the adolescent, for example, to defer his quest for emancipation from the home until he attained economic independence, he would not only be a very unhappy and frustrated individual but would also be seriously retarded in overall personality development. Hence, because either alternative presents major difficulties and disadvantages, some form of compromise is usually adopted, depending on the urgency of the needs connected with the early-maturing function and on the severity of the penalties following premature utilization. Thus, the middle-class adolescent male in our society has tended to settle for both substitutive sexual outlets and partial emancipation from parents. This compromise avoids completely neither the conflict and the incompleteness of self-expression associated with one alternative nor the frustrations and retardation of psychosexual and personality development associated with the other alternative. It does, however, spare the adolescent from the more drastic consequences that would follow from the choice of either extreme position.

WHAT PRECIPITATES PSYCHOLOGICAL TRANSITION?

A crucial general problem of psychological transition is understanding the conditions that bring it about. When an individual's personality is in a state of developmental equilibrium—true to the principles of homeostasis—it tends to maintain the existing equilibrium until forces sufficiently prepotent to render it untenable intervene. Changes of ordinary magnitude, however, can be easily assimilated within the current framework of personality structure without disrupting homeostatic balance. Thus, the stability and general constancy of personality organization are assured unless the individual is confronted by changes in his biosocial status that are so overwhelming that basic structural reorganization is necessary.

This being true, under what conditions does psychological transition become "a relevant possibility"? What types of changes are likely to be effective in overcoming the inertia inherent in this developmental situation? This problem becomes somewhat less formidable if we bear in mind first that the conditions necessary for precipitating a transitional stage of development are not necessarily synonymous or coextensive with the conditions required for carrying it forward to a successful conclusion. The circumstances, for example, that make childhood personality status completely untenable and initiate beginning adolescent progress toward adult maturation do not in any sense ensure the eventual attainment of adult personality status. Second, under precipitating factors we shall include both (1) conditions operative for a relatively long period of time, that is, those which exert a preparatory or predisposing influence but are inadequate in themselves to effect transition; and (2) factors with a more dramatic and explosive impact that not only supplement and consummate the changes initiated by the predisposing conditions but also serve as catalysts in accelerating the rate of change to effect the inauguration of psychological transition.

Generally speaking, there are two main sources for the changes that compel psychological transition: (1) an urgent need within the culture for a fundamental modification of the social and personality status of an entire group of individuals who are in a given stage of developmental equilibrium; and (2) the occurrence of marked changes within the individual—changes in physical makeup, basic drives, competencies, perceptual ability—which are so crucial that present status becomes incompatible with his altered appearance, capacities, needs, and perceptions (Ausubel, 1950b). Both types of precipitating factors are important in adolescence.

The social needs for restructuring childhood personality status originate in the unwillingness and inability of parents to assume responsibility indefinitely for their children's economic support, and in society's recognition of the fact that because of the limited duration of life a new generation of individuals must be constantly trained and equipped to take over the task of maintaining and perpetuating the culture. Hence, it becomes a matter of deliberate social policy to develop in adolescents those personality traits that are most important for ensuring not only the physical survival of the individual and the group but also the cultural survival of the particular values and traditions to which the social order subscribes.

Operationally, cultural needs for modifying the direction of personality development are mediated both through specific training institutions and through the more subtle and pervasive device of confronting the individual and everyone responsible for his welfare with a new set of social expectations. Hence, parents of their own volition and under the pressure of new social expectations begin to withdraw derived status from their adolescent children; the adolescents in turn are influenced by the depreciated social value of their derived status in contrast to the increased emphasis placed on the acquisition of earned status.

The individual factors that help precipitate adolescent transition originate less from any startling new advances in intellectual, perceptual, social, or adaptive capacity than from a cluster of interrelated physiological changes with far-reaching implications for bodily appearance, drives, and emotions. Thus, the combined effect of attaining (1) the outward appearance of adult body form, (2) the reproductive capacity for creating his own family unit, and (3) the biological sex drive and emotional repertory of a mature adult apparently "releases a powerful drive within the individual for establishing himself as a person in his own right" (Ausubel, 1950b). It would be highly unnatural for him to react to his newly acquired physical and biological attributes of adulthood in any way other than by striving for the status prerogatives that they seem to imply. More important, however, than the individual's reaction to his own pubescence is the social response that his sexual maturation elicits, since almost universally, for reasons that are apparently self-evident in the light of its symbolic significance, it constitutes a mandatory and unchallengeable indication for the social termination of childhood personality status.

Two different forces, therefore, converge to precipitate the period of adolescent transition. A long-standing social need is the predisposing condition, whereas the impact of pubescence must be accounted the more crucial precipitating factor. For not only do the physiological changes of pubescence generate important internal needs for reorganizing personality more independently, but they also provide the impetus for releasing latent social pressures directed toward the same end. That is, the conversion of implicit, undirected needs into explicit expectations capable of effecting developmental change is not a spontaneous or self-determined phenomenon but occurs in response to appropriate and well-defined cues, supplied in this instance by the individual's sexual maturation. Although the interval between the occurrence of pubescence and the cultural recognition of it (in the form of altered social expectations) is generally brief, this is not invariably true. Sometimes, as in Samoa (Mead, 1939)*, several years may elapse before any social notice is taken of

---

* It should be realized, however, that the Samoan situation is the exception to the rule. Many writers, such as Benedict (1934) and Kuhlen (1952), have overgeneralized the significance of this fact to mean that puberty institutions are purely social phenomena unrelated to the occurrence of biological pubescence. This view is not supported by the weight of cross-cultural evidence. The content of such institutions is socially determined but in the vast majority of cases the precipitating factor impelling cultural recognition is biological.

what in most other cultures is a highly dramatic event eliciting considerable reaction from both parents and the community.

Hence, although there may be some delay between the attainment of pubescence and the initiation of adolescent transition, the
important thing is that the former event always precedes and never
follows the latter. This is nowhere better illustrated than in those cultural environments in which "economic necessity imposes mature,
economic and social tasks upon preadolescent boys and girls." Despite their obligation to assume adult responsibilities and to make
adult adjustments in certain areas of life, these individuals still fail to
shed their childhood personality status in the eyes of their parents or
of society (Sherif & Cantril, 1947). Thus, although "situations such as
these do contribute to the early development and sharpening of the
ego" (Sherif & Cantril, 1947), it is apparent athat the inauguration of
adolescence becomes a relevant possibility only in a setting of sexual
maturity; for only in such a setting does society perceive the individual's strivings for emancipation, volitional independence, and equal
social membership as having any self-evident legitimacy.

Further proof of the crucial role of pubescence in precipitating
adolescent development is the fact that the social needs for altering
childhood personality status as well as the important individual pre-
conditions (in terms of social and intellectual maturity) for doing so
have already been operating for several years without effecting psychological transition. Pubescent children do not suddenly become
economic burdens, nor do they suddenly loom as potential replace-
ments for dying members of the adult community. Furthermore, their
attained level of sheer adaptive ability in relation to the actual amount
of intelligence and social skill required for adequate independent adjustment to the physical and cultural environment has long since
qualified them for a more mature personality status. The validity of
this proposition is substantiated both by the responsible economic
tasks successfully managed by children in rural communities and in
most primitive cultures, and by the successful adjustments that
slightly retarded individuals (who never surpass the preadolescent
level of intellectual or social maturity) are able to make even in complex urban environments. Evidently, then, in contrast to the situation
in other transitional periods of development, we cannot ascribe the
onset of adolescence to marked and sudden changes in motor, intellectual, perceptual, or social capacity.

We do not wish to imply by this that the preadolescent gains in
biosocial competence have no implications for personality development or receive no recognition from parents or society. The fact is
that parents and other social agencies do demand more mature and

responsible behavior as children become older; and the latter in turn exercise their newly acquired competencies in acquiring some sources of independent earned status and of mature role-playing experience—whether in school, playground, farm, or newspaper route. As a result of this wider social experience and the independent, nonparental source of ego support that it provides, children view their homes more objectively and begin devaluing their parents. However, until the advent of pubescence these changes take place within the framework of childhood personality status; and in the total economy of ego organization, the parental hearth still remains the major source of current ego status.

PREVENTION OF DEVELOPMENTAL REGRESSION

Once adolescent transition is inaugurated, what prevents a reversal of the change and a restoration of the developmental equilibrium that formerly prevailed? Considering all of the difficulties associated with psychological transition, the adolescent not infrequently—and understandably so—wishes for a return to his childhood personality status. Counteracting this tendency, however, are the very same pressures, social and individual, that precipitated the period of transition. These include the factor of transitional anxiety, which begins to operate as soon as the adolescent loses his former status, internalizes aspirations for a new status, and reacts with fear to the uncertainty surrounding the eventual attainment of the latter. This anxiety can be reduced only by making continued progress toward adult personality status. Hence, developmental regression tends to be avoided both because of the high level of striving maintained to minimize anxiety and because the very contemplation of regression is anxiety producing.

But again we must emphasize that the pressures that counteract regression—like the factors that precipitate adolescent transition—are not adequate in themelves to result in or ensure the attainment of adult personality status. As we shall point out in detail later, the relevant variables affecting the latter outcome are the degree of social recognition as an adult that the adolescent receives, the availability of adult status and role-playing experience, the opportunities for acquiring economic and social independence, the quality of earlier parent-child relationships, and various constitutional factors affecting goal structure. However, the blocking of the road back does guarantee that in the event of maturational failure the individual becomes an unsuccessful, immature adult rather than a re-created, successfully adjusting child.

STAGES OF ADOLESCENCE

It is customary to divide the adolescent period into various stages on the basis of chronological intervals. Thus, Cole (1948) distinguishes between "early," "middle," and "late" stages of adolescence, using different age ranges for boys and girls to allow for the earlier onset of pubescence in girls. In our opinion, a more defensible and less arbitrary criterion for demarcating stages of adolescence is the degree and type of adjustive stress experienced by the individual during this transitional period. However, regardless of the criterion used, a given classification of stages cannot hold true for all cultures, since the relative length and difficulty of adolescence tend to be socially determined. The following discussion, therefore, will apply only to adolescent development in our own and similar cultures.

For several reasons the initial stage of adolescence presumably involves the greatest amount of stress. First, the individual must contend with the disorientation produced by the abrupt loss of childhood status. Second, in the light of the unrealistic expectations of preadolescents about the status prerogatives enoyed by adolescents in our culture, the discovery that (despite their close physical resemblance to adults) they are rejected by adult society and have almost no opportunities for acquiring adult status comes as a rather rude and traumatic awakening. Third, it takes a certain amount of time for adolescents to anchor themselves in the peer culture that will furnish the major portion of their interim status.

In the second stage of adolescence, therefore, once these initial adaptations are made, there is a substantial decrease in the amount of adjustive stress experienced by the adolescent. As he gradually recovers from the initial shock of disorientation, as he begins to appreciate that his original expectations were unrealistic, and as he becomes reconciled to a prolonged period of interim status, he reacts less acutely to the deprivation of his needs for adult status. In addition, various substitutive satisfactions are available in the peer culture to compensate for the frustration of the adolescent's self-assertive drives. Although the total load of frustration in the second stage of adolescence is reduced by the development of more realistic aspirations and of compensatory sources of status, fluctuations in the level of stressfulness are characteristic. For example, somewhere past the midpoint of this period an accumulation of transitional anxiety and chronic frustration (with no immediate relief foreseeable) may give rise to profound feelings of discouragement and despair; whereas only a few years later with the end in sight, the same degree of deprivation can be borne with greater equanimity and cheerfulness.

We are forced to take exception to the view expressed by Dollard et al. (1939) and others that the peer group activities of adolescents represent sublimations (or other types of compensatory derivatives) of frustrated sex drives. We have pointed to evidence (Kinsey et al., 1948) that shows that male adolescents in our culture either practice no sex repression at all or, if they do, obtain compensation directly in slightly watered-down forms of sexual expression. The function of the peer culture, therefore, is to provide a source of interim status and an opportunity for adult role-playing experience, and not to compensate for nonexistent psychophysiological sex frustration. Furthermore, even if such frustration were a prominent feature of adolescence, it would still be more logical to conceive of the peer group and other interim status activities as autonomously derived from other needs and experiences rather than as direct derivatives of the blocked energies of a single fountainhead of drive (Allport, 1937). In these circumstances, without in any way meeting the accepted criteria of sublimation, they could still counterbalance the effects of sexual deprivation by providing gratification in other significant areas of personality need.

4

Physiological Aspects of Pubescence

THE NATURE OF PUBESCENCE

Pubescence refers to the characteristic group of bodily changes associated with the sexual maturation of the human individual. As we have already indicated, it covers only a restricted portion of the entire field of adolescent development. Adolescence, on the other hand, includes not only the physical phenomena of pubescence, but also all of the behavioral, emotional, social, and personality changes occurring during this developmental period.

Genic considerations

In the broader sense of the term, pubescence is a phylogenetic phenomenon. As a result of common racial inheritance, pubescence in man shares all of the major aspects of sexual maturation generally found in mammals, and especially in primates. In addition, if we examine the content of these pubescent changes from one individual to the next and the sequence in which they occur, we find a remarkable degree of constancy (Ausubel, 1954; Ramirez, 1973; Tanner, 1962).

This constancy, not a matter of accident, is determined by the genic constitution of each individual. Whenever we deal with development that is phylogenetic in nature, that is, common to all members of a biological species of individuals, two valid generalizations about the genic factors involved can be made: (1) *Very little variability between individual members of the species is provided for genically*. Hence, the course and outcome of development typically tend to be uniform, rather than characterized by a range of individual differences. For example, with relatively few exceptions human infants tend to be born with one head and two eyes, and to creep before they walk, largely because the single genes determining these factors are practically identical for all individuals. (2) *The directional influence exerted by these genic factors is so potent that it is virtually unmodifiable by environmental conditions for all practical purposes.* Thus, two individuals, exposed to radically different environments, tend to reach practically identical developmental outcomes insofar as the acquisition of phylogenetic traits is concerned. Constancy, therefore, is virtually guaranteed both by the absence of genic variability and by the preclusion of environmental differences because of prepotent genic influences. We might profitably consider the operation of this latter factor in somewhat greater detail.

It is generally accepted today that heredity *alone* never shapes the ultimate course and outcome of development. From the very moment of conception, when genic endowment is fixed, its influence on growth is always modified by the environment. This proposition is especially relevant to pubescence in which many years intervene before the effects of hereditary factors are exhibited phenotypically. During the interim, environmental conditions might reasonably be expected to exert considerable unopposed influence on the direction of development. However, the relative contribution of heredity or environment to the development of a given trait is always proportional to the strength of the infuence either factor exerts on the *particular* growth process. Therefore, when genic factors happen to be prepotent (as they are where phylogenetic development is concerned, i.e., sequence and content of pubescent changes), environmental differences are, for all practical purposes, incapable of effecting any significant degree of variability in developmental sequence (Ausubel, 1952a; Tanner, 1962).

The same degree of constancy, however, is not to be expected for those aspects of pubescence that are not phylogenetic in nature, such as age of onset and rapidity of completion. The very same genic considerations as above apply here, but in reverse. Thus, variability between individuals in this instance is predetermined by a certain range of differences in genic endowment. For example, in a group of girls sharing a relatively homogeneous environment in Western culture, the age of first menstruation typically varies from 10 to 17 and tends to be normally distributed (Boyd, 1961; Tanner, 1962, 1975). The genic determination of these individual differences is confirmed by the fact that the daughters of late-maturing mothers tend on the average to experience their first menstruation at a later age than the daughters of early-maturing mothers (Donovan & Van der Werff Ten Bosch, 1965; Gould & Gould, 1932; Ramirez, 1973).

An additional source of variability inheres in the fact that the genic factors influencing the chronology of pubescence (e.g., age of onset) are not sufficiently prepotent to preclude the influence of environmental differences. Thus, possibly because of improved standards of health and nutrition, the age of menarche seems to be lowering in the present generation of girls (Tanner, 1962, 1975).

We can, therefore, summarize this discussion of the genetics of pubescence by noting that changing environmental conditions (malnutrition, improved nutrition) modify nonphylogenetic aspects of pubescence such as chronology,* but leave phylogenetic aspects such as sequence† unaltered. This difference in susceptibility to environmental influences tends to increase genically determined variablility in the first (nonphylogenetic) instance and to maintain genically determined invariability in the latter (phylogenetic) instance.

In all probability the sequence and content of pubescence changes have not changed for thousands of years, and girls have always become pubescent approximately 2 years earlier than boys. However, the age of onset of pubescence has been declining in most Western countries for the past century (Tanner, 1975). A good or optimal environment has a leveling influence: the age of onset is earlier, on the average, for all cultural and socioeconomic groups, since the environmental determinants (e.g., general health and nutrition) are improved for most chidlren. Individual differences, therefore, in the nonphylogenetic aspects of pubescence are determined today predominantly by genic factors (Tanner, 1975). Thus, the difference that prevailed in England 50 years ago between high and low socioeconomic groups in age of menarche has been virtually obliterated today (Tanner, 1975).

Pubescence as a psychobiological problem

The physical changes associated with pubescence result in psychobiological consequences as soon as they affect the emotions, drives, behavior, or personality organization of the pubescent individ-

---

* At this point it should be noted that culture per se does not influence the chronology of pubescence, but only insofar as it is related to such relevant factors as health and nutrition.

† Tanner and Marshall's data (1969, 1970) may indicate that very slight variability in sequence of pubescent traits may rarely occur.

ual. When this point is reached, it becomes appropriate to speak of the entire complex of changes as adolescence. And since the pubescent infrahuman mammal also undergoes psychobiological changes in both his individual and his interpersonal behavior, it is erroneous to restrict the use of the term *adolescence* to the human species. It would be more precise to state that at the infrahuman level adolescence is *purely* a psychobiological phenomenon that is, the behavioral changes induced by pubescence are not regulated or differentiated by social institutions. If the same criterion is used, the frequent statement that individuals in primitive cultures undergo only pubescence rather than adolescence (because adult status is achieved so rapidly) is even more erroneous; for in addition to the inevitable psychological reactions to pubescence, there is in every culture, no matter how primitive, some degree of institutionalization of the adolescent period.

At the human level, pubescence is the cause of psychobiological problems insofar as it has certain general effects on behavior which are universal in distribution and which transcend specific cultural differences in form and content. Some of these common factors include: (1) feelings of bewilderment in relation to the strangeness and suddenness of these physical changes; (2) the need for the first time since infancy to socialize new drives and emotions of physiological (hormonal) origin; and (3) the direction of regulation from the relatively diffuse to the more highly specific. We have also stated that the occurrence of pubescence is universally a precondition for the initiation of adolescent transition and almost invariably is the critical or consummatory precipitating factor.

In Chapter 6 we shall discuss in detail the various psychological consequences of pubescence. The task of this chapter and of Chapter 5 will be to describe and explain the physical changes that take place. Underlying this approach is the assumption that a proper understanding of the behavioral implications of pubsecence depends on an appreciation of the bodily changes to which they are related. Although in some cases this relationship is clear enough, it must be admitted that most of the physical changes usually cataloged have few if any psychological implications but are included nevertheless to provide a more complete picture of adolescent development. In these two chapters, therefore, we shall strive for selectivity rather than for completeness. Even so, the psychological relevance of many explanatory physiological data will be questionable. Nevertheless, they will be included on the theory that even if they are intrinsically irrelevant for understanding the relationship between physiological events and behavior, they make the former category of events more meaningful and hence easier to understand and remember.

Types of pubescent changes

The physical changes that occur at puberty may be grouped into three levels by the antecedent factors that bring them about. At the first level, initiating all of the subsequent changes, is the activation (or increased activity) of the *gonadotropic* and *corticotropic* hormones of the anterior pituitary gland. The antecedent physiological stimulus for this initiation is believed to be of genic origin and is mediated by the hypothalamic activation of the pituitary gonadotropic hormones (Donovan & Van der Werff Ten Bosch, 1965; Tanner, 1975; Weiland et al., 1971). It seems that the low blood levels of sex hormones found in the prepubescent individual inhibit this hypothalamic action on the anterior pituitary gland. At pubescence, on the other hand, the hypothalamus becomes less sensitive to this type of inhibition and thus activates the production of pituitary gonadotropic hormones (Donovan & Van der Werff Ten Bosch, 1965; Tanner, 1975), thereby stimulating the gonads to secrete functional quantities of androgens and estrogens (with their consequent primary and secondary sex characteristics). At the second level are the immediate consequences of the secretion of these two hormones: (1) the production of mature ova and spermatozoa and the secretion of gonadal hormones as a result of gonadotropic stimulation; and (2) the increased secretion of adrenal cortex hormones as a result of cortiocotropic stimulation. Both of these latter hormones are responsible for the group of third-level changes: (1) the development of primary sex characteristics (e.g., enlargement of penis, testes, uterus); (2) the development of secondary sex characteristics (e.g., maturation of breasts, voice changes, growth of pubic hair); (3) changes in other (nonsexual) physiological functions (cardiovascular, respiratory); and (4) changes in size, weight, and body proportions, and related changes in strength, coordination, and skill.

Figure 4-1 represents these different types of physical changes and their interrelationships schematically. The growth hormone of the anterior pituitary gland is included in this diagram because it undoubtedly continues to function and to stimulate skeletal growth during pubescence. However, unlike the gonadotropic hormones, which first become functionally active at pubescence, growth hormone has been regulating the rate of growth throughout the entire postnatal existence of the individual. The corticotropic hormone, as shown by the

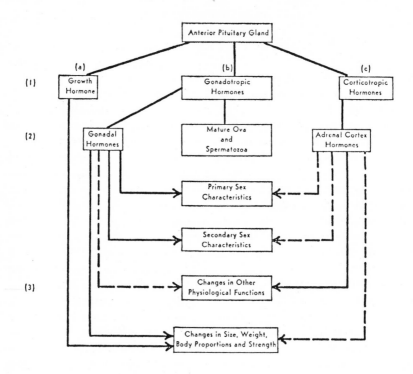

Fig. 4-1. Types of physical changes occurring during pubescence and their interrelationships.

growth curve of the adrenal gland (Harris et al., 1930; Ramirez, 1973; Tanner, 1975), is probably secreted in minimal quantities during childhood, but at pubescence production is markedly increased. In the illustration of the effects of the gonadal and adrenal cortex hormones, respectively, a solid line indicates that the endocrine gland is chiefly implicated in the particular set of changes shown; a dotted line indicates that in comparison to the other gland it plays only a subsidiary role.

In this chapter it will be convenient to discuss the hormonal changes of pubescence and their effects on sexual maturation (reproductive capacity, primary and secondary sex characteristics) and on other physiological functions. In Chapter 5, the changes in height, weight, body proportions, and strength will be summarized and related to motor development.

THE INITIATION OF PUBESCENCE:
HORMONAL CHANGES

The relationship between endocrine factors and the initiation of pubescent phenomena is well established by many parallel and mutually reinforcing lines of evidence. In general such evidence has been obtained in five different ways (Best & Taylor, 1973; Ramirez, 1973): (1) experimental extirpation of endocrine glands in animals, or surgical removal in human beings; (2) injection of hormonal extracts into humans or animals; (3) determination of the quantity of hormonal substances in the urine of individuals at different age levels—either by chemical analysis or by observing their effects on the sexual maturation of animals; (4) correlation of precocious puberty with hypertrophy of certain endocrine glands and increased quantities of their hormones in the urine, and the correlation of delayed or absent puberty with destructive lesions of these same glands and diminished hormonal excretion in the urine; and (5) observation of changes with age in the weight and output of endocrine glands, the growth and function of which are known to be regulated by "tropic" hormones. It would serve no useful purpose in this book to present the detailed evidence on which the following outline of the functions of the various hormones in pubescence is based. Nevertheless, the reader should at least be aware of the different methods for ascertaining the function of the glands of internal secretion as they influence pubescent changes.

Although there is an *absolute* difference between pubescent and nonpubescent children in the overt manifestations of pubescence (i.e., in the presence of primary and secondary sex characteristics), a corresponding absolute difference in the endocrinological basis of pubescence does not prevail between these two groups. That is, physiologically speaking, prepubescent boys and girls are not completely asexual. Sex hormones are present in the bloodstream, but in insufficient quantities to give rise to either functional or structural changes; and just as important, no significant difference exists between boys and girls in the ratio of male (androgenic) to female (estrogenic) sex hormones that they produce (Donovan & Van der Werff Ten Bosch, 1965; Ramirez, 1973; Tanner, 1975). The proximate causes responsible for initiating pubescence lie in *critical* changes in the quantitative levels and ratios of these hormones to each other; in the decreased inhibition of the hypothalamus brought about by the rising level of gonadal hormones; and in the degree of responsiveness of the target tissues stimulated by gonadal hormones to the catalytic influence of these hormones (Shock, 1944; Tanner, 1975).

The more detailed picture would appear to be something like this: In prepubescent children the adrenal cortex, under minimal stimulation from the corticotropic hormone of the anterior pituitary gland, secretes whatever androgenic and estrogenic substances are present in the bloodstream. These hormones are functionally identical with the estrogens and androgens produced by the gonads (ovaries and testes, respectively) Donovan & Van der Werff, Ten Bosch, 1965; Ramirez, 1973). In either sex, the adrenal cortex produces both hormones, in each more androgens than estrogens; but the androgenic-estrogenic ratio is only slightly higher in males than in females (Donovan & Van der Werff Ten Bosch, 1965; Ramirez, 1973). The important thing to note, however, is that normally these hormones are not present in sufficient quantities to initiate pubescent changes. But in hypertrophic tumors of either the pituitary cells secreting cortiocotropic hormone or the adrenal cortex itself, sufficient amounts of sex hormones are produced to lead to precocious puberty in young children of either sex (Best & Taylor, 1973; Shock, 1944). In girls, however, pubescence is accompanied and followed by masculinizing changes because of the preponderantly androgenic content of the adrenal cortex hormones (Best & Taylor, 1973; Shock, 1944).

Biochemically, therefore, prepubescent sexuality seems to be a function of the cortiocotropic hormone and of the gonadal-like hormones produced by the adrenal cortex. There is no evidence to indicate that the gonads themselves secrete androgens or estrogens before pubescence; and it is definitely established that they do not produce mature sperm or ova. This leads to the conclusion that the gonadotropic hormone that regulates both of these functions is not functionally active before puberty (Hall, 1973) for the reasons explained above. As a matter of fact, Greulich et al. (1942) and Hall (1973) could find no gonadotropic hormone in the urine of nonpubescent boys.

In the normal course of events, three factors change to bring about the structural and overt functional manifestations of sexual maturation: (1) The various genital tissues (e.g., penis, uterus, Fallopian tubes) become more sensitive to the stimulation provided by the estrogenic and androgenic hormones of the gonads and adrenal cortex; and these glands, in turn, become more responsive to stimulation by their respective "tropic" hormones secreted by the anterior portion of the pituitary gland (Greulich, 1944; Hall, 1973; Ramirez, 1973; Tanner, 1975). (2) The output of corticotropic and gonadotropic hormones increases markedly. This is shown by the presence of the gonadotropic hormone in the urine for the first time (Greulich et al.,

1942; Hall, 1973), by the phenomenal growth in the size and weight of gonads and adrenals just prior to and during puberty (Harris et al., 1930; Ramirez, 1973), and by the large increase in the secretion of androgens and estrogens by these glands (Ramirez, 1973; Shock, 1944). (3) Gonadotropins are secreted for the first time because the hypothalamus becomes more resistive to the inhibitory influence of prepubescent sex hormones, and this stimulates the pituitary to secrete gonadotropic hormones (Hall, 1973; Ramirez, 1973; Tanner, 1975). Not only do the total quantities of male and female sex hormones present in the bloodstream increase for both sexes (because of increased adrenal cortex output), but the androgenic-estrogenic ratio also rises for boys and falls for girls. This differential hormonal pattern for the two sexes is established because the male or female gonad, unlike the adrenal cortex, secretes only one kind of sex hormone, i.e., the sex-appropriate hormone in each case.

We can also infer reasonably that factors known to be correlated with individual differences in age of pubescence, ie., heredity, climate, nutrition, general health, prepubescent height and weight, are either causally or indirectly related. At any rate, once critical levels of gonadal and adrenal cortex hormone production are reached, primary and secondary sex characteristics appear relatively quickly, as well as physiological changes in other organ systems. Also, unless repressed by cultural influences, psychophysiological sex drives result from the increased presence of estrogenic or androgenic substances in the bloodstream. These relationships have been unequivocally confirmed by changes in the expected direction produced by injection of the hormones, by surgical castration, and by destructive lesions of the gonads (e.g., mumps, tuberculosis) and adrenals (Addison's disease). The production of mature sperm and ova, on the other hand, is not dependent on hormonal stimulation by the gonads but is regulated by specific fractions of the gonadotropic hormone (Ramirez, 1973; Shock, 1944).

PRIMARY SEX CHARACTERISTICS

The primary sex characteristics consist of the actual sex organs involved in copulation and reproduction. During the entire period of childhood the growth of these organs lags behind that of all other organ systems (Harris et al., 1930; Tanner, 1962). For all practical purposes, such growth is negligible in comparison with the skeletal changes that take place before puberty and the genital growth accompanying pubescence. The reason for this relative stunting has already been made clear. The genital organs grow only in response to an adequate level of gonadal stimulation, an event which does not take place until the age of puberty (Donovan & Van der Werff Ten Bosch, 1965; Ramirez, 1973). Skeletal and visceral growth, on the other hand, is regulated by the growth hormone of the anterior pituitary gland, which is produced in functional amounts even before the birth of the child. As a matter of fact, the genital organs may be larger at birth than they are in subsequent years of an infant's life because of the stimulation to which they are subjected by maternal hormones during intrauterine life.

The growth of the major sex organs of the male is a matter of considerable psychological importance because their location is external; hence, in contrast to those of the female, they afford a basis for comparison with the genitalia of other males. Because of the firmly rooted belief in our folklore that the size of the external genitalia is closely correlated with and symbolic of masculine virility, potency, and attractiveness to women, boys (as well as their parents, teachers, and peers) are deeply concerned with the growth of their external sex organs. Generally speaking, three general sources of variability in the size of the male genitalia exist: (1) individual differences in genic factors limiting the maximal growth attainable regardless of the adequacy of hormonal stimulation; (2) individual differences in androgenic output; and (3) individual differences in the age of pubescence. Unfortunately, however, adolescent boys are bound by the "tyranny of the norm" and have little regard for individual differences (Gallagher & Harris, 1976; Stolz & Stolz, 1944). Their parents and teachers also tend to set unreasonable standards of masculine development (Schonfield, 1950; Stolz & Stolz, 1944). Hence, because textbooks on anatomy and adolescence tend to show surprising prudery in treating the growth and dimensions of the male sex organs, these topics, which are of considerable practical importance to parents, teachers, physicians, and counselors, are discussed briefly below. Their psychological implications are considered in Chapter 6.

The growth curves for (1) volume of testes, (2) length, and (3) circumference of the fully stretched flaccid penis are practically parallel, although the slope of the last-mentioned characteristic is somewhat less steep than that of the first two (Schonfield, 1950; Schonfield & Beebe, 1942). [Measurements of the unstretched, flaccid penis are misleading because they correlate poorly with measurements of the erect penis. However, the stretched flaccid penis is about the same length as and 0.77 times the diameter of the erect penis (Schonfield, 1950; and Schonfield & Beebe, 1942).] Before the age of 12, growth in all three measurements is negligible. The testes begin to grow first, followed by growth in the length and then in the circumference of the penis. At 13 the median volume of the testis is 4.8 cm^3 (range: 1.5 to 20 cm^3), the median length of the fully stretched flaccid penis is 8.8 cm (range: 5.5 to 15.5 cm), and its median circumference is 5.8 cm (range: 4.2 to 9.5 cm). At 15, the corresponding measurements for volume of testis are 11.8 (range 2 to 27), for length of penis 11.8 (ranges: 6.5 to 17.5), and for circumference of penis 7.7 (range: 5.5 to 10.5). At maturity (age 17 to 25) these measurements are 16 (range: 7 to 33), 13.5 (range: 8.5 to 19.5), and 8.5 (range: 6.5 to 12.5), respectively (Schonfield, 1943; Schonfield & Beebe, 1942).

In evaluating a case of apparent genital underdevelopment, one should keep in mind the three factors making for variability. The diagnosis of delayed puberty is self-evident (complete absence of all primary and secondary sex characteristics), and unless caused by some endocrine disturbance, the condition will eventually right itself; the genitalia will reach their intended size only at a later age. When pubescence is not markedly delayed in onset but appears arrested, underdevelopment of the male sex organs may be due either (1) to genic factors governing structural limitations or (2) to insufficient androgenic stimulation referable to gonadal or pituitary insufficiency. In the first situation the small size of the genitalia presents a sharp contrast to the otherwise normal development of secondary sex characteristics. In the second, however, retardation in these subsidiary physical indices of masculinity is a distinctive accompaniment of small genitalia, since their development is also dependent on adequate androgenic stimulation. An example of this condition is provided by Fröhlich's syndrome, which occurs in lesions of the pituitary gland. It is marked by hypogenitalism, adiposity, and female body type.* The crucial distinguishing feature between these two different varieties of underdeveloped genitals for therapeutic management is the fact that only the type caused by hormonal insufficiency responds significantly to the administration of gonadotropic or androgenic hormones (Best & Taylor, 1973; Donovan & Van der Werff Ten Bosch, 1965).

In girls, variability in the primary sex characteristics naturally occurs but is psychologically unimportant because the major sex organs are internal, and the external genitalia are relatively inconspicuous and hidden from view. Physiologically, however, individual differences are determined by the same three factors making for

---

* It is important to differentiate this disease from ordinary obesity, in which normally sized genitalia may appear unduly small as a result of being imbedded in suprapubic fat.

variability in the size of the male genitalia. But even if the female reproductive organs are not open to direct inspection, fairly reliable inferences regarding their relative state of maturity can be drawn from the establishment of the menstrual cycle. Menstruation does not occur in the absence of sexual maturity, and usually the failure to initiate menstruation is prima facie evidence of sexual immaturity. It may sometimes happen, however, that sexually mature women who have borne several children have never menstruated. Also, although ovulation is usually part of the menstrual cycle, either event (ovulation or menstruation) can occur in the absence of the other (Best & Taylor, 1973; Tanner, 1975). Thus, the establishment of menstruation is not absolutely correlated with reproductive capacity since it does not necessarily guarantee that a particular girl also ovulates. Menstrual cycles tend to be highly irregular in the beginning but become more regular with increasing age (Hartman, 1936; Sturgis, 1976; Tanner, 1975). A period of physiological sterility also exists for one or more years after the occurrence of the first menstruation (Ashley-Montagu, 1946; Tanner, 1975).

The physiology of menstruation is a highly complex matter, which cannot be entered into fully here. Note, however, that the menstrual cycle involves a series of interrelationships among the gonadotropic hormones, the ovaries, and the uterus. As a result of cyclical gonadotropic stimulation, the ovary produces two kinds of hormones (estrogens and progesterone), the latter effecting hypertrophic changes in the internal lining of the uterus. Sometime past the midpoint of the menstrual cycle, ovulation occurs (Hartman, 1936). If the ovum is fertilized, the uterine changes that have taken place in the meantime become the maternal contribution to the formation of the placenta, and menstruation does not occur. If ferilization does not occur, the preparatory thickening of the inner wall of the uterus becomes superfluous and is sloughed off. The discharge of this necrotic tissue, mixed with mucus and blood, constitutes the chief overt manifestation of the menstrual cycle (i.e., menstruation).

Hence, the occurrence of the first menstruation is generally accepted as an indication that the primary generative organs of the female have reached functional maturity. The event is comparable in physiological significance to the first ejaculation of semen by the pubescent male except that it is more definite and dramatic; hence, the exact date of its occurrence can be fixed with greater assurance. This definiteness is further highlighted by the fact that menstruation is frequently accompanied by unpleasant physical symptoms such as abdominal cramps, headache, backache, flatulence, nausea, and fatigue. The attention of the pubescent girl may therefore be unduly drawn to this cyclical event, which in her mind becomes symbolic of all the physical changes that have occurred during pubescence. Thus, psychologically speaking, menstruation is more comparable in significance to the enlargement of the male genitalia in the recognition it receives both from the individual and from her parents, teachers, and contemporaries. It provides a distinct dividing line between girls who are socially accepted as sexually mature and girls who are still regarded as prepubescent.

SECONDARY SEX CHARACTERISTICS

The secondary sex characteristics include subsidiary physical features that serve as indices of masculinity and femininity. Since their development is dependent on stimulation by functional quantities of androgens and estrogens, they too do not appear until puberty, overlapping in time of appearance with the emergence of the primary sex characteristics. In terms of significance for heterosexual adjustment, however, the former are even more important than the latter. First, secondary sex characteristics are more readily observable and socially accessible as criteria of sexual maturity and sex appropriateness, especially to members of the opposite sex. Second, unlike the primary sex organs, they play an important role in determining the physical attractiveness and hence the heterosexual effectiveness of adolescents and adults.

Another important difference between the primary and secondary sex characteristics is that the latter are not dichotomous in distribution. That is, in terms of his or her primary sex organs an individual is either male or female and not something in between. Whatever variability exists with respect to the primary sex characteristics must be expressed within the framework of this dichotomy. Hence individual differences are always *intra*sexual and never *inter*sexual in nature. The genitalia of a boy may be large or small, but they can never be placed on the same qualitative scale with female sex organs. Under no circumstances (excluding rare instances of hermaphroditism) can overlapping between the sexes occur.

All of the secondary sex characteristics, on the other hand, are truly continuous in their distribution. No absolute boundary line exists between the two sexes. Male and female can be placed at opposite ends of the same continuum because all differences are quantitative in nature. The same structures (e.g., breasts, pubic hair, facial hair) are present in both sexes varying only with respect to such factors as size, quantity, and extensiveness. Hence, although there is a distinct and unmistakable difference between the mean measurements of boys and girls regarding all of these variables, overlapping does occur at the center of distribution. For example, in a late-adolescent group of 77 boys and 79 girls rated by Bayley and Bayer (1946) in terms of androgyny (maleness) of body build, the scores of each sex were normally distributed with a large difference between the means of each group. However, there was overlapping of scores at the low end of the male distribution and the high end of the female distribution.

Just as commonality of structure provides the anatomical basis for bisexuality in the secondary sex characteristics, the hormones of the adrenal cortex provide the physiological basis. At puberty the adrenals in both sexes secrete larger quantities of both estrogens and androgens (more of the latter in each sex). However, when the gonads are functioning adequately, the quantity of sex-appropriate hormone they produce tends to overshadow the effect of the opposite sex hormone secreted by the adrenals. In cases of gonadal insufficiency, on the other hand, this effect may be sufficient to result in highly undifferentiated or even multiple inappropriate primary and secondary sex characteristics (e.g., Fröhlich's syndrome).

The appraisal of a given case of sex inappropriateness of the various physical criteria of masculinity and femininity requires careful consideration of the same three sources of variability listed above for the primary sex organs. The diagnosis of late pubescence presents no difficulty. Cases of hormonal insufficiency are marked by small genitalia and by a general lack of appropriateness in *all* of the seconday sex characteristics. However, if the primary sex organs are normal in size, and only one or two physical traits are inappropriate, the condition may be attributed to specific genic factors regulating the structural development of the trait in question.

Development of breasts

Enlargement of the breasts is the earliest and most important social criterion of sexual maturation in girls. Because of their conspicuousness, which is only slightly affected by clothing, they are even more significant in this respect than the male genitalia. During prepubescence and prior to the first menstruation, the first change that is observable is an elevation of the pigmented area surrounding the nipple (the areola). This is often referred to as the "bud stage." It differs from the characteristic form of the breast in early childhood (after the age of 3) in which only the nipple projects above the level of adjacent structures (Greulich, 1944; Tanner, 1975). The next change that occurs, beginning before the menarche and continuing well into adolescence, is a gradual enlargement and protrusion of the area surrounding the areola. For the most part, this is caused by the deposition of fat tissue (Greulich, 1944; Tanner, 1962). No striking increase in glandular tissue itself takes place until pregnancy ensues.

The growth of the breasts from rudimentary childhood structures to full-sized adult organs is dependent on genically determined limitations on absolute size and on adequate hormonal stimulation from the gonads. Growth will not take place in girls who suffer from gonadal insufficiency. For the same reason, the breasts of men normally persist as rudimentary organs. Mammary enlargement does occur in newborn male infants because of the stimulation provided by maternal hormones, and sometimes in male adolescents in response to the initial increase in estrogenic production by the adrenal cortex. Also in certain diseases of the liver, in which the usual amount of deactivation of estrogens fails to take place, an embarrassing degree of mammary development (gynecomastia) may occur and persist in adolescent boys and men (Best & Taylor, 1973; Donovan & Van der Werff Ten Bosch, 1965).

Body build

Characteristic changes in body build take place during pubescence. These changes tend to follow a typical pattern in each sex, thereby giving rise to male and female body types. Standards of maleness and femaleness of body form have been developed for 17- to 18-year-olds by Bayler and Bayer (1946) and Stolz and Stolz (1951) from rear-view nude photographs. The distribution of *somatic androgyny* scores based on these standards for a group of adolescents in the California Growth Study has been discussed above. According to Bayley (1951),

> variations in form are of two principal kinds. There is the *degree* of differentiation ranging from the neutral childhood form. . . to the extreme or exaggerated characteristics of either sex. . . . There is also variation in the extent to which an individual has physical characteristics of the opposite sex. . . . These two variables, of degree and kind of differentiation, seem to be partially independent.

In our classification of sources of variability in secondary sex characteristics, differences in *degree* would be attributable to gonadal functioning, whereas differences in *kind* would more likely be determined by genic limiting factors relating to structure.

Salient features of masculinity and feminity include flaring and rounding of the hips in girls, and broadening of the shoulders in boys with a concurrent accentuation of muscular development in the shoulder girdle, arms, thighs, and calves (Greulich, 1944; Tanner, 1975). There is also a characteristic sex difference in the distribution of fat. In girls with a feminine body form, fat is generally deposited in the buttocks, thighs, and upper arms. In boys who are masculine in body build, the more usual location for the deposition of fat is the anterior abdominal wall.

Hair

Puberal changes in hair occur in both sexes. From the standpoint of microscopic structure, these changes are identical for both boys and girls. And in many parts of the body such as the head and axilla, even the location of these changes and the approximate quantity of hairs involved are similar. However, in other parts of the body, such as the pubic region, face, abdomen, arms, legs, and shoulders, characteristic differences between the sexes occur in the quantity, location, and proportion of the hairs undergoing structural modification from the childhood to the adult type.

Variability among individuals in this particular secondary sex characteristic is extremely great, and overlapping between the sexes is not uncommon. Although gonadal insufficiency invariably gives rise to sex inappropriateness in the distribution of mature hair, there is still considerable room for genically determined differences between individuals who are otherwise comparable in sex hormone output as indicated by general degree of sexual maturity.

During infancy and childhood the dominant variety of hair is called *vellus* or down. Microscopic examination shows that it lacks a core (*medulla*) and contains relatively little pigment. Beginning with the hairs on the head, vellus is gradually replaced by *terminal* or adult hair, which is longer, thicker, more highly pigmented, and medullated (i.e., has a core). This replacement occurs at an accelerated rate during puberty in both sexes. But in many parts of the body the rate of replacement is less rapid for girls than for boys, and in some parts (for example, the face) replacement does not occur at all.

PUBIC AND OTHER BODILY HAIR

In girls, because of the inconspicuousness of the external genitalia, the growth of pubic hair is an important social criterion of pubescence. It generally follows the initial changes in breast development but is fairly well established by the time the menarche occurs. In boys, pubic hair first begins to develop after the testes have started to grow. The sequence of changes is the same in both sexes. First, there is an increase in the quantity of unpigmented and straight downy hair. This is followed by an intermediate type of course down, which is longer, thicker, more abundant, and slightly pigmented. With increasing age, all of these changes become accentuated, and in addition the hairs become kinky and cover a wider area. In most girls the area is trangular in shape, with the base or upper border formed by a broad horizontal line running the width of the pelvis. In boys, growth continues from this horizontal line in an upward direction, describing another triangle the apex of which is at or above the umbilicus. Thus, the area covered by pubic hair tends to be rhomboidal in men; but exceptions to this rule are numerous and not of great significance (Greulich, 1944; Tanner, 1962).

Axillary hair does not usually appear until the growth of pubic hair is almost complete (Greulich, 1944; Tanner, 1975). By this time the menarche has occurred in girls and first ejaculation in boys. Sex differences are not apparent in quantity, texture, or distribution of axillary hair. However, in males, beginning with middle pubescence, pigmented hairs appear on the forearms, arms, legs, and thighs, and finally around the areola of the nipple and on the chest. In girls, if terminal hairs grow in these areas at all, the growth tends to be scantier and less pigmented. But individual differences in this respect are marked. It is not unusual to find women who are more "hairy" than the average male (Greulich, 1944; Tanner, 1962).

FACIAL HAIR

Sex differentiation in hair is most marked on the face. Prior to puberty no sex difference whatsoever exists; but the development of the beard is one of the most significant of all the secondary sex characteristics in adolescent boys. It indicates that the period of sexual maturation is finally drawing to a close.

The growth of facial hair follows a characteristic sequence of events (Greulich et al., 1942; Stolz & Stolz, 1951). First, a juvenile type of mustache develops from an increase in the length, thickness, and pigmentation of the downy hair on the upper lip. These same changes then occur in order on the upper cheeks, lower lip, chin, and mandibular regions of the face, and lastly on the submandibular portions of the neck (Greulich et al., 1942; Stolz & Stolz, 1951). When these intermediate hairs are finally replaced by coarser and more highly pigmented terminal hairs, shaving becomes necessary (mean age of 16 to 17).

Generally speaking, terminal facial hair does not develop in girls

(Greulich et al., 1942; Tanner, 1962). Sometimes, however (more frequently in dark-skinned girls), an intermediate type of growth occurs, especially on the upper lip. But unless there are other obvious signs of sex inappropriateness, hormonal disturbance is not involved. Slight hirsutism (overgrowth of facial hair in women) is usually an anatomical peculiarity of genic origin. When it is pronounced, other signs of masculinization are generally present, and further investigation usually leads to the diagnosis of hyperactivity of the adrenal cortex (Best & Taylor, 1973).

Sweat and sebaceous glands

In addition to the pubescent changes in the hair follicles, two other important developments take place in the skin: (1) enlargement of the *apocrine* sweat glands and (2) increased activity of the *sebaceous* (oil-producing) glands. These changes are not differentiated according to sex, but are general indices of sexual maturity in either sex. Their chief significance lies in their relation to body odor [more pronounced in boys according to Tanner (1975)] and to the cosmetic appearance of the skin, both of which are highly important for social and heterosexual adjustment during adolescence.

The growth and activity of the apocrine (in contrast to the *merocrine*) sweat glands are closely related to sexual maturity and functioning. Unlike the merocrine glands, which are distributed over the skin of the entire body, the apocrine glands are found only in areas of the skin having special significance for sex functions or development (e.g., the armpits, breasts, genital and rectal regions) (Greulich, 1944; Tanner, 1975). Their enlargement during puberty is responsible for "the characteristic odor of axillary perspiration," which is not observable prior to this time (Greulich et al., 1942; Tanner, 1975). In sexually mature girls and women the activity of these glands is increased during the premenstrual phase of the menstrual cycle. The function of these glands, therefore, seems to be comparable to that of the scent glands of other mammals (Greulich et al., 1942) and to bear little relation to the heat-regulating function of the ordinary merocrine sweat glands.

The sebaceous glands enlarge and become more active during puberty, producing increased quantities of their oily secretion. But since the excretory ducts of these glands do not enlarge proportionately to accommodate the increased secretion, drainage is poor. The ducts frequently become blocked with hard plugs of waxy material to which dust particles adhere. These are the familiar "blackheads," which occur most commonly on the sides of the nose and on the chin and forehead. Since the blocked sebaceous glands easily become inflamed and secondarily infected, this condition is frequently associated with acne (Strauss & Pochi, 1976). Few individuals are fortunate enough to escape completely this common skin disturbance of puberty, which, from the standpoint of psychological trauma, is one of the most serious of all the somatic complications of adolescent development. Since androgens stimulate functioning of the sebaceous glands, acne is more frequent in adolescent boys than girls.

Voice

Voice changes constitute a rather conspicuous feature of pubescence in boys because the suddenness with which they take place frequently causes "cracking" or loss of control. The vocal chords become much longer resulting in a marked lowering of pitch. But since anatomical growth proceeds at a more rapid rate than neuromuscular control, an embarrassing loss of ability to regulate and maintain constancy of pitch occurs in almost all boys.

This accelerated period of vocal growth is usually a feature of late adolescence (16 to 18) (Tanner, 1971), although the first signs of deepening may generally be noted soon after the appearance of the first pubic hair. In girls, the growth of the vocal chords is both less marked and more gradual. Hence, the lowering of pitch does not proceed as far, and loss of control rarely occurs.

Variability in depth of voice—just like variability in quantity of body hair and density of beard in men—is largely a function of genic factors regulating the growth of the vocal chords. Only in extreme cases (male sopranos) does there appear to be a relationship between depth of voice and gonadal insufficiency. Eunuchoidism—produced by either castration or disease—is invariably accompanied by absence of pubescent voice changes. In fact, castration of certain prepubescent males has been practiced by various ethnic and religious groups for just this purpose.

TEMPORAL ASPECTS OF PUBESCENCE

In studying the temporal relations of pubescence, it is important to distinguish, as we did above, between *chronology* and *sequence*. Chronology refers to the *age range* in which the changes of pubescence begin and end; sequence refers to the *order* in which the component physical changes of puberty take place. Differences in chronology reflect the operation of genic variability and environmental influences. Sequence, however, as a phylogenetic phenomenon, tends to be almost devoid of individual differences as a consequence of both genic invariability and lack of sensitivity to relevant environmental factors. Closely related to the problem of chronology is the question of which criterion of pubescence shall be used in establishing the age at which it occurs. Moreover, the problem of sequence is complicated by the fact that each component change takes place not instantaneously but over a variable period of time that differs from one physical trait to the next. Thus, change X may *begin* before change Y, but the latter may reach completion first (Marshall & Tanner, 1969, 1970).

Age range for onset of pubescence

The age at which puberty actually occurs cannot be determined with any exactitude since it differs when the averages of different groups are taken and also when different criteria of sexual maturity are used. For our purposes, however, only two facts are important: (1) there is a wide range of normal variability within each sex group (10 to 18 in girls, 12 to 18 in boys); and (2) it is reasonable to infer that on the average girls reach sexual maturity approximately 2 years before boys.

When the menarche is used as the criterion of sexual maturity in girls, different studies place the mean age of puberty from 12.5 to 13.6 (Shuttleworth, 1939; Simmons & Greulich, 1943; Tanner, 1975). When the criterion of straight, pigmented pubic hair is used for boys, typical averages are 13.1 to 14.4 (Boas, 1932; Tanner, 1962). Thus, if these two different criteria were truly comparable, little difference between the sexes would exist. However, a more comparable criterion (since it can be used for both sexes) is mean age at which the maximum yearly increment in height takes place. Shuttleworth (1939) found this to be 2 years later in boys (14.8) than in girls (12.6) in the New England region, and Tanner (1975) reported comparable findings in other Anglo-Saxon areas.

Hence, for purposes of convenience, we may place the average age of pubescence at 13 for girls and 14.5 for boys if we realize that these are estimates rather than true values, and that much variability takes place around the mean. This sex difference in age of pubescence in favor of girls is confirmed by the greater maturity of girls as judged by their social and heterosexual interests between the ages of 12 and 15. However, this does not mean that girls mature earlier than boys in terms of sexual *experience* and *activity*. Kinsey et al. (1948), for example, found that practically all boys experience orgasm by the age of 15, whereas fewer than a quarter of girls do so; and although this difference is probably less marked today, it is undoubtedly still in favor of boys. Nevertheless, the earlier sexual maturation of girls (in a physical and social sense) is one of the most important facts of adolescence; and its implications for social and emotional development as well as for education will be fully discussed in later chapters.

Criteria of pubescence

The choice of an adequate criterion of sexual maturity in determining the age of pubescence is in many ways a pseudo-problem. First, pubescence by definition refers to a *constellation* of typical bodily changes associated with sexual maturation, and not to any particular change. The choice of reproductive capacity as the most crucial and representative of the physical changes that take place is purely arbitrary and is hardly defensible on either biological or behavioral grounds. Second, each of the component bodily changes occurs over a period of time rather than all at once (Tanner, 1975). Hence, when the physical phenomena of pubescence are considered as a whole, it is meaningless to conceive of a definite *age* of puberty. It is more reasonable to think of an *interval* of several years embracing a series of changes that are initiated in characteristic sequence and progress to completion at different rates of development. Only for convenience in research, and in the day-to-day handling of boys and girls, does it become worthwhile to estimate "when" puberty really occurs; and to do this it is necessary to select arbitrarily one or more criteria of pubescence.

Obviously, different criteria will differ in validity, definiteness, convenience, presence in both sexes, and accuracy with which they can be measured. In girls the menarche is a convenient index of sexual maturity, the occurrence of which can be definitely and accurately determined (providing one does not rely on retrospective reports). But although menstruation is unequivocally indicative of maturity of the primary sex organs, the converse does not necessarily always hold true. Also as pointed out above, menstruation and ovulation are not absolutely correlated. Another difficulty is the absence of a completely analogous event in boys. The emission of semen is only approximately similar in significance, and is a poor criterion besides, because the date of initial occurrence is less definite and more subject to retrospective errors of memory.

Pubic hair is a convenient, definite, and accurately measurable bisexual criterion. However, its validity for assessing the pubescent status of a given individual is questionable in view of large individual differences unrelated to sexual maturity. The same holds true for age of maximum growth. But for comparing the pubescent status of different groups (boys versus girls), these individual differences are unimportant if a large enough sample is employed. For research purposes, therefore, both of these criteria are quite serviceable.

In nonresearch settings, parents, teachers, and contemporaries of either sex use whatever combinations of criteria are most accessible. For example, boys tend to be most influenced by the factor of breast development in assessing the sexual maturity of girls, whereas girls rely unduly on such factors as height and facial hair in making comparable judgments of boys. On the other hand, parents, teachers, and peers of the same sex frequently have more complete and valid data (e.g., menarche, pubic hair, seminal emissions, enlargement of male genitalia) on which to base an estimate of sexual maturity. At any rate, serious mistakes in assessing pubescent status are rarely made in actual practice regardless of the criterion that is used. But when errors are made, they are usually in the direction of underestimates because of a tendency to set unreasonably high standards of sex appropriateness (Gallagher & Gallagher, 1976; Schonfeld, 1950).

SEQUENCE OF PUBESCENT CHANGES

The relative phylogenetic invariability of the sequence of pubescent changes has been confirmed by several lines of evidence. Different investigators working with different populations report different mean ages for various events, but there is substantial agreement on sequential appearance.* Furthermore, in cases of precocious or retarded puberty—whether that within the normal range of differences or that caused by endocrine abnormality—the same sequence of changes is followed as in the instances of more typical chronology. Apparently, then, there is a genically determined order (that is the same for almost all individuals) in which the various body tissues implicated in sexual maturation become sensitive to the influence of estrogenic and androgenic substances. The order in which the changes once initiated reach completion is also predetermined. But since these two varieties of sequence are somewhat independent of each other, considerable overlapping occurs.

By pooling data from the various studies discussed, we arrive at

---

* Marshall and Tanner (1969, 1970) report occasional variation in sequence of pubescent changes that is not substantiated by American studies.

the following sequential picture of pubescence: In girls (Marshall & Tanner, 1969, 1970; Reynolds, 1948; Shuttleworth, 1939) the order of onset is initial enlargement of the breasts; appearance of straight, pigmented pubic hair; age of maximum growth; appearance of kinky pubic hair; onset of menstruation; and growth of axillary hair. In boys (Greulich et al., 1942; Kinsey et al., 1948; Marshall & Tanner, 1969, 1970; Schonfeld & Beebe, 1942; Shuttleworth, 1939) the corresponding order of pubescent phenomena is beginning growth of the testes; appearance of first pubic hair (straight, pigmented); early voice changes; first ejaculation; growth of kinky pubic hair; age of maximum growth; appearance of axillary hair; marked voice changes, and development of the beard.

OTHER PHYSIOLOGICAL CHANGES IN PUBESCENCE

In addition to the bodily changes that are integrally related to sexual maturation and functioning (primary and secondary sex characteristics) practically every organ system of the body is affected by the endocrine developments of pubescence. Skeletal and muscular changes are considered in Chapter 5. In this section we shall consider the significant changes occurring in all other nonsexual organ systems.

Types of physiological changes

Two main types of nonsexual physiological changes occur during pubescence: (1) the completion of physiological maturity; and (2) the disturbance of physiological equilibrium (as a result of new hormonal activity) and the gradual process of adjustment and establishment of a new equilibrium.

Shock (1944) refers to the first type of change as "physiological 'learning.' "

Just as pediatricians have discovered that the young child is not simply a miniature adult, so students of human development have come to the realization that the adolescent is neither child nor adult in his physiological reactions. In the adolescent many new physiological adjustments are being made which were unnecessary in the young child and which become stabilized in the adult.

As an example, the regulation of body temperature may be cited. The rather wide fluctuations in body temperature observed in young children give way to a more stable regulation of temperature by the beginning of the second decade. Thus the growing organism has "learned" to utilize and coordinate the numerous mechanisms involved in temperature control.

Other examples include the attainment of adult respiratory capacity and the adult pattern of cardiovascular dynamics.

The second kind of change—initial hormonal disequilibrium followed by gradual adaptation and restoration of equilibrium—is reflected in the disturbances of the sebaceous glands referred to above (adolescent acne). Spontaneous recovery from this condition with age is indicative both of tissue adaptation to hormonal inbalance and of eventual stabilization of the total endocrine picture. Its partial responsiveness to hormonal therapy also adds credence to this interpretation of its etiology (Strauss & Pochi, 1976).

OTHER ENDOCRINE GLANDS

The main endocrine changes related to pubescence occur in the anterior pituitary gland, the gonads, and adrenals. The sudden increased functioning of these glands leads not only to important changes attributable to the effects of their own enhanced output but also to a disturbance of the entire endocrine balance.

The growth of the thymus gland is inversely related to that of adrenals during puberty (Best & Taylor, 1973; Donovan & Van der Werff Ten Bosch, 1965). Preliminary investigation indicates that the thymus gland inhibits sexual maturation and facilitates skeletal growth, but these results are far from conclusive. It is definitely known, however, that the thymus gland will not shrink in size until the adrenals become more active. In atrophic diseases of the adrenals (Addison's disease), the thymus remains prominent; in hypertrophic tumors of the adrenals, the thymus begins to degenerate prematurely. The functions of the thymus and adrenals are reciprocally antagonistic, at least in lymphatic if not sexual development. The shift in thymus-adrenal balance is partly responsible for the decline in lymphoid tissue during puberty and the diminished lymphatic response to bacterial infection. The thymus gland also probably exerts an inhibitory influence on muscular tonus, since hypertrophic tumors of the thymus result in excessive muscular relaxation and weakness. Hence, the large gain in muscular strength that occurs with pubescence may possibly be related, in part, to the decline in the size and importance of the thymus gland.

Changes in the thyroid gland are largely mirrored by alterations in basal metabolic rate (which provides an index of body heat production in a state of physical, gastrointestinal, and mental rest). Although basal metabolic rate (expressed as calories per square meter of body surface per hour) is largely a function of thyroid activity, other important variables are also involved. Relatively less heat, for example, must be produced per pound of body weight if less heat is lost either through better temperature control or because the ratio of body surface area to body weight is declining. Both of these facts become increasingly true with age from infancy to adult life. Hence, during adolescence, the thyroid gland enlarges and more *total* heat is produced by the individual (because he becomes heavier); but since less heat tends to be lost, the basal metabolic rate expressed as above declines in both boys and girls (Best & Taylor, 1973; Shock, 1944). At all ages, however, basal metabolism is higher in boys than in girls.

CARDIOVASCULAR CHANGES

During pubescence the cardiovascular system undergoes tremendous expansion in volume and physiological capacity (Maresh, 1948; Tanner, 1975). The heart especially increases in size and in the thickness of its muscular walls. Hence, with each stroke it can pump a much larger volume of blood through the circulatory system, thereby increasing systolic blood pressure (the pressure of blood within the arteries accompanying each heartbeat) (Tanner, 1975). Diastolic blood pressure, the blood pressure between heartbeats, also rises because of the heightened resistance to blood flow provided by increased vascular tonus (Shock, 1944; Tanner, 1975). Both changes are undoubtedly brought about by enhanced functioning of the adrenal cortex; but since systolic blood pressure rises more rapidly, "pulse pressure" (the difference between systolic and diastolic pressures) tends to rise during puberty. Also beginning with puberty, systolic blood pressure rises more rapidly in boys than in girls, accounting perhaps, in part, for the sex difference in athletic capacity (Shock, 1944; Tanner, 1975).

An immediate consequence of this increase in cardiac capacity is a drop in pulse rate. Since more blood can be delivered in a single stroke, the heart need not beat as rapidly to pump the same volume of blood through the vessels in the space of a minute. Pulse rate drops "eight to nine beats per minute" for both sexes during adolescence, but at all ages is "two to six beats per minute faster" for girls (Shock, 1944; Tanner, 1975), the sex difference increasing somewhat with age. This sex difference in pulse rate parallels the sex difference in systolic blood pressure, but naturally is in the opposite direction.

The pattern of circulatory adjustment to maximal physical effort changes in a comparable fashion during pubescence. The increased needs of muscle tissue for oxygen and glucose are met more by a rise in cardiac output (as reflected by systolic blood pressure changes) than by a rise in pulse rate (Shock, 1944; Tanner, 1975). As one might anticipate, the compensatory increment in blood pressure is greater in boys than in girls, and the sex difference tends to become even greater with age. On the other hand, girls respond to exercise with a greater rise in pulse rate, which also takes a longer time to reach the basal level during the recovery period. Hence, it is clear that pubescent individuals are physiologically capable of doing a greater amount of work than younger children, but it is not yet clear whether more or less physiological strain (as measured by recovery time) is involved for an equivalent amount of work (an amount of work adjusted for body size).

Because of the greater increase in number of red blood corpuscles and in hemoglobin, adolescent boys are better able to mobilize the delivery of oxygen to muscles during exercise (Tanner, 1975). Boys also have a greater capacity for metabolizing and thus disposing of the lactic acid formed in working muscles (Tanner, 1975).

RESPIRATORY CHANGES

In terms of absolute units (liters per minute), there is a large increase in respiratory capacity during pubescence (Shock, 1944). The chest cavity enlarges and the lungs increase in size and weight. The rate of breathing also declines. However, if respiration volume is corrected for body size, it is easily seen that respiratory capacity does not keep pace with general body growth. Throughout the adolescent period there is a steady decline in respiratory volume expressed as liters *per square meter* per minute (Shock, 1944).

The most significant fact about respiratory changes during adolescence is the large difference in lung capacity that develops between boys and girls. This is probably both a cause and a consequence of the sex difference in athletic activity and prowess. Prepubescent boys and girls have nearly the same respiratory capacity, but with increasing age the difference becomes increasingly greater in favor of boys.

Health and disease in adolescence

Health and disease are relevant topics for adolescent development for two main reasons. First, different age periods are marked by characteristic patterns of disease. In terms of both the pathological processes and the kinds of tissues involved, these differential patterns reflect significant changes in physiological status and development (Ausubel, 1954). It is not a matter of coincidence, for example,

that the site at which rickets occurs changes with age; that certain infectious diseases are most common in childhood)* that tuberculosis,†
endocrine disorders, and acne figure so prominently in adolescence;
and that atherosclerosis and other degenerative diseases occur mostly
in middle and old age. The diseases of adolescence mirror the physiological stresses and strains as well as the disturbances in physiological
equilibrium that occur during this particular stage of development
(Ausubel, 1954).

Second, physical illness and defects become more important for
personal adjustment during adolescence. Because of the increased
social premium placed on physical attractiveness and conformity to
group physical norms, both the individual and his group tend to be
more concerned by injury and disfigurement. Disease, therefore,
constitutes a much greater hazard to normal personality adjustment
during the adolescent period. And since at this time the body also
tends to become a more important part of the individual's psychological field, both in terms of its social significance and in terms of
his own self-concept, physical disturbances are more likely to arise as
complications of emotional disorder.

MORTALITY AND MORBIDITY RATES

In terms of mortality rate, adolescence marks the beginning of an
ascending trend that is maintained for the rest of the life span. The
death rate is very high in infants under 1 year of age; it drops precipitously between the ages of 1 and 4 and then more gradually until the
ages of 10 to 14 (Heald, 1976). In the age group from 10 to 19 the mortality rate for adolescent males is 85, more than double (45) that of the
10 to 14 age group (Heald, 1976). For white females, the comparable
figures are 40 and 30 for the corresponding two age groups (Heald,
1976). The hazards of life during adolescence, therefore, are approximately twice as great as during preadolescence, and about twice as
severe in males as in females. The greatest single cause for the increased mortality rate is the spectacular rise in violent deaths, i.e., the
number of fatal accidents, homicides, and suicides. The other major
causes of death in this age group are neoplasms, cardiovascular and
renal disease, diabetes, congenital malformations, and asthma (Heald,
1976), but these diseases still account for only 40 percent of the
number of deaths caused by accidents (Heald, 1976).

---

* This difference is currently masked by the availability of vaccines for most of the
infectious diseases of childhood.

† Tuberculosis has become a much less common disease in adolescence since the
advent of effective chemotherapy.

The health picture during adolescence is much brighter if we use morbidity rather than mortality rates as our criterion of freedom from illness. When one uses such indices of incidence as total number of illnesses, physicians' calls, number of days in bed, number of hospital days, and number of days of absence from school, the adolescent appears to have an advantage over the preadolescent child (Heald, 1976). We may conclude that neither the incidence nor the mortality of disease increases during adolescence if we exclude accidents and injuries from consideration. It is in the *kinds* of illnesses that are most prevalent that the greatest contrast between the two age groups is found. The common childhood disease rheumatic fever declines in incidence during adolescence (Wittemore, 1976), whereas tuberculosis, endocrine disorders, and acne become increasingly more frequent (Gallagher et al., 1976; Heald, 1976).

COMMON MEDICAL PROBLEMS OF ADOLESCENCE

Infectious diseases

Adolescents are not immune to the common childhood diseases (measles, mumps, etc.). They are just as susceptible to these diseases, except for chicken pox, as younger children, but contract them less frequently merely because these are so contagious that few persons can escape them as children.* In fact, a disease such as diphtheria is actually becoming more common in adolescents and adults than in children because the former have been immunized against it less recently. Mumps is a much more serious disease in adolescents than in children when it occurs because of testicular swelling, which takes place in almost one-third of the cases. If bilateral, it may even lead to sterility.

The incidence of new cases of rheumatic fever declines during adolescence but is still quite substantial (Whittemore, 1976). In addition, there are the residual cases of heart damage remaining from childhood attacks. The restriction on physical activity which this necessitates creates serious problems of emotional and social adjustment for many boys and girls (Berenberg, 1976; Josselyn, 1949). Preliminary experimental work with animals indicates that increased susceptibility to tuberculosis is partly a function of gonadal secretion (Lurie, 1949).

---

*This, of course, is less true today because of the availability of vaccines against many of these diseases.

Endocrine disorders

Disturbances related to the establishment of sex functions naturally first become prominent during the adolescent period. Early or late sexual maturation is usually a function of genically determined variability, providing that it occurs between the ages of 10 to 17. Beyond this normal range, endocrine disorder or nutritional deficiency should be suspected. The most common cause of precocious puberty is overactivity of the adrenal cortex or of the basophilic cells of the anterior pituitary gland which produce gonadotropic and corticotropic hormones (Cushing's syndrome) (Kenny, 1976; Lowrey & Brown, 1952). Delayed puberty (including general signs of sex inappropriateness) is induced by atrophic lesions of these same glands (e.g., Addison's disease, Fröhlich's syndrome) or of the gonads themselves (e.g., tuberculosis, mumps) (Kenny, 1976). But regardless of whether puberty is chronologically displaced because of normal genic variability or because of organic disease, the same consequences in skeletal growth and psychological disturbance take place.

Menstrual irregularities are almost universal during the first year of puberty until normal rhythm is established (Sturgis, 1976; Tanner, 1975). The menarche is delayed in instances of late puberty caused by any of the hormonal conditions described above, and sometimes in instances of nutritional deficiency, narcotic addiction, and emotional trauma. But even after menstruation is well established, various difficulties—pain, distress, irregularity, excessive or insufficient flow—are very common (Sturgis, 1976). Some of these cases are attributable to gonadal imbalance, liver dysfunction, thyroid or nutritional deficiency, or organic disorder of the uterus, and respond to treatment directed along these lines (Sturgis, 1976). In many other instances, however, minor disturbances are either consciously or "unconsciously" exploited for psychological reasons, for example, to avoid distasteful physical or social activity, to gain sympathy from others, or to rationalize poor performance.

When pregnancy occurs in adolescence, labor is apt to be shorter in duration, cesarean section is less frequently necessary, and infant and maternal mortality are lower (Marchetti & Menaker, 1950). Psychiatric care, however, is extremely important for unwed adolescent mothers because of the shame and fear involved in the experience of childbearing.* The greater frequency of toxemia (a complication of

---

* The degree of shame experienced tends naturally to vary with the degree of stigma attached to birth out of wedlock in different ethnic, subcultural, and cultural settings.

pregnancy marked by high blood pressure, convulsions, swelling of the extremities, and other symptoms) among adolescents has been attributed in part to this psychological trauma.

Two other endocrine disturbances are also more common in adolescence than in childhood: diabetes and goiter (enlargement of the thyroid) (Selenkow & Thep, 1976). General hormonal imbalance is probably a factor in both diseases. Diabetes in adolescents is more severe than in adults and much more difficult to control, partly because of its relative refractoriness to insulin treatment and partly because of the resistance of adolescents to dietary regimentation (Cabell, 1976). A good deal of the thyroid enlargement that occurs in adolescence is probably a reflection of the greater need for iodine in the diet that arises at this time because of increased body heat production. If the iodine content of the drinking water is barely adequate to supply childhood needs, compensatory enlargement of the thyroid takes place. This is shown by the greater incidence of goiter in the Great Lakes region where iodine deficiency is much greater than in any other part of the country (Cabell, 1976).

Although acne is not an endocrine disorder per se, its relation to hormonal imbalance* has already been discussed. It is in all probability the most common disease of adolescence (Strauss & Pochi, 1976) and by any criterion the most serious in terms of its psychological consequences. Its chronicity and refractoriness to treatment are especially troubling to adolescents because of their limited time perspective. In the image that they have of their own bodies, this defect occupies a very prominent place and is projected almost indefinitely into the future. Adults tend to minimize the seriousness of this condition because they prefer to forget the concern that they manifested over it as adolescents, and because pride makes their own adolescent children and acquaintances simulate indifference. Time (the regaining of physiological equilibrium) is the most important therapeutic factor, although scrupulous cleanliness, x-ray therapy, topical treatment, minor surgery, antibiotics, psychotherapy, and estrogens have all proven beneficial (Strauss & Pochi, 1976).

Nutritional disturbances

The nutritional disorders of adolescence are a reflection of the unusual needs for proteins and certain vitamins and minerals during this period of development (Johnston, 1948; Young, 1976). The

---

* Androgens are a prerequisite for the development of acne. In adolescent girls the disease is caused by the increased production of adrenal cortex androgens, which stimulates secretion of the sebaceous glands. Acne does not occur in eunuchs.

requirements of tissue growth demand a protein intake about three times that of the adult period. Similarly, larger amounts of calcium and vitamin D are needed for skeletal growth than at any other time of life with the possible exception of early infancy (Johnston, 1948; Young, 1976). The large increase in blood volume also creates a greater need for iron, especially in girls, who lose menstrual blood periodically (Young, 1976). It is in these requirements that nutrition is most likely to be deficient rather than in total caloric intake; and experience shows that where these nutritional deficiencies occur, an insufficiency of the B complex vitamins is frequently present. Reference has already been made to the increased need for iodine.

The chief cause of nutritional disturbances in adolescence is the lack of knowledge of adolescents and their parents about these special dietary requirements. A contributing cause is indiscriminate dieting by girls intent on losing weight. Less important are the peculiar food habits popularly attributed to teenage boys and girls. Indulgence in soft drinks, candy, and hot dogs is a social rather than a physiological phenomenon of adolescence, and tends to supplement rather than to replace the conventional three meals a day. Anorexia nervosa, a psychogenic disorder that frequently begins with excessive dieting, is becoming more common and occurs particularly in adolescent girls. It is marked by extreme and sometimes fatal weight loss and aversion to food (Bruch, 1976).

Obesity is a common medical problem in adolescence and one with important psychological and social implications. In girls it is a serious handicap to heterosexual relationships, and in boys it frequently simulates an apparent underdevelopment of the genitalia. As in other periods of life, the main cause of obesity is overeating and insufficient exercise in persons constitutionally predisposed to gaining weight. Obesity attributable to thyroid deficiency or to adrenal and pituitary disturbances (Fröhlich's syndrome, Cushing's syndrome) is relatively rare (Kenny, 1976). A more important cause of adolescent obesity is compulsive overeating, which serves as a defense against anxiety or as a compensation for social inadequacy.

Accidents

It has already been noted that accidents constitute the greatest single cause of death in the age group of 15 to 19 and account for the greater part of the increase in the mortality rate over the preceding half decade (Heald, 1976). This rise in the frequency of accidents can be attributed to greater freedom of movement away from the home, to participation in more violent physical activity, to poor judgment and irresponsibility, to recklessness stemming from aggressive defiance of adult rules and regulations, and to repressed aggressive tendencies. The major causes of accidental death are automobile mishaps, drowning, falls, and injuries from firearms. As one might easily anticipate, fatal accidents are much more frequent among boys than among girls (Heald, 1976).

The psychological implications of bodily disease and injury are discussed in Chapter 6.

5

Physical Growth and Motor Development

Maturational changes in the skeletal tissue (bone, muscle, and fat) are among the more important physical developments of pubescence. These changes are significant for two main reasons: (1) they alter such crucial aspects of body form and appearance as height, weight, and body proportions, which figure so prominently in social and individual concepts of adult physical maturity; and (2) they are crucially related to changes in skeletal mass, strength, and coordination, which have important implications for the development of motor skills.

Skeletal maturation is part of the pubescent cycle because it is intimately related to the endocrine developments that give rise to the primary and secondary sex characteristics and to maturational changes in other organ systems (Ausubel, 1954); Tanner, 1975; Weiland et al., 1971). It consists both of quantitative dimensional changes, such as growth spurts in height and weight, and of qualitative changes in tissue composition and function. Like the secondary sex characteristics, these changes occur in both sexes, differing only in degree for boys and girls.

The relationship between the endocrine phenomena of pubescence and the gross as well as the qualitative changes that take place in the skeletal system is exceedingly complex. A discussion of this relationship will be reserved until a more descriptive account of the internal skeletal changes and of the adolescent growth spurt is given.

FACTORS DETERMINING SKELETAL GROWTH

It is important to realize at the outset that pubescence is, relatively speaking, only a minor factor in determining an individual's terminal adult height. Typically the significance of the age of sexual maturation lies chiefly in its relation to *when* the pubescent growth spurt occurs, that is, to the relative height of an individual at various points in his adolescent career. As long as the age of pubescence falls within the normal range of individual differences, postpubescent height can be predicted from prepubescent and even from early childhood height with a reasonable amount of accuracy (Shuttleworth, 1939; Vandenberg & Falkner, 1965). Pubescence, in other words, does not significantly affect the ultimate height an individual will eventually attain, provided it does not occur extremely early or unusually late.

Heredity is the principal variable determining skeletal growth (Vandenberg & Falkner, 1965). A close relationship exists between the stature of parents and the adult height of their offspring (Harris et al., 1930; Tanner, 1975; Vandenberg & Falkner, 1965). The influence of genic factors is mediated through the growth hormone of the anterior pituitary gland and operates with considerable uniformity and regularity over the age span from antenatal existence to maturity. A child who is tall at birth also tends to be tall at the ages of 6 and 19 (Vandenberg & Falkner, 1965). But since height is an idiosyncratic rather than a phylogenetic trait,[*] it is relatively susceptible to the influence of environmental factors. Nutrition—especially the intake of protein, calcium, and vitamin D—seems to determine whether the individual will attain the maximum height possible within his genic limitations. This is the most plausible explanation we have for the mean increase in stature of approximately 3 inches that has taken place over the hundred-year interval between 1830 and 1930 in Eastern college women and Harvard undergraduates (Bowles, 1932), and over the past century in most parts of the Western world (Tanner, 1975). It reflects both rising standards of national nutrition and the earlier age of pubescence, which is correlated positively both with prepubescent as well as with final adult height (Ausubel, 1954; Tanner, 1975). Terminal adult stature is also being reached 6 to 7 years earlier now than a century ago (Tanner, 1975).

---

[*] It is true, of course, that the *range* in which human stature occurs is a *species* characteristic. Consistent differences are also found among the mean heights of children of different racial stocks growing up in the same environment, e.g., Chinese, Japanese, Hawaiian, South European, and North European on the islands of Hawaii (Wissler, 1930). However, considerable overlapping between racial groups makes individual prediction on the basis of these differences worthless.

QUALITATIVE CHANGES IN SKELETAL TISSUE

An important change that takes place during pubescence is an alteration in the relative proportions of the various skeletal tissues that constitute the total breadth of an extremity. In the calf, for example, there is a sharp rise in the breadth of bone and muscle tissue for both boys and girls, a rise that is greater for boys than for girls (Reynolds, 1946; Tanner, 1975). This sex difference is possibly related to the general muscular hypertrophy which androgenic hormones induce in laboratory animals (Papanicolaou & Falk, 1938). The amount of fat tissue, on the other hand, decreases more for boys than for girls (Reynolds, 1946; Tanner, 1975). That these changes are a function of pubescence rather than of age is shown by the greater growth of bone and muscle tissues in early-maturing girls in contrast to late-maturing girls (Reynolds, 1946).

More important is the change that takes place in the composition and structure of the bones. As the skeleton becomes increasingly more mature, the proportion of osseous to cartilaginous tissue increases. First, cartilage is replaced by osseous matter; then the process of ossification is completed by the deposition of calcium. Vitamin C is necessary for the first step, and vitamin D is required for the latter step (Best & Taylor, 1973; Hall, 1973). The "skeletal age" of an individual is an expression indicating the percentage of his total wrist area that is ossified (as determined by x-rays), in relation to the mean values of various age groups. Hence, a child of 10 with precocious skeletal maturity may have a skeletal age of 12. In terms of skeletal age, girls are consistently more mature than boys over the entire age span. At the age of 6 the difference is only about 1 year; but at 14, girls and boys are 2 years apart (Pyle et al., 1971; Tanner, 1962; Todd, 1937) on this index of skeletal maturity, and the gap is not closed until the termination of the adolescent period.

Skeletal age is an extremely useful index of physiological maturity. For one thing, it is closely related to growth in stature. During pubescence final adult height can be predicted more accurately if the individual's skeletal age is known (Crampton, 1944; Greulich, 1950; Shuttleworth, 1939; Tanner, 1962). Second, it is highly correlated with other criteria of sexual maturity (Greulich, 1950; Tanner, 1975) and can be used as an objective index of pubescent status. The age of menarche is more closely related to prepubescent skeletal age than to height, weight, or annual increments in height (Simmons, 1944; Weiland et al., 1971).

In order to appreciate the relationships between bone structure, skeletal maturation, and longitudinal growth, it is necessary to trace

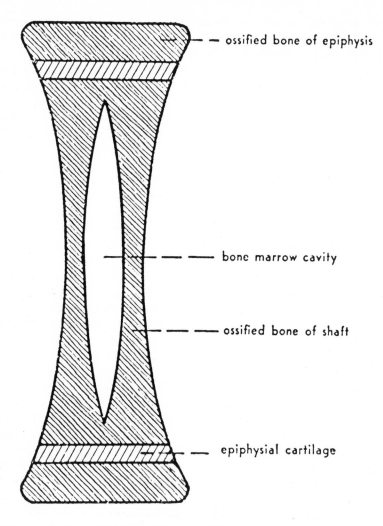

— — ossified bone of epiphysis

— — — bone marrow cavity

— — — ossified bone of shaft

— — epiphysial cartilage

Fig. 5-1. Schematic diagram of frontal section of a long bone of the lower extremity during the pubescent period.

the development of a typical long bone such as the femur or tibia of the lower extremity. As illustrated schematically in Fig. 5-1, a long bone consists of a *shaft* containing the bone marrow cavity and a wider portion at either end called the *epiphysis*. At birth the entire bone is composed of cartilage except for small centers of ossification in the epiphyses. During infancy and childhoood the epiphyses and the shaft gradually undergo ossification, except for a strip of cartilage situated at their junction known as the *epiphyseal cartilage*. It is here that all longitudinal growth of the bone takes place during adolescence. As long as these cartilage cells remain unossified, they are able to multiply and lengthen the bone (Ausubel, 1954; Little, 1973). The hormonal developments responsible for initiating the rapid growth spurt during preadolescence and early adolescence and for terminating growth at the end of adolescence (by leading to ossification of the epiphyseal cartilage) are extremely complicated and are discussed in a later section.

THE ADOLESCENT GROWTH SPURT

Skeletal growth takes place over an interval of approximately 18 to 20 years. The rate of growth, however, is far from constant. It is marked by two spurts, each of which is succeeded by periods of very slow growth. The first spurt occurs in early infancy and is followed by a long period during which the yearly increments in stature are small and relatively constant. The second growth spurt begins 1 to 2 years before pubescence, about the age of 11 in girls and approximately 2 years later in boys (Shuttleworth, 1939; Tanner, 1962, 1975). Shuttleworth (1939) found the mean age of maximal growth to be 12.6 in girls and 14.8 in boys. For girls, this is 6 months to a year before the occurrence of the menarche; for boys, it is slightly more than a year after the appearance of first pubic hair and initial ejaculation of semen. Tanner (1975) places the age of peak velocity of height in Anglo-Saxon countries at 12 in girls and 14 in boys. Thereafter, a period of gradual deceleration sets in until the ages of 18 to 20 when growth ceases completely.

The adolescent growth spurt, although beginning before the onset of other criteria of sexual maturation, is definitely related to the endocrine changes that initiate pubescence (McCloy, 1938; Richey, 1937; Tanner, 1975; Weiland et al., 1971). To begin with, the age at which the period of accelerated growth starts is a function of the age of pubescence (Richey, 1937; Weiland et al., 1971). The earlier onset of sexual maturation in girls is reflected in the fact that between the ages of 11 and 14 girls for the first and only time tend to be taller than boys. Second, characteristic differences exist between the growth patterns of

individuals who show different rates of maturing. For both sexes, the faster maturing children have more intense spurts of rapid growth with the period of acceleration both starting and stopping abruptly, while the late-maturers have less intense periods of ac-

celeration and with a subsequent growth which is longer continued, more even, and gradual. (Bayley & Tuddenham, 1944,
pp. 46–47)

Finally, as shown by the data of Crampton (1944) and others, only a
small percentage of prepubescent individuals are as tall as the
average postpubescent.

Not only do children who mature sexually at an earlier age undergo the adolescent growth spurt sooner, but they also hold a consistent advantage over late-maturing children in height and weight
long before any signs of puberty are evident (Bayley & Tuddenham,
1944; Richey, 1937; Shuttleworth, 1939; Tanner, 1975). That is, early-
maturing children are found to be taller and heavier than slow maturers even at the age of 6 (Richey, 1937; Shuttleworth, 1939). In addition, they tend to be "broad-built with relatively wide hips" in contrast to the latter who "are more likely to be long-legged and slender"
(Bayley & Tuddenham, 1944; Simmons, 1944).

Age of pubescence in relation to adult height

It is clear that early-maturing children are taller at all ages (at least
from 6 onward), and both enter and complete the adolescent growth
spurt at an earlier age than their late-maturing contemporaries
(Richey, 1937; Simmons, 1944; Tanner, 1975; Vandenberg & Falkner,
1965). It is less clear, however, whether the age at which pubescence
occurs affects an individual's ultimate adult stature. In general, the
statement we made earlier holds true: a positive and predictable relationship prevails between prepubescent and postpubescent height
(Vandenberg & Falkner, 1965) [estimated at 0.8 by Tanner (1975)] providing that sexual maturation does not occur extremely early or extremely late. This means that the age of pubescence (within normal
limits) affects only the age at which the growth spurt begins and that
at which it terminates, and does not affect the individual's ultimate
stature. A tall prepubescent child tends to mature earlier and, therefore, has an earlier occurring growth spurt (Tanner, 1975; Vandenberg & Falkner, 1965). But he also becomes a taller adult than the
shorter prepubescent child. Hence, early-maturing children tend to
develop into taller adults and vice versa (Tanner, 1975; Weiland et al.,
1971). The remaining 30 percent of the variance in adult height that is
not determined by the correlation between pre- and postpubescent
pubescent stature is determined both by age of onset of pubescence
and by genic factors governing variability in the growth curve (Ausubel, 1954; Tanner, 1975).

At the extremes of the distribution—in examples of precocious or retarded puberty—postpubescent height can no longer be predicted from prepubescent height. Here an inverse relationship prevails between age of sexual maturation and ultimate adult height. If puberty occurs precociously, not only does the growth spurt take place precociously, but it also ceases long before normal adult height is attained, resulting in a form of dwarfism (Greulich, 1942, 1944). If, on the other hand, the onset of pubescence is abnormally delayed, growth continues for too long a time and a very tall, long-legged adult develops (Greulich, 1944). The same condition is produced by prepuberal castration (Greulich, 1944).

Somewhere between these extreme conditions and the more typical age sample of sexual maturation the data are somewhat equivocal and interpretation is difficult. The situation is somewhat clearer for boys than it is for girls. Various investigators agree that either there is no significant relationship between earliness of pubescence and the terminal adult height of boys (Bayley & Tuddenham, 1944) or the relationship is positive (Bayley & Tuddenham, 1944; Shuttleworth, 1939). For girls, on the other hand, some workers report no significant relationship (Richey, 1937), whereas others (Bayley & Tuddenham, 1944; Shuttleworth, 1939) report an inverse relationship (early maturers end up shorter and vice versa). The latter differences may be a function of just how early- or late-maturing these various groups of girls are. For example, Shuttleworth (1939) determined the adult height of three groups of girls whose mean ages of maximal growth were 10.5, 12.5, and 14.5, respectively. In order of adult stature at age 19, these groups differing in age of sexual maturation ranked as follows: middle, early, and late. It seems possible, therefore, that relatively early (although not precocious) pubescence may limit final height in girls but not in boys. In this connection, Bayley and Tuddenham (1944) suggest that "the female sex hormones are more potent than the male sex hormones in terminating physical growth."

Endocrine aspects of the adolescent growth spurt

We have already shown that the occurrence of the adolescent growth spurt is closely related to the onset of sexual maturation and to structural changes in bones that determine the individual's skeletal age. The formidable task still remains of explaining how the cells of the epiphyseal cartilage are stimulated to multiply at this time, and how their multiplication is finally terminated by ossification during the decelerating stage of growth in late adolescence.

The most generally accepted hypothesis in the past was that the prepubescent growth spurt is initiated by a sudden increase in the production of the pituitary growth hormone. The gonadal hormones were believed to account for the decelerating phase and for the eventual termination of growth by causing "a gradual reduction in either the amount or the effectiveness of the growth hormone" (Greulich, 1944). As the secretion of gonadal hormone increased, a turning point was reached (age of maximal skeletal growth), and thereafter the rate of growth diminished until it ceased completely. In precocious puberty, growth was believed to be stunted because the influence of the growth hormone was prematurely cut short by the abnormally early appearance of the gonadal hormone. If, on the other hand, puberty was delayed, the growth hormone operated unopposed on the expansion of the epiphyseal cartilage for too long a period, and a long-legged eunuchoidal individual resulted (Greulich, 1944).

This theory accounts satisfactorily for the termination of growth and for the sequence of events in precocious and retarded puberty. However, it explains less adequately (1) the initiation of puberty, (2) the positive relationship between earliness of sexual maturation and adult height within the normal range of pubertal onset, and (3) the demonstrable fact that adrenal cortex and gonadal hormones stimulate bone growth* (Little, 1973).

There is no evidence to support the view that the growth hormone becomes more active in prepubescence. Furthermore, if this theory were true, (1) why should rapid growth continue into early pubescence when gonadal secretion increases, (2) why should early-maturing individuals grow more rapidly and (except in extreme instances in girls) end up just as tall, and (3) why should injections of gonadal hormones induce skeletal growth as well as sexual maturation (Little, 1973; Schonfeld, 1950)?

To overcome these difficulties the senior author (Ausubel, 1954) proposed the following alternative hypothesis that is now supported by the sequential histological changes (from cartilage proliferation to ossification) found in the epiphyseal cartilages of laboratory animals in response to gonadal hormones (Little, 1973). Estrogenic and androgenic hormones have two effects on cartilage: (1) like the growth hormone they stimulate cartilaginous proliferation (Little, 1973; Wei-

---

*In cases of precocious puberty it is true that the individual does not attain normal adult stature. Nevertheless, he is considerably taller than children of comparable chronological age. And what is more significant, as shown by Greulich's (1950) own data, he is far advanced in skeletal changes. This is presumptive evidence that androgenic hormones stimulate cartilaginous growth rather than oppose the action of the growth hormone.

land et al., 1971); but (2) they also accelerate, at a certain critical level, the process of ossification which terminates bone growth. According to this view, the prepubescent growth spurt would be initiated as increasing amounts of estrogenic or androgenic substances are produced and add to the existing stimulation supplied by the growth hormone (Weiland et al., 1971). The initiation of this event would precede the occurrence of other signs of sexual maturation because of the greater sensitivity of the epiphyseal cartilages of the long bones of the lower extremity to sex hormone stimulation. Then, as the level of gonadal secretion increased, skeletal growth would reach a critical maximum level and finally begin to decelerate since more and more cartilage would simultaneously be ossified. If puberty were markedly retarded, the growth hormone would have a longer time in which to function before both the adolescent growth spurt and ossification would supervene, resulting in a tall, long-legged individual; and if it took place prematurely, the early ossification would deprive the epiphyseal cartilage of the benefit of several years of growth hormone stimulation during the childhood period, resulting in an abnormally short adult (Richey, 1937).

Within the median range of distribution of age of pubescence, the positive genically determined relationship between earliness of maturation and terminal skeletal height is not disturbed. As long as the epiphyseal cartilage is open for a reasonably long time (and hence subject to stimulation by the growth hormone), final adult height is not differentially influenced by the age at which puberty and intense gonadal stimulation commence. The latter factor merely affects the age at which the adolescent growth spurt occurs. Thus, the boy who is tall at 6 tends to mature earlier than his shorter contemporary, undergoes an earlier growth spurt, and becomes a taller adult (Vandenberg & Falkner, 1965). Earliness of pubescence is thus positively correlated with terminal stature because both factors are similarly related to initial height.

Operating antagonistically to this relationship is the inverse relationship between earliness of maturation and ultimate height that prevails when there is a marked increase or reduction in the total length of time during which the epiphyseal cartilage is open (retarded or precocious puberty). Somewhere between the extremes and the normal limits of the distribution of age of pubescence, these two factors counterbalance each other and result in a relationship that follows neither pattern. This point of equilibrium seems to show a sex difference since the inverse relationship sets in earlier in girls (Bayley & Tuddenham, 1944), leading to the hypothesis that estrogenic hormones surpass male sex hormones in their propensity for stimulating ossification of epiphyseal cartilage.

CHANGES IN BODY WEIGHT

An adolescent spurt in weight is as regular an accompaniment of sexual maturation as a spurt in height (Greulich, 1942, 1944). Like the spurt in height, it occurs earlier in children who enter pubescence at a younger age and tends to precede other signs of sexual maturation Greulich, 1944). In girls it usually takes place between the ages of 10 and 14, whereas in boys it occurs 2 years later (Tanner, 1962). Between the ages of 12 and 15 girls for the first time become heavier than boys, but thereafter boys regain their superiority. Crampton (1944) found no prepubescent boy who was heavier than the mean postpubescent boy in his sample of 361 cases. The heavier child, just like the taller child, tends to become pubescent earlier (Greulich, 1944). We have already referred to sex differences in the distribution of fat. The best current device available for assessing the adequacy of growth in weight (according to the individual's own idiosyncratic growth pattern) is the Wetzel grid technique, which rates maturity in terms of "the percentage level reached with respect to ultimate level" (Wetzel, 1944).

CHANGES IN BODY PROPORTIONS

Concomitantly with the growth spurt, a change in body proportions takes place. The most important change, occurring in both sexes, is a reversal of the ratio of trunk to leg growth, which alters "the proportion of sitting to standing height" (Bayley & Tuddenham, 1944). In contrast to the preadolescent years, the trunk begins to grow more rapidly than the legs until the ratio stabilizes as growth is completed (Bayley & Tuddenham, 1944; Tanner, 1971). The upper portion of the face, particularly the nose, grows at a faster rate than in childhood, giving rise to a marked change in facial appearance. According to Krogman (1939), growth of the face during adolescence occurs primarily in length (depth) and least in height, with growth in width occupying a middle position. This is precisely the opposite of the situation in preadolescence.

The relative growth of various organ systems may be compared in Scammon's grouping of their growth trends under four general types: lymphoid, neural, general, and genital (Harris eta al., 1930). Genital growth increases most spectacularly during adolescence, and there is a substantial but not as great an increase in general (skeleton, musculature, internal organs) growth. Neural growth tapers off, nearing completion at age 4; and lymphoid tissues actually decrease in weight. Growth of the respiratory and vascular organs tends to keep pace with growth in skeletal (bone and muscle) tissue (Maresh, 1948; Tanner, 1975) thereby obviating the possibility of physiological imbalance in meeting the enhanced nutritive needs of an enlarged body frame with larger muscles.

Other changes in adolescent body proportions are either sex linked or related to "velocity of maturation." In girls the most prominent change is a relative widening of the hips, and in boys a corresponding increase in the breadth of the shoulders (Bayley & Tuddenham, 1944; Tanner, 1975). These differences, together with characteristic sex differences in muscular development and distribution of fat, constitute the basis for standards of male and female body build. The chronology of their occurrence (as well as the changes in trunk-limb ratio and in facial proportions) is naturally a function of the age of pubescence. In addition, however, characteristic differences exist between early- and late-maturing individuals. Late-maturing boys and girls tend to be relatively long-legged and to have shorters trunks than their more rapidly maturing contemporaries. Early-maturing boys also tend to be relatively broad hipped and narrow shouldered in comparison to late-maturing boys (Bayley & Tuddenham, 1944).

Stolz and Stolz (1944) refer to these shifting patterns in the rates of growth of various body parts as "asynchrony of development." Since the resulting changes in body proportions take place within a relatively short space of time, they are quite noticeable and call for some form of psychological adjustment.

GROWTH IN STRENGTH

A striking consequence of skeletal maturation during pubescence, with important implications for motor development, is a marked gain in strength (H. E. Jones, 1947; Tanner, 1975). In part, this reflects the increase in the size of long bones, of the shoulder and pelvic girldes, and of the musculature in general. In part, it may reflect an increase in the strength of individual muscle fibers as a result of a shift in the endocrine (thymus-adrenal-gonadal) balance and an increase in androgen level (Papanicolaou & Falk, 1938). However, that growth in streńgth should lag behind growth in muscle mass (Stolz &

Stolz, 1944; Wilgoose, 1950) is not at all surprising since the acquisition of structure generally precedes the acquisition of function. Time is needed before new structural capacities can become functional. A clear illustration of this principle is found in the vocal chords, which increase greatly in size during early pubescence but not correspondingly in degree of control.

When strength of grip is plotted against age, an increase in the rate of growth is noted for both sexes during the years of pubescence (H. E. Jones, 1944; Tanner, 1975). That this gain in strength is mostly a function of pubescence rather than a function of age is shown by the significantly greater scores made by pubescent as compared to prepubescent boys and girls (H. E. Jones, 1944, 1946b, 1947). The average pubescent boy exceeds 97 percent of prepubescent boys in strength (Crampton, 1944). Precocious development of strength is also a characteristic of premature puberty.

More important for their motor and social implications than the gain in strength made by both boys and girls are the differences between the two sexes. In girls, the growth spurt begins earlier, reaches a maximum more quickly, and then begins to taper off at about the age of 13 or 14 (H. E. Jones, 1947). In boys, the gain in strength does not reach a maximum until age 16 and tapers off more slowly. Hence, the sex difference in strength tends to be widened during adolescence (H. E. Jones, 1944, 1947; Tanner, 1975).

Sex differences in strength are no doubt at least partly a function of cultural conditioning. Muscular development depends to a large extent on opportunity for use and exercise, which, by virtue of our cultural tradition, is heavily weighted in favor of boys. However, there are good reasons for believing that anatomical and physiological factors are also involved. Androgens, as already suggested, may exert a differential effect on muscular development. Because of their greater height and weight, the greater breadth of their shoulders, and the greater length of their bones, boys have a decided advantage in terms of leverage. In locomotor activities boys are also favored by the more advantageous angle that the neck of the femur makes with the pelvis. Physiologically, as pointed out above, boys also have greater tolerance for physical exertion because of a greater respiratory volume, a greater ability to compensate for increased work load through a rise in systolic blood pressure, a lower pulse rate, a superior oxygen delivery system (more hemoglobin and red blood cells), and quicker disposal of lactic acid.

As Jersild (1946) and his associates suggest, the social implications of this sex difference in strength are "that joint participation by boys and girls in the more robust athletic activities after the age of about fifteen will not function primarily in the nature of a competitive contest between or among equals. Such participation will mainly serve the social purpose of enabling the members of the two sexes to be together."

MOTOR DEVELOPMENT DURING ADOLESCENCE

The subject of motor development during adolescence may be most relevantly considered in relation to the growth in size, strength, and body proportions described in the preceding pages. These events provide the underlying basis for whatever changes take place in physical performance during this period. In personality development, however, such objective shifts in motor capacity are less important in themselves than in relation to the changed biosocial status of the adolescent. Hence, we shall be primarily concerned with the implications of adolescent motor development for social and vocational adjustment rather than with motor development per se.

The motor ability of an individual during adolescence, just as in earlier stages of development, constitutes an important component of his feeling of competence in coping with the environment. It enables him to feel either executively competent and capable of looking after many of his own needs or relatively dependent on the physical assistance of others. In addition, it continues to provide an important source of personal satisfaction, pleasure, relaxation, and leisure time activity. But in many ways it acquires new significance for personal and social adjustment.

First, during adolescence motor competence enters more crucially into the matter of the individual's earned status.* Throughout childhood, the capacity for self-help is something which the individual acquires largely in response to parental pressures and in order to retain parental approval; motor ability serves as a source of earned status chiefly in relation to his peer group. Now, however, it becomes a significant consideration in his quest for earned status in the adult world. For this reason it figures prominently in his deliberations about choice of a vocation.

The second major difference is that the prestige and "social esteem" associated with "competitive athletic skills" become for boys a major rather than a secondary source of current status during the adolescent period (H. E. Jones, 1946a). This is not to say that physical prowess is socially unesteemed in the age period preceding puberty.

---

* For the distinction between earned and derived (attributed) status, see Chapter 7.

In the earlier stage, however, the earned status achieved by the child through his own competence still is subsidiary to the derived status he enjoys at home. Success in competitive physical skills becomes much more eagerly sought after by the adolescent since it constitutes a more crucial determinant of his self-esteem.

Finally, because of the greater significance attached to the body during adolescence, noticeable physical incompetence or awkwardness becomes a more acute source of self-consciousness, embarrassment, and social ridicule. Thus, for this reason alone, motor handicaps are more likely to result in serious damage to the individual's self-concept.

Gross motor skills

The developmental picture for dynamic strength (running, jumping, throwing) is similar in some respects to the situation already described for static manual strength (strength of grip), and different in others. The two abilities are significantly correlated during the adolescent period (Wilgoose, 1950). The differences are attributable to the fact that dynamic strength is more closely related to the *functional utilization* of strength as involved in athletic performance. In addition to strength, the factors of speed of movement, coordination, agility, and dexterity are implicated in dynamic strength.

The parallel of growth in dynamic strength to growth of strength of grip is much greater for boys than girls. In boys, dynamic, like static, strength is more highly correlated with physiological than with chronological age* (Cunning, et al., 1972; Espenschade, 1940; Espenschade & Eckert, 1967). It also grows slowly, reaching a maximum after the age of 15; but the gain is relatively less than that in static strength. In girls, on the other hand, dynamic strength tends to show an actual *decrease* (rather than merely to decelerate in rate of growth as in strength of grip) in most functions (broad jump, 50-yard dash) after the age of 13. Thus, although sheer strength remains a function of maturational status in girls, cultural factors influencing interest and inclination become more important after this point in determining whether increased strength will be used in the gross motor skills. Hence, during adolescence the divergence between the sexes in these abilities tends to become even greater than in strength. How-

---

* It should be noted, however, that scores on the Brace test of *motor aptitude* (in contrast to dynamic strength as measured by athletic ability) are negatively correlated with pubescent status. Prepubescent boys, in other words, make better scores than pubescent boys on this test (Dimock, 1937).

ever, overlapping does occur and an occasional girl exceeds the average boy in both respects. Girls who are stronger and more physically fit participate more in physical activities (Van Dalen, 1949), which demonstrates the interrelationships between strength and skill on the one hand and exercise on the other.

Therefore, to those biological causes of sex differences in strength listed above, we must add factors of "cultural expectation. . . motivation and practice" in explaining the ever-widening gap between boys and girls in competitive athletic skills after the onset of pubescence (H. E. Jones, 1944). These sex differences are obviously important for their social implications in the peer group. However, in modern industrial society, with the gradual elimination of the need for physical strength and gross motor skill in most occupations, they are becoming increasingly less significant as relevant factors affecting vocational choice and aptitude.

Mechanical abilities

Fine motor and mechanical abilities follow still another growth pattern than strength and gross motor skills. Involving as they do limited, swift, and precise movements of the small muscles of the hand rather than gross movements of large muscle groups, they are not implicated in the characteristic pubescent changes in muscle mass, strength, and coordination (Jones & Seashore, 1944). The aspects of motor development most specifically related to sexual maturation involve the long bones and the muscles that are attached to them. Hence, development of fine motor and mechanical abilities pursues its own growth pattern in relation to chronological age and seems to be relatively independent of the influence that pubescence exerts on other functions.*

In accordance with the principle of "developmental direction" (which states that muscles closer to the midline of the body mature earlier), manual coordination lags behind that of the wrist, elbow, and shoulder in the order stated. Hence, fine motor skills are acquired relatively late in comparison to abilities involving the larger muscle groups (Jones & Seashore, 1944). When compared to the growth curve for intelligence, which is similarly unaffected by the

---

* Jones and Seashore (1944) in discussing the development of these abilities among subjects in the California growth study report that "there are some indications. . . that the early-maturing boys and girls tend to show somewhat steeper growth curves in early adolescence and tend to reach an earlier plateau. The differences however are smaller and less consistent than in the case of strength and gross motor performance."

physiological events of pubescence, the growth in mechanical ability during the adolescent period is not only less in magnitude but also terminates at an earlier age.

Another important difference between gross and fine motor abilities is the geater degree of intercorrelation among the former. The fine motor abilities are much more specialized, so that if an individual is superior in one mechanical ability it is no indication that he is likely to be superior in another. Jones and Seashore (1944 pp. 133, 136, 137) conclude:

> We find practically no evidence for. . . a general factor in fine motor skills, but a great deal of evidence for rather narrow group factors, and always for at least some specific factors in each test. . . . The group factors are not only relatively narrow as to the tests included within each group, but they often exclude tests which at first glance seem logically related. Also the group factors are only slightly related among themselves. . . . [Thus] in view of the specific nature of motor skills it is misleading to speak of a "general motor ability."

If, as these findings suggest, fine motor abilities are highly specific, and there is no such thing as *"general* mechanical ability,"* it becomes necessary to reevaluate the predictive value of various test batteries designed to measure manual dexterity and aptitude. Although it is conceivable that a particular subscore on such a battery may be highly predictive of success in a closely related occupation, the *composite* score is not likely to be very meaningful or to have much predictive value. We should also remember that success in any specific mechanical vocation depends on factors other than mechanical aptitude, such as general intelligence, previous experience, motivation, and quality of technical training (Jones & Seashore, 1944). These additional factors may explain

> why highly skilled workers in a mechanical occupation make higher test scores than do lower-skilled workers. . . . The only conclusive evidence for the aptitude nature of a mechanical test is to administer it to a group of subjects before training and to show that the test scores do predict success as measured by rate of learning or by final levels of achievement after considerable experience in practical work. (Jones & Seashore, 1944, p. 141)

Sex differences in mechanical abilities tend to be inconsistent in direction. Under conditions of relatively equal opportunity for practice, differences are small and in most instances statistically unreliable [for example, reaction time to sound, spatial eye-hand coordination,

bimanual coordination, manual steadiness (Jones & Seashore, 1944).]
In "temporal eye-hand coordination" boys are consistently superior
to girls, whereas the reverse is true in a test "requiring the selection
of an appropriate finger movement in response to a series of
numbers visually perceived" (Jones & Seashore, 1944).

In everyday mechanical skills, however, as we might suspect from
the specificity of these skills, relative superiority is almost completely
a function of differential opportunity for practice. Boys, for example,
tend to outdo girls in skills involving the use of carpentry tools,
whereas girls show to advantage in skills such as sewing and dress-
making (Jersild, 1946). Certainly, a legitimate vocational implication
that can be drawn from consideration of these data is "that there can
be much more latitude of vocational choice notably for girls than conventionally has been allowed" (Jersild et al., 1946). It would seem
more reasonable and less wasteful of talent and ability, as Jersild et al.
suggest, to relate vocational opportunity to the "actual potentialities"
of boys and girls than to purely arbitrary considerations of sex appropriateness dictated by cultural tradition.

Interest in physical activities

With adolescence begins the increasing trend toward sedentary
habits that is perhaps the most characteristic psychological datum of
the aging process. A sharp decline in both interest in and volume of
physical activity occurs (M. C. Jones, 1944). "Children who earlier
were on the go much of the time now do more sitting or standing
around. There is a decline in participation in vigorous sports and a
relative increase in the time spent as a spectator of sports" (Jersild et
al., 1946).

This change is much more thoroughgoing and abrupt in girls
since, as we have noted, competitive physical activities continue to
play an important role in determining the peer group status of adolescent boys. This loss of interest among girls also accounts for the
decline in their performance in gross athletic skills. It is largely a
response to cultural standards of sex-appropriate behavior reinforced
by a fear that vigorous physical activity will induce masculine bodily
characteristics (for example, bulging muscles). Hence, even the most
confirmed preadolescent tomboy generally mends her ways with the
advent of puberty.

In both sexes the decline in physical activity is partly a function of
the competition offered by new social interests (extracurricular clubs,
dancing). To an unknown extent, also, it is probably a normal accompaniment of aging, since as individuals become older there appears

to be a noticeable loss of pleasure in sheer exertion and a noticeable increase in the disposition to avoid bodily activity.

A related change is

> a decrease in the number of different or separate play activities [which] begins even during elementary years. It occurs, in part, . . . by reason of occupation with more highly organized games which combine many operations into one large activity (a well-organized baseball game, for example, combines running, dodging, chasing, throwing and the like). (Jersild et al., 1946)

The implications of this shift toward a more sedentary existence are uniformly undesirable. It is not only unnecessary in terms of actual physical capacity at this stage of life, but it is also unhygienic. From the standpoint of losing a good source of "pleasure, relaxation, . . . release from boredom" and leisure time activity, it is equally unfortunate (Jersild et al., 1946). It has also been observed informally that an adult will seldom pursue as a hobby a motor skill that has not been learned during childhood and early adolescence.

Part of the responsibility for this unsatisfactory state of affairs must be laid to the physical education program of schools, which emphasizes varsity sports and the type of athletic team activity that adults can continue only with difficulty after leaving school (football or baseball in contrast to handball, tennis, and swimming) (Jersild et al., 1946). The writers can thoroughly endorse the following statement by H. E. Jones (1944, p. 119): "The student of child development is inclined to believe that in this field our chief objectives should be conceived, not in terms of providing new and larger stadia for champions, but in terms of providing informed guidance and wholesome physical activities for students in general."

A special problem of guidance arises for high school or college athletes who later enter sedentary occupations. During the years of active athletic participation, the heart muscle hypertrophies to accommodate the increased needs of the skeletal muscles. If physical activity is abruptly discontinued, a certain portion of the hypertrophied cardiac tissue becomes superfluous and is no longer used; and, as so frequently happens when tissues are no longer functional, "disuse atrophy" sets in. In the heart the most common form of atrophy is fatty degeneration, which leads to impaired cardiac capacity. To avoid this unfortunate sequence of events it is necessary for athletes to undergo a gradual tapering off program when they contemplate retirement from strenuous physical activity.

Adolescent awkwardness

Much controversy has prevailed over the years over the issue of whether or not awkwardness in adolescence is biologically or socially determined. Both Dennis (1946) and Kuhlen (1952) cite investigations that purport to show that in the Brace test of gross motor aptitude, there is for boys a consistent gain with age over the adolescent period. Thus, they attribute the apparent awkwardness to various social factors. These include lack of experience in common social situations, i.e., making introductions, applying for a job; "razzing" from others when the adolescent first attempts to exercise such adult functions as dancing; and the replacement of automatic action in gait and posture with embarrassed self-consciousness. Dennis (1946) also points to the "size-age illusion" as a contributing cause. The early-maturing child who undergoes an early growth spurt "is perceived as older. . . [and hence] arouses expectations of agility and skill above average for his age."

We will not attempt to deny that these social factors are responsible for much of the awkwardness of adolescence. However, biological variables are also relevant. We have noted from the growth curves for different structures and functions that the gain in muscle mass precedes the gain in muscle strength, which in turn precedes the gain in gross motor skill. This is an expression of the familiar biological principle that functional capacity is not attained concomitantly with but subsequent to structural growth. This principle is especially evident in the neuromuscular system where practice and learning are such important factors. It is also understandable that simple functions such as strength involving a single set of muscles will be acquired before complex functions requiring coordination of several muscle groups, either concurrently or in a given temporal sequence.

If structural changes take place gradually, "the young boy or girl can adjust his coordination to his new bodily dimensions as rapidly as they are achieved" (Dennis, 1946). But this does not describe the situation during pubescence when growth in size and strength takes place in spurts and "precipitates too sudden a need for acquiring new patterns of physical coordination consonant with increased physical capacity" (Ausubel, 1950b). Many of the eye-hand coordinations built up over the years of childhood may be rendered obsolete by these changes (Frank, 1944a). The sudden shift in body porportions contributes still another biological reason for adolescent awkwardness.

During adolescence the growth curves for speed of movements involving the elbow, wrist, and fingers are all *parallel* (Jones & Seashore, 1944) even though rate of growth in size and strength in the larger muscle groups is much greater. Also, when the growth curves on the Brace test are plotted *separately* for pubescent and prepubescent boys, the prepubescents are found to be superior (Dimock, 1937) in the age range of 12.5 to 14.5. H. E. Jones (1944) reports that "boys tend to show a lag or even a recession in [motor] growth at around the skeletal age of fourteen years." Also, the argument that mechanical skill and manual dexterity improve during adolescence is not relevant since these functions are not particularly affected by pubescence. The significant skeletal changes of adolescence are principally in the long bones and in the large muscle groups; and it is here that we should look for disproportions in the rate of growth to result in possible dysfunction (defective coordination, awkwardness).

Motor ability and personal-social adjustment

We have pointed out that an adolescent's motor development cannot be isolated from broader issues of personal and social adjustment.

Particularly among adolescent boys the ability to take part in playground games and to play a normally lively role in various physical activities is more often than not an important factor in the development of successful social relationships. . . . With the coming of pubertal changes, girls tend to lose interest in active games and in the display of various forms of athletic prowess. . . . Among boys, however, competitive athletic skills are among the chief sources of social esteem. . . . These relationships would seem to be due not merely to the high premium which adolescents place upon athletic proficiency, but also to the fact that strength and other aspects of physical ability are closely joined to such favorable traits as activity, aggressiveness and leadership. (H. E. Jones, 1944, pp. 101, 117, 118)

H. E. Jones (1944) documents this statement with data from a study by Bower, who showed that in seventh- and ninth-grade boys, "popularity was unrelated to intelligence, height, home ratings, or school adjustment, but was significantly related to strength and to physical ability as measured by a series of track-event tests." Presenting data of his own collected over a period of 6 to 8 years, H. E. Jones (1946a) found significant differences in personal and social adjustment between boys making high and low scores, respectively, on tests of strength. The former were superior on ratings of popularity, "emotional buoyancy," social adjustment, and family adjustment, whereas the latter were rated higher on such items as "generalized tensions," "personal inferiority," and "physical symptoms." In general, these differences between the two groups tended to become more marked over a 6-year period.

Retardation in motor competence is the beginning of a vicious cycle in social maladjustment that is difficult to break. Boys with poor physical ability tend to enjoy low social prestige in the group. They thus have reasons to shun both physical activities and group participation because both are associated with failure.

The child with negative and withdrawing traits is unfavorably regarded by his classmates; his failure to participate in physical activities increases his poor reputation and at the same time, through lack of practice, he falls further and further behind his classmates in those very characteristics that are needed to maintain status. Moreover, the child who seeks to participate but is unable to do so because of lack of skill may be forced to take refuge in withdrawal as his only defense against conspicuous social rejection. (H. E. Jones, 1944, p. 118)

It is possible, of course, that as a consequence of inferiority in physical skills, an individual may be motivated to develop other abilities from which he can derive compensatory satisfaction or prestige. But as Jones (1944) points out, "it is a critical question whether in so doing, he will lose contact with his classmates, or, on the other hand, will find a socially adequate use of such favorable traits as he may possess." If the compensatory outlet does not tend to result in social isolation, it may legitimately be encouraged as an activity that possesses as much as or greater intrinsic value than athletic pursuits. In any event, however, the potential adjustive value of direct guidance (individual coaching) in motor skills should not be overlooked. Jack et al. (1934) showed that as a result of such individual guidance socially timid children become more ascendant and self-assertive in their peer relationships.

The feasibility of guidance in physical skills is enhanced by their specificity and their susceptibility to improvement as a result of practice guided by instruction directed toward

the detection and elimination of the particular difficulties of each individual which constitute his 'bottleneck' toward progress in learning that skill. . . . A person who has a poor initial score in a motor activity is in many cases only temporarily handicapped, and if the skill is important to him he can often attain at least normal levels of proficiency by means of remedial training adapted to the nature of his difficulties.

If it is desirable for [the] best performers to receive special coaching in their activities it should be at least equally desirable and perhaps even more important to provide even larger amounts of such coaching for the lower ranking members of the group.

This, of course, does not assume that every person should attempt to develop a high degree of skill in every type of motor activity, but simply that there should be facilities to encourage those who have initial handicaps to develop at least far enough to be able to play a normal role in everyday activities or in informal competition within their groups. Emphasis upon the general principles of good form in an activity can be taught in groups, with special attention to those for whom still more intensive training is necessary. (Jones & Seashore, 1944, p. 142)

In the case of boys who are temporarily retarded in growth, informed guidance implies an understanding of their individual growth patterns and potentialities. (H. E. Jones, 1944, p. 119)

6

Psychological Accompaniments of Bodily Change

Chapters 4 and 5 reviewed the physiological events of adolescence: the endocrine changes and their consequences for primary and secondary sex characteristics; the physiological changes in organ systems; and skeletal changes and their implications for height, weight, body proportions, strength, and skill. In this chapter we shall examine the psychological phenomena that accompany these physiological changes. But in contrast to the approach in Chapter 7 (where we are concerned with pubescence merely as the major change in the individual's biosocial status responsible for *precipitating* the adolescent reorganization of personality structure), we shall be concerned here with the more *direct* behavioral consequences of the new physiological happenings.

In addition to the contribution of pubescence to the altered biosocial status of adolescents, physical changes influence psychological accompaniments in several other ways. (1) Endocrine substances and changes in hormonal balance are capable of lowering the general threshold of behavioral reactivity and of altering (in a nonspecific fashion) the intensity and feeling tones of emotional responses. Through this facilitating effect, general changes in emotional expression—in range, depth, specificity, direction consistency, and stability—are induced. (2) Hormones are able also to provide a physiological substrate for the generation of more *specific* drives, interests, emotions, and states of awareness. The sex hormones, for example, furnish the nucleus and the raw material from which a large part of the heterosexual feelings, motivations, and interests of adolescents are fashioned. This relationship is exceedingly complex, is by no means inevitable, and depends on the interaction among physiological events, individual psychological experience, and cultural influences. (3) On a purely perceptual basis, both the individual and the group observe and react to the bodily changes that have taken place. These changes are perceived not in isolation but in relation to the similarities and differences that arise between one person and the next by reason of variation in rate and pattern of maturing (Ausubel, 1950b, 1952; Jersild et al., 1946). The individual is obliged to alter the mental image of his own body form, and various members of the group regard his body in a new light, as an object with a positive rather than neutral sex valence. (4) The individual responds to the social reactions that his own bodily changes elicit. To the social responses of approval or disapproval, admiration or ridicule, acceptance or rejection, he makes corresponding reactions in his own self-estimate and self-defense systems.

CHANGES IN INTERESTS

The influence of pubescence on the interests of adolescents is customarily measured by correlating the maturity level of their interests with various physical indices of sexual maturity. However, even when a positive correlation is found, a direct causal relationship need not necessarily be assumed. It is true that hormonal factors may directly create a differential sensitivity to stimuli of a heterosexual nature. But at the same time, much of the increased interest in heterosexual activities is generated indirectly through a process of social identification; that is, the pubescent individual tends to identify with and be accepted by his pubescent peers in the community, and to associate himself with their interests. This latter mechanism is also a more plausible explanation of relationships between physiological maturity and shifts in interests that are either unrelated to sex activities (athletics) or related in only a culturally determined sense (criteria of masculinity and femininity).

When the maturity of boys' interests was expressed in the form of "developmental age," Sollenberger (1940) found a moderately high correlation between that index and the quantity of androgens excreted in the urine. Postmenarchial girls achieve scores indicative of greater maturity on the Pressey Interest Attitude Test (Stone & Barker, 1937) and also show more interest than premenarchial girls in grooming, heterosexual activities, and daydreaming but less interest in athletic activities (Stone & Barker, 1939). Terman and Miles (1936) found that early-maturing boys and girls obtained higher masculinity and femininity scores, respectively, than their late-maturing counterparts of corresponding chronological age. The only reliable difference in play interests between pre- and postpubescent boys of similar age is in automobile driving (Dimock, 1937).

RECASTING THE BODY IMAGE

The body image is the mental picture that each individual has of his own appearance in space. It includes such factors as height, weight, body build, facial appearance, the hair, eyes, and voice (Schilder, 1935).* Ordinarily, during most periods of life, the body image changes imperceptibly because the body itself changes in this way. Especially during the childhood years growth is slow and gradual. The small changes in appearance and quantitative increments in height are easily absorbed in the prevailing image the child has of his own body; no radical revisions are necessary.

During adolescence such rapid changes take place in size, body proportions, primary and secondary sex characteristics, and facial appearance that minor adjustments in the body image are no longer sufficient. "The old body-image becomes incompatible with the new perception of the physical appearance and bodily dimensions of self." Nothing less will do than a conscious and wholesale restructuring of the outmoded body image. However, there is a drastic change not only in the structure of the body image but also in its importance.

Changes in body contours, new sensory experiences from developing sex organs, the upsurge of energy, new as well as heightened emotional responses—all tend to focus the attention of a boy or girl on his body. . . . This focusing of attention on the body is probably a concomitant of those periods in human life when the velocity of physical change is rapid, as in infancy and adolescence. . . . As changes in growth bring changes in sensations or appearance, interest in the body is renewed and concepts of self undergo revisions. . . .

These bodily experiences are the not-to-be-ignored signs of growing up and become in a certain sense the symbol, not only

---

*For a complete discussion of the body image concept, see Schilder (1935), who introduced this concept in personality theory, developmental psychology, and psychopathology. Schonfeld (1966) applies this concept more specifically to the role of the family in the development of the adolescent's body image and to adolescent personality and behavior disorder.

of being different from last month or last year, but of a new attitude toward self, toward others, toward life. (Stolz & Stolz, 1944, p. 83)

The body image, of course, is not of uniform significance and importance to adolescents throughout this entire period of growth. When junior high school students were asked what they liked and did not like about themselves, they mentioned physical characteristics more frequently than they did social relationships or intellectual status (Jersild, 1952). This trend was much less marked in senior high school. In all probability adolescents attach more importance to their own physical shortcomings than their age mates do, although it must be admitted that this concern has considerable basis in objective fact.

SEX DRIVE AND SEX AWARENESS

The activation of the sex hormones creates an emergent problem of adaptation during pubescence. For the first time since early infancy a powerful, new, physiologically conditioned drive appears on the psychological scene, requiring initial regulations, direction, and socialization. In this respect at least, the problem of personality maturation during adolescence is more comparable to that of infancy than of childhood. If at this time the individual is older, is more responsive to social norms, and has more compelling reasons to control hedonistic impulses, it is also true that he stands at the threshold of a new era of self-assertion and desire for volitional independence.

Preadolescent sex interests and activities

There is abundant evidence from the behavior of preadolescent subprimates (males only) (Ford & Beach, 1951), primates (Ford & Beach, 1951), and humans in our society and in primitive societies (Blos, 1941; Ford & Beach, 1951; Kinsey et al., 1948; Malinowski, 1929) to indicate that sex interest, curiosity, and activity prior to puberty are natural and frequently occurring phenomena. Such activities and manifestations of sex interest include masturbation, "peeking," mutual exhibitionism and genital manipulation (Ford & Beach, 1951; Kinsey et al., 1948), interest in obscene talk and pictures, flirtation, and attempts at intercourse (Ford & Beach, 1951; Kinsey et al., 1948). In some cultures, such as our own, preadolescent sex play is frowned on and suppressed, but nevertheless it is indulged in surreptitiously. In other cultures such as the Alorese, Lepacha, Trobriand, Hopi, and

Ifugao, adults take "a completely tolerant and permissive attitude toward sex expression in childhood" (Ford & Beach, 1951). Not only do some of these peoples "permit children free sex play. . . [and] also allow them opportunity to observe adult sexual behavior," but they also encourage experimentation in heterosexual intercourse. Ford and Beach (1951) conclude:

> After reviewing the cross-species and cross-cultural evidence, we are convinced that tendencies toward sexual behavior before maturity and even before puberty are genetically determined in many primates, including human beings. The degree to which such tendencies find overt expression is in part a function of the rules of the society in which the individual grows up, but some expression is very likely to occur under any circumstances.

Despite this evidence of prepubertal sex activity, there are good reasons—both theoretic and empirical—for believing that postpubertal sex behavior is qualitatively different from that which takes place prior to puberty. The matter of sexual expression assumes such compelling new urgency and so many rich new feeling tones during adolescence that qualitatively the problems of control and direction are no longer recognizable as those present during childhood. Hence, it is to be expected that regardless of the various types of outlet (or lack of outlet) provided for this drive in different societies, the stirring of sexual instincts (resulting from the increased production of sex hormones within the adolescent's own body) will give rise to universal feelings of uneasiness and bewilderment in relation to the emergent needs for their control and direction. Whether he feels shame or pleasure, guilt or joy, is another matter which is determined by family or cultural conditioning.

Adult (or postpubescent) sexuality can only be conceived of "as a form of self-expression (functionally or historically related to hormonal stimulation) which is related to the individual's experience of himself in a biological sex role" (Ausubel, 1950b; Ausubel & Kirk, 1977). Adolescent sexuality does not begin where childhood sexuality terminates. There is a qualitative difference, a definite break between the two. Childhood sexuality consists primarily of erogenous sensuality, of exploratory and manipulative activity, of curiosity about the anatomy and physiology of sex and reproduction, and of imitative attempts to simulate adult romanticism and sex play. It is "more or less a part of his other play. . . and usually sporadic" (Kinsey et al., 1948). After pubescence it becomes "an end in itself, frequent and regular" (Kinsey et al., 1948). In at least half of the instances of childhood history of sex activity preadolescent play ends well before or with the onset of adolescence, and more adult sexual activities must start from new points, newly won social acquirements, newly learned techniques of physical contact. In many cases, the newly adolescent boy's capacity to ejaculate, his newly acquired physical characteristics of other sorts do something to him which brings child play to an end and leaves him awkward about further sexual contacts. (Kinsey et al., 1948)

Malinowski (1929), after observing the uninhibited sex play (including attempted coitus) of Trobriand Island children, reached the same conclusion as Kinsey:

As the boy or girl enters upon adolescence, the nature of his or her sexual life becomes more serious. It ceases to be mere child's play and assumes a prominent place among life's interests. What was before an unstable relationship culminating in a exchange of erotic manipulation or an immature sexual act becomes an absorbing passion and a matter for serious endeavor.

Relationship between sex hormones and sex drives

Having concluded that sex hormones make for a qualitative difference between pre- and postpubescent sex behavior, we shall examine this relationship in greater detail. Exactly what role does any hormone or organic condition of the body play in generating a drive?

For a long time psychologists have spoken about "primary" or "innate" drives that are physiologically determined, and "secondary" or "acquired" drives that are developed as a product of experience. However, this distinction is really gratuitous since there are really no innate drives; all drives are the outcome of experience. The notion that there exist at birth ready-made and preformed drives capable of energizing behavior is a relic of Hippocratian psychology. It was carried to an extreme by psychoanalytic theorists who attributed to these "innate" drives complex structure and patterning in content, goal-object, and mode of gratification.

It requires fewer untenable assumptions to postulate that man is born neither with drives nor with emotions but with a *capacity* to develop both. There is no storehouse where drives are kept before birth. At birth even a hunger drive does not exist. It develops as a result of the experience of having the stomach empty for approximately 3 hours so that hunger contractions take place in response to hormones released by lowered blood sugar level.

Sex hormones are physiological. The sex drive, on the other hand, is a psychological state or condition (conscious or "unconscious") that arouses the organism to seek and be selectively receptive to sexual experience. As a result of the facilitating influence that gonadal hormones exert on the nervous system, sex drives may be generated under certain conditions. But the conversion of sex hormones into sex drives is by no means inevitable, and in no way can the former be conceived of as drives* in themselves.

In subprimate mammalian species, the relationship between sex hormones and sex drives seems to be relatively invariable. Experience is still necessary for the one to be translated into the other, but it contributes little more than the necessary opportunity in time. That is, in these species there tends to be relatively little sexual behavior that is independent of hormonal stimulation, especially in females (Ford & Beach, 1951). In the primates, however, sexual behavior to a large extent acquires freedom from hormonal regulation.

If we turn our attention to monkeys, apes and other animals of higher evolutionary status we find that the. . . relation between sex hormones and sex behavior has become less precise. The full-grown female chimpanzee with constant opportunity for sexual contact displays an obvious cycle of sexual desire that correlates fairly well with the rhythm of ovarian hormone secretion. Nevertheless she may, under certain conditions invite or permit copulation by the male at times when she is not fertile and when the estrogen concentration is low. In contrast to the tendencies of lower mammals the female ape engages in sex play long before the first menstrual cycle or puberty.

For the majority of women the greatest degree of sexual reactivity is experienced just before or just after the period of menstrual flow. . . . In women as in females of other species, the secretion of estrogen is greatest at or about the time of ovulation, that is, somewhere near the midpoint between the two points of menstrual flow. Yet relatively few women feel their highest sexual drive at this time. Peaks of sexual desire that occur near the time of menstruation cannot be accounted for in terms of high estrogen levels. Factors other than hormonal ones have become maximally important in determining the level of sexual responsiveness in females of the human species.

---

*It has been customary in the past to define a drive as a stimulus, usually internal, that arouses persistent mass activity. Typically, such intense external stimuli as pain are also included in the definition.

The conclusion is substantiated by observations to the effect that surgical or natural menopause need not produce a decrease in the sexual activities of healthy, emotionally well-balanced women. Although ovarian hormones are no longer present in the system most individuals continue to experience sexual desires and to participate in sexual relations. (Beach, 1951)

Once sex drives are generated in primate species (after pubescence), it is evident that the presence of sex hormones is no longer required for their continued existence and functioning. Many men castrated after puberty show little loss in sex drive or in copulatory activity (Beach, 1951; Shock, 1944). Further proof of the relative lack of dependence of human sex behavior on hormonal control is the noteworthy fact that male and female sex hormones do not stimulate heterosexual or homosexual behavior, respectively, in homosexuals, but will stimulate either pattern depending on other psychological factors involved (Ford & Beach, 1951).

Nevertheless, the degree of freedom from hormonal control is far from absolute. Some contact with an adequate level of sex hormone stimulation is necessary for adult sex desires to develop. "Studies on humans surgically deprived of their sex glands have indicated that when the operation is performed prior to puberty, interest in individuals of the opposite sex fails to develop."* (Shock, 1944) Oriental potentates have relied on this fact for centuries in selecting eunuchs to manage their harems. Dennis (1946) has presented a summary of the literature about men with retarded sexual development who did not experience sex desire and potency until treated with male sex hormones.

There is no longer any doubt that sex hormones play a significant facilitating role in the generation of sex drive. Besides the evidence from normal pubescence, we have referred to the effect of administering sex hormones to castrated and hypogonadal individuals. A review of cases of precocious puberty also suggests that early "endocrine changes greatly increase the strength of the sexual drive" (Best & Taylor, 1973; Dennis, 1946), making it comparable to that found in adults. However, the mechanism whereby "the chemical compound androgen exerts its effect upon behavior still remains to be identified" (Beach, 1951). Undoubtedly, the nervous system is

---

*It should be noted, however, that prepubertal castration "does not necessarily prevent the development of strong sexual reactions in male chimpanzees" (Beach, 1951).

chiefly implicated, but as Beach has shown, androgens may influence sex behavior in at least one other way. An adequate level of male sex hormone is necessary to prevent deteriorative changes in the skin of the glans penis of the male rat. These changes reduce tactile sensitivity of the glans and probably contribute to the "inhibitory effect upon copulatory performance" (Beach, 1951).

Under favorable psychological conditions the inherent *potential* drive in sex hormones becomes actualized. The most important variable affecting this outcome is cultural tolerance toward the initial sex interest and desire induced by the hormone acting with various perceptual stimuli. Other factors contributing to erotic feelings are tactile sensations from the sex organs and the sight of the primary and secondary sex characteristics of others. Provocative stimuli mentioned by adolescent boys in a questionnaire study were female nudity, daydreaming, obscene pictures, motion pictures, sex conversation, burlesque shows, dancing, and nude art* (Gianturco & Smith, 1974; Ramsey, 1943b).

However, if the cultural environment completely denies the existence of the sex drive, it remains latent and unactualized. Nothing need be repressed because nothing is generated in the first place. If for 13 years it is impressed on a girl that girls do not experience sex drives, the facilitating effect of sex hormones on the nervous system comes to naught. No sex feelings enter her psychological field because of the potent negative influence of family and cultural prestige suggestion. We cannot perceive what we already know not to exist. In Chapter I we discussed several examples of this phenomenon. Both Manus girls and puritanically reared girls in our own culture fail to develop any sex drive. And Arapesh boys and girls both fail to develop sex desires apart from a specific affectional object.

Once sex drives are generated and enter the psychological field they become too insistent, on the whole, ever to be completely repressed. In instances of apparent complete repression, it is more precise to speak of the drives as never having been formed in the first place. We have referred already to the definitive evidence obtained by Taylor (1933), Kirkendall (1940), and Kinsey et al. (1948) showing that middle-class adolescent males in our culture are typically unable to repress their sex urges successfully; and if they cannot express

---

*For a more complete discussion of normal psychosexual development and of predispositions, established by aberrant psychosexual experience in childhood and early adolescence, toward deviant sexual behavior in later adolescence and adult life, see Rutter (1970).

them in sexual intercourse, they do so through other substitutive sexual outlets (masturbation, petting, etc.) rather than "sublimate" them into intellectual, peer group, artistic, or other pursuits.

Psychophysiological and psychoaffectional sex patterns

A qualitative difference between preadolescent and adolescent sex activity has been postulated on the association of adolescent sex activity (functional or historical) with sex hormones. A further distinction remains to be drawn between two different kinds of hormonally inspired sex desire. If sex urges are directed toward a specific affectional object, they may be regarded as *psychoaffectional*. If they exist apart from feelings of love and affection for a given person, they may be termed *psychophysiological*. Any combination of these two components of sex behavior may be found.

In most cultures, including our own, the two patterns exist concomitantly, varying in relative importance at different stages in the life cycle. The psychoaffectional pattern requires greater emotional maturity and generally appears later, especially among boys at the lower educational levels. Indiscriminate sexual promiscuity, involving no emotional attachments, is a good example of psychophysiological sex activity. The psychoaffectional pattern by itself is more common among women in our culture,* and is the only type of sex activity recognized for both men and women among the Arapesh. On the other hand, some individuals never develop anything but psychophysiological sex desires, and women in some societies (i.e., Manus) repudiate both patterns of sex behavior.

FORMULATING A BIOLOGICAL SEX ROLE†

Sexual maturation and the generation of sex drives create another urgent problem for the adolescent: the necessity of accepting a biological sex role. The need is precipitated not only by his reactions to his own changed physical appearance and the intensification of his sex awareness, but also by the reactions of others to him as an adult sex object. Even if he does not become intensely aware of the devel-

---

*In more recent times, as a result of the feminist movement, the trend toward equal social rights for women, and of sex and biological education in the schools, girls are beginning to acknowledge that they too are endowed with physiological sex urges.

†For a more complete review of significant factors in formulating a biological sex role, the interested reader is referred to Rutter (1970).

oping opposite sex, he is obliged to cope with the attention and sex desires of age mates directed toward his own body. When a preadolescent girl undergoes changes in hip and chest contours, older boys look at her with different eyes and she cannot help but notice. Along with this comes a more formal but implicit acceptance of the individual by society at large as a member of an adult sex clan. The insistence of this social expectation cannot be long ignored!

Sex role in preadolescence

The preadolescent child undoubtedly identifies strongly with his own sex group and develops intense feelings of loyalty to it. But this identification occurs primarily for purposes of social grouping and play interests; it carries none of the implications of biological sex role that are associated with membership in an adult sex clan. In our culture, as in many others, the preadolescent peer group is based on a social segregation of the sexes.

We have already concluded that individuals cannot assume a biological sex role until they both (1) become capable of adult sexuality, and (2) receive cultural recognition as sexually mature individuals. Neither condition can be met prior to pubescence. This does not mean, however, that preliminary experimentation with adult sex roles does not take place in prepubescents.* Besides the motivation of curiosity and sensuality, preadolescent sex play is largely motivated by the desire to experiment with biological sex roles. This largely accounts for much of the imitation of adult romanticism, for the flirtation that occurs with the parent of opposite sex, and also for the attempts at heterosexual intercourse. In addition, the preadolescent assimilates much of the cultural folklore (four-letter words, "dirty" stories, and so forth) and moral values about sex: that sex is ugly or natural, that it is to be expressed or repressed, that it is permissible and enjoyable—for men but not for women, etc. He elaborates in fantasy many unshared misperceptions and half-truths that remain conceptually and socially immature because they are not subject to social validation. And in our culture he bears his share of the social guilt surrounding sexuality because of his sexual curiosity, activities, and fantasy.

---

*Evidence of such preadolescent sex interest and activity (e.g., Ford & Beach, 1951; Kinsey et al., 1948) is of course completely incompatible with psychoanalytic assertions regarding a "latency" period in sex drive and interest between the "genital phase of psychosexual development" (ages 5 to 6) and the onset of puberty.

Facilitating factors in adolescence*

The incorporation of an appropriate (heterosexual) biological sex role is facilitated by several factors in childhood and adolescent experience: (1) a model of happy marital relationships provided by parents; (2) strong positive identification with the sex role of the like-sexed parent; and (3) favorable initial experience with members of the opposite sex (Gundlach, 1969). The hormonal changes of adolescence do not (as was formerly believed) strengthen heterosexual impulses; they merely intensify the expression of the existing sex role (homosexual or heterosexual) (Ford & Beach, 1951). Gender role is the sex membership the individual adopts from the gender role attributed to him, and conceives of himself as exhibiting, even if it is in conflict with his anatomical and hormonal sex characteristics (Money, 1965).†

The attitudes of parents can exert a strong facilitating influence. It is helpful if the parent of the opposite sex reacts to his son or daughter as an individual with a biological sex role. This is especially important in preadolescence, since the normal segregation of the sexes precludes a good deal of the potential experimentation that would otherwise take place. "A girl needs her father's overt approval and outspoken admiration of herself as a young woman to help her to clarify and accept the feminine role" (Frank, 1944b). Similarly, a boy's mother should not make him feel that the "male's interest in sex is repulsive to a woman" (Frank, 1944), or cling to him so that he is prevented from making normal contacts with girls of his own age (Gianturco & Smith, 1974). If parents are able to accept as normal the adolescent's preoccupation with sexual concerns and fantasies, the latter does not feel nearly so guilty about sex. On the other hand, a parental attitude (implicit or explicit) to the effect that "my daughter is too pure to have such thoughts" interferes with the acceptance of a biological sex role, or, at the very least, induces unnecessary guilt feelings.

|

---

* Gender role refers to the biological sex clan an individual identifies with and exhibits behaviorally in social situations. Subjectively, it is also the sex membership role incorporated in his self-concept.

† Additional data and discussion of facilitating and retarding factors in formulating a biological sex role identification can be found in Gundlach (1969), Hetherington (1965), and Money and Ehrhardt (1972).

Retarding factors in adolescence

Hindering the adoption of an appropriate biological sex role is the absence of many of the facilitating factors mentioned above: the lack of suitable adult model of the same sex with whose sex role the adolescent can identify, unhappy marital relations between his parents, and unfavorable initial experience with the opposite sex (Gundlach, 1969; Hetherington, 1965; Money & Ehrhardt, 1972). As Frank (1944b) and Gianturco and Smith (1974) point out, if the parent of opposite sex deprecates the sex role of his adolescent child, the child finds it extremely difficult to identify with that role. If the father, for example, belittles girls and women, his daughter is more likely to reject the feminine sex role. Many cases of female sex delinquency start precisely in this way. The belittled girl uses sex as a means of obtaining power and revenge from the sex group that wronged her (Frank, 1944; Gianturco & Smith, 1974).*

Clinically, homosexuality is found most frequently in instances in which the child overidentifies with the sex role of the parent of opposite sex, for example, the boy identifying with his mother's sex role. Another common cause is narcissism, or a superfluity of self-love. Next to loving oneself, loving a person who is like oneself is the most satisfactory possible substitute (Ausubel, 1952a; Bieber, 1967; Gianturco & Smith, 1974; Gundlach, 1969).

Hence, the adolescent, depending on the psychological climate, may adopt one of three possible attitudes toward his appropriate biological sex role: (1) accepting, leading to heterosexuality; (2) rejecting, leading to homosexuality or asexuality; and (3) ambivalent, leading to an alternation of attitudes (bisexuality) or to sex delinquency. It should not be thought that rejection of heterosexuality always leads to homosexuality. The other possible outcomes are asexuality (a complete renunciation of sexual expression), bisexuality, and sex delinquency.

CHANGES IN EMOTIONAL EXPRESSION

Very little that is definitive is known about the emotional concomitants of pubescence. The empirical data bearing on this subject are fragmentary, inadequate, contradictory, and equivocal. Also, as

---

*For a developmental study of the effects of father or mother dominance on sex role identification, see Hetherington (1965). In general, the developmental research findings support the clinical impressions cited here about the causes of homosexuality as well as studies of gender role (e.g., Frank, 1944b; Gianturco & Smith, 1974; Gundlach, 1969; Money, 1965; and Money & Ehrhardt, 1972).

Kuhlen (1952) points out, "most of the studies contrast older children with younger children, but fail to study the situation in the years following adolescence." However, the lack or unavailability of positive evidence does not necessarily enable us to conclude that no relationship exists between pubescence and emotionality. It may mean only that the research designs of previous studies have been inadequate for the problem under investigation, and that final judgment must be reserved until truly adequate data are available for evaluation. It should be evident that more sensitive and subtle instruments than paper-and-pencil personality tests and questionnaires are required to throw light on a matter as complex and resistive to measurement as emotional expression. More fruitful approaches include extended longitudinal observations, clinical interviews, projective techniques, and physiological indicators of emotionality. In the meantime, we can best rely on theoretical considerations and logical inferences from related data.

Nonspecific changes in emotional reactivity

The existence of a syndrome of nonspecific behavioral changes associated with a pattern of emotional instability is a well-accepted principle of modern experimental psychopathology. The medical evidence for the emotional concomitants of hormonal imbalance (e.g., thyroid dysfunction, hyperinsulinism, the menopausal syndrome) is unequivocal. From the experimental studies of Pavlov (1927), Masserman (1946), Maier (1948), and Hamilton (1925), there are positive indications in psychopathology that chronic frustration, states of prolonged confusion, perceptual disorientation, and unresolved conflict lead to a similar condition of altered emotional reactivity. This consists of the following clearly defined behavioral syndrome: a greater magnitude of response to a weaker stimulus; a response which is more generalized, undirected, perseverative, and unadaptive, frequently in reaction to a less specific stimulus; sometimes complete blocking of activity; aggressive responses; subjective feelings of anxiety, insecurity, inadequacy, and depression; and, finally, a facilitation of various compensatory, substitutive, or indirect adjustive mechanisms such as withdrawal (flight), rationalization, displacement of affect, and regression.

Adolescence is characterized by a host of psychobiological and psychosocial conditions that make for just such a heightened capacity for emotional reactivity: the state of physiological flux and disequilibrium, the increased hormonally inspired sex consciousness and sex drive, the lack of experience in controlling and directing the latter;

the abrupt loss of childhood ego status, the sudden lack of stable ego links and anchorages, discrepancies in rate of growth, transitional anxiety over proving oneself; problems related to somatic variations and to early or late maturation; too sudden needs for revising body image and incorporating a biological sex role; and tensions relevant to emancipation and parent-child conflict. The same results may also be brought about by a number of psychosocial factors: prolonged deprivation of status, confusion concerning socioeconomic sex role, inconsistencies and discontinuities in the social order, and the pressures that come from living in an aggressive competitive society.

A cross-sectional study of Rorschach responses shows that the affective energy available to the child is at a maximum during adolescence (Ames, et al., 1971; Thetford et al., 1951).

Greater emotional reactivity depends on a general lowering of the threshold for emotion-producing stimuli. As a result, emotional reactions become more intense and occur in response to a wider range of stimuli, which are more subtle and less specific in nature. Until this new capacity for emotionality is brought under control and appropriately modulated (a task requiring considerable learning experience), inconsistency, flightiness, instability, and lability of mood are inevitable. Moodiness, giggling, exaggerated emotional responses, irritability, indolence, and disorganized desultory activity have been described by Tryon (1939a), Hurlock and Sender (1930), and Gallagher and Harris (1976) in studies based on observation of adolescents. In the study by Hurlock and Sender, however, we have no comparable data for the preceding or succeeding periods of growth, and are therefore unable to relate these behaviors specifically to the adolescent period.

Other less convincing evidence of increased emotional instability in adolescence is found in the greater incidence of fingernail biting (Gallagher & Harris, 1976; Wechsler, 1931); in the higher ratio of unpleasant to pleasant items listed by older children in a 20-minute interval (Thompson & Kepler, 1945); and in the greater number of themes of anxiety, discouragement, and fear produced by adolescents in response to a series of pictures (Symonds, 1945).

Several studies and most clinicians seem to agree that girls manifest greater emotional instability than boys during adolescence (e.g., Gallagher & Harris, 1976; Tryon, 1939a). This sex difference is in part reflective of greater cultural tolerance for emotional display by the female sex. However, it may also be indicative of actual greater emotional stress during the adolescent period which is a result of more rapidly changing and more ambiguous norms for biological and social sex roles, greater parental repression of strivings toward independence, and less developmental continuity in the factors accounting for status in the peer group.

Changes in specific emotions

Specific categories of emotion also undergo change during adolescence. This is especially true of the emotions of aggression, affection, and fear. The causes of these changes are partly biological and partly social.

In addition to the cultural expectations leading to greater self-assertiveness in adolescents, hormonal factors also play a role.

> Androgen treatment of hypogonadal men often. . . [augments] aggressive tendencies [which] may be expressed in social relations. . . . A similar correlation between androgen and aggressive behavior exists in many animal species. . . . Fighting is increased in fishes, reptiles and birds by androgen administration. Male rats and mice fight less frequently and vigorously after castration, and normal or even hypernormal aggressiveness can be evoked in castrates by administration of large amounts of male hormone. Female mammals and birds become increasingly likely to fight with each other or with males if they are treated with male hormone. . . .
>
> Female chimpanzees that are socially subordinate to their masculine partners often become temporarily dominant during the period of estrus. If two female apes are kept together in the absence of males, a fairly stable dominance pattern emerges; and this is frequently reversed when one or the other animal comes into estrus. Similar reversals can be induced in spayed apes by the injection of ovarian hormone. (Beach, 1951)

Sex hormones also undoubtedly influence the quality and intensity of affectional responses that the adolescent is capable of making. These new feelings enter into the psychoaffectional sex drive. However, the methodological difficulties of obtaining direct empirical evidence on this relationship are practically insurmountable. What evidence we do have is only inferential. Prolactin, a hormone of the anterior pituitary gland, induces maternal behavior when injected into virgin or male animals (Beach, 1951). Levy (1942) has brought forth evidence indicating a positive relationship between degree of motherliness and length of menstrual flow.

Hormonal changes at adolescence probably have less influence on fear reactions, although it is well known that the anxiety and depression frequently found in menopausal women are related to a decrease in gonadal hormones and an increase in pituitary gonado-tropins (Beach, 1951). The changes that occur in adolescence, how-ever, seem to be more closely related to social factors and intellectual development. Fear of specific physical hazards declines, but worries associated with social and economic concerns become more promi-nent. The influence of cultural tradition on this trend can be seen in the fact that girls lose their fear of physical dangers less completely than boys do, acquire worries about social relationships earlier, and develop fewer anxieties about vocational aptitude and opportunity (Tryon, 1939b). This is in accord with evidence of a shift in adoles-cence toward social, intellectual, and religious stimulus words as the chief causes of blocking and muscular tension in word association experiments (Sharp, 1938).

PROBLEMS REFERABLE TO EARLY OR LATE MATURATION *

Large differences prevail "in the rate at which different individ-uals approach maturity" (Gallagher et al., 1976; Stolz & Stolz, 1951). There are wide differences in rate of maturation that are still compati-ble with normality, each individual developing at his own optimal rate. Unfortunately, however, children and adolescents never seem to adopt this viewpoint spontaneously, and hence, torture themselves and their age mates over trivial deviations from the norm. This atti-tude springs largely from the exaggerated need for conformity that is basic to the structure of the adolescent peer group.

The seriousness of this problem depends largely on the degree and conspicuousness of the deviation, that is, on the number of years of acceleration or retardation. The slow maturer is at a great disadvan-tage because of the uncertainty of his situation and the limited time perspective characteristic of adolescents. He has no way of knowing when his pubescence will eventually occur. In the meantime, he begins to wonder if he is a biological anomaly and frequently enter-tains serious doubts that he will ever mature (Ausubel, 1950; Tanner, 1971). He is also at a serious disadvantage socially (M. C. Jones, 1957). In athletics, he is hardly in a position to compete with boys of his own age who are much taller, heavier, and stronger. His position on the

---

* For an excellent review article of this topic, including some original research data largely confirming the earlier work of H. E. Jones (1949), M. C. Jones (1957, 1958), M. C. Jones and Bayley (1950), Mussen and Jones (1957), and Stolz and Stolz (1951), see Weatherly, 1964.

social dance floor is equally untenable. Ostracism from the peer group, therefore, is not a rare or unlikely occurrence under these circumstances; and it is hardly surprising that in order to prove himself he sometimes resorts to behavior which is far from socially acceptable to adults (M. C. Jones, 1957; Stolz & Stolz, 1951).

Late-maturing boys are described by adults as unattractive in physique, more tense and eager, more intemperate, and less well-groomed. Their peers describe them as more restless, less reserved and grown-up, more "bossy," and less involved in extracurricular activities (M. C. Jones, 1957, 1958; M. C. Jones & Bayley, 1950; Mussen & M. C. Jones, 1957). They have more negative self-concepts, greater feelings of inadequacy and rejection, and feelings of dependency alternating with rebelliousness and self-assertion. These differences are also maintained after adolescence into adult life (M. C. Jones, 1957, 1958). Self-consciousness about their retarded physical development may also cause them to develop "greater or lesser degrees of shyness or timidity in his behavior" (Stolz & Stolz, 1951). According to H. E. Jones (1944), late pubescence may result in a loss of previously held status in the group, and "when the biological innovations of adolescence are at last clearly avowed, a turning point may be reached. . . in social recognition and in feelings of personal security." Such an outcome, of course, presupposes that the individual had not isolated himself completely from group participation during this interval.

Early maturation is much less of a handicap and in a certain sense may even be considered an advantage, except perhaps initially in girls. Once the initial embarrassment of being a physical misfit is overcome, the early maturer has all of the advantages of superior height, weight, strength, and heterosexual effectiveness on his side. In addition, as a result of his early maturation he obtains greater opportunity to enact more mature roles and acquire mature role playing and leadership experience (Mussen & Jones, 1957). On the other hand, he may find himself embarrassed by the disproportionate expectations of adults (Ausubel, 1950b). The early-maturing boy also is closer to the girl's body build than the later-maturing boy, and also endures a longer period of frustration of his sex drives and of his needs for volitional and economic independence. Bayley and Tuddenham (1944) conclude: "The poorest adjusted among the four extreme groups [are] the early-maturing girls and the late-maturing boys [since in a] coeducational school in which grade placement [is] largely [determined] by chronological age [these] two groups would stand out in a school room as physically the most different."

The effects of early maturation are greater in girls than in boys because girls are more conspicuous in a chronologically homogeneous classroom. They are inordinately tall and stocky and tend to

have a muscular physique (Mussen & Jones, 1957), with resulting embarrassment and self-consciousness. This difference, of course, diminishes with increasing age. The late maturers are judged by adults
and peers as more sociable and as possessing more leadership ability,
cheerfulness, and expressiveness (H. E. Jones, 1949). In later adolescence these differences in favor of late-maturing girls tend to diminish (Weatherley, 1964) or even be reversed (M. C. Jones, 1958), as
shown by projective test data, in the case of such traits as maturity of
thought processes and positive self-concept (Mussen & Jones, 1957).

We must also consider here the psychological readjustments necessary when sudden shifts in relative size, weight, and physical attractiveness are a consequence of early or late maturation. For example,
the individual who matures very early stands head and shoulders
above his prepubescent age mates. But by the time he is 15 or 16 the
reverse situation may prevail. Similarly, the late-maturing individual
must adjust to the realignment in physical and social status when his
delayed pubescence finally occurs.

ADJUSTING TO NORMAL SOMATIC CHANGES

In addition to the reactions leading to an alteration of the "body
image" (Schilder, 1935), the adolescent displays other perceptual responses to the physical changes of pubescence. Some of these perceptual reactions result in feelings of uneasiness, self-consciousness,
and embarrassment. Nevertheless, we must agree with Jersild (1952)
that

> we should not overdo our compassion. In some accounts of
> physical development it has been the fashion to paint a highly
> lugubrious picture. If the child is fat he is miserable; if he is
> skinny he is sad. If he is tall for his years, he staggers under the
> responsibilities that fall upon him; if he is short, life is a bitter
> pill. The woe that goes with a big bosom is equaled only by the
> misery that comes with a flat chest.
>
> Actually, of course, adolescent growth has both its dark and
> bright aspects. The changes that mark the transition to adult
> status not only present problems but also bring occasion for joy
> and pride.

Interest in grooming and adornment

One of the more obvious psychological reactions to bodily
changes is an increased concern with grooming and personal appearance, despite the fact that standards of dress have generally become

more informal among all age groups during the past 25 years. This increased concern is true (even if the standard costume of adolescents happens to be blue jeans) and is in marked contrast to the preadolescent indifference to such matters. Preadolescents (notably boys), as a matter of fact, seem to pride themselves on being dirty and slipshod. However, beginning with adolescence there is an abrupt change in attitude. As already noted, Stone and Barker (1939) found statistically reliable differences between pre- and post-menarchial girls in interest in grooming and appearance. Among their concerns are hair, facial appearance, fingernails, and clothes.

Three kinds of motivations seem to underlie the development of these new interests: (1) The adolescent desires to increase his heterosexual effectiveness without alienating or provoking the criticism of his own sex group. (2) He desires to assert his right to adult status by assuming the prerogatives associated with adult physical appearance; hence, the desire for cosmetics and more adult dress styles. Silverman (1945) found that the use of facial cosmetics by girls increases steadily after the age of 12. (3) A third motivation is the need for conformity to peer group standards. The adolescent peer group desires to establish its unique individuality and its recognizability from adult society. It is able to do this and still mimic adult society by adopting extreme forms of adult dress and grooming (extreme styles, excessive use of cosmetics). When a conflict exists between adult and peer group standards, however, the adolescent can usually be depended on to cast his lot with his age mates.

Reaction to normal somatic changes

In contrast to the somatic *deviations* that occur in some adolescent individuals, but not in others, are a group of bodily changes that constitute general characteristics of pubescence. How does the adolescent react to them?

The mere attainment of adult physical stature is a source of serious misperception by adolescent boys and girls in our culture. Because of it, they often feel that they are entitled to the rights and privileges which they have always associated with adult physical form. It takes considerable time and many bitter disappointments before they appreciate that the achievement of adult personality status involves more than the acquisition of physical maturity. But if growth in stature is a cause for ego enhancement, the typical history of asynchrony in skeletal development is also a cause for serious concern. Adolescents do not and cannot realize in advance that temporary disproportions in body dimension will be corrected in due time.

Perhaps the most disturbing of all instances of asynchrony is the early and sudden spurt in the growth of the nose (Krogman, 1939; Stolz & Stolz, 1951). Although the initial prominence of the nose is frequently corrected by corresponding growth in other facial features, its disproportionate size is one of the more common causes of homeliness in both men and women, as well as in adolescents.

The development of primary and secondary sex characteristics is for the most part a source of pride rather than of psychological disturbance. This conclusion can be inferred in part from the fact that lack of normal development of these characteristics is one of the most serious categories of somatic problems mentioned by adolescents (Gallagher & Harris, 1976; Stolz & Stolz, 1944). Even the onset of menstruation, a phenomenon associated with considerable shame, embarrassment, secrecy, and dread in our culture, is accepted unemotionally or eagerly by a majority of girls. Because of the relative degree of prominence of the changes, primary sex characteristics are more important for boys, and secondary sex characteristics are more important for girls (see Chapter 4).

A group of secondary sex characteristics involving the skin and associated structures elicit particularly strong emotional reactions from adolescent boys and girls. Boys are extremely eager for the dense growth of body and facial hair, whereas girls are equally concerned that these hairs fail to develop. Another skin phenomenon about which adolescents are particularly sensitive is body odor. This sensitivity is a product of cultural factors: the high premium placed on cleanliness in the United States and the influence of commercial advertisements stressing the terrible social consequences of body odor or bad breath. From a purely biological standpoint, there is also reason to believe that certain body odors reflect increased sexual functioning and play some vestigial role in arousing the sexual sensibilities of the opposite sex (see Chapter 4).

The most important and prevalent source of emotional disturbance associated with the somatic changes of adolescence is acne. The seriousness of this problem is generally underestimated by parents, teachers, and counselors because adolescents find it too traumatic to even admit their concern to themselves, much less express it to others. The actual importance of the problem, however, is revealed in the number of hours spent in front of the mirror, and in the willingness of adolescents to experiment with every conceivable remedy suggested in pulp magazines, advertisements, and by age mates for the disguise or amelioration of the condition. Although actual empirical evidence is lacking, many persons who work with adolescents feel that severe acne is an important determinant of social unpopularity (and even ostracism) during adolescence. The individual's response to this social reaction consists of damage to the self-concept (loss of self-esteem) and withdrawal from social activities. Because of the greater importance of facial beauty in girls, the occurrence of acne in them is probably more traumatic than in boys. However, girls have the advantage of using cosmetics to conceal blemishes.

Adjusting to somatic deviations

The relationship between physical defect and behavioral maladjustment is two-sided and recriprocal. Either condition almost inevitably gives rise to the other, which in turn reinforces and tends to perpetuate the original state of affairs. A vicious circle is established; and it often becomes difficult indeed to ascertain which component existed first (M. C. Jones, 1965).

In adolescence the psychosomatic (and somatopsychic) relationship is more important than in childhood because of the more significant role played by the body in the individual's social status and self-concept (Ausubel, 1950b, 1952a; Gallagher & Harris, 1976; M. C. Jones, 1965). Physical attractiveness and sex appropriateness become crucial determinants of individual status within the peer group and also of heterosexual effectiveness. Thus, the increased social disadvantage of physical deviancy has important repercussions on the self-concept and the deviant manifestations of behavior disorder (M. C. Jones, 1965).

The characteristics of behavior disorder also tend to be more somatic during adolescence than during childhood. Clinical experience with different age groups demonstrates vividly that the area in which behavioral response to frustration or conflict is most likely to occur is that region of the psychological field that is most central at a given stage of development. In infancy and early childhood, when the feeding situation is so crucial to mother and child, interpersonal friction leads to feeding problems. At a later stage, when the child's conformity to parental training demands becomes the most crucial issue, behavior disorder often takes the form of negativism. And in adolescence when bodily changes play so prominent a role in the changing self-concept, it is understandable that the physical (psychosomatic) components of the emotional and behavioral response to frustration will be correspondingly enhanced. Similarly, the emotional response to somatic deviation or physical disability (somatopsychic) will be greater (Ausubel, 1950b, 1952a; Harris, 1976).

Psychological concomitants of somatic defects *

Physical defects first of all constitute an objective limitation to the individual's capacity to adjust to his environment. Cardiac and orthopedic disabilities, for example, restrict participation in athletic and social activities. Sensory (visual and auditory) defects restrict the range of sensitivity and responsiveness to important intellectual and social stimuli. When unsuspected and uncorrected, therefore, they make school learning difficult and simulate mental deficiency. Indirectly, also, they may lead to failure in school by placing too great a strain on the individual's capacity for attentiveness. Rather than contend with the continual burden of this strain and failure, he may prefer to disengage himself from the entire painful situation and develop an attitude of either indifference to or active dislike for the frustrating school environment.

A number of physical conditions also give rise to behavioral disturbance by lowering the general threshold of reactivity. When this happens, the individual manifests undue irritability, restlessness, and distractibility, and responds to trifling stimuli with exaggerated, undirected, inappropriate, and frequently aggressive responses. Some of the more common causes of this altered state of behavioral reactivity in adolescence are fatigue, chronic physical strain, pain, hunger, and hormonal imbalance. Hormonal imbalance, of course, is characteristic of all adolescents, and chronic strain, pain, and excessive fatigue may be associated with any number of physical and sensory defects or situational stresses that occur during adolescence.

More important than the objective handicap inherent in physical defects, especially during the adolescent period, is the social disadvantage at which they place the deviant individual (M. C. Jones, 1965). Deviancy from group physical norms elicits a highly negative response from his peers and almost guarantees that he will be treated differently from his fellows. The least common denominators of this differential treatment are devaluation, avoidance, rejection, and accordance of lower status. Regardless of verbal statements of sympathy, or of verbal claims that they are uninfluenced by another's physical disability, adolescents in their *actual* behavior accord highly discriminatory treatment to persons with physical handicaps. These persons tend to enjoy lower status in the group, are frequently ostracized, fail to receive their share of attention from the opposite sex,

---

* For a review of psychological concomitants of physical handicaps, see Berenberg (1976).

and are often treated with open contempt and hostility (H. E. Jones, 1944, 1946a). It would be an understatement to say that adolescents take competitive advantage of the physical shortcomings of their rivals in the competitive race for status in the group and for favor in the eyes of the opposite sex.

The individual's response to his own physical disability is largely a reflection of the social reaction to it. During adolescence, when he is so dependent on the peer group for status, he tends to accept as real and valid the value that the peer group places on him. Because the group's opinion was less important in childhood, on the other hand, it was possible for him to retain a more flattering self-image, provided that he was intrinsically accepted and valued by his parents. Hence, disability in adolescence almost inevitably leads to damaged self-esteem. At the very least, it results in hypersensitivity and self-consciousness about the defect. The individual imagines that the eyes of everyone are focused on his disability and that it constitutes the chief topic of conversation when he is absent. This is especially true of persons with sensory impairment, who normally tend to feel suspicious because so much of what goes on around them must remain a matter of conjecture. Another manifestation of this hypersensitivity to physical defect is the resistance displayed by so many adolescents to physical examination (Ausubel, 1950b; Gallagher, 1960). They are diffident and embarrassed about revealing their physical inadequacy or sex inappropriateness to physicians whom they believe to be especially sensitive (by virtue of training) to the slightest degree of abnormality or deviancy in these respects.

The situation becomes more serious when ego damage becomes severe enough to lead to a significant withdrawal from social life. Interpersonal relationships acquire a negative valence in the individual's psychological field since they are associated with traumatic ego-related feelings. Avoiding social interaction thus becomes a self-protective device which may lead to irreversible defects in the socialization process. Deprived of the experience required for learning the elemental techniques of social adjustment, he may incur a developmental deficit that permanently incapacitates him for normal interpersonal relations in adult life. For this reason, any of the compensatory or aggressive forms of compensatory ego enhancement are far less serious than withdrawal as a reaction to the ego-deflating implications of somatic defect.

Somatic concomitants of psychological stress

For the same reason that somatic defects are an important cause of psychological disturbance during adolescence, psychological disturbance, in turn, is more frequently mediated through physical manifestations. As a more prominent component of the ego, the body becomes more intimately implicated in disturbances involving this core constituent of personality structure. The adolescent individual is more apt to respond to frustration of any kind with physical symptoms and disability than he did as a child (Ausubel, 1950b, 1952a; Harris, 1976).

The simplest variety of psychosomatic manifestation consists of the ordinary physiological (autonomic) accompaniments of emotion or anxiety: sweating, rapid heartbeat, palpitations, vasomotor disturbance, rapid breathing, muscular tension, and dry mouth. One of the more common consequences of emotional stress in this category is a subjective feeling of overwhelming fatigue or exhaustion. These symptoms acquire secondary adjustive value when they are used by the individual as a justification for failure, poor performance, or avoidance of a disagreeable situation (rationalization). A related adjustive use to which they can be put is to serve as convenient foci for the displacement of anxiety. That is, it appears to the adolescent that the real cause of his anxiety is not concern over his studies, peer group relations, or his vocational future, but rather some less ominous physical condition (Harris, 1976; Stolz & Stolz, 1944). This may be an actual somatic defect, such as obesity or acne, rather than a physiological consequence of anxiety. At any rate, it is less anxiety producing for the individual to believe that the source of the threat to his self-esteem is something tangible and physical, such as obesity, rather than an unflattering personal characteristic, such as low intelligence or lack of social acceptability.

In addition to the physiological concomitants of emotion, and existing somatic defects of independent origin that are used for rationalization, withdrawal, and displacement purposes, one type of physical injury is an indirect consequence of psychological stress. "Accident proneness" in adolescents is not an uncommon outlet for aggressive proclivities (Dunbar, 1938). "As a means of expressing their resentment against parents and elders, [and] of provoking guilt feelings in the latter, adolescents may unconsciously expose themselves to danger" (Ausubel, 1950b).

But regardless of whether disturbance originates in the somatic or in the psychological area, the effects are almost invariably circular and reciprocal. Obesity of physical origin, e.g., endocrine dysfunction, induces psychological feelings of inferiority, which may, paradoxically enough, worsen the original condition by leading to compensatory overeating. On the other hand, the origin of the obesity may lie in inadequate social adjustment, which leads to an attempt to secure nonspecific substitutive gratification.

Types and frequency of somatic deviations

By definition, somatic deviations consist of departures from culturally established norms of physical appropriateness for men and women. Individuals are generally regarded as ugly or attractive insofar as they conform to or deviate from the median anatomical measurements of their own sex group in a given cultural setting. Because of the multiplicity of factors in the determination of physical attractiveness, few individuals escape deviancy in at least one bodily characteristic. And almost invariably, for reasons to be discussed below, the most serious deviations are those that are related to norms of sex appropriateness and to physical standards of masculinity and femininity. The nicknames resented most by boys are those which make reference to inadequacies in masculine physique (Habbe, 1937).

PRIMARY SEX CHARACTERISTICS

As noted in Chapter 4, deviations in the primary sex characteristics, such as smallness of the external genitalia, are of psychological significance in boys only. But just as for acne, the seriousness of this problem cannot be validly estimated from the verbal reports given by adolescents to parents, teachers, and counselors. Few individuals who are vitally troubled by such actual, or imaginary, defects are willing to undergo the ego trauma involved in even admitting this concern to themselves, although their actual behavior may belie this apparent unconcern. And here, because of the vital implications for masculinity, the "tyranny of the norm" is even more unreasonable and inflexible.*

---

*This situation is compounded in the case of an adolescent with a relatively small flaccid penis. Since he typically views the penises of other adolescent boys in the same flaccid condition in making judgments of comparative size, and does not realize that there is little or no correlation between the size of the flaccid and the size of the erect penis (see Chapter 4), he tends to exaggerate his real or imagined deviation from the norm. As any psychiatrist can testify, the vast number of men who go through life with a "small penis complex" (avoiding men's locker and shower rooms, and even men's toilets, because of self-consciousness and embarrassment) would be truly astounding to lay persons.

The size of the male external genitalia is actually correlated with psychological aspects of sexuality (sex drive, masculinity) only in unusual cases of insufficiency. The reason for this has been made clear in Chapter 4. Genic variables determining structure are more important determinants of variability in size than hormonal stimulation, except in extreme cases (hypogonadism or hypergonadism of endocrine origin).

In helping adolescents adjust to this somatic deviation, much can be accomplished by exposition and interpretation of the relevant facts. Simple assurance from a physician that the range of normal variability is wide, that penis size is negligibly correlated with sex drive, that (except in extreme cases) copulation is not seriously affected, and that heterosexual effectiveness and attractiveness to women are not impaired has a great deal of therapeutic value (Ausubel, 1950b; Gallagher & Harris, 1976; Schonfeld, 1950). In cases of serious hormonal inadequacy, endocrine therapy is indicated and may effect evident improvement in a matter of weeks. Pseudohypogenitalism due to obesity can be cured by correcting the latter condition.

BODY BUILD

Shortness of stature is a genuine social handicap in our culture which naturally has its reflections in ego feelings.

A short man seems to have greater difficulty in commanding the attention of strangers or casual acquaintances; at the level of superficial social reactions we are apt to associate size with masculine dignity. When we look for leaders among a group of boys whom we do not know very well, we tend to try the larger boys. . . . More specifically shortness is a real handicap to a junior or senior high school boy who seeks prestige through athletic prowess in the popular team games. In none of the sports most popular among adolescent boys do short boys succeed in achieving representation proportionate to their incidence.

In following the appropriate adolescent urge to establish satisfying social relations with girls, the short boy often finds his lack of size a handicap. This handicap arises partly from the culturally developed preference of girls for men who are 'tall and handsome', and partly as the result of the special precocity of girls in relation to boys at this particular stage in their development. At a time when girls tend to seek the companionship of boys older than themselves they are most apt to snub the advances of contemporary boy friends who still both look and act like small boys.

In social dancing, both girls and boys much prefer a partnership in which the boy is at least as tall as the girl. (Stolz & Stolz, 1944, p. 88)

In girls, precisely the opposite condition prevails. Tallness is not an accepted cultural criterion of femininity and represents "a genuine emotional hazard" (Stolz & Stolz, 1944). Shortness in girls or tallness in boys does not become a problem except in extreme divergence from the norm.

Obesity is a common somatic deviation with wide variability in psychological outcome. Some boys and girls are extremely disturbed by it and are willing to institute strict dieting regimens to ameliorate the condition. Other adolescents seem to be completely unconcerned.

Comments and humorous allusions to getting fat are so frequent in casual conversation, especially among women, that too much significance must not be attributed to verbal protestations about the matter. Avowed disturbance over slight deviations from the fashionable dress-model figure may serve as convenient conversational camouflage to cover other more important dissatisfactions with self. (Stolz & Stolz, 1944, p. 89)

On the other hand,

excessive fat is both cumbersome and unsightly at any age. It interferes with graceful and effective performance of any locomotor activity. . . and is, therefore, particularly unwelcome to the adolescent boy who seeks social recognition through athletic achievement. In early adolescence this is to some extent true for girls also, but their disturbance over being fat is more closely connected with the fear of being unattractive in terms of our current cultural ideals. . . .

In any case, the nicknames and thoughtless derogatory comments which, before the adolescent period, may cause the fat boy or girl only rather vague discomfort or no discomfort at all, take on a new penetrating quality for the physically self-conscious and socially sensitive juvenile in the less friendly atmosphere of the junior high school. (Stolz & Stolz, 1944, p. 90)

With respect to "sex-inappropriate physical traits," the adolescent boy is most disturbed by a syndrome consisting of a:

. . . considerable increase of fat around the hips. . . combined with small external genitalia, scanty pubic hair, narrow shoulders and an unusual development of subcutaneous tissue about the nipples. In such a case the feeling of sex inappropriateness arises not merely from a lack of what is considered acceptable male development, but also from the superficial similarity of the whole pattern to that popularly associated with female development. . . .

During the adolescent period girls, also, are sometimes concerned because their bodily size and configuration do not correspond closely enough to their ideals for themselves. . . . Some of the commonly occurring physical traits which in our culture may combine to give adolescent girls a feeling of sex-inappropriateness are: unusual tallness, squattiness, large hands, large feet, clumsy ankles, undeveloped breasts, pigmented facial hair, extreme thinness, moderate or extreme fatness, heaviness of lower jaw, hairiness of arms and legs, general massiveness of body build. (Stolz & Stolz, 1944, pp. 91–92)

Hormonal therapy, when indicated, "falsies," and cosmetic (plastic) surgery can do much to ameliorate the agonizing of many adolescent girls who exaggerate the heterosexual handicaps posed by flat-chestedness or who are unduly disturbed by it emotionally.

Why somatic deviations are important during adolescence

Somatic deviations become so crucial during adolescence because of the increased importance of the body in the individual's self-concept.

"One obvious reason for this is the enhanced awareness of their bodies which adolescents acquire, partly from the consciousness of their own physical development, and partly from their increasing identification with culturally determined ideals concerning appropriate physical characteristics for men and women. . . . Thus each boy and girl in our culture gradually cumulates into self attitudes toward his body a mixture of identification and rejection, of pride and embarrassment, of concern and ignoring. . . . [And since] all human beings are most vulnerable in those areas where lie their strongest drives, it can be assumed that any condition which cuts across vital urges or endangers their fulfillment becomes a hazard for an individual and a potential source of basic frustration" (Stolz & Stolz, 1944, pp. 84, 85, 87).

Concern with cultural standards more specifically entails sensitivity to the norms of the peer group. Since the peer group becomes the chief source of his status and prestige, the adolescent desires to conform to "the specific 'norms of body proportions and growth' prevailing in his own limited circle" (Ausubel, 1950b). Now, for the first time, physical attractiveness becomes a crucial determinant of the girl's sociometric status among her peers of both sexes. In similar fashion, a boy's sociometric status is largely governed by his relative degree of masculinity and athletic prowess.

These same characteristics are also important for heterosexual effectiveness, but more so for boys than for girls. A girl who is unattractive to and unpopular with other girls can still be very attractive to boys. But for boys to be popular with girls, they must first win recognition of superior masculine attributes among their sex (Tryon, 1944). For this reason somatic deviations are more serious for boys than for girls during adolescence even though girls "are far more apt to do something to relieve their frustration than boys are. In the improvement of face or figure they are willing to spend time, forego pleasure, withstand the demands of hunger, endure pain and discomfort" (Tryon, 1944). However, it seems much more likely that this greater disposition to "do something about it" is more a result of the greater availability of corrective measures, and of greater cultural tolerance for such ameliorative procedures, than of stronger motivation from greater frustration or ego damage. In adult life, on the other hand, there is no doubt whatsoever that the effects of somatic deviation on heterosexual adjustment are much less disastrous for men than for women. Even in the present feminist era, men can more easily compensate for physical unattractiveness to the opposite sex through vocational success.

"The greater significance which these bodily variations assume at adolescence is partly due to the fact that they are now associated with a sense of finality that was not present during childhood" (Ausubel, 1950b). As the Stolzes (1944) so eloquently put it: "In childhood, years of growth stretch indefinitely ahead and growing-up, adequate in every respect, is taken for granted. But during puberty, boys and girls begin to realize that the years of growth are numbered and they are faced with the reality of permanent differences of size in relation to other people." The impact of this sense of finality is compounded by "the notoriously limited time perspective of adolescents. . . since it is imagined that conformity to peer standards will *always* be as important. . . . [Hence] the traumatic effect of somatic variations during adolescence must be evaluated in terms of the act that the 'ego lives' less in the future than is customarily its wont" (Ausubel, 1952a).

Factors determining the seriousness of outcome

All adolescents do not react in the same way to somatic deviations.

> How serious such problems may become for any boy or girl will depend upon how strong the drive is and how drastically the condition interferes with the satisfaction of his urges. How each person "takes" these frustrations will be determined by previous life experiences, and will be modified by the extent to which he is finding genuine satisfactions in other basic areas of life which may lessen the strains in the frustrated areas. (Stolz & Stolz, 1944, p. 85)

It need not be imagined, for example, that self-depreciation is an inevitable accompaniment of organic defects or disabilities. After cataloging the major somatic deviations of adolescence, Stolz and Stolz (1951) conclude, "of all the items mentioned, acne seems to be the only one which almost universally causes emotional difficulties for an adolescent boy or girl."

Numerous other factors affect the seriousness of the problem: the extent of the deviation, both from the norm of the peer group and from the child's ideal; its "probable duration," and its obviousness to others; its relation to other physical defects and to problems of adjustment arising from nonsomatic sources (Stolz & Stolz, 1944); and the attitudes of the individual, his parents, and his peers toward the condition. In most instances the individual tends to magnify the seriousness of his defect out of all proportion to the actual impression it makes on his associates. Yet in view of the premium that our culture places on beauty, especially in girls, this is hardly surprising. We tend, for example, to take for granted that good-looking persons can "get away with murder." It is also important to remember that objective fact is completely irrelevant in such matters. "For the practical purposes of individual guidance, problems of adjustment exist only when an individual says that he is disturbed or acts as though he were disturbed" (Stolz & Stolz, 1944, p. 97).

The matter of becoming reconciled to limitations in physical form and appearance thus becomes one of the major adjustment problems of adolescence" (Ausubel, 1950b). It is not "an easy thing to accept an ugly, unattractive body as the final physical representation of self" (Ausubel, 1952a). Hence, adolescents in trying to accept

> the reality of their appearance, [strive] to make that reality as pleasant as possible. Not all boys and girls succeed in mastering this developmental task. This is evidenced in everyone's experi-

ence by individuals in adult life who continually struggle with their appearance or in some way or another try to compensate for real or imagined defects. (Tryon, 1944, p. 223)

The different modes of adjusting to such somatic defects are legion in number. As a last resort ugliness may even be perceived as a virtue.

Many guidance procedures can be used to supplement medical treatment in helping adolescents adjust to somatic variations (Gallagher & Harris, 1976).

In one case this may consist of persuading the adolescent that he is exaggerating the differences which are really unimportant. Another adolescent may need assurance that the differences are but a passing phase of normal development. Sometimes a boy or girl can be helped by learning techniques of dress or grooming which render an undesirable physical variation less obvious. Sometimes they need help in developing compensatory assets which will gain for them social acceptance in spite of their physical peculiarities. (Stolz & Stolz, 1944, p. 98)

Conditions exist, however, in which there is no possible hope for effecting any physical improvement. In such cases (e.g., patients with incurable congenital defects or chronic disabling diseases), adjustment is furthered best by having the individual accept the reality of the poor prognosis as early as possible. A certain amount of stoicism is necessary, after which the building of self-acceptance along other lines can be attempted (Gallagher & Harris, 1976; Schonfeld, 1950).

Finally, in evaluating the significance of psychological reactions to bodily disturbance, it is important for the counselor not to be misled as to the *actual* source of the emotional stress in many cases. Through the common mechanism of displacement of affect, anxieties of entirely different origin may be ascribed to a somatic defect.

7

Personality Maturation During Adolescence

CHILDHOOD AS A PERIOD OF DEPENDENCY

Our cross-cultural survey of preadolescence has brought us to the conclusion that childhood is inevitably a period of biosocial dependency. The reasons for this inhere partly in the child's relative incompetence in the motor, intellectual, and social skills necessary for survival, and partly in the universal cultural tendency to deny equal social membership to sexually immature individuals regardless of their capacity for environmental adaptation (Whiting & Child, 1953).

The actual developmental situation is far more involved than this simple statement of dependency indicates. Three other variables complicate the picture. First, there is never a complete correspondence between objective biosocial realities and parents' attitudes. In early infancy, for example, when the child is most helpless and dependent, he is treated with considerable deference by his parents. They make few if any demands on him and usually accede to his legitimate requirements.

This is true to a greater or lesser degree in most cultures. Infancy is invariably the period of life accorded most indulgence. The Navaho, for example, are even more extreme in these practices than we are.

Children are highly valued by the people and are almost invariably wanted—all Navahos make a fuss over babies. They receive from the start a very great amount of attention and a great deal of facial stimulation by touch. . . . The child is nursed whenever he cries. Only occasionally is there any delay. . . . The baby himself determines not merely when he wishes to suck but also when he is finished. . . .

To the Navaho baby. . . other persons must appear warm and dependable, for every time he cries something is done for him. Every step he takes toward social participation is rewarded. . . . The child runs from person to person and is petted by each in turn or consoled if it has met with some small accident. . . . Older persons are almost always quite tolerant of displays of aggression and little temper tantrums. When a two-year-old has something taken from him or fails to get what he wants, he will scream, arch his back, brace himself, and be quite inconsolable until his elders give in [which they often do] or somehow distract him.

The child is under much less pressure to hurry up and walk than white children, and the Navaho mother counts it no disgrace that the child takes his time to grow up. . . . All training in the first two or three years of life is delayed, gradual and gentle. Not until he can talk and understand is pressure put on a child to learn Navaho conventions of excretion. . . . A child at this age is almost never cuffed or even spoken harshly to. . . . The positive side of child training in this period is mainly a matter of constant encouragement in the acquisition of language and other skills. (Leighton & Kluckhohn, 1947a)

Although the infant is *executively* helpless to gratify his own needs, he tends to perceive himself as *volitionally* independent and relatively omnipotent (Ausubel, 1952a). That is, he perceives his own inability to satisfy his wants, but this dependency is only a small part of the larger gestalt of perceived volitional power characterizing the self. Executive dependence detracts not a whit from the feeling of omnipotence since a volitionally omnipotent individual has no need for executive competence as long as others are at his beck and call. In fact, it may even enhance the child's notion of his own power that success in need gratification takes place despite the manifest handicap of executive incompetence. He might, therefore, legitimately conclude: My will must be powerful indeed if a tiny, helpless creature like myself can compel omniscient adults to gratify my desires.

A second complication lies in the discrepancy between objective reality and subjective perceptual content. It is obvious that a large number of environmental and social situations are complex and subtle enough to require considerable experience and sophistication before realistic perception is possible. Maturation of perceptual capacity is a regular feature of psychological development. There is, for example, a steady progression with age in children's ability to perceive accurately their own and others' sociometric (Ausubel & Schiff, 1952) or social class (Stendler, 1949a) status. The infant possesses sufficient perceptual ability to distinguish between the deferential behavior of his parents and the matter-of-fact or competitive attitudes of his siblings. What he is not mature enough to perceive is the motivation underlying his parents' overt subservience (Ausubel, 1952a; Shaffer, 1963). From this arises the misperception that the parent is obliged to defer to his powerful will rather than that the deference is altruistic in the face of his helplessness and limited frustration tolerance. A similar lack of perceptual maturity underlies the expansiveness and "out-of-bounds" aspects of 4-year-old behavior. The child overestimates his executive competence and believes himself capable of managing his own affairs without direction or supervision (Ausubel, 1952a).

Finally, the dependency of childhood must be qualified in degree. The neonate cannot even perceive that he is executively dependent since a notion of dependency cannot arise before he has both a perception of his own helplessness and an appreciation of the causal relationship between the actions of others and the satisfaction of his needs. At first, the parent is merely a conditioned stimulus that happens to be present when his needs are being gratified (Escalona, 1969). Later, as the child becomes mature enough to appreciate that he is dependent on the parent for physical survival, he concomitantly develops a notion of volitional omnipotence. This phenomenon necessarily awaits the development of a concept of volition, which is an outgrowth of the observation that the unlearned adaptive response of crying (when he is hungry or uncomfortable) is almost invariably efficacious in relieving his distress.

The notion of executive dependence becomes but a subsidiary part of the self-concept of volitional omnipotence. It merely imposes qualifying constraints on this independence. That is, omnipotence is perceived as not unlimited but in relation to the availability of a specific executive arm (the parents) subservient to his will and devoted to his interests. Thus, the infant's sense of security—"his level of confidence with respect to the future beneficience of his environment insofar as his safety and the provision of his basic needs are concerned" (Ausubel, 1952a)—becomes a function of his executive dependence. Sudden separation of the 9-month-old infant from his mother leads to strong feelings of insecurity accompanied by severe disturbances of mood and behavior (continuous crying, depression, apathy, loss of weight, eczema) (Spitz, 1946). The infant's sense of adequacy on the other hand—"his feeling of personal worth, impor-tance, and ability to control and manipulate the environment to his own needs"—is derived from a misinterpretation of early parental subservience to his needs and desires as a result of which he vastly exaggerates his volitional power and independence (Ausubel, 1952a).

This situation usually exists until about the age of 2 or 3. In the meantime, the child acquires more executive competence and be-comes more capable of responding to parental direction. The parent, desiring to assume the volitionally ascendant role in the relationship and to train the child in the traditions of the culture, begins to make demands on the child. The environmental supports for the belief in volitional independence now collapse. As perceptual maturity ad-vances, the child begins to perceive that his parents are free agents, not obliged to defer to him; that he is dependent on them volitionally as well as executively; that he is relatively impotent and dependent on their good will for the satisfaction of his wishes; that executive in-competence is the basis of his volitional impotence rather than the proof of his omnipotence.

How reminiscent of our own culture, for example, is the situation of the Navaho [also the Chamorro (Joseph & Murray, 1951)] toddler in contrast to his idyllic infantile existence:

Except for ill health, the Navaho child's troubles may be said to begin only at the weaning period. . . . [He] comes to learn that the world around him makes demands and imposes restrictions in addition to giving reassurances and rewards. . . .

The Navaho weaned child must face keenly felt depriva-tions. . . . Weaning means less and less of the mother's atten-tion. Deprivation of the breast is merely one sign of a general loss. For the weaned child is no longer allowed to sleep every night by the mother's side. His sleeping place is now under the blanket which also covers the two or three other children nearest him in age. The mother surrenders to these older children most of the care of the weaned baby. . . .

Latterly he had been accustomed to nurse as much for comfort as for nourishment. Now this solace is denied him even when he is tired, angry, cross or frightened. . . . Crying is less immedi-ately responded to and less fully tolerated. A weaned baby who gets in the mother's way may be rather roughly jerked aside. . . .

Moreover the mother starts to make demands on him. . . . No longer is everything done for him with hardly any effort on his part; instead he must learn to feed, wash and dress him-self. . . . Serious demands for bladder and bowel control usually coincide with weaning or come shortly thereafter. . . . Soon performance of simple chores, such as bringing in sticks for the fire or snow to be melted for water, comes to be expected. Ne-glect of these, or getting into mischief, will bring a harsh scolding or a cuff or, a little later, a mild switching. . . . The weaned child . . . finds that no longer are almost all his responses re-warded, no longer does his mother devote herself mainly to his pleasure. After the child really begins to talk he finds that all responses and rewards are made much more *selectively* by his elders—he has to do the right thing for attention and praise. (Leighton & Kluckhohn, 1947b)

The crisis in ego development that results requires a complete reorganization of ego structure on a greatly devalued basis. The most acceptable and least traumatic alternative is for the child to adopt the role of satellite to his parents. By doing this he acquires a *derived* sta-tus, which he enjoys vicariously by the mere fact of their accepting and valuing him for himself, regardless of his competence or perfor-mance ability. A much more reliable feeling of adequacy can develop from this type of status, conferred by fiat, than from a mere earned type of status, which he would have to earn by virtue of his ability to manipulate the environment. At this stage, volitional and executive dependence are not perceived as unrelated phenomena; executive is perceived as a necessary prerequisite of volitional independence. The child is dependent in both aspects and derives from the new satelliz-ing relationship his feelings both of security and of adequacy.

It is apparent that satellizing will not occur in just any type of home environment; it is necessary that the child be accepted and val-ued for his own sake. Obviously, if derived status is a function of these two conditions, it cannot be acquired in an atmosphere of ei-ther rejection or extrinsic valuation (when the parent values the child as an extension of his own ego, in anticipation of the child's eventu-ally gratifying his own frustrated ambitions). And lacking the advan-tages of instrinsic security and adequacy associated with derived sta-tus, the child has little incentive for relinquishing the notions of volitional omnipotence and independence and of becoming subservi-ent to the will of another. Even when parents accept and intrinsically value him, the child finds the crisis of ego devaluation difficult to ac-cept. He submits only after a state of negativism: the grandiose fea-tures of his infantile ego structure are asserted in a last show of defiance before acknowledging that the advantages of derived status offer him a more tenable biosocial position (Ausubel, 1952a, White, 1960).

The consequences of satellizing for the future course of personality are profound. Extensive devaluation of the notions of ego importance (the centrality of self in a given interpersonal environment), of omnipotence, and of volitional independence takes place. But to compensate for this, the child acquires a guaranteed source of derived status from which he obtains intrinsic feelings of security and adequacy. In addition, as he accepts a volitionally dependent and subordinate role in relation to his parents, it becomes more and more important for him to obtain and retain their approval; only in this way can he feel sure that the status he enjoys by the fiat of acceptance will continue. Thus, his sense of security and adequacy becomes increasingly dependent on conformity to parental standards and expectations of more mature and appropriate behavior. In almost all cultures this means that he will acquire greater executive independence, more ability to forego immediate hedonistic satisfactions for the sake of long-range objectives, and a new sense of obligation to abide by internalized parental values.

Finally, as a result of satellization the child acquires a frame of reference for assimilating values and attitudes. He acquires a strong motivational set to perceive the world in the light of the values and expectation of his parents. His security depends on this ability. Later this learning orientation is reinforced by personal loyalty and by the desire to avoid the guilt feelings we know will ensue if he repudiates parental values. Learning, in other words, is primarily a by-product of identification (satellization) with the person on whom he is dependent; the actual content of the value or goal that is assimilated is of secondary importance. The renunciation of a value so learned is tantamount to an act of personal disloyalty and may, therefore, produce guilt feelings.

However, no sooner is the dependency of satellization achieved than new conditions are created which undermine it and alter the shifting balance of dependence-independence. At the same time that he enjoys the derived status of dependent child in the home, he begins to acquire an earned, performance-based status in the peer group and in school.* Here he is valued not for himself but primarily

---

* In primitive cultures and rural communities, the dependent child finds his source of earned status in the home more than in school or peer group. Especially in primitive societies, life is usually hard, and "children start working as soon as they are able, helping more and more as they grow older" (Leighton & Kluckhohn, 1947b). The quality of

for what he can do and how well he can perform in comparison with his fellows.* As he makes vast strides in executive competence through expansion of motor, intellectual, and social capacities he begins to perceive himself in a less dependent light. His parents loom less omnipotent and less omniscient in relation to his own abilities. He fancies himself entitled by virtue of his new capacities to greater volitional independence, to greater extrinsic status, to a more responsible role in the social order.

But the extrinsic status of childhood—even if achieved in economically significant activities, as in primitive cultures and rural environments—can constitute only a subsidiary source of status. The sexually immature individual can nowhere acquire adult personality status no matter how vital his contribution to the economic life of the home or community. The earned status he enjoys must inevitably play a subordinate role in the larger gestalt of volitional dependency and derived status, which characterize the biosocial position of children the world over.

EGO DEVELOPMENT AMONG BLACK CHILDREN

The ego development of black children and youth in the United States manifests various distinctive properties, both because blacks generally occupy the lowest stratum of the lower-class subculture and because they possess an inferior caste status in American society (Ausubel, 1958b). Their inferior caste position is marked by an unstable and matriarchal type of family structure, by restricted opportunities

---

their performance then becomes a factor in determining whether they are to be rewarded. At 9 years of age, Navaho girls are "already capable of taking entire care of the house and younger children in their parent's absence. Their reward would be the approval of their relatives and perhaps a gift of lambs or new clothes from the trading post if the family could afford them" (Leighton & Kluckhohn, 1947b).

* This competitive aspect of earned status is almost inevitable in our culture, but it is not a necessary component of such status in all cultures. "The Navaho is completely unaccustomed to an explicitly stated hierarchal ranking of persons such as is carried out in the grading system in white schools. At first, at least, being singled out from one's fellows for superior performance is embarrassing or actively disturbing rather than rewarding" (Leighton & Kluckhohn, 1947b). The essential feature of earned status is that it is gained through an individual's own efforts (rather than vicariously by virtue of a dependent relationship to others) and depends on the quality of his performance. It is always ego-enhancing but not necessarily ego-aggrandizing. That is, the rewards associated with earned status may be the achievement of personal satisfaction, group approval, or feelings of safety and security (as among the Navaho), rather than of prestige, "success," or competitive advantage. Paradoxically, therefore, self-enhancing earned status may be best directed toward the welfare of others.

for acquiring educational, vocational, and social status, by varying degrees of segregation from the dominant white majority, and by a culturally fixed devaluation of their dignity as human beings. The consequences of this regrettable state of affairs for black children's self-esteem and self-confidence, for their educational and vocational aspirations, and for their character structure, interpersonal relations, and personality adjustment constitute the characteristic features of their ego development.

Beginning in the preschool period, the black child gradually learns to appreciate the negative implications of dark skin color for social status and personal worth (Erikson, 1964), and he resists identifying with his own racial group. This reluctance to acknowledge his racial membership not only results in ego deflation, but also makes it difficult for him to identify with his parents and to obtain from such identification the derived status that universally constitutes the principal basis of self-esteem during childhood. Much of the derived status that white children obtain from their parents is made available to the black child by virtue of his membership in an unsupervised peer group, which accordingly performs many of the socializing functions of the white middle-class home. This is especially true for the black boy who often has no adult male with whom to identify in the frequently fatherless black family, and who finds maleness deprecated in his matriarchal and authoritarian home. Early experiences in fending for himself result in precocious social maturity, independence, and emancipation from the home (Broderick, 1965).

During preadolescence and adolescence, black youth characteristically develop low aspirations for academic and vocational achievement (Rosen, 1959). These low aspirations reflect existing social class and ethnic values, the absence of suitable emulatory models, marked educational retardation, restricted vocational opportunities, lack of parental and peer group support, and the cultural improverishment of the black home. Because of loyalty to parents and rejection by the dominant white group, black adolescents develop ambivalent feelings toward middle-class achievement values and the personality traits necessary for their implementation. In many instances they use the objective facts of racial prejudice and discrimination as a rationalization for personal inadequacies, apathy, lack of striving, and antisocial behavior. The seeming hopelessness of attaining adequate vocational and social status in the wider American culture induces many black youths to withdraw from contact and competition with whites, and to seek the psychological shelter of their own segregated subculture (Himes, 1961). The detrimental effects of segregation and inferior caste status on black ego development naturally vary from one child to another depending on ability, temperament, and the degree of intrinsic self-esteem and ego maturity that can be acquired within the home environment. The effects of the black revolution on black ego development are discussed on pages 300–302.

WHY PERSONALITY STRUCTURE MUST BE
REORGANIZED IN ADOLESCENCE

In terms of the needs arising out of the child's dependent biosocial status, satellization is the most felicitous of all possible solutions to the crisis of ego devaluation. In response to the various pressures at the close of infancy,

> it effects a reorganization of infantile ego structure that is more stable and tenable under the changed environmental and perceptual conditions of childhood. However, beginning in later childhood and extending throughout adolescence, a second major shift in biosocial status precipitates a new crisis in ego development, the maturation crisis which demands a reorganization of comparable scope and significance. (Ausubel, 1952a)

With changed conditions confronting him, the child finds the satellizing organization of personality just as untenable and unadaptive as the omnipotent organization was at an earlier date. Thus, whereas satellization may constitute "the surest foundation upon which a healthy personality structure is built, ego maturation represents the essential ingredient of the superstructure which is the immediate functional organ of personality in adult life" (Ausubel, 1952a).

Although a good deal of cultural uniformity characterizes the personality changes of adolescent and adult maturation, different cultures provide diverse varieties of specific content to these changes; even within a given cultural setting parents differ in the precise manner of executing the cultural prescription. Nevertheless, the goals of personality maturation are remarkably similar in all cultures because of the operation of the same principles of individual development and societal organization (the needs of individual and group survival, the necessity for transmitting cultural traditions).

Hence, the concept of maturation can be defined only in terms of a pan-cultural norm indicating the direction in which certain aspects of personality structure must change if the [desired goal] of an acceptable adult member of society is to be realized. This cultural ideal of personality maturity influences in turn prevailing expectations relative to changes in goal structure during adolescence, the latter being inevitably fashioned in terms of enhancing the former. (Ausubel, 1952a)

The essence of this concept of maturation, that is, acquiring the motivation to achieve greater volitional independence and a more earned source of ego status, is obviously incompatible with a relationship of satellization. The satellizing orientation must be weakend before the individual will strive to seek status on the basis of his proficiency in the virtues and competencies valued in his particular culture. This orientation when applied to the learning of goals and values has been called "incorporative" (Ausubel, 1952a).

Once these basic maturational goals are internalized, they can be implemented only if a number of other personality attributes are simultaneously modified in the appropriate direction.

> For example the enhancement of extrinsic status requires that an individual pay less attention to the immediate gratification of hedonistic needs and concern himself more with planning for long-range prestige goals; that he acquire greater competence in implementing decisions by himself; and that he at least give the appearance of conforming to the moral standards of his social group. . . .
>
> The adolescent is required to give greater self-reference to considerations involving his own competence and his status in the group. Accordingly he finds it necessary to adopt much more of the incorporative orientation in the learning of more mature goals and values—because only within the framework of this learning orientation can he efficiently enhance the objective of extrinsic status. . . . [When related to this goal] the criteria of blind loyalty, personal allegiance and craving for personal approval cannot be very reliable motivations for the acceptance of new values. More efficacious and realistic in this situation are such criteria as expediency and perceived superiority in expediting the gratification of particular status needs. The overt satellizing orientation is also frowned upon socially because it conflicts with the maturational ideal of greater volitional independence which is so crucial for the success of the new approach to status problems. (Ausubel, 1952a)

ATTRIBUTES OF ADOLESCENT PERSONALITY MATURATION

The typical course of personality development in our culture—and the one least calculated to generate internal stresses leading to neurotic anxiety and its complications or to the consequences of inadequate ego maturation—is a history of childhood satellization followed by desatellization in preadolescence and adolescence. The following list is a summary of the characteristic features of ego maturation that appear in related contexts in preceding or succeeding sections of this volume:

Ego Maturation Tasks During Adolescence*
  A. Acquisition of greater volitional independence.
      1. Independent planning of goals and reaching of decisions.
      2. Assimilation of new values on the basis of their intrinsic validity of their relation to major goals or the individual, rather than on the basis of loyalty to parents or parent surrogates.
      3. Greater reliance on nonparental (that is, societal) sources of ego support.
      4. Aspiring to more realistic goals and roles—adopting a level of ego aspiration that is more consonant with ability and environmental possibilities.
      5. Increased frustration tolerance, the ability to withstand more intense and prolonged experience with frustration, without marked loss of self-esteem, collapse of aspirational level, or deterioration of performance.
      6. Emergence of an adequate self-critical faculty—the ability to evaluate own performance critically, to perceive deficiencies and inadequacies in this performance, to become cognizant of discrepancies between an objective standard and own efforts to attain it.
      7. Abandonment of special claims on others' indulgence.
  B. Reorganization of goal structure on a less devalued basis.
      1. Greater need for obtaining earned (as opposed to derived) status.
      2. Heightened level of ego aspiration.
      3. Increased self-valuation.
  C. Replacement of hedonistic motivation by long-range status goals.
  D. Acquisition of increased executive independence.
  E. Acquisition of moral responsibility on a societal basis.

_____

* Adapted from D. P. Ausubel, 1952a.

The centrality of self during adolescence

There are a number of reasons for believing that the self-concept occupies a more prominent place in the individual's psychological field during adolescence, and that considerable upward revision of self-estimate and level of ego aspiration takes place (Elkind, 1967). In contrast to the carefree and extroverted self of later childhood, the adolescent self becomes a more crucial and clearly delineated object of awareness (Montemayor & Eisen, 1977). The adolescent appears concerned with more precise verbalization of his feelings about himself. For all practical purposes, diaries are almost an exclusive adolescent (and feminine) phenomenon (Kuhlen, 1952). Daydreaming is more common in postpubescent than in prepubescent youth (Stone & Church, 1973). Increased awareness of and interest in other traditional symbols of selfhood such as the body (Clifford, 1971; Schachter et al., 1971) and one's name (Eagleson, 1946) are also characteristic of adolescence. Concern with intellectual status and social relations have considerable self-reference and are important sources of self-esteem in the adolescent (Jersild, 1952). Finally, adolescent preoccupation with dating can be partly explained by the usefulness of the opposite sex as a contrast medium for self-expression and sharper definition of individuality.

Adolescence is a period of inflation of ego aspirations and self-estimate. In contrast to the early crisis of devaluation, it may be regarded as a time of ego revaluation. All of the maturational tasks of adolescence—acquisision of volitional independence and earned status, emancipation from parents, achievement of economic independence, release from dependence on parents in assimilating values, learning a biological sex role, emphasis on executive independence and long-range status goals, and acquisition of adult body form—have ego-inflationary implications. This supposition is confirmed by analysis of the content of adolescent fantasy, which casts the ego in heroic and amorous roles (Singer, 1966). The fact that the vocational goals of adolescents tend to be at a higher level than is justified by a realistic consideration of aptitude and job opportunities (Hurlock, 1973) leads to the same conclusion.

ADOLESCENT PERSONALITY COMPARED TO THOSE OF INFANCY AND CHILDHOOD

The tasks of adolescent personality development overlap sufficiently with those of infancy and childhood to make a more detailed comparison profitable.

To begin with,

> the crisis of maturation just like the crisis of devaluation precipitates an extended period of developmental disequilibrium. All of the difficulties attending a transitional stage of ego development must be endured again. A secure and established biosocial status is exchanged for a new status which is unsettled, marginal, conflictful and uncertain of attainment. A highly differentiated and familiar psychological field must be abandoned for one that is uncharted, ambiguous, undifferentiated, and fraught with unknown implications. The quest for orientation must be begun anew. It is no wonder then that resistance to change will come from within as well as from without. (Ausubel, 1952a)

Second, adolescence resembles infancy more than childhood in that a new biological drive (sex) must undergo initial socialization. This emergent phenomenon presents a problem that has not arisen since early infancy, and the control of this new source of hedonistic motivation is comparable in many ways to the early regulation of hunger, thirst, and bladder and bowel evacuation.

Third, there is reactivation of the issues of dependence versus independence and of self-assertion versus subservience, which have lain relatively dormant since the crisis of devaluation.

> Again violent fluctuations in these dichotomous needs are the order of the day until a new equilibrium is found. But the general trend is change in the opposite direction. The pendulum swings closer to the infantile goals of volitional independence and mastery of the environment than to the subservient attitude of childhood. This does not mean that the young adult is back in the same place which he left at the close of infancy; for behind this shift in ego development is considerable growth in perceptual ability and executive capacity, and fundamental changes in social pressures and expectations. Thus, the positions which were abandoned as untenable after the fierce resistance from three to five are given a new basis in reality which turns the tide of battle and enables them to be held permanently following the equally turbulent struggles of adolescence. (Ausubel, 1952a)

Reference has been made to the shift in the independence-dependence balance during adolescence. This shift, however, is in and of itself not coextensive with the process of adolescent personality maturation; it is only one component aspect of the more general constellation of changes cataloged in this section, and can not be appreciated properly apart from them. For example, the need for greater volitional independence is accentuated by higher ego aspirations, greater self-valuation, and increased demands for earned status. The adolescent individual who (1) has more modest ego demands, (2) values himself more modestly, and (3) is more content with vicarious status can also tolerate considerably lower levels of volitional independence with much greater equanimity than his more ambitious contemporary with a more grandiose self-concept.

As in the crisis of devaluation, negativism is a prominent aggressive response of the individual to the insecurities and anxieties of the rapid transition in biosocial status. In devaluation, however, the general direction of change is toward a decrease in status, whereas in the new situation the reverse holds true.* More important is the difference in the cause of the disproportion between status and capacity that gives rise to much of the conflict-provoking negativistic behavior. In the earlier period, the 2- and 3-year-old demands volitional freedom far out of proportion to his executive capacity. The adolescent, on the other hand, receives too little volitional independence in relation to his ability (Ausubel, 1950a). Status deprivation exists in both instances; in the first case this is attributable to the unrealistic aspirations of the child, but in the second to the inability or unwillingness of parents or social order to provide status commensurate with capacity.

The same difference underlies a general similarity between infancy and adolescence in still two other areas. The adolescent like the presatellizing child is more concerned with achieving earned (in contrast to derived) status, but has a more realistic claim in actual executive competence. Similarly, the adolescent's higher self-valuation is more realistically grounded in environmental supports.

Finally, the adolescent resembles the presatellizing child in owing to personal loyalty relatively few (in comparison with the satellizing child) of his feelings of accountability to parental moral standards. But unlike the situation in infancy, these feelings are based on more abstract propositions, are directed by societal sanctions and guilt feelings, and do not owe their force to more tangible applications of reward and punishment.

On the other hand, adolescence is in several respects more nearly continuous with the direction of personality development during statellization. The childhood trends toward greater executive independence, increased reliance on long-range goals, greater overall moral responsibility (despite the shift in the basis for these) (Ausubel,

---

*However, the status of the infant is heading toward greater stability and security in childhood, whereas the transition from childhood to adolescence involves a comparable loss in these areas.

1952a; Kohlberg, 1968, 1973), and greater conformity (Costanzo & Shaw, 1966) are extended during adolescence. Hedonistic motivation is further attenuated. "But this time the motivation is different, it reflects a need for attaining recently internalized more mature goals which would be frustrated by preoccupation with pleasure-seeking activities, rather than a need to gain parental approval" (Ausubel, 1952a). And although the adolescent shift toward earned status is more reminiscent of infancy, there is continuation of the childhood trend to seek such status on the basis of actual executive competence.

CONTINUITY IN PERSONALITY DEVELOPMENT

In this chapter we are primarily concerned with those aspects of continuity in personality development which have special relevance for the unique maturational tasks of adolescence. However, it is necessary to consider in a more general way the nature of and the factors responsible for longitudinal consistency in the patterning of personality.

In the discussion of the similarities and differences between adolescence and earlier stages of personality development, it became clear that "as in every evolutionary process, continuity although less striking and dramatic goes hand in hand with modification. The consequences of previous modes of ego organization leave a permanent residue in personality structure which play an important directional role in future developments" (Ausubel, 1952a).

Numerous evidences of continuity in personality development can be cited (Ausubel & Sullivan, 1970). For example, analysis of the life histories of over 90 anti-Nazi German refugees both before and after Hitler's accession to power led Allport, Bruner, and Jandorf (1941) to conclude:

Very rarely does catastrophic social change produce catastrophic alterations in personality. Neither our cases nor such statistics as are available reflect any such number of regressions, hysterias or other traumatic neuroses as the gravity of the social crisis might lead one to expect. On the contrary, perhaps the most vivid impression gained by our analysts from this case-history material is the extraordinary continuity and sameness in the individual personality. . . . Resistance to social catastrophe is the outstanding characteristic of our cases. . . .

Personalities studied by independent investigators working a full year apart in a period of serious disruption are seen by a new set of judges to be recognizably the same. Where change does take place, it seems invariably to accentuate trends clearly present in the preemigration personality. Radical transformations do not occur, selective reinforcement and partial inhibition accounting for what change there is. In no case does the alteration correspond to the complete upset in the life space.

These data by no means point to the invariability of the personality pattern once it is laid down. As Leighton and Kluckhohn (1947b) point out,

> In spite of the fact that Navaho infants receive a maximum of protection and gratification, when they grow to be adults they are very moody and worry a great deal. . . . The theorists. . . claim too much for the earliest years and do not pay enough attention to later events and to the total situation in which the mature person finds himself. Infantile indulgence probably does constitute the firmest foundation upon which, if later circumstances are reasonably favorable, a secure and confident adult personality can be built. But it affords only a possible basis; it does not, in and of itself, promise fulfillment. The high degree of tension observed among adult Navahos may be traced partly to the exceedingly grave pressures to which Navaho society is at present subject, and also to the conflicts caused by weaning, other experiences of later childhood and beliefs about supernatural forces.

Satellization alone will not predispose toward the attainment of normal adult personality unless it is followed by desatellization in later childhood and adolescence (Ausubel, 1952a). Favorable infantile experience may be appreciably vitiated by later experience with chronic or crippling disease, later rejection by parents, and delayed onset of adolescence (H. E. Jones, 1943). Parent attitudes or their perception by the child may undergo drastic change as the child advances in age. The adolescent child's emergence from either a highly benevolent or a highly rejecting home into a more neutral peer environment may release latent introversive or extroversive trends (previously masked by their respective opposites) which had been more appropriately evoked in the social climate of the home.

Psychological basis of consistency in personality
development

Developmental consistency in personality patterning is a consequence of numerous psychological factors. These factors may be classified roughly as those emanating from (1) the child, (2) the environment, and (3) self-perpetuating psychological mechanisms associated with various dimensions of personality structure.

Persistence in personality patterns undoubtedly inheres partly in certain genic and constitutional prepotencies. These predispositions may be strong enough to resist intensive training in the opposite direction by parents and teachers (Shirley, 1941). Thus a large measure of the consistency in the parent-child relationship is a function of the child's constitutional makeup. Differences in this makeup evoke different components of the parent's repertory of possible behaviors. A particular parent will respond differently toward an active or passive, toward a docile or self-assertive child (Bell, 1971). Likewise, different children, depending on their constitutional predispositions, will behave differently in response to a particular pattern of parental behavior, thereby tending either to change or perpetuate the pattern (Schaffer & Emerson, 1964). Thus, in some instances, dominance in the child may intensify an attitude of rejection in the parent, whereas in other instances it may hold it in check.

The parent adds to the consistency of the child's personality development by providing a continuing environment that tends to remain relatively constant during the important formative years of the child's growth. This constancy, of course, is an expression of the parent's own general consistency in personality structure from year to year. Its effect is enhanced by the necessarily restricted nature of the child's environment during the early years (which isolates him from possible counterbalancing influences outside the home) and by the tremendous power of the parent in regulating the child's life during this accelerated stage of development.

During the periods of middle childhood, preadolescence, and adolescence, the parent continues to provide more or less the same quality of training for personality maturation; but by this time his influence is diluted by other forces in the culture. However, the growing child navigates primarily within the restricting confines of a limited social class environment, which resembles his home in many aspects and which is also characterized by substantial continuity in value systems over a score of years.

Finally, consistency in personality development is a function of both (1) the stability of certain central dimensions of ego structure, and (2) the self-perpetuating nature of some of the mechanisms of personality construction. As a result of characteristic ways of interacting with significant persons in the environment, more or less permanent constellations of ego needs and habitual modes of self-evaluation arise. Examples of such constellations are differential feelings of security and adequacy and needs for ego status and independence that emerge in crucial developmental experiences such as satellization or failure to undergo devaluation. These constellations give rise to propensities for characteristic modes of learning, aspiring, socialization, ego defense, and attitudes toward authority and group demands. Such propensities are, with situational factors, the immediate variables in most current behavior. They affect behavior in two ways: (1) as *proximate* determinants entering directly into the formulation of learning and socialization patterns at the level of current biosocial status, and (2) as *substrate* or background factors that contribute more indirectly to the operations of current biosocial status.

The difference between these two types of propensities may be illustrated as follows. An adolescent with a previous history of satellization derives most of his current biosocial status from earned rather than from derived sources. Nevertheless, he continues to display subsidiary satellizing patterns in his learning orientation and approach to group functions; these furnish a subsidiary derived source of status. On the other hand, certain residual products of his satellizing history provide a substrate which does not function concurrently as a subsidiary source of derived status, but affects the *major* current type of status (earned status). For example, our ex-satellizing adolescent has residual intrinsic feelings of security and adequacy which permit him to acquire and gain ego satisfaction much more readily than the nonsatellizer, and hence has less need for and is not as highly motivated to attain high extrinsic status. He can become reconciled more easily to failure and downward revision of his level of ego aspiration.

Finally, the longitudinal continuity of individuality can be attributed to the fact that certain central dimensions of personality (e.g., satellization or nonsatellization) play a crucial integrative role in its development and organization. It would be surprising indeed if the prior existence and operation of such salient aspects of individual uniqueness did not leave some functional residue in personality structure. The latter could affect directly the kind of current biosocial status an individual seeks and the basis on which he assimilates values. "Thus, for example, although an adult who satellized as a child obtains most of his current status from earned rather than from derived sources, some satellizing patterns still remain operative in adult life and furnish a subsidiary source of status, e.g., satellizing-like relationships with boss, spouse, pastor, physician, membership group, etc." (Ausubel, 1957). In addition, a residue of prior satellizing experience could conceivably constitute an inner core of self-acceptance which would be independent of situational success and failure. Although this would not function as a subsidiary source of currently generated status, it could exercise a substrate influence serving to keep his ego aspirations within realistic limits and to protect him from catastrophic impairment of self-esteem (Ausubel & Sullivan, 1970).

PREPARATORY ASPECTS OF PERSONALITY MATURATION

From the standpoint of ultimate criteria of maturity, the satellizing era of middle and late childhood is a period of mixed progress. The attenuation of hedonistic motivation, the gain in executive independence, and the enhancement of feelings of moral responsibility are all steps toward adult maturation. But in relation to other, more crucial characteristics of mature personality structure, such as volitional independence and reliance on earned status, satellization constitutes at least a temporary setback. It is true that realistic progress toward these goals also occurs; but as already pointed out, whatever earned status is achieved occupies only a subsidiary position in the total gestalt of biosocial dependency.

Childhood may be regarded as a period of apprenticeship in acquiring the *qualitative* aspects of personality maturity that are necessary for individual and cultural survival. Adolescence, on the other hand, is more a period of apprenticeship in attaining the prerogatives and behavioral capacities associated with volitional independence and earned status. Thus, much of the personality development necessary for maturity is achieved before adolescence or exists at a near-threshold level, and is, therefore, a function of the quality of training for maturation provided during this period.

FACTORS BRINGING ABOUT PREPARATORY MATURATION

First among the factors impelling change toward personality maturation is the cumulative impact of progress in cognitive and executive capacities, which in turn induces modification of parental and societal expectations. During middle childhood, there is an increase in the child's ability to comprehend abstract relationships, to reason, and to generalize (Piaget, 1926, 1952, 1964). Hence, the first precondition for acquiring more mature behavior patterns, readiness for learning, is satisfied.

Although Piaget is an interactionist, emphasizing both maturation and learning, he is sometimes mistakenly interpreted as believing that development is solely a spontaneous process, generated from within the child. The application of external pressures, so this view goes, is held to be unnecessary and unwise, and productive of resistiveness. But, although the removal of external coercion eliminates negativism, it also obviates the possibility of growth.

> Gains in maturity do not arise spontaneously and automatically out of the needs of the child. They are more than a reflection of increased readiness to undergo training as a result of increased capacity proceeding from growth, although this factor must also not be ignored. Involved in every noteworthy maturational advance relative to ego structure is some change in the expectations of significant persons in the child's environment which is enforced by some coercive form of pressure. (Ausubel, 1952a)

Just as important for maturation as appropriate revisions in expectations is sufficient opportunity for learning mature and responsible behavior. Without the requisite experience and practice, maturation could evolve no more readily in response to altered external expectations alone than by spontaneous generation from changed conditions of internal readiness.

Parents play a strategic role in the changing environmental expectations inducing personality maturation in the child. The new demands they set reflect their own needs and desires as well as their changed perceptions of the child's growing capacities for responsible behavior. "Also channeled through them are changing cultural expectations of appropriately mature behavior at various stages of development" (Ausubel, 1952a). And in either case it is they who apply whatever coercive measures are required to effect the necessary degree of conformity. The parent is "unwilling to serve indefinitely as the executive arm of his offspring's will. . . . At the termination of infancy he welcomes the increased self-sufficiency of the child since it frees him for other tasks, and approves of the shift in ascendence-submission which gives him greater control and direction of the latter's activities" (Ausubel, 1952a).

To enforce conformity to his new expectations the parent can rely on reward and punishment, approval and disapproval, prestige authority, moral restraints imposed by the child's guilt when he strays from his parents' values, and the power to extend or withhold the appreciation which chiefly motivates the child's early bids for extrinsic status. Although it is true that external controls and extrinsic considerations (reward and punishment) generally tend to be replaced by some form of self-discipline, "the process of internalization is a very gradual one and by definition presupposes the original existence of external controls, since obviously nothing can be internalized which does not first possess an external form. . . . [And] even after internalization is fairly well established, the presence of external controls in the background serves a salutory effect" (Ausubel, 1952a).

In the new face he presents to his child, the parent is for the most part playing the role of cultural representative. "Reality training is important. . . among all people who survive" the usual conditions (Leighton & Kluckhohn, 1947b). Under an economy of scarcity, everyone must develop certain minimal skills and a willingness to work. When life is more abundant, the child's actual economic contributions to family survival may be deferred until early adulthood, but in many cases he is no longer permitted the self-indulgence and irresponsibility of earlier years. At the very least, a large share of self-help is demanded.

> As in the post-weaning period the [Navaho] child learns that he cannot indefinitely continue to have his way, so between five and eight, he has to acquire a sense of responsibility. Every society has to teach its members that they cannot always indulge themselves and that they have duties toward others. The difference lies in when, and how, and by whom the child is disciplined. White society's training in some types of self-restraint. . . comes early. The Navaho child is "beaten down" later after he is sure of the fundamental affection of his relatives. (Leighton & Kluckhohn, 1947b)

The sanctions for appropriate behavior are eventually referred to some social norm. Parents in our culture appeal to children not to shame them by their misbehavior in the eyes of the neighborhood, but the Navaho parents say, "If you behave like that people will make fun of *you*."

In contrast to the extreme indulgence with which they are treated in infancy and early childhood, Navaho

> children are severely rebuked and even whipped if they take shelter during a storm while out herding and lose track of the sheep. Neglect or abuse of livestock is the least forgivable of

childhood misdemeanors. When children first begin to help with the herding at six or seven, they tend to ride and chase the sheep and goats and otherwise disturb and distract them from feeding. Harsh scoldings break them of these habits quite quickly. . . . The culprit is dressed down properly, and an effort is made to shame him into more responsible conduct. . . .

The growth of a sense of responsibility is facilitated by the custom of setting aside each year a sheep or two which, with their increase, belong to the child himself. The young herder feels, then, that he isn't just doing a job for his mother and father—he is also looking after his own property. His own interests become involved in his learning to care properly for the flock. . . .

The period from six through the early teens is a time for learning skills as well as for developing responsible behavior. Besides the chores of chopping and bringing in firewood, emptying ashes, hauling water, husking corn, etc., instruction in more specialized tasks begins. From about the age of eight on, children of the two sexes tend to be separated a good deal of the time. Each group is trained in certain skills by their elders of the same sex. (Leighton & Kluckhohn, 1947b)

The culture not only regulates (1) the general direction or preparatory maturation, which is typical of most human societies, and (2) the more specific aspects that are idiosyncratic to its particular values and traditions, but also places "limits upon the personal punishments and even the scoldings which may be imposed on children" (Leighton & Kluckhohn, 1947b). Within this general pattern, however, there is considerable room for individual family differences, both in the emphasis placed on different goals of maturation and in the type, severity, and feeling tones behind the controls used to effect their realization.

ESTRANGEMENT OF PARENT AND CHILD IN URBAN CULTURES

In rural and primitive cultures, the home serves as both the source of subsidiary extrinsic status and the training institution for developing more mature and responsible behavior.

In modern urban cultures, however, children have little opportunity for exercising independence, responsibility and identification with the world of adult concerns. . . necessitating a complete separation of the activity and interest systems of child and adult. Such children are given no responsibilities in the work-a-day world of adult concerns, and hence, evolve a complete set of prestige-giving values of their own. (Ausubel, 1952a)

In almost all spheres of life,

our culture goes to great extremes in emphasizing contrasts between the child and the adult. . . . The child must be protected from the ugly facts of life, the adult must meet them without psychic catastrophe; the child must obey, the adult must command this obedience. These are all dogmas of our culture, dogmas which, in spite of the facts of nature other cultures commonly do not share. . . .

We think of the child as wanting to play and the adult as having to work. . . . But in many societies. . . when the child can run about it accompanies its parents. . . doing tasks which are essential and yet suited to its powers; and its dichotomy between work and play * is not different from that its parents recognize, namely the distinction between the busy day and the free evening. The tasks it is asked to perform are graded to its powers, and its elders wait quietly by, not offering to do the task in the child's place. (Benedict, 1938)

This absence of absolute dichotomy between child and adult prevails among the Navaho.

Children and adults do not belong to two separate worlds. The same set of standards prevails in most things for all ages, from the child (as soon as he can talk) to the old people. . . . [At the same time] Navaho practice is to expect only so much from children at each age level. The white tendency is to project adult standards down into all except the earliest childhood. (Leighton & Kluckhohn, 1947b)

Ruth Benedict (1938) reports essentially the same situation for the Cheyenne Indians:

The essential point of such child training is that the child is from infancy continuously conditioned to responsible social participation, while at the same time the tasks that are expected of it are adapted to its capacity. The contrast with our society is very

---

* The distinction between work and play is also less marked in primitive cultures. Curle (1949) suggests that segmentation of life in modern civilization as a result of rapid social change, the greater availability of leisure time, and the greater freedom of individual choice in heterogeneous societies has brought this about.

great. A child does not make any labor contribution to our industrial society except as it competes with an adult; its work is not measured against its own strength and skill but against high-geared industrial requirements. Even if we praise a child's achievement in the home we are outraged if such praise is interpreted as being of the same order or praise of adults. . . .

At birth the little [Cheyenne] boy was presented with a toy bow, and from the time he could run about serviceable bows suited to his stature were specially made for him by the man of the family. . . . When he finally killed a buffalo, it was only the final step of his childhood conditioning, not a new adult role with which his childhood experience had been at variance. (Benedict, 1938)

Among the Canadian Ojibwa,

the boy accompanies his father [on hunting trips] and brings in his catch to his sister just as his father does to his mother; the girl prepares the meat and skins for him just as his mother does for her husband. . . . The young child is taught consistently that it has only itself to rely upon in life, and this is as true in the dealings it will have with the supernatural as in the business of getting a livelihood. This attitude he will accept as a successful adult just as he accepted it as a child. (Benedict, 1938)

Such training in responsibility inevitably brings with it some subsidiary earned status and volitional independence.

The techniques. . . by which a child is conditioned in a responsible status role. . . depend chiefly upon arousing in the child the desire to share responsibility in adult life. To achieve this, little stress is laid upon obedience, but much stress upon approval and praise. Many American Indian tribes are especially explicit in rejecting. . . any dichotomy according to which an adult expects obedience and a child must accord it. . . . [Maternal uncle] and child share reciprocal privileges and obligations which in our society can only develop between age mates. . . . Such kinship conventions allow the child to put in practice from infancy the same form of behavior it will rely upon as an adult; behavior is not polarized into a general requirement of submission for the child and dominance for the adult. (Benedict, 1938)

In urban societies, on the other hand, the culture is not organized to provide children with many important opportunities for extrinsic status. Mature roles must be learned by a course other than gradual participation in family or communal responsibilities. "Denied a place in adult reality they [children] must find other outlets for the independence and mature interests which personality growth has stimulated" (Ausubel, 1952a). They are obliged to find sources of earned status in peripheral activities (school, peer group athletics) far removed from the main current of status in the adult world (Ausubel, 1952a; Bronfenbrenner, 1970). They supplement this with the vicarious status that can be obtained through identification with the glamorous exploits of prominent figures in public life, and with whatever satisfaction can be gained by carrying on covert guerrilla warfare with adults and adult standards.

Thus, the child's interests and concerns become "oriented more toward his contemporaries than toward his parents." In his peer group he is given a chance to obtain the mature role-playing experience from which adult society excludes him and which his parents are unable to furnish. Identification with this group also provides a substitute source of derived status, providing him with this ego support which reduce his dependence on parental approval. And "by attributing the prerogatives of judgment, decision, choice and initiative to a group fashioned in his own image, he. . . . effectively demolishes his exclusive association of these powers with parental figures and thus paves the way for eventually assuming them himself" (Ausubel, 1952a).

School serves a similar function. It provides both a new subsidiary source of earned status based on academic ability and a fresh source of derived status which challenges the parent's monopoly of this commodity and of omniscience as well.

All of these factors—availability of other sources of derived status, reduction of absolute dependency on parents for ego support, need for going beyond the home for extrinsic status, increased competence of the child, and emergence of a new authority to challenge his parent's omniscience—tend to break down "the deified picture" he nurtures of his parents. And as the parent's omnipotence declines, his power to confer by fiat an absolute intrinsic value on the child begins to ebb. This stimulates an intensified quest to satisfy status needs beyond the home.

The net effect of this urban displacement of the home as a training institution for personality maturation is threefold: (1) Desatellization from parents is undoubtedly accelerated by their devaluation, although not until adolescence is over is the child "sufficiently free of the attitude of subserviance to evaluate them with critical detachment" (Ausubel, 1952a). (2) The lack of actual role-playing experience in the adult world cannot be completely compensated for by the various substitutes available in school, peer group, and hero-worship activities. Lacking the stimulation of genuine social expectations of mature behavior in the adult sense, and sufficient opportunity for suitable practice, the individual must inevitably lag in ego maturation (Ausubel, 1950a). (3) Finally, this situation

> inaugurates a long period of estrangement between children and adults which persists until the former attain adulthood themselves. Insurmountable barriers to commonality of feeling, to mutual understanding and to ease of communication are built up. This alienation is not unaccompanied by resentment and bitterness. Although outright resistance to adult authority is usually withheld until adolescence, there is reason to believe that the preadolescent's apparent conformity is only a veneer which hides the smoldering rebellion from view. This is revealed by the often contemptuous and sneering remarks he makes about adults in his own company, and by the studied indifference to adult standards which he professes out of earshot of the latter. (Ausubel, 1952a)

PUBESCENCE: CONSUMMATORY FACTOR
IN PERSONALITY MATURATION

The preparatory changes in personality maturation cataloged above, as well as the factors bringing them about, are not to be minimized in evaluating the total maturational change from the close of infancy to the beginning of adult life. Yet the transition cannot be consummated merely by the cumulative impact of these same factors: i.e., parental and cultural needs for personality maturation; increased executive competence of the child; new sources of derived status and ego support; the weakening of dependency ties on parents; the deflation of parents and the continued progress toward desatellization; the achievement of an independent, subsidiary source of earned status. This is true even where children are not relegated to a separate and discontinuous world of status opportunity, but contribute to the economic sustenance of the family. The conclusion is inescapable that whatever independence and earned status children can earn before pubescence can occupy only a subsidiary role in the larger gestalt of biosocial dependency. The gains in these areas are primarily a by-product of the training in responsibility and the attenuation of hedonistic impulses that constitute the main maturational business of childhood.

The personality maturity of adolescence and adulthood are qualitatively different from the maturity of childhood. In our own culture this qualitative difference is explicitly recognized in the dichotomy characterizing the types of status activities and opportunities for independence available to children and adults respectively. In cultures which do not erect such dichotomies, this qualitative difference prevails nevertheless as a result of a transcendental leap that becomes effective at a crucial transitional point on a continuous quantitative scale. This point is reached when in the total economy of ego organization, earned and derived sources of status exchange positions as subsidiary and dominant (or peripheral and central) figures in the gestalt.

Pubescence plays the role of crucial catalytic agent in shifting the direction of the source of status, and hence in inaugurating the consummatory aspects of personality maturation. It is the cue for reversing social expectations about the major type of status that the child may appropriately seek. Hence, for the pubescent individual,

the social value of derived status depreciates while the corresponding value of extrinsic status increases. The adolescent, thus, not only finds that he is increasingly expected to establish his status through his own efforts, but also that the latter criterion tends to displace the childhood criterion (i.e., of derived status) as the chief measure by which his social milieu tends to evaluate him. Simultaneously, social pressure is put on the parents to withdraw a large portion of the emotional support which they had hitherto been extending to him by way of conferring intrinsic status. (Ausubel, 1952a)

In addition to the fact that of his own volition and under cultural pressure the parent acts to provide less derived status, his power to do so is also impaired. Continued widening of the child's social horizon tends to effect an increasing devaluation of the parent's stature. This process is accelerated by (1) the now more glaring inability of the parent (in comparison with other cultural agencies) to furnish an extrinsic source of status, and (2) the more critical and objective appraisal the child can make of his parent when the child is freed of the bias and "halo effect" implicit in an attitude of subservience.

Pubescence also exerts a catalytic effect on the child's strivings for personality maturation. In the face of the altered cultural expectations that puberty induces, he feels that his aspirations for greater status and independence are more legitimate. But even apart from these social sanctions and pressures, his reactions to his newly attained adult physical form, reproductive power, and biological sex drive cannot do otherwise than generate aspirations for the status with which these attributes are patently associated.

MECHANISMS OF DESATELLIZATION

This discussion obviously relates to children with a history of satellization during the childhood era. The mechanisms whereby nonsatellizing individuals undergo personality maturation are treated separately.

Desatellization through resatellization

Within the satellizing orientation itself we have delineated two different patterns of maturation. The more familiar type, characteristic of modern urban civilization, involves gradual replacement of parents by age mates as the essential socializing agent. The age mates not only supply the child's needs for extrinsic status and the opportunity for mature role-playing experience, but also displace the parents as the persons in relation to whom any residual remnants of the satellizing orientation are maintained (resatellization). This pattern, as already pointed out, involves considerable devaluation of and desatellization and alienation from parents, yet also carries with it relatively slow and inefficient maturation during preadolescence and the middle years of childhood. But

> although this substitution of age-groups standards for home standards is often regarded as a phenomenon rooted so deeply in the psychology of maturation as to be inevitable, cross-cultural investigations show this is not so. In Samoa the young boys and girls are given increasing status in the community as they reach and pass adolescence, but there is no period when they rebel against the authority of the head of household and substitute instead a set of counter and antagonistic standards. (Mead, 1940)

Frank (1944b) makes the same observation: "In a static, tradition bound society, the process of emancipation does not necessarily imply a supplantation of the family as the principal medium through which the culture operates." "Here the family could still serve as the primary source of goals and standards while the adolescent's position in relation [to parents] merely shifts from a dependent to an independent role" (Asubel, 1950a). "That is, the adolescent could still learn most of what he needs to know as an adult from his parents, but would assimilate this knowledge for use in the role of an independent person in his own right" (Ausubel, 1952a).

In addition to the factors already mentioned as contributing to devaluation of parents and renunciation of their standards is the fact that the

> role we give to parents that they must pose as better and more complete representatives of their culture than they really are also exposes growing children to almost inevitable disillusion. Furthermore the notion that children are different in kind from adults fosters attitudes in children's and adolescents' groups which are qualitatively different from the attitudes of the adults. (Mead, 1940)

The gap thus created between children and parents under these circumstances is further widened by the rapid rate of social change. Adding to the psychological and social distance already present are the very different worlds in which the two generations grow up, producing an actual discrepancy in the content of the values each accepts. Hence, "the children who continue to adhere to the standards set up by their parents carry the stigma of being 'old fashioned,' or 'out of date' " (Mead, 1940).

What are some of the outstanding consequences of this substitution of age mate for parental socialization? Besides inducing more complete devaluation, it also accelerates desatellization. The mere fact that individuals of their own generation assume the function of setting standards, a power that had always been regarded as the prerogative of omniscient elders, serves to devalue parents as suitable foci for satellization, and to sanction the legitimacy of their own assumption of this power. But this same factor leads also to another quite different result:

> There is a difference in the positive self-valuation of the individual who is attempting to meet standards represented by remote and highly respected persons. . . and the individual who is striving hard to meet the standards of persons who inspire no great respect. . . . The rejection of parental standards in favor of late-recognized and antagonistic age-grade standards results, therefore, in an attenuation of self-respect and a weakening of the internalized standards of behavior upon which the operation of our culture is still postulated. (Mead, 1940)

According to Margaret Mead, age-mate socialization has important reciprocal repercussions on social change. An entire revolution of standards becomes possible merely by appealing to the readiness of youth to reject parental ways in favor of a new set of mores (Mead, 1970). Such change, however, which is founded on no other basis than the need to conform to group norms, does not necessarily bring progress. "The quantity of the surrogates replaces their quality, for a single individual or pair of individuals, who are highly respected as different in kind and better than the child, is substituted the number of age mates who approve and follow a certain course of behavior" (Mead, 1940).

Thus is lost an important potentiality for social progress inherent in the older system of socialization by parents, namely, the "striving to avoid the self-reproach of failing to realize an unobtainable ideal, the picture of the parent. . . conceived in childhood" (Mead, 1940).

The repudiation of parental standards in favor of less idealistic age-grade norms also makes youth reared on an earlier diet of satellization more susceptible to demagogic influence. As Mead (1940) points out, this readiness to accept alien doctrines is not unaccompanied by feelings of guilt in rejecting prior loyalties. "And it is this element in their character structure which leaves room for the leader, a parent surrogate who will lift their conformity to the mob on a higher level again and make them feel less guilty of apostasy toward their own infantile acceptance of their parents' dictated systems of morality" (Mead, 1940).

As we shall see later, however, the greater readiness of the adolescent to accept age-grade in preference to parental norms does not necessarily make for a complete overthrow of the standards previously accepted; for the new norms presented by the peer group tend to hew more closely to the values of the social class in which the adolescent claims membership than to the alien values of a different social class. The same values that the child rejects because they are proposed by the parent are eagerly accepted when advocated by the peer group in slightly different form but with essentially the same content.

Desatellization through the achievement of earned status

More important for the outcome of desatellization than the issues of who is the basic socializing agent and who (parents or peer group) becomes the focus of residual satellizing trends is the mode of acquiring earned status. The satellizing orientation is abrogated primarily by the displacement of derived by earned status as the chief source of self-esteem in the adolescent individual. However, the major socializing agent must inevitably constitute the source of the extrinsic status in question. Hence, we find the same split between rural and primitive cultures on the one hand, and urban cultures on the other, in the manner in which extrinsic status is attained.

Generally speaking, adolescence is less prolonged in cultures in which adolescents gain extrinsic status by participating in the same types of economic activities as their parents. But in cultures characterized by age-mate socialization, parental sources of status are not available to adolescents, adolescence is extremely prolonged, and earned status is achieved in peripheral functions far removed from the main economic currents of the social order. We have already referred to the latter situation as *interim status*. Although from a long-range standpoint the goals of this type of status have only temporary "stop-gap" significance, they do constitute distinctive objects of striving in their own right during the adolescent period.

Here arises another source of discontinuity between children and adults. Three discrete value and status systems must be learned before adult life is reached. And during adolescence the individual is obliged simultaneously to satisfy the need for immediate age-mate status while keeping an eye toward the more long-range goals of adult status.

In either setting it is important to realize that earned status does not necessarily mean individual success, prestige, power, or preeminence. It may just as well be competence that is not compared with another's, modest security, safety, approval for group mindedness, maintenance of "face." Thus, among the Navaho,

the youngster is not urged to strive for individual achievement. There is no promise of personal success for the able and hardworking or the good and righteous. On the other hand, a sense of worthlessness is never drummed into a child so that his whole subsequent life is a stuggle to justify himself. . . . To accept authority over his fellows or to take initiative in any obvious fashion has for the Navaho the psychological meaning of separating him from the social group to which he looks for both support and regulation. . . . But a sense of responsibility is none the less real for being divided and shared, for being—to the white person— vague and unfixed. . . . The majority seem to be only interested in safety. . . . They themselves will sometimes say, "All we want is enough to eat for ourselves and our families." . . . The predominant drive is for moderate material well-being. (Leighton & Kluckholn, 1947a)

A somewhat similar situation exists among the Maori of New Zealand where there is a greater emphasis on derived status and on the task-oriented and group welfare features of earned status rather than on the self-aggrandizing aspects of earned status (Ausubel, 1965). The Maori is less concerned with achieving occupational prestige and is, therefore, less willing than the *pakeha* (European) to internalize traits important for implementing achievement goals, i.e., to practice self-denial and self-discipline and to persevere in the face of adversity. Valuing personal relationships, derived status, and kinship ties above material possessions and occupational prestige, the Maori strives for helpfulness, generosity, hospitality, and sociability more than for punctuality, thrift, and methodicalness.

> Greater stress was laid on mastery of skills for its socioeconomic importance, on pride of craftsmanship, and on the personal satisfactions of meritorious accomplishment; on kinship obligations and on *intertribal* competition; and on the satisfactions associated with working together in an intimate, personal context of reciprocal psychological support. These characteristics of primary status and the continued importance of derived status engendered and made valuable in turn traits of mutual helpfulness and cooperative effort in bearing economic burdens, generosity, hospitality, and concern for the welfare of kinsmen. Because of the greater availability of derived status, the attainment of primary status was a less compelling necessity for the maintenance of self esteem. (Ausubel, 1960)

In recent times this situation has been modified to some extent as the Maori have been subjected to the acculturation pressures of modern New Zealand society. Most young Maori adolescents have assimilated the *pakeha* pattern of educational and vocational aspirations. However, these aspirations are not generally shared by the adolescents' parents who identify with the traditional Maori orientation toward earned and derived status. Hence, the parents do not really encourage and support the implementation of the aspirations fostered by the educational system and the modern society. This lack of consistency has forced many Maori adolescents to develop a kind of double standard in order to satisfy both home and school.

Since the *pakeha* standards are never adequately internalized or developed, it is only a matter of time before the influence of Maori cultural values, as mediated through parents and peers, begins to prevail. In addition, Maori adolescents also become progressively more aware of the obstacles standing in the way of their vocational success because of *pakeha* prejudice and discrimination. This perception of the relative unavailability of the promised rewards of self-denial and striving similarly disposes them to abandon or modify their earlier aspirations (Ausubel, 1960).

From this we may conclude (1) that the magnitude of residual intrinsic adequacy feelings available to adolescents and adults is partly a function of a societal norm the mean value of which varies from culture to culture, with considerable room for individual family differences; (2) that the drive for extrinsic status is inversely related to the magnitude of these residual feelings of adequacy; and (3) that the particular orientation of the goals toward which earned status is directed (competitive and individualistic or cooperative and group-related) is conditioned by the prevailing value system of a culture or subculture.

In both types of socialization patterns (age grade and parental) a transitional variety of earned status is evident. That is, the child's initial quests for extrinsic status are largely bids for parental approbation, and as such must be considered modified manifestations of satellization. If they elicit appropriate signs of appreciation from parents, their continuation as ends in themselves is encouraged.

Desatellization through exploratory orientation

Two modes of assimilating values, the satellizing orientation and the incorporative orientation, have already been discussed as characteristic of childhood and adulthood, respectively. The incorporative is naturally an accompaniment of the quest for greater extrinsic status since it uses a criterion of ego enhancement as the preparatory set in reacting to new value experience. The satellizing orientation, on the other hand, is predicated on personal loyalty and the need to retain parental approval (or to avoid the guilt engendered by repudiation of parental standards). Common to both orientations, however, to a greater or lesser degree, is a subjective bias favoring the generation and perpetuation of a given type of status (earned or derived), and a relative indifference to objective considerations impinging on the empirical or logical validity of the value in question.

A third type of learning orientation (exploratory) is not status oriented in either sense, but is directed toward objective problem solution regardless of the status implications involved.

In every person's psychological world there is a. . . sphere of value-laden, ego-involved learning experience in which the task itself and not its relation to ego status is the primary focus of concern. Where task-oriented goals or values are concerned, levels of aspirations operate, success or failure is experienced, but self-esteem is not necessarily affected since ego status is not at stake. The basis of the exploratory [orientation] lies in the active curiosity which is manifested by human beings from the earliest days of infancy. (Ausubel, 1952a)

The use of the exploratory orientation is obviously limited during childhood, "for as soon as the implications of independent objective investigation are pursued to their logical conclusion, the danger always exists that they will conflict with values tied to primary allegiances, and hence precipitate an avalanche of guilt feelings" (Ausubel, 1952a). But as subservience to parental values wanes, the exploratory orientation can be used more freely, and continued use promotes desatellization by deemphasizing considerations of personal loyalty in value assimilation.

Unfortunately, however, the development of the exploratory orientation is severely curtailed in the course of age-mate socialization. The adolescent's marginal status and his dependence on the peer society for status permit little deviation from group values, and hence little opportunity for independent exploration. On the other hand, when the adolescent owes his opportunities for extrinsic status to his elders, there are similar pressures to make him adhere to traditional values. In both instances, the exploratory orientation tends to be sacrificed because of the adolescent's need to conform to the standards of the agents who control the sources of his earned status. The very operation of this factor, in other words, is merely another manifestation of the incorporative orientation.

FACILITATING AND RETARDING FACTORS IN MATURATION

Factors that serve either to advance or impede the progress of maturation may be conveniently divided into (1) conditions relating to familial or parent-child relationships, and (2) cultural arrangements impinging on the acquisition of status by adolescents.

Familial factors

The existence of a general set of cultural imperatives and expectations for the course of personality maturation does not necessarily ensure that the maturation will take place as culturally anticipated. For the actual implementation of these policies, the culture must rely on the individual family. And since parents in a given culture differ among themselves, and since different children react in different ways to the same parental practice, maturation depends largely on various dimensions of the parent-child relationship. The parental attitudes or behaviors that are particularly relevant to maturation are (1) degree of protectiveness (care, solicitude), (2) dominance (self-assertiveness or deference to child's will), and (3) appreciation (recognition) of child's competence.

These parental attitudes affect maturation by promoting or discouraging (1) the child's freedom in obtaining extrinsic status or in attempting the incorporative and exploratory orientations in value assimilation; (2) the development of "multiple sources of security and adequacy through satellization with persons and groups outside the home"; and (3) the development of "skills in independent planning and goal-setting by providing opportunities for practice, and appropriate conditions for learning realistic roles and goals, adequate frustration tolerance and realistic self-criticism" (Ausubel, 1952a).

For children to develop "the skills that are necessary for competent exercise of volitional independence," they require "opportunity for exercising choice, making plans and decisions, practicing self-direction, and learning from [their] own mistakes" (Ausubel, 1952a).

Adequate freedom for exploration, for trial-and-error learning, and for manipulating a variety of social situations is needed. Mature volitional behavior can only be learned [through] actual role-playing experience. Hence, overdominated children whose parents make all their decisions, and overprotected children who are never exposed to the possibility of making an independent decision lest they [injure themselves, experience frustration or] make a fatal error, are inestimably handicapped in the learning of volitional maturity. (Ausubel, 1952a)

A mature capacity for volitional independence is also characterized by a capacity for (1) bearing frustration without unduly abandoning level of aspiration, self-esteem, self-criticism, independence of decision, or performance ability; (2) setting goals and aspiring to roles that are realistically possible; (3) acquiring a reasonably accurate estimate of own status, abilities, and performance; and (4) making demands on others that are legitimate and tolerable. The realization of these goals is largely dependent on

direct experience with frustrating and restrictive aspects of [the] environment. It presupposes acceptance of the barriers and limitations imposed upon the free, unhampered exercise of will by the inherent structure of the social order and by the prevailing social expectations and prohibitions surrounding individual behavior. . . . The irreducible condition for achieving these objectives is to confront the child consistently, firmly and unambiguously. . . with the unadorned realities that define his biosocial position at home and in his culture. (Ausubel, 1952a)

There is no other way to learn to handle frustration than to have first-hand experience with it. "Purposeful and persistent avoidance of frustration creates for the child a conception of reality which is so distorted that he becomes exclusively conditioned to living in a hedonistic environment" (Ausubel, 1950a).

Development of frustration tolerance, therefore, requires that a child be encouraged to solve his own problems. . . that his course through life not be continually smoothed by systematic elimination of the problems which confront him. He must learn to take responsibility for the consequences of his behavior when mistakes are made and failure ensues. Parental "whitewashing". . . reinforces the immature tendency to cope with failure and misbehavior by rationalization, disclaiming of responsibility, and abandonment of even minimal standards of self-criticism. (Ausubel, 1952a)

The overly permissive parent fails to develop frustration tolerance in the child by acceding to the child's demands for help whenever he encounters difficulty. He fails also to structure realistically the limiting and restrictive aspects of the child's world, thereby making difficult the setting of realistic goals and the accurate perception of self-role.

The conditions under which self-role can be realistically learned require a clear appreciation of what can be legitimately included within the appropriate age-sex subculture role, and what must perforce be excluded from it. The attitude of unvarying permissiveness fulfills neither condition. By advocating unrestricted freedom for the child in setting his goals, by refusing to impose limitations on behavior which is socially unacceptable, and by denying the legitimacy of status differences between children and adults, the overly permissive parent or teacher makes it impossible for the child to perceive the boundaries of his role. . . .

Extreme. . . exposure to this variety of child-rearing [may] lead to extreme unrealism regarding the demands which an individual can legitimately make on others. . . . He develops the notion that he is a very precious and privileged person. His parents *have* to do things for him and have to help him. . . because he has a special claim on this indulgence. [And] eventually this orientation is extended to the world at large. (Ausubel, 1952a)

Desatellization and the utilization of learning orientations other than satellization are also facilitated if the child is accepted unconditionally, that is, if obedience and conformity as ends in themselves are not made the price of acceptance. Navaho parents never demand socially acceptable behavior as the condition of parental love and protection or say to a child, "If you do that, mother won't love you anymore" (Leighton & Kluckhohn, 1947a). Hence volitional and moral independence becomes less fraught with dangerous consequences.

Similarly, the more impersonal the basis on which obedience and conformity are required, the less likely is the desire for independence to be inhibited by feelings of personal loyalty and guilt. Navaho parents do not demand obedience as a personal right or regard disobedience as "bad," but point out "the advantages of obedience [and] the value in taking advice and instruction from more experienced persons" (Leighton & Kluckhohn, 1947a). Threats are not warnings of personal reprisal for insubordination but objective predictions of disaster for children who fail to heed prudent admonition. The authority for discipline is depersonalized and referred to supernatural forces or to agencies "outside of the immediate family circle" (Leighton & Kluckhohn, 1947a). If a plea for good conduct is made by appealing to shame-avoidance, the plea for deflection of shame is made from the child rather than from the parent (Leighton & Kluckhohn, 1947a). In all of these ways, the overly dependent and personal aspects of satellization are minimized.

The dangers of extreme satellization are also avoided

if the child can find derived status in multiple sources rather than in his parents alone. Under such circumstances the one source is no longer so precious. He need not tread so warily to avoid arousing disapproval. Fortified by the ego support he receives from friends, grandparents, older siblings, teachers, group leaders, etc., he can afford more often to assert his independence and risk arousing parental ire. (Ausubel, 1952a)

The part that the peer group plays in this process in our culture is played by the "extended family" in many cultures such as the Navaho, in which the child is reared more by a group of relatives than by parents. This results in an attenuation of attachment and loyalty to a single person or pair of persons. Similarly, the greater diffusion of authority results in fewer manifestations of personal resentment and rebellion.

Even when parents are not overprotective or overdominating, inherent factors in the parent-child relationship make them ambivalent toward the child's emancipation. They tend to fear the loss of love that removal of his dependency creates (Meyers, 1946).

> They have a vested interest to protect—the satisfactions, the ego supports, the feelings of power and importance that go with having another individual dependent upon them for guidance and direction. "Emancipation requires much sacrifice by parents. They must relinquish authority" and "learn the patience and restraint required to develop the capacity for self-direction in the child." This is naturally a much more difficult task for parents who are exploiting the dependent aspects of the child's attachment for them as a substitute source of status and affection in instances of vocational or marital maladjustment. (Ausubel, 1952a)

Such feelings of ambivalence naturally give rise to parental inconsistencies in behavior and expectations which confuse the child and compound the retarding influence the ambivalence exerts on maturation.

Feelings of rivalry, often only dimly perceived, also complicate the parents' attitudes toward the child's maturation. They cannot help comparing their waning powers and motivations with the child's growing competencies and naively sanguine aspirations. If these are a source of pride, they also represent a threat which, with each passing day, brings the shadow of eventual displacement closer. "Unconsciously," therefore, they may be motivated to slow the progress of maturation. However, the resentment which these attitudes provoke in the child may bring about the opposite effect (desatellization) by deepening the estrangement which already so frequently exists.

Not to be ignored in this picture is the possibility of serious lag between alteration of attitudes and appropriate modification of related behavior. It is a commonplace observation that underlying attitudes may remain unaltered despite formal changes in outward behavior. Less frequently recognized is the equally important tendency for old behavior patterns to persist out of sheer inertia despite modification of the attitudinal substrate. It takes time to learn the appropriate gestures, mannerisms, and inflections of a new role even if one has mastered the required shift in feeling tones. And even then the phenomenon of perceptual constancy in the child may force altered parental behavior into the same perceptual molds because of the prepotency of habitual expectations.

Hence, the child frequently fails to respond appropriately to changes in parental expectations of greater maturity because he cannot reorganize into a new gestalt what to him can have only a fixed and constant perceptual meaning despite manifest changes in stimulus content. He thus withdraws from parents "for no other reason than the fact that they always are the ones to whom he has always *been* a helpless child" (Zachry, 1944).

Personality maturation also suffers from ambivalence of the child. He is naturally reluctant to part with the protection and security of dependency and a familiar biosocial role for the anxiety and insecurity inevitably associated with any transition in development. And, "unfortunately, sufficient ambiguity prevails regarding the biosocial role considered appropriate for adolescents, and the period of transition is sufficiently prolonged" to offer considerable support for the yearning to return to the "good old days" of childhood (Ausubel, 1952a). This regressive alternative has a more powerful attraction for children with strong needs for hedonistic gratification (who find long-range striving difficult), and for sedentary, shy, "thin-skinned," and introverted individuals to whom self-ssertion comes painfully.

Desatellization, therefore, is, even under the best of circumstances, "a difficult and inevitably conflictful phase of ego development." The child must contend with ambivalence, rivalry, the inertia of habitual attitudes and behavior patterns in his parents, and his own ambivalence and perceptual constancy. If he becomes too independent he provokes parental resistance and internal feelings of guilt. On the other hand, if he remains too dependent and submissive, he "loses face in his own eyes and in the eyes of his peers, feels inadequate for failure to gain extrinsic status, and develops feelings of hostility and resentment toward parents for thwarting his growth" (Ausubel, 1952a).

Cultural factors

There is no doubt that the cultural availability of extrinsic status is the crucial variable affecting the rate, duration, and difficulty of adolescent maturation. Almost all of the distinctive characteristics of adolescent development in Western civilization are derivatives of the fact that the pubescent children's greater executive competence can receive no social recognition in terms of adult status-giving activity. On the other hand, in primitive rural cultures such as the Navaho, "there is no period of several years when the individual is neither child nor an adult as the adolescent in White American society today. The Navaho's physical maturity and social maturity are more nearly coincidental" (Leighton & Kluckhohn, 1947a). Our adolescents must customarily look forward to an 8-year period of subadulthood that provides a marginal, interim status in peripheral activities and a good deal of uncertainty regarding the eventual attainment of adult status.

Such a situation is more or less inevitable in any complex culture requiring extended education and apprenticeship. The peer group is obliged, then, to provide compensatory sources of status and to assume responsibility as the major training institution of adolescence. But this dichotomy need not be as absolute as it is presently. With some intelligent social engineering, adolescents even as apprentices could be provided with a good deal of status-giving experience and responsibility in projects involving the community as a whole.

The reasons for the prolonged adolescence in our culture and its grosser behavioral consequences are discussed at length in Chapter 11. Here we are concerned only with what at first glance seems to be a purely self-evident phenomenon, namely, "the precise nature of the mechanisms whereby socio-economic conditions necessitating a prolongation of the transitional period of sub-adulthood become translated into an actual process of retardation in the sphere of psychological development. The relationship between social status on the one hand and ego valuation on the other is a fundamental problem of ego psychology" (Ausubel, 1950a).

The most important intervening variables in this process of transmutation—"the level of social expectations regarding rate of maturation and the availability of mature role-playing experience"—are intimately related. The former, in fact, is almost completely a function of the latter, which depends on socioeconomic factors influencing the need for adolescent manpower. In accordance with fluctuations in this need, society keeps shifting its view of the urgency with which adolescent maturation should take place.

> This relationship is never a one-to-one affair since a certain minimal level of status change is anticipated on the basis of pubescence alone, and a certain amount of time lag is inevitable between the onset of changed economic conditions and the evolution of new social attitudes. Nevertheless the correspondence is quite close; and in the more usual type of economic situation in our culture, conditions are such that little sense of urgency is felt regarding the rapidity of maturation. Thus, although the adolescent may desire to gain status more rapidly than he is allowed to, he feels no pressure to do so—at least from the adult segment of society. (Ausubel, 1952a)

Having no other frame of reference as a guide than prevailing social expectations, "his level of aspiration with respect to the proper rate of maturation generally corresponds to the relative urgency with which society regards the problem. Most adolescents would believe any other course to be virtually impossible, since like children, they tend to believe that prevailing social arrangements are absolutely given and hence immutable" (Ausubel, 1950a).

Why do adolescents base their levels of aspiration regarding maturational progress on cultural expectations? First, as in any unstructured field, these expectations undoubtedly exert considerable influence in the form of prestige suggestion. Second, they have motivational properties emanating from their capacity to generate *transitional anxiety*. The mere existence of these expectations constitutes a threat. Adolescents are expected to mature at a certain rate or else face the possible loss of "status advantages otherwise accruing from successful maturation." The feelings of anxiety and insecurity instigated by this threat can be reduced only by suitable evidence of maturation, thereby giving rise to appropriately pitched motivations (levels of aspiration) (Davis, 1944).

Culturally induced low levels of aspiration for maturational progress actually result in developmental retardation by "making the adolescent disinclined to seek out. . . role-playing experiences propitious for personality development" (Ausubel, 1952a). And the most proximate variable involved in this chain of events, the one directly responsible for the lagging rate of maturation, is deprivation of the necessary experience required for personality growth.

When the cultural unavailability of adult status becomes extreme, it retards personality maturation even more directly. By ruling out access to needed experience to individuals who would otherwise obtain it by high endogenous motivation (despite social discouragement), it exerts a leveling influence negating motivational variability of other origin.

In addition to status deprivation, other social factors largely idiosyncratic to our culture, such as various types of cultural discontinuities and discrepancies in attaining adult status, also tend to retard adolescent personality maturation. These are discussed in Chapter 11.

PERSONALITY MATURATION IN NONSATELLIZERS

The preceding picture of personality maturation is characteristic of all children who undergo devaluation and subsequent satellization. But not all children present this typical developmental history; and since mode of maturation is largely a function of childhood personality structure, we must consider this problem separately for the nonsatellizers.

The prerequisite parent attitudes necessary for devaluation and satellization and the parent attitudes leading to nonsatellization (rejection and extrinsic valuation) have already been discussed. It is true that different cultures vary in the degree of socially sanctioned acceptance and intrinsic valuation that parents are expected to extend to children; but familial *intra*cultural differences are a much more striking source of variance than *inter*cultural variability in parent attitudes.

The child who fails to satellize also fails to undergo ego devaluation. The infantile personality structure that is not presented with appropriate conditions for reorganization tends to persist despite various changes in the child's biosocial status. Unable to achieve feelings of security and adequacy on a derived basis, he continues to operate on the basis of their extrinsic counterparts. And under these auspices he is not obliged to surrender the volitional independence and the grandiose level of ego aspiration, renunciation of which is implicit in the self-subordination of anyone who satellizes, who derives his status vicariously by the mere fact of relationship to or acceptance by an omnipotent figure.

Reasons other than failure to satellize also tend to prevent devaluation. (1) Reconciliation to an earned status that the child would be realistically entitled to on the basis of actual biosocial competence involves too drastic, abrupt, and traumatic a shift from the previous ego organization to be acceptable. (2) In the absence of any intrinsic source of adequacy, extrinsic status serves a compensatory function; and hence the need for it is greater and less easily relinquished than among satellizers. (3) Other factors in the parent-child relationship operate against devaluation. The rejected child reacts with bitterness and vengeful fantasies to the humiliating depreciation to which his self-esteem is subjected; and implementation of the vengeance and self-vindication he seeks requires the attainment of more than ordinary success. The home environment of the extrinsically valued child, on the other hand, continues to support the grandiose properties of infantile ego organization. The parent intends to aggrandize his own ego through the child's attainments, and hence does all in his power to maintain the fiction of the child's infantile omnipotence by maintaining a worshipful and deferential attitude. It will be convenient, therefore, to refer to the extrinsically valued child as "overvalued."

Hence, during childhood both varieties of nonsatellizers remain undevalued with these main differences between them: The rejected unlike the overvalued child suffers from impaired self-esteem and has no opportunity for the exercise of volitional independence or for the satisfaction of exalted ego needs. The rejected child also is usually overdominated and obliged to adhere to stringent standards of mature behavior, to develop executive independence, capacity for postponing hedonistic gratification, and a sense of responsibility. The overvalued child, on the other hand, is usually underdominated and under less pressure to acquire these attributes of maturity. With either, however, the only basis on which the child accepts the desirability of maturation is not the satellizer's need for retaining derived status, but the perception of mature behavior *from the very beginning* as a necessary precondition for the attainment of earned status in the community; and in rejected children there is the additional consideration of submitting to the exacting demands of persons on whom they are economically dependent for survival.

Later impact of nonsatellization on maturation

Desatellization, as represented by the tasks of acquiring greater volitional independence, primarily striving for extrinsic status, raising the level of ego aspiration, and adopting the incorporative and exploratory learning orientations, is ordinarily the main business of adolescent maturation. Since in nonsatellizers these tasks are accomplished in advance, it follows that maturation involves a less comprehensive change and is more likely to be successful. The nonsatellizer with his high ego aspirations and his exaggerated needs for earned status has always regarded dependence disdainfully, as symbolic of defeat in his quest for these goals. "Volitional independence had never been really surrendered, and hence does not have to be regained" (Ausubel, 1952a).

Other aspects of maturation take place for the express purpose of implementing the acquisition of earned status—provided there are "no overwhelming contraindications emanating from the non-satellizing situation itself" (Ausubel, 1952a). For example, goal frustration tolerance, self-critical ability, executive independence, and long-range goals are acquired easily enough.

> But the imperious need for superior accomplishment and preeminent extrinsic status effectively prevents the setting of realistic goals in many cases. Although level of ego aspiration is uniformly high in non-satellizers and is extremely resistant to lowering in the face of frustration, there is no reason for believing that the distribution of ability in this group is [uniformly high]. . . . Aspirational level will, therefore, be persistently and unrealistically high except in the small minority of individuals whose abilities are commensurate with their ambitions. (Ausubel, 1952a)

It would be reasonable to expect also that the attenuation of immature personality traits on the basis of expediency (ego enhancement) is a much less stable arrangement than attenuation on the basis of satellization. In satellization there is implicit and unquestioning acceptance of the desirability for change. In the former instance, on the other hand, "where changes are made with specific ends in view," (1) abandonment of ends leads to reversal of change, and (2) incompatibility of the change with underlying ends often leads to sabotage of change. Thus, should either the goals of ego enhancement be abandoned (as in periods of severe personality disorganization), or any of the goals of ego maturation be perceived as in conflict with the ends of ego enhancement, maturational regression could easily take place. The most vulnerable aspect of this type of maturation lies in the durability of feelings of moral accountability under conditions that are prejudicial to personal gain and advantage. Lacking the satellizer's implicit acceptance of the duty to abide by all internalized moral values, the nonsatellizer is sorely tempted to let these values "go by the board" if the stakes are sufficiently high and the chances of apprehension and retribution sufficiently low. As we shall see later, these factors facilitate "reactive" maturational failure in nonsatellizers.

If maturation is more often successful in nonsatellizers it is also more stressful. The satellizer's extrinsic self-esteem* is damaged by status deprivation during adolescence, but this injury tends to be peripheral because of a residual core of intrinsic self-acceptance. The nonsatellizer's self-esteem, on the other hand, is "wholly a creature of the environmental vicissitudes which deny or gratify" the exalted ego aspirations on which he has "staked his value as a human being" (Ausubel, 1952a). Hence, the absence of intrinsic feelings of adequacy makes the damage wrought to the only type of self-esteem he knows (extrinsic) central rather than peripheral. In addition, only when intrinsic self-esteem is lacking do threats to extrinsic self-esteem have the power to induce neurotic anxiety (Ausubel 1952a).

The destructive impact of status deprivation on self-esteem and potential for anxiety response is greater in nonsatellizers for still another reason besides lack of intrinsic adequacy. Because of their exaggerated needs for ego enhancement (which are highly resistant to discouragement), they find the same degree of status deprivation

---

*In this discussion, the term "feelings of adequacy" is used synonymously with "self-esteem." When "extrinsic," such feelings are referable to earned status; when "intrinsic," they are referable to current or residual derived status. Anxiety is a tendency to respond with fear to anticipated situations which threaten self-esteem. Neurotic anxiety exists when the basis of this tendency inheres in already impaired self-esteem rather than in an objectively hazardous situation. Neurotic anxiety thus appears to be an "overresponse." Clinical observations have led to the hypothesis that only persons who lack intrinsic feelings of adequacy are vulnerable to sufficient loss of self-esteem to be subject to neurotic anxiety (Ausubel, 1952a).

much more deflating to self-esteem. They are denied also the current source of derived status that adolescent exsatellizers enjoy by maintaining a part in a satellizing orientation* toward peer group, teachers, and employers. They are unable to experience the "ego support and 'we feeling' that is derived from the act of dependent identification with and self-subordination to group interests" (Ausubel, 1952a).

MATURATION OF REJECTED CHILDREN

Although rejected children find adolescent status deprivation more stressful than do satellizers, adolescence often presents them with quite a few more opportunities for status than childhood. The decreased importance of the rejecting home in comparison with the importance of school and peer group is in itself an ego-inflating factor. The fact of rejection becomes less catastrophic as the importance of the rejecting figures in the psychological world diminishes. Also, in comparison with childhood many new opportunities of achieving extrinsic status present themselves.

Rejected children do have a latent capacity for forming satellizing-like relationships to nonthreatening individuals. Their original failure to satellize was due to the absence of suitable parental figures in the home rather than to disinclination. When these children are removed from the home, the possibility of satellization is increased, although fear of repetition of rejection makes them move cautiously.

Neurotic anxiety is almost invariably present in rejected children from the very beginning. Self-esteem is sufficiently impaired, both by (1) the absence of intrinsic feelings of adequacy and (2) the catastrophic injury to extrinsic adequacy feelings implicit in the rejecting situation, to constitute the major source of threat in any adjustive situation.

The socialization of the rejected child is made difficult by his inability to assert himself adequately and to protect himself from the aggression of others. This is a consequence of a learning deficit acquired in the course of having to submit so long and helplessly to parental aggression that he cannot master the roles necessary for adult self-assertion. Aggression by others evokes a habitual response of helpless submissiveness.

What other persons usually fail to recognize, however, is that this aggression and domination are only outwardly accepted; that

---

* It might be noted here that nonsatellizers also use the incorporative and exploratory orientations exclusively in value assimilation.

quite unlike the overdominated satellizer who genuinely accepts the subservience to which he is subjected, the overdominated non-satellizer gradually accumulates a reservoir of resentment and hostility which eventually overflows with such violence as to rupture existing relationships beyond repair. (Ausubel, 1952a)

Typically, the rejected child tends to be taken advantage of, appears to accept the situation meekly, and then to the amazement of others erupts violently and impulsively. To avoid this sequence of events he prefers to withdraw from conflict situations and to intellectualize his aggression. Either course of action, however, does little to promote effective interpersonal relationships.

MATURATION OF OVERVALUED CHILDREN

In contrast to its effect on the rejected child, adolescence usually brings a marked loss in extrinsic status and self-estimate to the overvalued child. He can hardly expect the same flattery and adulation in school and peer group that he was accustomed to receiving at home. In fact, adolescence frequently marks the onset of neurotic anxiety; for only now is the impairment to his extrinsic self-esteem sufficiently catastrophic to predispose him to this personality disorder. But unlike that of the rejected child, his anxiety is not offset by the possibility of obtaining some derived status (and, therefore, some intrinsic self-esteem) through the belated establishment of satellizing-like relationships.* His failure to undergo devaluation and satellization was less a compensatory reaction of self-defense than an outcome of the parent's active fostering the infantile ego organization. Thus, he tends to find satellization too degrading and is usually too obnoxiously selfish, self-centered, and narcissistic either to inspire genuine love in others or to be capable of relating himself emotionally to them.

The overvalued child differs from the rejected child also by manifesting no incapacity for self-assertion and aggression. In fact, his socialization is hindered by an excess rather than by a deficiency of these qualities. He tends to alienate associates initially by his overbearing, domineering, and importunate behavior.

But in his case the motivation is available to modify the strategy of his interpersonal relationships and to learn more acceptable social behavior, since he recognizes the importance of good social relations in the struggle for power. Through assiduous study

---

* Neurotic anxiety may be allayed in the rejected child by his achievement of intrinsic status per se, and by the reduction of frustration which this permits through a lowering of level of ego aspirations.

and intelligent application of self-control he is able to acquire an agreeable set of formal manners and a superficial veneer of good fellowship to mask his formerly offensive aggression and self-seeking. . . . Hence. . . he is able to learn a highly effective form of self-assertion in interpersonal relationships. (Ausubel, 1952a)

Last, because of his excessively permissive upbringing, the over-valued child experiences more initial difficulty than the rejected child in acquiring goal frustration tolerance, long-range goals, self-critical ability, and executive independence, and in relinquishing hedonistic motivations. But unlike the underdominated satellizer, his lack of intrinsic self-esteem and his exaggerated needs for ego enhancement and genuine volitional independence motivate him more strongly eventually to acquire those attributes of maturity.

8

Parent–Child Relationships in Adolescence

THE MEANING OF EMANCIPATION

"Throughout the entire animal kingdom where parents play an altruistic role in the rearing of their young, 'emancipation seems to be quite a natural process' " (Ausubel, 1950b). But neither among animals nor in human societies can emancipation be considered "synonymous with the more general problem of achieving adult personality status. It is merely that component part of the latter which depends upon a readjustment of the parent-child relationship on a basis that is more compatible with the [growing child's] increased capacity to fend for himself" (Ausubel, 1950b). The achievement of full adult personality status requires a degree of social recognition that transcends the mere alteration of intrafamilial relationships.

Parents at the infrahuman level cease to exercise responsibility for their young even before the young acquire sexual maturity. Animal society, however, does not recognize adult status until the onset of pubescence. Once this point is reached, acceptance as an adult depends only on various interpersonal determinants of intragroup structure, such as sex, strength, number of individuals in the group, relative dominance, and newness in the group.

In human societies, total emancipation rarely if ever precedes pubescence; and the interval of time between emancipation and the achievement of adult status is always culturally institutionalized. That is, this achievement is not merely a function of interpersonal relationships within the group, but is a product of social regulation based

197

on traditions, values, beliefs, and institutions transcending individual differences and the specific population characteristics and dominance hierarchy of a given group. In primitive cultures the time lag between these two phenomena tends to be relatively short. But

> in our society a large degree of emancipation is achieved relatively early compared to the delayed acquisition of adult social status. Through emancipation the adolescent establishes himself as a person in his own right, apart from his parents, prepared to strive for adult goals and willing to assume responsibility for the direction of his own affairs. But it is one matter to achieve this preparatory state of resolution and independence in a family setting, and still another to achieve that degree of social recognition as an adult which will afford the necessary experience in playing actual adult roles that is required for the attainment of this new personality status. Also since it is quite impossible even [in a family setting] to conceive of oneself as an independent adult ready for mature tasks and responsibilities in the face of prolonged socioeconomic dependence, adolescents can only achieve a certain limited measure of emancipation until their economic independence is an accomplished fact. (Ausubel, 1950b)

Thus, emancipation is an important aspect both of personality maturation and of the achievement of adult personality status. A large share of personality maturation is achieved in the home in relation to parents. Although much of this maturational change in the home antecedes pubescence, emancipation remains incomplete without it. The final transition between emancipation and the achievement of adult status, on the other hand, is a function of cultural arrangements that are initiated by pubescence but depend for their consummation on other socioeconomic factors. And, finally, emancipation and the attainment of adult status influence each other reciprocally: an unemancipated individual is inevitably handicapped in the quest for social recognition as an adult; conversely, deferment of recognition as an adult necessarily delays the completion of emancipation.

The specific developmental tasks implicated in emancipation have already been cataloged. The universality of these tasks and of the general direction of personality change in relation to them during adolescence enables us to regard emancipation as one of the basic psychobiological problems of adolescence.

FACTORS INFLUENCING THE NATURE AND ATTAINMENT OF EMANCIPATION

Age trends

The course of emancipation in our culture is typically marked by two periods of slow and gradual growth, each of which is followed by a period of acceleration. The first period, which begins with the child's entrance into school and his absorption into a peer group, is climaxed by a spurt induced by pubescence. Prior to this time any gains in self-help and independence are primarily executive advances and are accompanied by a tightening of parental volitional control. After the initial acceleration of emancipation in response to pubescence, the rate of growth is slow again until adult status is achieved as a result of financial independence, marriage, or induction into military life.

The empirical research on emancipation, or as it is variously referred to in the study of adolescence, the development of autonomy or independence, suggests that the degree of emancipation from parental standards gradually increases between childhood and adolescence but that even at age 18 adolescents still possess strong emotional ties to their parents. Meissner (1965) noted an increase in rebelliousness and alienation from parents between the early and late years of high school. Douvan and Adelson (1966) found that for a national sample of girls, independence increased sharply between ages 11 and 18 for such behaviors as dating, job-holding outside the home, access to independent funds, and spending most of leisure time with friends instead of parents.

However, when we look beyond these rather superficial and specific aspects of behavioral independence to the more deeply felt and enduring emotional bonds between adolescent and parent, we find that the developmental changes are more modest. For instance, Douvan and Adelson (1966) found only slight changes for girls between childhood and adolescence in the following measures of emotional independence: belief that relationships with friends were more important than relationships with parents; choosing as an advisor someone outside the family rather than a parent; increase in disagreements with parents. Even when a majority of 18-year-olds make choices that indicate a high degree of emotional independence, a large minority of girls make choices that suggest a continuing strong attachment to their parents.

Bowerman and Kinch (1959) distinguish three aspects of the parent-peer situation: (1) *identification,* e.g., does the adolescent feel that his parents or friends understand him better; (2) *association,* e.g., which group does the adolescent prefer to spend time with; (3) *norm orientation,* e.g., with respect to questions of right and wrong, whose ideas does the adolescent feel are more like his own. Questionnaires were administered to students between grades 4 and 10, and the results suggested that during this time span students markedly shifted their association from parents to peers, although they continued to identify more closely with their family and showed only a moderate change in norm association. These and other studies suggest that adolescents may be happy enough to settle for such ritual signs of emancipation as holding a job, dating, etc., while maintaining an attachment bond to parents at least until full adult status is achieved (Bowerman & Elder, 1962; Westley & Elkin, 1957).

MECHANISMS OF EMANCIPATION

The mechanisms by which emancipation is achieved are no different from those already described for personality maturation: (1) gradual replacement of parents by peers as the essential socializing agent; (2) the achievement of earned status.

In urban culture, in which the peer group constitutes the chief training institution of adolescence, emancipation

is largely the outcome of positive changes in the relationships between adolescents and *non-parents,* rather than the result of any positive modification of the parent-child relationship itself. Seldom is there any planned or deliberate determination of policy. There is merely the deterioration of a relationship as it is replaced by new loyalties, new standards, and new sources of status. Parental influence and prestige wane to the point where the peer culture is even obliged to take over the functions of transmitting and enforcing class attitudes, aspirations and standards of behavior. (Ausubel, 1952a)

Thus, desatellization or emancipation from parents is to a large extent a product of resatellization. Values and goals are still acquired by intellectual satellization, that is, as by-products of subservience to others on whom the individual is dependent for derived status; but now personal loyalties have been transferred from parents to age mates.

Other writers, commenting on adolescence in America, have suggested that the increased importance of peers as socializing agents for the developing child may be due less to the attractiveness of the peer group than to the deterioration of the parent-child relationship. Bronfenbrenner and his coworkers interviewed sixth-grade children who were classified as either peer- or adult-oriented and concluded that "the peer-oriented youngster was more influenced by a lack of attention and concern at home than by the attractiveness of the peer group" (Bronfenbrenner, 1970, p. 101). Bronfenbrenner is concerned about the implications of his findings for future generations of Americans and pessimistically concludes that "the peer-oriented child is more a product of parental disregard than of the attractiveness of the peer-group—that he turns to his age-mates less by choice than by default. The vacuum left by the withdrawal of parents and adults from the lives of children is filled with an undesired—and possibly *undesirable*—substitute of an age-segregated peer group" (Bronfenbrenner, 1970).

The strength and pervasiveness of this newly felt peer loyalty are indicated by the development of conformity to peer pressures. Costanzo and Shaw (1966) investigated conformity in individuals between the ages of 7 and 21 using a procedure developed by Asch (1956). The results indicated that conformity increases between ages 7 and 12 and declines thereafter; this inverted *U* pattern was found for both males and females, although females conformed somewhat more than males at all ages. The authors suggest that the explanation for this pattern has to do with the adolescent's difficulty in adjusting to puberty and with his ambiguous and marginal social status. Presumably the early adolescent experiences a good deal of confusion and uncertainty over his recently occurring sexual maturity and his new marginal social status, and therefore looks to his peers as models for what is appropriate and correct behavior.

This increasing conformity to peer standards is not an all-or-nothing proposition, however, since whether or not an adolescent conforms to his parents or his peers depends on the particular issues under consideration. Brittain (1963, 1969) studied possible situational differences in conformity by presenting hypothetical parent-peer dilemmas to a group of adolescent girls. The findings indicate that adolescents were more likely to accept the advice of their parents on issues concerning the future and the adult world, although they looked to their peers for answers to questions about school and the peer culture.

The expansion of the child's social horizon during adolescence, as his physical mobility increases, also plays a role in emancipation.

The widening of his social contacts makes him realize that his parents' home embodies only one specific representation of the culture, that other and perhaps better patterns of values are possible. For the first time he may gain insight into "the discrepancies between [parental] pretensions and actual situation" (Frank, 1944b). Adolescents may thus

> become concerned about their own families, sensitive and worried about family customs and patterns and ways of living which now appear peculiar, different and embarrassing. . . . The boy or girl especially of foreign-born parents or of some conspicuously minority group may want to conceal his family from his contemporaries as a social liability. . . . [The parents in turn may] find it difficult to understand such apparent disloyalty. . . . [They] cannot see that their adolescent boy acts and speaks in such a manner just because he is so concerned about his family. . . and so eager to have them appear better than they are. It is a reversal of parent-child positions [with respect to the source of pressure for improvement]. (Frank, 1944b)

However, the impact of increased social awareness on emancipation cannot be attributed solely to the wider knowledge it provides for making invidious comparisons. Equally important is the newly acquired ability to use this information critically in appraising parents, a result of liberation from the unconditional acceptance of parental dicta.

It should be realized that important as these new sources of derived status are in displacing the parent and inducing desatellization via resatellization, their efficacy in emancipation depends largely on their ability to provide earned status to the adolescent. And since this status becomes increasingly important with the progress of adolescence, this second mechanism through which allegiance is deflected from parents must be accounted the major emancipating influence on adolescence in urban cultures. In support of this interpretation is the indisputable fact that emancipation is successfully accomplished in rural and primitive cultures in which parents and elders retain control of the socializing process and of the extrinsic status available to adolescents. The only essential factors necessary for emancipation are (1) pubescence, (2) the withdrawal of derived status by the parents, (3) the existence of parental and social expectations that adolescents shall seek earned status, and (4) the availability of adult role-playing experience.

FACILITATING AND RETARDING INFLUENCES ON EMANCIPATION

In general, the same factors promote and retard emancipation as affect personality maturation, and in the same ways. The availability of freedom of movement and of adult role-playing experience, sources of security outside the home, unconditional parental acceptance, withdrawal of derived status by parents, and heightened social expectations of achieving adult status all facilitate emancipation. On the other hand, residual habits of parental interference, rivalry, ambivalence about relinquishing control, and lack of appreciation for progress in achieving executive or volitional independence discourage emancipation. Particularly detrimental are over-protective and overdominating parent attitudes which inhibit the learning of self-reliance (Rehberg et al., 1970).

Various other factors also influence the course of emancipation. We have already mentioned the ambivalent attitude toward the need for personality maturation and the phenomenon of perceptual constancy. The individual's attitude, in childhood, toward authority is also important since it tends to predetermine in large measure what it will be in adolescence: blindly accepting, conditionally accepting, accepting under protest, overtly rebellious, resentful. Physical maturity is another important determinant of rate of emancipation since parents and teachers scale their expectations of mature behavior in terms of physical development rather than in terms of chronological age. Finally, many important cultural factors affect the rate of emancipation such as the availability of extrinsic status for adolescents, and the degree of discreteness characterizing the status roles available to children and adults, respectively.

Research evidence indicates that boys achieve emancipation from parents more rapidly than do girls. For instance, Douvan and Adelson (1966) found that boys develop moral autonomy and moral standards based on internally generated principles sooner than girls do. In terms of personal decisions, 16-year-old boys indicate that their own standards are more important than their parents' and that the standards of peers are least important. Girls continue to rely heavily on their parents' judgments, and they are more dependent on their peer group for validation of their self-concept (Douvan & Adelson, 1966; Solomon, 1961).

The unevenness of emancipation

In no other task of adolescence is the characteristic unevenness of growth in a transitional phase more apparent than in the acquisition of emancipation. Parents in our culture are much quicker to withdraw emotional succor than to relinquish their traditional authority, and are more readily disposed to retract derived status than to provide earned status. Their expectations of greater responsibility and maturity of behavior are far in excess of their willingness to grant their adolescent children autonomy of decision and recognition as adults. This discrepancy between expectations and demands, on the one hand, and prerogatives and privileges on the other, is much greater than the comparable situation confronting the adolescent in the peer group, but is considerably less disconcerting than the discrepancy in the culture at large. The lag in attaining emancipation is shorter than the lag in acquiring social status as an adult.

> Although the home, like society in general, offers little in the way of status-giving activities, its greater structural flexibility allows for greater modification of [interpersonal] relationships than do other social institutions. Thus, the adolescent can achieve a considerable measure of emancipation from the home in the way of self-assertion and independent activity even though he fails to acquire much status. His changed physical appearance makes complete perpetuation of the old parent-child relationship difficult. Society, on the other hand, is protected from the impact of individual pubescence by buffers of impersonality and emotional distance. (Ausubel, 1952a)

But "since the family unit cannot be set apart or insulated from the larger society of which it is a part, we may expect the process of emancipation to reflect" the major characteristics of the adolescent's position in the culture (Ausubel, 1950b). Thus, it is inevitable that the "unusual prolongation of adolescence in our society results in an extended period of partial emancipation" (Ausubel, 1950b).

> Being supported tends to keep the adolescent a child in his parents' house—a child whose opinions don't count, whose judgments are overriden, who is expected to seek and follow advice. And he is no longer a child. But neither is he grown up enough to comprehend. To him his inability to earn a living and to accept responsibility are a reflection, a sign of inadequacy. He is a failure. If the pressures become too great, the adolescent boy unable to stand the feelings of humiliation and the sense of guilt

arising from the unbearable realization that he is a burden on his parents, runs away from home. (Zachry, 1944)

PARENT–YOUTH CONFLICT IN ADOLESCENCE

We have already discussed the fact that there is little evidence to suggest that a state of war exists between adolescents and their parents. The stereotyped notion that the relationship between parents and their adolescent children, especially their male children, is characterized by conflict, disagreement, and disharmony does not seem to be borne out by the facts. In a national survey concerning the "generation gap," 57 percent of the adolescents questioned indicated that they got along fine with their parents and enjoyed their company. Only 4 percent of the adolescents said that they did not enjoy spending time with their parents (Yankelovich, 1969b). Other studies have suggested that although there is a certain amount of conflict between adolescents and their parents, the magnitude and intensity of these disagreements have been exaggerated by the mass media (Banks, 1969; Harris, 1971). The purpose of this section is to describe those areas of adolescent-parent disagreement and to examine the nature of this conflict.

Overt issues

The overt issues that result in disharmonious relationships between parents and adolescents are not necessarily the actual or crucial causes of the conflict. In some instances they do provide a clue to the underlying issues. In others, they are quite trivial in themselves, serving merely as the battleground for hostile feelings engendered by causes quite remote from the points at issue.

Payne, Summers, and Stewart (1973) investigated disagreement across three generations consisting of undergraduates, their parents, and grandparents. A questionnaire assessing possible areas of concern was administered to the three groups and the questions were factor analyzed with the following three factors emerging: (1) Conventional Morality, e.g., patriotism; (2) Personal Failure, e.g., getting caught cheating on an exam; (3) Embarrassment, e.g., having an unexpected guest drop in when you home is messy. Overall, the data indicated that there were greater differences between undergraduates and their parents than between parents and grandparents, with the largest difference between undergraduates and their parents in the area of conventional morality. Today's parents seem much more concerned than their adolescent sons and daughters about violation of norms in such areas as obscenity, patriotism, sexuality, and drugs. Other studies have also found that adolescents tend to be more liberal than their parents about contemporary social issues (Boshier & Taylor, 1972; Friedman et al., 1972).

Although generational differences certainly exist on issues of contemporary morality, in fact, Lerner et al. (1972) found that adolescents and their parents disagreed on almost half of such issues, the disagreement is mainly one of quantity or intensity rather than quality or direction. Adolescents may indeed be more liberal than their relatively conservative parents, but few adolescents could be classified as radical.

In regard to issues more specifically concerned with the day-to-day interaction of adolescents and their parents, LoSciuto and Karlin (1972) found that adolescents perceive most conflict between themselves and their parents to take place around the areas of homework, money, and hair style. Most adolescents appear to perceive their beliefs as generally similar to their parents' although certain specific differences are seen to exist in areas that we would consider to be concerns about emancipation and autonomy. The magnitude of these differences was found to be greater for older adolescents than for younger, and for males than for females.

Sex differences

The process of emancipation and the degree of adolescent-parent conflict that occurs as a result of this process differ markedly for boys and girls. In general, boys in our culture appear to experience more intense conflict with their parents in more areas than do girls (Douvan & Adelson, 1966). In a nationwide investigation of adolescence, boys were found to be more "actively engaged in establishing independence from parental control" than girls. In comparison to girls, boys were found to be less likely to accept parental regulations as appropriate. In areas other than conflict within the family, adolescent males show a similarly greater degree of problem behavior in comparison to girls. For example, more boys than girls are involved in such delinquent behavior as truancy and vandalism (Kelley & Pink, 1975).

Two broad classes of factors may be responsible for these characteristic sex differences. Males have been found to be generally more active and aggressive than females at all ages, including infancy, and this difference may be biologically based (Maccoby & Jacklin, 1974). It is possible that the hormonal changes occurring at puberty may produce intense sexual and aggressive feelings in males and result in a higher level of conflict with parents and authorities in general. Of course, environmental factors may also be important, for as many observers have pointed out, girls in our culture are not punished for dependency and compliance, whereas boys are more likely to be rewarded for independence and assertiveness (Schaeffer, 1971).

Underlying causes

The most important single cause of parent-youth conflict is the preservation of parents' attitudes that interfere with the adolescent's greatly expanded need for volitional independence. In his analysis of the development of individuality, Boszormenyi-Nagy (1965) suggests that the child progresses from a state of mother–child symbiosis to "individuation" to actual separation from his family. The last and most complete phase of individuation, which we would call emancipation, corresponds to adolescence and occurs only if the family system as a whole allows it. Since individuation means a partial end to the symbiotic family togetherness, the emancipation of the adolescent from the family results in a painful loss to every member of the family. The adolescent's need to fly with his own wings must be accompanied by his parents' willingness to allow his flight to occur. According to Boszormenyi-Nagy, the parents' inability to let go, their attempt to control their adolescent beyond the point where it is appropriate or even possible, is often the underlying cause of adolescent- parent friction.

Morton, Alexander, and Altman (1976) argue that the root cause of adolescent-parent conflict revolves around the mutual need of both parties to redefine their relationship in the light of the adolescent's increased abilities and new social status. The family crisis that occurs during the adolescent period involves the necessity of replacing the hierarchical parent-child relationship with an egalitarian parent-adolescent one. Recent family interaction research reveals that the adolescent period is, in fact, characterized by decreasing parental dominance and increasing child dominance (Alexander, 1970, 1973). Furthermore, this change occurs through an increase in the adolescent's potential ability to influence his parents (Jacob, 1974; Mischler & Waxler, 1968), although the parents continue to maintain greater power throughout. Alexander (1973) suggests that if the adolescent's efforts at establishing a more equal parent–adolescent relationship are accepted by his parents, then the more dramatic and unfortunate consequences of adolescent change are avoided. If, in contrast, parents attempt to maintain the modes of exchange and unequal distribution of influence characterizing the earlier parent–child relationship, "then nonmutuality may be sustained, resulting in continued conflict and even runaway or ungovernable delinquency" (Morton et al., 1976).

A direct corollary of the overly restrictive attitude of parents that is responsible for much friction during adolescence is the lack of respect they show for their children.

> It is very humiliating for one aspiring to be an adult to be castigated like a child, to be nagged, yelled and shouted at. But even worse are the scorn, the ridicule and the condescending attitudes that greet physical awkwardness, faltering or confused articulation of political views, and clumsy efforts at heterosexual expression. Even if he cares little about everything else, every adolescent—just because he is first aspiring to adult status—cherishes an ideal about the essential dignity of a human being, which, if respected, would leave him decidedly less provocative and resistive to guidance. (Ausubel, 1950b)

"Perceptual constancy" on the part of the adolescent may also generate parent-youth conflict. Even though the parents' attitudes and behavior toward the adolescent may *actually* undergo considerable change (e.g., become less controlling and less restrictive), the adolescent nevertheless fails to perceive this change because he has been overhabituated to regard himself in the past as a dependent child in relation to his relatively omnicent and omnipotent parents. On the other hand, although a parent's attitudes may change extensively in the appropriate direction, his (the parent's) acutal behavior may fail to exhibit corresponding change just because of the inertia generated by overhabituation to his former parental role ("behavioral lag").

Misunderstandings are also more or less inevitable because parents cannot help but approach the problems of their children in the light of their own conflicts and anxieties at a similar age. They find it difficult to appreciate that "adolescents develop their own standards and codes to guide their behavior, and what is more confusing, these standards shift and change as children mature" (MacKenzie, 1944). And in addition to this cognitive block to understanding caused by projection, the rearousal of forgotten conflicts leads to anxiety that can be most easily allayed by arbitrarily ruling out of bounds for the child the same impulses that in adolescence created difficulty for the parent.

In another sense, however, the memory of parents seems too

short rather than too long. Not only do they project their own experiences where these are no longer applicable, but they fail to profit by experience that is relevant.

> They tend to forget that as adolescents they, too, found it necessary to defy their own parents for just and adequate cause. Hence, it not rarely happens that the parent, who himself was most rebellious as an adolescent in defense of his legitimate rights of self-determination, becomes the most ruthless in suppressing his own children when they demand the same rights. (Ausubel, 1950b)

And, finally, the parent generates conflict not because of what he does or feels, but simply because he is, in the eyes of his child, a representative of the adult society that is denying him status and equal membership. The parent inevitably "becomes the undeserved target for the child's resentment against the deprivations, the frustrations, and the prolonged withholding of adult status to which the latter is subjected" (Ausubel, 1950b).

The adolescent is also largely responsible for the generation of parent-youth conflict. To begin with, he cherishes unrealistic expectations of achieving complete emancipation at the onset of pubescence.

The most serious cause of parent-youth conflict emanating from the child is the fact that the adolescent cannot escape "challenging parental authority as the price of his own individual maturation and of acceptance in his own age group" (Frank, 1944b).

> What actually happens in most cases is that the adolescent mimics the stylized and stereotyped attitude of hostility toward adults that is fashionable in his peer group; and whether he believes in it or not [he] is obliged to act the part, at least in public. Being forced in this way to satisfy at the same time the conflicting norms of home, school, and friends, it is inevitable that loyalty to the home will give way first, since the adolescent derives the least portion of his status from the home situation. This conflict is brought to a head if the parents adopt a hostile, "either-or" attitude toward the values of the peer group (Blos, 1941). Gardner (1947) refers to an "untouchable phase of adolescence in which the adolescent looks for confirmation or denial of his ideas to someone—almost anyone—beyond the home. It is the age of the girl chum or boy pal whose knowledge of facts and values and estimates of worth are inevitably taken to be truer than those of the parents." (Ausubel, 1950b)

The adolescent, therefore, orients himself to a social norm that anticipates and even requires a certain amount of defiance of parents. In the light of these expectations, bravado and hostility, if felt, can be expressed more easily than affection (Blos, 1941).

An inevitable and ubiquitous cause of parent-youth conflict, one that has always been with us and that probably always will be, is a condition known as "generation gap." This refers to the misunderstandings, difficulties of communication, and conflict of interests that necessarily arise simply because of the difference in age between individuals of two generations. Merely on the basis of temperamental differences related to developmental status, we would anticipate a certain amount of friction. Those on the ascending limb of life in terms of vigor and level of aspiration tend to have a different outlook on life from those on the descending limb. It is the contrast between the physically active, impulsive, hopeful, and idealistic individual who still has to experience many of the hard realities of life, and the more sedentary, inflexible, cautious, realistic, and perhaps embittered individual whose optimism has been tempered by a wider range of sobering experience.

In addition to differences attributable to developmental status, generation conflict is also induced by differences in the value system of each age group. The extent of such disparity is obviously a function of the rate of social change. In periods of rapid change, such as that following the introduction of industry into a rural community, it is inevitable that wide discrepancies will exist between the value systems of parents and children. A similar cleavage is commonly seen between immigrant parents and their native-born children.* And since an adult tends to think in terms of the values of his youth and to evaluate the behavior of his children in terms of the norms that prevailed when he was growing up, misunderstandings are not an inexplicable outcome.

Finally, parent–youth conflict is enhanced by any socioeconomic event, such as economic depression, which prolongs emancipation and thereby increases both intrafamilial contact and the adolescent's emotional instability. This situation is further aggravated if the father is unemployed. Under such conditions intrafamilial tension is increased by the father's loss of morale and prestige (especially if his children are working) and by his lowered threshold of irritability (Komarovsky, 1940).

---

* Any type of social mobility, such as from urban to rural living or from a lower to a higher social class, produces the same result.

Prognosis of parent–youth conflict

Just because parent-child conflict increases during adolescence, we should not exaggerate its significance or ignore the many positive aspects of this relationship.

Friction in various forms is almost inevitable if the home is peopled by real persons. . . . The normal home has its quota of bickering and disagreement. One of the functions of a good home is to serve as a place where husbands, wives, and children can become annoyed with each other without suffering dire consequences. The more solid the affection between members of the family the more will each feel free to be himself. . . .

While the adolescent is striking off on lines of his own, his parents and his home continue to be of great importance in his life. He needs the anchorage which the home affords. It is important to him to be able to count on his parents as persons who regard him with disinterested affection and in whom he can confide without fear of ridicule or betrayal.

He needs the home as a base of operations that is stable when other things are in flux. He also needs the home as a place where he can relax, let down his hair, so to speak, and give way occasionally to petulance, complaints and childish behavior which he would not allow himself to display in his relations with his peers or with adults outside the home. (Jersild, 1946)

Serious parent-youth conflict is not inevitable, even in urban cultures where the peer group is the chief socializing institution. And in rural cultures such as the Navaho,

the feelings of a child for his parents are much likely to be seriously mixed than is the case among white people. . . . Instances of open aggression against the mother even in stories and dreams are exceedingly rare. . . . The relationship of children and fathers is also dominantly a warm one. The stereotype of the harsh, tyrannical father is lacking in Navaho culture. (Leighton & Kluckhohn, 1947)

Although there is a strong positive relationship between the relaxing of parental controls and the attainment of emancipation, the two are not necessarily coextensive. "The absence of parental control [per se] should not be considered an indication of maturity. The task of equipping the child for self-direction is no less formidable than the problem of getting parent and child to let go of each other in a progressive fashion" (Dimock, 1937). Many overly permissive parents avoid conflict by abandoning all controls precipitately. In the long run, however, although conflict may be avoided, such emancipation is less complete than in instances in which parents take an active part in the upbringing of their adolescent children. Avoiding friction, in other words, is not an end in itself. No genuine progress can be accomplished painlessly.

The frequency with which adolescents are brought to guidance centers "because they manifest an exaggerated need for independence, because they delight in being perverse and contrary, and because they defy parental authority" requires that we establish prognostic criteria. Parents are understandably concerned about this situation and want to know how it will turn out. Clinical experience with disturbed adolescents has led one of the writers to classify all cases of parent-youth conflict into two broad categories: First, in the prognostically hopeful group, the condition is a transitory phenomenon brought on by factors specific to the developmental problems of adolescence. It

> may be an exaggerated response to status deprivation or to the parents' ambivalent attitude; it may be incited by the militancy of the child's peer groups, or it may represent a distorted idea of the very meaning of emancipation in the mind of the adolescent. Under these circumstances the problem can often be quickly solved by interpreting parent to child or vice versa, or by favorable manipulation of the environment. (Ausubel, 1952a)

Second, in the prognostically unfavorable group, the disturbed emancipation process is rooted in a fundamental distortion of the parent-child relationship that is in no way specific to the tasks of adolescent maturation. The three most common types of disturbed adolescents, and the parent-child relationships responsible for their unsatisfactory situation, are (1) the dominant, self-assertive child who has been harshly rejected; (2) the overvalued child who has been rejected in later childhood or adolescence; and (3) the overdominated and over-motivated child who rebels openly against parental domination. "Such conflict may lead to serious consequences, i.e., delinquency, running away from home, impulsive marriage, abrupt withdrawal from school, with the likelihood that the conflict will persist into adult life" (Ausubel, 1950b).

These clinical impressions were tested by comparing from 20 of the most serious cases of parent-youth conflict in the above writer's retrospective study (Ausubel, 1951a) 10 individuals who showed little residual conflict as adults with 10 other individuals who showed considerable residual conflict. Both groups manifested significantly greater conflict with parents during childhood than the population at large, but the nonimproving group reported significantly less favorable parental attitudes before adolescence than the group that eventually improved. Another significant difference was a change for the better in the parental* attitudes of the improving group in the post-adolescent period (Ausubel, 1951).

Parents can, therefore, be "given assurance that if their relationships with their children had been established on a basis of mutual respect and affection, it is reasonably certain that the same relationships will be reestablished once the turbulent period of adolescence is over" (Ausubel, 1950b).

His acute sensitivity with respect to self-determination now laid aside, once the question of his adult status is finally settled, the child—now adult—can meet his parents with a new sense of ease. He can afford to listen attentively to their advice, neither accepting nor rejecting it because of its source, but evaluating it on the basis of its intrinsic merits and assuming responsibility himself for making the final decision. (Ausubel, 1950b)

Thus, the products of "the emancipated situation should include a retention of mutual trust between parent and child. It should include a continuation of respect and honor for parents and of genuine devotion and concern by the parents for the offspring" (Meyers, 1946).

DISCIPLINE IN ADOLESCENCE

Need for changed methods of control

It is evident that methods of parental control must be adapted to meet changing conditions of personality organization and maturity. Physical restraint, parental approval, uncritical obedience, and personal loyalty are no longer appropriate measures for exacting conformity from the desatellizing individual. New methods must recognize the adolescent's need for greater volitional independence, his greater capacity to respond consistently to more abstract and rational principles of conduct, and the changes in his learning orientation.

---

*Parental attitudes refer to the attitudes of the parents of the subjects in this study and not to the attitudes on parenthood of the subjects themselves.

Discipline must necessarily be less authoritarian. Obedience can no longer be demanded for its own sake, and once this untenable position is abandoned, many "supposed occasions for punishment melt away." Navaho parents, as already pointed out, never expect this type of obedience. They regard disobedience not as intrinsically "bad," but as dangerous because of its consequences. However, some parents of adolescents in our culture still insist on unquestioned obedience as an inalienable right. They make it clear that they will "stand for no nonsense" and will "put the child in his place" (Zachry, 1944).

Such discipline may be temporarily effective and achieve a certain outward conformity to visible authority by employing the repressive measure of fear, pain, ridicule and deprivation (Zachry, 1944). What it fails to achieve, however, is that *inner* control based upon an acceptance of the moral authority of society which underlies adult as contrasted to childhood moral behavior; and in addition it carries the danger of provoking further aggressive defiance and encouraging further sabotage or repudiation of adult goals. (Ausubel, 1950b)

The consequences of overstrict, authoritarian control are to produce adolescents who are hostile and rebellious, and who are unlikely to identify strongly with their parents (Douvan & Adelson, 1966; Elder, 1963). Parents are salient models for their children and it is not surprising that children attempt to control others in a way that is similar to how they themselves have been controlled. Parents generally do not tolerate aggression directed toward them from their children, although the parents' use of authoritarian and punitive disciplinary methods may encourage their child to attempt to use these types of methods with his peers. Research suggests that parents who use physical punishment have children who are aggressive with their peers and in many cases delinquent (Feshback, 1970).

The very nature of adolescence, as a period of emancipation, requires a nondirective type of discipline that relies more on explanation, discussion, and opportunity for individual decision than on appeal to dogmatic sanctions. "Reasons contributed by other people seldom mean a thing to [the adolescent]; he has to be helped to work things out for himself in his own mind."

Several features of Navaho discipline are especially suited to the requirements of adolescence. The Navaho concept of punishment, for example, is less personal and less vindictive. The authority for discipline resides in the group rather than in a single powerful figure (Leighton & Kluckhohn, 1947a). Discipline, therefore, provokes less resentment and rebellion in an individual who is trying to emancipate himself from parental control. Parents in our culture could emulate with profit the Navaho practice of achieving control of the individual by

"lateral sanctions" rather than by sanctions from above. That is, the Navaho from childhood on is brought into line more by the reactions of all the people around him rather than by orders and threats of punishment from someone who stands above him in a hierarchy. "Shame" is the agony of being found wanting and exposed to the disapproval of others, as opposed to the fear that some single superior person will use his power to deprive one of rewards and privileges if specified tasks are not carried out according to instructions. (Leighton, 1947)

The peer group, as a matter of fact, does achieve this type of control over adolescents in our culture, but parents usually work in opposition to it rather than in collaboration with it.

Need for discipline in adolescence

Advocating changed methods of discipline in adolescence does not mean that *no* discipline is required. As already pointed out, "spontaneous maturation" is a myth in human development, except perhaps in certain aspects of physical growth with a strong phylogenetic component. Personality maturation is largely the outcome of responding to a body of very explicit social expectations, reinforced by appropriate sanctions. Unrestricted freedom

leaves little room for the development of moral responsibility or of respect for the rights of others. Secondly, it frustrates the adolescent's need for definite and unambiguous standards of social reality with the aid of which he can control and orient his new emotional urges and ego demands. It is one of the main functions of both home and school, as representatives of the social order, to make certain very firm, definite and consistent demands on adolescents. (Ausubel, 1950b)

The removal of all pressures for conformity eliminates immediate interpersonal conflict, but also leaves an immature, insecure, and disoriented individual who acquires little frustration tolerance and self-critical ability, and is unable to aspire to realistic roles and goals.
One can control adolescents by relying more heavily on reward

motivation unreinforced by appropriate punishment than one can with younger children. That is, principles of conduct are now established on a level abstract enough that rewarding the "good" alternative implies simultaneous condemnation of the "bad." But this implication is never completely thorough-going since it requires "a level of logical consistency that is rare in the typical person's organization of values and attitudes. . . . Hence, consistent and unambiguous discipline requires explicit definition of the limits of unacceptable behavior, reinforced by tangible evidences of disapproval" (Ausubel, 1952a).

Also, even though one can rely more on self-discipline in adolescents, it is still necessary to keep external restraints visible. Such restraints are not the chief support of acceptable conduct, but they are necessary to discourage "the temptation to test the limits of tolerance for unacceptable behavior, i.e., to see how much one can 'get away with' before incurring retribution." Needless to say, tendencies such as these are "present in all of us, irrespective of whether a generally wholesome conscience is operating," and make us thankful for the presence of the policeman on the corner (Ausubel, 1952a).

MATURATIONAL FAILURE ATTRIBUTABLE TO FAULTY CHILD REARING PRACTICES

Maturity is only a relative term. That is, an individual may be characterized only as *more* or *less* mature, depending on the degree to which he exemplifies the composite virtues of the ideal of maturity in a given subculture. Considering all of the variables that enter into the attainment of maturity, we realize that few persons can expect to reach adult life without incurring one or more maturational defects of varying severity. In this section we shall be concerned only with maturational defects that are both (1) attributable to some serious derangement of the parent-child relationship, and (2) gross and disabling enough to warrant a diagnosis of "maturational failure."

Appraising the seriousness of maturational defects is extremely important in child guidance work. The problem of differential diagnosis is the same as that in evaluating the significance of parent-youth conflict. Parents are rightly concerned when their children present evidence of maturational retardation. They want to know what the prognosis is. Hence, the most useful classification of problems of maturation uses prognosis as the chief nosologic criterion.

Just like parent-youth conflict, maturational retardation may be divided into (1) a transitory, prognostically favorable type that is merely symptomatic of the general stress of adolescent development in our culture; and (2) a more serious, prognostically unfavorable variety (maturational failure) that does not clear up with adolescence and is reflective of deep-seated disturbance of the parent-child relationship. The transitory type is partly an expression of the ambivalent attitude that both parent and child adopt toward maturation. The greater portion of it, however, springs from a reluctance to part with the interim values and status built up so painstakingly in the peer group. This reluctance represents more than the usual resistance to developmental change; it is also a form of group defiance and revenge for the earlier insult of being excluded from the adult orbit of status operations.

The permanent kind of maturational retardation (failure) can be divided into two subcategories: (1) maturational failure in satellizers that is simply an outgrowth of parent attitudes unfavorable for desatellization; and (2) maturational failure, especially in nonsatellizers, that is an aggressive, vengeful response to harsh, rejecting, or overdominating parent attitudes. We will refer to the first type as "developmental" and to the second type as "reactive" failure.

"Developmental" failure

Maturational failure attributable to inappropriate parental attitudes is the "terminal phase of a progressive developmental condition" (Ausubel, 1952a). It is a "relatively rare extreme form of a phenomenon which in varying degrees of lesser severity is a quite common occurrence" (Ausubel, 1952a). Other variables relating to social conditions and individual personality differences among satellizers are also contributing factors. In the more complete forms of failure (in overprotected and underdominated children), the major tasks of maturation—acquisition of adult volitional independence, striving for earned status, attenuation of hedonistic motivation, attainment of increased executive independence and societal moral responsibility—are not accomplished. In overdominated and underappreciated children, the degree of maturational failure is less complete and less severe.

The *overprotected* child fails to gain volitional and executive independence because he is shielded from necessary experience with mature roles, from choice-making decisions (lest he injure himself by unwise choices), and from frustration of any kind. His parents differentially reward behavior that makes him more dependent on them and make no demands that he surrender derived status, seek earned status, or relinquish hedonistic motivations. Peer group socialization, frustration tolerance, and self-critical ability are lacking because of inadequate experience in social situations and in overcoming frustration through his own resources and ingenuity. Concepts of moral responsibility remain tied to specific parental contexts and acquire no social generality; the individual is unable to conceive of himself as an independent entity functioning in a community and therefore responsible to its moral authority.

Underdominated children, on the other hand, have considerable experience in self-assertion and choice making. But as a result of growing up in an undemanding, indulgent, and unrestricted home, they do not develop those personality attributes that implement volitional independence on an adult level: frustration tolerance, self-critical ability, and capacity for setting realistic goals. They too are under no pressure to relinquish hedonistic motivation, to strive for earned status, or to acquire executive independence. Accustomed to their parents' submission, they are unable to accept authority (Symonds, 1939), make unreasonable demands on others, and expect special consideration (Levy, 1943). Not required to curb their hedonistic impulses or to develop any responsibility toward the ethical values of their parents, they uncritically accept them as valid, but behave as if they "were exempt from the usual moral restraints governing most people" (Ausubel, 1952a).

> The net result of this curious imbalance in volitional development, in which the desire for volitional independence is totally unmatched by capacity for same, is that the individual *wills* to be dependent on the will of others. . . . As long as the outward appearance of self-assertion is preserved—a need which is too basic to be relinquished—it can actually serve the purpose of establishing and reinforcing a relationship founded on volitional dependency. . . . What he mainly demands from others. . . is that they accept responsibility for planning his future and smoothing his way. (Ausubel, 1952a)

When a parent's *overdomination* is benevolent, consistent, and acceptable to the child, neither rebellion nor complete maturational failure results. "Under the circumstances 'continued acceptance of authority on the child's part' (Meyers, 1946) can be maintained even into his old age" (Ausubel, 1952a). The authoritarian parent sets high standards and does not countenance immature behavior. Overdominated children, therefore, are industrious, highly motivated, responsible, and self-critical (Symonds, 1939). What they lack is experience in and opportunity for self-assertion and independent decision making. They are excessively docile and submissive, and lack spontaneity and self-confidence (Symonds, 1939). Making decisions seems to them a prerogative of parents and those in authority. Also, they acquire moral responsibility on a societal basis with considerable difficulty because their ethical values "are so completely dominated by the personal figures of parents" (Ausubel, 1952a). In extreme examples, incapacity for freeing themselves from parental domination is so marked that marriage even becomes unthinkable.

The *underappreciated* child is discouraged early in life from seeking earned status. As an accepted satellizer, he has no lack of derived status, but he finds that his parents take his accomplishments for granted. He sees little purpose in striving, since regardless of his efforts, the only reward that means anything to him, parental approval, is not forthcoming. Because it is a very unrewarding process, maturation is undertaken half-heartedly; and without later motivation provided by the appreciation of parent surrogates, it is very likely to proceed irregularly and terminate at a subadult level (Ausubel, 1952a).

"Reactive" failure

In "reactive" failure, the necessary conditions for maturation are present, but the child deliberately chooses failure as an instrument for revenge on parents. Under ordinary circumstances, nonsatellizers are strongly motivated to achieve a high degree of maturity since they perceive that it is a precondition for attaining the long-term ego enhancement they desire. The motive of revenge, when present, is more important to overvalued than to rejected children, since the parents of the rejected child cannot be hurt by the failure of a career about which they are unconcerned.

Maturational failure in overvalued children is precipitated by a sudden replacement (in late childhood or preadolescence) of overvaluing attitudes by authoritarian control. The parent may grow tired of his obsequious and adulatory role, or of the child's arrogance, which he formerly thought "cute" or portentous of future greatness. He may finally perceive that the child will never be a "genius" or even a "great man," or that a younger sibling has greater potentialities. Sometimes, especially with girls, the parent seeks to regain control at adolescence simply because he is concerned about sexual experimentation or aggression. The child, who is completely unprepared for this sudden about-face and is quite incapable of submitting to authoritarian control, becomes understandably resentful and rebellious. His resentment is increased by the fact that his friends are winning greater freedom while his is being curtailed. Hence, despite the tremendous need for ego enhancement,

the desires for achieving absolute independence and for wreak-
ing vengeance on the resented parent become the dominant motives in life. Both aims can be best served simultaneously by
adopting an attitude of obstinate perverseness, by repudiating
the entire process of adult maturation, and by choosing goals and
standards of behavior which are diametrically opposite to those
advocated by the parent. . . . Motivational immaturity and childish irresponsibility are combined with inflated ambitions and an
exaggerated need for volitional independence (which is often in
marked disparity to the individual's actual executive dependence). In extreme cases this pathological need for independence is generalized to include freedom from control of any sort
whatsoever. The individual then sets himself up as being above
any criticism or moral censure, and acknowledges no responsibility to be bound by the moral authority of society. (Ausubel,
1950b)

The overvalued child may sometimes undergo temporary maturational retardation even in the absence of traumatic reversal of parental attitudes. In spite of high prestige aspirations, the overvalued child
tends to be hedonistic, self-indulgent, and undisciplined because of
parental underdomination. Systematic work outside his immediate
realm of interests is distasteful. If, before he is reconciled to the "sacrifices" of mature behavior for long-range ego enhancement, he is
confronted with the necessity of conforming to an exacting program
of schoolwork, he may reject maturation and choose a less irksome
alternative. Instead of overcoming his distaste for systematic application to uninteresting tasks, he may choose always to cast his plans in
grandiose terms that stamp him as "being different," but nevertheless
fail to provide the sustained effort needed for completion. There is
enough ego satisfaction in merely evolving such high-flown plans and
in "being different" to gratify his needs for extrinsic status. And he ra-
tionalizes his obvious lack of accomplishment: "I'm so superior to ordinary mortals that I don't have to bother following through on my
plans."
    Rejected children, even the thick-skinned, extroverted, self-as-
sertive ones who rebel against overdomination, are less apt to choose
reactive failure as a weapon against parents. To do so would hardly
constitute adequate revenge since the parents would not be greatly
hurt. In fact, such failure would justify their rejection of him; whereas
the child desires to reverse their original judgment that he is not
worth bothering with. At the very worst, his exaggerated need to free
himself from "hatefully regarded parental authority" leads to extreme

parent-youth conflict and to a permanent rupture of relationships with parents (Ausubel, 1952a). The rejected child also finds the tasks of maturation less onerous than the overvalued child since he has never been conditioned to an excessively permissive environment. He is less likely to balk at the self-discipline that maturation requires or to regress to immaturity when "the going is rough."

Reactive failure sometimes occurs in overdominated satellizers who find themselves eventually unable to tolerate parental authority. This reaction is relatively rare since enough affection for parents is usually generated in a satellizing relationship to preclude the need for such extreme vengeance. It is more likely to occur when the parent's discipline is harsh and inconsistent (Symonds, 1939). Under these circumstances the more self-assertive child may rebel openly and repudiate the goals of maturation. The less aggressive child will more likely sabotage the ambitious goals his parents set for him, and defer outright rejection of maturity until the parents' death.

9

Moral and Religious Development

Part of the process of personality maturation involves various shifts in the individual's organization of moral (and religious) values and behavior. Our first task in this chapter will be to review certain *general* changes in the nature, organization, and psychological basis of moral values, changes attributable to adolescent development. Second, we shall be concerned with personality and social factors accounting for individual and subcultural differences in moral values. Third, we shall examine some of the determinants and consequences of the social estimate of an adolescent's character, i.e., his reputation. Last, we shall make inventory of some of the specific moral and religious beliefs of adolescents in our culture and of their relationship to behavior.

GENERAL DEVELOPMENTAL CHANGES DURING ADOLESCENCE

The term *conscience* is an abstraction referring to the cognitive-emotional organization of an individual's moral values and to the psychological processes on which that organization is based (Ausubel, 1952a). Conscience presupposes an internalization of moral values from standards in the social environment, and the acceptance of a sense of obligation* or responsibility to conform to them (Ausubel,

---

* The sense of obligation is itself a moral value and must undergo internalization in order to be stable and effective in regulating behavior. But it is also the core value of an

1952a). Also necessary for the functioning of conscience is the ability to anticipate the consequences of behavior, and to exercise inhibitory control to bring these anticipated consequences into line with perceived obligation. When behavior is not appropriately regulated to conform to moral obligation, a special kind of negative self-evaluation occurs known as *guilt*. Guilt consists of feelings of shame, "self-disgust, self-contempt, remorse, and various characteristic visceral and vasomotor responses" (Ausubel, 1952a). Since guilt is an extremely uncomfortable, self-punishing, and anxiety-producing phenomenon, guilt avoidance is a strong motivating force to keep behavior consistent with moral obligation. However, guilt cannot be experienced in the absence of the capacity for realistically appraising one's intentions and behavior in the light of internalized moral principles. Conscience, therefore, remains at a rudimentary level until the self-critical faculty is developed (Ausubel, 1952a).

But conscience is no more an inherent given than any other aspect of personality. It shifts with changes in the parent-child relationship, in social expectations, perceptual ability, and cognitive organization, and with maturational advances in biosocial competence and goal structure; and in turn it has an important influence on all of the latter aspects of ego development (Ausubel, 1952a; Sherif & Cantril, 1947).

The nature of conscience necessarily changes with personality development since all of its component psychological processes undergo developmental change. Intellectual growth affects the generality, consistency, and abstract quality of moral values, and sharpens the self-critical faculty. The widening of the social horizon, and various shifts in allegiance and dependency modify values and the basis on which moral obligation is sustained (Ausubel, 1952a). In this section we shall examine several major developments in the organization of conscience that begin with the onset of desatellization and are consummated during the adolescent period.

Greater independence in assimilation of values

The increased importance of the incorporative and exploratory orientations during adolescence brings about a change in the basis on which moral values are accepted. Personal loyalty to parents becomes a less impelling motive to accept and abide by moral values than con-

---

individual's moral system which not only makes possible the implementation of other values but also gives generality to moral bevavior. For example, the disposition to refrain from committing an act of dishonesty depends on more than the strength of the value of honesty in a given context. Equally important is the strength of the moral obligation to abide by *all* internalized values (Ausubel, 1952a).

siderations of equity and ego enhancement; and satisfaction of these considerations demands much more critical examination of values and much less reliance on prestige authority (Ausubel, 1952a). This is reflected, in part, in the greater liberality, tolerance, and flexibility of moral outlook that takes place during adolescence (Kay, 1969; Pressey, 1944; Rosander, 1939; Schneider & Vanmastrigt, 1974), indicating some degree of liberation from uncritical acceptance of dogmatic teachings (Ausubel, 1952a). Fewer adolescents than sixth graders disapprove of activities traditionally regarded as wrong by stern or "old-fashioned" moralists (Pressey & Robinson, 1944). Experimentation with smoking, for instance, increases with age, and adolescents express less negative attitudes about smoking than preadolescents (Schneider & Vanmastrigt, 1974).

Essentially, however, there is a change in the basis on which moral values are accepted. Adolescents place equity in interpersonal relationships above instrumentality or considerations of expediency (Ausubel, 1952a; Kay, 1969), but the moral values of a culture are inculcated in the early years, and hence show little variability in degree of acceptance from childhood to adult life (Eberhart, 1942; Frederickson, 1972; Thetford et al., 1951). A longitudinal study of normal adolescent boys' identity, heterosexual relationships, relationships with parents, drug experiences, and social action revealed that independence was being achieved gradually. Although the subjects were shifting their object relationships, they were not simultaneously discarding their parents' basic value systems (Offer et al., 1970). The authors consider their subjects to be representative of a significant segment of today's youth. Haan, Smith, and Block (1968) describe similar results in their studies of moral reasoning of young adults. However, adolescents and young adults consider the basis of their values their own. Thus, in the sixties the shift from utilitarian to expressive concerns and concerns for people (Havighurst, 1975) became more pervasively identified with youth as voiced in their protests, but analyses of these protests showed an affinity between the outlook of the protesters and that of their parents (Haan et al., 1968; Keniston, 1970).

Continuity in moral structure (despite desatellization and shifts in allegiance) is maintained by the tendency of the peer group to adhere closely to the basic values of the social class in which it holds membership (Ausubel, 1952a; Keniston, 1975; Sherif & Cantril, 1947; Sugarman, 1973). Furthermore, values assimilated on the basis of satellizing loyalties are remarkably durable and resist displacement. To meet the requirements of emancipation it is enough to give acceptable and independent reasons for holding these values rather than to reject them outright (Ausubel, 1952a).

And, finally, the adolescent's real independence in the choice of moral values is highly limited. It is true that he is liberated from slavish conformity to parental standards. But at the same time he gains a new master who demands even greater conformity and has the power to enforce it, i.e., the peer group (Ausubel, 1952a). The difference is that he conforms to peer-group expectations because he consciously recognizes the expediency of so doing rather than because he implicitly believes in the validity of the values he espouses (Ausubel, 1952a).

Values acquire a wider social base

Concomitant with resatellization (in cultures characterized by age-mate socialization) is a gradual broadening of the source from which values are acquired. Increased exposure to new social environments, coupled with a loss of subservience to parental values, enables the adolescent to perceive the standards of his home as merely special variants of subcultural norms (Ausubel, 1952a). With increasing age, his values tend to become more typical of the culture at large but less typical of the values held by his parents (Webster, 1958), particularly during college years (Bengston & Starr, 1975; Keniston, 1975; Webster, 1958). "As several observers have pointed out, the similarity in orientations between parents and children may stem not so much from explicit socialization (involving teaching or modeling) as from their sharing the same socio-economic location and being exposed to similar cultural aspects of the broader social structure" (Bengston & Starr, 1975, p. 230).

The degree of resemblance between attitudes of parents and those of adolescents, however, varies considerably depending on the issues in question. Thus L. E. Thomas (1974) in his review of the literature on the "generation gap" used a modified version of Rokeach's (1974) typology of belief system examining evidence for a generation gap on three levels of belief: (1) central core of beliefs (value orientation), (2) intermediate beliefs (authority), and (3) peripheral beliefs (attitudes) for high school and college populations and their parents. He found little evidence of generational differences in peripheral beliefs involving attitudes. There appeared more possibility of generational discontinuity in intermediate values (authority), especially in relation to legitimacy of national institutions. Little research is reported on the central core of beliefs (value orientation), but several studies on political attitudes reveal higher agreement on partisan attitudes than on political orientation. There are also striking differences in time perspectives. Thomas claims that the generation gap proponents such as Friedenberg, Mead, and Roszak have focused on central core of beliefs, whereas "no gap" proponents have dwelled on peripheral beliefs or attitudes.

Thus, interpersonal relationships in adolescence as value bases are tentative. Adolescents commonly discover that their parents are not flawless and move away toward other visible adults and historical and public figures (Havighurst et al., 1946) as well as peers. However, in later adolescence or youth, a more mature assessment of parents as complex personages, of wishes, conscious and unconscious, and of historical situations is grasped. Consequently, although the parents' influence on attitudes diminishes with age, there is an increase in conformity aspects of the adolescent's personality (Thetford et al., 1951). Keniston describes incisively the wider social base for values in adolescence that has a propelling power triggering curious phenomena in later years of adolescence or youth.

In youth, the question of whether to live one's parents' life, or to what extent to do so, becomes a real and active question. . . a compulsive need to live out for oneself the destiny of a parent, as if to test its possibilities and limits, experience it from inside, and [perhaps] free oneself of it. In the end, the youth may learn to see himself and his parents as multi-dimensional persons, to view them with compassion and understanding, to feel less threatened by their fate and failings, and to be able, if he chooses, to move beyond them. (Keniston, 1975, p. 18)

Changes reflective of intellectual maturation

Growth in cognitive capacity alone accounts for several significant changes in character organization during adolescence. For one thing, moral concepts, like all other concepts, become more abstract. This enables moral behavior to acquire greater generality and consistency from situation to situation, since abstraction presupposes the identification of essential common elements (Hartshorne & May, 1930; Hoffman, 1963; Kohlberg, 1964, 1968).

Growth in intellectual ability also makes possible the more critical, objective, and rational approach to moral values that distinguishes the incorporative and exploratory orientations from the satellizing orientation (Ausubel, 1952a). And by sharpening the self-critical faculty* (making possible the perception of finer discrepancies between precept and conduct), it leads to overall strengthening of moral obligation through the guilt-avoidance mechanism (Ausubel, 1952a). It is obvious, however, that the growth of the self-critical faculty depends on more than intellectual capacity, since the ability to

---

*Dimock (1937) found a marked increase in the self-critical attitudes of boys from ages 12 to 16.

criticize others antecedes the development of self-critical ability. The capacity for judging one's own behavior on the same terms as the behavior of others represents a signal degree of liberation from infantile egocentricity.

Declining moral absolutism, increasing reciprocity, and emergence of universals

Earlier we referred to conscience as the cognitive-emotional organization of moral values. The capacity to make moral judgments constitutes an important feature of conscience development.

Jean Piaget's pioneering work on the development of moral judgment in children (Piaget, 1932) pointed the way to thinking about the normative qualities of moral development.

Using his now well-known "clinical method" of interviewing children, Piaget presented them with paired short stories focusing on moral issues and asked them to make judgments as to the naughtier action.

Piaget delineated two stages of moral development. In the first stage of *heteronomy* (from approximately 4 to about 8 years of age), the child is governed by an ethic of authority. This stage begins with "moral absolutism," by which Piaget means the tendency of the young child to accept rules as self-evident, axiomatic givens rather than as human contrivances to facilitate interpersonal relationships. This inherent sacredness of moral standards depends in part on a perception of parents as infallible and omniscient beings. It begins to break down as parents become devalued, as the child realizes that there are other authorities, various moral alternatives, and different versions of the truth. As he joins older peer groups in which roles and relationships are clearly differentiated and in which he himself takes part in the formulation of rules, a functional rather than a "sacred" concept of moral law emerges. Because the group is never dignified by the same halo of sanctity surrounding his parents, the child can adopt the exploratory orientation in his peer group long before he dares to do so at home (Ausubel, 1952a).

Piaget's second stage, the *autonomous stage*, starts at approximately 8 years of age and is characterized by egalitarianism and democracy. The notion of moral law as a system of reciprocal obligation arises as the individual assumes various roles in communal and group enterprises. Piaget (1932, 1951) found that as children grow older they become increasingly desirous of interpersonal relationships based on mutual respect and reciprocity. Such relationships can, of course, be established much more easily with peers than with elders.

Research following Piaget's work has been unable to clearly validate Piaget's proposed relationship between heteronomous morality and unilateral respect for authority (Boehm, 1966; Kohlberg, 1963a).

The principle of reciprocity involves more than an expectation of bilaterality, that others have moral obligations toward oneself and vice versa. The individual must free himself from the egocentricity that does not enable him (1) to criticize himself on the same basis as he criticizes others; (2) to approach questions of equity on a detached, objective, and task-oriented basis; (3) to argue from the standpoint of another, or of an abstract proposition; and (4) to be aware of the needs and interests of others. There is general agreement that these capacities are expanded during the elementary school years and during adolescence, but most American researchers disagree with Piaget's view that older and younger children are qualitatively different in their egocentricity. There is little doubt, however, that true liberation from egocentricity requires mutual respect and freedom to criticize in a climate of equality (Ausubel, 1952).

Once the individual conceives of himself as an independent entity operating in a social community, and acquires a sense of reciprocal obligation, he completes the process of transferring his feeling of moral accountability from parents to the moral authority of society (Ausubel, 1952).

Kohlberg's longitudinal, and his cross-cultural work (1963b, 1969) in particular, has demonstrated that a two-stage theory of morality development is too global to encompass all of the developmental nuances. Kohlberg studied moral judgment in childhood and adolescence. He presented 10 hypothetical situations involving conflicts between particular kinds of values (e.g., a conflict between "legal-social rules" or the "commands of authority and the needs and welfare of other individuals") to carefully controlled subjects of varying ages and different cultures and arrived at three levels of moral judgment (Kohlberg, 1963a).

He distinguished these levels as follows: level I—preconventional or premoral; level II—conventional; and level III—postconventional, autonomous, or principled. Each level has two stages of development yielding six moral stages. The first four stages are substantially equivalent to Piaget's stages. Kohlberg's last two stages emerge at or after adolescence at the postconventional, autonomous, or principled level. The first of these two latter stages, stage 5, the social-contract legalistic orientation, is motivated by a desire for community respect. Emphasis is on the "legal point of view but with the possibility of changing law on the basis of rational considerations of social utility" (Grinder, 1973, p. 342), instead of freezing it at the "law and order"

level. Stage 6, the conscience or universal ethical principle orientation, is motivated by self-condemnation for lapses.* The governing
factor here is a comprehensive, universal, and consistent principle of
justice, reciprocity, and equality of human rights (Kohlberg, 1973).

Stage 3 ordinarily emerges in adolescence, when *universalizable
and reversible* † principles become operative (Baier, 1966). Conscience
then becomes more rational‡ depending on internal standards, moral
obligation, and cognitive abilities capable of the highest levels of
abstraction.

The age-related changes in Piaget's and Kohlberg's theories of
moral development depict qualitative changes in the cognitive
aspects of conscience. Their theory of cognition, however, similar to
that of Dewey (1909), G. H. Mead (1934), and Baldwin (1906), depicts
no dualism between intellect and affect (Kohlberg, 1971; Piaget &
Inhelder, 1969). This point is often overlooked in discussions of the
relationship between Kohlberg's moral judgment and moral conduct.

Absence of dualism is evidenced in the similarities between
moral and ego development theorists in whose view conscience is independent of a superego construct, and moral development is
regarded as a subset of general ego development. These theorists
espouse a three-stage developmental process (Ausubel, 1959; Kohlberg, 1969; Loevinger, 1966).

> This three-level process in moral and ego development implies:
> (1) a first level at which rules and the expectations of others are
> external to the self; (2) a second level at which the self is iden-
> tified with or equated with the rules, stereotypes, and expecta-
> tions of others, especially authorities; and (3) a third level at
> which the self is differentiated from conventional rules. (Ausubel
> & Sullivan, 1970, p. 479)

In our ego development framework, level 1 is the presatellizing ego,
level 2 involves early and late ego satellization, and level 3 is the
desatellizing stage (Ausubel & Sullivan, 1970).

---

*For discussion of empirical evidence on Kohlberg's moral stages, see Beck et al.
(1971); De Palma, D. J., and Foley, J. M. (Eds.). *Moral development: Current theory and
research.* New York: Wiley, 1975; and Solso, R. L. (Ed.). *Contemporary issues in cognitive psychology: The Loyola symposium.* Washington, D.C.: Winston, 1973.

†Acceptable to the person whether he is on the "giving" or "receiving" end of it.

‡For a fuller discussion of the role of rationality in moral development see Ausubel
(1971).

Greater expediency in moral standards

Adolescence marks the period of developing more elaborate understandings of the naturalistic relationships between cause and effect, reciprocal relationships, and principled morality. These qualities, in conjunction with the acquisition of identity as a central task of development during this period, make the adolescent sensitive, critical, and dependent on his ego strength and the moral order of his society* (Cantwell & Svajian, 1974).

During this period of desatellization, however, in his struggles for earned status, marked by internal conflicts (Turiel, 1973), and facing societal inconsistencies (Erikson, 1950, 1965; Keniston, 1970), the adolescent develops relativistic outlooks on values (Turiel, 1973) which make it easy to resort to ego-enhancing actions. Greater compromise of principle and reliance on an approach of expediency occur. If conformity to group norms is the price of social acceptance, adherence to absolute standards of morality is extremely unrewarding. If "getting ahead" requires cutting moral corners, most individuals will yield to the pressure and develop a less stringent code of ethics. Two-thirds of junior high school students are willing to condone stealing under certain conditions (for example, from a public utility corporation), and only one-tenth are unqualifiedly opposed to it (Stendler, 1949b). From the fifth to the twelfth grade there is a sharp rise in the percentage of children who justify "social lies" (Tudor-Hart, 1926). In a sample of 1,629 high school students, of which 515 were in college preparation and 744 were in general curriculum, 40% of college preparation and 43% of general curriculum students said they would cheat if the only way to pass a course was cheating (Schab, 1972).

In some cases this behavior is indicative of the naiveté, inexperience, and impulsiveness of adolescents, and of the initial reaction to the shock of disenchantment on being initiated into the corruption existing in certain areas of public life formerly believed to be sacrosanct. In other cases, however, it has the same significance as exaggerated cynicism, namely, as a form of aggression against adult society, in which strong motivational "set" exists to perceive all adult behavior in an unfavorable light. The cynical adolescent, then, proceeds to emulate and outdo the behavior he purports to perceive in

---

*Kohlberg and Kramer (1969) found that principled thought, especially stage 5, emerges in adolescence, but that stage 6 principled thought tends not to become crystallized until the early twenties.

adults, while the perfectionist in an orgy of self-righteousness sets himself up as a champion of truth and virtue against a hopelessly wicked world (Ausubel, 1952; Keniston, 1970; Light & Laufer, 1975).

Guilt feelings in relation to age-mate socialization

In recent years several cultural anthropologists have advanced the notion that a different type of relatively guiltless conscience operates under conditions in which an omnipotent parent does not personally administer the moral sanctions of the culture. Leighton and Kluckhohn (1947a), for example, assert that among all Navaho age groups, "sensitivity to shame largely takes the place that remorse and self-punishment have in preventing anti-social conduct in white society." And Mead (1940, p. 105), in describing the moral behavior of adolescents in our culture who undergo peer-group rather than parent-regulated socialization, states: "Shame, the agony of being found wanting and exposed to the disapproval of others, becomes a more prominent sanction behind conduct than guilt, the fear of not measuring up to the high standard which was represented by the parents." (Mead, 1940, p. 105.)

This point of view is based on the psychoanalytic premise that a guilt-enforced conscience (superego) can develop only under certain specified conditions of the parent-child relationship; that the culture assigns qualitatively different roles to parent and child; that the parent or parent surrogate personally enforces the moral code with appropriate rewards and punishments; and that the parent demands obedience as an inherent right and punishes disobedience as morally wrong rather than as dangerous or inexpedient. It makes the further assumptions that: (1) guilt feelings can arise only in response to an acknowledged violation of moral standards developed under the above conditions; (2) "true" conscience is not operative unless moral behavior is enforced only by internal sanctions such as loyalty or fear of guilt; and (3) guilt and shame are dichotomous (Ausubel, 1955).

Our analysis of the development of the satellizing, guilt-centered conscience has shown that only three developmental conditions are absolutely necessary: the internalization of moral values, the internalization of a feeling of obligation to abide by them, and the ability to perceive a discrepancy between one's conduct and one's values (Ausubel, 1955). Despite Leighton and Kluckhohn's denial of internalized moral values and obligations among the Navaho, their own descriptions of typical Navaho behavior assume that the individual strongly identifies with the moral code of his culture and recognizes obligations to conform to this code which are not wholly dependent on social sanctions of reward and punishment (Ausubel, 1955).

A satellizing bond can also be established in relation to a group (peer group or extended family) as well as to single individuals. Although less intense, such bonds are nevertheless potent enough to induce guilt feelings when recognized moral values and obligations internalized from the group are violated. Neither is it necessary for the child to perceive the parent or the group as qualitatively superior or as entitled to implicit obedience, as long as they are endowed with sufficient prestige authority to structure an otherwise undifferentiated moral field (Ausubel, 1955).

As pointed out above, at no time are internal sanctions ever unreinforced by external restraints. Throughout life, from early childhood to old age, conscience is buttressed by external controls, the importance of which fluctuates from one developmental level to the next. Hence, the assumption that true conscience cannot be operative if such other external sanctions as shame, expediency, ego enhancement, physical punishment, and supernatural retribution are simultaneously present is purely gratuitous (Ausubel, 1955).

Mead's depreciation of the role of guilt in adolescence assumes that guilt feelings can arise only in an omnipotent parent–subservient child type of relationship. She ignores the facts that: (1) the satellizing history of the individual is perpetuated by substrate representation in current personality organization; (2) ex-satellizers continue to form satellizing relationships during and after adolescence; and (3) guilt can be experienced apart from a satellizing relationship provided genuine moral obligations are internalized (Ausubel, 1955).

The claim that shame replaces guilt as the chief moral sanction behind conduct in adolescence is based on the assumption that shame and guilt are mutually incompatible and dichotomous. Actually, shame is part of every guilt reaction, although types of shame exist apart from guilt. The shame component of guilt is the negative self-evaluation that arises from an acknowledged violation of internalized moral obligation. Shame, however, can take place under any condition involving self-depreciation vis-à-vis the group. An individual may experience shame for violating a group norm (although no internalized moral obligations are involved) simply because he is exposed to public scorn and ridicule. But the mere fact that guiltless shame is invoked as a moral sanction does not mean that guilt and the shame of guilt are not also operative in this same situation (Ausubel, 1955).

FACTORS INFLUENCING INDIVIDUAL DIFFERENCES IN
ADOLESCENT MORAL DEVELOPMENT

The preceding review of changes in moral development in adolescence does not take into account differences among individual adolescents. Even though developmental pressures are uniform for all individuals sharing a common social environment, "character is formed differently in different personalities" (Havighurst & Taba, 1949). In the first section we shall be concerned mainly with personality differences that influence different types of moral development, and in the following section shall consider some socioeconomic factors relevant to the same relationship.

There are no adequate reasons to believe that pubescence per se influences the course of moral development. Stone and Barker (1939) did find significant differences in maturity of moral judgments between pre- and postmenarcheal girls; but these differences undoubtedly reflected the spurt in social maturity accompanying pubescence rather than any physiological correlate of pubescence itself. Dimock (1937) did not find any correlation between physical maturity and moral knowledge in boys.

Personality type

"Good character (or bad character) may have a very different meaning in the lives of two individuals when seen in the total configuration of their personalities. . . . It is influenced by a different set of causative factors and by a different set of learning experiences" (Havighurst & Taba, 1949, p. 182). We may reasonably expect to find important differences in moral development between satellizers and nonsatellizers, and between the various subtypes making up each of these primary personality types.

The nonsatellizer obviously fails to undergo the various changes in conscience development associated with satellization, and he is similarly spared the changes resulting from desatellization (Ausubel, 1952a). His moral development, therefore, involves more continuity from one stage to the next. During early and middle childhood, instead of developing a sense of obligation in relation to a general attitude of value subservience, loyalty, need for approval, and retention of derived status, the nonsatellizer continues to conform to parental standards for the same expediential reasons as during infancy. He is sensitive to prestige suggestion at the hands of parents, but only because he recognizes the latter's objectively greater knowledge and competence—not because he is motivated by a strong need to unconditionally reflect their value judgments. Fear of deprivation and loss of succor rather than guilt avoidance keeps him in line and checks the overt expression of his hostility and aggression. Moral obligations are assimilated on a selective basis only, that is, if they are perceived as leading to ego enhancement (Ausubel, 1952a).

During late childhood, the nonsatellizer becomes capable of internalizing moral values and obligations on the basis of the exploratory orientation. Unhampered by satellizing loyalties, he finds it easier to grasp functional concepts of moral law based on equity and reciprocal obligations. In this way, too, he acquires the prerequisites for a guilt-governed conscience. But the stability of moral obligations that circumvent a preliminary history of satellization (prior to assimilation in final adult form) is highly precarious because (1) infantile irresponsibility has never been attenuated by strong, emotionally charged feelings of obligation in relation to significant individuals in the child's interpersonal world; and (2) powerful needs for ego enhancement are often in conflict with the content and goals of ethical norms (Ausubel, 1952a).

Under such conditions, moral obligations are seldom repudiated outright; this would require direct and inexpedient conflict with cultural sanctions. However, two less drastic alternatives are available: (1) indirect evasion of the demands of conscience and of the punishment of guilt when the needs of ego aggrandizement are too strong to be denied; and (2) buttressing conscience by the mechanism of reaction-formation when moral obligations are too solidly entrenched to be circumvented (Ausubel, 1952a).

Moral obligation can be evaded in two ways: (1) by selectively inhibiting the self-critical faculty so that, when convenient, even glaring discrepancies between precept and practice cannot be perceived; and (2) by claiming superior status so that one is above the law for ordinary people (Ausubel, 1952a). This concept has been institutionalized in justifying the exploitation, enslavement, and extermination of "inferior" races.

Reaction-formation rigidly suppresses motives that are at variance with internalized moral obligations and substitutes more acceptable motives. Nevertheless, many loopholes for surreptitious circumvention are still present. Suppression does not imply rejection and can never be wholly complete. Antisocial trends can also be expressed under the guise of lofty ideals. At the very best, the moral behavior of the nonsatellizer becomes unspontaneous, stereotyped, and unduly circumscribed (Ausubel, 1952a). Awareness of the underlying strength of his unacceptable attitudes encourages the erection of exaggerated defenses. Afraid to trust himself at all, he seeks iron-clad security in rigid taboos instituted against the undesirable behavior, accompanied by a self-conscious overemphasis of the antithetical moral trait. Moral judgment passed on others' conduct tends to be formal and absolutistic rather than related to the relevant situational and personality context in which the behavior could be more fairly evaluated for genuine ethical merit (Ausubel, 1952a).

The overvalued child who has never felt much pressure to conform to parental standards frequently regards himself as immune from ordinary moral obligations (Ausubel, 1952a). The rejected child, on the other hand, is not likely to claim such unique exemptions since he has been subjected to rigorous discipline. In most instances he will acquire a strong rational conscience, buttressed by reaction-formation, and permitting occasional moral lapses through impairment of the self-critical faculty (Ausubel, 1952a). However, the concomitance of harsh rejection by parents and extreme self-assertiveness in the child may result in the child's repudiating the entire pattern of parental moral values; this type of delinquent child is known as the aggressive antisocial psychopath. When rejection is expressed in parental neglect and self-love, the child displaces the hostility he feels for his parents onto others. Such behavior is reinforced by the parents' tendency to condone it as long as they themselves are not disturbed (Ausubel, 1952a). Delinquents report more often than normal children that their parents are neglectful and lacking in solicitude and affection (Glueck & Glueck, 1950).

On the positive side, however, the rejected child possesses a latent capacity for forming satellizing-like relationships which enable him to experience the type of guilt feelings that occur in normally satellizing children (Ausubel, 1952a).

Among satellizers, aberrations in conscience development are generally less severe. The most serious problem is presented by the underdominated (overpermissively handled) child who has great difficulty acquiring a sense of moral obligation (Ausubel, 1952a). To begin with, he is not required to inhibit hedonistic motivations or to curb aggressive impulses. The limits of unacceptable behavior are poorly defined and inadequately or inconsistently enforced. Second, like the overvalued child, he is treated as a specially privileged person, exempt from the usual responsibilities toward others, and is not encouraged to develop a realistic self-critical faculty. Fortunately, however, unlike that of the overvalued child, the underdominated child's motivation for immoral behavior is more likely to lie in hedonistic self-indulgence than in unprincipled ego enhancement at the expense of others. Also, there is always the possibility of his forming satellizing relationships to teachers and group leaders who are able to provide greater firmness and consistency of discipline (Ausubel, 1952a).

The chief difficulty for overprotected and overdominated children lies in transferring feelings of moral obligation from parents to society and in arriving at independent value judgments. The situation leads to no serious consequences as long as the parent is alive and does not subscribe to antisocial attitudes or behavior. However, if the parent is a moral deviant, uncritical loyalty of the child can lead to delinquent behavior; whereas the death or removal of the parent can create a vacuum in moral responsibility. But again this is not apt to be serious since infantile irresponsibility has been attenuated in satellization, and there is no driving need to further ego enhancement at any price, as in the case of the excessively ambitious nonsatellizer (Ausubel, 1952a).

Sociocultural factors

In addition to having differences in character development attributable to personality makeup, individuals differ depending on the "value systems of the social groups" to which they belong or to which they relate themselves positively or negatively (Havighurst & Taba, 1949; Kohn, 1963). The values held by the family, by the dominant groups and institutions in the community, and by persons in positions of authority and high status constitute the "moral climate" in which a young person grows up. These groups and persons are in a position to punish undesirable conduct and to reward desirable conduct, and their expectations have much to do with the standards of behavior developed by the individual (Havighurst & Taba, 1949).

Sociologists are aware of the influence of social class membership on moral development, of "each sub-grouping having its characteristic mores" (Bull, 1969, p. 37).

Within a given social class environment, the attitudes toward aggression, honesty, thrift, community responsibility (Havighurst & Taba, 1949), specific issues and institutions—law and police, for instance (Kohlberg, 1969), helpfulness, and altruism (Berkowitz, 1968; Sugarman, 1973) have a certain consistency. But, naturally, complete social class homogeneity in moral belief or behavior never exists (Ausubel, 1952a; Graham, 1972). Considerable interaction and diffusion among classes occur. Social class differences with respect to certain aspects of moral development appear to have been diminishing over the past 20 years (Bronfenbrenner, 1962). In some cognitive aspects of conscience development, as a matter of fact, recently obtained differences are negligible (Boehm & Nass, 1962). This phenomenon may reflect the diminution of class differences, over this period of time, in child rearing practices (Ausubel & Sullivan, 1970).

Some of the homogeneity in moral outlook among different social classes, however, is more apparent than real. The gap between practice and professed belief is probably smallest in middle-class children since parents, school, church, and community agencies all cooperate in enforcing the official ideology. Thus children "from higher-status homes have an interwoven complex of advantages over those from a poor background. Their greater security, both economically and emotionally, gives them freedom from temptations that beset less fortunate children" (Bull, 1969, p. 37).

The phenomenon of moral confusion is not restricted to any social class, but is a general characteristic of our rapidly changing culture. Genuine concern for traditional moral values is disappearing at an alarming rate as greater cultural emphasis is placed on achieving immediate material advantage at any price (Ausubel, 1952a). Precept and practice drift farther apart when expediency, opportunism, and conformity become the chief passports to success. Under such circumstances, formal appearances become more important than content, and the letter of the law replaces its ostensible intentions. Anything goes which can be provided with a veneer of legitimacy that protects the individual from legal reprisal (Ausubel, 1952a).

Why can such a "selective morality" (which condemns an unethical practice that is illegal, yet sanctions a similar practice that violates no existing statute) be so easily assimilated despite its glaring inconsistencies? Simply because our modern youth have developed an extremely high tolerance for moral ambiguity and confusion (Ausubel, 1952a). Because of the prestige suggestion inherent in the operation of social norms, they are assimilatable in such a way that their incompatibility is never even perceived; the perceiver presumes that inconsistency in cultural values is inconceivable, and therefore an advance "set" exists to perceive such values as consistent regardless of manifest content—even if logic-tight compartments must be constructed to prevent critical comparisons from being made (Ausubel, 1952a).

Enough is known about primitive cultures such as the Dobu (Benedict, 1934), Manus (Mead, 1939), and Betsileo (Kardiner & Linton, 1939) in which comparable moral practices have been institutionalized to predict that human beings can perceive such a state of affairs as perfectly natural and can adapt their value systems to conform to it. But in cultures that face a transition to social revolution in moral values, considerable variability prevails in the reaction of particular individuals, depending, in part, on their perceptual acuity, their susceptibility to prestige suggestion, their need for ego enhancement, and the strength of their moral convictions. It is significant that Kohlberg's research (Kohlberg & Kramer, 1969)* shows that even at age 24, only 10% of the middle-class urban male population has reached the "personal principles" phase (stage 6), while another 26% are at the social contract (stage 5) phase. The study showed no clear increase in stage 5 thinking beyond high school. Perhaps even more significant is the fact that during the student activism of the Sixties, a study of University of California students at Berkeley showed a marked difference between the protesters and the nonprotesters. The greater number (56%) of the protesters were at the postconventional levels of morality, while only 12% of the nonprotesters had reached the same level. The overwhelming majority (85%) of the nonprotesters were in the conventional stage (Haan & Block, 1969a, 1969b; Haan et al., 1968; M. B. Smith, 1969a, 1969b).

Thus many individuals fail to see that any problem of moral inconsistency exists, while others are acutely disillusioned; but the degree to which they adapt to the requirements of the situation depends on the kind of conscience they possess and on their need for extrinsic status. This type of moral climate is in a sense made to order for the ego needs of the nonsatellizer, except when he happens to have a strong rational conscience (Ausubel, 1952a). The satellizer (or the nonsatellizer with a strong rational conscience), on the other hand, who perceives what is going on, is unable to make the required adaptations without experiencing feelings of conflict, guilt, self-reproach, and resentment toward a culture that requires such moral compromises for the sake of survival and legitimate ego enhancement. He feels impelled to crush all vestiges of moral feeling in himself because he perceives them as a handicap in a jungle, "dog-eat-dog" society. But try as he may, he cannot stifle his conscience completely. In desperation he may adopt a double moral code: one for his friends and family, another for his colleagues and competitors. But in any case guilt feelings exercise considerable restraint over his behavior so that his violations of the moral code are generally less flagrant and more defensible than the nonsatellizer's. His immorality more usually serves the interests of survival rather than catering to the predatory needs of aggressive ego aggrandizement (Ausubel, 1952a).

Moral beliefs of adolescents

Expressed belief is probably a more valid reflection of an individual's moral structure than is reputation. Since expressed beliefs obviously do not correspond completely to actual beliefs because of un-

---

* As was pointed out earlier in this chapter, stage 5 starts in adolescence.

derstandable desires for self-embellishment, there is a widespread tendency to regard them as inferior to conduct as indices of character (Ausubel, 1952a). But are not most persons highly motivated to obtain "good" reputations, which means that they frequently *behave* in accordance with perceived expectations rather than with their own moral values? As a matter of fact, many individuals often express their true feelings verbally, whereas in situations calling for translation of these feelings into action they are constrained by fear of reprisal and other considerations of expediency (Ausubel, 1952a).

General characteristics of moral values

Although in stable and relatively homogeneous cultures moral values assimilated in the family, community, and peer group fail to show startling changes in adolescence, in heterogeneous urban cultures undergoing rapid change, and manifesting inconsistencies between different sectors and between belief and conduct, adolescents become critical and sensitive as evidenced in student civil rights and antiwar protests in the 1960s mentioned earlier. But moral values of our culture are implanted early in life. Hence studies of developmental changes in beliefs do not always show startling changes as children enter adolescence. When change does occur it is more striking in actual conduct than in mere verbal statements of belief (Rosander, 1939). Traditional beliefs need not be changed* when they require no supporting behavior, even if they are not in accord with actual sentiments. But when such beliefs demand self-denial (e.g., abstinence from alcohol, church attendance), developmental shifts toward greater liberalism take place (Rosander, 1939).

There is a fair amount of generality among moral beliefs. Yet many inconsistencies between beliefs point up the lack of a sufficiently generalized code of ethics. Aside from the influence of the general climate of moral expediency in the wider culture, this trend stems also from the ubiquitous tendency in the adult world to solve moral conflicts by appealing to platitudinous slogans and dogmatic doctrines, and from the fact that the teaching of what is right and wrong is done with reference to isolated, concrete acts of behavior. Thus an effort to help the adolescent develop a coherent moral philosophy is for the most part absent (Ausubel, 1971; Havighurst & Taba, 1949; Kohlberg, 1958, 1963a, 1971).

---

*The Yankelovich (1972) study of the college scene during 1968–1971 shows a high degree of positive sentiment among college students with regard to the various choices of life offered by society.

Beliefs, knowledge, intelligence, and conduct

Since values obviously have a cognitive aspect, we could reasonably anticipate that they would be influenced both by intelligence and by moral knowledge. However, these two factors become significantly related to moral beliefs only when they fall below a critical minimal level. Beyond this minimal degree of intellectual ability required for acquiring acceptable values, personality and motivational factors are the truly important variables.

Intelligence correlates positively (but lowly) with moral maturity scores obtained from Kohlberg and Piaget type tests (Boehm, 1962a, 1962b; Kohlberg, 1963a, 1964, 1968; Whitemen & Kosier, 1964). Kohlberg (1964, pp. 404–405) points out, however, that "moral judgment is [only] moderately correlated with IQ, but is quite highly related to age, with intelligence controlled. . . . Intellectual development, then, is an important condition for the development of moral thought, but level of moral thought can be clearly distinguished from intellectual level." Thus, neither IQ nor school achievement is highly correlated with measures of moral belief (Havighurst & Taba, 1949). Moral knowledge bears a similar relationship to beliefs and is related to intelligence, socioeconomic status, and the moral knowledge scores of associates (Dimock, 1937; Kohlberg, 1964).

The actual moral beliefs of an individual are the truest measures of his character. If they could be validly ascertained it would certainly be found that they are significantly related to conduct (Ausubel, 1952a). The widespread opinion that belief and conduct are unrelated springs from: (1) the confusion between moral belief and moral knowledge; (2) the confusion between expressed and true beliefs; and (3) the confusion between deliberate insincerity on the one hand and actual lack of discriminative ability on the other, as a determinant of the discrepancy between belief and conduct (Ausubel, 1952a).

Moral knowledge is only one aspect, and a relatively minor aspect, of moral belief. It is true that a certain minimal amount of intelligence and social experience is required to learn acceptable moral values. The latter, however, become transformed into ethical beliefs only when they are interiorized or invested with sufficient emotional and intellectual conviction as to constitute genuine dispositions to behave in certain ways in particular moral situations or dilemmas. Immoral behavior in persons of normal intelligence who are exposed to acceptable moral beliefs is an outcome not of insufficient moral knowledge, but of either lack of a feeling of obligation to conform to these values or selective impairment of the self-critical faculty in relation to ethical aspects of their own behavior (Ausubel, 1952a).

The negligible significance of moral knowledge as a variable in moral behavior is borne out by the low correlations which Hartshorne and May (1930) found between moral knowledge and performance. There is also little difference between delinquent and nondelinquent boys in ability to identify the correct ethical alternative in hypothetical moral problems (Bartlett & Harris, 1936). Curiously enough, intelligence correlates much more highly with moral conduct than it does with moral knowledge (Hartshorne & May, 1930). Intellectually "superior" children surpass their "average contemporaries" in such traits as conscientiousness, perseverance, prudence, and truthfulness (Kohlberg, 1968; Terman, 1925). This superiority, however, prevails mostly in regard to moral traits that either depend on moral knowledge or are important for achieving individual success, rather than in regard to traits reflecting moral attitudes (Hartshorne & May, 1930; H. E. Jones, 1954). This can be interpreted to mean that intelligence influences moral behavior not (as might be expected) through determining moral beliefs, but in an extraneous manner; that is, intelligent children have less reason than others to cheat in order to do well in schoolwork, and are more apt when cheating to perceive the conditions that might prove hazardous. One difference between delinquent and nondelinquent youth (within a given socioeconomic class) is that the latter's greater mean intelligence enables them to avoid participation in illegal activities when the chances of apprehension are great (Ausubel, 1952a).

A second reason for the seeming disparity between beliefs and behavior is that expressed beliefs are not necessarily actual beliefs. Avowal of conventional and socially acceptable beliefs is considered to be judicious in any society, although during adolescence youth often delight in expressing cynical and antisocial viewpoints which exceed by far their actual behavioral manifestations in this direction. On the other hand, in relation to peer-group activities, adolescents tend to be highly conforming in their beliefs.

Specific beliefs and attitudes

PREJUDICES

By the time children reach adolescence, racial and ethnic prejudices are well established. Although it is true that preferences of school children for racial and ethnic groups increase from the first to sixth grade, considerable variability is present (Koch, 1946; Minard, 1931; Moreno, 1934). After the sixth grade, however, homogeneity of attitude gradually increases (Koch, 1946; Kutner & Gordon, 1964) and becomes increasingly similar to the prevailing adult norms in the respective communities of different adolescents (Blake & Dennis, 1943; Zeligs, 1938, 1948). Thus Wilson (1963) asserts that a review of the literature on the development of ethnic attitudes reveals several tendencies: (1) there is a tendency for level of prejudice to be stable over the later ages of adolescence; (2) there is a tendency for perceived norms to become stabilized at some time in adolescence; and (3) there is a tendency toward an increase in the degree of consistency in an individual's response to a given ethnic group during adolescence.

The primary effect of adolescence on prejudices is to draw caste and class lines more sharply. Adolescents take on more of the actual interpersonal attitudes of their class reference groups and behave as their elders do. Before this time a certain amount of adult indulgence is shown toward manifestations of childish tolerance; children are still operating in their own world of values and are not, so to speak, "playing for keeps." Beginning with adolescence, however, they are expected to conform to adult social prejudices and to "watch their step" if they expect to succeed in life (Ausubel, 1952a). Parental admonitions about associating with the "wrong type" of children become more pointed and (especially in girls) are reflected in increased attitudinal intolerance (Bird et al., 1952). At the same time the supporting climate of public opinion is a crucial reinforcing factor from the wider community (Horowitz, 1936; Radke & Sutherland, 1949; Radke et al., 1949; Trager & Yarrow, 1952; Zeligs, 1938, 1948).

In relation to such pressures, considerations of rationality are totally irrelevant. At the same time that prejudicial behavior in choice situations sharply tends to exclude from social participation the groups subject to prejudice (Crisswell, 1939; Horowitz, 1936; Koch, 1946; Minard, 1931), the attitudes (intellectual judgments) of white children toward blacks become more tolerant (Brigham, 1974; Minard, 1931). Education does not reduce the incidence of anti-Semitic attitudes (Campbell, 1947), but the reasons given for intolerant attitudes toward national groups become more sophisticated and more highly rationalized with increasing age (Meltzer, 1941). Interfaith education on an impersonal and intellectual level does not reduce prejudices, but the discussion of personal experiences and attitudes is effective in reducing these (Kagan, 1952). The effect of the impetus of the civil rights movement remains to be seen. Evidence of change is emerging but is equivocal. Thus Brigham (1974, pp. 156–157) reports a study in which children in grades 4 through 12 in two segregated schools in the Deep South, asked to characterize whites and blacks on 50 "stereotype-relevant" traits, showed "the largest degree of between-race agreement in attributions in grades 7–11. . . . Perhaps the most encouraging findings are the widespread use of the No Difference response category and the very high agreement between races as to the favorability of these 50 traits." On the other hand, Lerner and Karson (1973) report a study of 406 white lower-middle class children in eighth and ninth grades who were asked to attribute each of 48 items from a verbal checklist to a picture of either a white or a black male. The results indicated that subjects held a predominantly unfavorable view of the black figure and a predominantly positive view of the white figure. The authors point out that their study suggests "that, when some white youth are forced to attribute a bad item to either a white or a black stimulus figure, a majority will choose the black figure. Thus, our results do not support the suggestion that the racial attitudes of white people toward black people are becoming more favorable" (Lerner & Karson, 1973, p. 382).

Rokeach (1974), in his study of value stability and change over a 3-year period (1968 to 1971) from a national area probability sample of Americans over 21, finds a significant increase in egalitarian attitudes toward race among American whites. He makes the following observation with regard to change in this attitude along with greater concerns for sexual egalitarianism, ecology, peace, and peace of mind: "It is not clear from these latter data, however, whether the changes between 1968 and 1971 actually occurred among adults in their twenties or, alternatively, whether they were a result of the movement of persons between 18 and 21 in 1968 into the 21–30 age category in 1971, or both. Future research with respondents under 21 years of age should help us answer this question" (Rokeach, 1974, p. 237).

It is generally assumed that prejudice is a multicausal phenomenon, involves intergroup learning, and is related to personality structure that is authoritarian (Adorno, 1950). Further, prejudice often reflects underlying insecurity, hostility, suspicion, punitiveness, and distrust of others (Ammons, 1950; Frenkel-Brunswik, 1951; Gough et al., 1950; Lyle & Levitt, 1955; Mussen, 1950; Radke et al., 1949; Tabachnik, 1962). In addition, adolescents who are more prejudiced than others appear to demonstrate lower level reasoning processes (Kutner, 1958; Kutner & Gordon, 1964).

Thus the nature of prejudice does not lead to ready or uniform solutions. Direct interracial contact increases racial prejudice in some individuals, as described above, whereas it reduces bias in children who are unaggressive and who hold favorable attitudes toward parents and age mates (Mussen, 1950). Under some intergroup conditions, intense conflict can be reduced if the children are confronted with a common and compelling problem which demands cooperative versus competitive action (Sherif, 1958). It is important for the development of positive ethnic attitudes, however, that the members of the different ethnic groups be cooperatively engaged in the pursuit of common objectives under equal-status conditions or as functional equals (Proshansky, 1966).

A diminishing prevalence of superstitious belief from the seventh to ninth grade (Caldwell, 1934), from high school to college (Lundeen & Caldwell, 1930), and from one level of college to the next (Dudycha, 1933; Valentine, 1936) reflects the increased intellectual sophistication accompanying adolescence. The decline in superstitious belief is a function of the general rise in level of intellectual sophistication paralleling school instruction, rather than a function of increasing chronological or mental age (Caldwell & Lundeen, 1934; Killen et al., 1974; Najarian-Svajian, 1966). Educated adults, unschooled in the physical sciences, make as many animistic and "magical" interpretations of natural phenomena as children (Oakes, 1947). High school students who prefer books on science also exhibit fewer superstitions than those who prefer fiction (Maller & Lundeen, 1933). Significantly, superstitions that are culturally anachronistic (beliefs in luck, charms, witchcraft, and evil spirits) are least often believed (Lundeen & Caldwell, 1930), whereas others less antagonistic to prevailing thought (animistic, supernatural, and teleological conceptions of causality; astrology; and phrenology) enjoy the greatest degree of acceptance (Lundeen & Caldwell, 1930; Ter Keurst, 1939).

STATUS OF RELIGION DURING ADOLESCENCE

Acceptance or rejection

Just as adolescence brings no great upheaval in moral structure, it effects no revolution in attitude toward religion, and, to a large extent, in religious beliefs or activities (Douvan & Gold, 1966). Contrary to widespread opinion, there is no rampant repudiation of religion during adolescence (Purdue Opinion Panel, "Ethical Values of High School Students," 1923–1965). Even though recent data from surveys (Yankelovich, 1972) suggest a trend away from conventional religion among college youth (Parker, 1971; Wuthnow & Glock, 1973; Yankelovich, 1972), "perhaps most significant has been the evidence that abandoning conventional religion (or an areligious perspective) for an alternative religion constitutes more of a break with the conventional than rejecting religion altogether" (Wuthnow & Glock, 1973, p. 175).

A great number of American adolescents belong to a church, usually the same church as their parents or elders (Bell, 1938; Myers, 1951), attend church services once a month or more* (Bell, 1938; Pixley & Beckman, 1949; Purdue Opinion Panel, 1965), and believe in a personal, omnipotent, omniscient, bodyless God (Dudycha, 1933; Gilliand, 1940; Nelson, 1940; Parker, 1971; Remmers et al., 1951). In his review of literature on changes in religious beliefs of college students over four decades, Parker (1971) concludes:

> The evidence would indicate there is an accelerated rate of change during adolescence when intellectual development is reaching a peak. In stable environments, religious change is minimal, but with the new environment in college, rapid changes occur during the freshman year. By the end of college, the rate of change has slowed once again.

The evidence by no means indicates homogeneity in the religious beliefs or practices of adolescents. As a matter of fact, significant differences exist between the sexes (Howells, 1928; Parker, 1971; Remmers et al., 1951), among age groups (Elkind, 1966; Harms, 1944; Jacquet, 1975; Kuhlen & Arnold, 1944; Remmers et al., 1951), among religious denominations (Allport et al., 1948; Bell, 1938; Howells, 1928; Jacquet, 1975; Kuhlen & Arnold, 1944; Parker, 1971; Remmers et al., 1951), and among social classes (Ausubel & Sullivan, 1970). It does indicate, however, that organized religion as a moral, philosophical, and social institution has not declined drastically for the greater number of American youth. A minority of students demonstrate religious defection by abandoning conventional religion for alternative religions. These students tend to be among the better rather than the poorer students. Referring to this and other findings of their study of a small and unique sample of students, Wuthnow and Glock (1973, p. 175) make the following observations:

> This finding in conjunction with the weak and inconsistent relationships between religious and economic status, and the experience of interpersonal problems, suggests that cognitive processes are probably among the more crucial factors for understanding current religious unrest. The evidence that religious de-

---

* "Religious participation is found to be at or near its highest peak during late childhood and early adolescence when children are under the most parental and church supervision. Then participation rates drop in the twenties" Strommen, 1971, p. 578).

fection and experimentation are associated with psychic stress is also revealing.

Religious observances

Among adolescents, not associated with particular religious unrest, there is a gradual trend toward decreasing church attendance (Katz & Allport, 1931; Rosander, 1939; Young et al., 1966) from early to late adolescence. Girls attend church more regularly than boys (Parker, 1971; Punke, 1936), and Catholics are more assiduous in this respect than either Protestants or Jews (Bell, 1938; Hassenger, 1967).

Religious beliefs

Changes in religious beliefs during adolescence show the same trends as those of moral values in general. As a result of the individual's intellectual maturation, his religious beliefs become more abstract and less literal (Kuhlen & Arnold, 1944; Parker, 1971). God is conceptualized as an omniscient power rather than as a corporeal being. Religious views also become more tolerant and less ritualistic; virtue is identified less with strict observance of specific denominational doctrine (Franzblau, 1934; Kuhlen & Arnold, 1944; Wuthnow & Glock, 1973).

For most adolescents, prayer serves to give thanks; less frequently it is used as a form of communion, to seek guidance or comfort, or to comply with habit (Pixley & Beckman, 1949). With increasing age fewer adolescents regard prayer as a form of penance or believe that prayers are answered (Brown, 1968; Goldman, 1964; Kuhlen & Arnold, 1944).

Religious doubts and conflict

For most adolescents, there is less acceptance of the more literal, ritualistic, and dogmatic aspects of religious belief—the literal interpretation of the Bible and belief in heaven, hell, and immortality (Kuhlen & Arnold, 1944; Parker, 1971). The typical adolescent today admits a certain amount of religious perplexity, especially about beliefs questioned by scientific discoveries, but he seems to accept this situation as more or less normal (Remmers et al., 1951). For the most part, such doubts are peripheral and do not seriously undermine the core of religious faith.

For a minority of students, however, especially at the college level, a critical attitude toward conventional religion leads to unrest. For these students religious and other forms of experimentation "show that religious defection is not an isolated matter but part of a broader—and apparently deep—dissatisfaction with the life that conventional society offers" (Wuthnow & Glock, 1973, p. 177).

Moral belief and religious belief or faith

Kohlberg (1974) points out that James Fowler's recent investigations of faith have yielded six stages of development roughly paralleling stages in moral development. In stage I divinity is believed to be an authority who is the ultimate dispenser of punishment and reward. At stage 2 the relation of man to God is one of exchange. Stage 3 children and adolescents entertain the notion of divinity as moral ideal, as an ideally good person, as the protector of goodness. At stage 4 divinity is first seen as lawgiver. At stage 5 divinity becomes identified with "or is the ground of inner freedom, individuality and responsibility" (p. 14).

Kohlberg suggests that the moral principles precede and do not require faith for their formulation or for their justification. "In some sense, however, to ultimately live up to moral principles requires faith. For this reason, we believe, the ultimate examples of Stage 6 morality appear to be men of faith" (p. 14).

Kohlberg further explains that stage 6 morality rests on autonomous rational morality but requires an ultimate stage of faith and moves men toward it. This faith orientation he calls stage 7, which forms a basis of a perspective on life's ultimate meaning. The question of "why be moral" raises the question of "how face death," which cannot be resolved on purely logical and rational grounds. The characteristics of stage 7 solutions are that "they involve contemplative experience of a non-dualistic variety. The logic of such experience is sometimes expressed in theistic terms of union with God but it need not be. Its essential is the sense of being a part of the whole of life and the adoption of a cosmic, as opposed to a universal humanistic (Stage 6) perspective" (p. 15).

Impact of adolescence on religion

INTELLECTUAL MATURATION

The cumulative impact of gradual progress toward intellectual maturity is responsible for most of the changes in religious belief occurring during adolescence. Increased ability to generalize results in more abstract religious concepts with less emphasis on the more literal aspects of religious doctrine. The general broadening of social experience, exposure to different doctrinal beliefs, and awareness of hypocrisy and inconsistencies in religious practice lead to greater tolerance and liberalness in religious outlook. Interest in religious questions is intensified by the newly attained capacity to pursue such abstract problems as the origin and purpose of life, the nature of truth, and the meaning of causality. And last, exposure to scientific teachings creates a certain amount of skepticism toward the literal interpretation of many theological doctrines.

PERSONALITY FACTORS

Part of the shift toward a more liberal and more highly rationalized concept of religion can be ascribed to the operation of the exploratory orientation with its emphasis on independently discovered reasons and its deemphasis of personal loyalty as an adequate explanation per se. The residual impact of the satellizing orientation and the importance of the incorporative orientation (its concern with consideration of extrinsic status) are also evident in the fact that for the most part the essential core of traditional religious belief remains intact through adolescence despite the multiplicity of factors that challenge faith. It strains credulity to believe that if choice of religious faith depended on reason and objective merit alone, the majority of adolescents would choose the denomination of their parents.

We have noted that in certain instances of parent-youth conflict, displaced aggression toward the parent may be directed against the church, resulting in a characteristic type of adolescent heresy. At the other extreme, increased identification with the church may represent (1) a compensation for the loss of security in the weakening of ties with parents; or (2) an anchor in the face of general value disorientation and the marginal status of adolescence. By the degree of resatellization thereby effected, the process of emancipation is furthered; and to the extent that conflicts and anxieties of other origins are displaced to the religious realm (where resolution of conflict is sometimes more easily accomplished than in other problem areas), preoccupation with religion may be regarded as an adjustive mechanism. Margaret Mead (1940) suggests that the adolescent's susceptibility to authoritarian religious influence may represent an expiation for the guilt engendered by repudiation of parental values.

Impact of religion on personality

There is evidence of a high relationship between "religiousness" and socially approved behavior with regard to such behavior as drinking, sex, and cutting classes. There is also evidence that "religious students" "live up to" the expectations of their parents to a much higher degree than nonreligious students. The "religious students" meet the academic and social expectations of the college environment to a greater degree than nonreligious students (Parker, 1971). Findings of this nature have raised the question as to whether the "religious" student's behavior is a result of his religious "beliefs" or his role expectations. At the same time evidence is adduced to confirm the hypothesis that degree of religious observance and Sunday school attendance are negligibly related to moral conduct (Betts, 1928; Goldsen et al., 1960; Hartshorne & May, 1930; Havighurst & Taba, 1949; Strang, 1929).

Neither type of evidence, however, deals with actual religious belief. The important thing to bear in mind is that evidence such as this proves only that formal religious observance makes for good character reputation but is only indifferently related to moral conduct (Ausubel, 1952a). It is apparent, however, that in the lives of many individuals religion plays a central role in the formulation of goals and values and in the enforcement of moral obligations. Thus Mennonite children ascribe religious values to more life situations and more moral authority to the church than do non-Mennonite children (Kalhorn, 1944), and adolescents in a particular closely knit Lutheran community have high reputations for honesty and reliability despite relatively low social status (Havighurst & Taba, 1949). It stands to reason that a person who really believes that moral uprightness is God's law, who feels obligated to practice the moral precepts of his religion in his everyday behavior, and who feels morally accountable to God for his conduct will be qualitatively different in his moral behavior from the general run of mankind. But when religion is practiced only formally on Sunday mornings, it is evident that it is little more than an institutionalized form of conscience balm for the immorality practiced on weekdays.

Religious orthodoxy may also be significantly related to mode of thinking and value assimilation as shown by its positive correlation with ethnocentrism and strong racial and ethnic prejudice (Adorno et al., 1950). On a priori grounds alone, one would anticipate that it would lead to avoidance of the exploratory situation and to rigidity of thought. Allen and Spilka (1967) postulated two distinct styles of religious belief and behavior. One of these, "Committed Religiosity," described a highly personal, diverse, clearly formulated, and flexible style. The other, "Consensual Religiosity," represented a concrete, specific, and rigid style (Parker, 1971). Allen and Spilka (1967) attempted to relate religious behavior with prejudice and with religious styles and they concluded as follows:

We have seen that Consensual Religiosity is tied to prejudicial attitudes, and a typologized, concretistic, restrictive outlook on religion. While verbally conforming to "traditional" values and ideals, these are vague, non-differentiated, bifurcated and neutralized or selectively adapted. In contrast, Committed Religiosity utilized an abstract, philosophical perspective; multiplex religious ideas are relatively clear in meaning and an open and flexible framework of commitment meaningfully relates religion to daily activities. (p. 205)

10

Intellectual Growth and Interest Patterns

Intelligence is considered as a measurement construct designating level of ability in performing a graded series of tasks implicating the component aspects of cognitive functioning at any given stage of intellectual development. For the most part, it is representative at adolescence and beyond of a general capacity for processing information and for using abstract symbols in the solution of abstract problems. Intelligence tests are valid to the extent that they measure this capacity. An intellectual ability, in other words, is really nothing more or less than a functional manifestation of a distinct and identifiable cognitive process as expressed in a range of individual performance or capacity differences.

In this sense, growth in intelligence is the least typical aspect of adolescent development. In all other components of growth—hormonal, skeletal, motor, personality, moral, and social—there is a discontinuous period of transitional development. The development of intelligence, on the other hand, follows a pattern very similar to the development of the fine mechanical abilities.

Of all the major tissues of the body and segments of the personality, also, it seems that only the small muscles and the intellect as a whole remain unaffected by the catalytic impetus to growth supplied by pubescence. The development of these aspects continues to respond to hereditary and environmental influences impinging on them, just as if pubescence were not taking place.

Intelligence test scores of adolescents generally show improvement over scores made by preadolescents, but this growth is part of a pattern that runs from childhood into the early twenties (Douvan & Gold, 1966).

In spite of the continuity in intelligence as a measurement construct, adolescence marks a qualitative change in the concrete-abstract and subjective-objective dimensions of intellectual or cognitive development. During adolescence discontinuous development in the capacity for abstract, objective, and hypothetical thinking is one of the primary features of intellectual growth. Thus cognitively the adolescent is a qualitatively different and more mature person than the preadolescent and the younger child. The ability to depart from the concrete and subjective thought of the child, characterized by relating tangible objects and events to self and the present, and to move toward abstraction, objectivity, and entertainment of possibilities plays an important role in thought, personality, moral, and religious development.

Many abstract concepts of government, interpersonal relations, characterology, and science become clear for the first time for a majority of individuals (Jersild, 1947). Hence more difficult problems of logic and reasoning can be handled (Jersild, 1947). Imagination is more "rational" and symbolic and deals less with manipulation of concrete images, even in such relatively nonabstract areas as spatial relationships (Michaud, 1949). Rorschach responses reveal greater ability to organize meaningful relationships (Thetford et al., 1951). All of these changes lead the child to a clearer and more comprehensive understanding of the nature of the environment in which he lives. He feels less awed by its complexity and more confident to navigate alone and unguided (Ausubel, 1952).

In the formation of judgments, greater objectivity can be brought to the weighing of evidence and less egocentricity and subjectivity are involved in arguing the validity of an abstract proposition. Both of these developments reflect the growing influence of the exploratory orientation and the sharpening of the self-critical faculty. In moral judgment this aids the development of functional and reciprocal concepts of moral obligation.

Expanded knowledge in many different areas has a noticeable effect in reducing the prevalence of misconceptions and superstitions. The validity of a perception of causality is largely dependent on the quality of the judgment about the relevance of an antecedent event for a particular consequence (Ausubel, 1954). This in turn depends on the individual's experience or sophistication in a given area (Ausubel, 1954; Oakes, 1947). Even when adults are required to provide explanations for events completely outside their sphere of competence, they tend to give answers that are remarkably similar to those of children (Oakes, 1947). When non-science teachers were shown some simple demonstrations of principles in physics, they tended to support the views they had once stated in its prediction or explanation, even when these were in conflict with the observation. There were striking instances of this reluctance to change even when the subject was looking at the phenomenon itself (Ausubel, 1954).

On the negative side, however, it is a fair inference that the judgments of adolescents are adversely influenced by their greater affectivity and by the lability and impulsiveness of their emotional responses (Thetford et al., 1951).

TRANSITION FROM CONCRETE TO FORMAL
OPERATIONS

Inhelder and Piaget presented considerable evidence indicating that "formal" (abstract) operations appear slightly before the onset of adolescence. On the whole their findings were corroborated by other investigators (Goldman, 1965; Jackson, 1965; Lovell, 1961; Yudin & Kates, 1963). Lovell's subjects attained this stage of development somewhat later than Inhelder and Piaget's, and Case and Collinson's (1962) somewhat earlier. Both Goldman and Jackson reported greater age variability, and Jackson less intertask generality, than did Inhelder and Piaget in the development of formal thinking. None of these findings, however, detracted from the essential validity of Piaget's conclusion that for the first time the child entering this stage of cognitive development thinks in terms of all-inclusive hypothetical possibilities (instead of "the here and now") or in terms of propositional logic ("second-degree operations" or "operations on operations"). "Instead of just coordinating facts about the actual world," states Piaget (1957, p. 19) "hypothetico-deductive reasoning draws out the implications of possible statements and thus gives rise to a unique synthesis of the possible and the necessary."

The elementary school child, according to Inhelder and Piaget (1958), is by no means dependent on immediate concrete-empirical experience in understanding and manipulating simple abstractions or ideas about objects and phenomena. It is true, of course, that the emergence of such ideas must always be preceded by an adequate background of direct, nonverbal experience with the empirical data from which they are abstracted. But once their meaning becomes firmly established as a result of this background of past experience, the child can meaningfully comprehend and use them without any current reference to concrete-empirical data.

The meaningful understanding or manipulation of *relationships* between complex abstractions without perceptible referents, or of ideas about ideas, on the other hand, is quite another matter. In this kind of operation the elementary school pupil is still dependent on current or recently prior concrete-empirical experience; when such experience is not available, he finds abstract relational propositions unrelatable to cognitive structure and hence devoid of meaning. This dependence on concrete-empirical props self-evidently limits his ability meaningfully to grasp and manipulate relationships between abstractions, since he can only acquire those understandings and perform those logical operations which do not go beyond the concrete and particularized representation of reality implicit in his use of props. Thus, when complex relational propositions are involved, he is largely restricted to a subverbal, concrete, or intuitive level of cognitive functioning, a level that falls far short of the clarity, precision, explicitness, and generality associated with the more advanced abstract stage of intellectual development.

Beginning with the adolescent period, however, children become increasingly less dependent on the availability of concrete-empirical experience in meaningfully relating complex abstract propositions to cognitive structure. Eventually, after sufficient gradual change in this direction, a qualitatively new capacity emerges: the intellectually mature individual becomes capable of understanding and manipulating relationships between abstractions directly, that is, without any reference whatsoever to concrete, empirical reality. He can now transcend the previously achieved level of intuitive thought and understanding and formulate general laws relating general categories of variables that are divorced from the concrete-empirical data at hand. His concepts and generalizations, therefore, tend to be second-order constructs derived from relationships between previously established verbal abstractions already one step removed from the data.

Careful analysis of the experiments performed by Inhelder and Piaget and by the other investigators cited above does not substantiate their view, as well as Lunzer's (1965), that the distinctive feature of formal or abstract (as opposed to concrete) operations is that the older child is able to deal operationally and verbally with ideas about ideas, to perform "second-order operations," or to go "beyond the framework of transformations bearing directly on empirical reality." The younger ("concrete operational") child can also do these things, as shown by the studies of Case and Collinson (1962) and Hill (1961). The latter demonstrated, for example, that most children ages 6 to 8 can easily draw correct inferences from hypothetical premises involving second-order operations. The preadolescent's and adolescent's ability verbally to manipulate relationships between ideas ("second-order relations") in the absence of recently prior or concurrently available concrete-empirical props is the distinctive attribute of formal operations.

GROWTH CHARACTERISTICS OF GENERAL INTELLIGENCE DURING ADOLESCENCE

Ljung (1965) described an "adolescent growth spurt" in mental development that is more marked in girls than in boys. The study included results from several factors of intelligence, some of which showed a much more definite spurt during the adolescent years than others. The spurt undoubtedly reflects the adolescent's greater ability to process information and solve abstract problems more efficiently that results from the shift to abstract cognitive functioning. It is not typically reflected in conventional intelligence tests but was in Ljung's tests because the measures he used were more comparable to academic achievement tasks.

The growth curve of general intelligence computed either from scaled* scores (Jones & Conrad, 1933; Wechsler, 1939) or from scaled scores transformed into percentages of adult performance shows a fairly steep rise in early adolescence, which tapers off in middle adolescence until ultimate capacity is achieved (Bayley, 1939; Freeman & Flory, 1937). The tapering off is so gradual that it is difficult to tell when growth actually ceases. The best estimates, based on testing a wide age sample of a relatively homogeneous population (Jones & Conrad, 1933; Miles & Miles, 1932; Wechsler, 1944), placed the age of terminal growth in the early twenties as scores decreased thereafter.

Although reports from these studies are at variance with the widely accepted finding by Terman and Merrill (1937) that mental age ceases to increase after the age of 16 on the revised Stanford-Binet test, the results of recent longitudinal testing of adults (Bayley, 1955, 1957, 1966; Bayley & Oden, 1955; Freeman & Flory, 1937; Owens, 1953) have challenged the concept that growth in intelligence stops at an early age and then declines. Bayley (1966, 1968a, 1968b) by extending the Berkeley Growth Study curves through 36 years found that Wechsler scores increased through age 26, after which they leveled off and remained unchanged through 36 years. However, there are

---

*The purpose of scaling is to make new scores from different tests and from different age groups comparable by expressing them in such a way that at any point of the scale the distances between units of measurement are equal in difficulty values.

increments after 26 years for male scores on the verbal scale. The female scores either actually drop (performance scores) or remain unchanged (verbal scores) between 26 and 36 years.

Cattell (1963) has reported the isolation of "fluid" and "crystallized" components of intelligence. As might be anticipated, the crystallized factor consists largely of process functions, presumably not much influenced by learning or educational experience, and reaches maturity at a relatively early age. It begins to decrease sometime between 18 and 38 years (Horn & Cattell, 1966). The fluid factor, in contrast, consists more of product functions which are appreciably influenced by education and experience, and therefore reaches maturity later in life and continues to show increases in adults to 30 years of age or older (Bayley, 1970). So-called culturally disadvantaged adolescents are naturally more deficient in the fluid than in the crystallized components of intelligence.

Because intellectual growth continues to the end of the high school period and beyond for all brightness groups, it would seem reasonable to insist on compulsory school attendance until the age of 18, which is well above the minimum required in most states (Segel, 1948). The growth curves for intelligence, as well as general adolescent cognitive development, also indicate that some school subjects, which a particular child may find too difficult at the beginning of adolescence, might easily fall within his capacity several years later. This would be especially true for less bright pupils (Jersild et al., 1946).

Effect of pubescence on the growth of intelligence

The most striking feature of the growth curve for intelligence as a measurement construct during adolescence is the absence of the typical growth spurt we have seen in other aspects of adolescent development. Although youngsters suffering from pathologically precocious puberty are considerably taller and stronger than their fellows, the intellectual tendency, if any, is for them to be retarded (Keene & Stone, 1937). And in the case of intellect and judgment the lack of growth spurt concomitant with sexual maturation is even more noticeable than in the case of intelligence; since, unlike the latter, not only do these functions exhibit an indefinite period of chronological growth, but they may also be adversely affected by the emotional instability characteristic of adolescence (Ausubel, 1950).

It is true, however, that postmenarcheal girls are slightly but significantly superior to premenarcheal girls on group intelligence test scores (Stone & Barker, 1937) and that "early maturing" boys and girls both tend to surpass later maturing adolescents in intelligence during the age range from 10 to 16 (Abernathy, 1936); but since this superiority is evident before pubescence (Freeman, 1936), it can hardly be attributed to the influence of sexual maturation per se. The most likely explanation is that both intelligence and age of pubescence are positively correlated with socioeconomic status and so with each other.

Although it seems self-evident that emotional instability would impair the exercise of judgment and the orderly acquisition of subject matter, there is no convincing evidence that it interferes with the growth of intellectual capacity. Despert and Pierce (1946) did find that fluctuations in the IQ correlated with changes in emotional instability, but these fluctuations were not outside the range of the error of measurement of the test used (Harris & Thompson, 1947).

Stability of general intelligence during adolescence

The question of stability of intelligence highlights the multiple nature of mental abilities. It appears that one general class of mental abilities, which may be referred to as verbal facility and knowledge, is more stable within individuals throughout growth (Bayley, 1970). This dimension falls into Cattell's crystallized category. Other abilities such as reasoning processes, arithmetic and verbal reasoning, perhaps attention span or short-term memory, and speed fall into the fluid category and appear to be "less stable over time" (Bayley, 1970, p. 1185).

In general, mental test scores indicate variability over time in the first 3 or 4 years but become increasingly stable after that age. When the child is at the age of adolescence, test scores of general intelligence acquire a fair amount of stability. The correlation of scores of intelligence tests given at the onset of adolescence with those given at the close of adolescence is in the neighborhood of 0.80 (Anderson, 1940). From year to year this correspondence is even greater (Thorndike, 1926). Thus, although some test scores fluctuate in individual growth curves, most individuals tend to retain the same relative position in the group throughout the adolescent period (Freeman & Flory, 1927). In extreme instances, of course, there are large fluctuations in test scores; but these fluctuations tend to be associated with unusual disorganizing factors in life history (such as illness) (Honzik et al., 1948) rather than with intrinsic irregularity of growth pattern or unreliability of the measuring instrument.

For purposes of individual guidance, however, a reliability coefficient of 0.80 is not too reassuring. In dealing with a particular individual it does not suffice to know that a majority of individuals at age 18 occupy the same relative position in the group in IQ as they did at age 13. There is sufficient variability in individual growth patterns to warrant frequent and periodic testing of intelligence if test scores are to be used at all for guidance purposes.

Distribution of adolescent intelligence

Intelligence tests continue to yield normal distributions during adolescence. Variability in test scores at any age or grade level is considerable. The distribution of mental ability among 14-year-old students in New York State is represented by a range of mental ages from 10 to 18 with the mode at 14.

Surprisingly enough, despite the tremendous increase in high school enrollment from 1916 to 1940 with a corresponding elimination of the intellectual selectivity that formerly operated when only one-third of the adolescent population attended high school, there has been no drop in the mean IQ of the high school population (Cole & Hall, 1970). This phenomenon may perhaps be accounted for by greater experience that present-day students have with tests, and by the closer correspondence between current methods of school instruction and the types of capacities measured by intelligence.

Differential aspects of growth of intelligence during adolescence

Girls show a slight superiority over boys in general intelligence during early adolescence (Conrad et al., 1944; Freeman & Flory, 1937), which is related to their more precocious sexual maturation. Differences between the sexes in particular cognitive abilities tend to be larger and more significant than in tests of general intelligence. Differences, however, in most areas are equivocal. A summary of 26 studies in sex differences (Oetzel, 1962) showed that the most consistent differences are in language development, verbal fluency, and spatial abilities. In language development and verbal fluency, girls showed higher scores in 23 studies; boys showed higher scores in one, and two studies failed to mark a difference between the sexes. In spatial abilities boys came out higher in 14 studies, there were no differences between the sexes in five studies, and the girls failed to show any superiority over boys. In vocabulary, 16 studies showed no difference for the sexes, four studies indicated higher scores for boys, and eight studies showed higher scores for girls. In reasoning and numerical reasoning boys' superiority appeared in 13 studies, girls obtained higher scores in four studies, and eight studies showed no difference between the sexes (Gallagher, 1964).

Boys exhibit greater variability in IQ than girls, achieving a larger proportion of extreme scores at either end of the distribution (Mc-Nemar & Terman, 1936). Terman's 25-year longitudinal study of intellectually gifted children showed that boys more frequently than girls retained their high intellectual status as they advanced in age (Terman & Oden, 1949). Differential factors of motivation and cultural pressure can perhaps explain part of the sex difference at the upper extreme of intelligence, but they cannot very well account for differences at the lower extreme.

Impact of socioeconomic status

The influence of environmental stimulation on the development of general intelligence is fairly well established. Prior to 18 months of age, zero or low negative correlations are found between scores on infant scales and various socioeconomic factors (Bayley & Jones, 1937). Thereafter, the magnitude of correlational indices increases rapidly. Many studies have reported correlation coefficients in the neighborhood of 0.50 between school-age children's IQ and parents' occupation and education (Bayley & Jones, 1937; Goodenough, 1927; Kagan & Moss, 1959; Marks & Klahn, 1961). The early absence of relationship simply indicates that intelligence tests cannot possibly measure the same cognitive abilities during infancy as in later years. The increasing correspondence between IQ and socioeconomic variables, as degree of test overlap increases, may reflect either the cumulative impact of environmental influences or an increasing manifestation of hereditary potentialities (Bayley & Jones, 1937; Jensen, 1968).

The interpretation of these social class differences in intelligence has led to much heated controversy between hereditarians and environmentalists. Actually three kinds of explanations based respectively on measurement, environment, and genic factors seem equally plausible, but the evidence currently available is not sufficiently definitive to establish their relative weight. The measurement argument stems from a certain amount of middle-class bias in the construction of most intelligence tests. This creates test disadvantage for the lower-class child and results in an underestimate of his true level of cognitive functioning. In order to derive a valid and fair estimate of intellectual capacity from test performance, it is necessary (1) that specific test items be based on experience and symbols equally available and familiar to individuals from all social class strata; and (2) that test materials arouse comparable degrees of interest and motivation in persons of different social class origins (Davis, 1948; Eells et al., 1951).

Most present-day intelligence tests are heavily weighted with specific items that are more familiar and appealing to middle-class environments.* The tests are thus "unfair" in the sense that their specific item content does not give the lower-class a fair opportunity to demonstrate his attained level of cognitive capacity. But since intelligence tests do not purport to measure either genic potentialities per se or noncognitive abilities, they are unfair neither because they fail to measure level of functioning in those noncognitive abilities in which lower-class children excel nor because the middle-class environment is experientially or motivationally more propitious for the development of native cognitive endowment. The very fact that these tests favor middle-class children demonstrates that the environment can operate selectively to develop certain aspects of intellectual endowment. This conclusion is compatible with the findings that intelligence becomes more and more differentiated with increasing age (Garrett et al., 1935; Segel, 1948), and that the sex differences in many specific intellectual functions increase or reverse themselves as children grow older (Kuhlen, 1952).

Acceptance of the test-bias explanation of social-class differences by no means rules out the genic or environmental interpretations.† Insofar as environmental factors contribute to some of the variance in intelligence test scores, it would not be unreasonable to expect that differential social class levels of stimulation and motivation affect extent of actualization of genic environment. Evidence for this type of mediation of environmental influence comes from the finding that children's IQs are more highly correlated with parents' education than with the economic status of their homes (Bayley, 1970; Loevinger, 1943). More specifically, Lesser, Fifer, and Clark (1965) have reported some relevant class and ethnic differences in school-age children for different mental abilities. On verbal ability Jewish children scored highest, Negroes second, Chinese third, and Puerto Ricans fourth. On reasoning, the rank order was Chinese, Jews, Negroes, and Puerto Ricans. On numerical ability, the ranks were Jews, Chinese, Puerto Ricans, Negroes. On space, the order was Chinese, Jews, Puerto Ricans, Negroes. These findings raise the question of the extent to which the ethnic differences result from innate potentials or from differences among the groups in cultural value systems and hence in differential rewards for skills in mental abilities tested (Bay-

---

* Large socioeconomic differences, however, prevail also for other nonverbal tests.

† The finding that approximately the same social class differentials appear on the Davis-Eells "Culture Fair" test as on the Kuhlmann-Finch test (Coleman & Ward, 1955) casts doubt on the claim that the Davis-Eells test is culturally more fair, but does not necessarily invalidate the test bias hypothesis of social class difference.

ley, 1970). The environmentalist position with respect to social class differences in cognitive development is weakened, however, by the existence of large social class differences in the preschool period (Terman & Merrill, 1937), by the failure of social class differentials to increase with advancing age (Shuttleworth, 1940), and by the significantly greater correlation of foster children's IQ with true mothers' than with foster parents' educational status (Honzik, 1957; Skodak, 1939; Skodak & Skeels, 1949).

General level of environmental stimulation affects the growth of intelligence in a variety of ways. Children of parents in upper occupational levels maintain a constant superiority of about 10 IQ points over children coming from lower-class homes during the ages of 8 to 18 (Shuttleworth, 1940). And in instances of extreme deprivation (for example, Kentucky and Tennessee mountain children), there is a progressive decline in IQ level as the children advance from middle childhood to adolescence (Asher, 1935; Wheeler, 1932).

Closely related to socioeconomic differences in intellectual level is the impact of continued schooling on the growth of intelligence. Follow-up studies of children matched for IQ in the eighth grade indicate that even 20 years later reliable differences in intelligence test scores appear in favor of those who attended high school (Lorge, 1945). Nevertheless, schooling did not appreciably alter the relative positions of the individuals on the original ordering of IQs determined in the eighth grade. More impressive are the findings that in a number of subtests involving reasoning and abstract ability, improvement continues until the end of the college period (Hartson, 1936; Rogers, 1930; Shuey, 1948; Thorndike, 1948). Furthermore, the particular areas in which greatest improvement occurs (for example, verbal or numerical ability) seem to depend on the area of specialization in college (Hartson, 1936). It is therefore difficult to avoid the implication that schooling differentially influences the growth of the more complex components of verbal intelligence.

Growth differences between bright and dull adolescents

The growth curve for intelligence is not identical for bright and dull individuals. Although the terminal age of intellectual growth is the same for both groups (Conrad et al., 1944), the bulk of the evidence (based on studies of changes in the variability of the distribution of intelligence test scores with increasing age) indicates that the bright tend to grow away from the dull (Conrad et al., 1944; Richardson & Stokes, 1933; Turstone & Ackerson, 1927). In addition, there are qualitative differences between bright and dull adolescents of comparable mental age in several intellectual subabilities tested by various achievement tests. The bright surpass the dull on items requiring abstraction, a large vocabulary, differentiation of subtle shades of meaning, imagination, and generalization (Purvis, 1938). There is evidence that some kinds of intelligence increase well into middle age and perhaps beyond, not only for the bright but also for the dull (Bayley, 1970). Bayley (1936) found continued increases in scores through 36 years for the lowest scoring half of the Berkeley Growth Study sample. The increase was found for the lowest scoring males, whose IQs on the Wechsler scales increased from 64 at 16 years to 80 at 36 years. McCulloch (1957) found evidence of increased scores on verbal tests through 30 years or longer on mentally retarded institutionalized adults.

The implications of these findings are that "dull" students need not drop out of high school at the tenth grade as they frequently do at present, but could profit from schooling until the age of 18 and beyond. To maximize the benefit that such students can derive from continued instruction, the more difficult subjects could be placed at the end of the high school curriculum, and abstract materials could be concretized and made more meaningful in terms of life situations (Segal, 1948). Moreover, in order to recognize the peculiar capacities of these individuals and help them achieve success rather than failure, the school needs to provide for them a wide variety of learning activities (Segel, 1948).

Growth differences among separate intellectual abilities

Subtest analysis of various tests of intellectual ability shows that several important differences exist in the rate of growth, age of terminal growth, and rate of decline among the component subabilities.

Simple rote memory (memory span) reaches an earlier peak of development than general intelligence (Conrad et al., 1944), vocabulary, or arithmetical ability (Garrett et al., 1935), but this is not true of more perceptive and analytical types of memory (Jones & Conrad, 1933). During the preadolescent and adolescent periods, vocabulary and ability to dissect sentences grow at a more rapid rate than reasoning ability despite identical rates of growth during early and middle childhood (Conrad et al., 1944). Ability on the analogies test reaches an earlier terminal growth than on either the completions or opposites test. On the other hand, ability declines earlier for such functions as analogies and completions than for vocabulary and general information (Douvan & Gold, 1966; Jones & Conrad, 1933).

In conclusion, it appears that in general the more complex intellectual abilities have a more gradual rate of growth, reach maturity at a later age (Bradway & Thompson, 1962), but show evidence of decline earlier in life.

Differentiation of intellectual ability in adolescence

As already suggested, the concept of general intelligence is much less meaningful in adolescence than in childhood because of the increasing differentiation of intellectual ability that takes place. By the time an individual reaches adolescence, differential factors of interest, relative ability, specialization of training, motivation, success and failure experiences, and cultural expectation operate selectively to develop certain abilities and to leave others relatively undeveloped. Children with highly "differentiated" mothers (Dyk & Witkin, 1965) tend to undergo most differentiation. Original aptitude and experience seem to reinforce each other in circular fashion since children who are gifted in a particular area benefit differentially from instruction in that area (Lesser et al., 1962). However, inasmuch as considerable interrelatedness among different cognitive functions still remains (Schulman & Havighurst, 1947), evidence of increasing differentiation at the older age levels does not render the concept of general intelligence completely untenable. Furthermore, relatively high correlations between intelligence test scores obtained in the primary grades and retest scores obtained during adolescence indicate that there is much overlapping between the factors determining early level of general cognitive ability and later level of differentiated cognitive ability.

For practical purposes an intelligence test score has less utility after preadolescence than during the early elementary school years. The older child's and adolescent's relative standing in one ability has relatively little predictive value for their relative standing in another ability; and composite scores on intelligence tests are not very useful for predicting performance in a particular school subject. Much more meaningful than a total score is a profile showing the relative standing of an individual on a wide variety of basic intellectual abilities. Thurstone's test of "primary mental abilities," for example, provides such a profile. By expressing intelligence in terms of the smallest number of relatively "pure" and independent factors, it gives a much more definitive, convenient, and quantifiable qualitative analysis of cognitive ability than could be obtained from examination of the protocol of the more traditional Binet-type scale composed of batteries of heterogeneous subtests.

In conclusion, therefore, it can be stated that when differential aptitude batteries, purporting to measure only the relatively few and well-established "primary mental abilities" are used, they probably have more predictive value for the particular kinds of subject matter achievement for which they are relevant than do composite scores on tests of general intelligence or of general scholastic aptitude. However, the latter tests, as McNemar (1964) points out, are not completely without psychological significance or predictive value. In fact, they are more useful for predicting complex criteria of academic achievement, involving interaction among several abilities, than are even the well-established differential aptitude batteries, and are incomparably more useful than are differential aptitude batteries consisting of unvalidated factors of or factors manifesting little generality of function.

The increased differentiation of intellectual ability during adolescence is a general phenomenon, but also varies in relation to many differential factors. Segel's evidence (1948) shows that differentiation among intellectual traits is greater for bright than for dull adolescents. Intellectual abilities are also differentiated along social class and sex lines and as a result of prolonged or specialized education. Especially interesting are data indicating that superiority in a given function, reflecting higher general ability at a younger age level, may undergo reversal during adolescence as a result of differentiation. For example, girls have higher language and arithmetical ability than boys at the beginning of adolescence, but boys surpass them in arithmetical ability before the close of adolescence (Kuhlen, 1952). Children from upper socioeconomic groups are superior to lower-class children on tests of both verbal and mechanical ability at age 10, but at age 16 retain their superiority only on the verbal tests (Havighurst & Janke, 1944; Janke & Havighurst, 1945).

This progressive differentiation of mental ability requires a correspondingly increasing differentiation of curricular offerings. As Segel (1948) points out, a core curriculum is better suited to the intellectual organization of junior than senior high school students. Another consequence of this increasing differentiation apparent from studies of school dropouts is that between the ages of 10 and 14 maladjustment through lack of general mental ability is an item of importance among the factors causing youth to leave school. However, between the ages of 15 and 18 such maladjustment does not result in large numbers of youth leaving school.

Interaction between intellectual growth and personality

The impact of intellectual growth on adolescent personality development has been considered in large measure in the preceding three chapters. The acquisition of greater cognitive powers contributes to the need for more volitional independence, sharpens the child's perception of the environment, enables him to formulate more abstract and generalized moral values, and alters cultural expectations of the level of maturity appropriate for him. In all probability, the effects of intellectual growth on personality development are just as important as the changes they induce in cognitive organization per se.

Changes in personality organization also bring about marked changes in learning orientation. These changes in mode of acquiring values are also as significant as the increased capacity to assimilate more objective kinds of cognitive data.

Last, some relationship exists between intelligence and (1) interests, success, and adjustment, and (2) individual personality traits. The former relationship is probably a reflection of the fact that level of intelligence is one of many variables that influence the outcome of these other phenomena. The relationship to individual personality traits, on the other hand, is probably not indicative of any intrinsic association between intelligence and character but instead reflects the operation of certain relatively extraneous considerations.

Intelligence and personality

Numerous investigations concur in the finding that various personality traits such as reliability, perseverance, independence, and emotional stability are positively correlated with intelligence (Cattell, 1945; Terman & Oden, 1949). Striking differences between intellectually gifted and average children are found in these character traits. However, there is no reason to believe that the development of character and of intelligence are organically related in terms of the factors that impinge on their respective growth processes. Cattell's summary of the types of personality traits associated with intelligence sheds considerable light on some of the more adventitious reasons for this relationship: "It looks as if intelligence is directly more associated with character conceived in a narrow, self-conscious sense, and with regard to habits that are acquired later and through conscious ideals, rather than with basic emotional integration and goodness of character in the wider sense as might result from the emotional adjustment derived from the upbringing of the first few years or from relatively constitutional stability" (Cattell, 1945, p. 141).

The following factors probably contribute to the positive relationship between intelligence and some personality traits. (1) Brighter children are better able to perceive the expectations of their culture and to learn appropriate forms of conduct. They can also perceive more accurately which character traits are required for success. (2)

The personality traits that correlate most highly with intelligence are also most highly prized by middle-class homes; and, as already pointed out, intelligence test scores are positively related to social class status. (3) The wide variability in the degree to which the academic work output of children is responsive to an incentive of social prestige (Ausubel, 1951) suggests that this factor may influence in part the extent to which an individual's genetic endowment of verbal intelligence is functionally actualized. Highly motivated children tend to be persistent, stable, and responsible, on the one hand, and to make the most of their intellectual endowment in terms of IQ score.* That more intelligent children seem to be more honest is less a function of superior moral beliefs than of such relatively extraneous factors as less need to cheat to pass examinations, superior ability to avoid detection, and greater astuteness in estimating the chances of "getting caught."

Intelligence and interest patterns

Although intellectual achievement (as measured by subject matter achievement tests) tends to be unrelated to broad categories of interests (scientific, mechanical, pervasive, clerical) measured by such standard interest inventories as that of Kuder and Strong (Cronbach, 1970; Triggs, 1946), more subtle qualitative differences between the interest patterns of bright and dull adolescents have been uncovered. As could be reasonably expected, brighter individuals exhibit greater range and variability in their choice of hobbies and activities (Lewis, 1941; Sumpton & Luecking, 1960), participate more frequently in intellectual activities (Lehman & Witty, 1928; Sumpton & Luecking, 1960), and are more apt to acquire collections of objects demanding complex classification (Durost, 1932; Sumpton & Luecking, 1960). They also show greater interest than their duller contemporaries in solitary pursuits requiring serious cerebration (Lehman & Witty, 1927, 1928; Rice, 1974). Throughout adolescence and preadolescence they do much more extracurricular reading, and their reading interests achieve a higher level of maturity (Lehman & Witty, 1928; Scharf, 1973; Thorndike, 1941).

All of these differences in favor of bright individuals follow directly from their possession of sufficient intellectual capacity to support the interests. Everything else being equal, most persons naturally

---

*High motivation could conceivably raise IQ by actually stimulating the development of verbal intelligence and by yielding maximal performance in test situations (Ausubel, 1951b).

develop those interests that they can prosecute most successfully. Within a given individual quite a high relationship exists between hierarchies of interests and abilities (Thorndike, 1917), which results in mutual reinforcement and accounts in part for the greater differentiation of ability with increasing age.

Intelligence and adjustment

Intelligence level is obviously a factor contributing to the individual's ability to adjust to his environment. The brighter person has more resources in solving problems of adaptation and (other things being equal) is, therefore, less likely to experience frustration and failure. Intellectually gifted children* surpass children of average ability on all measures of adjustment (Lessinger & Martinson, 1961; Terman & Oden, 1949), whereas extremely dull children acquire many typical distortions of behavior that reflect the different ways in which they attempt to compensate for their school failure and social isolation.

Because of the high price that adolescents place on intelligence, as reflected in the things they mention as increasingly important in their self-estimate (Jersild, 1946) and in the attributes desirable in the opposite sex (Mather, 1934; Purdue Opinion Panel, 1961), inferior intellectual ability (just like physical unattractiveness) constitutes a definite handicap to which some adjustment must be made. One of the commonest forms of adjustment is self-delusion or inhibition of the self-critical ability. This is reflected in the fact that (1) high school students regard "lack of brains" as one of the least important causes of school failure (Gilbert, 1931), and (2) a larger percentage of students making poorer than better scores on academic aptitude tests are less inclined to believe that the test scores are truly reflective of their actual ability (Snyder, 1937).

Although a larger proportion of the low-scoring individuals are also opposed to reporting test results to students and deny that knowledge of score affects performance (Snyder, 1937), awareness of low standing apparently motivates increased academic efforts (Mitchell, 1934; Ross, 1938). However, with certain individuals who both lack intrinsic feelings of adequacy and entertain high opinions of their mental ability, knowledge of low or average IQ score may have considerable traumatic effect on self-esteem. Because of the almost su-

---

*Hollingworth (1942) points out, however, that children with extremely high IQs tend to be maladjusted by the social isolation that their intellectual superiority imposes on them.

perstitious awe in which the IQ is frequently held such reports are sometimes accepted as possessing the same reliability and catastrophic implications as a diagnosis of cancer or tuberculosis and therefore precipitate acute anxiety.

Increased intelligence creates as well as helps solve problems. The bright individual is sensitive to many disconcerting and threatening elements in the environment that do not disturb the equanimity of the duller person. The greater complexity of his existence provides an additional source of strain. On the other hand, the destructive potential of strain can only be estimated in terms of the capacity for resistance to stress. The possession of greater resources for coping with the environment offsets much of the strain that increased sensitivity would otherwise create for more able persons. Thus the bright and the dull tend to have distinctive types of adjustment problems (Levy, 1931; Wile & Davis, 1939) which differ both in level of complexity and in the sophistication of the adaptive resources brought to them.

Despite these characteristic differences in degree and quality of adjustment level for individuals near but not at the very extreme of the distribution of intelligence, there is little relationship between these two variables in the middle range of intelligence which accounts for 90 percent or more of the population (Conrad et al., 1944; Jersild et al., 1946).

> The reason for this is, of course, that the importance of intellectual status is usually relative to what is expected of a person and what he himself wants. . . . At least five factors are involved in the relation between intelligence and adjustment. These are the child's absolute level of intelligence; the level of intelligence required in the activities toward which he is being pointed through the ambitions of his family and friends; the social pressures which arise from such ambitions; his own "felt needs" and level of aspiration; and his actual achievment. These factors are interconnected in a variety of ways and a great variety of complex patterns may result. (Conrad et al., 1944, p. 180)

The complexity of the relationship between intelligence and adjustment is therefore not to be underestimated. It is apparent that a bright individual may have an overambitious level of aspiration, may be subjected to excessive family or social pressure, may underachieve for a large variety of reasons other than lack of intelligence, and may have little resistance to strain. On the other hand, other things being equal, it is also apparent that by virtue of greater ability such an individual is less likely than his less gifted contemporary (1) to aspire to goals far in excess of innate capacity, (2) to experience excessive failure and frustration, and (3) to lack the necessary resources to combat stressful and anxiety-producing situations. For these reasons he does not risk overtaxing his frustration tolerance as rapidly. Hence, complete lack of relationship between these two variables throughout the middle range of intelligence is somewhat surprising and suggests that the situation is at least in part a test of the inadequacy and grossness of available measures of adjustment. Given instruments capable of more subtle measurements of adjustment, the low but positive relationship that is theoretically indicated might conceivably emerge.

Another related problem is the relationship between intelligence and success. In academic achievement, success in various subject matter fields generally correlates near 0.5 with intelligence or academic aptitude test scores. Thus, although the two factors are obviously related, much room is left for the operation of personality variables.

As a group, intellectually superior individuals tend to gravitate toward professional occupations, to be more succesful vocationally, and to experience less unemployment (Pressey & Robinson, 1944; Terman & Oden, 1949). Within a group of gifted children (IQs over 140), however, Terman and Oden found that the adults successful 25 years later were as children more integrated in goal structure, more self-confident, and more persevering than the unsuccessful adults, but that the two groups were quite evenly matched in intelligence (Terman & Oden, 1949). We can conclude that better-than-average intelligence is undoubtedly a vocational asset, but that beyond this, unusual success in a vocation is more a function of special talent and of various personality traits than of extremely high general intelligence. There is no evidence that would indicate that creativity and general intelligence are positively related beyond this critical minimal point.

ADOLESCENT INTERESTS

Nature

The general topic of adolescent interests is introduced in this chapter because these are an important product of the interaction between intellectual growth and personality development. This was evident in the discussion of the relationship between intelligence and interests. We shall examine here only (1) certain general characteristics of adolescent interests and their determinants, and (2) those recreational interests with strong cognitive or intellectual components. Specific social, vocational, motor, and school interests are considered in appropriate chapters.

Meaning and importance

Interests can be legitimately regarded as motives in the sense that they are selective determinants of behavior and reflect the direction and relative strength of valences associated with different objects and activities in the individual's psychological world. Practically, however, since they reflect only the selective aspect of motivation, it is more convenient to regard them as organizers of the psychological field and to restrict the term *motive* to the discriminable properties of the goal attributes of behavior.

Viewed within this conceptual framework, then, the psychological field of any individual can be divided into different concentric zones reflecting varying degrees of intensity of ego involvement. The more central zones are areas of concern and importance to him. He has a vital stake in them. What happens in these areas is a source of pride or shame, of feelings of success or failure. Because of a selective perceptual and cognitive sensitization to these segments of the environment, they acquire a high degree of differentiation. Peripheral zones, on the other hand, are poorly differentiated and are regarded with indifference. Failure in such areas is easily sloughed off, and success does not inspire elation.

But this map identifies only the areas and activities (interests) with which the individual is concerned. It does not make explicit the reasons (motives) for his concern. The motivation for some ego-involved activities may in fact be entirely unrelated to ego enhancement, being energized solely by a need to acquire mastery or to discover a valid solution to a problem (exploratory orientation). The outcome is naturally attended by feelings of success or failure, but self-esteem is not primarily affected. Other interests may be prosecuted as a source of either derived (satellizing orientation) or earned (incorporative orientation) status. In the former instance, the underlying motive is to gain approval or vicarious status from the person with whom the satellizing relationship is established or to make manifest feelings of personal loyalty to him. In the latter instance, the underlying motive is the acquisition of extrinsic self-esteem by means of superior achievement. Social recognition or applause obviously enhances earned status, but self-enhancement can take place even when achievement is anonymous, through the simple expedient of an individual competing with himself (Ausubel, 1951).

In addition to their role as selective organizers of the psychological field, interests are also valuable indices of developmental maturity. In a given cultural environment interest patterns undergo characteristic shifts at different stages of development. Thus, despite considerable variability and overlapping between age groups (which reflect individual differences), fairly regular and predictable developmental changes occur. On the basis of interest patterns it is possible to make a general assessment of maturity that takes into account intellectual, social, and personality growth.

The selective process inherent in interests can also be put to another useful diagnostic purpose. Selectivity is never accidental. Particular interests (apart from limitations of capacity and opportunity) always reflect individual personality trends (introversion-extroversion, egocentricity-sociocentricity, subtlety or grossness of perception), and the relationship is invariably a reciprocal one. Participation in certain activities is, therefore, a determinant as well as a reflection of given personality characteristics.

General characteristics

Compared to those in preadolescence, interests during adolescence show both continuity and modification. Many of the activities of childhood are continued into adolescence but assume more complex or organized form: e.g., sports, games, reading, interest in mass media (Kuhlen, 1952; Lehman & Witty, 1927). Other activities are continued but for different reasons. Thus, during adolescence, interests become less ends in themselves and more means by which earned status, social prestige, heterosexual effectiveness, or prevocational competence is attained. Changes in interest patterns, however, lack the characteristic abruptness of the physical alterations of pubescence since they depend on more complex pheonomena than shifts in internal hormonal balance.

Although less abrupt in onset than physical changes of adolescence, interest patterns show a deceleration in rate of change. This is as true of vocational interests, which become moderately stable after age 17 (Cronbach, 1970), as of the more generalized interests. In general, stability during high school is perhaps as good as in college, points out Cronbach citing empirical evidence (Mallinson & Crumbine, 1952; Rosenberg, 1953; Tutton, 1955). Using a 98-item inventory (including Kuder and Strong inventories) eight times, Vallasekova (1971) at the Comenius University in Czechoslovakia found in her 4-year study of the patterns and changes of interests in ninety 11- to 13-year-olds at the beginning of the study that factors most saturated by sports, technical constructive activities, and manual and intellectual activities were fairly fixed as early as age 12, and represented an important part of adolescents' activities. Cunningham et al. (1968) studied 1695 males over a 16-year period. They tabulated 34 activities by age (16 to 29, 30 to 39, 40 to 49, 50 to 59, 60 to 69). In approximately half of the activities, participation decreased as age increased. However, the activities in which the younger men participated were similar to those in which the older ones participated. These statements and findings run contrary to earlier impressions that adolescent interests reflect short-lived fads and intense but transitory enthusiasms. Within the age span covered by the study of Cunningham et al., the strenuous leisure activities were low at all age levels.

The total amount of time available for recreation decreases during adolescence because of the encroachment of other responsibilities, such as study, work, and traveling to school or work. More important are changes in the content of recreational activities. Interests that promote social contact with the opposite sex (dancing, dating, parties) are increasingly valued, whereas interests requiring strenuous activity decline, as mentioned above. However, Dowell (1959) through an information checklist administered to 1830 college freshmen and sophomores concluded that college-age students tend to participate more often in physical activities than in sedentary activities. This finding is also in conflict with results of earlier empirical studies (Bell, 1938; Dimock, 1937; Lehman & Witty, 1927). Outdoor sports become more complex and highly organized and are motivated more by considerations of social prestige with members of both sexes. The loss of interest in physical activities is quite abrupt among girls.

The number of recreational activities indulged in drops markedly with increasing age. This is in part a reflection of (1) the trend toward increased selectivity, canalization, and differentiation of interests and abilities, and (2) the decreased availability of leisure time. In part, however, it is indicative only of the growing complexity and formalization of adolescent activities. Many "kid" games and "gang" activities are abandoned simply because they are too informal and so seem juvenile. Other simpler single activities, such as running, throwing, and dodging, become incorporated into more complex games involving both individual activity, such as swimming and bowling, and team activity, such as baseball, basketball, and football (Blumenfeld, 1965).

Determinants of interests

The foregoing changes in interest patterns characteristic of the adolescent period are attributable to the two major kinds of variables we have dealt with thus far—psychobiological and psychosocial. In the first category belong factors that are relatively universal in cultural distribution. These factors (pubescence, intellectual maturation) are responsible for the more general changes in direction and content of adolescent interests, namely, their increased reference to social sex themes and to earned status as the underlying motivation, their decelerating rate of change, and their increased complexity and lability. In the second category belong factors that are more specific to a given social environment and account for differences among cultures, subcultures, and social classes. These differences are the product of differential cultural expectations. Sex differences in interest patterns, for example, for the most part reflect institutionalized concepts of social sex role.

In this section we shall also consider determinants of differences between the interest patterns of individuals of comparable developmental status who share the same social environment.

IMPACT OF PUBESCENCE

Pubescence exerts both direct and indirect influences on adolescent interests. Directly—by lowering the threshold of awareness for sexual stimuli and by contributing to the evolution of sexual drives—it is largely responsible for the increased interest in social activities with heterosexual reference.* Indirectly—by modifying cultural expectations of appropriate behavior for children at this stage of development—it leads to the deemphasis of certain juvenile activities and to the encouragement of more mature interests. This influence is evident in the positive correlation between developmental age (maturity level of interests) on the one hand and height (Furfey, 1931) and androgenic content of boys' urine on the other (Sollenberger, 1940). Postpubescent boys and girls also achieve higher scores on tests of developmental age than their prepubescent contemporaries, (Carey, 1935; Stone & Barker, 1937) and postmenarcheal girls exceed premenarcheal girls of matched chronological age in their concern with adornment and heterosexual social activities and in their aversion to vigorous physical activity (Stone & Barker, 1939).

That pubescence alone is not responsible for all of the changes in adolescent interest patterns, especially those not relating to heterosexual social activities, is evident from the absence of significant differences between the play interests of prepubescent and postpubescent boys of similar chronological age (Dimock, 1937). Also, although

---

* Some of the differences in heterosexual social activities between pre- and postpubescent individuals are less a direct reflection of increased hormonal stimulation than of physical advantages associated therewith (height), which makes such activities as dancing, dating, and automobile driving more feasible and socially acceptable.

adolescent and preadolescent boys do differ in their play interests, the very gradual transition in interest patterns (in contrast to the relative abruptness of physical changes) suggests that other variables are involved in this developmental process. A large number of preadolescent interests that are not obviously inappropriate will survive because of the inertia from canalization. Once the psychological world of the individual is selectively organized into zones of different ego involvement, reciprocal channels of reinforcement increase differentiation in the same direction unless there are compelling forces of an antagonistic nature.

SEX DIFFERENCES

Differences in adolescent interest patterns of the sexes are influenced chiefly by the different cultural expectations of the appropriate social sex roles of boys and girls. To a lesser extent, they reflect differences in age of pubescence and in gross motor skills. Hence, although the general trends in social and physical interests are the same for both sexes, the heterosexual social interests of girls emerge at an earlier age, and the interests of boys in active sports do not begin to wane until middle and late adolescence. The greater concern of girls with matters of personal attractiveness and of boys with vocational and money matters reflects differential social pressures (Chabassol & Thomas, 1969; Symonds, 1936).

During adolescence, lines defining activities and roles traditionally considered appropriate for a single sex group were until recently more sharply drawn. The increased feminism, however, of recent years has decreased sex typing of adolescent interests.

SOCIAL ENVIRONMENT

The influence of gross social and cultural factors (differences in national culture, urban-rural differences) on the development of interests is self-evident. Differences in the physical environment, in the availability of recreational materials and participants, and, most important, in the prevailing values, conventions, and expectations of the cultural group impose many specific characteristics on the general developmental picture. For example, compared with their urban contemporaries, rural children participate more in solitary, outdoors, and collecting activities and are required by the low density of population to play less organized and less formal games embracing a wider age range of participants (Lehman & Witty 1928; Witty & Lehman, 1933).

Social class and race differences in interest patterns somewhat reflect discrepancies in purchasing power, but the differences in values have been considerably decreased. A study by Brough and

Reeves (1968) of 238 inner-city ninth graders and 382 ninth graders from a high socioeconomic suburb showed that the organizations, activities, and mass media to which these two groups of adolescents were exposed and of which they took advantage were surprisingly similar. The differences that did exist seemed to be related more to family income than to basic differences in the desires of the youngsters.

INDIVIDUAL DIFFERENCES

More important perhaps than differences among contrasting groups (racial, rural-urban, sex, educational, socioeconomic) are differences among individual adolescents with similar group affiliations. Such individual differences reflect variability in (1) the distribution of human abilities (motor, intellectual); (2) those aspects of personality organization determining selectivity in tastes; (3) the unique experiential background of every individual (in the types of activities to which he is exposed); and (4) the types of activities that are encouraged and rewarded by significant persons in each child's familial, school, and peer group environment.

Original proclivities for certain activities (based on differences in ability and personality makeup) perpetuate themselves by leading to successful and satisfying experiences, frequent practice, and hence to greater enhancement of the ability or trait. Through canalization, perceptual sensitization, and progressive differentiation of the psychological field, increasing selectivity in ordering ego involvements becomes a characteristic feature of psychological development. Relative degree of interest in a given activity is most likely a good criterion of level of ability in that activity—but only in the heirarchy of abilities within an individual, not within a group of individuals (Cronbach, 1970; Thorndike, 1917). Sometimes, however, such degree of interest more faithfully reflects differences in the hierarchy of rewards associated with different activities.

The relationship between interests and activities is a reciprocal one. Just as interests stimulate related activities, activities undertaken without any special interest may inspire such interest retroactively. Similarly, in the course of involvement, the motivation for an interest may change (the exploratory orientation may supplant or replace the incorporative orientation or vice versa).

During infancy and early childhood, as Jersild (1947) points out, what a child does and is interested in doing is almost completely a reflection of what he is able to do. Later, opportunity, stimulation, and differential reward become equally important. Thus, the older child or adolescent exercises only some of his potential capacities, and his expressed interests can no longer be considered coextensive with the potential range of interests he is capable of developing with appropriate stimulation. For these reasons, the tendency to regard the expressed interests of the individual at any given moment as "sacrosanct" and representative of his "true" needs and capacities is not defensible on logical grounds. Needs and interests do not simply "unfold" during development from the impetus supplied by internal maturational factors. At all times they represent the interaction between genic predispositions and environmental influences.

The teleological notions that only "endogenously derived" needs are genuine and worthwhile and that only the individual "knows" what is best for him and can suitably select what he truly needs are supported neither by logic nor by facts. They have been uncritically extrapolated from experiments with animals and human infants that indicate that in certain instances spontaneously selected foods best meet nutritional requirements.

Accordingly, an educational policy of using adolescents' interests should be aimed to help adolescents to cultivate and to acquire the most rewarding interests and should not be bound by the particular interests that adolescents happen to have acquired (Jersild, 1947).

RECREATIONAL INTERESTS

Some of the general changes in the interest patterns of adolescents can be illustrated by specific recreational activities that reflect both intellectual growth and characteristic shifts in the relative appeal value of different aspects of the cognitive field.

Reading

The adolescent does more reading than the preadolescent (Johnson, 1932), and reading among adolescents increases with grade. Seniors appear to read more materials on a regular basis (Scharf, 1973). The adolescent reads discriminately, critically, and purposefully (Lehman & Witty, 1927; Terman & Lima, 1927; Weintraub et al., 1974). His more critical and serious tastes in reading are illustrated by an increasing preference for nonfiction, for informational books dealing with politics and economics (Brink, 1939), for higher quality magazines (Elder & Carpenter, 1939), for magazine articles concerning world events and political news (Johnson, 1932; Jones & Conrad, 1944; Purdue Opinion Panel, 1959), and for the news, editorial, and society sections of the newspaper (Johnson, 1932; Scharf, 1973). At the same time he desires more adult fiction (Weintraub et al., 1974) and humor in books and magazines, and his interest in juvenile fiction and in magazine content dealing with westerns, detective stories, and motion picture stars declines (Jones & Conrad, 1944). All of these changes reflect (1) increased intellectual maturity, (2) expanding interest in the wider cultural environment embracing real persons and social problems, and (3) growing concern with self-improvement as an instrument for acquiring earned status.

Weitraub et al. (1974) point out that Johnson's summary of data obtained from the National Literature Assessment Survey revealed that females read more than males, whites read more than blacks, people in suburbs read more than those in the inner city, and those whose parents had higher education read more than those whose parents had lower education. Analysis of the last difference showed that the difference increased with age.

The New York Times fact-finding project (Freiberger, 1974) about reading by teenagers revealed a new trend. It showed that 24 percent of the readers evince a growing interest in the occult, witchcraft, magic, spiritualism, astrology, and the bizarre. Eleven percent are interested in problems of the 1970s. Ten percent are reading more serious advanced materials. Overall ratings by 7000 librarians and English chairmen of secondary and intermediate schools revealed that fiction-novel remains most popular, followed by mystery-suspense, science fiction, and biography-autobiography, with about 40 percent of the top 25 books having been written for adults.

Mass media

The recreational activities of the modern adolescent are increasingly dominated by the numerous varieties of mass media available (Lyness, 1952). During the junior high school period television watching rates higher than listening to the radio. However, during the high school years the popularity of the radio increases, and adolescents listen to the radio 1 to 3 hours each day (Hurlock, 1973), and even more extensively in conjunction with studying, reading, driving and talking. Baranowski's review (1971) of the research on television viewing time indicates that the "typical" high school student watches somewhere between 13 and 20 hours during any given week. Although competition of television and cost have reduced movie popularity, movies still are popular for dating and a welcome deviation from boredom from studies and other recreational activities available (Hurlock, 1973).

Major sources of news during adolescence are television, radio, and newspapers (Desjardins, 1972), and changes in movie, radio, and television interests closely parallel those for reading. Boys choose sports, car stories, mystery, and humor, whereas girls choose novels and historical romance (Desjardins, 1972). An abrupt increase in the popularity of dance music and popular songs on the radio reflects the intense absorption with heterosexual social activities.

The gain in critical judgment is reflected in tasks related to mass media as in reading, in greater insistence on subtlety in humor, and on plausibility, restraint, and ingenuity in the creation of suspense and dramatic plot (Abbott, 1937a, 1937b).

Hobbies

An analysis of the types of hobbies (constructions and collections) of adolescents gives another good index of the change in adolescent interest patterns. Construction and collecting interests, like reading interests, become noticeably more purposeful and discriminating during adolescence. Constructive hobbies (remaking cars, bicycles, musical instruments, furniture, and books for boys; and clothing, jewelry, and pottery for girls) lose their appeal for the adolescent as he grows older, as he takes a more critical attitude toward his workmanship and the hobbies' lack of functionality in relation to his social needs (Hurlock, 1973). The number of collections per individual diminishes, but those maintained are likewise related to actual interests and to envisaged needs. Changes in content are also consistent with the general trend of adolescent interests. Marbles, coins, stamps, and beads give way to letters, photographs, phonograph records, old magazines, and theatre or athletic programs. Girls add to the list costumes and jewelry, souvenirs of parties, and beauty aids (Hurlock, 1973; Kuhlen, 1963).

11

Adolescents and the Wider Community

Under the heading of psychosocial problems we shall consider the more specific aspects of adolescent development attributable to the unique social conditions within a given culture. These problems reflect differences rather than uniformities in the developmental process between cultures. The chief sources and categories of psychosocial problems are cataloged in Chapter 2. Problems such as these, characteristic of adolescent development in modern Western civilization, were at one time considered inevitable and universal consequences of man's biological heritage. Only relatively recently, since the emergence of cultural anthropology as a scientific discipline, have we come to regard these problems as unique by-products of the specific values, socioeconomic conditions, and training institutions presently current in our society. Viewed within the perspective of numerous studies of the comparative ethnology of adolescence, the specific problems confronting adolescents are apparently to a large extent culturally conditioned (Sherif & Cantril, 1947).

At this point it might be reasonable to inquire why the problems discussed in the preceding chapters on motor, somatic, personality, moral, and intellectual development could not be legitimately characterized as psychosocial. Is it not true, for example, that the very determination of the content as well as the significance of a somatic deviation is socially conditioned; that it is meaningless to consider the problems of emancipation or personality maturation apart from the matrix of social factors in which they are embedded? The answer is that a psychobiological problem is only a classificatory abstraction

that has no phenomenological existence. By definition it reflects commonality in process or principle which is universally true only when
expressed in such a highly generalized form that it corresponds to no
actual situation anywhere. That is, there are general principles of adolescent development which transcend cultural boundaries. But since
discussion of such principles in abstract form not only would be artificial, but also would present almost insuperable difficulties to comprehension, it has been convenient to consider them in the setting of
present-day American culture. We have so far discussed universal
problems of adolescent development—problems theoretically rooted
in a common culture-free base of physiological, personality, and intellectual change—as manifested in the particular social environment
that is most familiar to us.

How do such psychobiological problems differ from genuine psychosocial problems when given social reference? In the concluding
seven chapters of this book we shall be concerned with three main
categories of psychosocial problems. The first are problems that
possess very little universality because they do not stem from basic
features of adolescent development but owe their origin to the particular way in which a given society undertakes to handle or control the
period of adolescence. Such problems, e.g., schooling, vocational,
and peer group, are, in other words, essentially "handling" rather
than growth problems, and are not likely to exhibit any features in
common with those of dissimilar cultures. Emancipation from
parents, on the other hand, is a universal theme of adolescent development with specific variations in every culture. The second type of
psychosocial problems are those that do arise from universal developmental needs (for example, sexual expression) but depend almost entirely on specific social conditions for their mode of gratification.
Apart from the existence of the basic need, there is no developmental
uniformity from culture to culture at the level of implementation. In
addition to these two types of psychosocial problems, which arise
from directed social efforts to regulate the adolescent transitional
period—whether they consist of primitive initiation ceremonies or
complex educational processes—other general characteristics of a social order bear no specific or intended relation to the regulation of
adolescence but nevertheless affect its development profoundly. For
example, what effect do war, affluence, depression, rapid social
change, conflicting cultural values, and restriction of employment opportunities have on the nature of adolescence?

We shall, therefore, be dealing in the following chapters with the
unique problems of the American adolescent. We will not use his
problems to illustrate more universal developmental principles that

have widespread generality despite specific cultural patterning. This will be the story of adolescents who are denied membership in adult society, who create an elaborate, semi-independent interim subculture of their own, who undergo prolonged schooling and vocational apprenticeship, who live in a world of rapid social change and of conflicting moral ideologies, and who are often expected to submit to prolonged sexual control and postponement of marriage (Davis et al., 1949). We shall not be concerned with general attributes of personality maturation, with level of ego aspiration, with degree of volitional independence, with type of status sought, with the quality of striving, with the mode of assimilating values. Instead we shall try to ascertain how, within the framework of American culture, adult goals are differentiated with respect to cultural values and in terms of class and sex roles, because the adolescent strives "to stabilize his ego values. . . in relation to his reference group whatever this may be to him in his particular social milieu. . . He does his level best to incorporate [into his ego]. . . the norms of the group. . . in his particular social setting" (Sherif & Cantril, 1947, p. 276).

Since our culture is not a homogeneous one, we will have to give considerable attention to the impact of social stratification on the behavior of the various social groups to which our adolescents owe allegiance. Thus, it might be more accurate to characterize the task of this concluding section as an inquiry into the nature of the psychosocial problems confronting the several subcultures of adolescents in the total American population of this age group.

RELATIONSHIP OF ADOLESCENTS TO THE WIDER COMMUNITY

Increased contact with and awareness of the social order

With adolescence comes an inevitable widening of the child's social horizons. He grows away from the restricting confines of the family and of the neighborhood peer group. Through increased, broadened, and more direct contact with the wider community he acquires more first-hand knowledge of social institutions and of the differences in caste and class mores and values in our mosaic-like culture. This improved perspective of our cultural heterogeneity, however, depends on more than increased social experience alone. Also implicated are growth in ability to formulate abstractions and to perceive both hierarchical relationships in group structure (Ausubel et al., 1952) and the distinguishing symbols of social class status (Stendler, 1949).

The adolescent's enhanced social experience is itself a function of several changed factors. His greater size and appearance of maturity, plus the newly won emancipated status in the home, increase his physical mobility. He is more free to come and go as he pleases, to participate in activities at a distance from home, and to make friends beyond the radius of the neighborhood. Even overprotective parents must be reconciled to letting him travel to high school or to work. And, apart from the broadening influence of such travel, he is more likely to come into contact with associates drawn from a more diverse social class environment than his neighborhood elementary school.

The adolescent's increased social awareness creates a new and objective basis for evaluating his home and parents. This liberation from attitudinal and emotional subservience to parental dicta helps in his devaluation of parents and in his emancipation from home. At the same time it leads to a certain amount of social disenchantment. Direct and first-hand experience with the foibles of authority figures and with the inconsistencies and injustices in many social institutions leads to different and somewhat more tarnished perceptions of the social order than the idealized ones he naively accepted from Sunday school and textbook descriptions.

Increased awareness of the wider social environment is accompanied by increased interest and involvement in current events, politics, and social and economic issues. This was reflected in dramatic ways by student activism in the 1960s. The war in Indo-China, with its accompanying draft, along with the dehumanizing pressures of a highly technological society, turned students into an independent political force. Altbach and Peterson observe that prior to the 1960s the student movement generally followed political trends in society and in the adult radical movement (Bengston & Starr, 1975). That this pattern, however, gave way to enhanced political consciousness and social activism is widely documented in social science literature (Keniston, 1971; Yankelovich, 1974). Civil rights organizations in the forefront in the early 1960s crystallized community action in the latter part of the decade and engaged the participation of youth in the same period. Critical of the values of a technological society, students created new life styles (e.g., preindustrial life became fashionable); they affirmed the rights of each individual over utilitarian goals and technological efficiency (Light & Laufer, 1975) and substituted self-fulfillment in place of a conventional career.

Yankelovich (1974) points out, however, that the early 1970s mark "vast changes in the complexion and outlook of an entire generation of young people." He further points out that

some of the changes depicted—such as the renewed quiet on campus and the new seriousness of students in their pursuit of careers, may appear, at first glance, to reinforce the widely held view that the 1960s represented the odd aberration in our national history. The 1970s, it is said, have restored "normalcy," linking up in a chain of continuity with the 1950s and other more familiar periods in our national history. These observers point to the striking parallelism between the "privatism" of the 1950s when young people were preoccupied with their own personal lives and destinies, and the privatism of the 1970s with its similarly strong focus on self. (Yankelovich, 1974, p. 7)

An examination, however, of the "complexion and outlook" of youth in the early 1970s (Yankelovich, 1974) suggests that this latter assessment is a half truth. The war and the draft wove together radical political and life style values. With the end of the war and the draft, political beliefs moved in the opposite direction, away from their 1960 peaks. The vast majority of students, the 89 percent who do not identify with the New Left, adhere nevertheless to changing cultural values in marriage, authority, religion, work, money, career, sexual morality, and other aspects of the traditional ethic.

These new values, which were largely born in the struggle of the young to establish new institutions more responsive to their needs, surfaced in the form of a counterculture. Counteracting the prevailing moral absolutism of youth during the experimental years of the 1960s, a mere 10 to 15 percent of the college population led the attack on virtually every cherished institution, belief, and value. However, partly as a result of the experience of the following decade young people themselves came to see the futility of a preindustrial life style. The unprecedented combination of inflation and recession of the 1970s, following the affluence of the 1960s, contributed to the development of a synthesis of what is valid in both the old and the new. This is exemplified, for instance, by the shift in emphasis from a search for self-fulfillment in place of a conventional career, characteristic of the late 1960s, to how to find self-fulfillment within a conventional career emerging in the early 1970s (Yankelovich, 1974).

Two interesting features of the outlook of youth on the wider community speak for the greater readiness of the older adolescent for desatellization and abstract thinking. The Yankelovich studies (1972, 1974) show that value change has spread from college to noncollege youth in the 1970s, yet high school students generally "render a less critical diagnosis of our major social and political institutions. . . . In their personal values and moral outlook, high school youth hold more traditional moral views than the somewhat older group" (Yankelovich, 1974, p. 153).

Acquisition of adult status in modern society

The determination of when an individual attains adult status can be made only in reference to a social criterion. Among other things such a criterion must include equal membership in a given adult community, the right to assume accepted adult roles, and the privilege of equal access to activities that determine earned status on an adult level. In other words, the individual attains adult status in relation to the wider community and not in relation to the home or his peer group. The partial recognition as an adult that the adolescent receives in a family setting is too limited in scope and generality to confer adult status; and although the peer group offers complete equality of membership and unrestricted access to earned status, it does so only on a "sub-adult" level.

But the adolescent's need for earned status—"sub-adult" or otherwise—is so desperate that he is obliged to seek it wherever it is to be found. Denied membership in the wider adult community, he is forced to predicate his status needs on performance in school and peer groups. And the home—once so important for the regulation of the childhood era—is now caught between the vise of these two more important determinants of interim status and becomes reduced to a vestigial role, often serving as a mere boarding house until he can stand on his own two feet.

In most primitive cultures, adult status is attained more directly and expeditiously in relation to the occurrence of pubescence, taking place concurrently with the emancipation from parents. It is usually consummated as the result of initiation ceremonies involving various traditional ordeals and rituals. Then once these are successfully completed, the entire brief transitional period is happily and speedily brought to a close by the conferring of full adult status.

These rites mark definite shifts in the social and economic status of the individual. . . . Psychologically all of these steps, trials—ceremonies and preachings—which achieve the transition of the adolescent to the adult status, mean formation of attitudes related to his new relative role in society, his conformity in respecting property and sex rights of elders and interest groups, his settling down in the place assigned him by the established authority of his society. (Sherif & Cantril, 1947, pp. 212–213)

In most instances the puberty rites for boys are more complex than those for girls. In part this may represent an attempt to match the natural drama in the phenomenon of menstruation. In part, however, it may reflect the greater importance attached to the socioeconomic role of men in most cultures (Benedict, 1934). This interpretation is strengthened by Radin's observation (1937, p. 83) that the initiation ceremonies for the girl "become progressively more complex and differentiated as her economic functions become more important, after the introduction of agriculture, for instance. Occasionally, as in some West African tribes, puberty rites exist for her only."

Estrangement between the adolescent and adult society

It comes as quite an unpleasant shock to many adolescents that the achievement of adult status is not a direct consequence of attaining physical maturity. As children they fail to grasp the significant difference in status separating adults from the younger individuals who resemble them in form only. They nurture an idealized conception of the status, privileges, and prerogatives which are accorded adolescents in our society. Having this naive aspiration of graduating immediately to adult status, they are keenly disappointed to discover that they still have no standing in the adult world. In fact, in many respects they are still treated exactly as children, but without enjoying the secure, protected status of the latter.

Considerable time must still elapse before they completely understand the painful fact that adult status will be withheld for many years. They still have to learn that the achievement of adult status in our society is such a protracted process that it cannot be accomplished directly but requires instead the interposition of a complex interim status.

Because of the almost complete separation of the value and interest systems of child and adult in our culture, adolescents experience considerable discontinuity and hardship in abruptly scrapping the prestige-giving values of childhood and identifying with adult values. This is particularly difficult since not very long ago they had enjoyed the kingpin status of being the biggest children in the world of play and had reluctantly relinquished this status in the process of assimilating adult goals and standards of responsibility. The unexpected rejection only adds insult to injury. For now the adolescent must temporarily hold in abeyance and even reject these new value identifications for those revered in the adolescent peer society. Here he starts once more at the bottom rung of the ladder; and when, toward the close of adolescence, he reaches the top, he is sent hurtling down to the bottom again as a fledgling adult to start climbing yet another ladder of values.

Ruth Benedict has called attention to the fact that in many "age-graded cultures [which] characteristically demand different behavior of the individual at different times of his life," the trauma of discontinuity is softened by the practice of "graduating publicly and with honor from one of these groups to another" (Benedict, 1938, p. 165).

But in our culture, children no longer achieve adult status following the attainment of certain well-defined attributes of physical or sexual growth or after proving that they possess certain vocational and physical skills; and society has done away with the rituals and ceremonies which primitive peoples use to mark the accomplishment of various developmental tasks with their concomitant acquisition of more adult privileges and responsibilities. These "rites of passage" formerly gave a certain definiteness and continuity to the business of growing up and becoming adult. Adolescents knew just what was expected of them at each stage of development; and after achieving the expected tasks they were clearly and ceremoniously rewarded with the prerogatives of adulthood. Now, they are not only confused about the goals of maturation at any particular stage of the game, but also never seem to know what is coming next, since the sequence of developmental steps is vague and ambiguous and is subject to frequent change and even to individual preference. Deprived of the ceremonies and rituals, adolescents are always left wondering and unassured about what has already been accomplished and what has yet to be done.

Adolescents are alienated from the adult culture by still another discontinuity. This is "caused by the discreteness, the non-interrelatedness of the various institutions and agencies that deal with the child or the group during any one day" (Tryon, 1944, p. 237), the five or six different teachers, the parents, the church, the peer group, and the recreational agency.

The extreme heterogeneity of our society places a heavy strain on the task of identification; in fact, feelings of complete membership or belonging are probably no longer possible (Curle, 1949). And when to this is added the moral confusion and conflict of our society, the resulting disenchantment with the social order makes the prospect of identification with it not too inviting.

The adolescent, therefore, has sufficient reason to feel ambivalent toward the wider community—its unexpected rejection of his bid for membership, its prolonged withholding of status, its failure to provide signposts of progress and recognition, its fragmentation and compartmentalization of the training process, and its heterogeneity and moral confusion, which make identification difficult and unpalatable. He needs time to become reconciled to this stage of affairs and to find anchorage in his own peer culture. But until these compensatory adjustments are effected and the initial resentment wanes, hostility and aggressive reactions are the most appropriate mechanisms of defense available to the injured and threatened ego. A good part of the adolescent's exaggerated quest for independence and apparent contempt for established values can be attributed to his need for rejecting the norms of the adult culture which denies him membership. He responds with the attitude that what he cannot have is not worth having in the first place. To show just how little he cares about the adult world and his exclusion from it, he joins a peer subculture which strives to make itself as recognizably distinct and separate from adult society as possible; and as a further expression of his hostility he takes provocative delight in fashioning norms of behavior which are shocking to adult sensibilities.

Even after the bitterness wears off, the estrangement is perpetuated simply because the adolescent is now anchored almost completely in his own distinctive subculture. The goals and values of the interim status that it provides are partly ends in themselves, which are not held in common with the wider community. Nevertheless, throughout this entire period, regardless of how preoccupied he may appear to be with his peer culture, he keeps one eye focused on his future place in adult society. Ambivalence by definition is a two-sided feeling. What he rejects and purports to scorn, he also reveres and aspires to attain. How else could we explain his deliberately premature advocacy of certain external prerogatives of adulthood such as late hours, smoking, automobiles, and drinking? If adults were really beneath his contempt, would he strive so hard to imitate and distort their behavior, even if the object of his imitation were to express aggression and to arouse anger and grief?

In conclusion, we can summarize the adolescent's relation to the wider community. His contact with the social order is broader and more direct, and his insight into the workings of the culture is more mature and sophisticated. Through firsthand contact—instead of through the buffer relationship provided by the home—he acquires a more representative perception of cultural process than was possible from the biased interpretation by his parents. He also identifies more with broader social groups and becomes more concerned with social problems. But by no stretch of the imagination can the wider community be considered his primary social group. Rejected by the adult society he seeks to enter, he transfers his earned social affiliations from home to peer group. At first, resentment and various discontinuities inherent in this shift, and later, the very separateness of his own subculture contribute to the estrangement between him and the culture at large. Nevertheless, he never loses sight of the interim quality of his peer culture status and is preparing for his eventual entry into the adult world.

PROLONGATION OF ADOLESCENCE IN MODERN SOCIETY

Causes of prolongation

Generally speaking, the duration of infancy and the length of the dependency of the young on parents are proportional to the length of fetal gestation and of the life span in a given species. This proportionality, however, breaks down for the human species with its culture (Warden, 1936). Culture complicates and extends the process of psychological development. The more complex a given culture, the longer it takes for psychological development to be completed. Evidence in the previous chapter showed that growth in complex intellectual capacities extends into the college years. But apart from the necessity of continuing training and education to complete psychological development, the training period must be extended to ensure the continuity of the social order, which obviously depends on transmitting cultural values and traditions to the young.

This theoretical premise, in accord with the educational practice of advocating a broad academic background for all children and adolescents, although as much an instructional rationalization to "fill in" productively the extended period of adolescence bears its fruits in sensitizing youth to cultural values and sharpening their critical diagnosis of the fabric of the culture, its institutions, and its traditions, as mentioned earlier (Keniston, 1972).

Although the extension of education for a large percentage of youth may be desirable in itself, we should remember that the primary motivation has been the inability of society to provide jobs for adolescents. It is mere sophistry to pretend that they are psychologically too immature to find a place in our economy. Although it may be true that intellectual growth can continue past the high school period, this growth can frequently be fostered most advantageously by extended education that takes place supplementary to rather than in lieu of job placement.

Postponing the vocational problem by continued schooling provides some immediate feelings of status and social acceptance, but does not completely allay anxiety about occupational security. The majority of all youth regard economic security as their main problem. College students are apt to experience (1) feelings of inadequacy and immaturity referable to their dependent status, and (2) considerable apprehensiveness and uncertainty about the outcome of their schooling and the possibility of obtaining the job for which it supposedly prepares them. The latter was absent for the generation of the 1950s and the 1960s when opportunities for employment were available and offered options. Present-day youth, facing scarcity of jobs and lacking commensurate experiences of adversity in their earlier years, are particularly vulnerable to the impact of limited job opportunities.

The youth who forgoes continuing his education for the sake of immediate employment is more likely to regret his choice later in life than during adolescence. Achieving economic independence during adolescence adds greater enhancement to self-esteem than the pursuit of education. In not a few instances, however, college provides a welcome respite, an opportunity of escaping for several more years the frightening prospect of making a vocational choice, relinquishing economic dependence, or competing in the adult world.

SOCIOECONOMIC FACTORS

Adolescence is prolonged in modern society chiefly by the unique economic situation, in which the productive labor of adolescents is not only unnecessary for cultural survival but also represents a threat to the interests of adult workers. In practically all other cultures, adolescents participate vigorously in the economic life of the community or begin to prepare seriously for some occupational pursuit; and in many of the less favored cultures, the economic contribution of the child is demanded even before pubescence (Sherif & Cantril, 1947). But

in our industrial society conditions are such as to make it extremely difficult to provide youth with the work experience so essential for normal personality development, and it is even more difficult to open up for youth avenues leading to gainful employment of a kind that gives tone and zest to life. It is a significant fact that for most youth today creative labor must be had in factory, shop, or office instead of in communal family relations. But when youth turn from home and school to find part-time or full-time employment, they are faced by the ominous fact that our economy, in peace time, cannot make full use of their productive energy. (Edwards, 1944, p. 190)

The availability of gainful employment for adolescents is even less promising for future years because of the increasing tendency for persons in the middle and older age groups to constitute a greater proportion of the total population. And so long as full employment is denied older workers, youth will stand at the threshold of occupational life baffled and frustrated (Edwards, 1944). Trade unions understandably cannot tolerate adolescent competition in a labor market that is never fully depleted under normal peacetime conditions.

It should be noted, however, that whereas humanitarian concern for health and education has led to the elimination of abuses in unregulated child labor, society has given little thought to the harmful effects of status deprivation induced by an almost complete removal of opportunity for adolescent work experience.

Although the shrinking availability of work experience for adolescents is a general cultural phenomenon, there is considerable room for individual differences in inclination. Thus many enterprising young people in high school or college find part- or full-time employment, even during hard times, to take care of part or all of their expenses. Others are encouraged by their parents or choose on their own to concentrate on studies in preparation for future work rather than divert their energies.

In addition to the scarcity of job opportunities for adolescents, the available work lacks the qualities that facilitate personality development. Excessive specialization has made most jobs highly monotonous and routinized. There is little opportunity for exercising individual initiative for obtaining the personal satisfaction that comes with an integrated view of total accomplishment. Modern adolescents fail to derive from the employment that is available the same sense of personal importance and social usefulness that comes with greater individual participation in the planning and creative aspects of work. It is not, therefore, surprising that adolescent culture in the 1960s, as mentioned earlier, rebelled against the "work ethic" as it had come to stand; emphasized expressive and self-fulfillment values outside work; and is now returning to self-fulfillment in a career.

SPECIAL CULTURAL CONDITIONS

Since biosocial status is most fluid in adolescence, of all the developmental periods, society easily shifts its expectations of adolescents with the exigencies of the economic situation. In times of economic distress, adolescents' needs are the last to be considered, but when the need for manpower becomes suddenly urgent their participation is taken for granted without the benefit of any advance preparation. It is not at all unexpected, therefore, that the psychological effects of economic depression weigh heaviest of all on adolescents. At such times, children must live almost indefinitely with their parents. Full emancipation and marriage are postponed nearly beyond the point of tolerance. Education is lengthened even further, but is undertaken only half-heartedly, for seemingly it leads nowhere.

Under circumstances such as these the characteristic emotional instability of adolescence reaches its maximum intensity; for it appears to the adolescent as if all the organized power of society were arrayed against him in his legitimate quest for status.

Would it be possible to confront an ego already threatened by body changes, developmental tensions, and abrupt loss of status with anything more traumatic? Regardless of the basic strength of his intrinsic self-acceptance, there must be considerable ego deflation—at least in his extrinsic notion of ego adequacy (which is ordinarily a reflection of the value society places on him). Even if he does blame his environment for his misfortunes, he cannot avoid accepting the verdict that he is a stunted, developmental failure, a permanent subadult with marginal and indeterminate status.

The situation is precisely reversed, both quantitatively and qualitatively, during time of war. Vocational opportunities are almost unlimited. Numerous highly responsible jobs become available for relatively inexperienced youths when endurance, speed, agility, and boldness are at a premium in many military and war industry positions. Under such conditions economic independence is quickly acquired; adolescents virtually have maturity thrust on them (Davis, 1944).

This unaccustomed speed in transformation of status generates distinctive problems of its own. The inflationary value placed on human service—when adolescents are given jobs, responsibility, and salaries far out of proportion to their capacity for judgment and discretion—twists self-appraisal, appraisal of reality, and expectations from life completely out of focus. To a lesser extent, the same situation prevailed during the atypical affluent period of the 1950s and 1960s, with the abundance of relatively high salary, optimally choice jobs readily available to the young.

In these circumstances, the sudden intoxication of independence develops increased hostility toward adult authority. Youthful arrogance and conceit grow by leaps and bounds; and parent-youth conflict is intensified as parents feel that their children are "acting too big for their breeches."

The worst of it, however, come with the inevitable deflation of this new status when the nation settles down to a peacetime economy. For then the frustrations and deprivations formerly regarded as the normal heritage of adolescence become greatly magnified against the relatively "plush" background of the wartime era. For youth in the 1970s facing inflation and recession after the "plush" period of the previous two decades, frustrating experiences and a sense of deprivation assume even more magnified dimensions.

Effects of prolongation

NEGATIVE

The general adverse consequences of prolonged status deprivation on adolescent personality development (retardation of maturation, emancipation, and psychosexual development; delay of marriage and of social and economic independence; depreciation of extrinsic self-esteem; increase in level of anxiety) have already been discussed. We have also called attention to the role of status deprivation in bringing about emotional instability and have described the characteristics of this condition. Typical fluctuations in the level of emotional instability throughout adolescence have been related to changes in the total load of deprivation, to adjustments in the expectations of adolescents, and to the availability of substitutive sources of status. It has been suggested that the motivation underlying the adolescent's participation in new, status-oriented activities is independently derived from the ego needs generated by his new biosocial position and from intrinsic interest in these activities rather than "sublimated" from frustrated sex drives. Nevertheless, the development of new sources of status—even if autonomously derived rather than sublimated—tends to counterbalance the effects of deprivations in other spheres, making for a more favorable net balance of gratifications or for a reduction in the net total of frustrations.

In evaluating the general effects of status deprivation on personality development and emotional instability, it is important to bear in mind that in addition to being influenced by the environment, the individual is conditioned by the way he reacts to the same environment. His reaction in turn depends on his understanding of the environment and the enhancement he receives (Segel, 1951). Thus, there is extreme variability in reaction to status deprivation as a result of marked individual differences in level of ego aspiration, need for status and independence, frustration tolerance, availability of adaptive resources, and habitual modes of adjustment.

Aggression is the most direct and least sophisticated outcome of the adolescent's state of increased behavioral reactivity. Since it is apt to be diffuse, to contribute little toward goal attainment, and to provoke retaliation and counteraggression, it is usually used only when no other adjustive technique is available or when the need for immediate relief from tension is overwhelming. It is not directed against an indiscriminate object but generally relates to an important ego-involved area in the individual's psychological field. Due consideration is also given to the likelihood of and kind of retaliation. An extreme example of organized group aggression is found in the activities of the predatory adolescent gang. Such gangs arise in "disorganized" urban areas where transitory participation in delinquent behavior is considered a normal part of growing up. They are characterized by fanatical intragroup loyalty and by strict adherence to the proposition that their predatory activities are justified by society's indifferent or repressive attitude toward their aspirations for status. Such feelings are more commonly expressed by gang members from racial and ethnic minority groups who come to believe that the organized power of society is arrayed against them, that legitimate endeavor is hopelessly futile, and that organized aggression against society is the only path left open to them.

More usually, however, aggressive responses to status deprivation take the form of exaggerated demands for independence, rejection of the goals of adult maturation, and generalized contempt for established values and for adults; conceit, arrogance, and defiance of authority; and a stereotyped hostile attitude toward parents and elders. Not infrequently such aggression finds a pseudo-philosophical outlet in more introverted youth, expressing itself as a distorted and cynical materialism which denies any possibility of virtue or altruism, as a crass Epicureanism, or as nihilism.

Withdrawal is also a familiar adolescent response to deprivation. Milder forms are characterized by exaggerated introspectiveness, reserve, secretiveness, and stubborn disinclination to discuss personal problems. More serious manifestations of withdrawal are persistent retreat from social intercourse, asceticism, excessive intellectualization, running away from home, truancy, and suicide. Many early marriages among adolescents are merely desperate attempts to escape from conflicts and frustrations regarded as insoluble and unbearable.

Other common adjustive techniques of adolescents include: (1) displacement of affect from a genuine source of anxiety to a trivial, vastly exaggerated, or even imaginary somatic defect; (2) blustering denial of the existence of any problems, or an attempt to pass them off lightly by a disarming third-person reference to same, or by an air of swaggering indifference; (3) excessive indulgence in fantasies of a regressive or "superman" nature; (4) manic attempts to find security in frantic bursts of uncritical enthusiasm and undirected activity; and (5) overindulgence in accessible, hedonistic activity, such as compulsive overeating or sexuality.

POSITIVE

In contrast to these negative or maladaptive (but adjustive) reactions to status deprivation, a number of compensatory responses provide substitutive status. Chief among these is the peer society, which is discussed at length in Chapter 12. Another common status-seeking activity of adolescents is the attempt to identify themselves emotionally with the roles of glamorous individuals in public life. Thus, adolescent boys may become completely immersed in the minutest details of the lives and exploits of their heroes in the world of sports; while adolescent girls more frequently preoccupy themselves with the doings of movie, radio, and television personalities. Through this intense and intimate process of identification, a certain amount of reflected status is achieved. The same mechanism is involved in the "crushes" which adolescents "get" on idolized persons in their immediate environment, such as teachers or highly regarded age mates, usually of the same sex.

In certain individuals, extreme status deprivation ignites a burning ambition to rise above the limitations imposed by their environment, and sometimes, in exceptional cases, enough drive is generated in this manner to enable the individual to lift himself by his own bootstraps to levels of achievement which would ordinarily be thought impossible under the given handicaps. In contrast to the one who succeeds, however, hundreds make the attempt only to become discouraged and drop out along the way.

Unusual degrees of status deprivation may stimulate social reconstruction. In the United States, the extreme economic distress of the Depression in the 1930s created the Leftist movements, later drenched in the disillusionment created by Joseph Stalin. When the cold war following World War II and the devastation of the other industrial economies of Europe provided ingredients for continuing growth of American economy, the new affluence made the economic radicalism of the Depression superfluous. A whole range of new technologies and capital created bureaucracies that facilitated mobility. The new bureaucratic middle class looked for stability in hard work after the Depression, and with relatively radical and permissive outlooks raised a generation in the 1950s that experienced another unusual degree of status deprivation. The highly technological postindustrial society demanded a longer period of preparation, in many cases postgraduate schooling, for the world of work. This increased prolongation of status deprivation on the part of a "talented and unfettered generation had the social and historical setting for new movements" (Light & Laufer, 1975). The New Left engulfed the energies of youth sensitive to the discrepancy between their parents' liberalism and a work ethic that embodied enslavement to status and materialism, and made their ideology hollow. Dissatisfied with mechanized industrial and military bureaucracies, disillusioned in educational institutions caught in a technographic, dehumanizing establishment, and embittered by a government active in war and draft, they raised questions "that evoked critical images of apparently settled issues" (Light & Laufer, 1975, p. 94). The central question was: "Is it unAmerican to stop getting bigger, stronger, and wealthier in order to have larger cars, houses, missiles, guns, or body counts? How shall we as a society and as individuals find peace, security, love, and a place for ourselves and our children in this complex world?" (Light & Laufer, 1975, p. 95). While those coming from conservative families became hippies, children of liberal parents found expression in movements such as Students for a Democratic Society and civil rights activities (Light & Laufer, 1975; Wilkinson, 1975).

Scholars of the radical students' movements of the 1970s point out that the present-day quiet on the campuses does not signal a return to society of two decades ago. The new social values that grew on the campuses have now grown stronger, in some respects more mature, and have spread beyond the campus (Light & Laufer, 1975; Yankelovich, 1974).

DIFFERENTIATION OF THE SOCIAL CLASS ENVIRONMENT

Social class structure in the United States

In our heterogeneous society, there is no such thing as a uniform social environment determining in the same way the growth possibilities of the transitional period for all adolescents. Even though American democratic tradition and a stratified social system are not entirely compatible, and social class status differentiation is denied by many (Brown, 1965), it seems that "participation of any given individual in the culture of his society is not a matter of chance. It is determined primarily and almost completely as far as overt culture is concerned, by his place in society and by the training he has received in his occupying this place. . . . For the most complex industrial society of the United States, social class—the way people are ranked in the hierarchy of prestige and power—is but one way of defining the individual's place" (Clausen & Williams, 1963, pp. 67–68).

Each class to a greater or lesser extent has its own ideology, characteristic patterns of overt behavior, and ways of rearing children. Thus, within a given social class environment, not only are there distinctive educational and vocational aspirations and accepted forms of social participation, but also characteristic moral values relating to sex, aggression, honesty, responsibility, etc. (Clausen, 1968).

With respect to the various social institutions, youth, whatever their ethnic and racial attributes and environmental experiences, share some similarities among themselves as well as distinguishing features from adults in their exposure to educational systems and the labor force, peer group relationships, orientations to authority figures from parents to teachers to police, fashions, lifestyles, linguistic patterns, dating behavior, and general models of their social relationships. Yet they differ. They differ significantly along class lines as well as along racial and ethnic ones. (Wilkinson, 1975, pp. 285–286)

SOCIAL CLASS DIFFERENCES

Social class differences are pervasive in our culture, cutting across lines marking other systems of social rank, such as color, ethnicity, and religion. Although such differences are by no means vague or indefinite, there is greater flexibility or mobility between social classes than between the other systems of social stratification. Considerable variability also prevails within each class with respect to income, occupation, educational status, social participation, political beliefs, and aspirations for social mobility. Sociologists generally agree that there are three major social classes in our society—upper, middle, and lower—with two subclasses in each.

Members of the upper class come from old families with a long tradition of wealth, social prominence, and gentility. They place high value on family tradition, remain aloof from the community at large, and indulge expensive and esoteric tastes. Since they constitute a small minority in any locality, and usually refrain from direct participation in ordinary civic enterprises, the values of the middle class are more likely to constitute the official ideology of the community.

Middle- and lower-class differences have diminished in some respects. A review of the literature (Bronfenbrenner, 1958) indicates a trend in middle-class mothers toward more relaxed attitudes in child rearing and greater tolerance of impulse gratification. In addition, disillusionment with middle-class materialism, with the adaptive behavior of the organization man, and in general with what appeared to be hypocritical adult behavior led youth in the 1960s to a reexamination of professed and practiced values. The result was a downward movement in class values and mores, particularly in regard to sex, manners, speech, and in some respects attitudes toward work.

Nonetheless, members of the middle class are in a better position than others to see the adaptive value of high aspirations for earned status particularly in a society where educational achievement is not only necessitated by the demands of technological advancement but also serves as a means of control in the struggle between status groups (Collins, 1971). Supportive personality traits are therefore encouraged by parents in the form of initiative and responsibility; the deferred gratification pattern of hard work, self-denial, long-range planning, high frustration tolerance, prolonged education; and self-criticism, thrift, punctuality, orderliness, and respect for property (Ausubel & Sullivan, 1970).

The lower class contains a much larger percentage of individuals from minority ethnic groups and non-Caucasian racial stock. They earn their living through unskilled labor and live in depressed and overcrowded urban areas. Their children are apt to be poorly clothed and badly nourished and to receive inadequate medical care. Family life is less stable; separations and broken homes are frequent. Children drop out of school as soon as it is lawful to do so, and contribute to family income both before and during adolescence. The adaptive characteristics of lower-class families, in spite of diminishing class differences in mores, remain distinct. One basic adaptive characteristic is structuring relationships in terms of power (Hess, 1970) which is a realistic appraisal of their state in life. In work and in interaction with bureaucratic structures (welfare, police, hospitals, credit agencies), the central issue for them is who is in charge. Their "most characteristic and adaptive response is to comply and carry out instructions. . . . In line with this orientation the lower class father tends to equate respect from children with their compliance and obedience to his wishes and commands" (Hess, 1970, p. 467). Maas (1953) observed this orientation toward power in the relationship between members of adolescent clubs and their club leaders. It may underlie the greater frequency of physical punishment in working class families as opposed to the use of love and psychological control by middle-class families (Bronfenbrenner, 1958).

CASTE DIFFERENCES

Skin color is the chief criterion of caste membership. Despite outstanding changes in attitudes leading to greater interaction between social classes, caste membership remains as a most sharply drawn and rigidly enforced social rank. It is a lifelong form of rank that one can escape in approved fashion only by death (Davis, 1941).

Black children and adolescents face special problems of personality development as a result, largely, of the peculiar status of their elders in society and the disparaging evaluations of their color imposed by the white majority. In spite of differential involvement in the economic structure on the part of black Americans producing a diversity in ways of life among them, it is important to recognize that growing up black transcends status and class ranks (Deutsch, 1973; Ladner, 1972). "A disproportionate number of blacks are unemployed and poor even though there are many who are in the middle and working classes. Very few are in the upper classes. None is a member of the corporate rich. . . . Most remain in the low-income ghetto communities" (Wilkinson, 1975, p. 288).

Broken homes are even more common among black families than among white families, fathers are more frequently absent; matriarchal and negative family atmosphere more commonly prevails (Dai, 1949; Gordon & Shea, 1967; Moynihan, 1965; Rainwater, 1966). Thus the black child, like many other lower-class children, and even more often, is denied the benefits of biparental affection and upbringing; he is often raised by his grandmother or older sister while his mother works to support the family deserted by the father. When compared with black children with intact families, father-absent black children feel more victimized and feel they have less control of their environment (Pettigrew, 1964). Also, when the father is present, male identification suffers when the boy is faced with a role model while also confronted with an image of his future self (i.e., his father) as an economically inadequate male (Gordon & Shea, 1967; Rainwater, 1966). The black female child is in many instances more assertive (Proshansky & Newton, 1968), and, when compared with white children of the same age, is less conforming to pressures (Iscoe et al., 1964).

Blacks manifest several characteristic ways of adjusting to the inferior caste position imposed on them. These special adjustive techniques are a product of their unique cultural history (previous condition of servitude, fervent religious faith) and of the relative hopelessness of their position in the cultural hierarchy for social mobility and access to social and economic opportunity. Less insuperable handicaps confronting other unfavored minorities (Jews or Italians), on the other hand, are more likely to inspire increased striving or direct aggression. But the relative futility of striving and direct aggression for the black places a premium for some on withdrawing and escape.

Wilkinson (1975) points out that at the time of the Census Employment Survey, August 1970 through March 1971, the black youth population—16 to 24 years of age—represented nearly one-fourth of the total black population aged 16 and over in low-income areas. In October 1971 about 38 percent were not employed even though "significant numbers were seeking employment" (p. 388).

What is important to recognize here is that white youth of all ethnic groupings and in various socioeconomic groups never experience the structural handicaps and identity-negating philosophies which every black in the seventeen through twenty-four age range in America must face regardless of family social-class background. Some young blacks have expressed the view that within the economic system, they are no longer considered as instruments of production as they were during the era of slavery in America and the industrial explosion. They perceive themselves now as a stratum with a past—a heritage—which has left them outside the system of production and hence estranged from significant involvement in the economic arena. Employing a psychology of collective and defensive repudiation of a society which rejects them, many openly and actively oppose what they define as negative white patriarchal establishments and beliefs that not only deny them fair treatment and equal opportunities but inhibit their desire for self-expression and self-determination. (Wilkinson, 1975, p. 290)

Yet blacks are not a monolithic group. Even though they all experience the impact of a color-based caste system, the variations in economic, educational, and occupational statuses of families breed differential aspirations, values, choices of models, and goals in life.

Within the last two decades changed social and political conditions brought alterations of conceptions of roles and increased political consciousness among the blacks. Adolescents are at a new juncture in life chances (Frazier, 1967; Wilkinson, 1975). The 1960s transformed the earlier passive resignation and placatory attitudes to a redefinition of self-conceptions and identities exemplified by the slogan: "Black is Beautiful." Color distinctions, however, still affect their lives. In addition, too many youth like their elders have assimilated the biases of the dominant group with respect to imputing cultural and intellectual significance to color (Wilkinson, 1975).

There are greater numbers of black youth today in higher education and an increasing number seeking employment with advanced skills. Although their numbers are declining with the economic crunch, their new racial consciousness will promote the need for kinship as a requisite for collective action against institutional racism. The young blacks have replaced placatory attitudes with militance, and although the 1970s are less likely to bring the tumultuous behavior of the 1960s, young blacks are less likely to acquiesce about their future.

Impact of social stratification on adolescent development

The above differences in caste, class, and subcultural environment have been described in some detail, because by affecting the availability of status and the means of acquiring it, they obviously influence the difficulty, the length, and the mechanisms of adolescent personality development. In this section we shall discuss only the effect of social stratification on degree of status deprivation and motivational pattern. The impact of social class stratification on intelligence, interests, sex behavior, education, vocational choice, and peer group organization is described in the separate chapters devoted to these topics.

Economic necessity may force emancipation relatively early on a working class adolescent; on the other hand, wealth and education may prolong the period of dependency in an upper-class youth. Yet although the former may have to seek economic independence earlier, he is in no way sure of attaining his goal; whereas the latter knows that even if delayed longer, assured economic success will eventually be his. The position of the middle-class youth is somewhere in-between. Success is not assured in advance. He has to fight and stuggle for it; but the greater chances of succeeding give him more incentive to strive than his lower-class contemporary. He is thus more highly motivated, and his behavior is more persistently oriented than that of members of the status levels directly above and below him.

Although it is a mistake to stereotype disparities in child rearing practices between social classes without due cognizance of overlap (Hess, 1970), evidence points to the fact that middle-class parents

place greater stress than others on the maintenance of high aspirations for earned status and the achievement of high levels of educational and vocational success, financial independence, and social recognition. Middle-class children and adolescents are willing to
internalize these ego status goals, which lead to ego maturity in our
culture, because they perceive the eventual rewards attainable for
persons of their status (Ausubel & Sullivan, 1970).

Milner's (1949) case study data also support the proposition that
clusters of personality traits typical for a sex group within a given
social class can be isolated.

On the other hand,

> the social instigations and goals of the lower-middle-class are
> fundamentally unlike those of the lower-class. As the middle
> class child grows older, the effective rewards in maintaining
> learning are increasingly those of status; they are associated with
> the prestige of middle- or upper-class rank and culture. The class
> goals in education, occupation, and status are made to appear
> real, valuable, and certain to him because he actually begins to
> experience in his school, clique, and family life some of the pres-
> tige responses. The lower-class child, however, learns by not
> being rewarded in these prestige relationships that the middle-
> class goals and gains are neither likely nor desirable for one in his
> position. He discovers by trial-and-error-learning that he is not
> going to be rewarded in terms of these long-range goals, if he is a
> "good little boy," if he avoids the sexual and recreational explo-
> ration available to him in his lower-class environment, or if he
> studies his lessons. In this learning, he is often more realistic
> than his teacher, if one judges by the actual cultural role which
> the society affords him. (Davis, 1941, p.346)

This becomes particularly poignant in the light of recent studies
showing repeatedly that lower-class adolescents have higher vocational aspirations than expectations (Hess, 1970); they share the dominant values of the society but "stretch" them downward to suit their
behavior which is dictated by restricted resources. In this sense
members of the lower class have a wider range of values in certain
areas than middle-class individuals (Rodman et al., 1974).

In addition, each class must bear its characteristic time sequence
and total load of status deprivation. Total load varies inversely with
height of class standing; whereas periods of low and high load tend
to follow each other in ascending order for the lower group and in
descending order for the upper group.

There are also differences in the types of goals sought and in the approved manner of competing for them. In one group, direct physical attack is the preferred method; in the other, aggression is more polite and indirect, covered by a veneer of disarming amiability. As is to be expected, there are marked differences in the urgency with which adolescents of different class origins view the importance of preserving the status quo.

Because identifications with caste, class, and sex membership groups first become crucially important as ego supports during adolescence, we must reckon with their negative as well as their positive attributes. The fact that a given adolescent in the United States is white, Protestant, upper class, and can trace his ancestry back to the Pilgrims is a powerful brace to his marginal developmental status. But if he is of black, Puerto Rican, or Mexican descent, or lives on the wrong side of the tracks, what then? He must surely suffer an additional deflation in ego status, the traumatic potential of which must, as always, be evaluated in relation to the strength of intrinsic self-acceptance (Ausubel, 1952). It can be said, in addition, that there is sufficient time to build a quite stable system of intrinsic self-esteem within a familial setting before the impact of caste or class becomes a significant factor in the child's psychological field. Depending on whether or not this is done, the psychological trauma of identification with a stigmatized caste or class can assume either central or peripheral importance to the individual's self-esteem. The wide range of individual differences in reaction to this situation certainly lends support to this interpretation.

Interaction between social classes

It is obvious that interaction and overlapping between social classes has to occur in a culture such as ours, with its highly developed system of travel, communication, and mass media. The American emphasis on earned status based on performance criteria ensures downward and upward mobility between classes (Brown, 1965). Until recently, the dominant trend was a downward diffusion of middle-class ideology promoted by the prolonged exposure of all children to education, church, mass media, and youth organizations. Since the 1960s we have started witnessing an upward surge of some lower-class values and styles. Thus a broader spectrum governs social and moral values featuring some aspects traditionally identified with lower-class ideology (Yaneklovich, 1972, 1974). Social mobility is enhanced by a continuing trend toward higher working-class income and a wider dispersion of secondary school and college education.

Contemporary youth culture precludes the exclusivity formerly associated with the upper classes. The upper classes have become "democratized" since youth is less under the domination of parents (themselves afflicted by moral ambiguity) and more susceptible to influences outside the home (Vaz, 1969). In certain respects the two-way diffusion of ideologies has created uncertainties and confusions in values. Yet there are indications of syntheses emerging from the intermingling of social class values (Yankelovich, 1974).

However, enforcement of class boundaries has not disappeared. The enforcement becomes stricter as children approach adolescence and are still expected, for the most part, to reflect more closely the *mores* of their particular social class group, thus restricting learning environments in some measure.

The upper class provides a homogeneous social atmosphere for their children through the device of the private boarding school. Intermingling of different classes is further discouraged by factors of distance (neighborhood), clothes, and parental pressure. But even more important are feelings of class loyalty which are strongly developed by the time a child reaches adolescence (Ausubel, 1950; Mussen et al., 1974).

The two chief socializing agents of adolescence, the school and the peer group, work hand in hand in reinforcing the existing stratification of our society; although peer culture manifests some degree of difference from parental values, most peer groups show a fundamental continuity in many of the values and beliefs of parents and adolescents (Mussen et al., 1974). In schools, there is some infusion of lower-class members and individuals from black and Puerto Rican backgrounds now occupying a role as teachers, but by far the greater number are predominantly middle class in origin and outlook. The organization of the school is apt to favor middle-class behavior and penalize lower-class children.

TRANSMISSION OF SOCIAL CLASS VALUES AND ASPIRATIONS

Exposure to an appropriately restricted learning environment obviously facilitates the assimilation of differentially appropriate social class values and aspirations. It does not, however, explain per se the motivational auspices under which such internalization takes place. There is, furthermore, the difficult task of explaining how social class values can be effectively transmitted from adults to adolescents in the face of the serious conflict and discord between the two generations. How is it possible for an adolescent to repudiate the immediate authority of his parents and still retain their social class values?

In Chapter 7 we demonstrated how the culture at large engenders transitional anxiety as a means of motivating the personality development of adolescents. The transmission of differential class levels of aspiration in our society, on the other hand, is achieved by

> the maintenance in the individual of a certain level of anxiety with regard to the attainment of the required behavior for his status. This socialized anxiety plays a major role in propelling him along that cultural route prescribed by his family, school, and later by adult society at his cultural level. The anxiety which middle-status people learn is effective first because it involves the threat of loss of present status (and the severe social penalties associated therewith), and, second, because it leads as the individual may plainly see in successful persons to the rewards of power, of social prestige, and of security for one's children. . . . Anxiety leads to striving because only thus can anxiety be reduced to a tolerable level. (Davis, 1944, pp. 204, 214)

Long-range anxiety is an efficient taskmaster only if it is reinforced by more proximate contact with the pressures and threats which give it substance. If these are removed by virtue of a break in communication with parents and adult society, another more acceptable source of authority for the enforcement of class norms must be found. The peer society fulfills this function admirably since the adolescent does not feel that liberation from its standards is an essential requirement for emancipation. Quite the contrary, conformity to peer standards is one of his most cherished values. He can therefore assign with equanimity to his peer group the proximate power to enforce class aspirations without relinquishing the rebelliousness he deems essential for his development.

On the peer group, therefore, devolves the responsibility of maintaining, reinforcing, and transmitting to adolescents the appropriate motivational patterns that parents and adults favor but are unable to communicate and enforce effectively because of the estrangement that has grown up between them and their children. And with the power of social ostracism at its disposal, it sees to it that the values, associations, aspirations, and behavior patterns of its members adhere closely to the class reference group to which it owes allegiance. As Sherif and Cantril (1947, p. 247) point out, "no matter how serious the youthful rebellion and restlessness may be, adult-youth conflict in most cases will be an intra-family and intra-community affair. . . . An adolescent boy was strongly and at times openly critical of everything his parents did. Nevertheless he shared the major class delineations, political views and social distance norms of his upper-middle-class parents." The need of this boy was to "reject his elders, and not their class aspirations." When these aspirations were espoused and enforced by his peer group they were quite palatable and acceptable.

IMPACT OF SOCIAL CHANGE ON ADOLESCENT DEVELOPMENT

A condition of rapid social change compounds the difficulties of a person who himself is in a period of developmental transition. For added to the marginality and disorientation induced by the abrupt shift in biosocial status are the ambiguities and confusions of the new social environment to which he is required to make an adjustment. To be catapulted from a secure and charted psychological field into one that is virgin and unexplored is bad enough; but when the new field lacks stable landmarks and points of reference, the transition is even more traumatic. Thus, adolescents more than any other segment of the population are bound to suffer from the contradictions and anxieties inherent in a period of social transition. In fact, it is precisely these doubts and perplexities springing from the rapidity of social change which are in large measure responsible for the difficulties of adolescence in our society.

Rapid social change generates three special kinds of developmental difficulties. Most obvious is the accentuation of the disparity between generations that is responsible for much parent-youth conflict. A second difficulty is a function of the fact that when the social order is in a state of flux there is no stable system of values to which the adolescent can confidently anchor himself. A person who is floundering is desperately in need of values that are certain and tangible rather than permeated with inconstancy, doubt, and decay. The third and most serious difficulty, however, is an outcome of contradiction, ambiguity, and confusion. More threatening and productive of conflict than the existence of an unstable system of values are the irreconcilable demands and expectations that inevitably follow from contradictory social norms.

Ordinarily, when the rate of social change is not immoderate, there is a fair correlation between the social and economic conditions governing the organization of society and the kinds of values that govern the behavior of persons. But when the rate of social change increases, both the realities of social organization and the personal relationships they necessitate grow away from their ideological substrate. Although there has been little hesitation about accepting and using the new products of technology, there has been no corresponding willingness on the part of society to reorganize social institutions and to reorient value systems in accordance with the changed modes of living resulting from technological advances (Edwards, 1944).

Since the debris of outworn values has not been cleared but coexists with changed forms of social organization, a hiatus has developed between the official values of the culture and the actual practices that are realistically possible in interpersonal relations (Keniston, 1965). And since the child is taught that the world is constructed in the image of the official ideology, he is in for some disillusionment when he finally emerges from the sheltered orbit of childhood. Sudden exposure to the realities of life destroys his romantic and idealized conceptions of marriage, industry, and government.

The greatest developmental problem posed by technology has been the confusion in standards which it has created—standards of proper goals and methods of achieving them and standards relating to appropriate class and sex roles. Cultural lag has also resulted in an unusual amount of moral confusion making progressively less effective the historic carriers of the core values of society—family, church, and community. The adolescent, for example, had been taught the virtues of humility, forthrightness, and honesty. Yet all around him he sees the worldly triumph of dissimulation and aggressiveness. He had been led to believe that merit and virtue are inevitably rewarded with all of the good things of life; but in the actual struggle for position, he finds little chance of "climbing the ladder of success" except through favoritism, shrewd dealing, and inherited wealth and status. Under these circumstances what shall he do? Shall he hunt with the hounds or run with the hares?

> Shall youth be taught to lower their level of expectation, to abandon the ideal of social mobility for social adjustment? Are they to be encouraged to hold fast to the old ideal of social mobility even though most of them will experience failure in its realization? Or will they be encouraged to set their hands to the long and arduous task of so modifying the economy as to make possible the older ideal of equal opportunity in a mobile society? (Edwards, 1944, p. 193)

But again, individual reactions to moral confusion are extremely variable. Many adolescents fail to perceive that any inconsistency exists. Some experience severe psychological conflict, others are hardly troubled. To many the new moral practices are abhorrent and are accepted reluctantly and with reservations—for purposes of survival only. But to others these same practices are a welcome invitation to join in an unprincipled and ruthless quest for power at any price. Still others in their rebellion and protests highlight the need to recreate the living and relevant aspects of the past, and to create "new images of life which will provide constancy in a kind of rapid change" (Keniston, 1965, p. 220). For "identity and ideology are two aspects of the same process. Both provide the necessary condition for further individual maturation and, with it, for the next higher form of identification, namely, the solidarity linking common identities in joint living, acting, and creating" (Erikson, 1968, p. 189). Yet both hippie and New Left movements are nonideological. In the language of Keniston "postmodern youth displays a special kind of openness, flexibility and unfinishedness. In one sense, of course, identity development takes place; but in another sense, identity is always undergoing transformations that parallel the transformations of the historical world" (Keniston, 1971, p. 289).

12

The Adolescent Peer Culture

IMPORTANCE OF SOCIAL RELATIONSHIPS
DURING ADOLESCENCE

In Chapter 10 we noted the marked shift of interest patterns to social-sex activities and concerns. It is well known that adolescents are concerned with establishing social relationships with age mates of both sexes. The preadolescent "spends his social hours largely in sex segregated friendship and play groups. Around adolescence he begins his encounters and experiments with heterosexual social life" (Douvan & Gold, 1966, p. 497). Douvan and Gold (1966) report an important transition in the nature of boy-girl interaction in girls at 14. "Girls under fourteen share active team sports with boys and make no very sharp distinction between activities appropriate for like-sexed and co-ed clubs. Beyond fourteen, girls share individual sports (swimming, golf, tennis) and social activities with boys, but not team sports and they distinguish more sharply between all-girl and co-ed activities" (Douvan & Gold, 1966, p. 497).

The prepotency of group interests in the extracurricular whirl of adolescent activities is reflected in the exaggerated attention to nuances of interpersonal relationships, in spontaneous conversation, and in the dearth of references to school subjects or situations. The increased frequency, length, and gossipy flavor of telephone conversations during adolescence adds further testimony to the adolescent's passionate absorption with interpersonal relationships. There is also

311

increased interest in parties, dancing, and in the use of the automobile for social purposes.

The reasons for this intense preoccupation with social experience are apparent. It is true, of course, that group activity is facilitated by the adolescent's greater mobility and newly won emancipation from the home. Group activity also provides an opportunity for gratifying newly acquired heterosexual needs and interests. Much more important, however, is the adolescent's increasing concern with acquiring earned status as an independent entity. And since there can be no status apart from a system of relationships to a constituted social unit, adolescent peer groups are "formed spontaneously to serve the function of a social institution, to secure a status and a social identity for youngsters not genuinely provided with such an identity by society at large" (Sherif & Cantril, 1947, p. 291). Denied membership in the adult community that dispenses status roles in the central stratum of social interaction, he must create a substitutive albeit peripheral status-giving instrumentality of his own.

Hence, more out of necessity than out of inclination,

adolescents progressively turn to the closer company of agemates in their transition from childhood to adulthood. . . in an adverse adult-made world in which they are marginal in varying degrees. They interact in their own adolescent circles, limited and influenced, of course, by their particular social setting at large. . . . [Their] most intense strivings for status and approval take place within such groups. . . . This gives rise to certain norms of behavior, to fashions and fads of dress and amusement peculiar to various adolescent groups. During these years of transition, adolescents achieve immediate status through conformity to the norms of their age-mate groups. For the time being these peculiar adolescent norms of experience and behavior become the adolescent's own values, determining his personal relationships and attitudes to an important degree. (Sherif & Cantril, 1947, p. 251).

And since the peer group is almost the exclusive source of the extrinsic adequacy based on earned status that he so desperately seeks, it is hardly surprising that he immerses himself so intensely in group experience, becomes so conscious of his own and others' status in the group, and seems so willing to undergo personal sacrifices to render it loyalty and preserve its integrity.

THE ADOLESCENT PEER GROUP IN RELATION
TO THE WIDER COMMUNITY

Like the child, therefore, the adolescent continues to enjoy a buffered relationship to the culture at large. He is anchored in a peripheral subculture of his own making, which cherishes values and established criteria of status distinct from those of the adult community. But here the resemblance ends, and several important distinctions arise. First, although many of the adolescent's characteristic interim goals are discontinuous with those of adults, they more nearly approximate adult standards and level of behavior than do the child's. Also, the adolescent is more aware of their interim and substitutive nature and is simultaneously making plans for his inclusion in the adult world. Second, although isolated from the main currents of adult society, the adolescent has a more lively interest in and keener insight into its inner workings than does his younger contemporary. And last, the adolescent peer culture conforms more closely to the adult model of socialization: a group of nonrelatives outside the home determines and controls the individual's major source of current status.

It is clear that the social goals of adolescents are basically oriented toward the adult world and that the chief function of the adolescent peer group is to provide an interim status. This much becomes evident from the fact that it dissolves as soon as adolescents achieve anchorage and status roles in the wider community. It can also be inferred from the fact that the social experience of the peer group is hardly discontinuous with the types of social skills and attitudes necessary for adult socialization. In fact, one of the chief functions that both adolescents and their culture attribute to the peer group is the apprenticeship it provides for adult living. During the enforced period of waiting the adolescent develops the social skills he believes will aid him when he enters the adult arena. His elders are grateful for the opportunity to reassure themselves that he has internalized sufficiently well the appropriate attitudinal pattern of his social class reference group to be entrusted with equal membership in it.

Finally, it is important to realize that the adolescent peer group is related to the wider community in the very important sense that its nature, structure, norms, and purposes are largely conditioned by the characteristics of the particular adult culture or subculture in which it is embedded. As a survey of various types of adolescent peer groups shows, such group formations [fail] in the larger sense [to enjoy] any existence independent of the social milieu in which they are formed. For these groups are obviously, in turn, products of economic, ethnic, and other major social situations in the society at large. . . . The very factors which give rise to spontaneous groups are inevitably found as features of the larger social system. And by the same token, the particular activities, standards, and the like which provide individuals with social standing, status, or popularity in the larger society or in a particular stratum or locality of that larger society loom as important in the activities of these more or less well-structured subgroups. . . .

In the last analysis even the major established standards of success or failure of the gang or the gangster world are derived from the competitve, individualistic and financially hoarding standards of the society at large. . . . The major patterns of the gang world are derived from the social system in which it functions. (Sherif & Cantril, 1947, pp. 310–312)

GENERAL CHARACTERISTICS
OF ADOLESCENT GROUP LIFE

Emphasis on subjective experience

In contrast to the essentially more extroverted preadolescent who is typically content to participate in group activities, the adolescent is much more interested in the subjective analysis of group experience. He is vitally concerned with subtle overtones and elusive undercurrents in interpersonal relations and attempts through introspection to conceptualize them more precisely. To be accepted formally as an impersonal social entity is no longer sufficient. He craves intimate acceptance as a person and is much more sensitive to the feelings of acceptance and rejection directed both toward himself and toward his fellow group members (Ausubel, Schiff, & Gasser, 1952; Gordon, 1972).

It is at first glance difficult to reconcile this greater emphasis on subjective experience with the adolescent's more fervent participation in group experience and diminished expression of individuality. Why as a more introspective and introverted personality should he manifest so strikingly the characteristics of extroversion? The most plausible suggestion is that despite his greater procilivities toward introversion he is obliged to surrender himself more completely to group interests and to forego his individuality because the group and not the home is the major source of his status. The marginality of the adolescent's status, his dependence on peer group acceptance, and the greater structural need of the adolescent peer group for conformity to its standards all produce an apparent but spurious increase in extroversion. Nevertheless, although the adolescent is required to participate more intensively in group activities and to place greater restraints on his individuality, there are no restrictions on his introverted tendency to subjectivize experience.

This greater need for more subjective and personal group experience is reflected in the adolescent's disposition to abandon the larger "gang" for the smaller and more intimate "crowd" or clique. Except in disorganized urban areas where gangs fulfill a special compensatory function in response to the unique deprivations of boys and girls who live there, gang interests are more typically representative of the preadolescent era (Dunphy, 1963; Hartup, 1970; M. C. Jones, 1944; Thrasher, 1927; Wolman, 1951). Although preadolescent gangs were typically unisexual until recently, contemporary American society is showing a trend away from the severe sex cleavage which was heretofore characteristic of our culture (Kuhlen & Houlihan, 1965) and in this respect facilitates the adolescent's transition to the more typically heterosexual intimate "crowd" or clique.

Group consciousness

In distinguishing the peer groups of childhood from those of adolescence, Goodenough (1945) observes that the adolescent gang or club is characterized by a solidarity and feeling of group consciousness which in most instances the social groups formed by young children lack.

The factors responsible for this enhancement of group consciousness are threefold. First, both structurally and functionally the adolescent peer group is a more definite, cohesive, and perceptible social entity than the group formations of childhood. It is by far a more organized, stable, and distinctive institution than the loosely knit and casual groupings of children, and also serves far more important functions for status needs, training, emancipation, and resistance. If only because of the tremendous power it wields over their lives, adolescents have reason to be acutely aware of its existence. Second, group solidarity becomes a more important and meaningful concept during adolescence. The ability of the peer group to gain status and privileges for its members is clearly dependent on the extent to which it can maintain its unity and integrity as a distinctive organization. Every adolescent has a personal stake in enhancing and safeguarding the cohesiveness and influence of the group. Self-interest imposes group-mindedness on him. Third, the greater concern with power and status that adolescents characteristically manifest in and of itself makes them more self-consciously aware of the status-giving and "pressure group" functions of their group formations.

Stratification along social class lines

During adolescence there is greater selectivity in the organization and composition of peer groups than during childhood. Douvan and Gold (1966) point out that studies of cliques demonstrate that "the game of *inclusion* and *exclusion* is both fevered and deadly at adolescence. Younger children form groups and practice exclusion, but at adolescence the force of the identity quest invests these ritual forms with greater significance" (p. 347). Adolescents are considerably more conscious than children of such factors as social class status, ethnic and racial origin, and religious affiliation (Ausubel & Sullivan, 1970; Mussen et al., 1974). A number of studies have brought out the force of social classes in clique lines in particular (Coleman, 1961; Havighurst et al., 1962; Hollingshead, 1949).

During adolescence, caste and class lines are drawn much more sharply, and only rarely is there any serious overlapping of social strata in the organization of the adolescent peer group. As pointed out, the reason for this development is the decreasing tolerance that the adult world shows for deviations from the approved pattern of class values as children advance in age. Once they stand at the threshold of the wider community, "playing is for keeps" and sentimental notions of equality can no longer be indulged. This is not to say that individual differences in personality are no longer important in determining relative status among a heterogeneous group of adolescents. Such differences continue to operate, but only intraclique-wise, after differential factors of social class origin have selectively organized individuals into relatively homogeneous subgroups. With his and their increasing age it becomes decreasingly possible for a child with a winning personality to gain acceptance from his economically more favored contemporaries if he happens to come from the "wrong side of the tracks."

Heterosexual basis of organization

The organization of the adolescent peer group differs strikingly from that of its preadolescent precursor. It is predicated on heterosexual attraction and joint participation in activities suitable for both boys and girls. Sociometric studies uniformly indicate a fair amount of cross-sex choices in the primary grades, an almost complete dearth of such choices during preadolescence, and a rapidly increasing choice of members of the opposite sex during the junior high school and high school periods (Bradley & Newhouse, 1975; Kuhlen & Lee, 1943; Reese, 1966). One of the important implicit functions of the adolescent peer group is to provide suitable opportunities for gratifying new interests in persons of the opposite sex.

Their earlier sexual maturation directs girls' interests to such heterosexual social activities as dancing and parties before boys. During the junior high school period girls take the initiative in converting disinterested and somewhat reluctant boys into dancing partners, and in "dragging" them to parties of their own contrivance. Were it not for this pressure from girls the difference between the sexes in the emergence of these interests would undoubtedly be even greater than it is.

Changes during adolescence

In addition to the above trends in adolescent socialization, several characteristic developments take place from early to late adolescence. Structurally, adolescent groups undergo increasing differentiation into more selective and intimate subgroups (Cole & Hall, 1970; Dunphy, 1963); choices of "best friends" become more stable (Hartup, 1970); and the concept of mutuality becomes the focal point of friendship in which interaction replaces the preadolescent notion of parallel partnership (Douvan & Gold, 1966; Dunphy, 1963). Dating and "going steady" increase in frequency (Douvan & Gold, 1966), and social activities show greater formality and sophistication. Although earlier studies (Meek, 1940; Tryon, 1939a, 1944) concluded, as the thorough review of Hartup (1970) also confirms, that older adolescents are less susceptible to the influence of the standards and values of the peer group, more recent studies point to evidence in the opposite direction (Mussen et al., 1974) as an indication of increased behavioral autonomy from authority during adolescence (Douvan & Adelson, 1966). Thus Devereux (1970, p. 135) states: "Hartup's review cites many studies which appear to indicate that older children are less susceptible to peer influence than younger children. Our own results run consistently in the opposite direction: when peers are pitted against adults, older children are more likely to choose the peer-sponsored side of the dilemmas." Toward the close of adolescence marriage and family life are contemplated as more imminent possibilities. However, as Douvan and Gold (1966) point out, the review of research on premarital love involvement by Burchinal (1964) concludes that steady dating for social reasons is probably as important and as common as steady dating that is marriage oriented. This seems to apply to both high school and college students. Thus heterosexual attachments are no longer as commonly perceived to be related to problems of long-term affectional needs and mating as earlier studies (Kirkpatrick & Caplow, 1945) indicated. Serious attention is given to vocational choice and preparation.

STRUCTURAL CHARACTERISTICS OF ADOLESCENT PEER GROUPS

Adolescent peer groups use most of the organizational principles of adult societies. These groups resemble adult formations more closely than childhood groupings in formality, stability, complexity and differentiation of roles, and self-consciousness of hierarchical distinctions and interpersonal attitudes. Like adult groups, "they have group purposes, standards or values, and rules of behavior. . . . Such groups also have methods of securing conformity. . . . [Although] the individuals in any such group may remain constant over a long period of time, many changes [occur] in its objectives. . . its values. . . and its relation to the adult society" (Tryon, 1944, p. 220).

But despite the general similarity of the adolescent peer culture to adult groupings, the structural properties of the former are to a certain extent uniquely derived from the special needs of the youth group and are especially influenced through imitation of and initiation by members of the next older developmental level (Ausubel, 1950).

Although various adolescent groups have many functions in common, a fact which makes for generality in such structural characteristics as differentiation into subgroups, conformity requirements, and effectiveness of sanctions, it is clear that the structural properties of different groups will vary according to (1) the specific aspirations of individual group members, (2) their relative feelings of belongingness in the community as a whole, and (3) the particular or specialized goals and functions of a given peer group. These factors are demonstrably related to social class values, ethnic and regional traditions, degree of social mobility, and specific kinds of deprivations (Sherif & Sherif, 1964).

Origins of the adolescent peer group

According to psychoanalytic theory, the adolescent peer group (and, indeed, the major portion of the adolescent's preoccupation with group experience) is a simple derivative of the mechanism of sublimation. It is assumed that the energy of the culturally frustrated sex drive is directly channelled into group activities and, as a result, sex needs are vicariously satisfied. We have presented evidence that psychophysiological sex drives cannot be successfully repressed or satisfied by indirect means; that premarital intercourse in lower-class groups and more prevalent petting and masturbation in middle-class segments of our culture gratify these drives. The origins of the adolescent peer group can be more parsimoniously traced to (1) the practice, established earlier in childhood and preadolescence, of spontaneously forming age mate groupings for play purposes, (2) the catalytic effect of the urgent need for achieving anchorage and earned status, and (3) the impossibility of realizing these goals in adult society. Peer group activities undeniably reduce the total load of frustration; however, they do this not by vicariously gratifying blocked sex impulses, but by improving the adjustment picture in other important areas of ego needs.

Differentiation into cliques

Of the adolescent's greater need for more intimate and subjective social experience we can say that "the age-mate reference group. . . defines identification and personal preferences only in broad outlines and only for standards and fads common to all who relate themselves to these groups" (Sherif & Cantril, 1947, p. 261).

The adolescent clique is a more or less permanent, closely knit, selective, and highly intimate small group of individuals who share common secrets (sexual and otherwise), desires, attitudes, problems, interests, and aspirations such as those based on family background, school activities, and the like (Good & Good, 1974; Nash, 1973; Sherif & Cantril, 1947). Shared purposes, interests, and social class values, although prerequisite, are not sufficient for clique formation. More important are personal compatibility, congeniality, and bonds of mutual admiration and affection. A crowd is a larger social aggregation in which interpersonal feelings are less important and more impersonality prevails. A crowd need only be homogeneous in background, goals, interests, and ideals, and does not require unvarying homogeneity of social distance between members. An adolescent gang is similar in all these ways to a crowd, but it is usually unisexual, places greater emphasis on achieving a specific group goal (sexual, athletic, delinquent, aggressive), requires more solidarity and loyalty from its members, maintains a more hostile, rebellious, and conspiratorial attitude toward organized adult society, and resembles the preadolescent gang in its preoccupation with excitement, adventure, and the formal trappings of organizational secrecy.

Gang interests and activities are displaced by "crowds" and cliques during adolescence except when gang formation is specially favored by urban slum conditions. In accordance with their earlier physiological maturation, girls form such cliques earlier than boys and continue to operate within a more exclusive and secretive atmosphere. This greater proclivity for clique formation in girls may indicate that they have less access than boys to more formal and public criteria of independent status in the adolescent peer culture. It may also reflect the well-established sex difference in favor of girls to be more interested in people and in the subtleties of interpersonal relationships. Such interests can obviously be gratified more easily in cliques than in larger groups. In support of this interpretation is the fact that adolescent girls, but not boys, use their perceptions of the sociometric attitudes of their age mates toward themselves in furthering their status in the group (Ausubel & Schiff, 1955b).

> The reference-group concept permits specification of the particular group or set of people on whom the individual depends in appraising himself and others. In complex and changing societies, these people may not be readily identified by socioeconomic classification or group of people. The relative status of this group in the social organization and his own position within it serve as standards [anchors] for his appraisal of performance by himself and others. (Sherif, 1958, p. 156)

Studies of adolescent cliques continue to show that social class has at least some influence on clique differentiation (Barker & Lunn, 1970; Hargreaves, 1967; Hess, 1970; Lacey, 1970; Nash, 1973). Other factors influencing clique differentiation are sex (Collins & Thomas, 1974; Hollingshead, 1949), attitudes toward school, IQ, and favorable or unfavorable perceptions of teachers toward children in a class. This is true both in the primary school and in the secondary school (Nash, 1973).

In addition, other more personal criteria are applied. An important factor during early adolescence is degree of social maturity, which is usually a function of pubescent status. Retarded sexual development prevents an individual from being accepted in a clique of normally mature adolescents (H. E. Jones, 1944). Appropriateness of interests is a more important criterion for membership in a crowd than in a clique; in a clique it is a necessary rather than a sufficient condition. At the clique level, the most crucial selective factors are personality characteristics.

Although the personality characteristics that promote compatibility in a given clique vary, obviously, from one clique to the next, it is reasonable to suppose that an individual who enjoys high sociometric status in a particular "crowd" probably possesses the attributes of personality that would make him acceptable to most of its component cliques. The personality factors associated with high sociometric status at various stages of adolescence will be discussed subsequently.

Snobbishness and exclusiveness in adolescent cliques cannot be interpreted as wholly a result of increased need for more intimate and congenial interpersonal relationships. There are at least two other motivations. First, by derogating other groups of individuals, perceiving them as inferior or undesirable, and treating them with contempt and scorn, it is clearly possible to enhance one's own marginal status relatively without expending the effort or ingenuity required for positive self-enhancement. This mechanism undoubtedly accounts in part for the strong prejudices of college students toward minority group members, for the condescending attitudes of high-prestige cliques (Junior League, fraternity and sorority members) toward the nonelite majority, and for some of the general intolerance shown by adolescents for any kind of deviancy or alleged inadequacy. Second, through snobbishness and cliquishness, it is possible to both "corner" and limit the availability of status. By making status a scarcer commodity, one makes its achievement a more signal accomplishment; by creating a deprived and to-be-pitied out-group, one enhances considerably the advantages and enjoyment of in-group status. Furthermore, by adroit political maneuvering, cliques (fraternities) are able to acquire a monopoly on all important extracurricular posts and offices in high school and college.

It is interesting to note that "while the individual is highly dependent on his same-sex peers during adolescence, the awakening of heterosexual interests is not accompanied by a corresponding increase in sensitivity to unlike-sex peer pressure" (Collins & Thomas, 1974, p. 77).

That girls are more status conscious and disdainful of subgroup members than boys is probably related to the fact that they traditionally enjoy less social mobility and fewer opportunities for acquiring earned status, and seek to protect more jealously whatever status they do have. That is, even as adults, women depend more than men on derived status (the status that accrues from husband, family, or social group) instead of an earned status that results from individual accomplishment and which is capable of transcending the limitations of family and class origin. Women today, however, increasingly play the role of traditional mothers and at the same time conceive of themselves as independent women equal with men, form ego attitudes relative to different reference groups simultaneously, and experience uncertainty, conflict, and "confused search for resolution" (Sherif, 1968, p. 157).

Conformity aspects of the peer culture

From the preadolescent to the adolescent period of development, as the child's dependence on and stake in the effectiveness of the peer group increase, the latter's power to exact conformity is concomitantly enhanced (Campbell, 1964; Costango & Shaw, 1966; Schmuck, 1969).

This conformity assumes exaggerated patterns particularly relative to conspicuous aspects of behavior, such as musical tastes, fashions, and fads (Mussen et al., 1974), to such an extent that for the adolescent there can be no stronger argument for having or doing a thing than that "all the others are doing it." Opinions, prejudices, beliefs, likes, and dislikes are also determined by the group, and the boy or girl who differs is made to feel the force of group ostracism unless he or she has sufficient strength to gather his peers around him (Goodenough, 1945; Stone & Church, 1968). The adolescent turns increasingly toward agemate groups and sets. "Even though his parents be loved and valued, the result is reduced emphasis on parental capability and overestimation of the worth of age mate capacities, as Prado (1958) has shown experimentally" (Sherif, 1968, p. 157).

WHY THE PEER GROUP EMPHASIZES CONFORMITY

Despite the apparent self-evidentness of the proposition, it is still necessary to inquire why such exaggerated emphasis is placed on conformity in adolescent peer groups. Two different kinds of explanations may be plausibly advanced: (1) those relating to the structural requirements of peer groups and (2) those relating to the characteristics of adolescents.

No institution, especially if it has status-giving functions, can exist for any length of time without due regard by its members for uniform, regular, and predictable adherance to a set of avowed rules and traditions. Hence, in its efforts to establish a new and distinctive subculture and to evolve a unique set of criteria for the determination of status and prestige, the peer society must do everything in its power to set itself off as recognizably distinct and separate from the adult society which refuses it membership. If this distinctiveness is to be actually attained, it cannot admit the possibility of widespread nonconformity; since obviously if every adolescent were permitted to exercise his newly acquired craving for individuality, an unrecognizable medley of behavior patterns would ensue. Under such conditions, there would be no peer culture, and hence no compensatory source of status (Ausubel, 1950).

Conformity is also essential to maintain the group solidarity that is necessary to offer effective and organized resistance to the encroachments of adult authority. Obviously, if an appeal to precedent or to a prevailing standard of adolescent behavior is to be the basis for exacting privileges and concessions from adults, a solid and united front with a minimum of deviancy must be presented to the world. Once a precedent is established as the result of widespread and uniform acceptance of a given practice, each individual stands to profit from it. Johnny can now say, "I want to stay out until midnight on Saturdays; all the other boys do."

The principle of group conformity, therefore, is a self-protective device which arises from the needs of the peer culture to establish and maintain its identity as the chief adolescent status-giving institution in our society; and he who dares to defy its authority and thereby expose the group to possible extinction becomes an arch criminal, an enemy of peer society, worthy of receiving the supreme penalty in its arsenal of retribution—complete and unequivocal ostracism (Ausubel, 1950).

Apart from the structural needs of the peer group, various developmental characteristics of adolescents make them prone to overvalue the importance of conformity. First, any person with marginal status is excessively sensitive to the threat of forfeiting what little status he enjoys as a result of incurring the disapproval of those on whom he is dependent. To allay the anxiety from the threat of disapproval, he conforms more than is objectively necessary to retain group acceptance or to avoid censure and reprisal. Thus, many perfectly safe opportunities for the expression of individuality are lost.

Second, as pointed out, adolescents are partly motivated to perceive age mates as deviants, nonconformists, and out-groupers because by so doing they can enhance the value of their own conformity and in-group status. The larger the number of persons who can be perceived as outside the charmed circle, the more individuals they can perceive as inferior to themselves, the greater their own self-esteem becomes by comparison, and the more status value their in-group membership acquires. These ends can be most expeditiously effected by (1) elevating by fiat certain esoteric practices or character-istics into unique virtues, values, and symbols of status, (2) imposing these standards on others by having them accept them at face value, and (3) acquiring a very low threshold for the perception of deviancy from these standards so that few individuals can qualify for admission to the select circle of the originators and only "true" exemplifiers of the hallowed norms.

WHY THE PEER GROUP CAN COMPEL CONFORMITY

Pressures for conformity to peer group standards originate both from the group and from within the individual. The group implicitly and explicitly makes clear to the individual that it expects and de-mands conformity for the moral support, the feeling of belong-ingness, the anchorage, the derived status, and the opportunities for earned status that it extends to him. These pressures become evident when the adolescent finds he must win a place for himself in the group by conforming to their values and standards and by faithfully participating in their interests and activities (Packard, 1961; Phelps & Horrocks, 1958; Segel, 1951; Thompson, 1965). Conformity becomes the acknowledged price of acceptance, and full membership is care-fully withheld until the group feels reasonably assured of the can-didate's willingness to assume the obligations he incurs in return for the patent advantages he gains.

The adolescent has little choice but to accept the proposition that is offered him. He is dependent on the peer group for status, secu-rity, and anchorage during these hectic years of transition. Sherif and Cantril (1947) hypothesized that the degree of influence of agemate membership group varies directly with the degree of psychological weaning from grown-ups and the intensity of adult-youth conflict; and that the need for conformity to peer group standards is in direct proportion to the increasing marginality of the adolescent's status. Hartup's review of research (1970) on peer influences reveals among other things the extent to which the peer group serves as a reference function and points to the adequacy of family adjustment as a key fac-tor in determining peer influence. Devereux (1970, p. 132) in his re-view of several studies conducted at Cornell by Bronfenbrenner, De-vereux, and others over a period of 10 years, states that in several of their samples there is "clear evidence that the most peer-oriented and gang-involved children tend to come home from either highly permis-sive or highly punitive homes, and that adult-conforming children tend to come from homes with optimum combinations of adequate but not smothering support, firm but not rigid control, and moderate but not excessive punishment. . . there was also evidence that these intermediate, moderate ranges of parental behavior are related to autonomy in children."

After the adolescent wins an assured place for himself in the group, still other factors reinforce conforming tendencies. He learns that group approval brings a welcome "reprieve" from his transitional anxiety, uncertainty, and disorientation. If his group approves, he can feel absolutely certain of the correctness of his position. No longer need he be tortured by ambiguity or conflicting standards. With experience he also gains insight into the group's structural need for conformity if it is to survive and maintain its identity. It becomes easier for him to accept the burden of conformity when he perceives that his status and his privileges depend on it.

Last, the adolescent comes to render conformity automatically as a voluntarily assumed obligation growing out of the feelings of loyalty, belongingness, gratitude, and indebtedness generated in the very process of interaction.

In closely knit groups individuals will undergo much personal sacrifice to render each other mutual help or to prosecute group goals. For the sake of the group an adolescent may incur risks and face dangers that he would never dream of undertaking for his own benefit. Sherif and Sherif (1969) in their experiment confirm what they have repeatedly observed in the field, and state that proportional to the stability of a group, its norms are binding on members even when they are not face-to-face. As one experiment suggests so clearly, "this adherence is not blind conformity but a product of interaction with high affect for people who really count for one another. Unless this emotional nexus is clearly understood, there is little chance for adequate analysis of the phenomena of conformity-deviation during adolescence" (Pollis, 1964, p. 128).

Allegiance to group norms may under certain circumstances be carried to the point of participation in delinquent activities of which an individual adolescent might personally disapprove (Ausubel, 1950).

If the implicit pressures of the group and the internalized restraints and endogenously derived dispositions of the individual are insufficient to keep him in line, explicit sanctions are imposed. Depending on the seriousness of the offense and the nature and functions of the group, the punishment may vary from ridicule, censure, and rebuff to complete ostracism and even death. Shaming and ridicule are the most frequent and widespread forms of penalty used by peer groups. In addition to the privately felt self-depreciation before the group experienced in any feeling of shame (including the shame of guilt), such shaming practices involve pointed public attention to the infraction, publicly administered scorn or rebuke, and the exposure of the culprit to general ridicule, humiliation, and "loss of face." The mere fact that public shaming is resorted to does not necessarily eliminate the possibility that the offender experiences guilt feelings either before and subsequent to his offense or with and following his public humiliation.

INDIVIDUAL DIFFERENCES IN THE NEED TO CONFORM

The prevalence and strength of conforming tendencies during adolescence do not mean that there are no individual differences in the extent and quality of these traits. The highly self-assertive person, for example, can only restrain his individuality to a point; and the extreme introvert inevitably draws a line beyond which he refuses to participate in boisterous and exhibitionistic activities. The adolescent who has a highly developed set of moral or religious convictions may refuse to condone the practices of his group. Other individuals may have overwhelming interests that are regarded with scorn by their agemates. Finally, the nonsatellizer's need for ego aggrandizement and his lack of loyalty and "we-feeling" may cause him to betray group interests for personal advantage. If any of these personality traits are unusually strong they may lead to a sufficient deviancy either to make the individual unacceptable for peer group membership or to induce him to reject the desirability of identifying himself with his agemates.

Even apart from these deviancy-prone individuals, "what may be construed as a distinct group of adolescents are those who manifest quite autonomous and independent behavior, denoting a sense of self-sufficiency and competence in formulating their perceptions and lives" (Purnell, 1970, p. 238).

IMPACT OF GROUP STRUCTURAL NEEDS ON ADOLESCENT VALUES

It is hardly surprising that some of these unique structural characteristics of adolescent peer groups inevitably influence the value systems of adolescents. The need for conformity places a premium on loyalty and moral expediency, encourages snobbishness and intolerance, and deemphasizes the importance of moral courage and consistency. Devereux (1970, p. 137) reports that in the Cornell studies, subjects "who reported frequent association with peers consistently pictured themselves as more ready and willing to yield to temptation and go along with the crowd." He points to the "sobering set of findings" which indicate that the hold of the peer group increases from middle childhood to adolescence for peer-oriented children at the expense of the family.

That adolescents evolve extreme, unique, and esoteric values largely reflects the structural need to establish a distinctive subculture, recognizably different from those of adults and children. Respect for this structural need confines competition between groups and between individuals within a group to a struggle to outdo others in esotericism. From this arises a bewildering array of fads which change swiftly and capriciously; but while each is in vogue, woe unto him who dares to challenge the axiomatic superiority over all other possible alternatives with which it is invested.

Last, the undercurrent of stereotyped hostility and resistiveness to adults, which accounts for much of the peer group's solidarity, gives rise to an emphasis on norms of behavior that are deliberately perverse and shocking to adult standards. One manifestation of this rebellious attitude is an insistence on exemplifying, both prematurely and in extreme fashion, all of the external symbols of adult privilege and sophistication that under ordinary circumstances would be perceived as immoderate and in poor taste.

Devereux (1970) rightly questions whether data support the theories of Piaget, Parsons, and Kohlberg with regard to the positive role of peer experience for moral development. Is the road from middle childhood to adolescence one of continuous moral regression? He then points out that for autonomous moral judgment peer-group experience may play a crucial role. He reports that many of the high adult-scoring subjects fell easy prey to experimental pressure. "Autonomous or self-controlling children—those who were least influenced by our experimental pressures—typically scored in some intermediate range between either extreme adult or peer conformity" (Devereux, 1970, p. 137).

INTERPERSONAL RELATIONSHIPS WITHIN THE PEER GROUP

Up to this point, we have focused on the general characteristics of group experience during adolescence and on the structural properties of the adolescent peer group. But what about interpersonal relations among individual adolescents? Why do some individuals achieve high status and others low status within the group? Why are some rejected whereas others become leaders? Why do certain individuals choose each other as friends?

All of these are questions about the relationship between individual differences in personality, ability, and intelligence on the one hand, and the relative standing of the individual group member on the other. Also crucial to this relationship are differences between individuals in their approach to group experience and in their relative needs for status and prestige. Nor should we overlook the fact that as a result of interaction between individual differences in personality or between conflicting needs for superior standing in the group, tensions are generated that exert a disruptive influence on intragroup cohesion, the very factor which accounts for the social effectiveness of the peer group. Because the adolescent has no other alternative by which to measure his success, the greater success of some whose status is similar to his may threaten to disrupt the solidarity of those on whom he depends and appear to him a direct challenge to his own adequacy (Zachry, 1940).

Individual approaches to group experience

Although it is true that, in general, adolescents have greater need than children to acquire earned status, the relative magnitude and urgency of this need is inversely proportional to the strength of the residual intrinsic self-esteem that a given adolescent brings with him from childhood. The relative urgency of the need for earned status also varies inversely with the degree of current derived status that an adolescent is able to extract from his relationships with others. It follows that individual differences in the need for status in the adolescent peer group will depend, at least in part, on the extent to which satellization takes place during childhood. To the individual with a normal history of satellization, peer group membership provides derived status and constitutes an intrinsic ego support. He experiences a certain spontaneous joy and enthusiasm in group activity which follows from the "we-feeling" associated with group relatedness. To the nonsatellizer, on the other hand, the field of interpersonal relations is just another arena in which he contends for extrinsic status and additional ego aggrandizement. There is no identification with or self-subordination to group interests, and no possibility of deriving spontaneous satisfaction out of gregarious activity. Every social move is carefully deliberated for the possible advantages that may accrue from it, and the currency of social interchange is supplied by the synthetic manufacture of attitudes, remarks, and behavior which can be construed as conventionally appropriate for the specifications of a given situation.

We saw earlier that an individual's approach to adolescent peer group experience reflects the impact of the type of child-rearing attitudes to which he has been exposed and the type of relationships he enjoyed with his first socializers (his parents); in addition, the pattern of his earlier peer relations (popularity, leadership, conformity, cooperation, competition) plays a role.

Deep-seated personality defects rooted in the parent-child relationship influence many individuals to avoid interpersonal relations to varying degrees in preference to competing for status in the peer group. Rejected, overdominated, overprotected, underdominated, and overvalued children are heir to personality and behavioral traits that make their incorporation into the peer group difficult indeed. The peer group is ill-prepared to gratify the special social needs of one or another of these personalities, i.e., their needs for special protection, for continuous direction, or for invariable deference. Under the circumstances, group life must prove distasteful and unsatisfying, inviting retreat to the home.

The failure of rejected, overdominated, and overprotected children to learn adequate social techniques of self-defense and self-assertion because of the habit of deference to the will of others also disposes them to avoid the vicissitudes and pitfalls of group experience.

Furthermore, the overprotected child is oversensitized to the possibility of physical mishandling and unfair treatment at the hands of his age-mates, and the overdominated child (who has never learned to protect his rights) is continually fearful of being duped and exploited. The rejected child, on the other hand, is especially fearful of a repetition of the rejection he experienced at home. Hence, he finds it more agreeable and less hazardous (in terms of possible exploitation by others) to curtail his interpersonal relations to a minimum. The social isolation resulting from this withdrawal further limits the possibility of learning realistic social roles. And in the process of using withdrawal as an adjustive technique he usually acquires a habitual introversion and asociality which further restricts the scope of his social interaction with both boys and girls.

The prognosis for the eventual assimilation of underdominated and overvalued individuals into the adolescent peer group is somewhat more hopeful. Although they are disheartened by failure to receive the deference to which they are accustomed at home, and although they antagonize their associates by their excessively overbearing and obnoxiously aggressive self-assertion, they frequently learn by adolescence how to express their aggressiveness in more socially acceptable forms.

Surprising changes in introversion-extroversion and in general approach to group experience may occur at adolescence, when the individual is largely released from the influence of the home and enters the more autonomous, demanding, and status-conscious adolescent peer culture. The essentially "tender-skinned" individual, protected by a benevolent home, who had hitherto impressed others as extroverted, may now show greater introversion when his fate is more completely in the hands of less solicitous age-mates. Contrariwise, an intrinsically "thick-skinned" child, who appeared to recoil from interpersonal relations as a result of rejection or over-domination in the home, may become much more outgoing when his relatively more benevolent peer group plays the major role in his socialization.

Bases for relative status and prestige in the group

EVALUATION OF PEER GROUP STATUS

The preceding analysis of individual differences in the need for earned status and in approach to group experience has important implications for the evaluation of a given individual's measured status in the group. First, the adolescent's satisfaction or dissatisfaction with the status he enjoys is a function not only of its absolute magnitude but also of his aspirations for status. Second, this status can lead to feelings of success or failure, of adequacy or inadequacy, only to the extent that he is ego-involved in the group. If the status that the group can bestow lies completely beyond the sphere of his ego interests, it matters little to him whether it is low or high.

Equally important for evaluating an individual's status in the group is the methodological problem of determining it. Traditionally, sociometric techniques measure such status in terms of the weighted frequency with which an individual is chosen as first, second, or third choice by his age-mates for such roles as seat mate, friend, work mate, or fellow committee member. However, when the sociometric status scores of an adolescent group obtained in this way were correlated against corresponding scores derived by averaging the ratings of acceptance-rejection given an individual by all of the group members, the resulting correlation was only 0.46 (Ausubel & Schiff, 1952). Hence, it means one thing to achieve a relatively high level of popularity with most members of a group, and something quite different to be wanted frequently as a best friend. Which type of status is more meaningful can be determined only in reference to the needs and desires of a particular individual. An ostensibly popular adolescent in a "formed group" of casual friends may, in terms of his deep needs for intimate personal relationships, be no more than a "successful isolate" or "stranger in his group" who is compensating for rejection at the hands of the clique he truly wishes to join by participating vigorously in lower priority social activities. On the other hand, it is also possible for some individuals with little status in the group to survive fairly well because of one or two close friends.

FACTORS ASSOCIATED WITH HIGH PEER GROUP STATUS

In general, popularity among peers depends on the willingness of the individual, child or adolescent, to accept the group, and to make necessary compromises toward the peaceful and efficient operation of the group with its needs, purposes, and objectives (Fey, 1955; Hartup, 1970; Moore, 1967; Singer, 1951; Tryon, 1944). Since different groups have different goals and values, since changes occur in the needs, purposes, and personnel of a single group, and since an individual enjoys membership in many different groups and is even valued for different qualities by special subgroups (e.g., boys and girls) within a group, the factors associated with high peer group status are extremely variable. Research findings on this question can have reference only to the mean prestige value of various character-istics among different representative or special groups of adolescents, and not to the factors that actually account for high or low status in a particular group.

Numerous factors of personal background in different areas of adjustment have been found significantly related to sociometric status at three contrasting economic levels and for adolescents generally. Of great significance is the fact that "a basic commonness" was discov-ered in the background experiences predictive of social acceptability among the economic levels (Feinberg & Fryer, 1950). This indicates widespread agreement within the culture about desirable traits of personality. Hartup (1970) in his review of the literature states that a large number of studies show peer acceptance to be directly as-sociated with such personality traits as friendliness, sociability, social visibility, and outgoingness. Moreover, the results of these studies show that these particular characteristics hold across age levels—for preschool children as well as adolescents. Data for young adolescents also parallel those for younger children. "Peer acceptance between the ages of 12 and 16 is positively associated with sociability (Marks, 1954); lack of desire to change the behavior of other members of the peer group (Rosen et al., 1961); being helpful, good natured, and the 'life of the party' (Elkins, 1958); friendliness and enthusiasm (Grun-lund & Anderson, 1953); being 'good company' " (Hartup, 1970, p. 388). Among older adolescents positive correlations between sociability and peer acceptance are reported (Keislar, 1953). In fact, social participation and peer acceptance are positively related at all age levels, even though their reciprocal influence remains to be verified by other than correlational techniques employed to date by studies on the subject.

Adolescent studies indicate that social acceptance is positively related to conformity to peer group mores (Elkins, 1958); to good moral judgment as perceived by peers (Devereux, 1970; Porteus & Johnson, 1965) and to sensitivity to the feelings of others (Loban, 1953). However, popularity with peers is more important for girls than for boys (Simmons, 1975). Keislar (1953) reported positive correlations between sociability and both peer acceptance and prestige. For girls, however, sociability was correlated more highly with acceptance than with prestige. In both sexes, on the other hand, prestige was more highly correlated with marks, school effort, and other achievement-oriented characteristics than was peer acceptance. Peer acceptance, therefore, appears to have somewhat different correlates during adolescence than does prestige (Hartup, 1970).

SEX DIFFERENCES IN THE BASIS OF PEER STATUS

The chief differences in the qualities admired in the opposite sex by adolescent boys and girls lie in the greater emphasis girls place on acceptance by parents and in the greater emphasis boys place on physical attraction and "good looks" (Purdue Opinion Panel, 1961). More important, however, is the greater continuity from preadolescence to adolescence in the qualities that make for high peer status among boys. Unlike boys, girls have no core value—such as athletic prowess—which persists in the peer culture as a significant determinant of status. Heterosexual effectiveness becomes for adolescent boys just another component of a previously defined masculinity; but in the case of girls it becomes an entirely new and almost solitary criterion for femininity and for feminine prestige in the adolescent peer society.

But if boys enjoy an advantage in this respect, girls are more fortunate in another. For a boy to be popular with girls he must first achieve popularity with his own sex on the basis of superior masculine attributes. But "girls who are most attractive to boys can be liked or disliked or even regarded almost with indifference by their own sex" (Tryon, 1944, p. 229). If a girl is not accepted by her own sex, another source of acceptance is open to her; whereas rejection by the peer group is more complete and devastating for boys.

CONTINUITY OF PEER STATUS DURING ADOLESCENCE

Because of the continuity in (1) the personality traits that are valued in the culture and in a particular subculture, (2) the personnel of a given peer group, and (3) the personality structure of individuals, it would seem reasonable to expect that relative status in the peer group maintains considerable stability over the adolescent years. Such stability is present even in the 3-year period between ages 7 and 10 when peer relations are much more fluid (Bonney, 1943). Between junior and senior high school, there is also considerable continuity in the individuals who provide leadership to the group (Levi, 1930). Sherif and Sherif (1969) in their observations of several dozen existing groups of adolescents in natural field conditions found in their analysis of observers' ratings of status over a period of 6 months to a year greater status consistency for the highest and lowest status positions and greater variability in the intermediate ranks.

On the other hand, changes in the membership and purposes of the peer group and in the pattern of personality traits that are admired at different stages of adolescence* lead to inevitable fluctuations in the relative status of individuals. Even in the highly structured street-corner gang, where positions in the group are relatively well defined and stable, status should not be viewed in static terms. When the pattern of interaction changes, the customary way of interacting with other members associated with one's status is altered. Then a change in position takes place (Whyte, 1943). Some people therefore have to cope with the problem of status deflation, whereas others have to learn how to handle new power that comes with higher status (Tryon, 1944).

However, in general, the status structure and the norms of the group "provide a remarkably accurate basis for predicting the behaviors of individual members" (Sherif & Sherif, 1969, p. 121).

Perception of status in the group

Realistic interpersonal relations and the smooth functioning of the group in terms of the differentiated status roles of its component members necessarily depend on the ability (socioempathy) of individ-

---

* A relatively frequent cause of loss in status lies in the fact that a particular role (e.g., clowning) successfully played at an earlier age may become inappropriate to the changing standards of the group. If an individual who excels in a role fails to perceive the diminished esteem in which it is held, he may continue to play or overplay it and thereby progressively undermine his status in the group.

uals to perceive to what extent they and others are accepted or rejected by the group. We have noted that this ability improves with increasing age and accounts in part for the greater complexity and
differentiation of older peer groups. At the adolescent level girls are
significantly superior to boys in predicting the ratings of acceptance-
rejection given them by their own but not by the opposite sex group.
The sociometric attitudes (acceptance-rejection) of girls are also more
accurately perceived by both sexes than those of boys. In perceiving
the sociometric status of others, boys are more accurate for members
of their own sex, whereas girls are equally well aware of the status
hierarchies within either sex group (Ausubel & Schiff, 1955b); their
superiority to boys in this respect inheres in their ability to perceive
more accurately the status of members of the opposite sex group.

The chief factor accounting for the relative accuracy of either an
adolescent's perception of another's acceptance or rejection of him
or of the other's status in the group is his own degree of acceptance
of that other person (Ausubel & Schiff, 1955b). Acceptance of another
results both in a more accurate perception and in an overestimate;
rejection leads to precisely the opposite consequences. Surprisingly
enough, there is no relationship whatsoever between ability to perceive own and others' status in the group. But in accordance with the
popular notion that women are more sensitive than men in perceiving
interpersonal attitudes, and thereby in furthering their social effectiveness in group situations, adolescent girls (but not boys) who have
superior socioempathic ability enjoy higher status in the group (Ausubel & Schiff, 1955b). On the other hand, controlling for sex and for
actual level of popularity, it is found that adolescents who perceive
popularity as more valuable are more self-conscious and less stable in
their self-pictures (Simmons, 1975).

Adolescent friendships with age mates of the same sex

Adolescent friendships are the ultimate consummation of the
progressive selectivity and differentiation of interpersonal relations
along a social distance scale that begins with crowd and clique formation. Although this final step generally occurs within the framework
of crowd or clique membership, it may sometimes (as with deviants)
be the sole form of positive social intercourse with age mates.

The purpose of adolescent friendships is not, as in preadolescence, merely to satisfy the need for a congenial but relatively impersonal playmate or companion in the prosecution of mutual interests,
but to obtain intimate interpersonal experience and mutual understanding and sympathy. With increasing age, children and adoles-

cents turn more and more to their age mates in sharing confidences and seeking advice about problems that trouble them. Unlike preadolescents, who are intensely eager for a large number of friends, adolescents desire to form fewer but deeper, more intimate friendships (Makaric, 1971; Meek, 1940). For similar reasons, "best friends" are almost invariably of the same sex, since it is practically impossible to overcome traditional barriers between the sexes in speaking freely about intimate personal problems, especially those concerning sex. Also, if a cross-sex relationship happens to become highly confidential, it is more than likely to lead eventually to affectional or marital ties.

BASES FOR THE SELECTION OF FRIENDS

The selective factors in the determination of adolescent friendships can be inferred from two related lines of evidence: (1) from the ways in which pairs of friends are similar, as well as from the extent of this similarity;* and (2) from the verbal statements of adolescents about the qualities they seek or desire in friends. It is clear that age, sex, and propinquity are determining factors in choice of friends among adolescents (Cole & Hall, 1970; Hartup, 1970; King & Easthope, 1973; Makaric, 1971). Hartup (1970) in his review of the literature stresses the fact that the role played by personality characteristics is far from being clear. Measuring devices currently available for ascertaining the resemblances between friends are too gross to give adequate insight into the subtle factors that obviously must be operative in generating mutual attraction between individuals.

The question of similarity or complementarity in friendship is not settled. Most studies dealing with this aspect of friendship have concentrated on adolescents but they are not extensive. Research results in similarity of friends are not in full agreement.

Haller and Butterworth (1960) found that occupational aspiration and educational aspiration were correlated within pairs of friends. . . . But Thorpe (1955) found no differences in the similarity existing between pairs of friends, pairs of partial friends, and pairs of nonfriends in terms of IQ, neuroticism, or popularity. Earlier studies yielded inconsistent findings with respect to IQ similarity in mutual friends. Bonney (1942) and Barbe (1954) found evidence of such similarity; Furfey (1927) and Challman (1932) did not. (Hartup, 1970, p. 403)

---

*Degree of similarity is customarily expressed as a coefficient of correlation between the paired scores of a sizeable number of mutual friends on a measure of a given trait.

Hilkevitch (1960) investigated in a group of 54 eighth grade boys and girls, all of whom were involved in reciprocal sociometric choices, the question of similarity and complementarity. The latter was evident in male pairs. For example, a large number of "attention seekers" sought friends who could share the limelight. Popularity with the opposite sex was the only reputation variable congruent among male friends. Girls' friendships were based more on congruence in variables measuring "labile, outgoing social behavior (e.g., reputed interest in having a good time, being fun, being a best friend). Thus common sociobehavioral traits appear to be aspects of friendship choice in girls, whereas complementary qualities seem to be more salient in the friendship patterns of boys" (Hartup, 1970, p. 403).

In comparing the profiles of 30 pairs of high school and college friends with the profiles of randomly selected individuals, Izard (1960) found no evidence of complementarity, and his data dealing with *Edwards' Personal Preference Schedule* showed significantly more similar profiles among friends than nonfriends.

Hartup also cites the findings of Byrne and Griffith (1966) showing that perceived similarity in attitudes draws people to each other. Makaric (1971) found that among 640 adolescents in 25 classes in their final year of secondary school in a socialist province of Vojvodina, moral qualities and character were the bases given in establishing and maintaining friendships.

Leadership in adolescence

In contrast to friendship and popularity, which represent the outcome of the feelings (like-dislike, acceptance-rejection) that group members develop toward each other, leadership is more closely related to the functional properties of groups. This does not mean that the leader's personality and the group members' feelings toward him are irrelevant to the achievement and maintenance of leadership. It means rather that those aspects of the leader's personality that affect the functional effectiveness of the group and those particular feelings of group members toward the leader that are related to his functional efficacy are most relevant to these problems.

The leader may be best described as the person who moves the group to action (Cunningham, 1951). Leadership status is a "hierarchical power dimension having to do with initiative and effective conduct of activities in the group and with control in *decision* processes" (Sherif & Sherif, 1964, p. 158). Leadership, therefore, will be bestowed by the group on that individual who in its judgment has the personality attributes, the experience, and the skills to organize, mobilize, and represent the group best in achieving its paramount needs and goals at a given stage of its development. It is significant that social insight is more an attribute of the leader than of nonleaders (Chowdry & Newcomb, 1952; Hurlock, 1973). However, ability to judge group opinion is more effective in familiar and relevant issues (Chowdry & Newcomb, 1952), and the longer the individual has been a member of a group, the more likely he will be to evaluate group opinion accurately (Creson & Blakeney, 1970; Gilchrist, 1959).

In friendship and popularity, however, affectional attitudes toward others operate more as ends in themselves. It is highly possible for a very ineffectual person to be popular; in fact, many easygoing individuals are popular for this reason. But although popularity does not necessarily guarantee leadership, leaders, by the nature of things, can seldom be unpopular for any length of time and retain their status (Hurlock, 1973). Although a leader is not obliged to form close friendships within the group, if he does he is more apt to "weather declining status" more satisfactorily (Tryon, 1944).

HOW LEADERSHIP IS ACHIEVED AND MAINTAINED

In accordance with its functional nature, leadership is conferred by the group as the top rank in the group structure and

> involves the shared expectations of other members for a particular individual occupying that position. These expectations vary markedly in terms of the kinds of activities the group engages in and qualities which count in their scheme of things. Invariably, however, they involve the supposition that what the leader approves of, what he suggests himself, or what he decides will be accomplished, will work out well. When his initiations to action and his decisions lead to failure in interteam competition, or result in social gatherings which bore and distress members, or get his fellow members into unnecessary trouble with authorities (parents, police, school)—then his word ceases to be effective. A new leader takes the initiative or the membership drifts away to other centers of interest. (Sherif & Sherif, 1964, pp. 159–160)

The popularly held belief that gangs are creatures of dynamic leaders is seldom true. Quite the contrary. The leader emerges out of the interaction of the existing gang (Thrasher, 1927).

The "group-given" nature of adolescent leadership is apparent from the fact that the leader cannot successfully disregard the established traditions of the group or the common purposes that he is chosen to advance (Thrasher, 1927). He cannot wield his power capriciously or abusively (Thrasher, 1927); and more than any other member of the group, he is required to honor his obligations scrupulously (Whyte, 1943). Nor can adult authorities impose a leader on the group by choosing a promising candidate and "training" him for leadership. If this is done, actual leadership power is withdrawn by the group, and the adult-imposed individual retains at best a nominal status out of deference to his sponsors (Cunningham, 1951).

The group-given nature of leadership can also be inferred from its situational character. The personality attributes or competencies that make for successful leadership in one culture, subculture, peer group, or even in one temporal phase or activity of a single peer group may lead to failure in another. To a certain extent, of course, the prestige of leadership ability in one area carries over without any objective justification to an entirely unrelated area ("halo effect"). Human beings in general feel more secure if they assume that a leader personifies the virtues his office requires. But the more experienced and sophisticated individuals become in group activities, the more they choose leaders on the basis of situational requirements, and the less they confuse the criteria for leadership with popularity or personal loyalty to friends (Clifford & Cohn, 1964; Cunningham, 1951).

Once attained, leadership in adolescence is maintained in various ways. Control through fear of physical prowess is much less important than in preadolescence, but it remains a significant factor in most lower-class gangs (Thrasher, 1927; Whyte, 1943). More important in adolescent "crowds" is the leader's ability to give or withdraw belongingness, to help the group achieve its aims by his special skills or general cleverness, to influence the group to place high value on the activities in which he excels, and to manipulate situations to gratify the special needs and allay the anxieties of insecure persons in the group (Cunningham, 1951). If he can succeed with these insecure persons he earns their loyalty and support; but first he must be perceptive enough to sense their difficulties and skillful enough to extend sympathy without incurring the wrath of the group for befriending deviants. Sherif and Sherif (1964, p. 180) referring to varying latitudes of acceptance and leadership conclude that "the more significant the activity for the identity and continued maintenance of the group and its central interests, the narrower the range of acceptable behaviors for all members, the latitude for the leader being narrowest. Conversely, the more incidental the activity to the foregoing concerns of the group, the broader the range of individual variation without the arousal of sanctions, the latitude for the leader being greatest."

The skillful leader also exercises control and influences his constituency through his lieutenants (Whyte, 1943). And when leadership changes, it generally passes on to one of these rather than to a peripheral member of the group (Whyte, 1943). One of the surest signs of the impending elevation of a person to leadership is his increasing degree of association with individuals of high status in the group (Tryon, 1944).

CHARACTERISTICS OF ADOLESCENT LEADERS

Although the characteristics of effective leaders vary depending on the requirements of the specific subculture, peer group, and situation, certain traits obviously have more leadership value than others in the majority of adolescent peer group situations within the general framework of the American culture. Research findings agree that the adolescent leader surpasses the nonleader in six broad areas of personality that are self-evidently related to leadership functions: (1) *physical appearance:* attractive, although not necessarily beautiful or handsome; appropriately clothed, judged by the standards of the group; acceptable body build and poise; athletic prowess (Cole & Hall, 1970; Hurlock, 1973); physical strength (Rosen et al., 1961); (2) *intelligence:* above average mental alertness and energy—how much above average depends on the nature of activities (Mitchell, 1970); (3) *decision-making ability:* discriminating judgment (Cole & Hall, 1970); firmness of decision (Carter, 1941; Thrasher, 1927); low suggestibility (Hunter & Jordon, 1939; Sherif & Sherif, 1964); self-confidence (Cole & Hall, 1970; Cowley, 1931); and imagination (Thrasher, 1927); (4) *interests:* maturity (Hunter, 1939); breadth of interests (Cowley, 1931); participation in social and leisure time activities (Pauley, 1958; Snyder, 1970); and conversation skills (Ahlbrand & Hudgins, 1970; Bretsch, 1952); (5) *socially relevant aspects of temperament:* extroversion, dominance (Rosen et al., 1961); unselfishness, fairness, flexibilility, and dependability (Hurlock, 1973); (6) *background factors:* better than average social status and income (Coleman, 1961; Karasick et al., 1968; Nelson, 1966).

STABILITY OF LEADERSHIP

Leadership fluctuates with changes in the needs of the group as determined both by social maturation and by various situational factors. Nevertheless, the basic pattern of personality traits associated with leadership ability must remain fairly constant beginning with adolescence. This is shown by the fact that although there is little continuity of leadership from elementary to junior high school, there is considerable continuity from junior to senior high school and from senior high school to college (M. C. Jones, 1965; Nelson, 1966; Pryer et al., 1962). Furthermore, high school leaders of both sexes are more successful in life after school than nonleaders (Havighurst, 1957; Marshall, 1957; Snyder, 1970).

The socially rejected or deviant adolescent

In the adolescent peer group, deviancy and social rejection are functionally synonymous. Whether the basis for the deviancy is active or passive and whether the deviant role is voluntarily assumed by the individual or forcibly thrust on him by the group does not alter the fact of social rejection, but it does have important implications for its interpretation, seriousness, and eventual outcome. At any rate, whatever the cause of the deviancy, because of the crucial role played by the peer group during adolescence, the deviant is placed at a terrible disadvantage in the struggle to emerge mature and adjusted at the conclusion of this period of development. By their own admission, at least 7 percent of adolescent boys experience serious difficulty in making friends, and 15 percent are seriously concerned by bashfulness (Fleege, 1945).

Socially rejected or deviant adolescents may be conveniently grouped into three main categories*: (1) individuals who by virtue of group-inappropriate personality traits, physical characteristics, or interests are rejected by the group; (2) individuals who reject group experience because they find it traumatic or unrewarding as a result of their personality makeup or social incompetence; and (3) individuals who neither reject nor are rejected by the group because of socially inappropriate or inadequate aspects of personality, but who are willing to accept ostracism from the group, if need be, to pursue other needs and interests. In the third category are opportunists who are willing to flaunt group standards to gain adult approval, highly self-assertive adolescents who are too individualistic to conform to group expectations, individuals with strong moral convictions who spurn any form of moral compromise or expediency, and adolescents with all-consuming interests in esoteric activities that enjoy low status in the crowd.

---

* In many instances, of course, all three factors operate in the same individual. The overprotected child, for example, is rejected by the group because of negative personality traits, withdraws from group experience because of social incompetence, and may develop strong nonsocial interests as a compensation for his social isolation.

CHARACTERISTICS OF SOCIALLY REJECTED ADOLESCENTS

The second and third categories of deviants have been discussed elsewhere. In this section we shall confine our attention to the characteristics of individuals who are socially unacceptable to their age-mates. Many such individuals (persons rejected or overdominated by parents) concomitantly reject the group because of asocial personality trends, social incompetence, strong nonsocial interests, or fear of rebuff. Others in this group also adjust to their outcast status by adopting a "sour grapes" attitude, by pretending that it is they who reject the group, that the group is beneath their notice, and that their isolation is voluntary, admirable, and indicative of special virtue.

Three main clusters of socially unacceptable personality traits have been found in adolescents who are rejected by their peer group. First are traits associated with the obnoxiously overbearing, aggressive, and egocentric individual who frequently gives a history of being underdominated or overvalued by his parents. Such adolescents are described by their associates as domineering (Mussen et al., 1974), interfering (Jennings, 1943), bullying (Dimock, 1937), conceited (Northway, 1944), exhibitionistic, attention-seeking and demanding, resentful of criticism, querulous, and irritable (Jennings, 1943). Another group of socially unacceptable personality traits characterize the adolescent who failed as a child to learn the give-and-take techniques of peer group play, who failed to develop social poise, skills, and effective methods of self-assertion and self-defense. This type of socialization history is typical of the overdominated, overprotected, or rejected child. Others regard him as excessively overdependent, fearful of being misunderstood, abused, or taken advantage of, and given to whining, nagging, and complaining (Dimock, 1937; Jennings, 1943). The third cluster of seriously unacceptable personality traits reflects a degree of introversion sufficiently disabling to interfere with spontaneous and uninhibited participation in group activities and social events. Included in this group are such characteristics as timidity, shyness, withdrawing behavior, preoccupation with introspective experience and intellectual interests, preference for social isolation (Dimock, 1937), a "wet blanket" approach to group activities, lack of social poise and skills (Kuhlen & Bretsch, 1947), and an apparent apathy and listlessness (Northway, 1944) which may indicate relative disinterest in the more immediate data of sensory and emotional experience.

Apart from these major personality configurations associated with social rejection in the peer group, individuals characterized as "nervous," "jumpy" (Dimock, 1937; Jennings, 1943), noisy (Northway, 1944), or prone to fabricate alibis and carry grudges (Dimock, 1937) enjoy low sociometric status. The merciless law of group conformity is also applied to the unfortunate somatic deviants—the short, the fat, the ugly, the puny, the awkward, the oversized, and the late-maturer (H. E. Jones, 1943; Stolz & Stolz, 1944).

EVALUATION OF SOCIAL REJECTION

In evaluating a given instance of social rejection during adolescence, one must consider many factors. First, it should be realized that seldom indeed is either acceptance or rejection completely unanimous in any sizeable group. Second, rejection is not as self-evidently obvious as it may seem. Frequently adolescents who perceive themselves as rejected are seriously in error. Teachers also are apt to be mistaken about the group's acceptance or rejection of an individual. The ability of teachers to perceive the sociometric status of their pupils diminishes rapidly with the increasing age of the pupils (Ausubel & Schiff, 1955b; Moreno, 1934), and it is quite low by the time pupils are of high school age (Bonney, 1947). Sometimes adolescents who are actually rejected are as unaware as their teachers of their status in the group.

Further appraisal of the seriousness of an individual case of rejection requires knowledge of (1) how widely shared the attitude of rejection is in the group, (2) whether it reflects active dislike of or passive indifference toward the person involved, (3) the modifiability of the factors on which the rejection is based, and (4) the availability of other compensatory attachments or interests. Finally, it is important to know whether the individual desires to be accepted by the group, and, if he does not, whether his expressed disdain for acceptance is genuine or the product of rationalization. Although unconcern with status in the group may, in rejection, be associated with relatively little immediate deflation of self-esteem, it may also be symptomatic of much graver defects in personality structure than the rejection of a deviant adolescent who craves acceptance by his age mates.

HELPING THE SOCIALLY REJECTED INDIVIDUAL

Teachers, counselors, and group leaders can do much to help certain types of socially rejected adolescents. With the aid of group members (nondeviants) who reject such individuals least, they can assist the rejected in gaining insight into the reasons for their rejection and in acquiring the skills that enhance status in the group. Smaller classroom subgroups and social gatherings of small groups can provide a social identity for persons who are unable to establish themselves in larger social units. Classroom and extracurricular situations can be manipulated to increase the social visibility of those particular competencies of the rejected individual that are compatible with the values of the group.

PROGNOSIS OF DEVIANCY

During adolescence deviants and socially rejected individuals are not in an enviable position. In varying degrees they all face social ridicule, abuse, and isolation. The fortunate ones achieve some measure of status and security by forming warm attachments to agemates of their own kind. Rarely, a sympathetic adult friend or teacher will offer them affection, direction, and encouragement. But more often they are left to flounder uncertainly, to drift farther and farther away from group living, to develop feelings of anxiety and inferiority, to withdraw deeper and deeper into themselves or into a compensatory world of unreality. The more seriously maladjusted may be claimed by suicide or schizophrenia.

With the coming of adulthood, the peer group begins to dissolve and adolescents are absorbed into the wider social community. And concomitantly, release comes for the majority of deviants. The recession of the demands for slavish conformity is one of the surest signs of approaching adulthood. Variability is then not only legalized, but, to a certain extent, also becomes desirable. Adolescents suddenly begin to notice the personal qualities of people. They evolve personal goals, personal tastes, personal interests, and personal preferences. The "hideous" deviant is then, for the first time, seen for what he really is—just another different human being. And after years of harrowing isolation, he dares again to lift his head and take his rightful place among his peers.

Adolescent gangs—varieties of deviant peer groups

Thus far in our discussion of the structural and functional properties of adolescent peer groups, we have been concerned only with the developmental characteristics that distinguish the group formations of adolescents generally from those of children and adults in the American culture. But we are also committed to the proposition that peer group behavior, like all other significant and value-laden activity of adolescence in our own or any culture, must inevitably reflect the distinctive influences of the subculture in which it is rooted. To avoid needless repetition, the preceding analysis of the adolescent peer culture has used as a model the peer groups sharing the typical middle-class values that dominate the school and the official ideology of the community. Requiring further consideration of specific subcultural differences are only those peer groups that deviate markedly from this pattern, those originating from upper- and lower-class strata in our society. And since detailed studies of upper-class peer formations (for example, the Junior League) are not presently available, this section will deal primarily with lower-class adolescent gangs found in disorganized urban areas.

For the purposes of this discussion, we can divide all adolescent peer groups into two main categories, deviant and nondeviant. Nondeviant groups (1) originate from and subscribe to the dominant middle-class ideology of the school and the community and (2) conform to the basic core of peer group values that characterize the adolescent segment of the middle class. On an informal basis, nondeviant groups function as cliques or crowds. More formally they are organized into unisexual societies (scouts, fraternities, sororities) or into bisexual extracurricular interest clubs.

Membership in a deviant group can no longer be relegated to particular neighborhoods, poorer classes (Kelly & Pink, 1975; Kratcoski & Kratcoski, 1975), or big cities (Sherif & Sherif, 1964). Deviant behavior, juvenile misconduct and crime, point out Sherif and Sherif (1964, p. 281), need to be recognized, and

> special categories for groups in different neighborhoods be dropped. . . . It is sometimes thought that the crowded neighborhoods of large cities are the only seats of juvenile misdeeds. In fact, two fifths of the court cases are contributed by suburban, small-town and rural areas, the noncity courts having the largest rate of increase in recent years. . . . Nor is the problem just one of particular ethnic or racial groups, although the ratio for many of the less favored are often higher. . . . If a city has a sizeable population in poor and crowded neighborhoods composed of an ethnic minority, the probability of a high delinquency rate for the minority is greater.

The distinguishing characteristic of the unisexual, highly structured deviant adolescent gang is nonconformity to the special values of the dominant (socially acceptable) peer group following the official ideology of the community. The middle-class youth who does not conform to the standards of his peer group remains a free-lance outcast, teams up informally with other outgroupers, or joins a more formal organization with highly specialized interests (art) or idealistic (religious, social reform) aims. The lower-class adolescent who subscribes to the social class ideology as well as to the adolescent values of the middle-class peer group remains on the fringe of acceptance in nondeviant groups. Usually denied full membership in nondeviant cliques, he settles for a respectable position in an acceptable but more formal interest group.

Street-corner gangs

Once a group is formed, the goals of its members—experienced by each with feelings of urgency—and the actions they impel are not isolated events. If the goals can only be realized through unacceptable activities, the knowledge that they are unacceptable need not prevent their performance. But if there are no protective adults to cover for the members in the event of detection, the members will face the wrath of hostile adults, even legal authorities. Thus, the facilities of the physical setting and adult resources combine to create conditions that Thrasher saw as conducive to the heightened solidarity and sense of loyalty among members, which characterize those groups formed in less fortunate circumstances called *gangs*. (Sherif & Sherif, 1964, p. 59)

Unlike other adolescent group formations, the street-corner gang is more continuous with and resembles more closely preadolescent peer groups. It differs from the high school "crowd" in having a more aggressive, predatory base, attributable to the need to compensate for deprivations other than those normally associated with adolescence in our culture. It is more of an action group functionally oriented toward the achievement of more concrete goals; as such it requires a more structured organization and greater group solidarity. Similarly, because of its special functions, it is usually unisexual, demands a higher standard of loyalty from its members, places greater emphasis on secrecy and physical prowess, comes into conflict with the law, and imposes more drastic penalties for disloyalty on its members.

The special deprivations confronting these adolescents consist of (1) material inadequacies associated with low socioeconomic status—lower standards of housing, food, clothing, recreation, economic security, and educational opportunity; (2) restricted social mobility—limited access to the more desirable vocational pursuits; (3) exclusion from the dominant peer groups of school and church, which provide other adolescents with a special identity and interim status (Sherif & Cantril, 1947); and (4) exposure to the snobbishness and patronizing attitudes of respectable society. In the gang, an organization of his own kind, the street-corner boy not only gains all of the status and security advantages of peer group membership, but also finds escape from the condescension of his "betters," a sense of brotherhood and power, and a measure of aggressive revenge against the society that rejects him.

ORIGINS AND OUTCOMES

Socioeconomic deprivation in itself is not sufficient for adolescent deviant gang formation in less fortunate circumstances. An additional indispensable condition seems to be the existence of a more or less segregated and deteriorating urban slum area providing sufficient isolation from the rest of the community for a separate subculture, adequate protection from the prying eyes of the law, and sufficiently close physical contact for the daily operations of the gang and the emergence of a communal sense of group solidarity (Thrasher, 1927; Whyte, 1943). The presence of unassimilated ethnic and racial groups in these areas further stimulates the formation of gangs since generation conflict is maximized in families of such groups. In addition to being excluded from nondeviant peer groups, these "second generation" adolescents are unable to identify with their parents and community, and commonly seek to disassociate themselves from the social stigma connected with their family background. The necessity for creating an entirely new social organization as the only means of attaining status is even more urgent. And under the protracted stress of such extreme status deprivation, adolescent gangs evolve quite spontaneously from the less structured play groups of preadolescents.

Adolescent gangs disintegrate as their members approach adulthood and attain status in more conventional ways, through marriage, raising a family, and earning a livelihood (Sherif & Cantril, 1947). In proportion to his gradually increasing involvement in the new status-giving functions, the adolescent's participation in gang activities and loyalty to gang standards diminishes. The tapering off process may take several years. In the meantime, the street-corner boy continues to "hang out" on the corner with the boys, but not with the same single-mindedness as previously (Whyte, 1943). Eventually, the vast number of such adolescents become incorporated into the folds of conventional society and observe the norms of the community at large (Thrasher, 1927; Whyte, 1943). Were it not for this shift in values, the typical slum boy's participation in delinquent gang activities would not merely constitute a characteristic transitory phenomenon of adolescent development in disorganized urban areas, but would lead to a permanent career in crime. Fortunately, however, this outcome is relatively rare.

Under certain conditions, however, the delinquent adolescent gang member fails to be assimilated to conventional society, and is inducted into the ranks of the adult criminal gang. Whether or not this happens depends on many individual personality factors associated with moral development. Two sociological factors, however, have an important bearing on the eventual outcome. (1) If, by virtue of frequent residence in correctional institutions an adolescent fails to establish rapport with the law-abiding elements of the community or is denied opportunity to engage in legitimate status-giving activities because of his "record," reorientation of his value system understandably fails to occur. (2) A similar lack of reorientation may occur if status deprivation is based not only on age and socioeconomic status, but is also associated with discrimination based on such permanent factors as racial or national origin. The predatory attitude tends to become fixed since the gang then views the problem of acquiring status as not being limited to adolescence—as in the case of other youth—but as a permanent struggle against overwhelming odds.

ORGANIZATION

The special organizational features of the gang related to its unique functions have already been mentioned. The superficial appearance of aimlessness and disorganization that strikes a casual observer is completely misleading (Thrasher, 1927). It is probably the gang's appearance of informality that is erroneously equated with planlessness and lack of structure. Actually, few existing groups can rival it in degree of differentiation of relationships between members, in stability of roles and status hierarchy, and in the group solidarity that permeates the membership. Years of extremely close association and comradeship in dangerous exploits and in fights with adult authorities, police, and other gangs weld an amazingly cohesive ingroup incorporating a complex system of mutually recognized obligations and loyalties (Thrasher, 1927; Whyte, 1943).

For the most part, criteria determining gang leadership conform to those outlined for adolescent leaders generally. To some extent, leadership in gangs is more despotically wielded and depends more on such factors as physical prowess, toughness, and fighting ability (Thrasher, 1927). However, these factors are more implicit than explicit in the leader's actual exercise of control. In daily operations, ingenuity and cleverness are more important assets (Whyte, 1943). The leader seldom has to resort to force; it usually suffices that he has earned a reputation for being able to take care of himself.

To some extent, also (probably because of the gang's functional orientation), the gang leader occupies a more central position in the group than most other adolescent leaders. Group members relate

more to him than to each other, and no decisions of any consequence are ever made in his absence (Whyte, 1943). The leader assumes full initiative and responsibility for carrying out group actions,
but legislative decisions are reached through group consensus; formal voting during meetings is a rarity (Whyte, 1943). Negotiations
with other gangs and with adults and officials are also conducted by
the leader, who thereby becomes more widely known than the ordinary gang member (Whyte, 1943).

However great his power, the leader cannot abuse or use it capriciously (Thrasher, 1927). Power comes solely from the group, and the
leader dares not ride roughshod over its acknowledged traditions,
goals, and mores (Thrasher, 1927). In accordance with his higher
status he is required to face hazards from which others shrink and to
be more scrupulous in meeting his obligations than less exalted
group members (Whyte, 1943). To a greater extent, also, he must be
loyal, fair-minded, and generous. He is expected to rise above personal vindictiveness, to settle amicably disputes between members
(Whyte, 1943).

NORMS AND ACTIVITIES

The norms, in such matters as honesty, aggression, and sexual
gratification, in adolescent gangs reflect in part the value system of
the lower socioeconomic groups from which they originate. But, in
addition, as befits a more rebellious group enjoying no status whatever in the adult community, the norms of such youth are more extreme, unconventional, and closer to those of the adult criminal
world than to the values professed by their parents. Through contact
with the school, the church, the courts, and various social agencies,
adolescent gang members have ample opportunity to learn that their
way of life is not sanctioned by conventional society. But "mere
knowledge of the norms of society" is a much less "potent determinant of behavior" than the status and other needs satisfied by the
peer group (Sherif & Cantril, 1947; Sherif & Sherif, 1964). At this point
in their development, the norms of the gang easily hold the field
against the conflicting standards of the world. Identification with gang
norms is also facilitated by the fact that home and family loyalties are
a minor matter to the street-corner boy. Furthermore, not too far
below the surface of their official ideology, his parents are in substantial agreement with the norms of his gang.

Being aware of the outlawed status of their value system leads
gang members to formulate justifications for their predatory activities.
They evolve an ethical code based on the premise that any behavior is
justifiable as long as it is intended to retaliate for unjust and repres-

sive treatment received at the hands of adult society. In this case, the entire body of criminal law is identified with the status-denying adult, and by lashing out at the former they are squaring accounts with the latter.

Despite the availability of such justifications, the gang boy frequently has serious doubt about the moral legitimacy of much of his behavior. This doubt added to his fear of the consequences of apprehension would be strong enough to inhibit delinquent acts were he committing these alone. For this reason the overwhelming majority of juvenile offenses are committed by groups of boys. The tangible presence of others reinforces identification with group norms, sets aside moral reservations, strengthens feelings of loyalty to the group, and allays fear of personal consequences. All of these factors create potentialities for aggressive, daring, and delinquent group behavior that do not exist when the gang member is operating as an individual.

The activities of adolescent gangs are extremely variable, running the gamut from nondelinquent athletic competition to various specialized forms of delinquent behavior (Thrasher, 1927). Within a given gang, a characteristic type of activity predominates, with a more or less fixed routine (Thrasher, 1927; Whyte, 1943). Geographically, also, to avoid conflicting interests, a gang restricts its operations to a carefully defined "sphere of influence," the violation of which leads to open warfare (Thrasher, 1927). Girls are customarily excluded from active membership in boys' gangs, but in late adolescence may acquire auxiliary status as lovers (Whyte, 1943). The number and proportion of cases of reported delinquency involving girls have been steadily increasing. "The percentage of cases involving girls. . . rose from 19% in the years 1958 through 1964 to 24% in 1970" (Kratcoski & Kratcoski, 1975, p. 84). Kratcoski and Kratcoski (1975) also point out that although earlier studies regarded delinquent behavior in girls to be limited almost exclusively to sex, recent Wise (1967) and Hindelang (1970) self-report studies showed no qualitative differences between males and females. The 1971 Uniform Crime Report statistics support the above-mentioned self-report study results. Wise (1967) reported that sex and alcohol delinquencies were committed equally by boys and girls, and "proportionately two of every three delinquencies of ungovernability, thought to be largely a female delinquency problem, were male offenses" (Kratcoski & Kratcoski, 1975, p. 85). In their study of 248 male and female students from 11th and 12th grades of three public high schools, using the self-report questionnaire, Kratcoski and Kratcoski (1975) found that male delinquency showed an effort to prove masculinity as it involved breaking into buildings, fist fights, destroying property, larceny of all types, joy riding, gambling, and premarital sex relations. However, distribution of items reflecting teenage culture orientation, such as drinking, driving without a license or permit, drug use, and skipping school, was about equal for boys and girls. There was also little difference in the mean number of offenses committed by males and females from different socioeconomic classes.

SUMMARY: FUNCTIONS OF ADOLESCENT PEER GROUPS

The significance of the peer group for adolescent development can be summarized most adequately by listing briefly the various functions it performs:

1. The most significant personality change during adolescence is a diminution in the importance of the status an individual derives from a dependent relationship to parents and a corresponding increase in the importance of primary status which he earns in his own right. Since the modern urban community is unable to provide the adolescent with earned status, peer groups are constituted to meet this crucial need.

2. The peer group is also the major source of derived status during adolescence. By achieving acceptance in the group, by subordinating himself to group interests, and by making himself dependent on group approval, the adolescent gains a measure of intrinsic self-esteem that is independent of his achievements or relative status in the group. This "we-feeling" provides security and belongingness and is a powerful ego support and source of loyalty to group norms.

3. The peer group provides a new frame of reference to relieve the disorientation and loss of anchorage from the abandonment of the childhood frame of reference when childhood biosocial status is surrendered. This disorientation is especially severe in early adolescence because of the adolescent's marginal position in the culture and his rejection by the adult community. The creation of peer group norms rescues him from his "no-man's-land" of orientation and provides relief from uncertainty, indecision, guilt, and anxiety about proper ways of thinking, feeling, and behaving.

4. In switching his primary allegiances to the peer group and in seeking a source of values outside the home, the adolescent makes great strides toward emancipation. He finds a new source of basic security to supplant the emotional anchorage to parents that had here-

tofore kept him confined within the dependent walls of childhood. By vesting in his peers the authority to set standards, he affirms his own right to self-determination, since he is patently no different from them (Ausubel, 1950; Zachry & Lighty, 1940). No longer need he implicitly subscribe to the belief that only parents and adults can determine what is right. As a result of the emotional support he derives from his peer group, he gains the courage to break the bonds of parental domination.

5. The peer group also serves as "a bulwark of strength in combatting authority. . . . By pooling their resistance in groups and throwing up barriers of one kind and another against adult authority and interference," adolescents manage to "exclude adults and protect themselves from. . . the coercions that the latter are prone to use" (Tryon, 1944, p. 220). By creating precedents and operating as a pressure group, the peer group gains important privileges for its members and emancipates itself from adult and institutional controls (Hollingshead, 1949).

Adolescents also use the peer group as an organized means of "rejecting completely the accepted standards of adult society" (Tryon, 1944, p. 238) and of repudiating the necessity for growing up. Even apart from delinquency, practically all resistance to acculturation in our society (Tryon, 1944) comes not from individual adolescents but from peer groups.

6. The peer group is the major training institution for adolescents in our society. The school's influence on adolescent development inheres largely in its capacity for providing "many of the occasions for adolescent boys and girls to receive the inculcation of adolescent culture—that body of attitudes, beliefs, and practices which is transmitted not by parents and teachers to children but by older to younger adolescents" (Frank, 1944b, p. 240). It is in the peer group that "by doing they learn about the social processes of our culture. They clarify their sex roles by acting and being responded to, they learn competition, cooperation, social skills, values and purposes by sharing the common life" (Tryon, 1944, p. 217). All of this is accomplished in an integrated way without self-conscious or self-important pomposity; "for unlike the adult-controlled training institutions and agencies in our society, the peer group does not regard itself as a training unit" (Tryon, 1944, p. 217). And in its role as a training institution the peer group transmits and enforces social class goals and values, since parents no longer enjoy sufficient control or rapport to carry out this function.

7. The peer group provides regularized media and occasions for

adolescents to gratify their newly acquired desires for increased heterosexual contacts, as well as a set of norms governing adolescent sex behavior.

8. As the chief source of adolescent interim status, the peer group reduces the total load of frustration and stabilizes the entire transitional period. It can offer compensations not only for the deprivations associated with adolescence per se, but also for the special deprivations that confront certain adolescents by virtue of their class, ethnic, racial, or religious affiliations.

13

Sexual Behavior in Adolescence

In previous chapters we have discussed the endocrine changes of pubescence and their more general psychological consequences in sex awareness, drive, and interests. We have also pointed to the existence of various psychobiological problems associated with gonadal maturation: the universal need to adjust to the perplexity and uneasiness generated by a strange and potent new drive; the necessity of subjecting for the first time since early childhood an emergent drive of physiological origin to initial control and direction in accordance with social expectations; the cultural pressures exerted on adolescent individuals to assume an appropriate biological sex role; and the general developmental trend for modes of sexual gratification to become increasingly more specific and differentiated with the progress of adolescence.

Our task in this chapter is fourfold: (1) to consider the extent to which the psychological consequences of gonadal maturation are culturally modifiable; (2) to assay the importance of sexuality in adolescent personality development and adjustment; (3) to examine various psychosocial aspects of adolescent sexuality; and (4) to formulate some principles of sex education and guidance appropriate for our culture.

PSYCHOSOCIAL ASPECTS OF SEXUALITY

In contrast to the psychobiological problems of adolescent sexuality that enjoy universal cultural distribution, psychosocial sex problems are culture-bound, reflecting the influence of the particular values, regulatory devices, and social conditions within a given culture. We shall be concerned here with five main categories of psychosocial sex problems: (1) peculiarities in psychosexual maturation that follow from the general cultural (or subcultural) orientation to sexuality—attitudes of acceptance or deprecation; of shame, guilt, and avoidance, or of naturalness and enjoyment; emphasis on psychophysiological or psychoaffectional aspects of sexuality; degree of sameness or difference in conceptions of male and female biological sex roles; (2) differences in patterns of socially provided opportunities for and restrictions on adolescent sexual gratification, and in the degree to which social sanctions are internalized by the adolescent; (3) differences in specific practices and varieties of sexual expression, in the frequency and types of sexual outlets available to adolescent boys and girls growing up in different social environments; (4) differences in means of regulating and formalizing the social and interpersonal aspects of erotic relationships between the sexes, for example, courting behavior and heterosexual activities in the peer group; and (5) differences in social sex role, in the personality attributes and socioeconomic functions customarily associated with masculinity and femininity.

In this section we shall consider the first two of these problems. It will be more profitable to reserve consideration of the remaining three problems until some attention is given to the modifiability of hormonally conditioned sex behavior and to the general importance of sexuality in adolescent development.

Different cultural orientations toward sexuality

Some idea of the tremendous variability in cultural orientation toward sexuality can be gained by comparing the sex attitudes of four primitive cultures in the South Seas (Mead, 1939) with those of our own culture.

Adolescent sex practices in Samoa reflect an elaboration of the physiological and sensuous aspects of sexuality, which are culturally emphasized, in contradistinction to the affectional components, which are relatively ignored. For both men and women, physiological sex urges are regarded as natural and pleasurable, although requiring more stimulation and having slower maturation in women. No unfavorable moral judgments are applied to sexual gratification on a physiological level, the only strictures being aesthetic, and directed against overt "unseemliness." No importance is attached to deep or permanent emotional attachments; the stability of marriage depends on social and economic factors. Adolescent premarital sex adventures mirror the general promiscuity and lack of deep emotion or ego involvement in sex relationships. No attempt is made to synthesize seriously the physiological and affectional components of sex. Whereas in our society comparable sexual behavior is regarded as more typical of adolescent emotional immaturity, in Samoa, adolescent sex conduct is not considered to be unrepresentative of the adult approach to sexuality. The Samoan attitudes toward virginity and fidelity are typical of their whole philosophy of sex: desirable in theory, intriguing in practice, but hardly credible considering the "sexual nature of man"—except where it is demanded by considerations of social status.

The Mundugumor attitude toward sexuality, like the Samoan, seems to reflect the characteristic personality constellation of the culture. Just as the easy-going Samoan expresses his casual style of life in the carefree and superficial emotional expression that characterizes his promiscuous sex activity, so the hard, aggressive, individualistic Mundugumor reveals his personality in the type of sex relationship that he establishes. Rigorous social taboos against promiscuity satisfy his passion for "keeping up appearances"; but these are in no sense internalized sufficiently to prevent the adolescent's vigorous, aggressive individuality from breaking through the frustrating barriers of adult-made social standards to gratify passionate physiological needs by skillful clandestine efforts. Like the Samoan, the Mundugumor accepts the desirability of the physiological aspects of sexual expression which also supersede the affectional components; the Mundugumor, however, is characteristically more vigorous, passionate, aggressive, and possessive in his attitudes and overt behavior. Also unlike their Samoan contemporaries, Mundugumor girls are more aggressive and take more initiative in arranging the clandestine liaisons. As one might imagine, the Mundugumor places more value on virginity than the Samoan, but this is not sufficient to discourage premarital sexual ardor.

Among the Arapesh, psychosexual development follows an entirely different pattern from that of either of the two cultures described. Because of long years during which husband and wife live together like brother and sister, actual sexual intercourse does not spring from a different order of feeling from the affection that one has for one's daughter or one's sister. It is simply a more final and complete expression of the same kind of feeling. And it is not regarded as a spontaneous response of the human being to an internal sexual stimulus. The Arapesh have no fear that children left to themselves will copulate, or that young people going about in adolescent groups will experiment with sex. The only young people who are believed likely to indulge in any overt sex expression are "husband and wife," the betrothed pair who have been reared in the knowledge that they are to be mates (Mead, 1939).

Both men and women find complete satisfaction of their sex needs in monogamous marriage. There is, however, this difference from monogamous marriage in our society: the physical component is not regarded as something inherently ugly and shameful (made tolerable by the marriage tie), but rather as a natural and acceptable accompaniment of an adult affectional relationship. Although sex is desirable affectional play in the mature relationship between man and wife, it is regarded as dangerous and antithetical to growth in those who have not yet attained their maturity.

If the Victorians had a felt need for a model of sexual behavior, it is a pity that they did not know of the existence of Manus society. Of all these four peoples, the Manus has approximated most closely the Victorian and dual standard of sex morality currently undergoing change in our culture. Only they carry their Puritanism one step further. They recognize, as we do, the strength and naturalness of the male physiological sex drive, and just as inconsistently as we apply strict taboos that aim at seriously outlawing its expression; but secretly, rape remains the ideal goal of sexual behavior. Women are not supposed to experience physiological sex drives; but whereas our Victorian morality concedes the right of women to enjoy marital sex relations on an affectional basis, so much shame and repugnance is attached to sex in Manus society that even in the legalized marriage relationship it is distasteful. This difference might partly be a result of the fact that the Manus marriage is from start to finish a pure business proposition with no affectional elements. In a very literal sense it corresponds to legalized prostitution. Men do not deny their strong physiological urges; but because they fear the wrath of the spirits, they confine their overt activities to enforced marital intercourse, enjoying rape mainly in fantasy.

Doctrinally and traditionally our own cultural orientation toward sexuality parallels the Manus. The sexual urge is regarded as an inherently evil and reprehensible drive which is tolerated only because it is necessary for the reproduction of the species. In the case of the male, a concession is made to the acknowledged strength of the sexual urge in that its existence is given a certain recognized status; but, nevertheless, it is formally expected that repression will be practised until marriage. In the case of the female, physiological sex drive is presumed to be nonexistent, and sexual expression is regarded as permissible only as part of her affectional duties as a wife. Since so many parents take the view that sex must be denied, and not even discussed, it is hardly surprising that children and adolescents have such distorted attitudes toward sexuality—attitudes that combine all the elements of shame, disgust, fear, guilt, mystery, and anxiety (Ausubel, 1950, p. 43).

But the status of sexuality in our own culture is much more complicated and confusing than that among Manus. For coexisting with our repressive doctrinal approach are lower-class norms that are comparable to those of the Samoans; scientific notions of the "naturalness" of sex expression; romantic ideals and affectional standards that are also applied to male sex behavior; and increasing acknowledgement of the legitimacy of psychophysiological sex behavior among women. When to this cultural repression, distortion, and confusion is added the abnormally slow pace of emotional and social development in adolescence, it is no wonder that psychosexual maturation proceeds so slowly, especially in girls. Thus, boys and girls are generally incapable at 16 or 18 of the deep emotional involvement that our culture regards as necessary and desirable for successful marital love relationships.

Cultural patterns of regulating adolescent sex activity

From this brief ethnological survey of sex behavior, it is evident that the social regulation of adolescent sex activity is closely related to the broader constellation of attitudes and values that the culture applies to sexuality in general. These regulatory practices can be classified on the basis of (1) the degree of tolerance or repressiveness toward adolescent sex expression, (2) the relative degree of emphasis placed on psychophysiological or psychoaffectional sex behavior, and (3) the extent to which different standards are set for boys and girls.

At one extreme of cultural permissiveness (Samoa), no restrictions whatsoever are placed on adolescent sex activity. At the other extreme (Manus girls, Puritanically raised girls in our culture), the prohibitions on sex activity are so severe that no sex drive at all, not even psychoaffectional, is developed. Between these extremes, in increasing order of repressiveness, are (1) formal prohibitions against sexual intercourse that are not seriously enforced and are not internalized by the adolescent; (2) social taboos against premarital intercourse that are not internalized but are enforced seriously and rigorously enough to require clandestine gratification of sex (Mundugumor boys and girls); (3) social recognition of the existence of physiological sex drives accompanied by serious cultural expectations of sexual abstinence until marriage that are effectively internalized by some adolescents (Manus boys, middle-class boys in our culture); and (4) social denial of psychophysiological sex drives modified by tolerance for psychoaffectional sex activity during marriage (middle-class girls in our culture). Among the Arapesh, the dimension of cultural permissiveness is somewhat irrelevant. It is true that no overt restrictions are imposed; but at the same time it is implicitly expected that adolescents will develop only psychoaffectional sex urges restricted to betrothed marital partners.

Regarding the relative emphasis placed on the psychophysiological and psychoaffectional aspects of sex, the Arapesh recognize only psychoaffectional sexuality, whereas the Samoan, Manus, and Mundugumor cultures primarily emphasize the psychophysiological. In our own culture both components are prominent and vary in importance with sex and class membership. The same types of sexual urges are attributed to both males and females in the Samoan, Arapesh, and Mundugumor cultures, whereas the Manus and until recently our culture make sharp qualitative distinctions between male and female sex drives.

From even the limited ethnological data reviewed above and in other parts of this volume (Leighton & Kluckhohn, 1947a; Malinowski, 1927; Whiting, 1941), it is apparent that primitive cultures cannot be contrasted to our own as having nonrepressive, matter-of-fact, and simple attitudes toward sexuality. Restrictions of varying degrees of severity against adolescent sex activity have been described for the Kwoma, Mundugumor, Navaho, and Manus cultures; and in the Manus culture, the rigorousness of the repression, and the aura of shame, ugliness, prudery, and sinfulness surrounding sex exceeds by far anything known in our own culture. Neither have we been alone in adhering to a double standard of sex morality, nor the furthest advanced in psychoaffectional standards of sex behavior. All we can say with definiteness is that in our own culture marriage is delayed longer and attitudes toward sex are more heterogeneous and more confused than in most other cultures.

Cultures also pattern the degree of acceptability of various forms of sexual behavior and at different stages of life.

In some societies such as the Revala Bedouins of Eurasia, homosexuality is so strongly opposed that both male and female offenders are put to death; in other societies, such as the Mbundu of Angola, it is simply considered immature and ridiculed; in still others, it is considered an essential part of sexual and social maturation. For example, among the Sievans of Africa, all men and boys engage in homosexual intercourse, and although assuming a feminine role is strictly limited to sexual situations, 'males are singled out as peculiar if they do not indulge in these homosexual activities.' (Mussen et al., 1974).

THE NATURE AND CULTURAL MODIFIABILITY OF SEX BEHAVIOR

True (adult or postpubescent) sexuality can only be conceptualized as a form of self-expression which is related to the individual's experience of himself in a biological sex role. The adoption of a biological sex role is dependent on: (1) the individual's ability to experience the unique feeling tones and psychological content that is either functionally or historically related to hormonal stimulation; and (2) cultural sanction of such experience, and recognition of the individual as a sexually mature adult. It follows that although biological sex role may be largely or (in certain instances of postpubescent castration) completely maintained by psychological stimulation, some degree of contact with functional quantities of gonadal sex hormones is necessary at some point in development.*

It is also apparent that gonadal stimulation can be regarded only as a necessary, not as a sufficient condition for the development of biological sex role. The mere presence of gonadal hormones does not guarantee the emergence of sex drives if the culture decrees that these are not to develop or that the individual is not yet sexually mature. Sex hormones never arouse sex drives in Manus girls, and several years elapse between Samoan girls' pubescence and the onset of their sexual activity (Mead, 1939). There is a similar lag for many girls in our own culture (Ellis, 1936; Smith, 1924). And among the Arapesh, gonadal hormones do not result in sex impulses without an affectional content.

Once the basis of biological sex role is laid, further differentiation inevitably occurs. One type of differentiation is in the distinction between psychophysiological and psychoaffectional sex drives. Other aspects of differentiation include the sex object desired, the type of activity or erogenous zone implicated, the degree of passivity or initiative displayed, and the appropriateness of the sex role adopted.

---

*Prepubescent castrates do not develop sex drives.

The factors that facilitate or retard the adoption of an appropriate (heterosexual) sex role and the various inappropriate outcomes have already been discussed. That the differentiation of appropriate biological sex roles depends on psychological factors over and above the hormonal substrate of sexual behavior is shown by the fact that injection of appropriate male or female sex hormones does not intensify heterosexual behavior, but merely reinforces the preexisting sex role, whichever it may be (Ford & Beach, 1951).

Preadolescent versus adolescent sexuality

Since the enactment of a biological sex role implies the existence of feelings and impulses in the individual that are dependent on gonadal stimulation and on social recognition of him as a sexually mature individual, it follows that there must be a qualitative difference between preadolescent and adolescent sexuality. There is considerable evidence of sensuous sex activity, sexual curiosity and exploration, and experimentation with and imitation of adult sex roles in prepubescent children; and although the extent of such activity varies from culture to culture, contrary to psychoanalytic theory, there is no evidence of a "latency period" during the years of middle childhood and preadolescence (Ford & Beach, 1951; Kinsey et al., 1948; Landis et al., 1940; Ramsey, 1943b).

But it is an assumption of quite another order to equate these activities with adult sexuality even if similar organs are involved in both instances. A child and biologist may both peer through a microscope, but one would hesitate to refer to the former as a scientist on this basis (Ausubel, 1952). Data of Kinsey and others, already cited, indicate that after pubescence, there is always a complete break in the qualitative meaning and significance of sex activity, and frequently considerable temporal discontinuity as well.

Such discontinuity, in no way incompatible with general principles of child or adolescent development, is certainly to be expected following the introduction of any new potent variable (functional levels of gonadal hormones). And since this discontinuity in experience is biologically inevitable, the culture can at best avoid discontinuity in training by refraining from inculcating in the child attitudes about sexuality that he must perforce unlearn before he can function effectively as an adult (Benedict, 1938).

The repressibility of sex urges

Strictly speaking, sex urges can be repressed only in the sense that as a result of extreme cultural denial they are never actualized from their hormonal substrate. Hence, agenesis would be a more precise designation for this phenomenon than repression. It occurs, as we have seen, among Manus girls and among Puritanically reared girls in our culture. Among the Arapesh, agenesis is restricted solely to the psychophysiological sex drive. The advocates of the sex repression theory of adolescent emotional stability have committed the double error (1) of minimizing in a general way the power of the culture to suppress or modify successfully the development of even basic potential drives, and (2) of assuming that sex drives are either preformed entities stored in the "unconscious" or inevitable consequences of gonadal stimulation rather than potential derivatives of sex hormones dependent on favorable experience for eventual consummation.

Once sex drives have been actualized from their physiological substrate they become much too urgent and insistent to be repressed in the majority of individuals. Several investigators have reported that in our own culture only rarely do postpubescent males have extremely low sexual outlets (Kinsey et al., 1948; Kirkendall, 1940; Taylor, 1933); and usually when this occurs special reasons (general apathy and incapacity to respond to sexual stimuli) exist for this anomaly (Kinsey et al., 1948). When social sanctions or moral scruples prevent sexual gratification through premarital intercourse, some direct substitutive outlet such as masturbation or petting is the general practice (Kinsey et al., 1948; Kirkendall, 1940; Taylor, 1933).

The psychoanalytic doctrine of sublimation, which proposes that the energy of frustrated sex drives provides the motivation for all of the constructive pursuits of adolescents and others and that through such pursuits vicarious sexual satisfaction is achieved, is hardly credible. Obviously there can be no sublimation if sex drives are not repressed but are gratified through premarital intercourse or through direct substitutive sex activity. Second, there is no reputable evidence to indicate that the same "blocked " energy of frustrated sex urges powers other activites, or that any of these activities yield vicarious sexual satisfaction. It is true that any constructive, self-enhancing activity provides compensation for frustration; but this does not necessarily mean that the compensatory activity is energized by the frustration or that the compensation makes up in kind for the specific deprivation.

It is more reasonable to conceive of motives as continually and independently generated in the course of reacting to new experiences and expectations rather than as derivatives of a single fountainhead of drive; and although frustration admittedly is a powerful spur to compensatory activity, positive impulses to know, explore, and master the environment, independent of frustration, can also motivate purposeful activity. During adolescence the individual is confronted by numerous status problems (apart from sexual frustration) that are sufficiently insistent to instigate adjustive efforts such as peer group activity; and the functional origins of these efforts are either freshly generated or rooted in adjustments found successful in the past (preadolescent group formations).

Detrimental effects of sex repression

Mead's Manus data (Mead, 1939), as well as psychiatric experience with Puritanically reared women in our own culture, indicate that suppression of nonaffectional sexuality (Arapesh) or the imposition of either rigorous (Mundugumor) or merely formal (lower-class American) prohibitions on premarital intercourse are not attended by psychological stress. As long as the adolescent does not internalize moral obligations to abide by these taboos, and as long as opportunities for clandestine gratification are available, no more mental conflict is generated than under conditions of unrestricted freedom, as in Samoa.

Serious psychological stress from sex develops in middle-class boys because of (1) the ideological confusion that results in attempts to rationalize the logically incompatible cultural position (which the culture refuses to acknowledge as illogical) that psychophysiological sex urges are "natural" but at the same time must be repressed on ethicoreligious grounds until marriage; and (2) the psychological impossibility of repressing a drive that they are morally obligated to repress. They are placed in the unenviable forced choice situation in which self-denial leads to unbearable psychophysiological tension, and self-indulgence gives rise to strong guilt feelings. The only realistic solution to this dilemma is to relieve the psychophysiological tension through autoeroticism and petting, and to find moral comfort in the fact that by refraining from intravaginal intercourse, they preserve technical virginity. But they still cannot avoid guilt feelings resulting from the substitutive equivalence of these activities with the interdicted goal of complete sexual intercourse; and the chronic existence of such guilt necessarily plays havoc with self-esteem.

The frustration of acknowledged sexual goals has other deleterious effects on self-esteem. Incomplete self-expression sexually comes to symbolize the adolescent's subadult status in society and causes pervasive and gnawing feelings of deprivation, inferiority, and demoralization. He becomes preoccupied with this frustration, overvalues its importance, and lets it distract him from other activities. Some adolescents find in masturbation a preferred escape from rather than a substitute for normal heterosexual reality; and others become fixed at the level of sexual satisfaction that can be derived from petting and regard intercourse as an anticlimax.

Not to be ignored either are the exaggerated defenses which some adolescents erect against their sexual impulses. This may result in asceticism or in an overintellectualization of all the emotional problems of living. It is possible to explain in such a fashion some cases of adolescent preoccupation with philosophical, social, and political problems.

Middle-class girls reared in traditionally Victorian or orthodox religious environments are spared most of these consequences. Theirs is not the difficult task of reconciling the idea of moral guilt with the seemingly overpowering strength of a natural biological impulse. They don't face the temptation that if they transgress only occasionally—especially if they are not caught—they can probably get away with it. Instead, the matter is settled very simply for them; they are told, and usually accept the fact, that they simply do not have these urges.

But times are changing for girls. As a result of recent trends in sex education, girls are beginning to wonder if they too are endowed with physiological sex urges. And as they wonder they are forced to wrestle with the moral problem of repression. There is evidence of higher level of guilt among girls compared to boys of the same degree of religious activity, for instance, which is inversely related to sex activity (Langston, 1973). In any case, there is considerable overlapping. The late-maturing boy suffers less than the early-maturing boy since he has less need for sexual outlet.

For the adolescent girl, however, sex repression creates marital problems that usually do not arise for boys. To effect a successful marital adjustment, she will have to harmonize her own feelings and attitudes with their less inhibited correlates in her husband. Total repression results in frigidity; and even for those girls who eventually accept a psychoaffectional sex role, the idea of sex may be associated with such odium and repugnance that even in connection with affectional purposes there are strong inhibitions that are only gradually overcome. According to Kinsey's data, one of the two most important sexual factors which most often cause difficulty in the upper-level marriage is the failure of the female to participate with the abandon necessary for the successful consummation of any sexual relation (Kinsey et al., 1948). The other factor listed by Kinsey—"the failure of the male to show skill on sexual approach and technique"—may also be attributed in part to the effects of extreme sex repression (Kinsey et al., 1948).

THE IMPORTANCE OF SEXUALITY IN ADOLESCENT
DEVELOPMENT AND ADJUSTMENT

Relationships between sexuality and adolescent
personality maturation

The hormonal changes, the alterations in body form, and the psychological correlates of both naturally play a major role in adolescent personality development. We have referred to these characteristics of pubescence as the consummatory factors in precipitating the transitional personality phase of adolescence. They accomplish this not only through their effect on cultural expectations, but also endogenously by their impact on the individual. The adolescent reacts to his adult body form, his newly acquired reproductive capacity, and his mature sexual drives by raising his aspirations for volitional independence and earned status. However, just because pubescence is the crucial catalytic agent that initiates the adolescent period of development, sexuality cannot be regarded as the central problem of adolescence.

Newly acquired sexual urges pose a significant obstacle to personality maturation also since they are the chief source of hedonistic need during adolescence. The control and regulation of a new physiological drive creates an emergent problem of adaptation that has not arisen since early childhood. It is true that the individual is now older, more experienced in self-control, more responsive to moral obligations, and more highly motivated by status considerations to postpone the need for immediate hedonistic gratification. But by the same token he is also more self-assertive and resistive to adult standards and direction.

Insistent sex needs not only threaten other long-range goals, but also, as the Rankians point out, threaten the individual's newly acquired volitional independence (Hankins, 1943). Genuine affectional relationships imply considerable self-surrender and limitation of personal autonomy. These can be avoided either by asceticism or by entering into numerous and superficial psychophysiological sex relations (promiscuity).

Sexuality and adolescent adjustment

Sexuality is an important area of adolescent adjustment. Whether existing sex needs are gratified or denied affects the total balance between frustration and satisfaction and, hence, the overall stressfulness of adolescence. Stressfulness is also influenced by conflict or guilt feelings about sex, and impinges on the individual's behavioral reactivity or emotional stability. Frustrations of sex needs may result in preoccupation with and overvaluation of sexuality, bothersome distractions, and compensatory attempts at self-enhancement in other directions. By symbolizing his subadult status or by instigating guilt-producing substitutive sex outlets, these frustrations may impair self-esteem.

Because of the intense psychological conflict until recently about sex in middle-class boys in our society and because of the unrealistic cultural "avoidance and deprecation of the subject of sex in the face of their positive knowledge of its actual importance," these adolescents subjectively overvalue the relative importance of sexuality in the total scheme of things. But regardless of its actual intrinsic importance, there is no gainsaying the phenomenological reality of this overvaluation to these adolescents. In a much different category is the social scientists' interpretive overvaluation of the importance of sexuality in adolescent adjustment.

Much of this interpretative overvaluation can be attributed to deficiencies in the type and sources of information about sex behavior that have in part been remedies. Before Kinsey and coworkers' (1948) monumental study* of the sexual expression of the American male, most available conceptions of adolescent sex activity were conjectural.† Previous studies were superficial and did not sample large or representative enough segments of the population. And in keeping with their psychoanalytic orientation, many psychologists and psychiatrists were too liable to overgeneralize from case histories drawn from middle-class patients and from their own middle-class backgrounds.

Among those who are concerned with interpreting adolescent psychology in our culture, the point of view has been steadily gaining ground that the American adolescent owes the greater part of his characteristic emotional instability to the inordinate amount of sex frustration he experiences. This opinion is customarily bolstered by citing Mead's Samoan data, which are overgeneralized to support the hypothesis that an invariable, one-to-one, casual relationship prevails

---

* "Kinsey's data have been subjected to statistical attack on the grounds that they are not adequately representative of the lower educational levels. It has also been suggested that the median rather than the mean would be a more valid measure of sexual outlet [since it would be less distorted by] the inclusion in the data of high outlets conceivably due to compulsive sexuality. Nevertheless this study remains the most representative and exhaustive performed to date" (Ausubel, 1950).

† Kinsey's differential findings by social class were foreshadowed in various studies of social stratification (Davis & Dollard, 1940; Lynd & Lynd, 1937).

between the stressfulness of adolescence and the degree of cultural repression of adolescent sex activity.

When we consider all of the evidence, however, it becomes apparent that sex frustration is only one of many factors in adolescent status deprivation, and one of the less crucial factors leading to a stressful adolescence. First, there is no simple relationship between the severity of cultural restrictions on sexual expression and the degree of psychological conflict from sex. Such conflict develops only when simultaneously sex drives are generated and moral prohibitions against their expression are internalized. In our society, therefore, psychological conflict about sex is hardly characteristic of adolescents generally, since as early as 1948 studies led by Kinsey established that 85 percent of American male adolescents accept premarital intercourse as natural and desirable, and despite the existence of formal expectations to the contrary, exercise this conviction almost as freely as Samoan adolescents (Kinsey et al., 1948). Twenty-eight studies of premarital sex behavior conducted since Kinsey's report in 1953 indicate that there has been an increase in the percentage of young people engaging in premarital sexual intercourse. Moreover, this change has been more revolutionary for women to the extent that today there is almost no difference between the proportions of young men and women who engage in such behavior (Dreyer, 1975). Psychological stress from sex is relatively impressive only in some middle-class youth, and not because of psychophysiological tensions produced by repression per se (since such tensions are relieved by masturbation, petting, and sexual intercourse) but because of the psychological ambiguity of the situation, the guilt feelings engendered, and the invidious reflections on self-esteem.

Second, there is little relationship between experienced degree of conflict about sex and the total stressfulness of adolescence because other nonsexual factors are more crucial in determining that stressfulness. Depending on the operation of these other factors, absence of sex repression and lack of psychological conflict about sex can coexist with either a relatively unstressful adolescence (as in Samoa) or an extremely stressful adolescence (as among present-day youth in our own culture). Whenever adolescence is simultaneously nonstressful and unaccompanied by little mental conflict about sex, other more compelling reasons unrelated to sexuality can usually be found for the idyllic nature of adolescent development. Samoans, for example, adopt an extremely casual approach to life and do not engage in any frantic struggle for status; and Arapesh adolescents are warmly accepted and eagerly integrated into a benevolent noncompetitive culture.

On the other hand, in primitive cultures in which a stressful adolescence coexists with considerable conflict about sex, there are also other reasons for the experienced difficulty of adolescence. In the Mundugumor, Manus, and Kwoma cultures, greater emphasis is placed on status, the culture as a whole is more competitive and aggressive, the adolescent has a more marginal position in society, and status is more persistently withheld from him. Hence, although sexual problems undoubtedly add to the stressfulness of adolescence in the Manus (Mead, 1939) and other primitive cultures (Malinowski, 1927), greater weight must be given to the traumatic potential of these nonsexual factors.

If this proposition holds true for primitive cultures, it can be applied with even greater validity to our own culture; for the differences among primitive cultures in nonsexual determinants of adolescent stress are relatively minor in comparison with the corresponding difference between primitive and complex cultures. When so many important variables contributing to a stressful adolescence are simultaneously operative, the presence or absence of sexual conflict is a relatively negligible factor. Thus, although the lower-class adolescent male in our society is spared the trauma of psychological conflict about sex, his adolescence on the whole is no less stressful than that of his middle-class contemporary.

ADOLESCENT SEXUAL EXPRESSION IN OUR CULTURE

The "sexual revolution" among adolescents

Prominent in discussions of sexual behavior among adolescents in our culture is the question of a "sexual revolution" among youth. Dreyer (1975) summarizes the debate as follows:

There have been enough studies to begin to answer the question about whether there has been a "sexual revolution." As reviewed by Cannon and Long (Cannon & Long, 1971), Kantner and Zelnick (Kantner & Zelnick, 1972, 1973), and Sorenson (Sorenson, 1973), the results of twenty-eight studies of premarital sex behavior conducted since Kinsey's report in 1953 clearly indicate that there has been an increase in the percent of young people who engage in premarital sexual intercourse, but that this change has been more "revolutionary" for women than for men. In general, the percent of white men aged fifteen to twenty-five who have had sexual intercourse before marriage has not increased very much in the last twenty-five years, but the number of white women aged fifteen to twenty-five having premarital sexual intercourse has risen dramatically until today there is virtually no difference between the proportions of young men and women who engage in such behavior.

The recent survey by Hunt (1973) of 2026 people of all ages in the United States showed that about 80 percent of the single men under 25 and 75 percent of the single white women under 25 had had sexual intercourse. Compared to Kinsey's findings in 1953 this shows a slight increase for men and a large increase for women, about 30 percent of whom had reported premarital intercourse in 1953. The incidence of premarital sexual intercourse among non-college men under the age of 17 was reported to be 66 percent in 1953 and 75 percent in 1972. However, 18- to 24-year-old men who reported having relations with prostitutes dropped from about 33 percent in 1953 to 3 percent in 1972 (Dreyer, 1975).

Similarly, young married men under 25 show a slight increase in extramarital sexual relationships with 32 percent of young husbands reporting such behavior; whereas married women of the same age group present a marked increase—24 percent in Hunt's sample compared to 9 percent in Kinsey's sample reporting such behavior (Dreyer, 1975).

There seems to be relatively little change in the past few decades in the incidence of either male or female masturbation, according to recent studies (Bardwick, 1971; Pomeroy, 1969a&b; Simon et al., 1972; Sorenson, 1973). Anxiety, conflict, and guilt, however, have decreased and there is more scientific information and objectivity (Mussen et al., 1974). Masturbation is the chief sexual outlet of early adolescence and shows a marked increase in incidence with the onset of puberty (Kinsey et al., 1948; Ramsey, 1943b). Heterosexual petting, which increases in frequency and in intimacy of contact with increasing age (Kinsey et al., 1948; Ramsey, 1943b), eventually involves as many as 88 percent of all boys (Kinsey et al., 1948). Thirty percent of Kinsey's adolescent male population reported petting to orgasm. Premarital intercourse constitutes 25 percent of the total male sex outlet before the age of 16, and 40 percent of total outlet between the ages of 16 and 20 (Kinsey et al., 1948). As adolescence progresses, the average boy's frequency of orgasm increases, "reaching a lifetime peak of about 3–4 times per week between 16 and 17 years of age" (Mussen et al., 1974, p. 572). This frequency tends to persist with only slight dimunition until the age of 30, after which there is reported gradual tapering.

Girls report much more variability in frequency of masturbation than boys. Some girls report in Kinsey's studies of 1948 and 1953 never masturbating, others report a frequency of masturbation as low as once or twice a year; still others masturbated as many as 10 to 20 times a week.

Dreyer (1975, pp. 199–200) points out that homosexuality among young people shows little change in the last 20 years.

> Approximately 20 percent of the men and 10 percent of the women aged eighteen to twenty-four in the Hunt study reported ever having had a homosexual relationship. These figures were very similar to those presented by Kinsey in 1953. Such findings are difficult to interpret, since for many of the subjects there had been only one brief homosexual contact in early adolescence, suggesting experimental trial rather than a long-range preference for homosexuality.

Attitudes and values

According to the Yankelovich Survey (1972), a substantial minority of students have begun to reevaluate conventional constraints related to marriage and family life. Although 71 percent disagreed with the proposition that "the traditional family structure no longer works" and 61 percent were "looking forward to being married," there is a sizeable departure from the traditional moral position on the subject. For instance, 43 percent did not consider extramarital relations morally wrong; 58 percent did not consider planning and having children without formal marriage morally wrong; 34 percent thought marriage was obsolete; and 36 percent expressed interest in living in a commune.

Starr points out that the moral acceptance of premarital coitus seems to have increased even more rapidly than its actual evidence.

> In the Christensen and Gregg (1970) study 55% of the males and 38% of the females reported approval of premarital coitus in 1968 as compared to 47% of the males and 17% of the females in 1958. Bell and Chaskes (1970) found significant decreases in the proportion of Temple coeds who felt that they had "gone too far" by engaging in premarital intercourse—from 65% to 36% between 1958 and 1968 among those in a dating relationship, from 61% to 30% among those going steady, and from 41% to 20% among those engaged to get married. (Starr, 1974, p. 89)

Starr (1974) also refers to the Leidy and Starr (1967) report of the Purdue Public Opinion survey of high school students revealing a strong trend toward the relaxation of sexual morals among American youth from the early fifties to the middle sixties.

> Presented with the hypothetical situation of some friends "not following the morals or rules related to the behavior of un-married people" 46% of the boys and 67% of the girls stated in 1952 that they "would not consider them good friends any more." By 1965 the proportions had dropped to 22% and 38% respectively. A survey by Yankelovich (1969) found 88% of parents of noncollege youth and 74% of parents of college youth agree-ing with the statement that "premarital sexual relations are mor-ally wrong" as opposed to 57% of noncollege youth and only 34% of college youth. (Starr, 1974, p. 89 & 90)

SUMMARY

On the whole, studies conclude that the rate of increase in higher level of sexual activity has been moderate for male adoles-cents, particularly since World War II (Godenne, 1974; Vener & Stew-art, 1972; Vener et al., 1972), but the "sexual revolution" has taken place in the behavior of the female in terms of her participation in premarital intercourse with virtually as great frequency as the male (Cannon & Long, 1971; Dreyer, 1975; Kantner & Zelnick, 1972; Soren-son, 1973; Vener & Stewart, 1972), and in both male and female atti-tude toward sex. The largest changes seem to have occurred in the decade of the sixties (Starr, 1974, p. 174).

An increasingly less exploitative attitude toward sex seems to prevail (Starr, 1974). "In place of what Waller (1937) described as the mutually exploitative, thrill-seeking and antagonistic 'rating and dat-ing complex,' among high school and college students, Riesman (1959) has perceived 'more desire to share' and 'less desire to im-press' than in bygone days (Starr, 1974). Sexual attitudes appear more liberal than in past decades (Finger, 1975). There does not appear to be as great a gap between ideals and actual practice" (Nutt & Sedla-cek, 1974, p. 351). There is general agreement that on the whole men and women feel that premarital sex experience is acceptable "within the framework of an emotionally involved relationship, and the extent to which they agree that such behavior is acceptable is directly related to the intensity of emotional involvement" (Dreyer, 1975, p. 204). Both male and female students attach greater importance to the meaning of the relationship than to arbitrary social norms (Mussen et al., 1974). Thus in one large study, high school and college students agreed that premarital intercourse when the couple is engaged or in love is more acceptable than petting in the absence of affection (Reiss, 1964).

There has been a marked decline in involvement with prostitutes. There is little evidence of promiscuity in the majority of cases. Most of them limit intercourse to one or two partners, and in most cases with a boy or girl of their own social group with whom they are seriously involved (Packard, 1970).

Group differences

There is general agreement in the current data that along with a "sexual revolution" there has been a general reduction of differences among sex, social class, and racial groups. For instance, the concept of a double standard of sexual behavior that made it more acceptable for men than women to engage in premarital sexual intercourse has practically disappeared. Recent studies reveal that the percentage of women engaging in premarital sexual experience is equal to that of men.

Similarly, social class differences in sexual behavior do not appear to be as great as reported in studies made in the 1940s and 1950s.

> In the past it was often noted that lower-class youth began sexual activity earlier than middle- and upper-class youth and that larger proportions of lower-class youth were sexually active before marriage than either middle- or upper-class youth. The recent data seem to show that in terms of the age at which sexual activity begins, the percent of men and women engaging in sexual intercourse, and the variety of sexual acts practiced, the middle and upper classes are not much different than the lower classes. (Dreyer, 1975, p. 200)

In fact, in line with other manifestations of the youth revolution or counterculture, the available evidence indicates that the greatest percentage increase in premarital sexual intercourse in recent years has been among higher socioeconomic adolescents and especially among better educated middle- and upper-class girls (Sorenson, 1974; Zelnik & Kantner, 1972).

Another trend supported by available data is that racial differences in sexual behavior appear to be disappearing also. "Black women aged fifteen to nineteen tend to begin having sexual intercourse at an earlier age than white, with 80 percent of the blacks and 40 percent of the white women reporting having had sexual intercourse by the age of nineteen. This racial difference tends to decrease and level out after age twenty" (Dreyer, 1975, p. 200).

However, in spite of the lessening of differences in sexual behavior patterns along sex, social class, and racial lines, regional differences remain. Thus, Packard found that college women in the East were more active sexually than midwestern men but less active than southern men (Packard, 1968). In another study of the sexual behavior of black and white men at high schools and colleges in New York and Virginia, Reiss found that in both states black men were more active sexually than white men, but that white men in New York were more active sexually than black men in Virginia (Dreyer, 1975; Reiss, 1967).

Evaluation of the major sex outlets *

MASTURBATION

In recent years there has been a violent swing in the direction of informed professional opinion about the detrimental consequences of masturbation. Most investigators today agree that the chief damage caused by masturbation comes from experiencing (1) related feelings of guilt and impaired self-esteem, and (2) anxiety about incurring the manifold forms of physical, mental, and moral deterioration popularly associated with the practice. Although this position is essentially sounder than the earlier one, since no physical or psychological damage has ever been traced to the effects of masturbation per se,† the implications of the practice as an escape from heterosexual reality must be considered. From what we know about canalization, the danger always exists that through conditioning it may become more than a substitute for heterosexual activity and evolve as an end in itself.

On the positive side, as an outlet for accumulated psychophysiological sexual tension which might otherwise interfere with the satisfactory performance of the adolescent's school and other responsibilities, it fulfills a useful function, especially in the case of those individuals who have compunctions about sexual contact with the opposite sex on any other but a psychoaffectional basis.

---

* This evaluation of sex outlets is based only on psychological criteria. Complete evaluation must also take into account the relevant moral issues. These are discussed on pages 389–391.

† Kinsey points with justice to the fact that most medical writers help to perpetuate such anxieties by virtue of their unwillingness to make this statement unequivocally (Kinsey et al., 1948).

PETTING

The same dangers—guilt feelings, anxiety, and canalization—exist for petting. However, since it is closer to the goal of heterosexual activity, and, under any circumstances, is a more meaningful and emotional sexual experience, it must be regarded as preferable to masturbation. An exception to this statement applies when, on idealistic grounds, an adolescent feels obliged to refrain from interpersonal sexual outlets unless he entertains feelings of genuine affection for the person involved.

In addition to involving less moral conflict for middle-class adolescents, petting also offers certain practical advantages to individuals who are either ignorant about prophylactic measures regarding birth control and venereal disease, or who are very alarmed about these possibilities. It also probably serves a desirable function by reducing autoeroticism, and by releasing some of the unnatural inhibitions about sexual expression, especially in the female. The nervous tension presumably aroused by petting has been grossly exaggerated (Kinsey et al., 1948). If orgasm results there is no residual tension. If orgasm does not occur, any tension which does not subside spontaneously is frequently relieved by masturbation, the event which would otherwise have transpired in the first place.

PREMARITAL INTERCOURSE

Provided it is not productive of moral conflict, premarital intercourse is undoubtedly the most satisfactory sexual outlet of the three. The precise outcome depends on the type of partner, the degree of acceptability without conflict, the conditions under which it occurs, and the worries about pregnancy and venereal disease that are generated. Kinsey et al. (1948) report that few males ever regret premarital intercourse, but this is probably less true of females, as most psychiatrists can testify from clinical experience.

DIFFERENTIATION OF SOCIAL SEX ROLES

Components of social sex role

In contrast to biological sex role, which refers to feeling tones, behavior, and impulses functionally or historically dependent on gonadal stimulation, social sex role refers to the differential functions, status, and personality traits that each culture traditionally assumes to inhere in the very fact of sex membership.

Social sex roles in a given culture are generally regarded as self-evident reflections of the essential nature of man and woman. That men and women perform social and economic functions that vary widely from culture to culture in degree of similarity is an anthropological commonplace; and to a greater or lesser extent, different cultures provide differential training for boys and girls that will equip them for the distinctive tasks they will perform as men and women. Such differential training takes place in our own culture as well as in more primitive cultures (Leighton & Kluckhohn, 1947b; Mead, 1949), but it is less thoroughgoing as a result of the greater discontinuity between the status worlds of children and adults. In our own culture, as Parsons (1942) points out, girls suffer less than boys from this discontinuity in training, since as children both are reared primarily by the mother who can provide a visible model of behavior as well as concrete experience with appropriate tasks only for the female sex role.

Another important aspect of social sex role is the hierarchical ordering of relations between the sexes in terms of (1) the relative values placed by the culture on maleness and femaleness, respectively, and (2) the degree of access each sex has to positions of social power and privilege. In most familial, vocational, and institutional situations in our culture, except for very recent changes, the male is trained for the superordinate positions. As in other types of inferior social rankings, however, the female position allows a certain degree of chronic aggression, sabotage, and cleverness against the superior rank (Davis, 1941).

From an early age boys learn to be contemptuous of the female sex role; and although girls resent and complain about the disrespect shown their sex (Remmers et al., 1950), Simmons and Rosenberg in their random sample of 1988 children from grades 3 through 12 in Baltimore found that girls are less likely than boys to believe it's "great" to be their own sex, they are more likely to perceive themselves acting like the opposite sex, and they are less likely to think it is important to avoid acting like the opposite sex. "Among the 15- and 18-year-olds, of their own sex, in contrast to 54% of the girls, 92% of the boys say they 'never' act like a girl, while only 50% of the girls say they never act like a boy" (Simmons & Rosenberg, 1975, p. 236).

The third important component of social sex role is the prevailing cultural conception of masculinity and femininity. This consists of a stereotyped, composite personality portrait of man and woman, defining the emotions, interests, moral attitudes, and character traits thought proper and desirable for each sex.

Our culture, for example, claimed until recently that men and women "are different kinds of people. Men are strong, bolder, less pure, less refined, more logical, more reasonable. . . . Women are more delicate, stronger in sympathy, understanding, and insight, less mechanically adept, more immersed in petty detail and in personalities, and given to 'getting emotional over things' " (Lynd & Lynd 1937). These notions of masculinity and femininity have deep and often obscure roots in the culture. In general, however, they are derived from the respective socioeconomic functions and statuses of men and women, and from the culturally determined characteristics of appropriate male and female body types and biological sex roles. The conventional differences between masculinity and femininity tend to decline as both sexes take on the same roles in the labor market (Bernard, 1969; Starr, 1974), as is apt to happen in a technologically sophisticated postindustrial society (Dreyer, 1975).

Impact of pubescence on social sex role

Studies (Kagan, 1964; Kohlberg, 1966) have shown that Americans develop a sex role identity by the age of 6 or 7, but during adolescence the youth in our culture acquire clear-cut and unambiguous conceptions of adult masculinity and femininity (Simmons & Rosenberg, 1975). The facilitating effect of adolescence on the emergence of social sex roles can be attributed in part to (1) greater perceptual sensitivity to social situations and interpersonal relationships, and to (2) the greater importance of social sex role at this stage of development.

During childhood social sex role is primarily differentiated for purposes of play. But in adolescence the aim of differentiation is more serious by far, involving a more or less permanent assignment of social, vocational, and family tasks and aspirations together with their appropriate personality traits.

But pubescence per se must be an important factor in the development of social sex role in view of the fact that pubescent individuals make higher scores on the M-F test than nonpubescent individuals of equivalent chronological age (Terman & Miles, 1936). This does not mean that sex hormones exert a direct influence on the individual's development of the appropriate masculine or feminine personality attributes. The immediate effects of sex hormones under favorable conditions are merely to increase sex consciousness and awareness of sex differences, and to develop distinctive characteristics of male and female body type. But as a result of increased sensitivity to sex differences, the individual becomes more aware of the social expectations and values attached to the male or female body.

As a result of reacting to his own changed body form, of reacting to the sexuality of others, and of being reacted to as a sexual object, he comes to identify with a given adult sex clan and to incorporate the personality characteristics compatible with the social expectations of membership in that clan. He thus acquires the complete constellation of differential personality traits associated with male and female socioeconomic functions, with the physical criteria of masculine and feminine attractiveness, and with the properties of male and female biological sex role.

The mere development of the body-type characteristics that follows from the sex-appropriate pattern of endocrine stimulation does not of itself result either in cultural norms of masculine or feminine attractiveness or in individual identification with and incorporation of the appropriate physical criteria of masculinity or femininity. The physical values that are culturally chosen as criteria of masculine or feminine physical attractiveness are not implicit in the sex differences themselves; they are arbitrarily selected from a large number of secondary sex characteristics and at arbitrarily designated points on a continuum of male and female body types.

The same holds true for biological sex role: neither its original emergence nor subsequent differentiation is implicit in pubescence. In cultures in which a sharp distinction is made between male and female biological sex roles (Manus, American), there is a correspondingly greater polarization of the concepts of masculinity and femininity; and when this distinction is not made (Mundugumor, Arapesh), the essential natures of man and woman are conceived as more alike.

Once learned, the concept of social sex role is continually reinforced by the availability of vivid perceptual cues, i.e., objective and culturally determined differences in the appearance, behavior, and presumed personality traits of the two sexes. Thus, not only the cultural existence of polarized concepts of masculinity and femininity but also the adolescent's identification with these concepts is facilitated by the presence of culturally defined differences in sex-appropriate physical traits, biological role, and socioeconomic functions. Biological and social sex roles are simultaneously differentiated in our culture, and each mutually reinforces the other.

Transitional social sex role of adolescence

Since the adolescent is not admitted to membership in society at large, he can play a social sex role only in his own peer group. It is inevitable that this role will be transitional and discontinuous with both its childhood and adult counterparts. The appropriate constellations of masculine and feminine traits associated with high peer group status have been discussed in detail earlier in this book. They are related, at least in part, to the unique interim goals and values of the peer group.

In relation to preadolescence, the social sex role of adolescence requires a break with the derived status inherent in the role of emotionally dependent son or daughter. Boys must primarily aspire to an extrinsic status based on their own performance abilities; and girls must aspire both to a derived status based on their husbands' careers and to an earned status related to their own homemaking abilities and their more circumscribed vocational roles. In relation to the adult social sex role, a similar degree of discontinuity prevails. In contrast to responsibility as a dominant characteristic of this role, the orientation of the youth culture is more or less specifically irresponsible.

In choosing its leaders, the youth culture places great emphasis on the importance of being an "all-round" personality, and relatively little weight on competence in a narrow field of specialization (Parsons, 1942). Male athletic prowess carries little prestige value in the adult culture; and sexual attractiveness or glamorousness in the female is a relatively minor component of the social sex role of adult women (Parsons, 1942).

Nevertheless, despite this evidence of discontinuity (just as in the transmission of major social class goals, values, and attitudes), the essential differential aspects of social sex role filter down into and are transmitted by the peer culture. It is true, of course, that in the middle and upper-middle classes there is up through college no sex differentiation in the process of formal education (Parsons, 1942); such differentiation takes place first at the postgraduate level where there is a "direct connection with future occupational careers" (Parsons, 1942). But despite the presumption of sex equality in future vocational roles that is initially engendered by this nondiscriminatory preparatory (high school and college) education, neither boys nor girls seriously doubt that eventually considerable differentiation of occupational status will take place on the basis of sex membership. Girls adopt a more ambivalent and less ego-involved attitude than boys toward expressed vocational choice because in anticipation of marriage the belief is still deep rooted that the husband must be the superior achiever in the occupational world and the wife the caretaker of young children (Komarovsky, 1973). Whereas the middle-class boy fully anticipates that he will be expected to create through his own vocational efforts and achievements the social status of his future family, relatively fewer girls in the same social class expect as married women to compete with men in their own fields or at occupational levels of equivalent social prestige (Parsons, 1942). They expect to fall heir to a derived status dependent on their husbands' station in life, and to acquire earned status in the roles of mother and housewife, supplemented perhaps by participation in cultural and community welfare activities (Parsons, 1942). Adolescent girls are less likely, even today, to envision future educational and presumably occupational opportunities as available to them. "While the boy emphasizes future opportunity, she is more likely to place primacy on interpersonal skills" (Simmons & Rosenberg, 1975, p. 256). It remains to be seen whether Women's Liberation will usher fundamental change.

Sex differences in the acquisition of social sex role

In some ways the acquisition of social sex role is more difficult for boys, but in other ways it is more difficult for girls. Boys are required to undergo greater personality change. The implications of emancipation—independence, self-reliance, striving for earned status—are applied more thoroughly in their case. For boys there is also less continuity from the adolescent to the adult social sex roles. Athletic ability and heterosexual effectiveness are less related to the adult male role than glamorousness is to the adult female role.

Girls, on the other hand, experience more difficulty in the transition between preadolescent and adolescent social sex roles since they lack a core value, such as athletic prowess, which persists from one stage to the next as a significant determinant of peer group status. The concepts of femininity and female sex role in our culture are also less stable and less consistent than the corresponding concepts for boys.

More recently, however, as noted earlier, especially children of working mothers see their own sex as having some of the traits usually associated with the opposite sex. Females feel more "aggressive and assertive and males more tender and warm," and when they are college students, they feel freer than their parents to engage in overlapping sex roles (Starr, 1974).

Yet studies (Simmons & Rosenberg, 1975) indicate that girls feel less positive toward themselves and their sex and more self-conscious about their role. They do not yet visualize themselves filling an important place in the adult world. They rate their sex role more harshly than boys. This is true even of black girls who, compared with white girls, hold a more favorable self-picture and a favorable position as females in their community.

The trend, however, is clearly toward feminism, notably in attitude. In a comparison of two samples between 1969 and 1975, Parelius (1975, pp. 151–152) noted the following shifts among women who were attending college as well as freshmen.

> Attitudes toward work, financial responsibilities, and the division of labor in the home showed the greatest amount of change. . . . attitudes toward the importance of marital and maternal roles changed also, but to a lesser degree. . . . few would sacrifice marriage or motherhood for occupational success. The far-reaching changes observed in the women's attitudes and expectations were not accompanied by equal shifts in their perceptions of men's willingness to marry feminist women.

Since most of these women are interested in marriage and motherhood, it is probable that they experience anxiety about their future.

Thus sex role definitions are shifting rapidly. Women, at least in certain segments of society, reject economic dependence and "unalleviated household responsibilities" of the traditional wife-mother role. Their goals therefore suggest restructuring of the family but not its dissolution.

Much research indicates that the experience of higher education tends to depolarize the sex roles among students.

> Terman and Miles (1936) long ago established that increased education has the effect of reducing the "masculine" score of men and the "feminine" score of women on the scale they devised to measure such differences. Carlsmith (1963) concluded from her research that sensitivity, aesthetic interests, and verbal ability seem to be valued for everyone in intellectual environments. Komarovsky (1972) reported from her research that "intellectual qualities are no longer considered unfeminine and. . . the imperative of male superiority is giving way to the ideal of companionship between equals (p. 876)". Riesman has observed that "greater femininity is being increasingly permitted to educated men in this country. . . there are many institutions throughout the country where men can without embarrassment be interested in art, in English, in dance, and in music (1959, p. 210)". In their study of college students, McKee and Sheriffs (1959) noted that men were willing to grant their "ideal woman" what are "probably the most basically masculine variables (action, vigor, and achievement effectiveness)", suggesting a change in the traditional female sex role stereotype. Moreover, men correctly perceived a pressure by women to be "more oriented to interpersonal relations" and to express more "human (feminine in the stereotype) feelings (1959, p. 362)". After a decade of research

using Rorschach sex-imagery cards on 1393 subjects, Brown (1971) concluded that men are responding increasingly more like women and women more like men. (Starr, 1974, pp. 86–87)

Parelius (1975) rightly observes that we do not yet know the extent to which new sex role definitions are being accepted by various segments of society. Attitudes do not necessarily translate themselves into behavior. Attitudinal shifts that develop on campuses may revert to former patterns particularly if not supported by reference groups.

The major shift is in the female sex role, which dictates modifications in the male role particularly in the family constellation. Yet girls are not really driven by the culture as are boys to prove their adequacy and maintain their self-esteem by their accomplishments. And lacking this powerful cultural instigation to achievement, in comparison to her average male counterpart, the career-oriented girl must either be motivated by an unusually high order of intellectual curiosity and creativity or have unusually great needs for ego enhancement that are rooted in her individual personality development.

Current trends, however, lend increasing social support for women who are adopting feminist perspectives. "Women's centers, communes, consciousness-raising groups, literature, and organizations extoll the virtues of feminist life-styles and provide some of the structure within which these life-styles might be realized" (Parelius, 1975, p. 152). Moreover, women seem ready to maintain feminist attitudes in spite of perceived male rejection of these attitudes. Comparing answers to the same questions given to college women in 1950 (Wallin, 1950) and in 1970 and 1971, Komarovsky (1973) found that women in the 1970s were much less likely to hide their ability than women in 1950 (Dreyer, 1975).

Biological or social determination of social sex role

Since the culture determines the socioeconomic functions, the relative status, and the biological sex roles of men and women, as well as the physical criteria of masculinity and femininity, social sex role is primarily a cultural derivative rather than an inevitable consequence of endocrinological differences. In all cultures social sex roles constitute institutionalized patterns of behavior that are transmitted to boys and girls by differential treatment, training, and expectations; and it is especially during adolescence, when physical changes in body form make identification with an adult sex clan possible, that these roles are effectively incorporated into ego structure.

All of this becomes much more evident when we look outside

our own culture and discover that its concepts of masculinity and femininity are not the only ones natural and possible in human societies. When the difference in the socioeconomic roles of the sexes lies in a direction opposite to that of our own culture, as among the Tchambuli, our notions of masculinity and femininity are precisely reversed (Mead, 1939); and, on the other hand, when little distinction is made between these roles, as in the Soviet Union, there is correspondingly less of a "dichotomy of personality characteristics between man and woman" (Sherif & Cantril, 1947). Similarly, when male and female biological sex roles are presumed to be more identical (Arapesh, Mundugumor), both sexes are expected to conform to similar ideals of character (Mead, 1939).

In taking this position it is not necessary to assume, as many social psychologists and anthropologists do, that biological factors play no role whatever in conditioning sex differences in personality. We have cited evidence in support of the proposition that gonadal hormones and prolactin can bring about significant changes in such temperamental characteristics as aggressiveness and motherliness. Nevertheless, personality differences that are conditioned by hormonal factors would not prevail unless they were supported by cultural variables operating in the same direction. And since cultural influences are able to negate and even reverse the consequences of biological conditioning, they must be accounted the prepotent factors in determining social sex role.

HETEROSEXUAL PEER GROUP AND COURTING BEHAVIOR

Our culture, like all other cultures, establishes formal and institutionalized practices and regulations governing the interpersonal relationships between the sexes. Invariably, the formality and rigorousness of these regulations increase as children reach adolescence; for beginning with pubescence, hererosexual relationships seriously impinge on such culturally important matters as biological sex role, social class status, and family organization. Whatever the mores that govern the approaches children of opposite sex can make to each other (physically or socially) they are almost invariably significantly different in relation to adults (Benedict, 1938).

Since in our culture the adolescent's social life and opportunities for sexual expression are almost entirely limited to his peer group, he is obliged to devise instrumentalities for formal heterosexual contact within its structural organization. In contrast to preadolescent group formations, adolescent peer groups are generally predicated on heterosexual membership and their activities are undoubtedly stimulated by gonadal maturation, as evidenced by their earlier appearance in girls than in boys. But the facts that an interval of a year occurs between pubescence and the appearance of these interests in girls and that a further interval of time interposes between the initial appearance of the interests and their translation into suitable activities (Jersild, 1946; Smith, 1924) shows that other factors (parental attitudes, identification with peer group activities, the learning of new social techniques) are also involved.

Courting relationships in the peer group serve several important functions. They provide for both sexes the major source of recreational activity during adolescence. For both boys and girls they are the source of most romantic and psychoaffectional sex experience and the basis for locating and choosing a suitable mate. They provide an important source of sexual gratification; and for both sexes, but especially for girls, they are a significant determinant of intragroup status and prestige.

Developmental changes in heterosexual relationships

The increasing depolarization of sex roles enhances possibilities of richer and more complex male-female relationships. There is evidence of an earlier peer relationship between boys and girls displacing the segregation of the sexes characteristic during the years of middle childhood and preadolescence.

Broderick and Fowler (1961) have found that although boys and girls 10 to 13 years of age still tend to prefer the company of their own sex, the old preadolescent pattern of cross-sex hostility and withdrawal appears to be declining significantly. In a middle-class southern urban school population 38% of seventh-grade children (approximately 12 to 13 years of age) chose at least one member of the opposite sex among their four closest friends. . . . Nearly half of both boys and girls preferred the companionship of a member of the opposite sex (as opposed to a member of the same sex or being alone) while eating, over two-thirds of both sexes preferred the companionship of a member of the opposite sex while taking a walk, and nearly three-fourths of the males and two-thirds of the females preferred the opposite sex as a movie companion. (Starr, 1974, p. 87)

The transitional heterosexual pattern thus manifests early. The same study (Broderick & Fowler, 1961) reports that of the 12- to 13-

year-old boys and girls 70% of the boys and 53% of the girls claimed to have had dating experience. These latter figures compare to 15% for boys and 20% for girls reported by Hollingshead (1949).

Another transitional form of development that does not markedly conflict with recognized preadolescent patterns and requires no new social learnings in relation to peers of the opposite sex is the early adolescent "crush." It involves strong attraction to and admiration of a peer of the same sex or an older person of the opposite sex. It is a well-suited substitutive outlet for heterosexual interests when adolescent boys and girls are still self-conscious and awkward about approaching each other.

The first type of "crush" is more common in girls than in boys (Hurlock, 1934), and, according to one study, involves the overwhelming majority of girls (Landis et al., 1940). This sex difference is compatible with the previously noted tendency for girls to be more concerned than boys with intimate interpersonal experience. However, such "crushes" are of relatively short duration and are replaced in almost all instances by normal heterosexual relationships as soon as these can be established with greater ease. Although these frequently involve very close association, some physical affection, and even intense jealousy (especially in girls), sexual connotations are seldom present and homosexuality is only a rare consequence (Landis, 1940). "Crush" behavior toward an older person of the opposite sex partakes more of romantic idealization and hero worship; and silent adoration is usually the only feasible way of expressing the felt devotion that is intense but quickly dissipated.

DEVELOPMENT OF THE ROMANTIC PATTERN

Once past the initial self-consciousness and bewilderment, when their status as adolescents is clearly enough established, boys and girls allow their heterosexual interests to come into the open frankly and unabashedly. Initially these overt manifestations are apt to be exaggerated, boisterous, silly, affectedly uninhibited, and randomly directed. Gradually, however, they become more restrained, dignified, patterned, and selective. Giddy interest in all members of the opposite sex gives way to a more concentrated interest in one person or in a favored few. Formal dating displaces diffuse, unorganized activity. With increasing age, "going steady" becomes more common, involving one fourth to one third of high school students and more than half of college students (Cole & Hall, 1970; Mather, 1934). The college group was also found to be more critical of their dates.

In addition to greater selectivity, other factors add to the growing stability of adolescent heterosexual relationships. As adolescents grow older, their relationships are more romantic and affectional, with greater depth of emotion (Kirkpatrick, 1936). As dating becomes increasingly oriented toward mating needs, these relationships necessarily become less casual.

The current romantic pattern of courtship involving the notions of voluntary selection of a mate, "special affinity" between the betrothed pair, and idealization of the loved one is neither typical of most cultures nor of very long standing in our own culture. To a large extent it is a function of our cultural concept of the traditional feminine sex role, of our official psychoaffectional orientation toward sexuality, and of the general aura of mystery surrounding sex. Psychoaffectional expressions of sexuality, however, need not be based on romantic love. Among both the Arapesh (Mead, 1939) and the Navaho (Leighton & Kluckhohn, 1947a), for example, marriages are "arranged" by parents and families. Also, "the Navaho theory is that one woman will do as well as another so long as she is healthy, industrious, and competent" (Leighton & Kluckhohn, 1947a). Nevertheless, in neither culture is there an absence of deep emotional content in the relationship between the sexes. It is interesting that despite the great emphasis we place on psychological compatibility in marriage, marriage partners are much more similar in social background factors than in personality characteristics (Burgess & Wallin, 1943, 1944).

Dating and courting beliefs and practices

In one study (Purdue Opinion Panel, 1961) of 2000 adolescents the typical age for beginning to date was judged to be 13 by nearly half of them and 15 or 16 by nearly the other half. "The actual facts, however, would indicate that dating starts somewhat earlier, certainly for girls, since they are more mature than boys. In one study of girls (Dixon, 1958) 20 percent under fourteen dated some, 70 percent over fourteen said they dated regularly, as did 90 percent over sixteen" (Cole & Hall, 1970, p. 364).

There is a growing consensus of opinion that a shift has occurred in the main purpose of dating (Collins, 1974). Whereas once dating was part of courtship, it has now become an end in itself (Hurlock, 1967). Every date now has an erotic component (Douvan & Adelson, 1967), providing the adolescent with a pleasant social experience and a socially approved outlet for heterosexual interests (Rogers, 1969; E. A. Smith, 1969). Hurlock (1968) believes that petting is so widespread during dating that it could truly be called a phenomenon of present-day youth. She contends that boys expect to pet on every date regardless of the circumstances, whereas Reiss (1969) contends that for girls "petting-with-affection is one of the most popular dating codes" (Collins, 1974, p. 318).

Some adolescents, but boys more than girls, date infrequently or not at all due to absorption in sports or other activities, physical immaturity, or unwillingness to accept such peer values as dancing, kissing, and necking. Adolescents who do not date are often socially maladjusted or reticent (Hurlock, 1973).

Feinstein and Ardon relate dating to adolescent development in the context of four stages. In stage I (ages 13 to 15) dating invitations are made by boys to girls to go to movies and parties "with public acknowledgement that they have a girl friend. Kissing and petting (making out) are indulged in as an indication of the heterosexual, nonplatonic aspects of the relationship" (Feinstein & Ardon, 1973, p. 160). Stage II (ages 14 to 17) is the practicing stage. The dating experience is not a critical one during the first 2 years of high school. Offer (1969) reports in a study of middle-class adolescents that by the end of the freshman year 53% had begun dating and by the end of the junior year 77% had started. However, the dating was described as irregular and not relished or thought to be important. Offer further states that those who did not date "did not feel abnormal or self-conscious. The only people in the study who seemed concerned were the parents, especially the mothers" (Feinstein & Ardon, 1973, p. 161). The main function of this stage seems to be the solidifying of sexual identification. Stage III (ages 16 to 19) leads to acceptance of the sexual role. "Experimentation with different dating models, becoming involved in longer-term dating relationships, increased experimentation with sexual relationships, and an increasing incidence of sexual intercourse as part of the relationship become the dominant trend" (Feinstein & Ardon, 1973, p. 162). Stage IV (ages 18 to 25) is for the development of a permanent choice leading to marriage.

Of the characteristics thought desirable in a prospective mate, physical and mental fitness, desire for a normal family life with children, dependability and trustworthiness, compatible interests, good personal appearance and manner, and pleasant disposition and a sense of humor are chosen most frequently in high school students (Cole & Hall, 1970; Purdue Opinion Panel, 1961; Remmers et al., 1950). These students are keenly aware that both partners must understand about the handling of money. The girl wants her prospective mate to have a job, and boys want their prospective wives to know how to manage a household.

Courtship problems and heterosexual adjustment

The courtship problems that bother adolescents most have to do with (1) the legitimacy of premarital sex intimacies—kissing, petting, intercourse (Butterfield, 1939); (2) dating practices—"blind," "pick-up," "girl-made" dates (Butterfield, 1939); (3) characteristics limiting the suitability of a prospective mate—age, religious, and educational differences (Butterfield, 1939); and (4) difficulties experienced in love affairs—quarrels, loss of interest, fear of overinvolvement (Kirkpatrick & Caplow, 1945b), the nature of "true love," "two-timing," long engagements, and terminating engagements (Butterfield, 1939).

Factors influencing the outcome of heterosexual adjustment

Whether or not heterosexual adjustment during adolescence will be successful is not a matter of chance. Depending on the personality characteristics of the individual and on the favorableness of his environment, he may either fail to adopt an appropriate biological sex role (sex perversion, sex delinquency, asexuality) or experience delayed or inadequate heterosexual maturation (Blanchard, 1944; Kinsey et al., 1948). The importance of learning experiences in achieving heterosexual adjustment is pointed up by the series of developmental changes in the relationship between the sexes during adolescence, by the relatively large number of love affairs of most individuals before choosing a mate (Hamilton & MacGowan, 1928; Landis et al., 1940), by the increasing degree of dissatisfaction from high school to college age with members of the opposite sex (Mather, 1934), and by the increasing degree of affectional success in successive love affairs (Kirkpatrick & Caplow, 1936).

Three main categories of unfavorable factors are implicated in heterosexual maladjustment during adolescence: (1) unfortunate parental attitudes and parent-child relationships—the example of an unhappy marriage in the home, the parents' deprecation of sex or of the sex of adolescents (Frank, 1944b), parental clinging to the adolescent child or preventing him from making heterosexual contacts with his peers, parental ridicule of early heterosexual ineffectiveness, unwholesome family relationships (Wolford, 1948); (2) personality traits associated with asocial tendencies [excessive introversion, timidity, insecurity, anxiety, impaired self-esteem (Wolford, 1948), asceticism, and overintellectualization] and with inappropriate differentiation of biological sex role (narcissism or overidentification with the sex role of the parent of the opposite sex); and (3) insufficient opportunity for learning experiences, from extreme physical unattractiveness, isolation from the peer group (Wolford, 1948) or members of the opposite sex (Willoughby, 1937), and lack of social skills.

The less serious of these influences, such as parental restrictiveness, asocial personality traits, and insufficient opportunity for heterosexual experience, usually only limit the rate and maximum extent of normal heterosexual maturation or lead to transitory aberrations in psychosexual development. In the latter category belongs the situational homosexuality associated with sexual deprivation (Kinsey et al., 1948; Willoughby, 1937). On the other hand, defects in personality traits directly influencing the appropriate differentiation of biological sex role may lead to permanent homosexuality; and extreme parental deprecation of sexuality or of a particular (male or female) sex role may lead to asexuality (frigidity, psychic impotence) or to sex delinquency.

SEX EDUCATION AND GUIDANCE

Adolescents' sources of sex information

Age-mates through friendship continue to provide the most frequent single source of sex information (Inman, 1974; Rockwood & Ford, 1945), but the family constitutes the most significant source (Inman, 1974; Remmers et al., 1950). In one study (Inman, 1974) of ninth through twelfth graders the majority of respondents had received first sex information during grade school from talks with friends or reading sexually oriented magazines with friends. Mothers alone provided much more information than did fathers. Schools were an important source of sex information, but the family (especially mothers) was the preferred information source. However, 22 percent of boys and 18.1 percent of girls said they would prefer both parents to dispense sex information rather than having one parent do it.

Both sexes said they were most comfortable discussing sex with peers of same or opposite sex.

The need for sex education in the schools

An increasing plurality of sexual attitudes, values, and life styles and an increased awareness of problems related to sexuality such as venereal disease, unwanted pregnancies among adolescents, and numerous yearly abortions make sex education in schools an urgent need. Over 50 percent of married couples have some sort of sexual dysfunction. One-third of all marriages end in divorce. Sexual anxieties are related to drug usage (Welbourne, 1975).

Services for venereal disease, unwanted pregnancy, and personal or marital problems, Welbourne points up, are provided in metropolitan areas. However, help in preventive measures is scarce. An increased concern even on the part of professionals and an awareness of the need for help are not coupled with adequate information and skills.

A program of general sex education

To be satisfactory and nonoffensive to parents of different moral beliefs and persuasions, the school can attempt to offer only a very general sex education. Such education would be concerned with the physiology and psychology of normal sexual development and with the emotional and ethical goals of sex expression. It would leave to individual guidance specific problems about various sexual practices.

Any effective program of sex education would also have to be geared to developmental "changes in the form of children's concern as they move from the early adolescent into the late adolescent period" (Jersild et al., 1946). L. K. Frank makes the following pertinent comment:

> It is. . . ironic to recall that when boys and girls are most eager to make an approach to each other, to discover what a man and woman mean to each other, and how they should act toward each other, we can only offer them sex education, i.e., teaching about procreation, which is the last thing they are really concerned about. They want to know not about babies, but what you can do with sex, what you can give and receive from the other, what love means. Instead of giving them our best knowledge and wisest counsel and helping them to direct these interests, the cautious parents may instead concentrate upon terrorizing them with the dangers of venereal disease. (Frank, 1944b, pp. 243–244; quoted by permission of the Society)

Thus, whereas instruction about reproduction, conception, the birth process, and the anatomy and physiology of sex is developmentally suited to the concerns of preadolescence, young adolescents are understandably more interested in the emotional and moral aspects of sex, in psychosexual development, and in problems of courting. Older adolescents have a more relevant interest in problems of marriage, homemaking, and the family.

Much of these materials could undoubtedly be learned with other established courses of study such as biology, hygiene, and home economics. It is extremely doubtful, however, whether the present preparation of teachers equips them to handle these problems properly.

ETHICAL ORIENTATION

The most vital aspect of the general program of sex education proposed is an insistence that sex education is meaningless unless it can be related to the meaning, the role, and the importance of sex in the modern world. To separate these questions from the province of sex education is to make of it a meaningless jumble of isolated facts, merely to substitute five-syllable for four-letter words. The writers, in other words, cannot accept the point of view that sex education must be only factual and descriptive in nature and must not presume to tell an individual how to behave in an activity that is primarily personal rather than social in nature.

What is forgotten in all such arguments is that every culture accepts an implicit set of ethical values for significant behavior and proceeds as a matter of self-preservation to educate the young to accept these values. Does anyone after all object to the "one-sided" advocacy of the virtues of democracy, honesty, truthfulness, and kindliness in our schools?

Since it is impossible to conceive of any directed behavior which is devoid of either purpose or moral content, how can guidance neglect either aspect? The individual still retains his right of self-determination by being free to accept or reject the goals and standards offered him, providing his behavior does not infringe on the rights or interests of others.

One position on the ethical orientation of sex education that could be taken but seldom is (at least explicitly), is that our culture should adopt the Samoan code of sex morality. This would be consistent with the widespread attitude that the stressfulness of adolescence is directly correlated with the severity of social restrictions on sexual expression. But we have already seen that there is no single, inevitable, or universal pattern of psychosexual development, and that the suppression of physiological sex urges is not invariably associated with psychological conflict. In the light of this finding it is possible to suggest a more realistic solution, which is also more appropriate to the emotional and aesthetic ideals of our society. And the finding that the Arapesh are able to prevent effectively the development of physiological sex drives merely through passive deemphasis and to channel all sex urges and consciousness along affectional lines lends credence to the belief that a psychoaffectional goal of sex behavior is neither unrealistic nor impossible (with proper sex education) in our culture.

The argument that "free expression of the psychophysiological component of sex" is more "natural" is psychologically irrelevant since practically every other "natural" drive in man has been drastically modified and channeled into highly differentiated and limited modes of expression. In advocating a psychoaffectional goal of sexual behavior, however, it need not be given the same negative connotations which it has acquired in our own Anglo-Saxon culture. In other words, our present-day acceptance of psychoaffectional sexuality need not be regarded as the lesser of two evils, as something intrinsically ugly and reprehensible, as "something to be relegated to the darkness of the night" but to be tolerated in relation to marital affectional needs. Instead, it can be given a more positive emphasis as in the Arapesh society where it is regarded as an added means of enriching and beautifying an affectional relationship between man and woman.

Sexual activity, then, could become but a component of the emotional expression of the total personality, instead of a partially repressed emotional outlet in women and a combination of physiological and affectional behavior in men (each of which is frequently pursued independently of the other). This concept of sexuality presumes a high degree of ego involvement which disallows a casual attitude toward sex activity, such as that which underlies sexual promiscuity, experimentation, and flirtation. The goal toward which it strives is the monogamous type of marital relationship which we have already adopted in our society. The difference, however, would be that marriage would be advocated as the best possible medium for enhancing a psychoaffectional sexual partnership rather than as the factor which in itself legitimizes something inherently shameful.

If our culture would adopt and teach this point of view, "psychosexual development would proceed accordingly," and adolescent boys and girls would really feel this way about sex. The problems associated with psychophysiological sex needs would for the most part vanish. And if marriage could occur at a reasonably early age, the sexual turmoil which now characterizes adolescent development in so many individuals would be a thing of the past.

Sex guidance

Such a program of sex education is concerned with general problems in sexual development and expression and with a long-range attempt to redirect psychosexual development in accordance with certain specified value judgments on the goals of sexuality. Sex guidance, on the other hand, deals with individual problems of sexual adjustment and can be handled effectively only within the framework of a counseling relationship.

This does not mean that guidance must take place in an amoral setting, that the counselor is concerned only with clarifying the sex problems of his client or with helping him adjust his inner sex needs to the limitations imposed by the environment. In the counseling relationship, sexual problems must be placed in an ethical context of meaning and objectives. It is the counselor's right (and duty) to communicate his own moral formulations and judgments to the client. He cannot, of course, insist that the client accept his position, but he can give him the benefit of reacting to a set of mature moral expectations representative of the culture at large. And in so doing he encourages the individual to approach his sex problems from the standpoint of some system of values rather than from the standpoint that one way is as good as another provided it reduces tension or yields satisfaction.

Two persistent ethical problems arise in modern sex guidance: (1) the management of existing psychophysiological sex needs, and (2) the management of psychoaffectional sex needs before marriage. Adolescents might very well be able to accept the proposition that society should so regulate psychosexual development in the future that individuals will develop only psychoaffectional sex drives. But what are they to do in the meantime with their own psychophysiological drives? The only answer consistent with the philosophy advocated is that the gratification of physiological sex tensions by autoeroticism is more in keeping with the psychoaffectional ideal than with the use of a "socio-sexual" outlet such as petting or intercourse. If this principle is acceptable, what then are we to tell adolescents who are genuinely in love but unable to marry about the ethics of premarital intercourse? To remain consistent we would have to admit that although premarital sex relations are obviously less satisfactory than marital relations, they are nevertheless compatible with a psychoaffectional approach to sexuality.

Realistic sex guidance, however, cannot ignore the social reality in which adolescents live. By the time they appear for guidance, depending on their social milieu, they have already incorporated a vast array of sexual attitudes, urges, inhibitions, taboos, and morally weighted opinions about the desirability and legitimacy of various forms of sexual activity. One can only present certain moral formulations to them and point out how they could be applied in practice. But because of the course which psychosexual development has already taken, one cannot expect that these precepts will be either acceptable or realistically applicable in every case. In practice, therefore, after a counselor has put the question of sexuality in its proper context of goal and purpose, the best he can do is to equip the boy and girl for intelligent self-determination. To do this one must supply precise and reliable information about the advantages and disadvantages, the issues and the implications of the various forms of sexual outlet. And to be meaningful and helpful, answers to such questions must be specific and related to the adolescent's actual problems.

14

Problems of Vocational Choice in Adolescence

Implicit in the foregoing treatment of diverse aspects of adolescent development has been the assumption that problems of vocational goals and placement are crucially significant both for personality maturation during adolescence and for the eventual attainment of adult status. We have seen that on the solution of these problems rest the possibilities for full emancipation from the home, economic self-sufficiency, social recognition as an equal member of adult society, complete psychosexual maturation, and the establishment of an independent family unit. And consistent with the increasing importance of occupational status for current and imminent adjustment, children manifest increasingly greater concern with problems of vocational choice and preparation as they proceed from preadolescence to early and late adolescence (Hurlock, 1973; Wattenberg, 1973). Despite challenges to the work ethic, vocational choice remains a primary and major concern for high school and college students (Cole & Hall, 1970; Hurlock, 1973; Van Til, 1976; Yankelovich, 1974). It is this unwavering preeminence of concern with vocational problems that offers convincing proof of the fact that, despite his apparent preoccupation with the immediate and often esoteric activities of his interim peer culture, the adolescent's primary goals are really predicated on inclusion in the adult world.

In all cultures, although varying degrees of emphasis are placed on the acquisition of superior status or competence, it is the individual's occupation, broadly conceived, through which earned status is attained or expressed. Whenever socioeconomic roles are differentiated by a functional division of labor or a hierarchy of social prestige values, the typical occupation of a man defines and symbolizes his relative position in the stratified social organization that almost inevitably results. In our own culture,

> the most fundamental basis of the family's status is the occupational status of the husband and father. . . . This is a status occupied by an individual by virtue of his individual qualities and achievements. But both directly and indirectly, more than any other single factor, it determines the status of the family in the social structure, directly because of the symbolic significance of the office or occupation as a symbol of prestige, indirectly because as the principal source of family income it determines the standard of living of the family. (Parsons, 1942, p. 609)

We have also observed that adolescents internalize the general level of status aspirations of their particular cultural or subcultural milieu and sustain this level of aspiration by experiencing an appropriate degree of "socially adaptive" anxiety about the status they are expected to achieve. As a result of this process of differential internalization of status needs, mean differences between cultures or subcultures in the relative importance of acquiring prestige, preeminence, or superordinate position in the social hierarchy are transmitted and maintained. Nevertheless, we are obliged to reckon with the universal fact that considerable variability is found in the relative status needs of different individuals within a homogeneous cultural setting, and that such differences in urgency and magnitude of need are largely a function of the presence or absence of intrinsic feelings of adequacy.

In various other contexts we have touched on additional psychobiological relationships between adolescent development and the acquisition of occupational status. Regardless of the extent to which children may contribute to the economic life of the community before pubescence, the significance of their occupational participation undergoes profound qualitative changes after they mature sexually and achieve recognition as adults. Social expectations of the quantity, imminence, initiative, and independence of occupational activity inevitably increase as the individual enters adolescence; and he himself views the problem of vocation with increasing seriousness and concern. But even more important than these changes is the fact that only after sexual maturation do the economic contributions of the individual make him eligible for initial consideration as an equal member of the adult community.

In considering the acquisition of adult status, we have also been obliged to discuss in previous chapters such psychosocial aspects of vocation as (1) the prolongation of adolescence and the period of subadulthood because of lack of the availability of work experience; (2) the effects of reduced social mobility, technological changes in the kinds of available work experiences, war, and economic depression on the rate of adolescent personality maturation; (3) the differentiation and transmission of social class aspirations for appropriate levels of vocational status; (4) social class differences in earliness of exposure to the vicissitudes of vocational life; and (5) vocational implications of social sex role.

In the present chapter we shall reexamine these general problems related to the acquisition of adult status in the more specific context of vocational choice. We shall attempt (1) to review the major developmental aspects of vocational choice—age of onset, rate of growth, stability, and relationship to pubescence; (2) to assess the influence of various individual and social determinants of vocational choice, such as intelligence, interests, special abilities, prestige needs, work experiences, economic urgency, social sex role, and social class membership; (3) to evaluate the occupational choices of adolescents in terms of compatibility with realistic possibilities, appropriateness of underlying patterns of interests and abilities, degree of factual knowledge about self and job entering into occupational decisions, awareness of underlying motivations, and outcomes of early vocational experience; and (4) to consider some of the issues in vocational guidance and work experience.

DEVELOPMENTAL CHANGES IN VOCATIONAL CHOICE

Since vocational choice reflects the selective operation both of interests and of motivational orientation, orderly developmental changes are inevitable in any cultural environment as the biosocial status of the child undergoes significant alteration from childhood to adolescence. In this sense it is possible to use an individual's pattern of vocational choices and interests as a rough index of his developmental maturity.

The principal impact of adolescence on vocational choices is a change in motivational orientation. As a result of the increased emphasis on the acquisition of earned status, vocational interests become less important as ends in themselves and more important as vehicles through which extrinsic status may eventually be attained. The child is less concerned with vocational matters as a source of status than as a source of imaginative and exciting play; and in expressing a vocational choice, therefore, he places more weight on the possibilities for glamor and excitement in a given occupation than on the prestige it carries in the adult world. But with increasing age, there is a steady increase in the percentage of boys and girls who renounce such glamorous occupations as cowboy, detective, and movie actress for the more realistically prestige-giving professional occupations which depend on education and require adeptness (Hurlock, 1975; Wattenberg, 1973).

The effect of pubescence on vocational choice is indirect rather than attributable to the direct influence of gonadal hormones. Through the adolescent's own reactions and the reactions of others to his changed bodily appearance, the physiological events of pubescence alter his pattern of vocational concerns. And because both the individual and his culture respond to the phenomenon of sexual maturation by expecting much more independence and earned status, the whole problem of vocational adjustment is suddenly pushed into the foreground of the psychological field, acquiring new significance, urgency, and anxiety-tinged imminence.

In accordance with their more precocious sexual maturation, serious vocational choices emerge earlier in girls than in boys (Finch & Odoroff, 1939; Hicks & Hayes, 1938). It is also significant that the "vocational interests of brighter children tend to develop earlier than those of duller children" (T. M. Carter, 1938; H. D. Carter, 1944). This difference undoubtedly reflects greater sensitivity to changing environmental demands and superior ability in directing adjustive efforts into more appropriate channels.

But although the onset of pubescence does invest the problem of occupational choice with new significance and urgency, there is reason to believe that the changes that do occur are less abrupt than the corresponding physical or emotional consequences of gonadal maturation. Other variables unrelated to the implications of pubescence for personality development must also be considered. Many preadolescent children, for example, have strong intellectual or mechanical interests that lack practicality or relevance to the world of adult status. Others have made strong emotional commitments to impractical occupational choices which they find difficult to surrender. In many instances, strongly canalized interests prove highly resistant to the influence of the new motivational orientation of adolescence. Redirection of vocational interest patterns along more appropriate lines may, therefore, be a very slow and gradual process.

In any event, it must be realized that the majority of the determinants of vocational choice—ability, interest, intelligence, personality, sex, family pressures, social class membership—operate before as well as after pubescence. Whatever changes occur in response to the altered social expectations associated with puberty are superimposed on an existing pattern of vocational preferences which is already highly determined in the possible directions it may take. The contribution of adolescence to vocational choice lies largely in the adaptation of preexisting occupational dispositions to the changed status needs that emerge at this stage of personality development. There is, therefore, considerable continuity from childhood to adolescence in the content and in the determinants of vocational choice. Discontinuity arises mainly in relation to the new gestalt of motivational orientation in which occupational problems become embedded at adolescence.

The stability of vocational interests and choices

In our 1954 edition of this book, we stated that there are few definitive data on how stable the vocational *choices* of adolescents are, but we can make reasonable inferences from comparable aspects of vocational *interests*. Flanagan (1973b), in his review of Project TALENT (the 1960 survey of interests, information, abilities, and backgrounds of more than 400,000 students in a random sample of all secondary schools in the United States), points out that the plans of twelfth grade boys proved to be very unstable. "For example, when asked about their career plans five years after they had graduated from high school, only 18.6 percent still planned the career they had chosen in 1960" (Flanagan, 1973b, p. 8). He states, however, that the high school students' scores on interest scales were fairly good predictors of the careers they were entering 5 years after graduation.

Super et al. (1963) suggest that there has been absence of a sharp focus as a basis of research. The widely recognized developmental nature of vocational choice (Cass & Tiedeman, 1959; Dysinger, 1950; Ginzberg et al., 1951; Norton, 1953; Super, 1942, 1953, 1954, 1955; Super et al., 1957) can be more helpfully used as a basis for interpreting data if an appropriate distinction is made between occupational preference and occupational choice (Super, 1968). The latter implies implementation.

To the 14-year-old it means nothing more than preference, because at that age the need for realism is minimized by the fact that the preference does not need to be acted upon until the remote future. To the 21-year-old student of engineering, on the other hand, "choice" means a preference which has already been acted upon in entering engineering school, although the final action will come only with graduation and entry into a job. No wonder that reality plays a larger part in choice at age 21, when, unlike choice at age 14, it is by definition a reality-tested choice. (Super, 1968, p. 124)

Thus analysis of the results of the 1960 Project TALENT found that there was a substantial lack of realism with respect to career plans. Nearly three times as many twelfth grade boys as could be expected to graduate from college indicated that they planned a career requiring at least a 4-year college degree. A substantial number of students planning careers as mathematicians, scientists, or engineers were in the bottom quarter of their high school class in reading, reasoning, and mathematical abilities (Flanagan, 1973b). In 1970, ten years after the initial survey, there was a definite increase in realism of career choices among high school boys. In 1960 girls showed more realism in their plans. However, girls showed less improvement over 10 years. In 1970 the girls were less realistic than boys in their plans.

Vocational preferences and competencies, the situations in which people live and work, and hence their self concepts, change with time and experience (although self concepts are generally fairly stable from late adolescence until late maturity), making choice and adjustment a continuous process. This process may be summed up in a series of life stages characterized as those of growth, exploration, establishment, maintenance, and decline; and these stages may in turn be subdivided into (a) the fantasy, tentative, and realistic phases of the exploratory stage, and (b) the trial and stable phases of the establishment stage. (Super, 1968, p. 128)

DETERMINANTS OF VOCATIONAL CHOICE

As already indicated, the factors that determine an individual's eventual vocational choice are operative from the very beginning of his developmental career. Even at the moment of conception, initial directional (genic) influences are brought to bear on such important determinants of occupational choice as intelligence, special abilities, interests, personality, and sex membership. And from the moment of birth he is subjected to differential parental and social class influences associated with his membership in a particular family group. By the close of childhood the cumulative selective impact of these various factors on occupational preference is extremely well established, although their actual influence is often masked by the special imaginative functions that vocational choices serve in the world of play. At adolescence, however, such diversionary influences are no longer operative, and whatever latent vocational predispositions exist come actively to the fore. These predispositions, modified and given new significance in the changed motivational context of adolescence, to a large extent determine ultimate occupational choice.

Apart from the intrinsic determinants of vocational preference, several other factors operate either to accelerate or retard the crystallization of an expressed occupational choice. "Merely by making a verbal statement of such choice, and advertising the fact," the adolescent can gain some prestige or standing in his crowd. The making of a definite choice also confers security and relieves anxiety by structuring the field and dissipating uncertainty, indecision, and ambiguity. It gives the adolescent an early start in his quest for economic security and independence by setting a tangible goal toward which he can immediately direct his efforts and training and thereby acquire appropriate competencies.

On the other hand, there are equally influential reasons for postponing as long as possible the formulation of an ultimate vocational choice. In view of the large number of possible vocations, his lack of first-hand knowledge about the vast majority of them, and the absence of adequate opportunity for comparing his qualifications with those of his fellows, the adolescent may quite understandably wish to await further maturity and trial-and-error experience before committing himself to such an important and often irrevocable decision. Thus, two mutually antagonistic sets of forces impinge on the advisability of reaching an early occupational choice. And although the ensuing conflict may itself be uncomfortable and produce tension, it probably exercises a beneficial effect by combatting both the anxiety-reducing tendency to make an immediate but possibly arbitrary or capricious decision and the natural inclination to avoid coming to grips with a difficult and frequently distressing problem.

Traditional sex roles have tended in the past to minimize competition between men and women. Increasing diffusion and flexibility in the roles of men and women in recent years, however, have weakened lines of demarcation and have created in some ways confusion and anxiety. "While Horner's study found that over 60 percent of the women in her sample showed 'fear of success,' as opposed to 10 percent of the men, a more recent follow-up study by Hoffman (1974), who studied the same variables at the same university, found that the same percent of women showed 'fear of success' (over 60 percent) but that a larger number of men (over 70 percent) also exhibited this fear" (Dreyer, 1975, p. 213). In men this is due primarily to a "belief that single-minded pursuit of success is not worth the sacrifices involved, rather than to fears of rejection or concern with sexual identity, which still characterize women" (Mussen et al., 1974, p. 582).

Komarovsky (1973) found that at an Ivy League college 55 percent of the male students said that they wanted their future wives to combine career and family in some way, and 40 percent said they did not want their wives to have careers outside the home. Even though these men, in general, held liberal attitudes toward women, their preferences in many cases for the role of their own wives remained in the traditional fold.

The studies in the 1960s showed that among women sex role preferences were changing "as more women than ever before expressed interest in a 'modern', 'instrumental', 'liberal', or 'career' role orientation. In addition, it was found that the contradictions in sex roles which Komarovsky described for college women (Komarovsky, 1946, 1953) were becoming more widely felt by all sectors of the population of women" (Dreyer, 1975, pp. 212–213).

This changing scene operates within a context where the dominating pattern has been for men to conceptualize themselves and be conceptualized by others as adequate males if they are providers; and for women to view themselves and be viewed by others as truly women if they have husbands who are adequate in their roles (Kraemer, 1974). Currently, therefore, some women, especially the less educated, are not geared to a full-time, long-term career (Rice, 1974). Some women want only to prepare for an occupation in which to work for a time before and after marriage, and for financial security in case of loss of their husbands (Gottlieb & Ramsey, 1964). Many highly intelligent and capable girls are willing to settle for secretarial and other positions below their level of ability because they are reluctant to work the rest of their life or because they are afraid of success as an unfeminine characteristic (Barnett, 1975; Horner, 1970; O'Leary, 1974; Rice, 1975; Schaeffer, 1971). A survey of 32,000 eighth, ninth, and eleventh grade students in 200 schools located in 33 states showed that over half of eleventh grade girls choose clerical and secretarial work, education and social services, nursing and human care (Prediger et al., 1974).

However, an increasing number of adolescent girls indicate a major, permanent interest in a career (Rice, 1975). Research on sex differences also shows that the emerging pattern of preferences for jobs rests less on intersex than on intrasex differences (Blum, 1975; Singer, 1974). Moreover, both male and female students are looking for jobs in which they can learn, accomplish something worthwhile, and work with friendly and congenial workers (Singer, 1974; Yankelo-vich, 1974). In spite of the women's liberation movement, however, studies of goals-expectation discrepancy indicate that women are not convinced that the opportunity structure of jobs is open to them (Berman & Haug, 1975; Olive, 1973).

Family pressures

The impact of family pressures on vocational choice is so pervasive and often so subtle and indirect that its precise influence is difficult to evaluate. If we examine the evidence for the specific and explicit influence of parents on the occupational decisions of adolescents, we are left with the impression that relatively few wish to pursue the vocations of their fathers (Kroger & Louttit, 1935) and that the majority both deny heeding the advice and suggestion of their elders (Anderson, 1932) and set their occupational aspirations at a higher level (Kroger & Louttit, 1935). This situation, however, is as it should be when we consider the prevailing estrangement between youth and their parents and the widespread acceptance of the tradition of social mobility. But there are several good reasons for believing that the actual influence of parents on their offspring's vocational choices is great indeed.

In the first place, parents are in a strategic position to orient the development of the child's interests throughout childhood in a given general or specific direction by the judicious provision of differential rewards and play materials; it is interesting, for example, that 43.6 percent of physicians' sons choose medicine and 27.7 percent of lawyers' sons choose law (Mussen et al., 1974). Similar results have been obtained about sons of social and physical scientists (Werts, 1968). Children, especially those who are unassertive or who have over-dominating parents, may implicitly accept their parents' plans for their vocational futures without even being aware of it. Second, parent attitudes are largely instrumental in determining the magnitude of the child's individual personality needs for earned status by affecting (1) the extent to which the child can acquire intrinsic feelings of adequacy, and (2) the extent to which his potential accomplishments are regarded as a vicarious source of parental ego enhancement. Parental motivation is significantly related to the aspirational level of adolescents, even when social class and IQ are held constant. "A working-class boy is likely to seek advancement in education and occupation if urged by his parents. He is unlikely to do so if his parents do not exert pressure in this direction" (Mussen et al., 1974).

Third, prior to adolescence, the parents serve as the chief agents of the culture in transmitting to the child differential social class aspirations for a given level of occupational prestige. The cumulative effect of years of subtle indoctrination along these lines, reinforced by peer group pressures during adolescence, leads to the assimilation of sufficient "socially adaptive" anxiety to ensure the maintenance of appropriate levels of striving.

Finally, during adolescence itself, the family's socioeconomic status makes possible or impossible the implementation of various high-level vocational goals through such devices as subsidizing technical education, furnishing capital or contacts necessary for launching a career, and offering a reprieve from the urgency of finding immediate employment. Thus, we can mainly credit the influence of the family for the fact that although adolescents are resistive to the specific vocational suggestions of their parents, in general, they achieve an occupational status commensurate with their family (and social class) background (Davidson & Anderson, 1937).

Social class factors and socioeconomic conditions

As the child approaches adolescence, social class pressures toward choosing a vocation commensurate with the occupational status needs and aspirations of his class reference group become more pointed and explicit. No longer can elders indulge expressions of vocational choice that reflect glamorous notions or imaginative fancies. The situation is comparable to the one we have already observed in changing standards of adult tolerance toward children's relative indifference to social class, ethnic, and religious distinctions in organizing their social groups. With the approach of adolescence, as the game begins to be played "for keeps," parents find "democratic" notions no longer amusing but downright threatening to their equanimity as they contemplate their offspring's future.

It is in relation to these differential social class pressures that "job prestige" becomes an important factor in the relative acceptability of various occupations to a given adolescent (Little, 1967; Rice, 1975). Widespread agreement exists at all socioeconomic levels about the general hierarchical ranking of different occupations along a gradient of social prestige. The factors accounting for relative rank on this scale are not always clear. Undoubtedly, income, educational level, supervisory control, and level of responsibility are important considerations. For our purposes, it is necessary to observe only that the stratification of occupations is socially determined and "is regarded in much the same manner by persons in various classes" (Carter, 1944).

This fact shows quite clearly that job prestige does not operate directly as a determinant of vocational choice, but only indirectly by defining a range of vocations that confer sufficient occupational status to be compatible with the socially instigated prestige needs of individuals from different social class levels. That is, the perceived hierarchy of occupations does not influence vocational choice as such, since persons at all social levels perceive this hierarchy in much the same way and yet make very different choices. An individual does not necessarily choose one job in preference to another because he perceives it as carrying more prestige. He uses his perceptions of the prestige hierarchy of vocations to select an occupation compatible with the needs for vocational status and prestige that he has internalized from his class reference group.

As will be pointed out later, the prestige rating of a job also helps determine its acceptability in terms of individual differences in needs for prestige within a given social class stratum. The stability of a vocational choice, therefore, is largely a function of its relatively stable position in the hierarchy of occupational prestige, which enables it to satisfy enduring and persistent needs for prestige determined both by individual personality development and by social class membership. The fact that the prestige attributes of jobs are seldom acknowledged by adolescents as important determinants of their vocational choices (Peters, 1941) does not belie their actual importance. In a democratic society, which officially denies the existence of any system of rank or privilege in the social organization of its members, it is more comfortable for such considerations to remain unformulated in explicit terms or at least not easily accessible to conscious awareness.

Another socially derived factor that adds to the occupational prestige needs of adolescents and hence to the stability of their occupational choices is our cultural tradition of social mobility. Young people wish to climb, to secure higher status, to receive higher rewards. Their hopes are often out of line with reasonable expectations. They are hardly to be censured for this. Their attitudes have been assimilated from the surrounding environment which bristles with expectations of climbing, of beginning at the bottom and working up, etc. There is, however, little evidence in our contemporary economy, in peacetime, to justify a belief in any widespread "upward mobility" with regard to occupations (Carter, 1944, p. 269). It is largely this vision of social mobility that causes adolescent boys from lower socioeconomic groups to aspire beyond the vocational attainments of their parents (Smelser, 1970). They start at least with a wide range of aspirations, wider than those of middle-class boys (Rodman et al., 1974), to allow themselves latitude in a world of greater social constraints for achieving their aspirations.

The findings on racial differences are of interest.

> Whites show a tendency toward a wider range of educational as-
> pirations, and blacks toward a wider range of occupational aspira-
> tions. This may stem from the greater importance of education
> for blacks as the major possible means for social mobility. In con-
> sequence, blacks are less likely to stretch their range of educa-
> tional aspirations downward, and they are more likely to hold a
> high level-narrow range of educational aspirations. At the same
> time, blacks realize that occupational advancement still might not
> match their educational attainment. As a result, despite their high
> level-narrow range of educational aspirations, blacks are likelier
> to stretch their range of occupational aspirations downward, and
> thus to have a wider range of occupational aspirations than
> whites. (Rodman et al., 1974, p. 195)

Social class membership acts in still another way besides its influence on occupational prestige needs to determine vocational choice.
The economic urgency of finding immediate employment and of contributing to his family's support may force the adolescent, regardless
of his actual inclinations, to adopt the short-range view and aspire to
a low-level occupation that is immediately available and requires no
further preparation. That this is actually the situation is shown by the
fact that adolescents from lower economic strata begin work at a
younger age and find initial employment at lower occupational levels
than their more economically privileged contemporaries.

Last, general socioeconomic conditions, apart from factors of social class membership, affect the character of vocational choice. Such
conditions include the general occupational outlook as determined
by a wartime economy or by economic depression and prosperity, as
well as more specific regional or industry-wide fluctuations in job
demand. They affect not only the relative attractiveness of different
occupations, but also the degree of social mobility and the disposition of the adolescent to aspire to higher levels of vocational status.

Individual differences

INTELLIGENCE

Generally speaking, the vocational choices of adolescents are
compatible with the intellectual requirements of different occupations (Byrns, 1939; Proctor, 1937; Terman & Oden, 1959; Welsh,
1971). That is, level of intelligence operates as a selective factor in
propelling brighter individuals toward vocations that demand more

intelligence, and in directing the vocational choices of duller individuals toward less intellectually demanding occupations. This relationship is also apparent in the "significant pattern of correlations" between inventoried interests and intelligence. Although such correlations are generally low, since vocational interest inventories are concerned with measuring areas of interest rather than with ascertaining occupational level within a given area, they are in the expected direction in relation to "the intellectual requirements of occupations" (Carter, 1944; Cole & Hall, 1970; Flanagan, 1973b; Welsh, 1971).

Evidence from performance of gifted adolescents suggests several trends.

There seems to be a positive relationship between nonverbal intelligence scores and scientific interests in the physical sciences and other vocations stressing methodical and rational approaches to their problems. Business interests, particularly in sales occupations and in vocations requiring social and personal contact with people, show negative relationship with nonverbal intelligence scores. Interests in the professional, biological sciences show a positive relationship to verbal intelligence scores, while interests in business detail and other occupations characterized by routine and systematic procedures seem to be negatively related. (Welsh, 1971, p. 163)

SPECIAL ABILITIES AND APTITUDES

The relative abilities and aptitudes of an individual undoubtedly affect his vocational interests just as they do his interests in general. Superior ability in a given field leads to success, which in turn inspires frequent participation and further development of the ability. The fact that corresponding interest and ability scores are negligibly correlated in a given population does not, as has been so frequently stated, contradict this statement of relationship. Since specialized interests and abilities are each affected by so many other genic and environmental variables, it is hardly reasonable to expect that there will be much correspondence from one ranking to the other between the relative positions of different members of a group when ranked in order of interest and aptitude, respectively. A much fairer method of testing this hypothesized relationship between vocational interest and ability is to correlate hierarchies of interests and abilities within a single individual. Related evidence bearing on this in scholastic interests and aptitudes (Cegelka, 1974; Thorndike, 1917) suggests, for example, that if computational interests were to hold the highest rank on an individual's vocational interest profile, the chances are good that his vocational aptitude profile would show a similar peak. At the same time, it is entirely conceivable that his actual computational ability would only be great enough to earn him median rank in relation to the national norms for his age and sex group.

The relationship between ability and vocational interests is further complicated by the fact that early statements of vocational preference are unrealistic and influenced by many factors extrinsic to the essential functions of a vocation. Furthermore, unlike most other expressions of interest that are based on some backlog of experience, expressed vocational choice can seldom be tested against any concrete experiences of success or failure in related tasks or activities. Hence, the adolescent must have considerable maturity, both in general level of sophistication and in the degree of relevant experience needed to make a satisfactory comparative appraisal of his pattern of aptitudes, before he can even take the factor of ability into account in selecting a suitable vocation. It is, therefore, not at all surprising that scholastic achievement seems to have little influence on the occupational choices of young adolescents (Hurlock, 1975). Significantly enough, however, with increasing age, considerations of ability play a much more important role in choosing an appropriate occupation (Flanagan, 1973b; Hurlock, 1975; Picou, 1973). Hence, to appreciate truly the influence of special abilities and aptitudes on vocational choice, it is probably necessary (1) to correlate hierarchies of interest and ability within a single person rather than paired interest and aptitude scores among a group of persons, and (2) to wait until vocational interest patterns become relatively stable before undertaking correlational studies of this nature.

MOTIVATIONAL FACTORS AND PRESTIGE NEEDS

We have shown how the character of vocational choice is influenced by group differences in needs for earned status and prestige that are related to sex, pubescent status, and social class background. Such differences primarily influence the level of occupational status to which an individual aspires. In addition, we must consider individual differences in needs for prestige and social recognition which play an important role in determining the nature of vocational ambitions. As pointed out in a previous chapter, the magnitude of such needs is a function both of constitutional factors and of the availability of residual feelings of intrinsic self-esteem from the parent-child relationship. It influences vocational choice in at least two different ways: first, in the selection of an occupation perceived as having a personally satisfying level of job prestige; and, second, in the differential selection of one of several vocations at the same level of prestige which differ in the degree of social visibility or administrative power they offer the individual. Together with their socially instigated counterparts, these personality-derived needs for occupational status and prestige are responsible for much of the stability and persistence of vocational choices, even in the face of highly adverse environmental conditions or of completely inappropriate abilities.

It is quite apparent that underlying motivations are not self-evidently given in the mere existence of vocational interests or preferences. Many different motivations can account for the same general kinds or levels of interests. We are not obliged to conclude, for example, that all individuals who have high vocational ambitions are necessarily motivated by prepotent prestige needs. In certain instances, such ambitions are mainly powered by unusually strong urges to explore challenging problems, by intellectual curiosity, by a high order of talent or ability, by devotion to ideals of social service. Only by careful motivational analysis, aided by complete knowledge of the life history of an individual and by certain objective measures of motivation (Ausubel, 1950; Lee & Thorpe, 1944), can we hope to appraise the relative influence of prestige needs in determining vocational choice.

OTHER PERSONALITY TRAITS

Since it is commonly accepted in our culture that different occupations require different constellations of personality traits, adolescents undoubtedly give some attention to temperamental compatibility in selecting their life work. In this sense personality structure acts as an important determinant of vocational choice.

One of the chief ways in which personality exerts this selective influence is by affecting the types of interests an individual develops. When adolescents are queried about the factors that enter into their selection of particular vocations, they place greatest emphasis on interest (Hurlock & Jansing, 1934). And it would seem that no other judgment of relative influence could possibly be made, since in this area of decision most opportunity apparently exists for the exercise of volitional choice and individuality. Most adolescents are either overtly bludgeoned or subtly coerced by socioeconomic pressures and conditions into striving for a given level of occupational status; and when influenced by the more individual aspects of prestige needs, they are rarely aware of their precise nature. It is mostly in the weighing of specific interests in the types of activities associated with different vocations that the opportunity for deliberate decision-making arises.

One aspect of the task of matching job requirements with suitable personality characteristics, therefore, can be resolved by ascertaining to what extent an individual's pattern of vocational interests conforms to that of successful persons in his occupation of choice (Anastasi, 1976; Kuder, 1946; Strong, 1943; Tyler, 1959). The validity of this approach is confirmed by the fact that the typical vocational interest profiles of different occupational groups, as determined by standardized inventories, differ systematically among each other and in logically predictable ways (Anastasi, 1976; Kuder, 1946; Strong, 1943; Tyler, 1959).

That interest profiles should reflect those aspects of personality that have relevance for vocational choice is hardly surprising. The differentiation of an individual's psychological field into areas of relative ego involvement (interest) is, after all, determined in much the same way as is his personality structure itself, i.e., by the interaction of the unique pattern of experiences, rewards, and values to which he has been exposed with his equally unique pattern of genically acquired predispositions to develop in certain designated directions. The types of interests that a person manifests are excellent indicators of his underlying personality traits; and it is only to be expected that if personality factors are to influence vocational choice, they will do so largely through the medium of differential interest patterns.

Holland (1966, 1973) regards occupational interests as the choice of a way of life reflecting the individual's self-concept and his major personality characteristics. Tyler (1959, 1974) regards the study of interests as a way of identifying the choices that the individual makes at various life stages. These choices are both a reflection of the kind of person he is and a forecast of what he is likely to become.

Other aspects of personality besides interests and motivation also influence vocational choice. Such products of personality maturation as an individual's needs for volitional independence and freedom from control, his frustration tolerance, his ability to postpone hedonistic gratification, his sense of responsibility, and his degree of executive independence are self-evidently related to the types of occupations he considers personally acceptable. For example, an inordinately strong need for emancipation from the home coupled with low frustration tolerance and inability to postpone hedonistic satisfactions may influence an adolescent to settle for a low-level job requiring little preparation. Other outstanding personality traits that obviously qualify or disqualify certain individuals for particular occupations are introversion-extroversion, anxiety level, egocentricity-sociocentricity, level of energy, and psychological sensitivity.

AN EVALUATION OF THE VOCATIONAL CHOICES OF
ADOLESCENTS

Realistic or unrealistic?

How realistic are the vocational choices of adolescents in terms of available job opportunities? All investigations of the occupational ambitions of youth both in and out of high school agree that the expressed vocational choices of adolescents are out of line with actual economic needs as measured by census reports of the distribution of the working population in different occupations. The discrepancy between desire and availability is in all instances caused (1) by too few adolescents wanting to enter the lower level occupations in which the need for manpower is greatest and in which the larger number of them must eventually find employment, and (2) by too many adolescents aspiring to prepare for professional and technical fields that cannot possibly accommodate all of the eager candidates for admission. For example, not one of the ten vocations most preferred by adolescent boys actually appears on the list of ten occupations they most frequently enter. We must conclude that the vocational ambitions of adolescents are unrealistic and overly sanguine in terms of the statistical probabilities of their ever gaining entrance into their occupations of choice. Under these circumstances, a large number of individuals are inevitably doomed to chronic frustration, job disillusionment, and general dissatisfaction with what life has to offer them.

Many writers are inclined to deny that the occupational choices of adolescents are truly unrealistic, or if they do admit this, are disposed to discount its significance. It is pointed out that although the vocational preferences of adolescents are excessively ambitious, their actual expectations of entering their occupations of choice are not greatly out of line with realistic probabilities. In considering whether this fact seriously qualifies the significance of the conclusion reached above, we must realize that the functional goal toward which an individual strives in his daily operations is more nearly reflected by his expressed occupational choice than by his level of expectation. Few persons actually aspire to a goal that is no higher than that which they probably expect to achieve or would be willing to accept if they had to. The individual's expressed statement of choice, not his prediction of ultimate outcome, constitutes his functional level of aspiration and determines whether or not he will experience feelings of success or failure, of adequacy or inadequacy in actual vocational achievement. This level of aspiration is an "action" goal "allied to practical motives" rather than an "ideal" goal. It already reflects considerable compromise with realistic considerations since it differs markedly from the "ideal" level of aspiration adolescents give when asked what they "would really like to do" if they were not required to heed environmental limitations on vocational choice (Ausubel & Schiff, 1955a).

It is also alleged sometimes that the vocational choices of adolescents are not really unrealistic but only reflective (1) of differential social class pressures for achieving high occupational status or (2) of prevailing notions of social mobility. The first factor can adequately explain why the vocational aspirations of upper- and middle-class adolescents are on the average more ambitious than those of lower-class individuals (Kroger & Loufitt, 1935; Little, 1967; Vigod, 1972). The second factor can likewise explain why young people from all social class backgrounds strive above the occupational levels achieved by their parents, and why this tendency is most pronounced among lower-class youth* (Kroger & Loufitt, 1935; Rodman et al., 1974). But by finding credible reasons for explaining why the vocational choices of adolescents are unrealistic, we are in no sense refuting the fact that they actually are so.

It is perfectly understandable why young people from all social class strata overaspire in relation to realistic probabilities of achievement, although it is true that in middle- and upper-class youth such aspirations for professional status are more realistically grounded. It is also understandable why the vocational wishes of young people and unemployed people are often impractical and often unrelated to the general demand, local opportunity, abilities, and assets (Carter, 1944; Flanagan, 1973a). And we are hardly blaming youth for being influenced by these factors. We are merely pointing out that one inevitable outcome of the operation of such influences is the generation of unrealistic vocational ambitions. The findings of Project TALENT (Flanagan, 1973b) indicate a trend toward greater realism. In referring to the survey and

---

*Under conditions of upward social mobility, the availability of greater "ceiling" necessarily makes for greater disparity between the occupational levels of fathers and the corresponding aspirations of their children at the lower as opposed to the upper end of the economic scale. Thus, although the vocational aspirations of lower-class adolescents are less ambitious (on an absolute basis) than those of their more privileged contemporaries, these aspirations are relatively higher when compared to the mean occupational status of the respective paternal groups.

follow-up of the 400,000 high school students in the study, Flanagan states:

> The unrealistic and unstable career choices characteristic of high school students throughout the country in 1960 were not typical of 1970's students. . . . An update of this 1960 national survey carried out in the spring of 1970 indicates that the proportions of 11th graders reporting plans for specific careers changed somewhat in the 10-year interval. For example, the percentage planning careers as engineers and physical scientists dropped nearly a third during this period, whereas the percentage planning careers as biological scientists, social workers, sociologists, and psychologists practically doubled. Half of the 11th grade boys in both 1960 and 1970 reported they planned to graduate from a four-year college training. It seems almost certain that about half of them will not complete this amount of training and will therefore be forced to modify their plans. (Flanagan, 1973b, pp. 92–93).

This movement toward realism may be partly due to the changing values of young people toward careers and success. They are concerned more with intrinsic than with extrinsic factors. Yankelovich (1974) in his surveys of college students between 1968 and 1971 specified an increasing valuation of "make a contribution to society," "challenge of the job," and "self-expression" as factors in career choice. In Project TALENT,

> In both 1960 and 1970 the most important factor influencing the choice of both boys and girls was "work which seems important to me." In 1970 nearly three-fourths of the boys and more than three-fourths of the girls reported that this factor was extremely important or very important to them. In both instances these proportions were slightly greater than in 1960. A factor which became more important for both boys and girls was "freedom to make my own decisions." The other three factors, "good income to start or within a few years," "opportunity for promotion or advancement in the long run," and "job security and permanance," all dropped substantially in the ratings of importance for the 1970 students as compared with the 1960 group. (Flanagan, 1973b, p. 94)

Relationship to factual knowledge of self and job

To what extent are the vocational choices of adolescents based on factual knowledge of the requirements and nature of different jobs and of the appropriateness of their own interests and abilities for these? The answer to this question is similar to the answer to the preceding question about the reality or unreality of occupational choice. Until recently there was not much evidence of adolescents' understanding of the necessary steps in preparing for the vocations they were to choose, the duties and tasks involved, the remuneration they expect to receive, and the job opportunities available (Ausubel et al., 1953; Ausubel & Schiff, 1955a; Flanagan, 1969; Jones, 1940; Thomsen, 1943). More recently Flanagan reports:

> the trend toward greater realism in the career planning of 11th grade boys is shown by an analysis of the average scores on the same reading comprehension test administered to groups of students planning specific careers in 1960 and 1970. The boys planning careers in mathematics, the biological sciences, psychology or sociology, political science or economics, law, and pharmacology in 1970 had average reading scores which were about the same as those entering careers in these fields as reported in the follow-up of students of the 1960 Project TALENT group. In contrast, the 1960 groups of boys planning such careers had average reading scores from 5 to 7 points lower than those of the groups entering these fields. In several fields, the average reading comprehension scores for the boys in both 1960 and 1970 indicated a lack of realism for their choice. These career fields included engineering, dentistry, armed forces officer, airplane pilot, and social worker. In both surveys the boys who indicated they planned such careers while in the 11th grade had average reading scores which were from 5 to 15 points below the reading scores of those who are actually entering those fields. (Flanagan, 1973b, p. 93)

Thus a substantial percentage of high school students still select occupations for which their level of abilities is not adequate. Many reasons can explain these facts.

In the first place, vocational choices are poorly grounded on pertinent information because of the pressures exerted on adolescents to reach an early decision about occupational preference. Such pressures emanate from the inescapable necessity of choosing between alternative curricula in high school and college, from the economic urgency of finding a job in the near future, or simply from the need to gain the security and reprieve from anxiety that are associated with the resolution of any uncertainty or ambiguity. Thus pressured into making a premature decision, it is hardly surprising that adolescents frequently make arbitrary or capricious choices.

Second, the prospects of reaching a sound and well-informed decision are not enhanced by the existence of countless numbers of jobs the requirements and relative attractiveness of which are constantly changing. Third, it is rarely possible for an adolescent to acquire any first-hand work experience in the occupation of his choice. Child labor laws, trade union practices, parental objections to early employment, and the complex forms of preparatory training required for modern specialized occupations make extensive sampling of different vocations highly impractical. To compensate for this deficiency in direct experience, greater maturity of judgment is needed, as well as more time to acquire related and vicarious experience that will provide more valid knowledge of jobs and of vocational aspects of self. But this extension of time is not available before decisions have to be made. When it finally does become available, it is frequently too late to scrap the investment already made in several years of training and to start anew in search of a more appropriate vocation.

Finally, accurate perception of the requirements and characteristics of jobs and of the personal qualifications necessary is frequently impeded by potent prestige needs—even when all of the necessary information for making a sound decision is at hand. Perceptions are notoriously selective. If the need is great enough, obvious environmental obstacles and hazards may be ignored or minimized, distasteful aspects of prestige-giving occupations may be overlooked, and glaring deficiencies in ability and temperamental suitability may be blithely disregarded.

It is therefore pertinent to inquire how much real "freedom of choice" exists in the selection of a vocation. The modern adolescent has a tremendously wider range of vocations to choose from than his grandfather had, but because he lacks access to the type of experience necessary for making a valid decision between alternatives, the greater number of choices only increases his bewilderment instead of genuinely adding to his sense of volitional freedom. Even if a sounder factual basis existed for reaching vocational decisions, true deliberative judgment could not be exercised without greater awareness of the underlying motivations entering into occupational choice. In the present climate of vocational decision-making, adolescents seem highly reluctant to acknowledge and come to grips with the factors influencing the types of occupations they select. Despite all of the presumptive evidence to the contrary, they consider such factors as "job prestige" and occupational status as relatively negligible when asked to rank in order of importance the factors that influenced their choice (Ausubel, 1955; Veress, 1972). Such conventionally acceptable reasons as "interest" and "ability" receive top mention.

VOCATIONAL GUIDANCE

The need for vocational guidance

The foregoing evaluation of the occupational choices of adolescents convincingly demonstrates that modern youth is confronted by extremely complex and baffling problems in the quest for suitable vocational placement. It leads inescapably to the conclusion that for a substantial percentage of youth the goal of vocational adjustment cannot be attained without some form of vocational education or guidance. Moreover, vocational education and guidance have become even more crucial in the 1970s due to certain new developments: (1) Unemployment has become once again large enough to create concern for the sheer necessity of getting and holding a job. (2) The benefits of education are increasingly evaluated in terms of occupational advantage. Cleary (1973, p. 42), referring to Jenks' work (1972), states: "It is no accident that this is the year in which a university professor has gained national notice by publishing a book which purports to show that education does not produce financial rewards." (3) Furthermore, models of education, particularly those of liberal arts and general education, that have facilitated the development of upper- and middle-class youth in the past have been questioned by new ethnic minorities both on cultural and utilitarian grounds. (4) The response to criticism of the current content and structure of formal education has been change, somewhat superficial and confused, but sufficiently upsetting to give room to "broadly-based new organizing ideas and approaches" (Cleary, 1973, p. 42).

Some like Cleary think that these developments demand a more fundamental approach to vocational guidance in the form of Career Education which can

force attention to systematic and sustained planning as a central activity of the student in the curriculum. . . . The reorientation of career development theory by Super and others (Super, Starishevsky, Matlin, & Jordaan, 1963) beginning in the 1950s has led to the recognition of occupational planning as a long developmental process involving increasing vocational maturation and emphasizing self-appraisal and conscious development of skills and decision making. (Cleary, 1973, pp. 46, 52)

Vocational education places orientation to economic life at the center of school life from earlier years. Information about occupations would begin in elementary schools, together with activities designed to develop positive attitudes toward work and achievement.

To an increasingly greater extent schools are becoming aware of preparing adolescents for vocations. Assistance in the choice of a suitable vocation is recognized as an essential activity of the secondary school in many countries (Fleming, 1949).

Short of a career education approach to curriculum, such assistance is being provided in the form of (1) vocationally oriented courses of "magnet" programs, (2) vocational counseling, and (3) various types of work experience programs.

All of these are steps in the right direction. They need in no way interfere with the unique responsibility of the school in transmitting our cultural heritage or in imparting a core body of knowledge and intellectual skills. In a broader sense the school is also one of the important agencies concerned with preparing young people for life. It cannot turn its back on the serious problems of vocational adjustment that its graduates will inevitably encounter. It cannot pretend that the transition from schoolboy to working man is easy, natural, or fraught with only ordinary hazards. And, as will be pointed out later, the school is in a strategic position to foster certain aspects of vocational guidance, such as work experience, which no other cultural agency could conveniently attempt to handle. A recent study (Prediger et al., 1974) of 32,000 eighth, ninth, and eleventh graders in 200 schools showed that the incidence of student-expressed needs far exceeded the amount of help students said they receive. Over half of the eleventh grade girls choose occupations in only 3 of the 25 job families: clerical and secretarial work, education and social services, nursing and human care. By contrast, 7 percent of the boys prefer occupations in these areas. Nearly half of the boys' choices fall in the technologies and trades cluster of job families, in contrast to only 7 percent of the girls' choices.

Vocational guidance versus psychotherapy

Since the typical adjustment problems of adolescence are developmental or situational in nature, i.e., products of the difficulties and uncertainties involved in acquiring adult status, many of the anxieties of adolescents and young adults would disappear entirely or be considerably alleviated if they could achieve the proper type of job placement. Hence in the more usual type of adolescent maladjustment, the psychotherapeutic possibilities inherent in vocational guidance greatly exceed those present in extended exploration of conflictful emotional material (Ausubel, 1950).

Even when adolescents suffer from serious personality disturbances, it is extremely important to focus attention on current problems of vocational adjustment while probing more deeply into etiological factors.

Only too frequently, however, does the latter goal become the main preoccupation of the psychotherapeutic session, while the immediate urgency for vocational adaptation is deemphasized so effectively that by implication it is regarded as almost irrelevant to the patient's psychological disturbance. It is hardly surprising then that, if in the course of extensive psychotherapy, substantial progress toward vocational progress is not simultaneously made (rather than postponed to await the solution of emotional conflicts), all the potential benefits of ventilation, catharsis, insight, and transference might be largely nullified by the patient's failure to possess the one practical instrument he needs to effect his maturation. And thus after completing several years of the treatment on which he had pinned his highest hopes, he emerges more crushed and forlorn than before; because not only does he still have his original emotional conflicts, but now he is also several years older, still a child in his father's house, and the prospect of vocational adjustment is still but a vague and intangible dream (Ausubel, 1950).

Vocational counseling does not imply that the counselor makes decisions for his client. Neither does it imply, however, that he must merely assist the client in clarifying his goals and attitudes without expressing any judgmental reactions regardless of how unrealistic or defeatist the client's approach may be. As we have emphasized so often before, maturation in no area of personality occurs spontaneously, but largely in response to perceived social expectations. The vocational counselor cannot afford to play only the role of neutral catalyst in helping the adolescent perceive and reorganize his vocational attitudes. He is also charged with the responsibility of representing the expectations of the culture about the direction in which mature occupational adjustment is perceived to lie. Hence, it is the counselor's constant duty to emphasize and to have the adolescent accept the imperative need for vocational adjustment as the core problem of adult maturation. In the event that an unsatisfying compromise must be accepted, it should be pointed out that vocational stabilization at any level of aspiration, if tangible and realistic, is preferable by far to grandiose but vaguer expectations, or to a complete absence of any adjustment. This proposition is not as self-evident as it seems, since the number of individuals with hypertrophied ego demands is legion who, on being denied their whole-loaf ambitions, seem to prefer no loaf at all to taking many proffered varieties of half-loaf solutions (Ausubel, 1950).

Foci of concern in vocational guidance

Vocational guidance is concerned with such tasks as providing factual information about jobs, clarifying and making more accessible to consciousness the motivations underlying occupational choice, ascertaining the occupational status or level to which an individual can realistically aspire, and appraising the kinds of jobs to which he is suited by his particular pattern of interests and abilities.

CLARIFICATION OF GOALS

The first task of vocational guidance is concerned not so much with narrowing down the field of suitable occupations as in widening the relevant field from which appropriate choices may be made, and in making the processes of choice more conscious and deliberate. The net result of these two operations is to increase the range, freedom, and rational and factual basis of vocational choice. Until these two steps are taken, there is no possibility of satisfactorily clarifying occupational goals and of proceeding to the next steps of choosing appropriate occupational levels and areas of activity.

The provision of relevant occupational information has a real place in a program of vocational guidance. When an adolescent knows such things as the requirements, duties, job opportunities, and remuneration of as many different kinds of occupations as possible, his range of choice has been tremendously extended, and a sound, factual basis for decision-making actually exists. The effectiveness of an informational approach, per se, however, is both variable and limited. It is more apt to be effective when the basic difficulty in occupational choice stems from lack of knowledge and experience rather than from unrealistic motivational pressures. The duller individual is more likely to benefit from the first stages of such a program since it supplies him with information that he would have difficulty in ferreting out for himself. The brighter person is more quick to perceive the relevancy of general information to his own situation.

Although the overall effect of vocational information programs is to make occupational choices more realistic, experience has shown that their beneficial influence can be greatly enhanced when the information is made personally relevant and meaningful, taken out of a general academic context, and applied specifically to the vocational problems of a given individual. It is at this point that vocational education becomes vocational counseling. Counseling, however, does more than individualize the meaning and applicability of information. It also clarifies and brings to the surface an individual's vague and unverbalized attitudes and motivations about occupations and occupational role.

Why is this process necessary and beneficial? In the first place, attitudes and goals that are private and unverbalized are not subject to the corrective influences of a shared social reality. Inevitably, therefore, they fail to measure up to social expectations or to reasonable standards of realistic planning. Second, such unformulated and often distorted attitudes unknowingly influence vocational decisions, and thus interfere to an undeterminable extent with the processes of deliberate choice. Genuine freedom of choice can exist only when there is substantial awareness of the underlying pressures and motivations, of the relative contributions of interest, ability, family and social class influences, individual prestige needs, and desire for job security or high financial returns to the eventual decision. But awareness of the existence of certain motivations does not necessarily guarantee insight into their effect on vocational choice; this relationship must be explicitly worked out before insight can be assumed. Neither does awareness of a motive necessarily negate its influence. It merely makes the latter more modifiable and brings it into the field of conscious determinants impinging on volitional choice.

OCCUPATIONAL STATUS

One of the first problems awaiting consideration after preliminary exploration and clarification of the field of occupations and occupational goals is the determination of an appropriate level of occupational status. The needs for vocational prestige that are engendered in the course of personality development, whether reflective of general social class pressures or of more intimate interpersonal relationships, are real and insistent. They cannot be ignored or lightly brushed aside. When clearly formulated and brought out into the open, however, they can be dealt with more rationally and related to realistic limitations.

It is a fairly safe assumption that, all other things being equal, vocational satisfaction will be maximal when an individual attains an occupational status commensurate with the magnitude of his prestige aspirations. Depending on this factor, and assuming again that other things are equal, a level of occupational status that is deemed appropriate for one person may be either too high or too low for another. Once the absolute level of occupational prestige needs is ascertained in the course of skillful interviewing,* it has to be brought into line with such realistic considerations as occupational demand, financial backing for education, capacity for sustained motivation, intelligence, and ability. If these factors do not support the existing level of vocational aspiration, a forthright attempt at lowering that level is indicated; and until the client can emotionally accept the desirability of taking this step it is exceedingly doubtful whether counseling can effect any further progress.

Although each case has to be considered on an individual basis, we have noted that in general the occupational aspirations of adolescents are unrealistically high; and in view of the persistent trend toward reduced social mobility, a general devaluation of vocational ambitions would seem to be indicated (Ausubel, 1950). Whenever possible, some degree of compensation can be effected within a given level of occupational status by giving preference to those vocations that offer greater possibilities of attaining supervisory control or public recognition.

DETERMINING SPECIFIC OCCUPATIONAL CHOICE

The second major problem in selecting a vocation is deciding on an appropriate area of occupational activity. This involves the choice of a general field of work or job family and the choice of a level of complexity within that job family. For example, both machinist and mechanical engineer belong in the same job family (machine trades) but at different levels of complexity. To a large extent, of course, level of complexity coincides with occupational status. Counseling about choice of occupational field involves such considerations as interests, intelligence, aptitude, and job availability.

Used judiciously in counseling situations, vocational interest inventories are valuable aids in selecting an appropriate field of work. Since they are reflective both of personality traits and of differential ego involvement relevant for occupational compatibility, they are useful for predicting educational choice and entrance into different occupations (Anastasi, 1976; Strong, 1935). For similar reasons they are predictive of occupational contentment (Anastasi, 1976) and so of

---

*A special instrument has also been designed to measure occupational prestige needs (Lee & Thorpe, 1944). The subject is presented with a list of 90 occupational activities arranged in groups of three which are relatively homogeneous with respect to kind of activity but which differ in degree of job prestige. In each group he indicates his preference. His total score, computed on the basis of differential weights assigned to different degrees of job prestige, is reflective of his mean level of prestige aspiration over the entire range of occupations presented.

vocational stability (Dyer, 1939; Strong, 1935), and of educational (Duffy & Crissy, 1940; Dunlap, 1935) and vocational (Strong, 1943) success. It stands to reason that individuals who are contented in a given job will over the long pull be successful in it, even though they may originally show less aptitude than other persons who manifest no particular interest. Also, as indicated above, an individual is usually able to do best what he is most interested in doing, although this does not necessarily mean that he will show more initial aptitude than a disinterested individual.

For determining level of job complexity within a given field of work, intelligence quotient is a very useful indicator. Although it is true that general intelligence is highly differentiated by the time of adolescence, differentiation occurs along the lines of major interest patterns. It is a fair assumption that intelligence will be differentially concentrated in areas related to high vocational interest and can, therefore, be used as a measure of the complexity of the problems an individual is equipped to handle in those areas.

Aptitude tests are sometimes useful in reinforcing impressions derived from interview and other materials, but, generally speaking, are not very helpful in selecting a particular field of work. Only when indicative of gross ineptitude are they likely to have much prognostic significance in individual cases. "There are, of course, many aptitude batteries available in well-designed forms conforming to good standards of test construction. But aside from verbal and mathematical ability—the two parts of what is often called scholastic aptitude—these multiple batteries have failed almost totally to be usefully related to vocational success, and, especially, to be helpful in assisting student planning" (Cleary, 1973).

The reasons for this unsatisfactory state of affairs are many. In the first place, most aptitude tests, particularly those in the psychomotor field, have very low validity coefficients (Cleary, 1973; Cronbach, 1949; Fleming, 1949; Super, 1949). A number of instruments usually have to be combined in a differentially weighted battery to approach even a respectable multiple coefficient of correlation with an independent criterion of occupational success; but such batteries are time consuming, difficult to administer, and even then rarely yield validity coefficients high enough to be useful for individual prediction (Fleming, 1949). Second, because mechanical skills are highly specific (Bennett & Cruickshank, 1942; Cronbach, 1949), it is practically impossible to construct a mechanical aptitude test that will predict success in a large variety of jobs involving different kinds of mechanical operations. To be even relatively efficient for guidance purposes, a mechanical abilities test would have to almost duplicate the specific tasks of a given job; but then, by definition, its predictive value would be highly restricted. Third, psychomotor aptitude tests, as usually administered, measure initial ability to adjust to a new task rather than ultimate capacity after practice has rendered the task familiar (Cronbach, 1949; Fleming, 1949), and the ultimate capacity is naturally more important for production and job success.

Finally,

> there is reason to believe that later skilled performance is related as much to interest, ambition, and general competence of methods of working as to anything which can fairly be described as initial mechanical aptitude. . . . Improvements in the kind of tuition given and in the attitude of the trainees as well as increases in the amount of practice appear, therefore, to be of greater practical usefulness in determining the final skill of a group of employees than excessive attention to refinements in the techniques of selection on the lines of any of the analytic aptitude tests of special abilities. (Fleming, 1949, p. 126)

Because the predictive value of achievement tests applied after actual trial of an occupation is higher than that of most skilled single testing of so-called aptitudes, vocational tryouts are extremely useful for occupational guidance. But such tryouts are not feasible for occupations involving long years of preparation. Work experience has other values for guidance apart from providing an index of relative ability; but since it also involves issues transcending vocational guidance, we shall consider it under a separate heading.

WORK EXPERIENCE DURING ADOLESCENCE *

Usefulness for vocational planning

One of the more important uses to which adolescent job experience can be put is in making occupational choices more realistic. Sustained firsthand experience with actual working conditions takes the glamor out of jobs. It also tests the genuineness of expressed interests, reveals to what extent contentment can be derived from a given field of work, and is a more significant indicator than aptitude tests of relative ability to succeed in a given job family. Diversified work experience, therefore, can be of great

---

* Much of this discussion is based on T. E. Christensen's *Getting Job Experience* (1949).

assistance in narrowing the field from which eventual vocational choice will be made.

For work experience to serve this function, it must be approached explicitly from the standpoint of finding out useful information about self in relation to the vocational world (Christensen, 1949). Merely working long hours or earning money as an end in itself without adopting this exploratory orientation only results in a set of specific learnings that cannot be applied to the more general problems involved in vocational choice.

Other values of work experience

Work experience can do a great deal to cushion the transition between school and work (Havighurst & Gottlieb, 1975; Land & Logan, 1949; Moss, 1951). School life obviously offers little indication of what lies ahead in the vocational world.

> Many adolescents nowadays leave school with the hopeful anticipation that they will find in the business world a kindliness and cooperativeness similar to those which they have met in the more or less child-centered school society of which they have formed a part. Disappointment often follows and the transition to adult status is consequently, in many cases, unnecessarily difficult. . . .
>
> New skills have to be learnt and insight into new situations has to be achieved. . . . The adolescent is a novice. . . . He is an outsider in a new group. . . . All the others know what is expected of them. The adolescent makes mistakes and experiences teasing as to clumsiness in work or inexperience in social relations. For all such reasons there is in the years of apprenticeship an element of insecurity and distress which is greater or less in proportion to the wisdom and the kindliness of all the members of the working community. (Fleming, 1949, pp. 197, 201)

Job experience also provides a "down-to-earth" opportunity for learning to get along with people—peers, superiors, and subordinates—in situations very different from any adjustive problem the adolescent has ever been confronted with before. It also makes possible for the first time the learning of work habits and attitudes that can be acquired only in an actual job. It is understandable why most employers demand such experience before they are willing even to consider an applicant for a position and why they are so reluctant to let him acquire it on their time. In addition to these patent advantages that work experience confers, it enables the adolescent to perceive more clearly the value and relevancy of many school subjects and provides invaluable practice in the management of earnings (Christensen, 1949).

The role of the school

If job experience is to become systematically available to a majority of adolescents and if it is to be optimally useful for guidance purposes, it seems that the secondary school will have to take the initiative in establishing suitable programs.* In the first place, under ordinary peacetime conditions, it is becoming increasingly more difficult for young people to obtain entry jobs requiring no previous training or experience. In addition, opportunities for work experience in the home are becoming more and more restricted (Christensen, 1949). Without some aid in getting job experience, it is hardly likely that many adolescents, except those who are driven by economic necessity or who display uncommon initiative, will be fortunate enough to obtain it on their own resources. Second, only the school is in a position to integrate satisfactorily work experience with a program of vocational guidance and to prevent it from making excessive demands on the time needed for academic and extracurricular activities. And last, the type of supervision that an agency such as the school can exercise is necessary to safeguard adolescents from exploitation and from exposure to hazardous or unhealthful occupations.

---

*It is not implied here that the responsibility for inaugurating work experience programs is solely the school's. Industry and various community agencies obviously have to cooperate if such programs are to be successful. However, it is not realistic to expect that any agency apart from the school will be sufficiently motivated to take the initiatory steps or to adopt a primarily educational orientation toward job experience.

15

Adolescents and the School

In common with all other institutions and the problems (and people) to which they relate, the channels of influence between school and adolescents invariably run in both directions. One direction is obvious. As a formally constituted agency dedicated to the task of training adolescents, the school in very deliberate fashion profoundly influences intellectual and moral growth. Less deliberately, but no less definitely, the interpersonal environment of the school impinges on many of the developmental tasks of adolescence—emancipation from the home, acquisition of earned status, and achievement of greater volitional independence in dealings with adults. Even more informally the school contributes to the growing social stratification that characterizes adolescent group life and provides opportunity for furthering peer culture activities and heterosexual adjustment.

The influence of adolescence on the school remained considerably less obvious for a long time. As a result of the personality changes and intellectual development during adolescence, important modifications occur in the cognitive, interpersonal, and motivational aspects of learning. These changes in the learning process actually influence what goes on in school by affecting what is learned and how learning takes place. In recent years there has been an increasing understanding of these factors and continuous attempts are in process for adjustments in teaching methods (Ausubel, 1962), curricular organization (Trump & Vars, 1976; Van Til, 1976), and in the social climate of the school (Havighurst, 1975). Institutional inertia and resistance to change, on the one hand, and increased heterogeneity of school population, on the other hand, creating a wide range of cognitive readiness and styles of learning and greater degree of variation in motivational patterns, complicate these attempts at adjustment and set in motion a variety of experiments in the name of alternative schools.

GENERAL FUNCTIONS OF THE SCHOOL DURING ADOLESCENCE

As a training institution, the school is primarily an instrument of cultural survival designed to perpetuate and improve a given way of life. Every culture implicitly accepts a set of values for significant aspects of behavior, interpersonal relations, and social organization. And if a culture is to survive, much of education must be concerned with inculcating these values in the young of all ages before they can be invested with adult status. This function of education has won so much explicit recognition and unqualified acceptance in such areas as aesthetics, character traits, and government that it is difficult to appreciate the position of those who contend that values are purely personal and that the sole business of schools is to "teach facts."

A second training function of the school, the value of which has only recently been challenged, is the development of various intellectual skills and the attainment of increased understanding in such cultural areas as art, science, literature, and mathematics. The value and importance of knowledge as an end in itself have been unduly deemphasized by certain educators who have been oversold on the virtues of "applied education," of gearing the curriculum to the expressed interests, current concerns, and problems of "life adjustment." A very extreme statement of this point of view would be that only intellectually superior or college-bound students should be exposed to academic subjects and that for all other adolescents the main purpose of secondary education should be preparation for vocational, family, and other forms of "life adjustment."

The third training function of the secondary school is to facilitate personality maturation in adolescents. As pointed out, whether by design or otherwise, the school cannot help but play a role in the personality changes of adolescence. Merely by providing an arena in which young people interact with each other and with adults, the school influences important aspects of personality structure at a time when these are undergoing significant change. And since the school has to play some role in this development, it might just as well be as constructive as possible. For to the extent that the developmental tasks of adolescents are or are not fulfilled, we acquire or fail to acquire mature citizens who are capable of carrying on and improving the culture.

It can also be convincingly argued that since the culture sets the standards by which adult maturity is judged and has so much to gain by the realization of these standards, it acquires the associated training responsibilities. From the standpoint of educational philosophy it is not difficult to defend the proposition that "education (in the broader sense) is also concerned with the development of personality, with the problems of individual adjustment" (Edwards, 1944, p. 195). There is no a *priori* reason for believing that the chief social institution charged with responsibility for training the young must necessarily be concerned with one exclusive aspect of development (the intellectual) rather than with the individual's total potentiality for growth. If pupils are to be equipped with symbolic tools to solve intellectual problems, there is no reason why they cannot also be prepared to meet other problems of adjustment. If the school does not assume this responsibility who else can and will?

The child-centered versus the subject-matter approach to education constitutes a pseudo-dichotomy that causes serious disagreement only among extremists at either end of the continuum. No realistic proponent of the subject-matter approach advocates that the curriculum should be taught without due regard for such relevant factors as readiness, motivation, and individual differences in intellectual ability; and similarly, constructive proponents of child-centered approach largely emphasize noncognitive determinants and outcomes of learning because of their importance in mastering subject-matter. (Ausubel, 1968, p. 30)

IMPACT OF THE SCHOOL ON THE DEVELOPMENTAL
TASKS OF ADOLESCENCE

Emancipation from parents

The school facilitates in several important ways the adolescent's emancipation from home and parents. By providing other parent-like adults (teachers) with whom he can satellize, it makes the relinquishment of emotional dependence on parents less abrupt and less traumatic. The home source of derived status seems more expendable when it can be replaced by another that is also more socially acceptable during the adolescent period. In

Theory and Problems of Adolescent Development

addition, the school progressively displaces the home as the major adult source from which the adolescent derives his normative values. It thereby devalues the parent's omniscience, infallibility, and monopoly on truth, and hence, his capacity for conferring derived status by fiat. Finally, by being able to offer the adolescent an important current source of earned status utterly beyond the resources of the urban home, the school enjoys an overwhelming advantage in competing for his loyalty.

The school is also in a strategic position as a respected neutral bystander to ease the tensions between parents and their adolescent children that are incidental to the struggle for emancipation. Merely by reestablishing broken lines of communication and interpreting one to the other, the school can alleviate much of the conflict that follows from misunderstanding.

The acquisition of earned status

During adolescence the importance of the school as a source of earned status naturally increases as this status assumes a central rather than a subsidiary role in the personality structure. This does not necessarily mean that the adolescent likes academic pursuits any better. Jersild (1963) points out that in a study by Johnson (1958) the majority of students liked high school better than elementary school, but the reasons they gave were not related to the academic program. As reasons for liking high school better, they mentioned more activities, more privileges, and an opportunity to meet more friends. Thus the motivational orientation underlying the adolescent's approach to learning subject matter and assimilating goals and values becomes progressively more dominated by the need for self-enhancement as a person in his own right.

The school offers two different but related kinds of earned status. The more current variety is merely a reflection of relative competence in mastering the curriculum and the relative class standing that accrues from this accomplishment. The second variety of earned status that the school offers has less current than "stepping stone" value. For example, certain courses of study and levels of graded school performance are prerequisite for college or vocational entrance. Similarly, vocational education and guidance and work experience programs have important implications for the *future* acquisition of earned status.

It is important to realize that the earned status that the adolescent can acquire in school has the same interim quality as the status available to him in the peer group. It relates to peripheral activities far removed from the mainstream of status-giving operations in the adult world. But rarely is achievement in these activities regarded as an intrinsically worthwhile goal in its own right as are, for example, many of the activities of the peer group. It has mainly "stop-gap" or substitutive value in lieu of real adult status; and in relation to future status aspirations it is largely perceived as part of an arbitrary sequence rather than as organically and logically related to the ultimate operations on which these aspirations are based. High school or college achievement can in no sense match the status that a full-time job can confer in terms of ego enhancement or maturational value.

Acquiring greater volitional independence in dealing with adults

One of the primary maturational tasks of adolescents is to acquire the volitional independence, the self-assertion, and the self-determination characteristic of adult status. In large measure this means adopting an entirely new orientation to adults and adult authority, learning how to resist adult domination, and learning how to react to adults as peers rather than as awesome beings with a qualitatively superior status. To be sure, all of these changes are only commensurate with the new biosocial status to which adolescents are aspiring, and their realization is motivated by the various pressures precipitating this transitional stage of personality development. Resistance to authoritarianism is also increased by the growing need for reciprocity in moral obligations and by diminished tolerance for nonfunctional moral absolutism. But the pressure of insistent needs is not alone sufficient to result in the acquisition of a difficult new behavioral role at variance with the cumulative impact of all previous experience. Youth can learn to be adults only through living and working with adults. The nature of their social behavior depends on the kinds of relationships which they experience (MacKenzie, 1944).

Since the school provides the larger number and the more important occasions and opportunities for adolescents to interact with adults, the types of adult-youth relationships established in the secondary school have a crucial bearing on the outcome of this basic developmental task. It will be necessary to examine the reactions that pupils make to teachers as persons, the perceptions that adolescents and teachers have of each other, and the varieties of social climates that exist in the school, and their impact on the attainment of volitional independence.

HOW TEACHERS PERCEIVE PUPILS *

In the past decade considerable literature has developed on teacher expectations. Stimulated by Rosenthal and Jacobson's study (1968) of the experimentally planted expectations of teachers and their effect on the learner, the hypothesis has been advanced that the teacher "for varied reasons perceives competencies and potentialities of children differently, and that these expectations are reflected in his interactions with children to produce differential performance among learners thus fulfilling his prophecy. 'Teacher expectation', 'self-fulfilling prophecy' and 'teacher faith' have been coined to imply this tendency for the teacher to create a reality commensurate with his perceptions" (Braun, 1976, p. 185). Studies both support and refute expectancy effects. One explanation of conflicting results lies in the distinction between induced or contrived and self-generated or natural expectations and perceptions. Braun (1976) points out that sources of input in teachers' perceptions or expectancies have been well documented. Among factors influencing teachers' perceptions are physical appearance, achievement, IQ scores, and general characteristics of older siblings and parents (Elashoff, Dixon, & Snow, 1971). There is some evidence that sex has an impact on teacher perceptions. Teachers express greater approval for girls than for boys (Davidson & Lang, 1960; Meyer & Thompson, 1956). LaVoie and Adams (1974) found that boys received lower ratings on attitudes and work habits than girls. Braun (1976) also cites studies (Freedman, 1972; Karlins et al., 1969) showing that race and socioeconomic status are powerful cues for shaping stereotype perceptions.

"There is some evidence that patterns of pupil-teacher and pupil-pupil interaction become a function of how both pupils and teachers perceive the individual child's status within the classroom social microcosm" (Braun, 1976, p. 198). Remedial classes and ability grouping generate perceptions and behavior commensurate to the status of the group (Stevens, 1971).

The implications of these findings are obvious. Braun (1976) points out that Rothbart, Dalfren, and Barrett (1971) and Cornbleth, David, and Button (1974) "found both quantitative and qualitative correlations between high school teachers' expectations and behaviors" (Braun, 1976, p. 199). Selective perception based on extrinsic factors such as attractiveness, sex, or "stereotype" judgment based on group

---

*This section is based primarily on Braun, C. Teacher expectation: sociopsychological dynamics. *Review of Educational Research,* Spring, 1976, *46,* No. 2, 185-213.

membership such as race or socioeconomic status fail to create an interpersonal climate in the school conducive to volitional independence. A study (Krause, 1975) of 13 social studies classes of inner-city sixth, seventh, and eighth graders and 5 social studies classes of suburban white seventh and eighth graders surveyed 474 subjects in 1968 to test the interpersonal transfer hypothesis for attitudes of trust, efficacy, and duty toward teachers generalizing to policeman, mayor, and president. The correlational findings lead to plausible explanations. "The student's sense of efficacy and duty toward his teachers are probably very dependent upon his trust of these teachers. Apparently the same dependency holds for duty toward and trust of policemen and even efficacy toward and trust of the mayor" (Krause, 1975, pp. 118–119).

Ability to empathize with adolescents free from discriminatory attitudes does not necessarily obligate teachers to adopt their values nor does it guarantee effectiveness in dealing with them. Understanding and nondiscrimination, however, are necessary, although not sufficient for skilled interpersonal relationships, since many other abilities and personality traits that are probably uncorrelated with psychological sensitivity (poise, self-assurance, sociocentrism, firmness, leadership qualities) are necessary for translating accurate perceptions into appropriate behavior.

HOW PUPILS PERCEIVE TEACHERS

The different ways in which pupils perceive the behavior and roles of teachers define and limit in much the same way, as teachers' perceptions of pupils, the kinds of interpersonal relationships that can be established in the school and their impact on personality development. The evidence is clear that pupils respond to teachers as persons and not only as dispensers of knowledge, although there is some evidence that pupils are primarily concerned with their teachers' pedagogic competence or ability to teach (Taylor, 1962). Nonetheless, they not only admire teaching skill, clarity, task orientation, and good classroom control, but are also highly appreciative of fairness, impartiality, patience, cheerfulness, and sympathetic understanding. In addition, they approve of teachers who are interested in pupils and who are helpful, kindly, and considerate of their feelings (Hart, 1934; Leeds, 1954). Krause (1975) cites studies (Aberbach & Walker, 1970; Easton & Dennis, 1969; French & Raven, 1959; Smith & Hudgins, 1966) which show that in the view of pupils, an unfair, inconsiderate, unhelpful, unreliable, or dishonest teacher is not entitled to full cooperation or respect.

Warmth in teachers is also a characteristic rated favorably by pupils, as well as principals, supervisors, and other observers (Cook et al., 1951; McGee, 1955; Ryans, 1960; Solomon et al., 1964). Teachers characterized by warmth are particularly appreciated by pupils who are highly concerned with their interpersonal relationship to and feelings for a teacher.

Another study of pupils' perceptions of teachers shows that teachers are seen as playing three major kinds of roles, as friends, opponents, and manipulators of status in learning situations* (Cunningham et al., 1951). As friends, they are "older and wiser" persons, helpful counselors, heroes, givers of security, and occasionally "pals." As opponents they are cast as "killjoys" who arbitrarily interfere with legitimate pleasures, as "enemies" to be "fought" and "outwitted," and as demons of power to be feared, respected, and placated. Much of this role obviously represents a displacement of hostile feelings from original parental targets. Teachers also share much of the brunt of adolescents' general antiadult orientation. In the learning aspects of the school situation they are perceived as "necessary evils" in the acquisition of knowledge, efficient organizers in the direction of work projects, "steppingstones" to future status rewards, dispensers of approval and disapproval, and moral arbiters who can absolve from guilt as well as point the accusing finger (Cunningham et al., 1951).

These pupil perceptions of teachers' roles naturally mirror the less desirable existing authoritarian practices as well as many commendable exceptions to these practices. What is more important, however, is their demonstration that pupils undoubtedly operate on the conviction that teachers are important interpersonal influences in their lives. Both their perceptions and their affective reactions indicate that they think it possible for teachers to play a more constructive role in helping them attain a peer relationship with adults. But before this change can ever be effected, teachers must not only become more accurately aware of the needs and aspirations of particular adolescents, but they must also become aware of the current roles their pupils assign to them.

---

* "A recent survey (Poole, 1975) conducted at a large eastern State University revealed that 95% of the students reported that during their educational careers they were victimized by testing and evaluation" (Poole, 1976, p. 342). Incidents cited attested to poorly constructed and administered classroom tests or evaluation instruments, misused standardized instruments, and improper grading policies and procedures.

IMPLICATIONS OF AUTHORITARIANISM FOR ADULT–YOUTH
RELATIONSHIPS

In most American secondary schools authoritarian controls have
been progressively liberalized to meet increasing needs for self-determination and growing capacities for self-direction and self-discipline.
Prevailing practice, however, in many schools still falls far behind
desirable standards of democratic classroom practice (Ausubel, 1969).

In general, overt compliance is the most common response that
preadolescents and adolescents make to excessive authoritarianism in
the classroom, especially if they are girls and if they come from
middle-class homes that place a great premium on success in school.
Adolescents from other backgrounds, however, may react with open
aggression and hostility to teachers, with negativism, or with passive
sabotage. Still others may drop out of school as soon as it is legal to
do so. Yet even those adolescents who apparently become overtly
reconciled to a continuation of an incongruously submissive childhood role probably do not really accept the authoritarianism to which
they outwardly defer, but respond with suppressed resentment and
variously negatively toned emotional reactions.

Older children and adolescents also do not satisfactorily internalize values that are indoctrinated in an authoritarian fashion if
the adult culture itself is organized along democratic and egalitarian
lines. Under these circumstances they feel unjustly treated and dis-
criminated against; and they tend not only to resent the authoritarian
discipline imposed on them, but also to conform to adult standards
only under threat of external compulsion. This is particularly true if
they perceive that many adults do not honor these standards but,
nevertheless, presume to punish them whenever they are guilty of
lapses. Hence, when adults preach the virtues of hard work, ambition, responsibility, and self-denial but do not practice these virtues
themselves in occupational life, children tend to emulate their example rather than their precepts. They become habituated to striving
and working hard under external pressure but fail adequately to internalize these values. Thus, when they finally enter the adult vocational world and the customary authoritarian demands for conscien-
tious effort are lifted, the tenuous structure of their disciplined work
habits tends to collapse in the absence of genuinely internalized
needs for vocational achievement.

Experimental studies of the impact of authoritarian leadership on
children's groups also point to various undesirable effects on group
morale and solidarity (Lippitt, 1940). In comparison with children in
democratically governed groups, pupils who are subjected to auto-

cratic control are more aggressive, direct their aggression against scapegoat group members rather than against the group leader, and adopt more submissive, placatory, and attention-demanding attitudes in dealing with the leader. They also manifest less "we-feeling," show less capacity for mobilizing constructive group effort in overcoming frustrating conditions, and are less capable of self-disciplined work and behavior when direct supervision is removed. H. H. Anderson (1943) obtained similar findings in studying the effects of "dominative" and "integrative" behavior by teachers.

There has been, however, a strong tendency on the part of educators to overgeneralize the significance of these findings. In the first place, the authoritarian leaders in the Lippitt study were hostile and unfriendly, and tended to give disruptive commands. Typically, authoritarian leadership tends to be more friendly, subtle, and benevolent, and thus has less damaging effects on social behavior and group morale. Second, the effects of autocratic and democratic classroom climate are relative, in part, to the personality structure of individual students. Students who have a strong need for direction and organization react favorably to a directive approach and very critically to a more permissive one (Wispé, 1951). Most important of all, it is undoubtedly ethnocentric to claim that only democratic teacher-pupil relationships are compatible with normal mental health and personality development. Many examples of authoritarian Western cultures (for example, Germany, Italy, Switzerland) exist in which all of the indices of mental health and mature personality development compare favorably with those prevailing in the United States. Hence, it is obviously not authoritarianism itself that has damaging mental health consequences, but rather the existence of authoritarian practices in home and school that are incongruous with the general pattern of interpersonal relations in the culture at large.

Children are able satisfactorily to internalize adult personality traits and mature attitudes toward authority, even in an authoritarian home and school environment, providing that: (1) personal, social, and working relationships among adults are similarly authoritarian, and (2) adults generally make as stringent demands on themselves as they do on young people. In countries like Germany and Switzerland these latter conditions prevail, and therefore authoritarianism in home and school has few adverse effects on mental health and personality development. In New Zealand and the United States, on the other hand, authoritarianism in the home and secondary school has more serious effects because it contrasts sharply with the egalitarian and generally relaxed character of vocational and social life in the adult world (Ausubel, 1965b).

In all cultures, however, even those which are generally authoritarian, there are credible grounds for supposing that an authoritarian classroom climate would generate the same effects on thinking and problem solving as does the authoritarian personality, and would lead to less effective group planning, teamwork, and self-direction. R. Spaulding (1963) found that punitive teachers, emphasizing shame as a technique of control, tend to inhibit pupil creativity. It also seems likely that an authoritarian and punitive classroom climate would increase the anxiety level of less able and anxious pupils and make them more defensive about exposing their inadequacies.

Partly as a reaction against traditional authoritarian practices, a small minority of schools and teachers under the influence of ultrapermissive doctrines of child rearing have instituted a laissez-faire social climate in the classroom. This approach permits pupils to do as they please, emphasizes freedom from restraint and discipline as an end in itself, strives for lack of structure and organization in school activities, and conceives of frustration as an unqualified evil to be avoided at all cost. Under such "catch-as-catch-can" conditions, aggressive pupils become ruthless, whereas retiring children become even more withdrawn. Observation of groups in which this pattern prevails shows that it leads inevitably to confusion, insecurity, and keen competition for power among group members (Cunningham et al., 1951). Pupils fail to learn the normative demands of society and how to operate within the limits these set, do not learn how to deal effectively with adults, and develop unrealistic expectations of the social structure of vocational life.

DEMOCRATIC DISCIPLINE IN THE SCHOOL SETTING

In contrast to the authoritarian and laissez-faire patterns of control, some schools have managed to create a democratic climate of adult-youth interaction that is more compatible with the developmental needs of adolescents. This kind of atmosphere has been achieved in part through various devices that enable young people to share in the planning and management of the curriculum and in the regulation of student activities and discipline. When properly paced and geared to actual capacities for self-determination, such attempts have been uniformly successful in improving group morale and in facilitating the development of mature, responsible, and realistically grounded volitional independence (Cunningham et al., 1951).

These procedures are in no way based on the assumption that individuals mature spontaneously without being confronted with the normative demands of society. Although the goal toward which they aim is the achievement of self-discipline, the need for external controls and for the explicit definition of the limits of socially acceptable behavior is not denied. They also take into account the cumulative impact of prior conditioning to anxiety reduction and other extrinsic motivations (examinations, grades, promotions) in the learning situation, and do not seek unrealistically to predicate all learning activity on intrinsic need for knowledge.

More important perhaps than effective administrative machinery in achieving a wholesome democratic atmosphere in the school is teachers' adoption of certain kinds of attitudes toward pupils.

In essence, these consist of respect for the dignity and feelings of students as persons, and care in avoiding techniques of condescension, sarcasm, or abuse of superior knowledge and position. They presuppose that hierarchical distinctions between students and teachers will be based on objective differences in knowledge and maturity rather than on such formal and arbitrary props as titles, degrees, and academic status.

Appropriate discipline in the secondary school is impersonal and matter-of-fact. It avoids recrimination and punitive implications. Whenever possible it is enforced by lateral (peer) sanctions rather than imposed from above. It respects the adolescent's greater need for rational and functional rules based on reciprocal obligation, and appeals more to logic than to loyalty or to the need for adult approval. And since more sophisticated social awareness enables youth to perceive more easily than children discrepancies between precept and practice, the moral principles on which discipline is based will be genuinely internalized only if verbal exhortations are reinforced by personal example (Hart, 1934).

Other developmental tasks of adolescence

In addition to its impact on the basic maturational tasks of adolescence described above (emancipation from parents, acquisition of earned status and volitional independence), the school also influences growth and adjustment in two other areas of personality that are crucially significant during this period of development—peer group and heterosexual relationships. As already pointed out, the peer group is for many reasons the chief training and socializing institution of adolescence. By bringing adolescent boys and girls together for so many hours a day, the school necessarily serves as the primary locus in which the peer culture operates. It is in an unusually strategic position to facilitate the social development of adolescents by providing a diversified and constructive framework of social and extracurricular activities in which boys and girls can socialize each other by practicing their biological and social sex roles in a peer setting.

Adolescents can also profit from more "direct instruction. . . in the basic skills required for every day social activity" (MacKenzie, 1944). They need training, for example, in "how to meet people, how to introduce friends to other friends and to parents, how to order food," in social dancing and ballroom etiquette, and in personal grooming. The need for school instruction in sex and courting problems and in boy-girl relationships has already been discussed.

IMPLICATIONS OF ADOLESCENT PERSONALITY DEVELOPMENT FOR SCHOOL LEARNING

Adolescent personality development is especially relevant to the motivational aspects of learning. It influences not only the way in which the individual assimilates goals and values but also his reasons for learning academic subject matter. Such motivations obviously operate not in a social vacuum but in relation to other persons both as individuals and as representatives of the culture. In assimilating values and implementing his learning orientation in the school environment, the adolescent reacts especially to the personality of the teacher. Depending on his particular motivational orientation, he responds in different ways to the type of person she is and to the different roles she plays—with acceptance or rejection, self-assertion or submission, feelings of dependent identification or of emulatory self-enhancement.

The teacher's behavior, therefore—her objectivity or subjectivity, her personal relatedness or detachment, the extent to which her practices are authoritarian or democratic—is an important variable affecting the motivational aspect of the learning process. Its appropriateness to a given adolescent's learning orientation can either facilitate or hinder the learning of values, goals, and subject matter. It can affect the development and differentiation of interests and ability and even the motivational basis of learning itself. The personality of the teacher induces different affective reactions to subject matter (Carey & Beary, 1938) and influences the adolescent's decision to either continue or terminate his schooling (Dillon, 1949; Jersild, 1963; Johnson & Legg, 1944; Penty, 1956). The motivational climate (praise, reproof, social recognition, competition) engendered by the teacher also influences learning outcomes (Hurlock, 1925, 1927; Rosenthal et al., 1974; Videbeck, 1960) and work output (Ausubel, 1951; Rubin, 1973) in an academic setting.

Recognizing the importance of interpersonal factors in school learning, studies are concentrating on the effects of teacher expectations (reviewed earlier in this chapter) on the learner. There is an increasing body of research on the effects of teacher anxiety on the learner which suggests that "at some level, anxiety in classroom teachers may become detrimental both to the teachers themselves and to the pupils" (Coates & Thoresen, 1976, p. 169). In addition much attention is being devoted to interaction analysis (Flanders, 1963).

We shall consider first the impact on school learning of personality changes characteristic of adolescents generally as an age group. Following this, it will be necessary to relate individual differences in personality development to differences in learning orientation and appropriate teaching practices.

Impact of general personality changes on learning orientation

As a direct consequence of the increased importance of earned status during the adolescent period, the incorporative orientation assumes a more centrally significant position in the individual's motivational approach to learning experience. In accepting the need for learning various skills, subject matter content, values, and goals, the adolescent recognizes as more relevant and important such considerations as self-enhancement, increased competence, social recognition, and status in the group; and correspondingly, need for parental and adult approval and blind loyalty to persons become less important motivational criteria since they are less effective in advancing earned status goals.

At the same time, it is also possible for the adolescent to make greater use of the exploratory orientation in learning situations. This is a more task-oriented, objective, problem-solving approach to learning, in which the individual disregards considerations of status (earned or derived) enhancement in setting his level of aspiration. Instead he places more weight on such intrinsic motivations as intellectual curiosity and pays more heed to such criteria as objective evidence and logical validity in determining the acceptability of values and beliefs. The adoption of the exploratory orientation is tremendously facilitated by the opportunity to carry the examination of controversial issues to their logical conclusion without fear of endangering the derived status from parental approval. It is also favored by the adolescent's greater need for volitional independence, his greater resistance to authoritarian indoctrination, and his greater capacity for approaching specific moral problems from a more self-consistent set of general propositions. On the other hand, full exploitation of this learning orientation is limited by the very marginality of his status, which disposes him to conform to the norms and expectations of those agencies (peer group and school) that control the source of his status.

The satellizing orientation to learning is by no means completely abandoned during adolescence. In general, however, it plays a less prominent role in the total motivational picture and is related to more socially acceptable sources of derived status than parents, that is, to teachers, youth, leaders, and peer group. In some cases deep attachments to authoritarian adult figures during adolescence may represent attempts by strong satellizers to compensate for the loss of satellizing ideological direction from parents; in other cases such attachments reduce guilt feelings from repudiation of parental values. And although the need for parental approval may cease to be an important factor in academic striving, scholastic achievement is still a significant determinant of an adolescent's character reputation and sociometric status.

These changes in learning orientation, together with a generalized antiadult attitude, make adolescents less disposed to accept the prestige authority of teachers in assimilating value judgments or in perceiving as meaningful and important learning tasks which impress them as trivial and pointless. They are more inclined to reject such subject matter content and to reject alien values that are forcibly imposed on them as soon as this is expedient, that is, after passing examinations and courses (Cantor, 1946; Segel, 1951). In general, they are less resistive to activity plans and administrative regulations if they are permitted to share in their development and in the processes of decision making.

Importance of current concerns

The problems of adjustment that adolescents face—emancipation from parents, somatic deviations, and relationships with peers, adults, and members of the opposite sex—are very real and important to them. Their importance is magnified by the limited time perspective of adolescence, which extends situational difficulties interminably into the future. When adolescents are actually queried about the types of subject matter they would like to include in the secondary school curriculum, these practical and immediate concerns figure prominently in their replies (Combs, 1976; Doane, 1942; Hopkins, 1940). The traditional high school not infrequently is concerned with teaching things which the student may have some use for in the future with little attempt to relate them to the interests of the students. Students therefore develop a dislike for academic studies (Jersild, 1963) and turn to interests and movements that are more satisfying to them (Cole & Hall, 1969).

Regardless of the compartmentalized approach that the school may adopt toward education, the adolescent relates the goals of academic learning to his current developmental tasks. Psychologically, these tasks are too urgent to be ignored. Hence, education must perforce be concerned with problems youth consider to be important. If young people perceive the school as uninterested in these problems, they react either by losing interest in the academic materials the school values or by feeling guilty for being preoccupied with supposedly trivial matters. If current concerns are not relieved, they inevitably serve as distractions from other constituted responsibilities.

To be related to present needs and purposes, learning tasks need not necessarily deal with problems of adolescent adjustment. Academic knowledge can have current experience value if its acquisition becomes a goal in its own right. It is unrealistic to expect that all school subjects will have even remotely practical implications. The value of much of school learning can be defended only because it improves an individual's understanding of important ideas in his culture. And if adolescents could be motivated to perceive knowledge in this light, it could conceivably constitute an important and exciting part of their current psychological field.

Nevertheless, many academic subjects do have actual relevance for future vocational goals. The difficulty is that these goals cannot be given vivid representation in current reality unless success in preparatory learning activities can be perceived as organically related to their attainment. As long as such activities constitute only formal and arbitrary hurdles barring access to distant goals, they have no current relevance other than as stopgap devices, as stepping stones to future status. A course in biology, for example, can be made very relevant to the present purposes of students aspiring to careers in the medical sciences only if the relationship between medicine and biology is made explicitly clear.

School marks can serve as immediate sources of earned status, as indicators that progress is being made toward an ultimate vocational goal, or as indices of success in mastering certain skills and understandings. All three purposes are useful in increasing the current relevance of school experience provided marks do not displace the achievement they symbolize as the actual goals of academic striving. This situation inevitably develops when school learnings are not accepted as intrinsically important or as organically related to vocational goals. Under such conditions marks become ends in themselves and interest in the subject matter terminates as soon as pupils know what marks they will receive (Segel, 1951). Although it is fashionable to condemn the use of school marks as an unqualified evil, it seems illogical to discard potentially useful devices merely because they are sometimes abused.

One might even assert the unfashionable view that aversive motivation, namely, the threat of those penalties associated with failure, is as necessary as the positive motivation stemming from anticipated rewards for sustaining the long-term academic achievement required for reaching professional goals. Although educators theoretically decry the use of aversive motivation, they implicitly rely on it to keep students studying regularly for their credits, degrees, and diplomas. They do this because they know that cognitive drive and anticipated reward for hard work are not sufficient to overcome both inertia and the typical human proclivity toward procrastination and aversion to sustained, regular, and disciplined work. Any teacher who imagines that the majority of his students would continue at their studies in the absence of structured programs, assigned work, deadlines, and examinations is living in a world of fantasy. The motivational force of an examination lies more in the fear of failure than in the hope of success. Thus, within reason, the threat of failure is a pedagogically legitimate form of motivation. Students study not only to avoid the actual consequences of failure but also to reduce both the anxiety which this threat generates and the guilt feelings that accompany lack of attention to academic duty.

We have repeatedly emphasized that adolescents are also vitally concerned with their future admittance to adult status as well as with the concerns of their interim peer culture. Such concerns can be alleviated in part if some portion of school activity can be perceived as organically related to progress toward the goal of economic independence. The need for vocational guidance and work experience is quite apparent when we consider that a large percentage of college graduates at the age of 22 "are less prepared to earn a living and actually have less earning capacity without further training than a commercial-school graduate" (Ausubel, 1949, p. 79).

Individual differences

Adolescents as a group display a different motivational orientation toward learning situations from that of preadolescents. In all probability, however, there are greater differences among individual adolescents than between adolescents and other age groups. Depending on individual differences in personality development, different motivational orientations toward learning (satellizing, incorporative, exploratory) receive varying emphasis over and above the influence exerted by general developmental trends. We must reckon with individual patterns of motivational orientations, which affect not only the mode of assimilating goals and values but also the motivations underlying the effort and activity of acquiring academic skills and knowledge.

Although incorporative and exploratory orientations generally become more important for adolescents, individuals who satellize as children continue in part to use the satellizing orientation in the secondary school. Nonsatellizers rely chiefly on the former two learning orientations. In varying degrees all three motivational components are usually present in most individuals. Not infrequently, as a result of continued successful experience, motivations that are originally absent in a given learning activity are developed retroactively. A socially rejected adolescent may seek originally to achieve superior competence in some academic field solely for compensatory ego enhancement. Eventually, however, he may develop genuine task-oriented interests that are functionally autonomous of his original motivation.

As the difficulty of schoolwork increases progressively, and as developmental changes in motivation occur, there may be marked shifts in the academic standings of certain individuals. A highly motivated child of only average ability finds it much more difficult to lead his class in high school and college than in elementary school. And conversely, a bright but poorly motivated child may improve his academic standing as a result of the increased developmental pressures for acquiring earned status.

THE SATELLIZING LEARNING ORIENTATION

In acquiring knowledge the motivation underlying the satellizing orientation is to gain the approval and acceptance of the person with whom the satellizing relationship is established. The assimilation of goals and values is, similarly, an expression of personal loyalty; dependent identification with another person is primary, and uncritical acceptance of his values regardless of their content is a secondary outcome. When satellizing relationships are strong, the learner is predisposed to perceive the world using the values and expectations of his preceptor since his derived status is dependent thereon. Prestige suggestion is "accepted because of the need of the individual to agree with the person making the suggestion. In such cases, the individual first accepts the suggestion, and then the perceptual qualities of the object are changed" (Krech & Crutchfield, 1948, p. 341). This perceptual set is reinforced by personal loyalty and by the need to avoid the guilt that would follow from accepting beliefs contrary to those of the person whose prestige authority is unconditionally accepted on a satellizing basis. The object of hero worship under such conditions is not to displace the hero or to emulate his attainments, but to identify in a subservient capacity and thereby to share vicariously in his status.

When values are accepted on a satellizing basis, resistance to new learning proceeds largely from conflicting ideological trends in the new set of values, which can only be accepted at the cost of repudiating prior loyalties and assuming the associated burden of guilt. Nevertheless, this must take place for resatellization to occur. "Learning. . . proceeds by a process of forming successive personal identifications each of which involves overcoming the resistance inherent in the necessity of repudiating a prior identification" (Ausubel, 1949, p. 179). The learner feels secure in his derived status only as long as approval is forthcoming. He finds disapproval threatening and when incurred through disloyalty productive of guilt feelings.

THE INCORPORATIVE LEARNING ORIENTATION

The motivation underlying the incorporative orientation toward the learning of skills and subject matter is enhancement of earned status through improving competence and achieving social recognition. Values and goals are assimilated on a comparable basis when they are perceived as contributing to the earned status of the individual.

"This learning process is strictly an act of independence requiring no subservience of self to others. . . . New values are incorporated, that is, taken bodily into his own value system, and regarded as his own without any implication of a dependent emotional bond arising between him and his preceptor. . . . The voluntary expression of dependence is inconceivable in such persons—since to them dependence is tantamount to admission of the inferiority against which all their strivings are directed" (Ausubel, 1949, p. 179). Prestige suggestion is not accepted blindly because of a need to agree with the person making the suggestion, but because the authority of the suggester is respected as relevantly influencing the outcome of the quest for earned status. The object of hero worship is to emulate and displace the hero, to use him as a guide and stepping stone to comparable achievements.

Since nonsatellizers "do not learn primarily by forming personal identifications, and, hence, in their system of values have no deep primary allegiances, the possibility of experiencing guilt by virtue of repudiating these loyalties is not present" (Ausubel, 1949, p. 179). New values are resisted because they constitute a potential threat to self-esteem by challenging (1) the existing system of values organized on an ego prestige basis and (2) various presumptions of independence, originality, infallibility, and omniscience. Because the nonsatellizer lacks "sufficient confidence in the ultimate outcome of the learning process, he is naturally reluctant to undertake new learning which could end in failure, or at any rate constitute a threat to his security while still incomplete and tentative" (Ausubel, 1949, p. 182). Resistance is eventually overcome when the "possibility of future ego aggrandizement by incorporation of the new value" is perceived (Ausubel, 1949).

Since nonsatellizers are more likely to suffer from impaired selfesteem and from anxiety, they are more likely to feel inadequate in new learning situations, to overrespond with fear, and to avoid improvisation. Initial failure in new learning tasks induces disproportionate lowering of self-esteem, panic, and impairment of performance ability. Disapproval does not threaten a relationship from which vicarious status is derived or provoke feelings of guilt; it serves as an objective index of failure with attendant consequences to selfesteem. The motivation for learning is generally higher in nonsatellizers because self-esteem is dependent solely on extrinsic considerations and is largely a function of superior accomplishment.

IMPLICATIONS OF LEARNING ORIENTATIONS FOR TEACHING
PRACTICES

If different pupils have different motivational orientations toward learning, teaching practices must necessarily be directed toward pupils as individuals rather than as members of an age group. Although it is apparent that pupils must be taught in a group, some opportunity always exists for individualization of the teacher's interpersonal role.

All three learning orientations are affected by what the teacher does as a person. But for the teacher to take the personality of the learner into account, he must necessarily be subjective in handling pupils and relate himself as a person to them. This type of interpersonal relationship is more important than the formal mode of communication between pupils and teacher (lecture, discussion, group process). The appropriateness of one or another of the formal methods largely depends on the teacher's own personality.

The teacher can not ignore the fact that to learners who adopt the satellizing orientation he is "more than an impersonal vehicle for the transmission of knowledge, that students. . . look to him as a sympathetic human being with whom they can identify emotionally" (Ausubel, 1950, p. 186). He must appreciate the basis of resistance to new ideas. And because of the obvious disadvantages of the student's tendency to accept ideas passively and uncritically, he should try to tone down the dependent aspects of satellization. . . . In the classroom this can be done by (a) objectifying discussion as much as possible, and by refusing to accept "blind" identification with the instructor's opinions; (b) by avoiding the use of praise when the student agrees with the instructor's point of view, and the use of disapproval when the student's reaction is critical; (c) by avoiding the use of paternalistic teaching despite the satellizer's responsiveness to same; and (d) by refraining from making agreement with the instructor the price of the personal emotional acceptance which he so eagerly seeks. (Ausubel, 1949, p. 78)

In relation to adolescents who learn more through the incorporative and exploratory orientations, "the role of the teacher should be that of a human catalyst—serving to objectify and clarify the data that are to be incorporated" (Ausubel, 1949, p. 184). It is more important for the teacher to use his subjectively derived insights in minimizing the resistance that nonsatellizers show to new learning materials. He can help do this by deemphasizing status differences between himself and the pupil,

by objectifying discussion as much as possible, and divorcing it from all connotations of a personal struggle between wills; by avoiding paternalistic teaching techniques; by bestowing as much approval as possible, and by avoiding disapproval, especially at the beginning, thereby bolstering self-esteem in the face of initial difficulties when it is apt to suffer unduly from deflation. He should recognize the panic which ensues upon confrontation with new situations and upon experiencing early defeat, and should allow the student to withdraw as gracefully as possible without taking advantage of this panic to drive home a point. (Ausubel, 1949, p. 185)

IMPLICATIONS OF ADOLESCENT INTELLECTUAL DEVELOPMENT FOR SCHOOL PRACTICES

The problem of meaningfulness

Learning is not entirely a matter of personality interaction between pupil and teacher. Many objective properties of ideas and the form in which they are presented influence the meaningfulness of subject matter and the outcome of school learning.

The process of learning may also be described *objectively* in. . . terms. . . of those inner structural and organizational changes which occur in ideas while they acquire individual meaningfulness. . . . At any given time when an individual is exposed to a new idea. . . a certain equilibrium prevails between that idea and the totality of his prevailing organization of concepts. . . . The process by which such new ideas are "imbedded" in the existing structure involves the mechanisms of leveling, sharpening, and assimilation. (Ausubel, 1949, p. 176)

During adolescence, developmental changes in the cognitive aspects of intellectual maturation require recognition from the school. As a result of these changes, the acquisition of meaningfulness depends more than ever on conceptual understanding, integration of knowledge, relevancy to perceived needs, and active learning.

Resistance to rote learning—the parroting of memorized phrases without any real conceptual understanding or perception of meaningful relationships—increases during adolescence. Many adolescents continue to memorize their way through the theorems of geometry without having any real grasp of their meaning, or to repeat dutifully in a literature class that a certain writer was a romanticist, another a realist, another full of "whimsy" without having a clear notion of why these labels are applied (Jersild, 1946, p. 230). But they probably learn less, forget more, and acquire more negative attitudes toward school as a result than they did under comparable circumstances as children. For one thing, this mouthing of meaningless phrases is more of an affront to minds that have a greater capacity to perceive and conceptualize symbolical relationships. For another, there is less disposition to accept at face value the prestige suggestion of teachers when they assert that such learnings are necessary and important.

An important factor in generating clear and stable meanings is achieving a proper balance between concepts and their supporting data. Concepts that cannot be related to illustrative experience or relevant examples soon become meaningless words. This is true of much teaching in the social sciences. On the other hand, most high school and college courses in mathematics and the sciences place undue emphasis on solving problems and performing laboratory exercises; and instructors seldom realize that students can solve complex problems in differential calculus or molar solutions without having the faintest notion of what calculus is about or what a molar solution is, simply by memorizing a series of procedural steps grouped under "type problems." Generally speaking, learning is more meaningful when it proceeds from lower to higher degrees of differentiation, when a student starts with a general conceptual overview that furnishes orientation and direction and then works "backwards" filling in details, specifics, and supporting evidence.

Because cognitive growth during adolescence results in thinking at a higher level of abstraction and self-consistency, a more integrated and less fragmented approach to knowledge is necessary for meaningful learning. Students are more concerned with obtaining an interrelated view of the various subjects within the school curriculum and with reconciling the content of school knowledge with life goals and perceptions of reality from other sources. Various kinds of "core" curricula have been devised to break down artificial subject matter boundaries and to correct the situation in which students take countless courses but succeed only in acquiring fragments of information, without any substantial competence in the narrow subject matter area, let alone an increase in their general understanding of things (Jersild, 1946, p. 229).

THE ROLE OF NEEDS IN MEANINGFUL LEARNING

For meaningful learning to occur, subject matter must be related to felt needs. Inability to see any need for a subject is the reason students mention most frequently for losing interest in high school studies (Combs, 1976; Young, 1932). Doing, without being interested in what one is doing results in little learning—since only that material can be meaningfully assimilated which is relevant to areas of concern and disturbance in the psychological field of the individual. It is unrealistic to expect that school subjects can be effectively learned until adolescents develop a felt need to acquire knowledge and understanding as ends in themselves rather than simply as tools for solving emotional problems or for meeting the ulterior demands of everyday life (Jersild, 1946). Once such a need is developed, learning naturally becomes more meaningful; but it is difficult to stimulate the development of such needs until subject matter can be presented meaningfully in the first place.

Few theoretical issues in psychology provoke more heated controversy than the role of motivation in learning. Positions vary all the way from the assertion that no learning whatsoever takes place without motivation to a complete denial that motivation is a significant variable in the learning process. The weight of the evidence indicates that although motivation is a highly significant factor in and greatly facilitates learning, it is by no means an indispensable condition.

The trend in recent research and thinking has been to place greater emphasis on the motivational power of such intrinsic and positive motives as curiosity (Berlyne, 1960), exploration (Montgomery, 1954), activity (Hill, 1956), manipulation (Harlow, 1950; Terrell, 1959), mastery or competence (White, 1959), and the need for stimulation (Butler, 1954). In addition, these latter drives have been elevated to the status of primary drives in their own right. Unlike other drives, they are, furthermore, gratified (reduced) by the very fact of successful learning itself. It is hardly surprising, therefore, that in many human learning situations the provision of explicit rewards makes relatively little (Abel, 1936) or no (Auble & Mech, 1953) difference in speed of learning or in performance level.

At the human level, cognitive drive (the desire for knowledge as an end in itself) is more important in meaningful than in rote or instrumental learning, and is, at least potentially, the most important kind of motivation in classroom learning.

The causal relationship between motivation and learning is typically reciprocal rather than unidirectional. Both for this reason and because motivation is not an indispensable condition of learning, it is unnecessary to postpone learning activities until appropriate interests and motivations have been developed. Frequently, the best way of teaching an unmotivated student is to ignore his motivational state for the time being, and to concentrate on teaching him as effectively as possible. Some degree of learning will ensue in any case, despite the lack of motivation; and from the initial satisfaction of learning he will, hopefully, develop the motivation to learn more. In some circumstances, therefore, the most appropriate way of arousing motivation to learn is to focus on the cognitive rather than on the motivational aspects of learning, and to rely on the motivation that is developed from successful educational achievement to energize further learning.

THE IMPORTANCE OF ACTIVE LEARNING

Since meaningfulness is largely a personal phenomenon, it can be achieved only if the individual is willing to expend the active effort required to integrate new conceptual material into his unique frame of reference. This means translating and rephrasing new ideas into his own terms and relating them to his own experience, personal history, and system of values (Cantor, 1946; Combs, 1976).

If learning is to be active, ultimate responsibility for its accomplishment must lie with the student (Cantor, 1946). Students, not teachers, need to ask more of the questions and to be more concerned with formulating perceived problems than with learning answers to questions where problems are not perceived (Cantor, 1953). The teacher cannot learn for the student nor navigate intellectually for him. He can only present ideas as meaningfully as possible—and more from a psychological than from a logical criterion of meaningfulness. The actual job of articulating new ideas into a personal frame of reference can only be performed by the learner. It follows that ideas forcibly imposed on students or passively and uncritically accepted by them cannot possibly be meaningful. "It is far too late to start making students responsible for the direction of their education when they reach the graduate level of instruction; it should be recognized from the start that real learning occurs only when there is active participation, when students have actual experience with the reality to which concepts refer instead of merely mouthing what is spoonfed to them" (Ausubel, 1950, p. 79).

All of this, however, is a far cry from demanding that they take complete charge of their own learning. The very nature of education as adequately guided instruction implies knowledgeable selection, organization, interpretation, and sequential arrangement of learning materials and experiences by academically competent and pedagogically sophisticated persons.

The school nonetheless can never assume complete responsibility for the student's learning. The latter must bear his full share by learning actively and critically, by seeking persistently to understand and retain what he is taught, by integrating new learning tasks with previously acquired knowledge and idiosyncratic experience, by translating new propositions into his own language, by putting forth the necessary effort to master difficult new subject matter, by asking significant questions, and by conscientiously undertaking the problem-solving exercises he is assigned.

The extension of schooling

Since intellectual growth continues longer than was previously thought—especially in the more complex mental functions—all adolescents could benefit from the extension of schooling beyond the teen years. Duller pupils could probably master several years later many subjects that are too difficult in early adolescence. However, the increasing differentiation of mental ability in late adolescence requires a corresponding diversification of subject matter if all pupils are to have optimal opportunities for further intellectual development and academic success.

The complexity of modern culture necessarily extends the period of adolescent training and indoctrination as well as the span of intellectual development. More time is needed to transmit the cultural values and the core of skills and knowledge that adolescents require to function optimally as adults in our society. But this development and training do not necessarily have to be completed before youth can win a respected place in the adult vocational world. Many young people can more profitably complete their education in the initial phases of their vocational careers. Ways of telescoping the educational preparation of youth "destined for the professions" should be considered to correct the disproportionate number of years spent in training in comparison with the actual time left for professional accomplishment.

Grouping versus individualization

The problem of effective teaching is tremendously complicated by the wide range of variability in knowledge, ability, interest, motivation, and social maturity typical of high school classes. To make possible greater homogeneity of teaching methods, rate of progress, and level of difficulty appropriate for the majority of pupils in a given class, and hence greater economy and efficiency of teaching and learning efforts, homogeneous grouping of pupils has been attempted by many school systems. Apart from such issues as the stigma attached to membership in a duller group and the beneficial effect of exposing duller to brighter pupils, inherent difficulties in the grouping approach have prevented the reduction of sufficient variability to justify the effort involved.

Because any one of a large number of relevant criteria could be legitimately chosen as the basis for grouping, the selection of a single criterion fails to control variability along other dimensions and may even increase it. If, for example, adolescents were grouped on the basis of physiological or social maturity, intellectual heterogeneity would be increased. Grouping on the basis of intelligence fails to eliminate the wide range of variability in academic achievement that is found within a narrow range of IQ scores; and grouping on the basis of achievement creates the same difficulty with respect to intelligence, and should, besides, be done separately for each subject matter field. In addition, neither of these two methods reduces the heterogeneity caused by differences in social maturity, intellectual curiosity, and other variables relevant to learning and peer relationships in the classroom.

But even if homogeneous grouping were feasible in the more identifiable and measurable of these variables, there is such wide variability in personality, experience, life goals, and motivational orientation to learning that the teacher would still have to treat pupils as individuals. Thus it is wiser to attempt a progressive adaptation of tuition to individual differences (and to encourage children by individualized activities to proceed as swiftly as they can) than it is to spend time first on classifying according to ability and then on mass teaching of supposedly homogeneous groups (Fleming, 1949).

Individualization is accomplished more effectively (while simultaneously preserving the advantages of group instruction) by bringing together children of diverse ability levels in one class, and by arranging for each pupil to progress at his own pace by means of varying the amount, nature, and difficulty level of the material he learns. In this way, differences in motivation, interest, and curiosity, as well as ability, are taken into account.

DIFFERENTIAL ABILITY GROUPING

If ability grouping is practiced at all, it should undoubtedly be based on the results of differential aptitude tests or on particularized measures of subject matter achievement (for instance, mathematics, science, language arts). In accordance with this point of view, a given pupil is placed in those particular sections of various school subjects that correspond to his relative aptitude or achievement standing in the disciplines in question. Many different kinds of administrative arrangements are compatible with this principle of grouping. One may set up separate sections of a given course or several subgroups within a given section. The Dual Progress Plan (Stoddard, 1961) places each pupil half of each day in his homeroom with his age mates and homeroom teacher for instruction in the "cultural imperatives." The rest of the day is devoted to various special subjects in which pupils are taught by specialist teachers in separate classes grouped to assure relative homogeneity of ability.

The Trump Plan (Trump & Baynham, 1961) involves greater flexibility of administrative arrangements in which the standard high school class of 30 is replaced by some very large demonstration and lecture classes (using, where advisable, either educational television or specialist "master teachers"), some small discussion groups, and much self-instruction with programmed learning devices. In any case, whatever the administrative pattern, differential ability grouping implies specialist teachers in the various specialty subjects, as well as teaching methods and instructional demands that are appropriate for the existing developmental readiness and subject matter sophistication of the groups in question.

Complementary to differential ability grouping is the provision of individualized instruction (differential assignments) within each group. For the greater part of the school day, each student works independently at his own optimal pace with sequentially organized programmed materials providing for self-testing. Such self-instruction is more efficient for most aspects of subject matter learning than is class instruction (Milton, 1962). As will be pointed out below, programmed instruction does not necessarily involve the short-frame and small-step-size formal characteristic of the typical teaching machine, but does provide for organizing, unifying, and explanatory ideas; for unusual lucidity of presentation; for early confirmation, clarification, and correction of newly acquired concepts and principles; for consolidation or necessary overlearning of existing knowledge before new material is presented; and for sequential organization of subject matter.

Those aspects of instruction in which knowledge is less well defined, and in which the acquisition of independent and critical thinking ability is a major goal, obviously require more class discussion and direct teacher participation. But teachers have more time to devote to these latter objectives, to cultivate a questioning attitude toward established knowledge, and to focus on the discovery aspects of acquiring new knowledge if the more stable and substantive aspects of a discipline are learned individually by means of programmed instruction.

Trump and Vars likewise suggest

> that the size of any group or the number of pupils that are assembled at any time should relate specifically to the purpose of the learning and teaching under way. . . . Some learning activities are best developed by the student working alone as a single individual. More frequently three or four students may work together around a table or in an area. At other times, however, groups of a different size may be assembled, according to the type of learning activity. For group problem solving and practice in discussion skills, the groups typically should be about twelve to eighteen. Much larger groups may be assembled to hear a teacher, a community member, a student presentation, or to view films or television programs. This kind of large-group instruction for specific purposes may occur either in the school or in the community. Most schools have found that groups of approximately 100 or so are easier to manage than extremely large groups. (Trump & Vars, 1976, pp. 230–231)

SOCIAL STRATIFICATION IN THE SCHOOL

The American secondary school quite naturally reflects the existing social stratification in the culture and in the adolescent peer group. It also reflects differential social class attitudes toward the school and motivations for academic success. Just as important is the fact that the school contributes to this stratification and helps perpetuate it by the type of curriculum it offers, the kinds of demands it makes on boys and girls, and the differential treatment it accords pupils from different socioeconomic backgrounds.

Social class bias of the school

The organization of the school in general is apt to favor middle-class behavior and penalize lower-class children. In the high school situation, there is a tendency to favor the retention of middle-class pupils and the earlier dropping out of lower-class pupils. A disproportionate number of the latter are placed in slow-learning sections—not only on the basis of low ability and motivation, but also, more informally, because of their social background (Havighurst & Neugarten, 1962; Hollingshead, 1949). Similarly, a disproportionate percentage of lower-class pupils are found in the vocational, commercial, and general high school curriculum rather than in the college preparatory curriculum. Thus, as a result of being typed and stigmatized as members of these low-prestige groups, and of enjoying relatively low scholastic morale, lower-class pupils are more disposed to drop out of school. Many urban schools, however, have specialized programs, sponsored by the United States Office of Education, to identify dropouts in order to persuade them back to school and to help lower-class students who have college potential.

The values of the dominant peer group in the socioeconomically heterogeneous high school are predominantly based on middle-class norms and standards, chief of which is acceptance of the importance of getting good grades (Havighurst & Taba, 1949; Hollingshead, 1949; Smith, 1945); and evidence suggests that pupils whose behavior conforms best to the extracurricular norms and expectations of the school also do better academically (Weinberg, 1964). More important perhaps are the subtle and intangible barriers to participation in the more intimate crowds and cliques. Very little crossing of social class lines occurs in clique organization (Hollingshead, 1949). Boys and girls from lower social class strata bitterly resent the patronizing and condescending attitudes of their more fortunate contemporaries. They feel snubbed, unwanted, and left out of things. When this situation becomes too intolerable it undoubtedly influences their decision to leave school (Havighurst & Taba, 1949; Johnson & Legg, 1944).

"Dropouts" as a function of social class status

The question of "dropouts" remains a major unresolved problem. "Each year for more than fifteen years (1958–1974) over one million youth have dropped out of school before high school graduation

(National Center for Educational Statistics, 1973). This situation is projected to continue at least through 1980, indicating that secondary education of all American youth is still far from a reality" (Smith & Barr, 1976, p. 154).

Many of the early school leavers come from homes low in socioeconomic scale where family tradition does not show education beyond elementary grades (Jersild, 1971). To begin with, it costs money to attend school (lunches, transportation, clothes, laboratory and activity fees) and to keep up with the adolescent crowd (Cole & Hall, 1970; Jersild, 1971; Wattenberg, 1973). Second, youth from lower-class homes are more urgently required to contribute to the family income. No less important are the reasons alluded to above—discriminatory attitudes of teachers and peers, lack of social class tradition recognizing the importance and desirability of education, and the absence of real rewards, current or future, for studying hard and conforming to middle-class standards. Low verbal intelligence to the extent that it is correlated with low socioeconomic status is also a minor contributing factor.

THE ADOLESCENT'S EVALUATION OF THE SCHOOL

From first grade through high school the child experiences an increasing degree of dissatisfaction with his school environment. The evidence unfortunately points to a gradual deterioration of his school morale as he climbs the educational ladder (Allen, 1960; Colemen, 1959; Demos, 1960; Jersild, 1949, 1952; Jersild & Tasch, 1949). The first grader is usually enthusiastic about school, his teacher, and academic achievement. With increasing age, however, his enthusiasm wanes and gives way to boredom, indifference, and complaint. School becomes a chore and a burden, fortunately punctuated by recess, sports, and holidays (Jersild, 1949)—something to be endured rather than relished. When an adolescent refers to a high school "activity" he generally means an extracurricular activity, not a school subject. In the spontaneous conversation of adolescents one hears little mention of the academic pursuits that fill the greater part of their working day.

When adolescents survey the high school curriculum, they express greater interest in courses of study related to current personal concerns and problems of adjustment than in the traditional academic subject matter (Doane, 1942; Hopkins, 1940; Jersild, 1949). A particular lack of interest is expressed in social studies (Jersild, 1949). And in accounting for their loss of interest in high school subjects, students emphasize such factors as inadequacy of teaching methods, dissatisfaction with teachers, and inappropriateness of content and difficulty level of subject matter (Bowman, 1960; Wattenberg, 1973; Young, 1932).

These very same reasons are prominent in the explanations that pupils give for dropping out of school (Dillon, 1949; Johnson & Legg, 1944; Wattenberg, 1973). Thus, although most adolescents today enter high school only slightly more than half are graduated. Economic and social class factors are related to survival in high school, but they tell only part of the story. Low intelligence, inferior school achievement, poor academic aptitude leading to school failure (Dillon, 1949; Segel, 1951), and poor reading ability (Grinder, 1973) account for an additional part of the mortality. The rest can be attributed to the fact that many adolescents are disinterested in what the school has to offer them and are disgruntled because the school refuses to provide help with problems that disturb and concern them (Wattenberg, 1973). In countries in which free participation in continued schooling is encouraged, the age of leaving school has been shown to be more directly related to school experiences of success than to the occupation of the parents, to socioeconomic level, or to initial performance in an entrance examination (Fleming, 1949).

What can be done?

The dissatisfaction of adolescents with the secondary school curriculum is not surprising. The implications of both adolescent development and a complex changing society for educational practice have not been satisfactorily realized. Nevertheless, they do not in the least imply "that secondary education should abandon the more strictly intellectual and cultural areas. To do so would be a denial of the adolescent's continuing capacity for intellectual horizons, to find new outlets for this curiosity, to add to his general information" (Jersild, 1946, p. 227). Since interest in ideas can with suitable stimulation be developed at all levels of intellectual ability, it is not necessary to suppose that there are groups whose potentialities are so one-sided that they must be left to the quite illiterate repetition of relatively simple mechanical manipulations (Fleming, 1949).

At least six major kinds of changes will have to be effected in the management of the secondary school before the goal of transmitting the ideas and ideology of our culture can ever be realized.

1. More use will have to be made of a psychological approach to cognitive learning that is developmentally appropriate for adolescents. In essence, this involves the methodology of maximizing meaningfulness—developing felt needs for acquiring knowledge in

various subject matter areas, emphasizing conceptual understanding as against rote memorization, increasing the interrelatedness of school subjects, and requiring adolescents to adopt a more active role in the learning process. In addition to making the acquisition of knowledge an end in itself, school can be given more current experience value by making more explicit whatever relevance courses of study have for future vocational goals.

2. Subjective and interpersonal factors in the learning process must receive greater recognition. Teachers cannot ignore individual differences in motivational orientation to learning. A more democratic social climate in the classroom is necessary to reduce resistance to learning, to foster more active and critical learning, and to help adolescents acquire greater volitional independence in dealing with adults.

3. Current problems of adjustment and future vocational concerns cannot be ignored without instigating negative attitudes toward school and creating distractions from academic pursuits. These problems are related in an important way to the outcome of personality maturation for which the school as a training institution has an undeniable responsibility.

4. Since the secondary school no longer caters to a highly selected social class group, it must be made more attractive to adolescents from all social class backgrounds. This means eliminating discriminatory practices by teachers and pupils, and making the academic rewards the school has to offer more real to lower-class adolescents by increasing the accessibility of college education and professional status to families of limited means.

5. Educators must devote more attention to studying the activity of teaching, in terms of strategies, teacher-student relations, observation systems, or conceptual analysis. Teachers, supervisors, and professors will need to study teaching by examining research on the theories of teaching (Hyman, 1976).

6. Secondary school leaders must consider carefully the hierarchical structure and horizontal relationships established by them for administrators, teachers, and students and devise alternative structures to facilitate innovations in teaching.

16

Behavior Disorders and Delinquency in Adolescence*

THE EVALUATION OF BEHAVIOR DISORDERS IN ADOLESCENCE

Behavior disturbances in adolescence are exceedingly common and often appear extreme in nature, serious, and alarming. On the other hand, in evaluating the seriousness of behavioral deviations during adolescence, we cannot apply the same yardstick that we would use at other stages of the life span. If the adjustments that adolescents achieve seem extreme and bizarre by adult standards, we should not forget that the developmental pressures to which they are subjected in our culture can hardly be regarded as mild or ordinary. As Blos (1941) and others (Ausubel 1950, 1952; Ausubel & Kirk, 1977) point out, even relatively severe deviations from acceptable behavioral standards in adolescence are not necessarily ominous in their prognostic implications. Adolescent maladjustment can be meaningfully appraised only in terms of adolescent norms.

The chief problem in diagnosing the behavior disorders of adolescence is determining whether the "abnormal" behavior of a particular adolescent is merely an exaggerated expression of the self-

---

*The purpose of this chapter is not to describe in detail the particular entities found in clinical psychiatric or psychological practice, but to consider, in general terms, how the distinctive personality, moral, emotional, and physiological characteristics of adolescents are related to the distinctive kinds of behavior disorders to which they are predisposed.

limited emotional instability characteristic of a transitional phase of development, or whether it is reflective of a more fundamental personality defect or predisposition rooted in childhood experience or ego development. Before such a decision can be reached, careful and thorough appraisal of an individual's complete developmental history is necessary. The observer who merely pays attention to the grossness of overt manifestations (symptoms) will almost certainly be misled. It is reassuring to appreciate at the outset that the greater part "of the so-called problems of adolescents have to do with normal reactions or normal phases through which the adolescent passes in his journey toward adulthood" (Gardner, 1947).

More recently Gallagher and Harris (1976) and Harris (1976) have reached similar conclusions. In fact, no other conclusion is possible "because certainly ninety per cent of adolescents do get through this stage of development without any serious emotional scars" (Gardner, 1947).

Role of emotional instability

We have already considered emotional instability as a generalized state of altered behavioral reactivity characterized by a well-defined syndrome of response tendencies and subjective reactions. This condition, which can be induced in animals and man by a large variety of physiological and psychological stimuli, is typical of adolescent adjustment because of the many psychobiological and psychosocial determinants of stress that operate during this period of growth. That adolescent development should be stressful and productive of emotional instability is a logical deduction that could defensibly be reached merely from consideration of the numerous and difficult developmental tasks and problems of adolescence presented in the preceding chapters. This logical impression, however, is also confirmed by observations of research and clinical workers, by results from projective tests and other indirect measures, and by some studies using adjustment inventories that are documented in previous chapters.

Many of the more nonspecific characteristics of adolescent emotional instability merely reflect a lowered threshold of behavioral reactivity—a tendency to respond intensely, diffusely, and in an undirected and unadaptive fashion to stimuli that would otherwise be too weak or too general to provoke any response whatever. Much of the exaggerated, flighty, labile, irritable, and apparently random behavior of adolescents belongs in this category. On the other hand, part of it can certainly be attributed to the undifferentiated state of their new biosocial status. Before habitual techniques of adjustment to new problems are evolved, before canalized modes of satisfying new needs are established, and before the requirements of new roles are learned, behavior must necessarily be fluid, exploratory, and experimental.

Whenever emotional instability is induced in part or in whole by frustration of goal-directed behavior, deprivation of need or status, or threat to physical integrity, the lowered threshold of behavioral reactivity is invariably accompanied by such subjective responses as rage, insecurity, inadequacy, and anxiety. These emotionally charged feelings occur in response to the threat to self-esteem, security, and ability to cope with the environment that is inherent in such situations. They provide additional incentive to the individual to remove or overcome the threat confronting him since they are uncomfortable, tension-producing affects; and the lowered threshold of behavioral reactivity facilitates the setting up of various adjustive mechanisms, the most direct and immediate of which is aggression. But because direct aggression is not very adjustive—since fear of retaliation and guilt feelings generate fresh threat—it is generally displaced by more devious, defense, compensatory, or escape adjustive mechanisms.

If feelings of inadequacy or anxiety become overwhelming (panic), disruptive behavior such as blocking or paralysis of activity, agitation, perseveration of unadaptive responses, apathy, or depression may occur, interfering with work and school responsibilities and interpersonal relations. Such reactions, which are in no sense adjustive, are too severe to be attributed to the transitional pressures of adolescence alone, and are generally caused by neurotic anxiety rooted in a nonsatellizing history of personality development.

The majority of behavior disorders during adolescence, therefore, are merely exaggerated manifestations of different aspects of the syndrome of emotional instability (i.e., adjustment problems of adolescence). They can be related to instances in which greater than ordinary developmental pressures that are situational in nature are operative over a period of years. In such cases a history of maladjustment is not usually present, either before or subsequent to adolescence. Improvement occurs over the course of adolescence as boys and girls become reconciled to an extended period of subadulthood, evolve anxiety-reducing adjustive mechanisms, and create compensatory interim status for themselves. Because of more severe conflicts associated with emancipation from parental domination and with acquisition of social sex role, girls, as pointed out previously, consistently show evidence of greater emotional instability than boys. Last, the intensity, course, sources, and manifestations of emotional instability vary in accordance with social class membership. Thus, before deciding whether any individual's behavior is normal or abnormal, one must first relate the adolescent's behavior to his social reality. Failure to take such considerations into account and generalization on the basis of clinical experience derived mainly from upper- and middle-class sources have resulted in some of the original misconceptions of psychoanalysis, particularly those relating to psychosexual development and to sexual repression.

Importance of childhood experience

One can only feel relatively sure that adolescent behavior disorder reflects only transitory emotional instability instigated by developmental pressures, provided there is no childhood history of serious personality defect or maladjustment. If, on the other hand, the behavior disorder or the predisposing conditions existed in childhood, the difficulties of adolescence can be blamed only for exacerbating, not for generating, the psycho-pathological trends a particular adolescent manifests.

Investigation of persistently serious or lasting behavior pathology in adolescents (neurosis, psychosis, character disorders, delinquency) shows that the origin of such disorder is almost invariably conditioned by constitutional or developmental factors in the home before the onset of adolescence (Redl & Wineman, 1951; Wittman & Huffman, 1945). In comparing the developmental, adjustment, and personality characteristics of psychotic, psychoneurotic, delinquent, and normal adolescents, it was found that the parent-child relationship was of crucial significance in determining the particular type of adolescent behavior disturbance that resulted (Redl & Wineman, 1951). Schizophrenic youths were extremely introverted and gave evidence of poor disciplinary, social, and emotional adjustment during childhood. "Psychotic patients [rated] their mothers as definitely below average in emotional stability, and definitely over-solicitous and over-protective. They [described] themselves on the average as dependent and with very strong emotional relationships [to] their mothers" (Wittman & Huffman, 1945).

Our analysis of personality development in Chapter 7 supports the same conclusion about the childhood origin of serious behavior disorder. The personality defects of nonsatellizers—lack of intrinsic self-esteem, susceptibility to neurotic anxiety and its complications, difficulties in peer group socialization, and vulnerability of moral obligations in the face of ego enhancement needs—are all products of parent attitudes of rejection or extrinsic valuation that are especially damaging in the preschool years. Similarly, the maturational deficiencies to which extreme satellizers are predisposed, as a consequence of exposure to overprotective, underdominating, and overdominating parent attitudes, begin in middle childhood and preadolescence. These attitudes interfere with the implementation of maturational tasks such as acquiring independent sources of status; increased frustration tolerance and self-critical ability; and greater capacity for postponing hedonistic gratification. Even "reactive" maturational failure in nonsatellizers is generally attributable to a change in parent attitude that occurs before adolescence. And when the development of behavior disorder is conditioned by such potent genic or constitutional factors as extreme introversion, asociality, or hedonistic needs that interfere with socialization and reality adjustment, on the one hand, and adult maturation on the other, there is evidence of their detrimental operation quite early in an individual's developmental history.

The role of adolescence

The incidence of behavior disorder and delinquency increases markedly during adolescence. Mental hospital admissions in the second half of the second decade of life show a tenfold increase over the first decade, and there is a corresponding increase in the frequency of delinquency (Freedman, 1967), "nervous breakdowns," suicidal attempts, alcoholism, and drug addiction (Ausubel, 1958; Freedman, 1967). But except for delinquency, and notwithstanding the fact that these rates would undoubtedly be much higher were there less stigma attached to the occurrence of mental disease, the incidence of serious behavior disorder requiring institutionalization is relatively low in comparison with that in subsequent decades of life. It would seem, therefore, that adolescence serves mostly as a rigorous testing and proving ground of the adequacy of personality structure laid down in the childhood years. Existing defects are more glaring but in most instances are not basic enough to lead to more than transitory developmental disturbances. Even when personality defects are more basic, adolescent experience acts mostly as an aggravating condition. The actual onset of most serious personality disorders is after rather than during adolescence.

The combination of psychobiological and psychosocial sources of emotional instability makes adolescence a difficult period of adjustment even for individuals with very normal personalities. The satellizer in addition has to "learn a new, independent way of life," and must contend with guilt feelings from the repudiation of primary loyalties to parents. His needs for earned status are not adequately met, thereby depressing his extrinsic self-esteem. But unlike the non-satellizer he has a basic fund of intrinsic adequacy to fall back on. The anxiety he experiences is typically transitional in nature and referable to environmental stress.

The same deprivations, on the other hand, are much more threatening to the nonsatellizer, who, possessing no intrinsic adequacy, reacts with more anxiety and sometimes with catastrophic impairment of self-esteem. His ego adequacy is wholly a creature of the environmental vicissitudes which deny or gratify the hypertrophied ego demands on which he has staked his value as a human being.

For prognostic purposes, therefore, it is important to differentiate ordinary transitional anxiety in adolescence from the actual or latent neurotic anxiety of nonsatellizers.

If nonsatellizers are more subject than satellizers to neurotic anxiety during adolescence, satellizers are more strongly predisposed to undergo maturational failure. Since they are required to effect a greater total change in personality structure, and "are less motivated by the need for extrinsic status" to do so, maturation in extreme satellizers is more drastically retarded by such unfavorable parent attitudes as overprotection and underdomination. As a result of maturational failure, adolescents fail to acquire the goal structure of adults. They do not aspire to earned status, to long-range goals, to volitional and executive independence. They lack adequate frustration tolerance, self-critical ability, and feelings of responsibility. Their adjustment to an adult world of reality is not very successful. Extreme introverts find it possible under such conditions to withdraw from social reality and find gratification of hedonistic needs in fantasy ("process" schizophrenia). More extroverted individuals try to satisfy childish, pleasure-seeking goals in reality, and at the same time hide their failure as adults from themselves by developing an adjustive impairment of the self-critical faculty. From the ranks of such persons are recruited vagrants, hobos, drug addicts, poolroom-hangers-on, confidence men, etc. Narcotic addiction is especially adjustive since it both gives rise to effortless and voluptuous sensations of pleasure and inhibits the self-critical faculty to the point where the addict becomes easily contented with his inadequate hedonistic adjustment to life, and is more easily able to evade and overlook responsibilities, and even in the complete absence of any actual accomplishments, he feels supremely satisfied with himself and his future (Ausubel, 1958). Addiction to barbiturates, cocaine, and the amphetamines has lesser but similar euphorogenous effects.*

---

*High doses of marijuana are also euphorogenous, but less reliably so and to a lesser degree. More typically, marijuana is used sporadically in social situations, rather

How, then, can we summarize the role of adolescent experience in relation to the behavior disorders of adolescence? Developmental pressures increase emotional instability leading to transitory behavioral disturbances in many adolescents who have quite normal personalities. But in the absence of intrinsic self-esteem, these same pressures may instigate neurotic anxiety and its complications; and because of increased social expectations of mature motivational behavior, maturational defects also become more glaring in adolescence, sometimes resulting in such extreme consequences as schizophrenia, long-standing drug addiction, and vagrancy. More commonly, however, the stressfulness of adolescence merely compounds existing predispositions to these disorders by exposing serious defects in personality structure. These defects make adjustment to adult social reality seem either difficult and unlikely because of inadequate goal structure or unduly threatening to self-esteem because of lack of intrinsic adequacy. The actual onset of serious behavior disorder necessitating institutionalization is usually postponed until adulthood. In either case the basic personality defects that are the primary etiological factors are essentially products of unfavorable childhood experience.

The meaning of frustration

Frustration is the common psychological denominator underlying the conditions that instigate emotional instability, precipitate more serious behavior disorder, and induce various adjustive mechanisms. Frequently, it is not appreciated that, by definition, frustration is purely a subjective phenomenon and not coextensive with the objective barriers or deprivations that most commonly bring it about. To be sure, magnitude of deprivation is not unrelated to the seriousness of the frustration that results. Everything else being equal, the longer and more completely adolescents are deprived of adult status, acceptance in the peer group, gratification of sex needs, and success in school, the more frustrated they are apt to become. But to ascertain how much actual frustration this situation produces in a given adolescent, one must first ask several subjectively oriented questions.

(1) To begin with, how ego involved is the adolescent in the particular goal, achievement of which has ostensibly been frustrated? We have already seen that ego involvement is a highly selective process and that success and failure occur only in areas in which there is ego

---

as a way of life in and of itself as is chronic heroin use; and among teenagers and young adults marijuana use is as pervasive as alcohol use was in previous generations and still is.

involvement. (2) How high is the adolescent's level of aspiration and how resistive to lowering in the face of initial failure? If aspirational levels are not high, or if they can be realistically adjusted to correspond to the difficulty of a task, the degree of frustration is not nearly as severe as when the reverse is true. (3) To what extent are goals overlapping, conflicting, or mutually exclusive? High achievement could conceivably be quite frustrating when success would preclude achievement of other more desirable goals. When conflicting goals are equally desirable, indecision could easily result in frustration of both goals, whereas choice of one goal would inevitably cause frustration of the other. (4) What resources does the adolescent have for coping with the problem? Whether or not a situation of given difficulty will result in frustration obviously depends on the availability of appropriate skills and resources. Depending on the nature of the problem, such factors as high or low levels of intelligence, creativity, health, energy, physical or social skills, and the availability of counseling assistance or financial backing may be very important in determining whether deprivation occurs and, if it does occur, how effectively it can be overcome or compensated for. (5) How much self-critical ability does the adolescent have? To experience failure, he must be able to perceive the shortcomings and inadequacies of his performance. As already noted, adjustive impairment of self-critical ability frequently occurs in immature and inadequate persons (e.g., drug addicts). (6) Finally, how much frustration tolerance does he possess? More important than whether frustration does or does not occur is the impact it has on behavior, which, in turn, is a function of various aspects of degree of tolerance to frustration. Operationally, this refers to how much frustration an individual can withstand without manifesting undue anxiety, loss of self-esteem, or unadaptive rage; without showing disorganization and impairment of performance or self-critical ability; without abandoning realistic goals; and without resorting to distortive adjustive techniques. Answers to these questions will be determined by differential factors of temperament, personality development, and resources available for adaptation.

In interpreting the meaning of frustration, it is necessary also to discount the widespread teleological notion that all behavior is motivated, goal directed, or adjustive in function. Frustration does not necessarily induce adjustive behavior. Most of the subjective responses accompanying frustration (feelings of inadequacy, anxiety, insecurity) as well as many of the behavioral consequences of the lowered threshold of reactivity (flightiness, irritability, emotional lability) are merely manifestations of apprehensive awareness of threat or of negative self-reactions, occasioned by such awareness, that have no adjustive value whatever. Furthermore, when these subjective responses become extreme, as in states of panic, behavior becomes disorganized and is characterized by blocking, blind aggression, rigidity, compulsiveness, unadaptive perseveration, and aimless agitation. Contrary to the assertions of some theorists (e.g., Maier, 1949), however, such reactions to frustration are not necessarily typical; they are only precipitated by catastrophic or unusually threatening situations. Under more ordinary circumstances, frustration gives rise to adjustive behavior in addition to milder nonadjustive responses indicating awareness of threat. The adjustive behavior may or may not be adaptive or constructive. Oftentimes, in fact, it leads to serious distortions of personality.

CLASSIFICATION OF ADOLESCENT
BEHAVIOR DISORDERS

The foregoing considerations lead to the following threefold classification of behavior disorders during adolescence. In the first group are disturbances, essentially unrelated to the tasks of adolescent development, that are merely residual from the childhood era. They consist of maladjustments which primarily represent a continuation of unresolved difficulties arising from failure to solve some of the developmental tasks of childhood which adolescence only aggravates further (Ausubel, 1950). These include the anxiety and delinquency disorders of nonsatellizers and the disturbances in peer group socialization attributable to unfavorable parent attitudes and genic or constitutional factors.

In the second group are disturbances that are more specifically relevant to the maturational tasks and adjustment problems of adolescence per se. It is convenient to divide this group into two separate categories: (1) transitory behavior disorders reflecting increased emotional instability, and (2) serious maturational failure largely conditioned by undesirable child rearing practices. Typical of the transitory disorders are the exaggerated adjustive responses to status deprivation cataloged in Chapter 11, sporadic delinquency, sporadic and nonaddictive drug use, and occasional repudiation of the goals of maturation. Maturational failure, on the other hand, refers to the more permanent and serious disorders of personality maturation, which predispose the affected individual to "process" schizophrenia, chronic drug addiction, and vagrancy (Ausubel, 1949, 1952; Ausubel & Kirk, 1977).

Both the residual and the maturational failure disorders, in contrast to the transitory group, are rooted in childhood experience, are resistive to treatment, do not materially improve with the termination of adolescence, and have an unfavorable or guarded prognosis. Further discussion of the residual disorders of childhood is beyond the scope of this volume and is properly treated in textbooks of psychopathology and child psychiatry. It should be mentioned, however, that overt pathological manifestations cannot always be found when childhood developmental history is reviewed. Since adolescence is such a rigorous test of the soundness of the foundations of personality laid in childhood, many earlier disturbances scarcely noted before, or thought to be benign, may suddenly flare up and become alarming during adolescence. Once removed from the protected environment of the home and required to compete on an equal footing with other boys and girls, once subjected to the multifarious stresses and strains associated with adolescent adjustment in our society, once mercilessly exposed under the dissection microscope of the peer society in its efforts to make him conform as closely to every other adolescent as one new penny to another, no boy or girl who has a basic personality defect could continue successfully to mask its presence.

Problems of differential diagnosis between the transitory and the two more serious categories of adolescent behavior disorder have already been discussed in relation to parent-youth conflict and maturational disturbances. Failure to differentiate between transitory and serious behavior disorders leads to much unnecessary pessimism in evaluating the adjustment status of youth. In 1951 and from the middle sixties to the present, for example, an outbreak of narcotic drug addiction among teenagers led to unfounded fears that a large percentage of adolescents, once initiated into this practice, would remain lifelong victims because of a "physiological dependence" on the drug. Totally ignored in all of this speculation was the fact that only adolescents who fail to undergo normal ego maturation are in any danger of becoming permanent addicts, since only for such persons do the opiates have lasting adjustive value; and that it is this psychological adjustive value of opiates rather than "physiological dependence" that is the essential cause of addiction (Ausubel, 1958). Most adolescents who sample drugs do so out of reckless bravado or because of high attitudinal tolerance (for using drugs) in the community or exposure to addicts and dope peddlers in slum areas of large cities. When "the rebellious, venturesome, 'try anything' adolescent boy who otherwise has a normal personality structure tries drugs, he finds that they have little adjustive value for him because he is really concerned with mature achievement in a real world" (Ausubel, 1952b).

For him it is sufficient that by having "his fling . . . he has served his purpose of asserting himself and defying adult authority" (Ausubel, 1952b). The main reasons for the teenage epidemic of drug addiction in 1951, for example, were (1) an intensification of normal adolescent thrill-seeking by the fatalism associated with prolonged international crisis and (2) an increase in the supply of illicit narcotic drugs coupled with a decline in the number of confirmed drug addicts (Ausubel, 1952b).

The more recent endemic proportions of drug abuse among urban slum youth are undoubtedly related to the protest movements of the Sixties, participation in the Viet Nam War, and the economic recession and loss of job opportunities in the seventies.*

DELINQUENCY IN ADOLESCENCE

Incidence

Criminal behavior is characteristically a youthful occupation. The incidence of delinquency rises slowly during the first half of the second decade and then climbs precipitously until age 19 (Shuttleworth, 1949; Stubblefield, 1967). During the early twenties, the rate of delinquency continues to increase, but less steeply, reaches a peak before age 25, and then declines rapidly thereafter. The incidence of juvenile delinquency is also increasing rapidly in most parts of the world (Friedman, 1967).

Why does delinquency differ from other serious behavior disorders, which do not typically reach their peak incidence until later in life? One suggestion is that aggression is the most direct and primitive response made to frustration and is subsequently displaced into more efficacious and need-satisfying adjustive techniques that are learned with increasing age. This phenomenon is especially evident in disorganized urban areas where, in addition, conditions of life favor the temporary alienation of the moral values of adolescents from those of conventional society. Another factor apparently inheres in the delayed or retarded personality maturation of certain individuals who, for this reason, reach at a more advanced age the same degree of moral development that most other persons attain in adolescence. Delinquency in sat-

---

* Recent reports from the Drug Enforcement Administration indicate an alarming increase of all forms of drug abuse among women, residents of suburbs and small towns and middle-class white youth (New York Times, June 19, 1975).

ellizers attributable to overdominating, underdominating, and overprotecting parent attitudes frequently follows this pattern.

To view the problem of adolescent delinquency in perspective, we must realize that only a small percentage (less than 10 percent) of all adolescents ever become legally delinquent. This is true even though the vast majority of college males retrospectively admit to sporadic offenses against the law. Actually, very few delinquent acts [3 to 5 percent according to Erickson & Empey (1963)] result in apprehension, formal arrest, and prosecution, especially when the offender is well-dressed and groomed, is white, enjoys high socioeconomic status, or lives on the right side of the tracks (Nye et al., 1958). In addition, many moral crimes and forms of antisocial behavior violate no existing statute. In interpreting statistics on delinquency, we have to bear in mind that the term refers only to habitual unlawful activity that is apprehended and results in judicial action.* It should be clear, therefore, that official incidence rates are always minimal estimates of the actual prevalence of delinquency during adolescence.

COMPARED TO PREADOLESCENCE

The probability of delinquency during adolescence is much greater if there is a childhood history of antisocial behavior (Ganzer & Sarason, 1973; Glueck & Glueck, 1933; Healey & Bronner, 1948). In fact, approximately two-thirds of adolescent delinquents begin their delinquent careers in preadolescence. Nevertheless, in addition to implicating a larger number of individuals, the adolescent period is characteristically associated with a more regular, serious, and organized kind of delinquency. One obvious explanation for this difference is the fact that "in adolescence the child often strikes back for the first time just because he is now strong enough or well enough integrated against a problem that has actually been quite as pressing for a number of years" (Plant, 1948). Greater freedom of movement and less adult supervision during adolescence also make it more possible to implement delinquent tendencies.

More important perhaps than greater opportunity and capacity for executing delinquent acts are the transitional pressures, the antiadult and aggressive attitudes, and the peer group sanctions that exist during adolescence. Prolonged status deprivation, superimposed on many other psychosocial and psychobiological problems,

---

* The distinction between delinquency and crime rests solely on the age of the offender which determines whether he comes under the jurisdiction of a juvenile court. The age jurisdiction of such courts varies considerably from one state to another.

increases emotional instability and lowers the threshold for aggressive response against the perceived frustrating agents or their symbolic equivalents. This reaction is bolstered by supportive antiadult peer group attitudes and sanctions for nonconformity to delinquent patterns of behavior.

Pubescence per se exerts no direct influence on the incidence of delinquency, which starts to increase at this time simply because the causal factors listed above do not commonly operate before a child attains sexual maturity. Furthermore, as already pointed out, delinquency generally has historical antecedents in childhood and reaches peak incidence in the late teens and early twenties rather than at the age of pubescence.

SEX DIFFERENCES

Important differences exist between boys and girls in the incidence, age of onset, etiology, and kind of delinquency practiced. Four to seven times as many boys as girls became delinquent in the past (Maller, 1937; Stubblefield, 1967), but the ratio of boys to girls has shown a steady decline over the past 75 years (Ganzer & Sarason, 1973). Boys also become involved in delinquency at an earlier age than girls, in more serious crime, and in more delinquencies against persons (Ganzer & Sarason, 1973). These differences are partly a reflection of the greater supervision to which younger adolescent girls are subjected, and partly a reflection of the fact that sex offenses constitute a more frequent category of delinquency among girls.* However, if these differences are culturally determined and reflect cultural attitudes toward male and female social sex roles, we can expect them to become increasingly less pronounced in the future as the "double standard" for sex morality continues to wane.

Sex differences in the kinds of offenses committed are even more striking. Stealing, mischief, traffic violations, truancy, and running away from home (Butler, 1973) are the major misdemeanors of adolescent boys (Nye et al., 1958). Delinquent girls, on the other hand, are most frequently charged with ungovernability, sex offenses, and leaving home.

Female sex delinquents "are not commonly driven by sex urges per se" (Healey & Bronner, 1948). Girls who fail to receive adequate affection and acceptance at home may resort to promiscuous sex experience as a way of obtaining warmth and acceptance from men or "for the secondary gains of attention, the pleasure of being taken to

---

* Sex delinquency generally presupposes anatomical sexual maturity, thus occurring rarely in prepubescent girls.

restaurants and amusement places, or the excitement of having other new experiences" (Healey & Bronner, 1948). In other similar cases, sex delinquency may be practiced in peer groups expressly organized for this purpose. Frank suggests that sex delinquency occurs in girls whose fathers adopt a hostile and deprecating attitude toward the female sex, and who then use their sexuality as a means of "exercising power over men," and in this way gaining "revenge for the years of humiliation they suffered as girls" (Frank, 1944b).

The greater frequency of sex delinquency among girls can be explained by several factors. First, because of prevailing cultural notions about sex differences in biological sex role, it requires less actual misconduct by girls to be charged with sex offenses. Second, since the social, emotional, and academic adjustment of delinquent girls is much superior to that of delinquent boys (Wittman & Huffman, 1945), there is reason to suppose that sex delinquency involves less pathological involvement of total personality structure than other forms of delinquency. Thus there is reason to believe that the maladjustment of delinquent girls is primarily related not to intrapsychic personality difficulties, but to difficulties of adjustment within the family group and to their general environment. Third, the use of heterosexual attractiveness as a means of obtaining earned or adult status is more widely accepted as an appropriate technique for women than for men. Adolescent girls, especially those who are sexually attractive or overdeveloped,* are thus more prone than boys to use their sexuality as a shortcut device for rapidly acquiring adult status. During World War II, this factor was probably responsible for the rise in sex delinquency among younger adolescent girls who were "left out" of the new world of more legitimate adult status that suddenly opened up for their somewhat older contemporaries.

The problem of culpability

Complicating the psychological assessment of delinquency are various moral and legal issues that do not arise in other forms of behavior disorder. And to make matters more complex, the various disciplines and professions that deal with delinquency adopt widely divergent approaches to these issues.

The legal point of view is closest to that of "the man in the

---

*Early or prominent sexual development occurs more frequently in delinquent than in nondelinquent girls (Burt, 1925). No data are available which indicate whether or not this relationship reported more than 50 years ago still prevails. It does, however, seem highly plausible that it does.

street." Since the law is primarily concerned with protecting the interests and safety of individuals, groups, and society, the most practical assumption is that in the absence of evidence to the contrary, unlawful acts are willfully committed and render the offender liable to punishment. The strict legal test for responsibility requires only that the accused person know right from wrong and be able to appreciate the nature and quality of his act.

Psychologists and sociologists, on the other hand, deny that the issue of moral accountability is relevant in delinquency. In line with the psychological determinism dominating the social sciences, the concept of moral accountability is held to be based on the discredited notion of "free will." The moral character of an individual is presumed to be shaped by forces beyond his control and, therefore, immune from any judgmental process with ethical implications. Immoral behavior is regarded as no different from any other kind of undesirable behavior.

The sociologist places greatest weight on social disorganization and conditions of socioeconomic deprivation in accounting for delinquent behavior. Psychologists and psychiatrists believe that delinquency is primarily a problem of disordered personality development arising from unfortunate relationships between the child and significant persons in his psychological field rather than a manifestation of disturbance in grosser patterns of social organization.

Sociologists and psychologists both agree, however, that since the causes of delinquency lie beyond the control of the individual, the prevailing judicial insistence on moral accountability is both inconsistent and based on archaic and unscientific notions of behavior. Typical of this approach is Zachry's (1944) statement that "to isolate certain forms of emotional disturbance and to label them with a term of opprobrium is both scientifically inaccurate and inimical to the interests of youth. It presupposes an attitude of sitting in moral judgment, of attaching blame for behavior which should be considered a symptom of disturbance."

In this dispute between the jurist and the social scientist, the writers are inclined to side with the jurist. Just because social and psychological causes can be identified as contributing to an individual's delinquency does not mean that he must forthwith be absolved from all moral accountability. There has been too great a tendency in modern psychological thinking about criminality toward divorcing all behavior of its ethical content. It seems just as one-sided to ascribe all antisocial behavior to underlying psychological disturbances as to see in it only a manifestation of basic immorality. From the standpoint of individual behavior, there is a moral aspect to most purposeful human activity, the psychological reality of which cannot be ignored. And although this aspect is so closely interwoven with the aspect of psychological disturbance that the two can hardly be separated, the relative significance of each in a given case of delinquency is usually clear enough to allow some judgment as to the individual's moral and legal accountability.

Acceptance of behavioral determinism, however, does not necessarily imply repudiation of the notion of moral accountability. Because we can satisfactorily explain the dynamics and the developmental history of antisocial attitudes, we are not obliged to regard the offender as free from blame. Regardless of events beyond his control that once transpired, if he can *presently* recognize a moral obligation and is physically and psychologically capable of exercising inhibitory control, he is accountable for his misdeeds. The vast majority of immoral and delinquent acts are committed under conditions where there is clear awareness of a moral issue and reasonable opportunity for exercising inhibitory control in conformity with the perceived direction of moral duty.

This concept of culpability goes beyond the formal legal definition. It refers also to acts of cruelty, injustice, and treachery which violate no statute or legal precedent. It does not preclude the application of rehabilitative, preventive, or therapeutic measures, or presuppose a spirit of vindictiveness. The notion of liability to punishment following misbehavior is an essential component of the concept of moral obligation which cannot be abandoned without jeopardizing the very basis of conscience formation. If therapy alone were instituted, culpable immoral behavior would not be distinguishable in any way from other behavior disorders. And in addition, punishment serves the necessary function of protecting society from its predatory members.

Differential diagnosis of delinquency

The operation of multiple causality in the development of behavior disorders is nowhere more striking than in delinquency. Seldom if ever is any single factor alone sufficiently prepotent to induce sustained or habitual antisocial behavior (Empey, 1967; Glueck & Glueck, 1950). Delinquency is in no sense a homogeneous category of behavioral disturbance. Underlying the least common denominator of overt unlawful activity are many different kinds of causal factors that often bear little or no relationship to each other.

This does not mean that classification is not possible. Causal factors can be grouped into major categories; and even if several factors operate simultaneously, experienced observers are usually able to agree on the one that is causally most crucial after careful study of the case history.

As in other adolescent behavior disorders, classification is not merely a matter of academic interest but is extremely important for prognostic purposes. The threefold classification used above can also be used here. On the one hand, there is the prognostically hopeful variety of delinquency that involves no serious abnormality in character development but reflects, for the most part, the transitory pressures of adolescent emotional instability and exposure both to the delinquent or ambivalent moral values of the neighborhood peer group and to the general subcultural milieu. Such delinquency is facilitated by the presence of certain temperamental traits (e.g., high impulsivity or suggestibility) but seldom becomes permanent unless reinforced by such factors as frequent institutionalization in "reform schools," inability to obtain legitimate employment, minority group membership, and strong identification with delinquent parents or siblings. On the other hand, two other categories of prognostically less favorable delinquency reflect (1) residual childhood defects in character development (in nonsatellizers) or (2) maturational defects in character referable to the developmental tasks of adolescence (especially in satellizers). These types of delinquency are more frequently associated with a childhood history of antisocial conduct, and are also facilitated by the possession of certain personality traits relating to the presence and channelling of aggressive responses and by the transitional pressures described above. But under ordinary circumstances neither of these factors by themselves leads to permanent delinquency.

Many lines of evidence support the validity of distinguishing between the less serious, transitory form of environmentally and situationally conditioned adolescent delinquency and the more serious, character-conditioned delinquency that is also aggravated by adolescence (Freedman, 1967; Stubblefield, 1967). In general, such evidence points to the inability of social factors to produce either transitory delinquency in the majority of adolescents growing up under unfavorable environmental conditions or permanent delinquency in more than a small percentage of such individuals (Empey, 1967; Ganzer & Sarason, 1973). Even in the worst slum districts, only a small minority of adolescents become habitually delinquent (Glueck & Glueck, 1950; Healey & Bronner, 1948). More young people choose to identify with the sanctioned value system of conventional society, which is transmitted by the home, school, church, and organized youth groups, than with the values of the delinquent gang. It is important to bear in

mind, however, that although the prevailing ideology of lower socioeconomic groups may differ in many important respects from those
of middle- and upper-class groups, it is in no sense essentially or predominantly at odds with the law. Even the majority of the members of
adolescent delinquent gangs eventually break their connection with
unlawful activities and settle down to a more conventional law-abiding existence. And finally, it should be pointed out that some adolescents from optimal social environments—many more than are ever officially charged with delinquency—become habitually wayward. Much
middle-class delinquency is due to characterological disorder, the
generation gap in values, the example of white-collar crime set by
parents and middle-class adults, and the post-World War II decline in
middle-class adult morality. It is inhibited, for the most part, by
higher aspirations for vocational and material success generated by
their social class milieu (and subsequently internalized during childhood in the home) and later by pressures emanating from middle-
class peer groups.

Etiological factors

TRANSITIONAL PRESSURES OF ADOLESCENCE

Several factors peculiar to the nature of adolescent development
in our culture contribute to the greater incidence of delinquency during this period. In the first place, delinquency is an aggressive response, and adolescents in the United States have a larger fund of
aggression than members of other age groups. This situation is both a
direct product of the prolonged status deprivation to which they are
subjected and a manifestation of the reduced threshold for aggression characteristic of all states of emotional instability. As suggested
earlier, aggression is the simplest and most direct response to frustration, and accordingly is displaced as other more adjustive techniques
are learned. Nevertheless, it is sustained over a period of several
years by the general antiadult orientation that crystallizes from the
identification of adults as the agents responsible for the thwarting of
their bid for independence and earned status.

"Moreover, an act of aggression sometimes results from the feeling that the world is hostile toward the aggressor" (Zachry, 1944).
Thus the adoption of a vindictive attitude toward young delinquents
may also instigate counteraggression. "To place the badge 'delinquent' upon them at the age when they are most sensitive, most easily wounded, only confirms them in their belief and consequently
tends to intensify the impulse toward aggression" (Zachry, 1944).

All that passes as aggression, however, does not conform to the behavioral definition. Much of the restlessness, thrill-seeking, and recklessness of adolescents that takes an unlawful turn (truancy, traffic violations, disorderly conduct, sampling of narcotics) is only a manifestation of generalized lowering of the threshold of reactivity or of high susceptibility to peer group pressures, and does not reflect any deliberately aggressive or antisocial intent. Also, much of the rebellious self-assertiveness of adolescents that appears to be a reactive form of aggression is, instead, a more positive expression of the developmental need for greater volitional independence. Finally, in assessing the significance of aggression in relation to delinquent behavior, it is important to realize that there are class standards regulating the overt expression of direct physical aggression; and, hence, what might almost be regarded as normal for one class might be viewed with alarm if occurring in another social setting.

The expression of aggressive behavior is facilitated in adolescence by the normative and coercive power of the peer group. Adolescents find aggressive group action much more efficacious in advancing their interests than individual acts of rebellion. Bolstered by group suggestion and moral sanction the individual adolescent will often participate in aggressive, antisocial behavior that he would never think of undertaking by himself. In participating in such activity he also responds to implied coercive threats of ostracism and to genuine feelings of loyalty to the group (Cloward & Ohlin, 1960; Sherif & Sherif, 1964; Short & Strodtbeck, 1965; Thrasher, 1963). Hence, most delinquent activity is committed by groups rather than by individuals (Healey & Bronner, 1948; Plant, 1948; Short & Strodtbeck, 1965). But because of the prevailing moral confusion, the weakening of traditional core values in our society, the widespread existence of corruption and lax morality in high places, and the cynical emphasis on expediency and material success that he sees all around him, identification with an upright way of life is not a self-evident alternative, (even in middle-class adolescents). He is thus tempted to experiment with various norms of ethical conduct, some of which are patently delinquent. Because of his marginal status and his vulnerability to group pressure, he is especially prone to swim with the tide and pursue a policy of moral expediency. Under such circumstances—when exposed to the influence of a delinquent peer group—the decision to cast his lot with delinquency can unfortunately be made more readily than we prefer to believe.

DISORGANIZED URBAN AREAS

The existence of special socioeconomic deprivations and of disorganized urban areas provides suitable conditions for the emergence of delinquent juvenile gangs (Empey, 1967; Glueck &

Glueck, 1952; Shaw & McKay, 1942). Such gangs make possible a more organized and sustained channeling of aggressive impulses into delinquent activities based on a predatory set of values. But although their antisocial values are continually reinforced by alienation from conventional society, and by close association with their fellows over a period of years in a cohesive action group (Cloward & Ohlin, 1960; Cohen, 1945; Matza, 1964; Sherif & Sherif, 1964), permanent delinquency is a relatively rare outcome (Empey, 1967).

Adolescent residents of urban slum areas naturally face all of the deprivations and developmental changes productive of increased aggression among youth in general. In addition, many other factors engender further hostility and antisocial attitudes. Such areas are characterized by overcrowding, substandard housing, large families, poverty, and inadequate nutrition and medical care; higher rates of physical and mental disease and unemployment; and the absence of suitable recreational facilities. They are populated by newly arrived and, hence, economically poorly established immigrants and minority groups (Blacks, Puerto Ricans, Mexicans) who are also harassed by racial and ethnic discrimination.* In school the children of these minority and lower socioeconomic groups are frequently exposed to condescending and patronizing attitudes and to the slurs, taunts, and discriminatory practices of age mates and teachers.† They soon learn that their educational and vocational opportunities are highly circumscribed. In their immediate environment they are daily witnesses of crime, vice, and violence. Shielded by the geographical isolation of the slum and the protection it offers from police and adult supervision, delinquent gangs can flourish with immeasurably greater ease than in homogeneous rural communities (Havighurst & Taba, 1949).

Psychological conditions within the home are equally conducive to the development of antisocial impulses. Parents quarrel more openly. Brutal beatings, drunkenness, illicit marital relationships, separations, and desertions are relatively common in this environment. The frequency of irresponsible, shiftless, incompetent, harassed, and overburdened parents incapable of providing adequate supervision for their children is also greater than in other environments. Parents often fail to provide suitable ethical training, sometimes furnish an example of delinquency by their own conduct, and not infrequently condone or show little concern over wayward behavior. Less emphasis is placed on school achievement, church affiliation, and partici-

---

* Delinquency rates for blacks, for example, are substantially higher than those for whites (Kvaraceus & Miller, 1959).

† These factors, of course, are less significant in segregated inner-city schools.

pation in community organizations (Conant, 1961; Havighurst & Taba, 1949; Plant, 1948; Rosen, 1959).

Once organized, the delinquent gang perpetuates itself through its closely knit, highly differentiated social structure, its system of mutual obligations and loyalties, and the adherence of its members to a delinquent code of ethics that is consciously chosen in preference to the sanctioned values of society (Healey & Bronner, 1948; Sherif & Cantril, 1947; Sherif & Sherif, 1964). Delinquents are generally very social individuals with a highly developed sense of comradeship and personal loyalty to their fellows (Healey & Bronner, 1936, 1948; Sherif & Cantril, 1947; Sherif & Sherif, 1964). They justify their predatory activity against society on the grounds that it is retaliatory for unjust and repressive treatment and that it is the only possible way of obtaining status and gratifying their needs.

RESIDUAL DEFECTS IN MORAL DEVELOPMENT

In contrast to the transitional and situational causal factors described above are residual defects in moral development. Such defects help explain why youths from even optimal social environments become involved in delinquency. They also account in part for the selective occurrence of chronic delinquency in only a small minority of exposed adolescent slum dwellers and for the small number of cases that terminate in permanent delinquency. The moral development of nonsatellizing children and the defects in conscience to which they are predisposed have already been elaborated in considerable detail.

It is not at all surprising that the incidence of delinquency is so much greater under conditions of child rearing that lead to an absence of satellization, when parents are rejecting and neglectful and make children feel unloved, unwanted, and insecure in affectional relationships. The delinquent pattern may first originate when such children discover that the only way they can obtain some attention is by participating in disapproved behavior. Delinquents more frequently judge their parents as lacking in solicitude, affection, and concern for their futures, and as harsh, unjust disciplinarians who abuse their power and authority (Glueck & Glueck, 1950; Healey & Bronner, 1948; Monahan, 1957; Wittman, & Huffman, 1945). Their family life is marked by conflict, hostility, and disharmony (Healey & Bronner, 1948; Monahan, 1957). They lack close emotional ties with parents, feel little regard for them, and tend to disavow the values the parents prize most highly (Zucker, 1943). They resent parental authority and training measures since they do not feel that their parents truly have their welfare at heart. But since aggression at home leads to swift reprisals, they transfer their rebelliousness and hatred of authority to other adults, turning on society for the revenge they seek against parents (Empey, 1967; Glueck & Glueck, 1950; Healey & Bronner, 1948; Monahan, 1957). In some instances the desired revenge is obtained merely by participating in disapproved activities. Not infrequently, however, rejecting, narcissistic parents are not at all concerned over the antisocial behavior of thier offspring as long as they themselves are not put to any trouble by it (Glueck & Glueck, 1950).

More basic to the delinquency of rejected children than the need for revenge is the unstable basis of moral obligation, the failure to abandon implicitly (on the basis of identification with parents) infantile notions of irresponsibility, and the failure to accept implicitly, in early childhood, parental values and personal responsibility to abide by parental dicta; the precarious dependability of a system of ethical controls that relies so heavily on external pressures and reaction formation when urgent considerations of ego enhancement are at stake; and the tendency to suffer selective impairment of the self-critical faculty with respect to moral lapses and to claim exemption from the moral code that applies to "ordinary" people. These same factors, especially the latter one, also operate in the overvalued child who is rejected in later childhood.

The aggressive, antisocial "psychopath" is an extreme and relatively rare example of this type of moral agenesis. For him harsh parental rejection is combined with an extremely self-assertive personality whose needs for counteraggression and vengeance are so great that considerations of expediency are cast aside, and complete and overt rebellion against parental standards takes place. Not only does a sense of personal moral obligation fail to develop, but also internalization of ethical values never occurs. The same hostile, rebellious attitude is later carried over in relation to social norms which the individual identifies with the hateful figures of his parents. Thus, there is no possibility of developing a sense of justice or obligation on rational grounds. Even the interests of self-aggrandizement are subordinated to the need for wanton destructiveness and aggressive retaliation against moral or legal authority.

From an early age this type of individual manifests ruthless, calculating, cruel, unfeeling, and remorseless behavior which appears to be incorrigible. In the underworld he is the conscienceless and unscrupulous criminal, the cold-blooded, egocentric murderer who shows affection and loyalty for no one.

MATURATIONAL DEFECTS IN MORAL DEVELOPMENT

Some instances of delinquency can be attributed to unfortunate parental practices (underdomination, overdomination, overprotection) which interfere with normal maturational changes in the conscience development of satellizers during preadolescence and adolescence. Overdominated and overprotected children experience difficulty in establishing moral obligations on a societal basis, in becoming responsible to the moral authority of society, as against the moral authority of parents, and in independently formulating generalized principles of conduct based on abstract principles of equity rather than on feelings of personal loyalty. If the parents themselves are wayward, this blind and personal identification with their specific code of values inevitably leads to delinquency. Death or physical removal of the parent may also favor the development of delinquency by creating a moral vacuum. In certain instances, originally acceptable authoritarian discipline may become less palatable with increasing age, resulting in overt rebellion or passive sabotage against parental standards.

The underdominated child develops more serious defects in moral structure. Because of lax discipline he fails to learn to curb aggressive impulses and to postpone immediate gratification of hedonistic needs. As a result, he may develop strong guilt feelings and an expiatory need for punishment, which he tries to provoke through flagrantly unacceptable behavior (Bettleheim, 1948; Freedman, 1967; Healey & Bronner, 1936; Jackson, 1949). In addition, inadequate external supports are available for the internalization of moral standards. Last, overindulgent parental behavior confirms his belief that he is a specially privileged person exempt from the moral obligations that apply to others, and interferes with the normal development of self-critical ability.

The writers take issue with the often expressed view that identification with parents (on the basis of their willingness to satisfy dependency needs) is both necessary and sufficient for children to acquire control over hedonistic impulses. In the first place, such control can be achieved on bases other than satellization. Non satellizers, for example, appreciate that self-denial is necessary to avoid punishment and gain ego enhancement. It is true that they may resent the restrictions imposed by parents, but unless the need for revenge is unusually great, their inordinately high ego aspirations ordinarily suffice to curb the desire for immediate gratification of pleasure-seeking goals. More commonly, the failure to learn self-control is an outcome of excessive permissiveness in the home environment.

The prognosis of delinquency conditioned by these maturational defects is fortunately better than that of the nonsatellizing variety discussed above. Attenuation of infantile irresponsibility and implicit acceptance of parental values in early childhood provide a more stable foundation for conscience. Delinquent behavior is less apt to be serious, ruthless, and vindictive since it is oriented more toward hedonistic self-indulgence than toward self-aggrandizement or obtaining revenge. Last, beginning with adolescence, the child comes less under the control of parents and is more exposed to influences (school, peer group, employer) that exert a less detrimental effect on moral development. Subsequent improvement of delinquent behavior in late adolescence and early adulthood substantiates the view that maturation in such cases is retarded rather than arrested.

OTHER PSYCHOLOGICAL FACTORS

Other temperamental traits and psychological variables unrelated to moral development as such may also play a role in the genesis of delinquency. These factors likewise help explain the selective incidence of delinquent behavior in only a minority of adolescents who suffer from moral defects or live in disorganized urban areas.

Organic brain injuries (postencephalitic parkinsonism, postconcussion syndrome) are only rarely related to delinquency (Bovet, 1951). Mental deficiency occurs more frequently among delinquents (Healey & Bronner, 1948); their mean IQ is also somewhat lower than that of nondelinquents. The significance of both facts must be qualified by the skewed distribution of IQs in slum areas. Delinquents do not compare unfavorably with their nondelinquent siblings on tests of mental ability (Healey & Bronner, 1948). Low IQ per se cannot be an important etiolgical factor in delinquency, but may constitute part of the larger constellation of variables associated with depressed socioeconomic conditions that contributes to the development of delinquent behavior. Intellectual deficit, for example, increases suggestibility, the tendency to take unwise chances, and the probability of apprehension. The school achievement of delinquents is also not commensurate with their verbal intelligence (Glueck & Glueck, 1950), thereby increasing the incidence of school failure and the inclination for truancy, which is one of the earliest and most frequent of juvenile offenses.

Apart from causes rooted in unsatisfactory parent-child relationships, delinquents may be more prone for other temperamental reasons to use aggression as a defense or status-gaining mechanism. In contrast to nondelinquents, they have been described as more restless and active, self-assertive, defiant, impulsive, suspicious, stubborn, crowd-minded, danger-loving, and destructive (Glueck & Glueck, 1950). All other things being equal, individuals possessing such personality traits are more likely to learn and habitually practice unacceptably aggressive ways of satisfying needs and reducing anxiety. It may also be that as a result of experiencing higher levels of frustration associated with physical, intellectual, and educational handicaps, they are more unhappy, discontented, and insecure than other adolescents, thereby having greater cause for aggression.

Preventive measures

It is universally agreed among authorities on juvenile delinquency that prevention is a much more feasible goal than treatment. To be effective, preventive measures must understandably be directed at the causal factors discussed above.

One of the more significant aspects of a preventive program involves measures to reduce the emotional instability of adolescence. Since psychobiological determinants of emotional instability cannot readily be influenced, attention must be directed toward minimizing the factors that prolong status deprivation, providing more work experience and earlier job opportunities, making earlier marriage possible,* and increasing social mobility. Much could be done merely by making school experience a more effective source of interim status and by reducing the amount of frustration that adolescents, especially those from lower socioeconomic backgrounds, meet in school.

The elimination of disorganized urban areas, and of such associated conditions as the segregation of minority groups, is an obvious aspect of any preventive program but is necessarily a long-range objective. Nevertheless, it seems highly unlikely that much progress can be made toward reducing the transitory, situationally conditioned delinquency of the urban slums until the underlying socioeconomic picture is improved. In the interim, programs of community action initiated and carried on by the concerted efforts of citizens and local residents interested in improvement of the community life in all its aspects can do much to improve the morale of the inhabitants. The use of local talent in delinquency areas for constructive purposes and the assumption of responsibility for and control of a community betterment program by the local residents constitute the basic features of the Chicago Area Projects which flourished a generation ago. The participants in such a program "achieve a sense of self-reliance, pre-

---

*This factor is less significant today than in previous generations because there is less social stigma directed against unmarried couples who live together.

serve their self-respect, and enhance their status among their neigh-bors by contributing time and energy to the creation of better oppor-tunities for children" (Shaw & McKay, 1942). Not only is such self-initiated effort more likely to result in constructive change, but also by avoiding the condescending attitudes of nonindigenous philanthropic institutions and by meeting potential delinquents on their own ground, it neutralizes the natural diffidence with which most crusaders and reformers have been greeted by disturbed and aggressive-minded boys and girls.

Last, a preventive program must be directed at reducing the in-cidence of deviant moral development. Essentially this involves im-provement of the mental hygiene of parent-youth relationships dur-ing adolescence (see Chapter 8), extension of parent education in child-rearing, establishment of more child guidance clinics, earlier identification and guidance of potential delinquents, and closer col-laboration between teachers and parents. In instances of particularly undesirable parent-child relationships, teachers and counselors can play a constructive role in moral development, as parent substitutes, by providing a more appropriate emulatory model and pattern of dis-ciplinary control. Considerable improvement in moral development could also be anticipated were there a restoration of greater uprightness and consistency of ethical standards in civic, business, and professional life.

17

Mental Hygiene and Guidance

Many specific aspects of mental hygiene and guidance in adolescence have been considered in the chapters on sexual behavior, vocational choice, and the school. In this chapter we shall consider only some general principles relevant to the mental health and guidance of adolescent boys and girls. More specific principles, schools, and techniques of counseling and guidance, of mental hygiene, and of various forms of psychotherapy can be found in specialized works in these fields.

THE IMPORTANCE OF PARENT-CHILD RELATIONSHIPS
IN PREADOLESCENCE

The crucial significance of parent-child relationships during childhood and preadolescence for normal personality maturation has been elaborated in great detail. The role of unfortunate child rearing practices in predisposing the individual toward both maturational failure and various defects in personality structure associated with nonsatellization has also been considered, as well as the relationship of each of these conditions to adolescent behavior disorders and delinquency. It follows that the most important aspect of the mental hygiene of adolescence is to minimize the incidence of undesirable parent attitudes and practices before the onset of this stage of personality development. And if such practices and their detrimental consequences on children's personalities do occur, it is unrealistic to hope for any substantial improvement following psychotherapy with children without some change in parental attitude or in the family situation. No other outcome is conceivable in view of the fact that children are largely under the immediate control of powerful adults who in most cases are responsible for the adjustive difficulties involved, and without whose cooperation, improvement in the interpersonal environment and implementation of insight would be impossible. Family therapy in which the family is considered as a "system," and treated as a unit, is now a flourishing form of psychotherapy (Ackerman, 1958; Boszormenyi-Nagy & Framo, 1965).

The difficulty of changing parent attitudes

The difficulties inherent in the task of modifying unfavorable parent attitudes certainly furnish little basis for rampant optimism in this direction. The sources of a parent's inadequacies as a parent are found in his own childhood and are, therefore, highly resistive to change. The personality trends that make a parent narcissistic, preoccupied, and hostile (rejecting) or over- or underdominating are quite stable by the time an individual reaches adulthood. If child rearing practices gratify important needs in the parent, if they provide compensatory ego enhancement (as in overdomination and overvaluation) or reduce anxiety (overprotection), they are especially resistive to modification. But even when these deep-seated personality factors are not operative, for the parent just to admit the need for drastic revision is tantamount to indicting himself as a parent. Mere awareness of attitudes that put him in an unfavorable light is often far less traumatic than directly pleading guilty to these failings by open admission, or indirectly by modification of his practices.

The difficulty of change is further compounded by the parent's subscription to a formal philosophy of child rearing. Sometimes this philosophy is merely an out-and-out rationalization of underlying attitudes, providing a supportive cognitive facade. Other times, it may have the status of an objective conviction relatively unrelated to attitudinal considerations. In such instances modification can be effected more easily since it is necessary only to convince the parent intellectually. The existence of an underlying attitudinal substrate, on the other hand, constitutes a more formidable challenge, which, if not met, often results in an unbridgable gap between theoretical understanding and practical application. But even without fundamental change in the underlying personality basis for parental practices, genuine intellectual convictions can considerably improve the parent-child relationship. They may do this just by opposing contrary personality trends and mitigating their severity without necessarily being potent enough to reverse them entirely. One should, therefore, never underestimate the potentialities of intellectual convictions for effecting personality change despite present-day psychological emphasis on the irrelevancy of all except emotional factors.

It is true, of course, that such superficial changes in parental practices have limited value since they are unspontaneous and are often betrayed in the smaller and less deliberate aspects of behavior. More can be expected from parent education and therapy in cases where detrimental parent attitudes stem from mere ignorance and misinformation rather than from severe distortions in personality structure. In either case one must reckon with the particular fads and fashions in child rearing which are in current vogue. Presently, this statement is just as applicable to excessive permissiveness as years ago (in the twenties and thirties) it was to an overly impersonal and highly controlled child rearing regimen.

Social pressure can also have a positive effect in overcoming undesirable parent attitudes (for example, overdomination). But although the rejecting parent tends to be socially frowned on nowadays, the same narcissistic preoccupation with himself that causes him to neglect his child provides him with a thick skin in the face of public or private criticism. The overvaluing parent, on the other hand, poses as a model of devotion.

IMPROVING PARENT–YOUTH RELATIONS

Although many aspects of parent–youth relationships are almost inevitably bound to be conflictful during adolescence, this does not necessarily preclude the simultaneous operation of more positive factors. Intimate and confidential relationships with parents are not only possible but are also definitely connected with good adjustment during adolescence. The importance of this confidential relationship is that it furnishes a natural basis for the child's seeking of guidance from the parent when he feels that he needs it. The ambivalence of the adolescent's attitude toward emancipation is such that "beneath the indifference and devaluation there is a strong inner need for parental aid and parental guidance" (Gardner, 1947).

But parent–youth hostility has been stereotyped to such a degree that the child is generally too ill at ease to approach his parents even when he would like to most. This is truly unfortunate since it adds to the abruptness of the adolescent transitional period, which, if made more gradual at the onset (although shortened throughout), might help to cushion some of the stresses and strains of adolescence. If parents, on the other hand, could accept the fact that emancipation does not necessarily imply cutting the child completely adrift emotionally as soon as he matures sexually, the painfulness of the adolescent's emotional marginality might be considerably reduced.

Measures aimed at minimizing parent–youth conflict—improving the balance between increased demands and responsibilities, on the one hand, and greater privileges on the other, recognizing the adolescent's (especially girls') greater needs for volitional independence, and using changed methods of discipline and control—have already been considered. In addition, it has been suggested that "giving the adolescent a place at the family councils would be a most constructive way both of showing respect for his developing adulthood and of adding dignity to his precarious status" (Zachry, 1944).

Parent–youth conflict would also be alleviated if parents could refrain from responding in kind to the aggressive provocations of adolescents since this only sets up a vicious cycle based on the *"either-or* proposition from which, unfortunately, neither the adolescent nor the parent can withdraw without serious loss of face" (Gardner, 1947). The former at least has the justification of emotional instability to excuse his behavior.

It has become fashionable to make parents assume the entire responsibility for strained parent–youth relationships. Actually, the blame is only partially theirs. Much of the discord can be attributed to "generation" differences in temperament, outlook, and values. Some of it is a function of the adolescent's exaggerated, unrealistic, and often unreasonable demands for independence, the antiadult orientation of his peer group, his ambivalence about the process of maturation, his tendency to hold his parents entirely responsible for all of the status deprivation he bears, and his frequent failure to perceive actual changes in parent attitude ("perceptual constancy"). Furthermore, the difficulty of the parent's position should be appreciated. It is not easy (even with the best of intentions) to relinquish control over children because of the heavy emotional investment involved in parenthood and the long-standing habit of interference. And if the parent interprets his adolescent children in the light of his own adolescence or resents the idea of eventual displacement, he certainly cannot be judged too harshly for these very human failings.

When parent–youth conflict is largely a function of transitional adolescent pressures and is superimposed on basically wholesome interpersonal relationships, simple mediation can be very effective. The improvement in adolescent behavior which often follows from merely interpreting the adolescent to his parents and teachers is truly astounding. Although there are many basic reasons for parent–youth conflict, there is no doubt but that the presence or absence of tolerance and understanding is the differential factor which makes a given relationship either tolerable and confidential or continuously explosive and acrimonious.

THE SOCIAL HYGIENE OF ADOLESCENCE

The premise underlying the suggestions in this section is that it is the responsibility of adult society to provide the proper conditions under which youth can develop and attain maturity. No help can be given "our restless and disturbed young people until we recognize our own responsibility in regard to them, and accept the fact that it is we who have failed them and not they who have failed us. Then and only then can we take measures to meet their needs" (Zachry, 1944).

The difficulties caused by the abrupt onset of adolescence could be considerably minimized by purposeful reduction of the present discontinuity in the value, interest, and status systems of children and adolescents. Unfortunately, because of the complexities of modern industrial civilization, more than token participation by children in the activities of adults would not be very feasible. Much more realistic is the possibility of shortening the period of status deprivation necessitated by present socioeconomic arrangements. Since the social order is being constantly altered under the impact of highly motivated pressure groups, there is no reason to resign ourselves passively to the immutability of this social situation insofar as it affects adolescents. It is possible for society to create conditions under which adolescents can achieve a large measure of status, responsibility, and importance in community projects and organization. In previous decades we have seen the establishment of such projects as the National Youth Administration and the C.C.C. camps. We have also seen what youth has been able to accomplish for the war effort in the civil liberty struggles of the Sixties and in the anti-Viet Nam War protests. There is no reason why adolescents cannot be assigned definite responsibilities in relation to community welfare projects and receive commensurate rewards and recognition.

The Veterans Administration (after World War II) revolutionized the social basis of late adolescence. By subsidizing education and vocational training, it accelerated the achievement of adult status by making possible early marriage and emancipation from parental economic support. Sooner or later, society will realize that the economic investment in such projects is trifling compared to the potential return in using youthful energies constructively, in facilitating adult maturation, and in reducing the harmful effects of emotional instability.

Unnecessarily severe transitional anxiety can be lessened by giving adolescents greater assurance of eventually attaining adult status. In essence, this means increasing social mobility. Nothing is more discouraging to the ambitions of youth than the fact that, as a result of the tremendous concentration and centralization of economic power which characterize our industrial society today, social mobility is decreasing, and in the struggle for status, inherited wealth and position are beginning to count for more than energy and capacity.

Although the problem of social mobility is more directly relevant to the existing aspirations of middle-class youths, it also affects the possibility of modifying the goals and value systems of lower-class adolescents.

> In order. . . to make low-status children anxious to work hard, study hard, save their money, and accept stricter sex mores, our society must convince them of the reality of the rewards at the end of the anxiety-laden climb. . . . Our society cannot hope, therefore, to educate the greater mass of lower-class people in any really effective way until it has real rewards to offer them for learning the necessary anxiety. (Davis, 1944)

As already pointed out, this anxiety need not necessarily be directed toward achieving money, power, and competitive position, but could be oriented more toward the goals of self-realization and social usefulness.

Because the peer group is undoubtedly fated to remain the major training institution of adolescence, society must do everything in its power both to further the establishment of a constructive peer culture and to see to it that every boy and girl makes some satisfactory emotional and social adjustment to it. The latter point is obvious since we can see all around us the unhappy position of the deviant who is ostracized for so many years from the company of his fellows. The former point is becoming increasingly more important due to the unprecedented amount of leisure time that is now available to the adolescent as a result of the diminution of farm chores and the postponement of gainful employment. The need for guidance in leisure becomes apparent when we witness the growth of spectator sports which "at best represent a shallow participation and little or no real development, either physical or mental, for those who participate" (Partridge, 1947). The failure of society to prepare youth adequately for enjoying the constructive use of leisure time is revealed even in a great city like New York where a startling number of adolescents not only do not participate in any athletic activity at all, but also belong to no organized social-recreational group and cultivate no hobby.

COUNSELING IN ADOLESCENCE

Because adolescence is a period of increased self-assertion and volitional independence, successful guidance must necessarily be as nonauthoritarian as possible.* Maximum emphasis must be placed on self-determination and free acceptance in the choice of goals rather than on forceful imposition of an alien set of values.

Nondirective therapists (e.g., Rogers, 1951, 1967) have made two significant contributions to the counseling of adolescents. First, they have emphasized the importance of a nonauthoritarian therapeutic relationship for the acquisition and emotional acceptance of insight and the minimization of resistance to change. Corollary principles stress the value of the client's self-discovery of his underlying attitudes and motivations, of endogenous stimulation of behavioral reorganization, and of the empathic ability and emotional relatedness of the counselor. Second, these therapists have focused attention on the importance of effecting adjustment to current situational problems, and have pointed out the disastrous consequences of ignoring such problems for several years while waiting for the client to acquire "depth" insight.

Both of these major nondirective principles constitute significant advances over previously accepted notions of counseling and psychotherapy. Unfortunately, however, they have been overgeneralized and have failed to take into account realistic limitations. For reasons that will be elaborated below, we cannot accept the gratuitous assumptions that (1) neither developmental aspects of maladjustment nor diagnostic considerations are relevant to the counseling situation; (2) counselors may only reflect or clarify the client's verbal productions but should not presume to express any expectations or judgments (moral or otherwise); (3) all insight must necessarily represent the product of self-discovery; (4) all behavioral change must be endogenously induced; (5) interpretation, supportive measures, and manipulation of the environment have no place in counseling; and (6) the counselor must have no authority and must not assume the initiative in or attempt to structure the counseling relationship.

---

*As will be pointed out later, it is impossible to avoid certain inevitably authoritarian aspects of the counselor's role.

The fact that in the final analysis only the individual himself can actually effect reorganization of his personality structure in no sense rules out the propriety or the relevance of external sources of insight or stimulation for behavioral change. In counseling, as well as in all life situations, perceptual and motivational reorientation occur partly under the impact of mature social expectations and within a realistic framework of interpersonal relations that does not ignore relevant moral problems. The expression of expectations and judgmental reactions by the counselor in no way violates the principle that the individual is primarily responsible for himself or that change cannot be imposed from without.

To the patient, the therapist represents the expectations of the social reality to which he has not yet succeeded in adjusting adequately. Much of the stimulus for change in motivation, attitude, and adjustive behavior during the treatment period will come from the expectations of the therapist in his role of social reality surrogate. However, if the therapist takes the position that it is the patient's prerogative to structure the framework of expectancy and set the limits in the relationship, the patient not only feels under no pressure to abandon his unrealistic, autistic, or immature frame of reference, but also feels justifiably encouraged to seek adjustment within such a framework with the tacit approval, support, and sanction of the therapist. Similarly, if the therapist articulates no moral expectations* and fails to express ethical judgments, the patient is justified in assuming that the former either approves of his immoral behavior or else considers that any type of ethical solution he (the patient) is satisfied with is also satisfactory to the therapist. In the latter case, therapy takes place in an amoral setting. Proper timing, good rapport, and tact on the part of the therapist are necessary as well as a constructive approach rather than an attitude of condemnation. However, if in spite of skillful handling the patient discontinues therapy simply because of the therapist's expression of moral judgment, it is problematical whether he could have benefited from it in the first place.

The degree of initiative, responsibility, and self-direction that a given client can assume in a counseling relationship cannot be dogmatically fixed at the start of therapy, but must be adapted to the requirements of his personality, the severity of his problem, and to fluctuations in his condition. An adolescent who is disorganized,

---

*The expression of moral values and judgments by the therapist does not necessarily mean that he expects the client to accept and conform to these particular moral values. It merely places the therapeutic relationship in a moral setting and encourages the client to formulate his own set of values.

panic-stricken, or hopelessly caught between the vicious cycle of anxiety and the fixed, perseverative, and maladaptive responses which it tends to engender obviously cannot be expected to take the initiative and rely on his own innate capacities for therapeutic change. At this stage he needs support, reassurance, interpretation, suggestion, practical advice, and whatever benefit can be derived from tranquilizers and environmental manipulation.

Even after the client is past the stage of panic, there is no reason why he cannot avail himself of the insights and reeducative assistance of the counselor in modifying his perceptual and motivational patterns and his adjustive techniques. Not only is self-discovery not an indispensable condition for the acceptance of insight or the initiation of change, but also it is frequently an impossible and unrealistic goal. Directed guidance in restructuring the client's environment and response repertory is also necessary in chronic maladjustments such as anxiety disorders if progress is to be made in solving current problems of adjustment, and if fixed and rigid defence mechanisms, which prevent efficient learning and working, are to be overcome. The anxiety neurotic who has acquired maladaptive ways of learning, perceiving, and setting goals is not free independently to select and use beneficial insights because of potent reaction sensitivities which predispose his behavior along rigidly channelized lines of a defensive nature.

The therapist is also obliged to take the initiative in those counseling relationships in which the client is withdrawn, hostile, or suspicious. Under such circumstances the therapist cannot passively allow the client to explore the situation by himself in order to ascertain whether or not it is threatening to him, since it is precisely in this area that his social maturity is most glaringly deficient. "Warmth and love" is also no magic formula that will automatically dissolve the aggressiveness of hostile adolescents. Such might be true in instances of reactive aggression induced by situational variables, but not where "character-conditioned hostility" is deeply ingrained as a fixed defense against anxiety.

It is equally unrealistic to deny the inherent authority residing in the role of the therapist and to set up the dictum that therapeutic benefit is limited in instances where the therapist is in a position of authority in relation to the patient. In the first place, the very fact that one individual appeals for help on the basis of another's expert knowledge inevitably injects an authoritarian aspect into the relationship. Secondly, if the therapist plays his necessary role of representing cultural expectations and defining limits for the therapeutic relationship, he automatically becomes invested with authority.

Lastly, the therapist's effectiveness depends on his being perceived by the patient as an individual of strength, someone to be respected rather than pushed around like an ineffective, overpermissive parent. Without authority he can set no realistic limits; and in the absence of such limits, therapy can only compound existing ego damage.

Finally, it should be pointed out that although attention to current concerns and therapy need not be postponed until a definitive diagnosis is made, permanent therapeutic change cannot be effected and prognosis cannot be evaluated in the absence of developmental diagnosis. Meaningful insight into the present adjustive situation cannot be gained by patient or therapist by examining only the end-product of development. Neither sequence nor process of growth is deducible from eventual outcome, although the latter necessarily reflects their operation. The practical clinical significance of this consideration enters into one of the first decisions that the therapist is obliged to make in every case he undertakes: are the adjustive difficulties of the patient an outcome of current transitional or situational pressures, or are they reflective of serious abnormalities in ego devaluation or maturation? Until this question can be answered, no intelligent decision with respect to prognosis, length, depth, urgency, and type of therapy indicated can be made.

To treat adolescents successfully, the counselor must have a good theoretical understanding of adolescent development and must have considerable first-hand experience with adolescent behavior at different social class levels and in different ethnic groups. The difficulties associated with the latter requirements have already been considered. In addition, he should be a sensitive, empathic individual capable of relating emotionally to others. These traits plus a constructive personality are much more important than formal adherence to permissive counseling techniques, which not infrequently are superimposed on an authoritarian and destructive orientation to human beings. In general, black counselors are preferable for black adolescent clients because of the inability of white counselors to perceive the world through the latter's eyes and because black children and adolescents understandably both distrust white power figures and find it difficult to identify with them.

SOME GENERAL PRINCIPLES IN GUIDING ADOLESCENTS

In concluding this section on the guidance of adolescents, it is necessary to mention four general principles not previously considered under more specific headings:

(1) There is a certain urgency about solving problems of maturation as they arise and about making definite progress in social and emotional growth from year to year. "Developmental tasks which are not accomplished successfully leave the boy or girl with a lack of readiness for further development and for the tasks which the school imposes. Those who are retarded are branded as out of step and queer" (MacKenzie, 1944).

(2) "The ideals of youth [are influenced] as much or more through the presence and behavior of teachers, clergy, and youth group leaders as through their verbal teachings" (Havighurst et al., 1946).

(3) The adolescent should be encouraged to adjust satisfactorily to current reality, even if it is inconsistent, and far from what it could or might be. Even while endeavoring to change them, it is necessary to recognize established laws and customs, irrational or otherwise. The adolescent must be prepared for the kind of world he is apt to face, not for the kind adults wish existed but as yet have been unable to create. To prepare him otherwise is to invite him to choose a life of continual maladjustment. This does not imply that the status quo must be accepted for what it is, but rather that a mature attitude toward social change be adopted, an attitude that does not "encourage the adolescent to batter his head against the wall of custom simply because these customs are inconsistent" (Partridge, 1947). However, this certain minimal and desirable degree of conformity to social custom is still a far cry from advocating a policy of "hunting with the hounds." Adolescents must be taught to express and courageously defend their moral principles if they are ever to develop into inner-directed autonomous adults.

(4) Finally, nothing is more important in the guidance of adolescents than maintaining that proper sense of perspective which is notoriously lacking in youth. As a transitional period in personality development, adolescence presents certain specific, transitory, and self-limited problems of adjustment.

It is only that the new demands for final adult status lend to the trial-and-error aspects and to the many varied but none the less normal phases of adolescent behavior—its bizarre, unpredictable, and. . . worrisome characteristics. My main therapeutic approach to the parents of adolescents—my main treatment, advice and prescription to them in the face of such behavior—is the tried-and-true phrase of the men of the ancient church who, when beset by the unpredictable and seemingly uncontrollable, comforted themselves and one another with the words, "It will pass. It will pass." (Gardner, 1947)

References

Abbott, M. A. A sampling of high-school likes and dislikes in motion pictures. *Secondary Education*, 1937a, *6*, 74–76.

Abbott, M. A. Children's standards in judging films. *Teachers College Record*, 1937b, *39*, 55–64.

Abel, L. B. The effects of shift in motivation upon the learning of a sensorimotor task. *Archives of Psychology*, 1936, *29* (No. 205).

Aberbach, J. D., & Walker, J. L. Political trust and racial ideology. *American Political Science Review*, 1970, *64*, 1199–1219.

Abernathy, E. M. Relationships between mental and physical growth. *Monographs of the Society for Research in Child Development*, 1936 (1, Whole No. 7).

Ackerman, N. W. *The psychodynamics of family life*. New York: Basic Books, 1958.

Adorno, T. W., Frenkel-Brunswick, E., Levinson, D. J., & Sanford, R. N. *The authoritarian personality*. New York: Harper, 1950.

Ahlbrand, W. P., & Hudgins, P. B. Verbal participation and peer status. *Psychology in the Schools*, 1970, *7*, 247–249.

Alexander, J. F. *Videotape recorded family interaction: A systems approach.* Paper presented at a meeting of the Western Psychological Association, Los Angeles, California, 1970.

Alexander, J. F. Defensive and supportive communications in normal and deviant families. *Journal of Consulting and Clinical Psychology*, 1973, *40*, 223–231.

Allen, E. A. Attitudes of children and adolescents in school. *Educational Research*, 1960, *3*, 65–80.

Allen, R. O., & Spilka, B. Committed and consensual religion: A specification of religion-prejudice relationships. *Journal for the Scientific Study of Religion*, 1967, *6*, 191–206.

Allport, G. W. *Personality, a psychological interpretation.* New York: Henry Holt, 1937.

Allport, G. W., Bruner, J. S., & Jandorf, E. M. Personality under social catastrophe: Ninety life-histories of the Nazi revolution. *Character and Personality,* 1941, *10,* 1–22.

Allport, G. W., Gillespie, J. M., & Young, J. The religion of the post-war college student. *Journal of Psychology,* 1948, *25,* 3–33.

Ammons, R. B. Reactions in a projective doll-play interview of white males two to six years of age to differences in skin color and facial features. *Journal of Genetic Psychology,* 1950, *76,* 323–341.

Anastasi, A. *Psychological testing* (4th ed.). New York: Collier Macmillan, 1976.

Anderson, H. H. Domination and socially integrative behavior. In R. G. Barker, J. S. Kounin, & H. F. Wright (Eds.), *Child behavior and development.* New York: McGraw-Hill, 1943.

Anderson, J. E. The prediction of terminal intelligence from infant and preschool tests. In *Intelligence: Its nature and nurture, Thirty-ninth Yearbook of the National Society for the Study of Education,* Part I. Chicago: The University of Chicago Press, 1940.

Anderson, J. E. The prediction of terminal intelligence from infant and preschool tests. In *Intelligence: Its nature and nurture, Thirty-ninth Yearbook of the National Society for the Study of Education,* Part 1. Chicago: The University of Chicago Press, 1975.

Anderson, W. A. Some social factors associated with the vocational choices of college men. *Journal of Educational Sociology,* 1932, *6,* 100–113.

Aries, P. *Centuries of childhood.* New York: Vintage Books, 1962.

Asch, S. Studies of independence and conformity: I. A minority of one against a unanimous majority. *Psychological Monographs,* 1956, *70* (9, Whole No. 416).

Asher, E. J. The inadequacy of current intelligence tests for testing Kentucky mountain children. *Journal of Genetic Psychology,* 1935, *46,* 480–486.

Ashley-Montagu, M. F. *Adolescent sterility.* Springfield, Ill.: C. C. Thomas, 1946.

Auble, D., & Mech, E. V. Partial verbal reinforcement related to distributed practice in a classroom situation. *Journal of Psychology,* 1953, *36,* 165–186.

Ausubel, D. P. The psychopathology and treatment of drug addiction in relation to the mental hygiene movement. *Psychiatric Quarterly Supplement, Part II,* 1948, 219–250.

Ausubel, D. P. Ego development and the learning process. *Child Development,* 1949, *20,* 173–190.

Ausubel, D. P. Negativism as a phase of ego development. *American Journal of Orthopsychiatry,* 1950a, *20,* 796–805.

Ausubel, D. P. Problems of adolescent adjustment. *Bulletin of the National Association of Secondary School Principals,* 1950b, *34,* 1–84.

Ausubel, D. P. Appraisal of current and residual parent-youth conflict in adolescence. Unpublished manuscript, 1951a.

Ausubel, D. P. Prestige motivation of gifted children. *Genetic Psychology Monographs,* 1951b, *43,* 53–117.

Ausubel, D. P. *Ego development and the personality disorders.* New York: Grune & Stratton, 1952a.

Ausubel, D. P. An evaluation of recent adolescent drug addiction. *Mental Hygiene,* 1952b, *36,* 376–382.

Ausubel, D. P. Relationships between shame and guilt in the socializing process. *Psychological Review,* 1955, *62,* 378–390.

Ausubel, D. P. The relationship between social variables and ego development and functioning. In M. Sherif & M. O. Wilson (Eds.), *Emerging problems in social psychology.* Norman: University of Oklahoma Book Exchange, 1957.

Ausubel, D. P. *Drug addiction: Physiological, psychological and sociological aspects.* New York: Random House, 1958a, 2nd edition (in press).

Ausubel, D. P. Ego development among segregated Negro children. *Mental Hygiene,* 1958b, *42,* 363–369.

Ausubel, D. P. *Maori youth.* New York: Holt, Rinehart & Winston, 1961.

Ausubel, D. P. Implications of preadolescent and early adolescent cognitive development for secondary school teaching. *The High School Journal,* 1962, *45,* 268–275.

Ausubel, D. P. The effects of cultural deprivation on learning patterns. *Audiovisual Instruction,* 1965a, *10,* 10–12.

Ausubel, D. P. *The fern and the tiki: An American view of New Zealand national character, social attitudes and race relations.* New York: Holt, Rinehart & Winston, 1965b.

Ausubel, D. P. *Educational psychology: A cognitive view.* New York: Holt, Rinehart & Winston, 1968.

Ausubel, D. P. Psychology's undervaluation of the rational components in moral behaviour. In C. M. Beck, B. S. Crittenden, & E. V. Sullivan (Eds.), *Moral education—Interdisciplinary approaches.* Toronto: University of Toronto Press, 1971.

Ausubel, D. P., & Kirk, D. *Ego psychology and mental disorder.* New York: Grune & Stratton, 1977.

Ausubel, D. P., & Schiff, H. M. The effect of incidental and experimentally induced experience in the learning of relevant and irrelevant causal relationships by children. *Journal of Genetic Psychology,* 1954, *84,* 190–123.

Ausubel, D. P., & Schiff, H. M. A level of aspiration approach to the measurement of goal tenacity. *Journal of Genetic Psychology,* 1955a, *52,* 97–110.

Ausubel, D. P., & Schiff, H. M. Some intrapersonal and interpersonal determinants of individual differences in socioempathic ability among adolescents. *Journal of Social Psychology,* 1955b, *41,* 39–56.

Ausubel, D. P., Schiff, H. M., & Gasser, E. B. A preliminary study of developmental trends in socioempathy: Accuracy of perception of own and others' sociometric status. *Child Development,* 1952, *23,* 111–128.

Ausubel, D. P., Schiff, H. M., & Zeleny, M. P. "Real-life" measures of academic and vocational aspirations in adolescents: Relation to laboratory measures and to adjustment. *Child Development,* 1953, *24,* 155–168.

Ausubel, D. P., & Sullivan, E. V. *Theory and problems of child development.* New York: Grune & Stratton, 1970.

Baier, K. *The moral point of view: A rational basis of ethics.* New York: Random House, 1966.

Baldwin, J. M. *Social and ethical interpretations in mental development.* New York: Macmillan, 1906.

Baltes, P. B. Longitudinal and cross-sectional sequences in the study of age and generation effects. *Human Development,* 1968, *11,* 145–171.

Baltes, P. B., & Schaie, K. W. (Eds.). *Life-span developmental psychology: Personality and socialization.* New York: Academic Press, 1973.

Bandura, A. The stormy decade: Fact or fiction. *Psychology in the Schools,* 1964, *1,* 224–231.

Banks, L. *Youth in turmoil.* New York: Time-Life Books, 1969.

Baranowski, M. D. Television and the adolescent. *Adolescence,* 1971, *6,* 369–396.

Barbe, W. B. Peer relationships of children of different intelligence levels. *School Society,* 1954, *80,* 60–62.

Bardwick, J. *Psychology of women.* A study of bio-cultural conflicts. New York: Harper & Row, 1971.

Barker, R. G., & Lunn, J. *Streaming in the primary school.* Slough: N.F.E.R., 1970.

Barnett, R. C. Sex differences and age trends in occupational preference and occupational prestige. *Journal of Counseling Psychology,* 1975, *22,* 35–38.

Bartlett, E. R., & Harris, D. B. Personality factors in delinquency. School and Society, 1936, *43,* 653–656.

Bayley, N. Mental and motor development from two to twelve years. *Review of Educational Research,* 1939, *9,* 18–37.

Bayley, N. Some psychological correlates of somatic androgyny. *Child Development,* 1951, *22,* 47–60.

Bayley, N. On the growth of intelligence. *American Psychologist,* 1955, *10,* 805–818.

Bayley, N. Data on the growth of intelligence between 16 and 21 years as measured by the Wechsler-Bellevue Scale. *Journal of Genetic Psychology,* 1957, *90,* 3–15.

Bayley, N. Developmental problems of the mentally retarded child. In I. Phillips (Ed.), *Prevention and treatment of mental retardation* (Part II). New York: Basic Books, 1966.

Bayley, N. Behavioral correlates of mental growth: Birth to 36 years. *American Psychologist,* 1968a, *1,* 1–17.

Bayley, N. Cognition in aging. In K. W. Schaie (Ed.), *Theory and methods of research in aging.* Morgantown: West Virginia University Library, 1968b.

Bayley, N. Development of mental abilities. In P. H. Mussen (Ed.), *Car-*

michael's manual of child psychology (3rd ed.), (Vol. I). New York: Wiley, 1970.

Bayley, N., & Bayer, L. M. The assessment of somatic androgyny. American Journal of Physical Anthropology, 1946, 4, 433–461.

Bayley, N., & Jones, H. E. Environmental correlates of mental and motor development. Child Development, 1937, 8, 329–341.

Bayley, N., & Oden, M. H. The maintenance of intellectual ability in gifted adults. Journal of Gerontology, 1955, 10, 91–107.

Bayley, N., & Tuddenham, R. D. Adolescent changes in body build. In Adolescence, Forty-third Yearbook of the National Society for the Study of Education, Part 1. Chicago: The University of Chicago Press, 1944.

Beach, F. A. Body chemistry and perception. In R. R. Blake & G. V. Ramsey (Eds.), Perception: Approach to personality. New York: Ronald, 1951.

Beck, C. M., Crittenden, B. S., & Sullivan, E. V. Moral education—Interdisciplinary approaches. Toronto: University of Toronto Press, 1971.

Bell, H. M. Youth tell their story. Washington, D.C.: American Council on Education, 1938.

Bell, R. Z. Stimulus control of parent or caretaker behavior by offspring. Developmental Psychology, 1971, 4, 63–72.

Benedict, R. Patterns of culture. Boston: Houghton Mifflin, 1934.

Benedict, R. Continuities and discontinuities in cultural conditioning. Psychiatry, 1938, 1, 161–167.

Bengston, V. L., & Starr, J. M. Contrast and consensus: A generational analysis of youth in the 1980's. In Youth, Seventy-fourth Yearbook of the National Society for the Study of Education, Part 1. Chicago: The University of Chicago Press, 1975.

Bennett, J. K., & Cruikshank, R. M. A summary of manual and mechanical ability tests. New York: Psychological Corporation, 1942.

Berenberg, W. The adolescent with physical handicaps. In J. R. Gallagher, F. P. Heald, & D. C. Garell (Eds.), Medical care of the adolescent (3rd ed.). New York: Appleton-Century, 1976.

Berkowitz, L. Impulse, aggression and the gun. Psychology Today, 1968, 2(4), 18–23.

Berlyne, D. E. Conflict, arousal, and curiosity. New York: McGraw-Hill, 1960.

Berlyne, D. E. The delimitation of cognitive development. In H. W. Stevenson (Ed.), Concept of development: A report of a conference commemorating the fortieth anniversary of the Institute of Child Development, University of Minnesota. Monographs of the Society for Research in Child Development, 1966, 31, 71–81.

Berman, G. S., & Haug, M. R. Occupational and educational goals and expectations: The effects of race and sex. Social Problems, 1975, 23, 166–181.

Berman, Y. Occupational aspirations of 545 female high school seniors. Journal of Vocational Behavior, 1972, 2, 173–177.

Bernard, J. Roles of modern women. New York: American Sociological Association, 1969.

Best, C. H., & Taylor, N. B. Physiological basis of medical practice (J. R. Brodbeck, Ed.), (9th ed.). Baltimore: Williams & Wilkins, 1973.

Bettleheim, B. The special school for emotionally disturbed children. In *Juvenile delinquency and the schools, The Forty-seventh Yearbook of the National Society for the Study of Education,* Part I. Chicago: The University of Chicago Press, 1948.

Bettleheim, B. The special school for emotionally disturbed children. In *Juvenile delinquency and the schools, The Forty-seventh Yearbook of the National Society for the Study of Education,* Part I. Chicago: The University of Chicago Press, 1975.

Betts, G. H. Religious attitudes and activities of university students: A report. *Religious Education,* 1928, *23,* 917–919.

Bieber, I. Sexual deviations. II. Homosexuality. In A. M. Freedman & H. I. Kaplan (Eds.), *Comprehensive textbook of psychiatry.* Baltimore: Williams & Wilkins, 1967.

Bird, C., Monachosi, E. D., & Burdick, A. Studies of group tensions: III. The effect of parental discouragement of play attitudes of white children toward Negroes. *Child Development,* 1952, *23,* 295–306.

Blake, R., & Dennis, W. The development of stereotypes concerning the Negro. *Journal of Abnormal and Social Psychology,* 1943, *38,* 525–531.

Blanchard, P. Adolescent experience in relation to personality and behavior. In J. McV. Hunt (Ed.), *Personality and the behavior disorders* (Vol. II). New York: Ronald, 1944.

Block, V. L. Conflicts of adolescents with their mothers. *Journal of Abnormal and Social Psychology,* 1937, *32,* 192–206.

Blos, P. *The adolescent personality: A study of individual behavior.* New York: Appleton-Century, 1941.

Blum, L. H. The discotheque and the phenomenon of alone-togetherness: A study of the young person's response to the frug and comparable current dances. *Adolescence,* 1966–67, *1,* 351–366.

Blum, S. H. The desire for security in vocational choice: A comparison of men and women. *Journal of Psychology,* 1975, *91,* 277–281.

Blumenfeld, W. Sports preferences of high school students as defined by reported participation. *Research Quarterly,* 1965, *36,* 205–206.

Boas, F. Studies in growth. *Human Biology,* 1932, *4,* 307–350.

Boehm, L. The development of conscience: A comparison of American children of different mental and socioeconomic levels. *Child Development,* 1962, *33,* 575–590.

Boehm, L. The development of conscience: A comparison of students in Catholic parochial schools and in public schools. *Child Development,* 1962, *33,* 591–602.

Boehm, L. Moral judgment: A cultural and sub-cultural comparison with some of Piaget's research conclusions. *International Journal of Psychology,* 1966, *1*(2), 143–150.

Boehm, L., & Nass, N. L. Social class differences in conscience development. *Child Development,* 1962, *33,* 565–574.

Bonney, M. E. The relative stability of social, intellectual, and academic status in grades II to IV, and the inter-relationships between these various forms of growth. *Journal of Educational Psychology,* 1943, *34,* 88–102.

Bordua, D. J. Sociological perspectives. In *Social deviancy among youth, The Sixty-fifth Yearbook of the National Society for the Study of Education,* Part 1. Chicago: The University of Chicago Press, 1975.

Boshier, R., & Taylor, A. J. The generation gap: Attitudinal differences between parents and their children in New Zealand. *New Zealand Journal of Educational Studies,* 1972, 7, 130–140.

Boszormenyi-Nagy, I. A theory of relationships: Experience and transactions. In I. Boszormenyi-Nagy & J. L. Framo (Eds.), *Intensive family therapy.* New York: Harper & Row, 1965.

Boszormenyi-Nagy, I., & Framo, J. L. (Eds.). *Intensive family therapy.* New York: Harper & Row (Hoedes), 1965.

Bovet, L. *Psychiatric aspects of juvenile delinquency.* Geneva: World Health Organization, 1951.

Bowerman, C. E., & Elder, G. H., Jr. The adolescent and his family. Unpublished manuscript, 1962.

Bowerman, C. E., & Kinch, J. W. Changes in family and peer orientation of children between the fourth and tenth grades. *Social Forces,* 1959, 37, 206–211.

Bowles, G. T. *New types of old Americans at Harvard and Eastern women's colleges.* Cambridge, Mass.: Harvard University Press, 1932.

Bowman, P., & Matthews, Ch. V. *Abstract of motivations for leaving school.* Quincy, Ill.: Quincy Youth Development Project, 1960.

Boyd, W. *A textbook of pathology* (7th ed.). Philadelphia: Lea & Febiger, 1961.

Bradley, F. O., & Newhouse, R. C. Sociometric choice and self perceptions of upper elementary school children. *Psychology in the Schools,* 1975, 12, 219–222.

Bradway, K. P., & Thompson, C. W. Intelligence at adulthood: A twenty-five year follow-up. *Journal of Educational Psychology,* 1962, 5, 1–14.

Braun, C. Teacher expectation: Socio-psychological dynamics. *Review of educational research,* Spring, 1976, 46, 185–213.

Bretsch, H. S. Social skills and activities of socially accepted and unaccepted adolescents. *Journal of Educational Psychology,* 1952, 43, 449–458.

Brigham, J. C. Views of black and white children concerning the distribution of personality characteristics. *Journal of Personality,* 1974, 42, 144–158.

Brink, W. G. Reading interests of high school pupils. *School Review,* 1939, 47, 613–621.

Brittain, C. V. Adolescent choices and parent-peer cross-pressures. *American Sociological Review,* 1963, 28, 385–391.

Brittain, C. V. A comparison of rural and urban adolescents with respect to parent vs. peer compliance. *Adolescence,* 1969, 13, 59–68.

Broderick, C. Social heterosexual development among urban Negroes and whites. *Journal of Marriage and the Family,* 1965, 27, 200–203.

Broderick, C. B., & Fowler, S. E. New patterns of relationships between the sexes among preadolescents. *Journal of Marriage and the Family,* 1961, 23, 27–30.

Bronfenbrenner, U. The role of age, sex, class, and culture in studies of moral development. *Religious Education,* 1962, *57,* (4), 3–17.

Bronfenbrenner, U. *Two worlds of childhood: US and USSSR.* New York: Russell-Sage Foundation, 1970.

Bronfenbrenner, U., & Devereux, Jr., E. C. Standards of social behavior among children in four cultures. *International Journal of Psychology,* 1968, *III,* 31–41.

Brough, J. R., & Reeves, M. L. Activities of suburban and inter-city youth. *Personnel and Guidance Journal,* 1968, *47,* 209–212.

Brown, C. *Manchild in the promised land.* New York: Signet Books, 1965.

Brown, C. Teacher expectation: Sociopsychological dynamics. *Review of Educational Research,* Spring, 1976, *46,* 185–213.

Brown, L. B. Some attitudes underlying petitionary prayer. In A. Godin (Ed.), *From cry to word.* Brussels: Lumen Vitae Press, 1968.

Bruch, H. Anorexia nervosa in adolescents. In R. Gallagher, F. P. Heald, & D. C. Garell (Eds.), *Medical care of the adolescent* (3rd ed.). New York: Appleton-Century, 1976.

Bull, N. J. *Moral judgment from childhood to adolescence.* Beverly Hills, Calif.: Sage Publications, 1969.

Burchinal, L. G. The premarital dyad and love involvement. In H. T. Christensen (Ed.), *Handbook of marriage and the family.* Chicago: Rand McNally, 1964.

Burgess, E. W., & Wallin, P. Homogamy in social characteristics. *American Journal of Sociology,* 1943, *49,* 109–124.

Burgess, E. W., & Wallin, P. Homogamy in personality characteristics. *Journal of Abnormal Social Psychology,* 1944, *39,* 475–481.

Burt, C. *The young delinquent.* New York: Appleton, 1925.

Butler, D. *Runaway house handbook.* Washington, D.C.: U.S. Government Printing Office, 1973.

Butler, R. A. Incentive conditions which influence visual exploration. *Journal of Experimental Psychology,* 1954, *48,* 19–32.

Butterfield, O. M. *Love problems of adolescence.* New York: Teachers College, Columbia University, 1939.

Byrne, D., & Griffith, W. B. A developmental investigation of the law of attraction. *Journal of Personality and Social Psychology,* 1966, *4,* 699–702.

Byrns, R. Relation of vocational choice to mental ability and occupational opportunity. *School Review,* 1939, *47,* 101–109.

Cabell, C. C. Diabetes. In J. R. Gallagher, F. P. Heald, & D. C. Garell (Eds.), *Medical care of the adolescent.* New York: Appleton-Century, 1976.

Caldwell, O. W., & Lundeen, Y. E. Further study of unfounded beliefs among junior-high-school pupils. *Teachers College Record,* 1934, *36,* 35–52.

Campbell, A. A. Factors associated with attitudes toward Jews. In T. M. Newcomb & E. L. Hartley (Eds.), *Readings in social psychology.* New York: Holt, 1947.

Campbell, J. B. Peer relations in childhood. In M. L. Hoffman & L. M. Hoffman (Eds.), *Review of child development research* (Vol. 1). New York: Russell-Sage Foundation, 1964.

Cannon, K. L., & Long, R. Premarital sexual behavior in the sixties. *Journal of Marriage and the Family*, 1971, *33*, 36–49.

Cantor, N. *The dynamics of learning*. Buffalo: Foster and Stewart, 1946.

Cantor, N. *The teaching-learning process:* A study in interpersonal relations. New York: Dryden, 1953.

Cantwell, Z., & Svajian, P. N. (Eds.). *Adolescence—Studies in development.* Itasca: F. E. Peacock, 1974.

Carey, T. F. *The relation of physical growth to developmental age in boys.* Washington, D.C.: Catholic University of America, 1935.

Carlsmith, K. K. Effect of early father absence on scholastic aptitude. Unpublished doctoral dissertation, Harvard University, 1963.

Carter, H. D. The development of interest in vocations. In *Adolescence, The Forty-third Yearbook of the National Society for the Study of Education,* Part I. Chicago: The University of Chicago Press, 1944.

Carter, T. M. Comparison of the attitudes of college men with the attitudes of college women in regard to fellowship behavior. *Journal of Social Psychology*, 1941, *14*, 145–158.

Case, D., & Collinson, J. M. The development of formal thinking in verbal comprehension. *British Journal of Educational Psychology*, June, 1962, *32*, 103–111.

Cass, J. C., & Tiedeman, D. V. Vocational development, the election of a secondary school curriculum, and public policy. Harvard studies in career development (No. 13). Cambridge, Mass.: Unpublished manuscript, Graduate School of Education, Harvard University, 1959.

Cattell, R. B. Personality traits associated with abilities. I. With intelligence and drawing abilities. *Educational and Psychological Measurement*, 1945, *5*, 131–146.

Cattell, R. B. Theory of fluid and crystallized intelligence. *Journal of Educational Psychology*, 1963, *54*, 1–22.

Cegelka, P. T., Omvig, C., & Larimore, D. L. Effects of aptitude and sex on vocational interests. *Measurement and Evaluation in Guidance*, 1974, *7*, 106–111.

Chabassol, D. J., & Thomas, D. C. Sex and age differences in problems and interests of adolescents. *The Journal of Experimental Education*, 1969, *38* (2), 16–23.

Challman, R. C. Factors influencing friendships among preschool children. *Child Development*, 1932, *3*, 146–158.

Chowdry, K., & Newcomb, T. M. The relative abilities of leaders and non-leaders to estimate opinions of their own groups. *Journal of Abnormal Social Psychology*, 1952, *47*, 51–57.

Christensen, T. E. *Getting job experience.* Chicago: Science Research Associates, 1949.

Clausen, J. A. (Ed.). *Socialization and society.* Boston: Little, Brown & Co., 1968.

Clausen, J. A., & Williams, J. Sociological correlates of child behavior. In H. W. Stevenson (Ed.), *Child psychology, The Sixty-second Yearbook of The National Society for the Study of Education,* Part I. Chicago: The University of Chicago Press, 1963.

Cleary, T. A. New directions for career planning. In L. McClure & C. Brean (Eds.), *Essays on career education.* Portland, Oregon: Northwest Regional Educational Laboratory, 1973, 39–55.

Clifford, C., & Cohn, T. S. The relationship between leadership and personality attributes perceived by followers. *Journal of Social Psychology,* 1964, *64,* 57–64.

Clifford, E. Body ratifaction in adolescence. *Perceptual and Motor Skills,* 1971, *33,* 119–125.

Cloward, R. A., & Ohlin, L. E. *Delinquency and opportunity.* New York: Free Press (Macmillan), 1960.

Coates, Th. J., & Thoresen, C. E. Teacher anxiety: A review with recommendations. *Review of Educational Research,* 1976, *46,* 159–184.

Cohen, A. K. *Delinquent boys: The culture of the gang.* Glencoe, Ill.: Free Press, 1955.

Cohen, Y. A. *The transition from childhood to adolescence.* Chicago: Aldine, 1964.

Cole, L. *Psychology of adolescence.* New York: Rinehart, 1948.

Cole, L., & Hall, J. N. *Psychology of adolesence* (7th ed.). New York: Holt, Rinehart and Winston, Inc., 1970.

Coleman, J. S. Academic achievement and the structure of competition. *Harvard Educational Review,* 1959, *29,* 330–351.

Coleman, J. S. *The adolescent society.* New York: Free Press, 1961.

Coleman, W., & Ward, A. H. A comparison of Davis-Eells and Kuhlmann-Finch scores of children from high and low socioeconomic status. *Journal of Educational Psychology,* 1955, *46,* 465–469.

Cole, R. *Erik H. Erikson: The growth of his work.* Boston: Little, Brown & Co., 1970.

Collins, J. K. Adolescent dating intimacy: Norms and peer expectations. *Journal of Youth and Adolescence,* 1974, *3,* 317–328.

Collins, J. K., & Thomas, N. T. Developmental study of conformity to unlike-sex peer pressure. *Perceptual and Motor Skills,* 1974, *38,* 75–78.

Collins, R. Functional and conflict theories of educational stratification. *American Sociological Review,* 1971, *36,* 1002–1019.

Combs, A. W. Fostering maximum development of the individual. In *Issues in secondary education, The Seventy-fifth Yearbook of the National Society for the Study of Education,* Part II. Chicago: The University of Chicago Press, 1976.

Conant, J. B. *Slums and suburbs.* New York: McGraw-Hill, 1961.

Conrad, H. S., Freeman, F. N., & Jones, H. E. Differential mental growth. In *Adolescence, The Forty-third Yearbook of the National Society for the Study of Education,* Part 1. Chicago: The University of Chicago Press, 1944.

Cook, W. W., Leeds, C. H., & Callis, R. *The Minnesota Teacher Attitude Inventory.* New York: Psychological Corporation, 1951.

Corey, S. M., & Beary, G. S. The effect of teacher popularity upon attitudes toward school subjects. *Journal of Educational Psychology,* 1938, *29,* 665–670.

Cornbleth, C., David, O. L., Jr., & Button, C. Expectations for pupil achievement and teacher-pupil interaction. *Social Education,* 1974, *38,* 54–58.

Costanzo, P. R., & Shaw, M. E. Conformity as a function of age level. *Child Development,* 1966, *37,* 967–975.

Cowley, W. H. The traits of face to face leaders. *Journal of Abnormal Social Psychology,* 1931, *26,* 304–313.

Crampton, C. W. Physiological age as a fundamental principle. *Child Development,* 1944, *15,* 1–42.

Creson, D. L., & Blakeney, P. M. Social structure in an adolescent milieu program: Implications for treatment. *Adolescence,* 1970, *5,* 407–426.

Crisswell, J. H. Sociometric study of race cleavage in the classroom. *Archives of Psychology,* 1939, *33* (235).

Cronbach, L. J. *Essentials of psychological testing.* New York: Harper, 1949.

Cronbach, L. J. *Essentials of psychological testing* (3rd ed.). New York: Harper & Row, 1970.

Cunning, G. R., Garand, T., & Borysk, L. Correlation of performance in track and field events with bone age. *Journal of Pediatrics,* 1972, *80,* 970.

Cunningham, D. A., Montoye, H. J., Metzner, H. L., & Keller, J. B. Active leisure time activities as related to age among males in total population. American Association for Health, Physical Education and Recreational Research Abstracts, 1968, p. 106.

Cunningham, R., Elzi, A., Hall, J. A., Roberts, M., & Farrell, M. L. *Understanding group behavior of boys and girls.* New York: Teachers College, Columbia University, 1951.

Curle, A. Incentives to work: An anthropological appraisal. *Human Relations,* 1949, *2,* 41–47.

Dai, B. Some problems of personality development among Negro children. In C. Kluckhohn & H. A. Murray (Eds.), *Personality in nature, society and culture.* New York: Knopf, 1949.

Davidson, H. H., & Lang, G. Children's perceptions of their teachers' feelings towards them related to self-perception, school achievement, and behavior. *Journal of Experimental Education,* 1960, *29,* 377–383.

Davidson, P. E., & Anderson, H. D. *Occupational mobility in an American community.* Stanford, Calif.: Stanford University Press, 1937.

Davis, A. American status systems and the socialization of the child. *American Sociological Review,* 1941, *6,* 345–354.

Davis, A. Socialization and adolescent personality. In *Adolescence, The Forty-third Yearbook of the National Society for the Study of Education,* Part 1. Chicago: The University of Chicago Press, 1944.

Davis, A. *Social class influences upon learning.* Cambridge, Mass.: Harvard University Press, 1948.

Davis, A., & Dollard, J. *Children of bondage*. Washington, D.C. American Council on Education, 1940.

Davis, A., Gitelson, M., Henry, W., & Ross, H. *Adolescents in American culture*. Chicago: University of Chicago Round Tables, 1949 (576).

Demos, G. D. Attitudes of student ethnic groups on issues related to education. *California Journal of Educational Research*, 1960, *11*, 204–206.

Dennis, W. The adolescent. In L. Carmichael (Ed.), *Handbook of child psychology*. New York: Wiley, 1946.

Desjardins, M. Reading and viewing: A survey. *School Libraries*, 1972, *21*, 26–30.

Despert, J. L., & Pierce, H. O. The relation of emotional adjustment to intellectual function. *Genetic Psychology Monographs*, 1946, *34*, 3–56.

Deutsch, C. Social class and child development. In B. M. Caldwell & H. N. Ricciuti (Eds.), *Review of child development research* (Vol. 3). Chicago: The University of Chicago Press, 1973.

Devereux, E. C. The role of peer-group experience in moral development. In J. P. Hill (Ed.), *Minnesota symposia on child psychology* (Vol. 4). Minneapolis: The University of Minnesota Press, 1970.

Dewey, J. *Moral principles in education* (1909). New York: Philosophical Library, 1959.

Dillon, H. J. *Early school leavers*. New York: National Child Labor Committee, 1949.

Dimock, H. A. *Rediscovering the adolescent*. New York: Association Press, 1937.

Dixon, M. M. Adolescent girls talk about themselves. *Marriage and Family Living*, 1958, *20*, 400–401.

Doane, D. C. *The needs of youth: An evaluation for curriculum purposes*. New York: Teachers College, Columbia University, 1942.

Dole, A. A., & Passons, W. R. Life goals and plan determinants reported by black and white high school seniors. *Journal of Vocational Behavior*, 1972, *2*, 209–222.

Dollard, J., Miller, N. E., Doob, L. W., Mowrer, O. H., & Sears, R. R. *Frustration and aggression*. New Haven: Yale University Press, 1939.

Donovan, B. T., & Van der Werff Ten Bosch, J. J. *Physiology of puberty*. Baltimore: Williams & Wilkins, 1965.

Douvan, E., & Adelson, J. *The adolescent experience*. New York: Wiley, 1966.

Douvan, E., & Gold, M. Model patterns in American adolescence, pp. 469–528. In L. W. Hoffman & M. L. Hoffman (Eds.), *Review of child development research* (Vol. 2). New York: Russell-Sage Foundation, 1966.

Dowell, L. J. Indoor recreation games of freshman and sophomore college men. Unpublished doctoral dissertation, University of Missouri, 1959.

Dreyer, Ph. D. Sex, sex roles, and marriage among youth in the 1970s. In *Youth, The Seventy-fourth Yearbook of the National Society for the Study of Education*, Part 1. Chicago: The University of Chicago Press, 1975.

Dudycha, G. J. The superstitious beliefs of college students. *Journal of Applied Psychology*, 1933, *17*, 586–603.

Duffy, E., & Crissy, W. J. E. Evaluative attitudes as related to vocational interests and academic achievement. *Journal of Abnormal Social Psychology*, 1940, *35*, 226–245.

Dunbar, H. F. Emotion and bodily changes. New York: Columbia University Press, 1938.

Dunlap, J. W. Preferences as indicators of specific academic achievement. *Journal of Educational Psychology*, 1935, *26*, 411–415.

Dunphy, D. C. The social structure of urban adolescents in peer groups. *Sociometry*, 1963, *26*, 230–246.

Durost, W. N. *Children's collecting activity related to social factors.* New York: Teachers College, Columbia University, 1932.

Dyer, D. T. The relation between vocational interests of men in college and their subsequent occupational histories for ten years. *Journal of Applied Psychology*, 1939, *23*, 280–288.

Dyk, R. B., & Witkin, H. B. Family experience related to the development of differentiation in children. *Child Development*, 1965, *36*, 21–55.

Dysinger, W. S. Maturation and vocational guidance. *Occupations*, 1950, *29*, 198–201.

Eagleson, O. W. Students' reactions to their given names. *Journal of Social Psychology*, 1946, *23*, 187–195.

Easton, D., & Dennis, J. *Children in the political system.* New York: McGraw-Hill, 1969.

Eberhart, J. C. Attitudes toward property. A genetic study by the paired-comparison rating of offenses. *Journal of Genetic Psychology*, 1942, *60*, 3–35.

Edwards, N. The adolescent in technological society. *Adolescence, The Forty-third Yearbook of the National Society for the Study of Education*, Part 1. Chicago: The University of Chicago Press, 1944.

Eells, K., Davis, A., Havighurst, R. J., Herrick, V. E., & Tyler, R. W. *Intelligence and cultural differences: A study of cultural learning and problem solving.* Chicago: The University of Chicago Press, 1951.

Eisenstadt, S. N. Archetypal patterns of youth. In E. H. Eriksen (Ed.), *Youth: Change and challenge.* New York: Basic Books, 1963

Elashoff, D. J., Dixon, J., & Snow, R. E. *Pygmalion reconsidered: A case study in statistical inference: Reconsideration of the Rosenthal-Jacobson data on teacher expectancy.* Belmont, Calif.: Wadsworth Publishing Co., 1971.

Elder, G. H., Jr. Parental power legitimation and its effect on the adolescent. *Sociometry*, 1963, *26*, 50–65.

Elder, V., & Carpenter, H. S. Reading interests of high school children. *Journal of Educational Research*, 1929, *19*, 276–282.

Elkind, D. The developmental psychology of religion. In A. H. Kidd and J. L. Rivoire (Eds.), *Perceptual development in children.* New York: International Universities Press, 1966.

Elkind, D. Egocentrism in adolescence. *Child Development*, 1967, *38*, 1025–1034.

Elkins, D. Some factors related to the choice status of ninety eighth-grade children in a school society. *Genetic Psychology Monographs,* 1958, *58,* 207–272.

Ellis, H. *Studies in the psychology of sex.* New York: Random House, 1936.

Empey, L. T. Delinquency theory and recent research. *Journal of Research in Crime and Delinquency,* 1967, *4,* 28–42.

Erickson, M. L., & Empey, L. T. Court records, undetected delinquency, and decision-making. *Journal of Criminal Law, Criminology, and Police Science,* December, 1963, 456–469.

Erikson, E. *Childhood and society.* New York: Norton, 1950.

Erikson, E. A memorandum on identity and Negro youth. *The Journal of Social Issues,* 1964, *20,* 29–42.

Erikson, E. Youth: Fidelity and diversity. In E. Erikson (Ed.), *The challenge of youth.* New York: Doubleday, 1965.

Erikson, E. *Identity youth and crisis.* New York: Norton, 1968.

Escalona, S. *The roots of individuality.* Chicago: Aldine Publishing Co., 1968.

Espenschade, A. Motor performance in adolescence. *Monographs of the Society for Research in Child Development,* 1940, *5,* (1).

Espenschade, A. A., & Eckert, H. *Motor development.* Columbus, Ohio: Charles Merrill, 1967.

Feinberg, M. R., & Fryer, D. H. An investigation of the background experiences of socially accepted and rejected adolescents at three economic levels. *American Psychologist,* 1950, *5,* 355 (Abstract).

Feinstein, S. C., & Ardon, M. S. Trends in dating patterns and adolescent development. *Journal of Youth and Adolescence,* 1973, *2,* 157–166.

Feshback, S. Aggression. In P. H. Mussen (Ed.), *Carmichael's manual of child psychology.* New York: Wiley, 1970.

Fey, W. F. Acceptance by others and its relation to acceptance of self and others: A re-evaluation. *Journal of Abnormal and Social Psychology,* 1955, *50,* 274–276.

Finch, F. H., & Odoroff, M. E. Sex differences in vocational interests. *Journal of Educational Psychology,* 1939, *30,* 151–156.

Finger, F. W. Changes in sex practices and beliefs of male college students: Over 30 years. *Journal of Sex Research,* 1975, *11,* 304–317.

Flake, M. H., Roach, A. J., Jr., & Stenning, W. F. Effects of short-term counseling on career maturity of tenth-grade students. *Journal of Vocational Behavior,* 1975, *6,* 73–80.

Flanagan, J. C. The need for improved vocational guidance. In U.S. Department of Health, Education, and Welfare Office of Education. Summary of papers presented at the Fourth Symposium for Systems under Development of Vocational Guidance. Washington: U.S. Government Printing Office, 1969, 1–2.

Flanagan, J. C. The first 15 years of project TALENT: Implications for career guidance. *Vocational Guidance Quarterly,* 1973a, *22*(September), 8–14.

Flanagan, J. C. Some pertinent findings of project TALENT. *Vocational Guidance Quarterly,* 1973b, *22,* 92–96.

Flanders, N. A. Teacher influence in the classroom. In A. A. Bellock (Ed.),

Theory and research in teaching. New York: Teachers College, Columbia University, 1963.

Fleege, U. H. *Self-revelation of the adolescent boy.* Milwaukee: Bruce, 1945.

Fleming, C. M. *Adolescence: It social psychology.* New York: International
Universities Press, 1949.

Ford, C. S., & Beach, F. A. *Patterns of sexual behavior.* New York: Harper &
Row, 1951.

Frank, L. K. Adolescence as a period of transition. In *Adolescence, The Forty-
third Yearbook of the National Society for the Study of Education,* Part
1. Chicago: The University of Chicago Press, 1944a.

Frank, L. K. The adolescent and the family. In *Adolescence, The Forty-third
Yearbook of the National Society for the Study of Education,* Part 1.
Chicago: The University of Chicago Press, 1944b.

Franzblau, A. N. *Religious belief and character among Jewish adolescents.*
New York: Teachers College, Columbia University, 1934.

Frazier, E. F. *Negro youth at crossways.* New York: Schocken Books, 1967.

Fredrickson, L. C. Value structure of college students. *Journal of Youth and
Adolescence,* 1972, *1,* 155–163.

Freedman, M. K. Sociopathic personality disorders. I. Sociological aspects of
juvenile delinquency. In A. M. Freedman & H. I. Kaplan (Eds.), *Comprehensive textbook of psychiatry.* Baltimore: Williams & Wilkins,
1967.

Freedman, M. K. Sociological aspects of juvenile delinquency. In A. M. Freedman & H. I. Kaplan (Eds.), *The child: His psychological and cultural development: II. The major psychological disorders and their treatment.*
New York: Atheneum, 1972.

Freeman, F. A. Intellectual growth of children as indicated by repeated tests.
Psychological Monographs, 1936, *47,* 20–34.

Freeman, F. N., & Flory, C. D. Growth in intellectual ability as measured by
repeated tests. *Monographs of the Society for Research in Child Development,* 1937, Vol. II (No. 2), Serial No 9).

Freiberger, Rima. *The New York Times report on teenage reading tasks and
habits.* New York: New York Times Co., 1974.

French, J. R. P., & Raven, B. The basis of social power. In D. Cartwright (Ed.),
Studies in social power. Ann Arbor: University of Michigan, 1959,
150–167.

Frenkel-Brunswick, E. Patterns of social and cognitive outlooks in children
and parents. *American Journal of Orthopsychiatry,* 1951, *21,* 543–558.

Freud, A. *The ego and the mechanisms of defense.* New York: International
Universities Press, 1946.

Freud, A. Adolescence. *Psychoanalytic Study of the Child,* 1958, *13,* 92–117.

Freud, A. Adolescence. In A. E. Winder & D. L. Angus (Eds.), *Adolescence:
Contemporary studies.* New York: American Book, 1968.

Freud, S. *The problem of anxiety.* New York: Norton, 1936.

Freud, S. *A general introduction to psychoanalysis.* New York: Washington
Square Press, 1952.

Freud, S. Three essays on sexuality. In *Standard edition* of the *Complete psy-*

chological works of Sigmund Freud (Vol. VII). London: Hogarth Press, 1953–1974.

Friedman, L. N., Gold, A. R., & Christie, R. Dissecting the generation gap: Intergenerational and intrafamilial similarities and differences. *Public Opinion Quarterly,* 1972, *36,* 334–346.

Furfey, P. H. A revised scale for measuring developmental age in boys. *Child Development,* 1931, *2,* 102–114.

Furfey, P. H. Some factors influencing the selection of boys' "chums." *Journal of Applied Psychology,* 1927, *11,* 47–51.

Gallagher, J. R. *Medical care of the adolescent: A textbook concerning the medical care and understanding of adolescents themselves and their disorders.* New York: Appleton, 1960.

Gallagher, J. R. Productive thinking. In M. L. Hoffman & L. W. Hoffman (Eds.), *Review of child development research* (Vol. 1). New York: Russell-Sage Foundation, 1964, 349–381.

Gallagher, J. R., & Harris, J. *Emotional problems of adolescents* (3rd ed.). New York: Oxford University Press, 1976.

Gallagher, J. R., Heald, F. P., & Garell, D. C. (Eds.). *Medical care of the adolescent* (3rd ed.). New York: Appleton-Century, 1976.

Ganzer, V. J., & Sarason, I. G. Variables associated with recidivism among juvenile delinquents. *Journal of Consulting and Clinical Psychology,* 1973, *40,* 1–5.

Gardner, G. E. The mental health of normal adolescents. *Mental Hygiene,* 1947, *31,* 529–540.

Garrett, H. E., Bryan, A. I., & Perl, R. E. The age factor in mental organization. *Archives of Psychology,* 1935, (January, no. 176), 5–29.

Gewirtz, J. L. Mechanisms of social learning: Some roles of stimulation and behavior in early human development. In D. A. Goslin (Ed.), *Handbook of socialization theory and research.* Chicago: Rand McNally, 1969.

Gianturco, D. T., & Smith, H. L. *The promiscuous teenager.* Springfield, Ill.: Thomas, 1974.

Gilbert, H. H. High-school students' opinions on reasons for failure in high-school subjects. *Journal of Educational Research,* 1931, *23,* 46–49.

Gilchrist, J. W. Social psychology and group processes. *Annual Review of Psychology,* 1959, *10,* 233–264.

Gilliand, A. R. The attitude of college students toward God and the church. *Journal of Social Psychology,* 1940, *11,* 11–18.

Ginzberg, E., Ginsburg, S. W., Axelrod, S., & Herma, J. L. *Occupational choice.* New York: Columbia University Press, 1951.

Glueck, S., & Glueck, E. T. *Five hundred criminal careers.* New York: Knopf, 1933.

Glueck, S., & Glueck, E. T. *Unraveling juvenile delinquency.* New York: Commonwealth Fund, 1950.

Glueck, S., & Glueck, E. T. *Delinquents in the making: paths to prevention.* New York: Harper, 1952.

Glueck, S., & Glueck, E. T. *Later criminal careers.* New York: Commonwealth Fund, 1973.

Godenne, G. D. Sex and today's youth. *Adolescence,* 1974, *9,* 33, 67–72.

Goldman, R. *Religious thinking from childhood to adolescence.* London: Routledge, 1964.

Goldman, R. J. The application of Piaget's schema of operational thinking to religious story data by means of the Guttman scalogram. *British Journal of Educational Psychology,* June, 1965, *35,* 158–170.

Goldsen, R. K., Rosenberg, M., Williams, R. M., Jr., & Suchman, E. A. *What college students think.* Princeton, N.J.: Van Nostrand, 1960.

Good, L. R., & Good, K. C. Similarity of attitudes and attraction to a social organization. *Psychological Reports,* 1974, *34,* 1071–1073.

Goodenough, F. L. The relation of the intelligence of preschool children to the education of their parents. *School and Society,* 1927, *26,* 1–3.

Goodenough, F. L. *Developmental psychology.* New York: Appleton-Century, 1945.

Goodenough, W. H. *Property, kin, and community on Truk.* New Haven: Yale University Publication in Anthropology, No. 46, 1951.

Gordon, C. Social characteristics of early adolescence. In J. Kagan & R. Coles (Eds.), *Twelve to sixteen: Early adolescence.* New York: Norton, 1972.

Gordon, C., & Shea, P. D. *Self-conceptions in family structures of disadvantaged youths.* An interim report for the Director of Upward Bound. Prepared for presentation during Session on Poverty at the Sixty-second Annual Meeting of the American Sociological Association in San Francisco, California, August, 1967.

Gottlieb, D. Activist youth today. In H. D. Thornburg (Ed.), *Contemporary adolescence: Readings.* Belmont, Calif.: Brooks/Cole, 1971.

Gottlieb, D., & Ramsey, C. E. *The American adolescent.* Homewood, Ill.: Dorsey Press, 1964.

Gough, H. G., Barris, D. B., Martin, W. E., & Edwards, M. Children's ethnic attitudes: I. Relationship to certain personality factors. *Child Development,* 1950, *21,* 83–91.

Gould, H. N., & Gould, M. R. Age of first menstruation in mothers and daughters. *Journal of the American Medical Association,* 1932, *98,* 1349–1352.

Goulet, L. R., & Baltes, P. B. (Eds.), *Lifespan developmental psychology: Research and theory.* New York: Academic Press, 1970.

Graham, D. *Moral learning and development—theory and research.* New York: Wiley, 1972.

Greulich, W. W. Physical changes in adolescence. In *Adolescence, The Forty-third Yearbook of the National Society for the Study of Education,* Part 1. Chicago: The University of Chicago Press, 1944.

Greulich, W. W. The rationale of assessing the development of children from roentgenograms of the hand and wrist. *Child Development,* 1950, *21,* 33–44.

Greulich, W. W., Dorfman, R. I. Catchpole, H. R., Solomon, C. I., & Culotta, C. S. Somatic and endocrine studies of pubertal and adolescent boys. *Monographs of the Society for Research in Child Development,* 1942, *7,* No. 3.

Grinder, R. E. The concept of adolescence in the genetic psychology of G. Stanley Hall. *Child Development,* 1969, *40,* 355–369.

Grinder, R. E. (Ed.). *Adolescence* (3rd ed.). New York: Wiley, 1973.

Grunlund, N. E., & Anderson, L. Personality characteristics of socially neglected, and socially accepted, socially neglected, and socially rejected junior high school pupils. In R. E. Muuss (Ed.), *Adolescent behavior and society: A book of readings.* New York: Random House, 1971. (Reprinted from *Educational Administration and Supervision,* 1953, *43.*)

Gundlach, R. H. Childhood parental relationships and the establishment of gender roles of homosexuals. *Journal of Consulting and Clinical Psychology,* 1969, *33,* 136–139.

Gustin, J. C. The revolt of youth. *Psychoanalysis and the Psychoanalytic Review,* 1961, *98,* 78–90.

Haan, N., & Block, J. Further studies between activism and morality. I. *The protest of pure and mixed moral stages.* Berkeley, Calif.: Institute of Human Development, 1969a.

Haan, N., & Block, J. Further studies in the relationship between activism and morality. II. *Analysis of cases deviant with respect to the morality-activism relationships.* Berkeley, Calif.: Institute of Human Development, 1969b.

Haan, N., Smith, M. B., & Block, J. Moral reasoning of young adults: Political social behavior, family background, and personality correlates. *Journal of Personality and Social Psychology,* 1968, *10,* 183–201.

Habbe, S. Nicknames of adolescent boys. *American Journal of Orthopsychiatry,* 1937, *7,* 371–377.

Hacker, F. J., & Geleerd, E. R. Freedom and authority in adolescence. *American Journal of Orthopsychiatry,* 1945, *15,* 621–630.

Haeckel, E. *Evolution of man* (Vol. 2). London: Kegan Paul, 1879.

Hall, G. S. *Adolescence* (Vols. I and II). New York: Appleton, 1904.

Hall, P. F. Gonadotrophic regulation of testicular functions. In K. B. Eik-Ries (Ed.), *The androgens of the testes.* New York: Dekker, 1973, 73–115.

Haller, A. O., & Butterworth, C. E. Peer influences on levels of occupational and educational aspiration. *Social Forces,* 1960, *38,* 289–295.

Hamilton, G. V. *An introduction to objective psvchobiology.* St. Louis: Mosby, 1925.

Hamilton, G. V., & MacGowan, K. *What is wrong with marriage?* New York: Boni, 1928.

Hankins, D. The psychology and direct treatment of adolescents. *Mental Hygiene,* 1943, *27,* 238–247.

Hanower, M. R. Social status and the moral development of the child. *British Journal of Educational Psychology,* 1934, *1,* 75–95.

Hanson, J. T., & Sander, D. L. Differential effects of individual and group counseling on realism of vocational choice. *Journal of Counseling Psychology,* 1973, *20,* 541–544.

Hargreaves, D. H. *Social relations in a secondary school.* London: Routledge, 1967.

Harlow, H. F. Learning and satiation of response in intrinsically motivated complex puzzle performance by monkeys. *Journal of Comparative Physiology and Psychology,* 1950, *43,* 289–294.

Harms, E. The development of religious experience in children. *American Journal of Sociology,* 1944, *50,* 112–122.

Harris, H. I. Psychologic and psychiatric problems. In J. R. Gallagher, F. P. Heald, & D. C. Garell (Eds.), *Medical care of the adolescent* (3rd ed.). New York: Appleton-Century, 1976.

Harris, J. A., Jackson, C. M., Paterson, D. G., & Scammon, R. D. *The measurement of man.* Minneapolis: University of Minnesota Press, 1930.

Harris, L. Change, yes—upheaval, no. *Life,* January 8, 1971, 22–27.

Harris, R. E., & Thompson, C. W. The relation of emotional adjustment to intellectual function: A note. *Psychological Bulletin,* 1947, *44,* 283–287.

Harrower, M. R. Social status and the moral development of the child. *British Journal of Educational Psychology,* 1934, *1,* 75–95.

Hart, F. W. *Teachers and teaching.* New York: Macmillan, 1934.

Hartman, C. G. *Time of ovulation in women.* Baltimore: Williams & Wilkins, 1936.

Hartshorne, H., & May, M. A. *Studies in the nature of character (Vol. I); Studies in deceit (Vol. II); Studies in self control (Vol. III); Studies in the organization of character.* New York: Macmillan, 1930.

Hartson, L. Does college training influence test intelligence? *Journal of Educational Psychology,* 1936, *27,* 481–491.

Hartup, W. W. Peer interaction and social organization. In P. H. Mussen (Ed.), *Carmichael's manual of child psychology* (Vol. 2), (3rd ed.). New York: Wiley, 1970.

Hassenger, R. (Ed.). *The shape of Catholic higher education.* Chicago: The University of Chicago Press, 1967.

Havighurst, R. J. *Developmental tasks and education.* New York: Longman, Green, 1951.

Havighurst, R. J. The social competence of middle-aged people. *Genetic Psychology Monographs,* 1957, *56,* 297–375.

Havighurst, R. J. Youth in social institutions. *Youth, The Seventy-fourth Yearbook of the National Society for the Study of Education,* Part I. Chicago: The University of Chicago Press, 1975.

Havighurst, R. J., Bowman, P. H., Liddle, J. P., Matthews, Ch. V., & Pierce, J. V. *Growing up in River City.* New York: Wiley, 1962.

Havighurst, R. J., & Gottlieb, D. Youth and the meaning of work. *Youth, The Seventy-Fourth Yearbook of the National Society for the Study of Education,* Part I. Chicago: The University of Chicago Press, 1975.

Havighurst, R. J., & Janke, L. L. Relations between ability and social status in a Mid-Western community. I. Ten-year old children. *Journal of Educational Psychology,* 1944, *35,* 357–368.

Havighurst, R. J., & Neugarten, B. J. *Society and education* (2nd ed.). Boston: Allyn and Bacon, 1962.

Havighurst, R. J., Robinson, M. Z., & Door, M. The development of the ideal self in childhood and adolescence. *Journal of Educational Research,* 1946, *40,* 241–257.

Havighurst, R. J., & Taba, H. *Adolescent character and personality.* New York: Wiley, 1949.

Heald, F. B. Morbidity and mortality. In J. R. Gallagher, F. P. Heald, & D. C. Garell (Eds.), *Medical care of the adolescent.* New York: Appleton-Century, 1976.

Healey, W., & Bronner, A. F. *New light on delinquency and its treatment.* New Haven: Yale University Press, 1936.

Healey, W., & Bronner, A. F. What makes a child delinquent. In *Juvenile delinquency and the schools, The Forty-seventh Yearbook of the National Society for the Study of Education,* Part 1. Chicago: The University of Chicago Press, 1948.

Hess, R. D. Social class and ethnic influences upon socialization. In P. A. Mussen (Ed.), *Carmichael's manual of child psychology* (Vol. 2), (3rd ed.). New York: Wiley, 1970.

Hetherington, E. M. A developmental study of the effects of the sex of the dominant parent on sex-role preference, identification and imitation in children. *Journal of Personality and Social Psychology,* 1965, *2*, 188–194.

Hicks, J. A., & Hayes, M. Study of the characteristics of 250 junior-high school children. *Child Development,* 1938, *9*, 219–242.

Hilkevitch, R. R. Social interactional processes: A quantitative study. *Psychological Reports,* 1960, *7*, 195–201.

Hill, S. A. A study of the logical abilities of children. Unpublished doctoral dissertation, Stanford, Calif.: Stanford University, 1961. (Abstract: *Dissertation Abstracts,* 1961, *21* (11, 3359).

Hill, W. F. Activity as an autonomous drive. *Journal of Comparative Physiology and Psychology,* 1956, *49*, 15–19.

Himes, J. Negro teenage culture. *The Annals of the American Academy of Political and Social Science,* 1961, *338*, 92–101.

Hindelang, M. J. Personality attributes of self-reported delinquents. Unpublished doctoral dissertation, University of California, Berkeley, 1970.

Hoffman, L. Fear of success in males and females: 1965 and 1971. *Journal of Consulting and Clinical Psychology,* 1974, *42*, 353–358.

Hoffman, M. L. Child rearing practices and moral development: Generalizations from empirical research. *Child Development,* 1963, *34*, 295–318.

Holland, J. L. *The psychology of vocational choice.* Waltham, Mass.: Blaisdell, 1966.

Holland, J. L. *Making vocational choices: A theory of careers.* Englewood Cliffs, N.J.: Prentice-Hall, 1973.

Hollander, J. W. Development of vocational decisions during adolescence. *Journal of Counseling Psychology,* 1971, *18*, 244–248.

Hollingshead, A. B. *Elmtown's youth: The impact of social classes on youth.* New York: Wiley, 1949.

Hollingworth, L. S. *The psychology of the adolescent.* New York: Appleton, 1928.

Hollingworth, L. S. *Children above 180 I.Q., Stanford-Binet.* Yonkers, N.Y.: World Book, 1942.

Honzik, M. P. Developmental studies of parent-child resemblance in intelligence. *Child Development,* 1957, *28,* 215–228.

Honzik, M. P., Macfarlane, J. W., & Allen, L. The stability of mental test performance between two and eighteen years. *Journal of Experimental Education,* 1948, *17,* 309–324.

Hopkins, L. T. Seniors survey the high school. *Teachers College Record,* 1940, *42,* 116–122.

Horn, J. L., & Cattell, R. B. Refinement and test of the theory of fluid and crystallized general intelligence. *Journal of Educational Psychology,* 1966, *57,* 253–270.

Horner, M. S. Femininity and successful achievement: A basic inconsistency. In J. M. Bardwick et al. (Eds.), *Feminine personality and conflict.* Belmont, Calif.: Brooks/Cole, 1970.

Horowitz, E. L. The development of attitude toward the Negro. *Archives of Psychology,* 1936, *28* (194).

Howells, T. H. A comparative study of those who accept as against those who reject religious authority. *University of Iowa Studies of Character,* 1928, *2*(No. 2).

Hunt, M. Sexual behavior in the 1970's. *Playboy Magazine,* 1973, *20,* 85–207.

Hunter, E. C., & Jordan, A. M. An analysis of qualities associated with leadership among college students. *Journal of Educational Psychology,* 1939, *30,* 497–509.

Hurlock, E. B. Value of praise and reproof as incentives for children. *Archives of Psychology,* 1925, *11,* (No. 71), 1–78.

Hurlock, E. B. The use of group rivalry as an incentive. *Journal of Abnormal and Social Psychology,* 1927, *22,* 278–290.

Hurlock, E. B. *Developmental Psychology* (3rd ed.). New York: McGraw-Hill, 1968.

Hurlock, E. B. *Adolescent development.* New York: McGraw-Hill, 1967, 1973.

Hurlock, E. B., & Jansing, C. The vocational attitudes of boys and girls of high-school age. *Journal of Genetic Psychology.* 1934, *44,* 175–191.

Hurlock, E. B., & Sender, S. The "negative phase" in relation to the behavior of pubescent girls. *Child Development,* 1930, *1,* 325–340.

Hyman, R. T. Teaching strategies for pluralistic teaching. *Issues in secondary education, The Seventy-fifth Yearbook of the National Society for the Study of Education,* Part II. Chicago: The University of Chicago Press, 1976.

Inhelder, B., & Piaget, J. *The growth of logical thinking from childhood to adolescence.* New York: Basic Books, 1958.

Inman, M. What teenagers want in sex education. *American Journal of Nursing,* 1974, *74,* 1866–1867.

Iscoe, I., Williams, M., & Harvey, J. Age, intelligence and sex as variables in the conformity behavior of Negro and white children. *Child Development,* 1964, *35,* 451–560.

Izard, C. E. Personality similarity and friendship. *Journal of Abnormal Social Psychology*, 1960, *61*, 47–51.

Jack, L. M., Manwell, E. M., Mengert, I. G., Berne, E. V. C., Kelly, H. G., Weiss, L. A., & Ricketts, A. F. Behavior of the preschool child. *University of Iowa Studies in Child Welfare*, 1934, *9*, No. 3.

Jackson, L. A study of sadomasochistic attitudes in a group of delinquent girls by means of a specially designed projection test. *British Journal of Medical Psychology*, 1949, *22*, 53–65.

Jackson, S. The growth of logical thinking in normal and subnormal children. *British Journal of Educational Psychology*, June, 1965, *35*, 255–258.

Jacob, T. Patterns of family conflict and dominance as a function of child age and social class. *Developmental Psychology*, 1974, *10*, 1–12.

Jacquet, C. H., Jr. (Ed.). *Yearbook of American and Canadian churches, 1975*. New York: Abingdon Press, 1975.

Janke, L. L., & Havighurst, R. J. Relations between ability and social status in a Mid-Western community. II. Sixteen-year-old boys and girls. *Journal of Educational Psychology*, 1945, *36*, 499–509.

Jenks, C. *Inequality: A reassessment of the effect of family and schooling in America*. New York: Basic Books, 1972.

Jennings, H. H. *Leadership and isolation*. New York: Longmans, 1943.

Jensen, A. R. Social class, race, and genetics: Implications for education. *American Educational Research Journal*, 1968, *5* (1).

Jersild, A. T. *Child development and the curriculum*. New York: Teachers College, Columbia University, 1946.

Jerslid, A. T. *Child psychology*. New York: Prentice-Hall, 1947.

Jersild, A. T. *In search of self*. New York: Teachers College, Columbia University, 1952.

Jersild, A. T. *The psychology of adolescence* (2nd ed.). New York: Macmillan, 1963.

Jersild, A. T., Chayer, M. E., Fehlman, C., Hildreth, G., & Young, M. *Child development and the curriculum*. New York: Bureau of Publications, Teachers College, Columbia University, 1946.

Jersild, A. T., & Tasch, R. J. *Children's interests*. New York: Bureau of Publications, Teachers College, Columbia University, 1949.

Johnson, B. L. Children's reading interests as related to sex and grade in school. *School Review*, 1932, *40*, 257–272.

Johnson, E. S., & Legg, C. E. Why young people leave school. *Bulletin of the National Association of Secondary School Principals*, 1944, *28*, 3–28.

Johnston, J. A. Nutritional problems of adolescence. *Journal of the American Medical Association*, 1948, *137*, 1587–1589.

Jones, E. S. Relation of ability to preferred and probable occupation. *Educational Administration and Supervision*, 1940, *26*, 220–226.

Jones, H. E. *Development in adolescence: Approaches to the study of the individual*. New York: Appleton-Century, 1943.

Jones, H. E. The development of physical abilities. *Adolescence, The Forty-third Yearbook of the National Society for the Study of Education*, Part 1. Chicago: The University of Chicago Press, 1944.

Jones, H. E. Physical ability as a factor in social adjustment in adolescence. *Journal of Educational Research,* 1946a, *40,* 287–301.

Jones, H. E. Skeletal maturing as related to strength. *Child Development,* 1946b, *17,* 173–185.

Jones, H. E. The sexual maturing of girls as related to growth in strength. *Research Quarterly,* 1947, *18,* 135–143.

Jones, H. E. Adolescence in our society. In *The family in a democratic society.* New York: Columbia University Press, 1949, 70–82.

Jones, H. E. The environment and mental development. In L. Carmichael (Ed.), *Manual of child psychology* (2nd ed.). New York: Wiley, 1954.

Jones, H. E., & Conrad, H. S. The growth and decline of intelligence. A study of a homogeneous group between the ages of ten and sixty. *Genetic Psychology Monographs,* 1933, *XIII* (3).

Jones, H. E., & Conrad, H. S. Mental development in adolescence. *Adolescence, The Forty-third Yearbook of the National Society for the Study of Education,* Part 1. Chicago: The University of Chicago Press, 1944.

Jones, H. E., & Seashore, R. H. The development of fine motor and mechanical abilities. *Adolescence, The Forty-third Yearbook Society for the Study of Education,* Part 1. Chicago: The University of Chicago Press, 1944.

Jones, M. C. *ICW Interest record: revised form for presentation of the cumulative record of an individual, with group norms by items for a seven year period.* Berkeley, Calif.: Institute of Child Welfare, University of California, 1944.

Jones, M. C. The later careers of boys who were early- or late-maturing. *Child Development,* 1957, *28,* 133–128.

Jones, M. C. A study of socialization patterns at the high-school level. *Journal of Genetic Psychology,* 1958, *93,* 87–111.

Jones, M. C. Psychological correlates of somatic development. *Child Development,* 1965, *36,* 899, 911.

Jones, M. C., & Bayley, N. Physical maturing among boys as related to behavior. *Journal of Educational Psychology,* 1950, *44,* 129–148.

Jones, M. C., & Mussen, P. H. Self-conceptions, motivations, and inter-personal attitudes of early and late-maturing girls. *Child Development,* 1958, *29,* 491–501.

Joseph, A., & Murray, V. F. *Chamorros and Carolinians of Saipan: Personality studies.* Cambridge, Mass.: Harvard University Press, 1951.

Josselyn, I. M. Emotional implications of rheumatic heart disease in children. *American Journal of Orthopsychiatry,* 1949, *19,* 87–100.

Kagan, H. E. *Changing the attitude of Christian toward Jew: A psychological approach through religion.* New York: Columbia University Press, 1952.

Kagan, J. The acquisition and significance of sex-typing and sex-role identity. In M. Hoffman & L. Hoffman (Eds.), *Child Development Research.* New York: Russell-Sage Foundation, 1964.

Kagan, J. A conception of early adolescence. *Daedalus,* Fall, 1971 *100,* 997–1012.

Kagan, J., & Moss, H. A. Parental correlates of child's I.Q. and height: A cross-validation of the Berkeley Growth Study results. *Child Development,* 1959, *30,* 325–332.

Kahn, M. L. Social class and parent-child relationships: For interpretation. *American Journal of Sociology,* 1963, *68,* 471–480.

Kalhorn, J. Values and sources of authority among rural children. *University of Iowa Studies in Child Welfare, 20* (No. 409), 11–14, 99–151.

Kantner, J., & Zelnick, M. Sexual experience of young unmarried women in the United States. *Family Planning Perspectives,* 1972, *4,* 9–18.

Kantner, J. F., & Zelnick, M. Contraception and pregnancy: Experience of young unmarried women in the United States. *Family Planning Perspectives,* 1973, *5,* 21–35.

Kapes, J. T., & Strickler, R. E. A longitudinal study of change in work values between ninth and twelfth grades as related to high school curriculum. *Journal of Vocational Behavior,* 1975, *6,* 81–93.

Karasick, B., Leidy, T. R., & Smart, R. Characteristics differentiating high school leaders from non-leaders. *Purdue Opinion Panel Poll Reports,* 1968, *27,* 1–18.

Kardiner, A., & Linton, R. *The individual and his society.* New York: Columbia University Press, 1939.

Karlins, M., Coffman, Th. L., & Walters, G. On the fading of social stereotypes: Studies in three generations of college students. *Journal of Personality and Social Psychology,* 1969, *13,* 1–16.

Katz, P., & Allport, F. H. *Students' attitudes.* Syracuse, N.Y.: Craftsman Press, 1931.

Kay, A. W. *Moral development: A psychological study of moral growth from childhood to adolescence.* New York: Schocken Books, 1969.

Keene, C. N., & Stone, C. P. Mental status as related to puberty praecox. *Psychological Bulletin,* 1937, *34,* 123–133.

Keislar, E. R. A distinction between social acceptance and prestige among adolescents. *Child Development,* 1953, *24,* 275–284.

Kelly, D. H., & Pink, W. T. Status origins, youth rebellion, and delinquency: A reexamination of the class issue. *Journal of Youth and Adolescence,* 1975, *4,* 339–347.

Keniston, K. Social change and youth in America. In E. H. Erikson (Ed.), *The challenge of youth.* New York: Doubleday, 1965a.

Keniston, K. *The uncommitted: Alienated youth in American society.* New York: Dell, 1965b.

Keniston, K. *Young radicals: Notes on committed youth.* New York: Harcourt, Brace & World, 1968.

Keniston, K. Student activism, moral development, and morality. *American Journal of Orthopsychiatry,* 1970, *40,* 577–592.

Keniston, K. Youth and dissent. *The rise of a new opposition.* New York: Harcourt, Brace, Jovanovich, 1971.

Keniston, K. Prologue: Youth as a stage of life. In *Youth, The Seventy-fourth Yearbook of the National Society for the Study of Education,* Part I. Chicago: The University of Chicago Press, 1975.

Kenny, F. M. Adrenocortical function in normal and obese abnormal conditions. In J. R. Gallagher, F. P. Heald, & D. C. Garell (Eds.), *Medical care of the adolescent* (3rd ed.). New York: Appleton-Century, 1976.

Kiell, N. *The adolescent through fiction.* New York: International Universities Press, 1967.

Killen, P., Wildman, R. W., & Wildman, R. W., II. Superstitiousness and intelligence. *Psychological Reports,* 1974, *34,* 1158.

King, R., & Easthope, G. Social class and friendship choice in school. *Research in Education,* 1973, *9,* 16–24.

Kinsey, A. C., Pomeroy, W. B., Martin, C. E. *Sexual behavior in the human male.* Philadelphia: Saunders, 1948.

Kinsey, A. C., Pomeroy, W. B., Martin, C. E., & Gebhard, P. H. *Sexual behavior in the human female.* Philadelphia: Saunders, 1953.

Kirkendall, L. A. *Sex adjustments of young men.* New York: Harper, 1940.

Kirkendall, L. A. Sex problems of adolescents. *Marriage Hygiene,* 1948, *1,* 205–208.

Kirkpatrick, C. A comparison of generations in regard to attitudes toward feminism. *Journal of Genetic Psychology,* 1936, *49,* 343–361.

Kirkpatrick, C., & Caplow, T. Courtship in a group of Minnesota students. *American Journal of Sociology,* 1945, *51,* 114–125.

Kirkpatrick, C., & Caplow, T. Emotional trends in the courtship experiences of college students as expressed by graphs with some observations on methodological implications. *American Sociological Review,* 1945b, *10,* 619–626.

Kitson, H. D. *Psychology of vocational adjustment.* Philadelphia: Lippincott, 1925.

Knepler, A. E. Adolescence: An anthropological approach. In G. D. Winter & E. M. Nuss (Eds.), *The young adult: Identity and awareness.* New York: Scott, Foresman, 1969.

Koch, H. L. The social distance between certain racial, nationality, and skin-pigmentation groups in selected populations of American school children. *Journal of Genetic Psychology,* 1946, *68,* 63–95.

Kohlberg, L. The development of modes of moral thinking and choice in the years ten to sixteen. Unpublished doctoral dissertation, University of Chicago, 1958.

Kohlberg, L. The development of children's orientation to the moral order. I. Sequence in the development of moral thought. *Vita Humana,* 1963a, *6,* 11–33.

Kohlberg, L. Moral development and identification. In *Child psychology, Sixty-second Yearbook of the National Society for the Study of Education,* Part I. Chicago: The University of Chicago Press, 1963b.

Kohlberg, L. Development of moral characters and moral ideology. In M. M. L. Hoffman & L. W. Hoffman (Eds.), *Review of Child Development Research.* New York: Russell-Sage Foundation, 1964.

Kohlberg, L. A cognitive-developmental analysis of children's sex role concepts and attitudes. In E. Maecoby (Ed.), *The development of sex differences.* Stanford, Calif.: Stanford University Press, 1966.

Kohlberg, L. Early education: A cognitive developmental view. *Child Development,* 1968, *39,* 1013–1062.

Kohlberg, L. Stage and sequence: The cognitive-developmental approach to socialization. In D. Goslin (Ed.), *Handbook of socialization theory and research.* Chicago: Rand McNally, 1969.

Kohlberg, L. Stages of moral development as a basis for moral education. In C. M. Beck, B. S. Crittenden, & E. V. Sullivan (Eds.), *Moral education.* Toronto: University of Toronto Press, 1971.

Kohlberg, L. The contribution of developmental psychology to education— Examples, from moral education. *Educational Psychologist,* 1973, *10* (Winter), 2–14.

Kohlberg, L. Education, moral development and faith. *Journal of Moral Education,* 1974, *4* (1), 5–16.

Kohlberg, L., & Kramer, R. Continuities and discontinuities in childhood and adult moral development. *Human Development,* 1969, *12,* 93–120.

Kohn, M. L. Social class and parent-child relationships: An interpretation. *American Journal of Sociology,* 1963, *68,* 471–480.

Komarovsky, M. *The unemployed man and his family.* New York: Dryden, 1940.

Komarovsky, M. Cultural contradictions and sex roles: The masculine case. *American Journal of Sociology,* 1973, *78,* 873–874.

Kraemer, H. *Youth and culture: A human development approach.* Monterey, Calif.: Brooks/Cole, 1974.

Kratcoski, P. C., & Kratcoski, J. E. Changing patterns in the delinquent activities of boys and girls: A Self-reported delinquency analysis. *Adolescence,* 1975, *10,* 83–91.

Krause, M. S. School children's attitudes toward public authority figures. *Adolescence,* 1975, *10,* 111–122.

Krech, D., & Crutchfield, R. S. *Theory and problems of social psychology,* New York: McGraw-Hill, 1948.

Kroger, R., & Louttit, C. M. The influence of father's occupation on the vocational choices of high-school boys. *Journal of Applied Psychology,* 1935, *19,* 203–212.

Krogman, W. M. Facing facts of face growth. *American Journal of Orthodontics and Oral Surgery,* 1939, *25,* 724–731.

Kuder, G. F. *Revised manual for the Kuder Preference Record,* Chicago: The Science Research Associates, 1946.

Kuhlen, R. G. *The psychology of adolescent development,* New York: Harper, 1952.

Kuhlen, R. G., & Arnold, M. Age difference in religious beliefs and problems during adolescence. *Journal of Genetic Psychology,* 1944, *65,* 291–300.

Kuhlen, R. G., & Houlihan, N. Adolescent heterosexual interest in 1942 and 1963, *Child Development,* 1965, *36,* 1049–1052.

Kuhlen, R. G., & Lee, B. J. Personality characteristics and social acceptability in adolescence. *Journal of Educational Psychology,* 1943, *34,* 321–340.

Kuhlen, R. G. *The Psychology of Adolescent Development.* New York: Harper, 1952.

Kutner, B. Patterns of mental functioning associated with prejudice in children. *Psychological Monographs*, 1958, *72*, (7, Whole No. 460).

Kutner, B., & Gordon, N. V. Cognitive functioning in prejudice: A nine year follow-up study. *Sociometry*, 1964, *27*, 66–74.

Kvaraceus, W. C., & Miller, W. B. *Delinquent behavior; culture and the individual*. Washington, Juvenile Delinquency Project, National Education Association of the United States (1959).

Lacy, C. *Hightown Grammar: The school as a social system*. Manchester: University Press, 1970.

Ladner, J. *Tomorrow's tomorrow: The black woman*. Garden City, N.Y., Doubleday, 1972.

Landis, C., Landis, A. T., Bolles, M. M., Metzger, H. F., Pitts, M. W., D'Esopo, D. A., Moley, H. D. K., Bergman, S. J., & Dickinson, R. L. *Sex in Development*. New York: Hoeber, 1940.

Langston, R. D. Sex guilt and sex behavior in college students. *Journal of Personality Assessment*, 1973, *37*, 467–472.

La Voie, J. C., & Adams, G. R. Teacher expectancy and its relation to physical and interpersonal characteristics of the child. *The Alberta Journal of Educational Research*, 1974, *29*, 122–133.

Lazar, M. *Reading interests, activities and opportunities of bright, average and dull children*. New York: Teachers College, Columbia University, 1937.

Lee, E. A., & Thorpe, L. P. Occupational interest inventory, intermediate form A. Los Angeles: California Test Bureau, 1944.

Leeds, C. H. Teacher behavior liked and disliked by pupils. *Education*, 1954, *75*, 29–36.

Lehman, H. C., & Witty, P. A. *The psychology of play activities*. New York: A. S. Barnes, 1927.

Lehman, H. C., & Witty, P. A. A study of play in relation to intelligence. *Journal of Applied Psychology*, 1928, *12*, 369–397.

Leidy, T. R., & Starr, A. R. The American adolescent—a bewildering amalgam. *National Educational Association Journal*, 1967, *56* (October), 8–12.

Leighton, D., & Kluckhohn, C. *Children of the people: The Navaho individual and his development*. Cambridge, Mass.: Harvard University Press, 1947a.

Leighton, D., & Kluckhohn, C. *Children of the people*. Cambridge, Mass.: Harvard University Press, 1947b.

Lerner, R. M., & Karson, M. Racial stereotypes of early adolescent white children. *Psychological Reports*, 1973, *32*, 3814—382.

Lerner, R. M., Schroeder, C., Ruvitzer, M., & Weinstock, A. Attitudes of high school students and their parents toward contemporary issues. *Psychological Reports*, 1972, *31*, 255–258.

Lesser, G. S., Davis, F. B., & Nahemow, L. The identification of gifted elementary children with exceptional scientific talent. *Educational Psychology Measurement*, 1962, *22*, 349–364.

Lesser, G. H., Fifer, G., & Clark, D. H. Mental abilities of children from different social-class and cultural groups. *Monograph for the Society of Research in Child Development*, 1965, *30*, 4 (102).

Lessinger, L. M., & Martinson, R. A. The use of the California Psychological Inventory with gifted pupils. *Personality and Guidance Journal,* 1961, *39,* 572–575.

Levi, J. J. Student leadership in elementary and junior high school and its transfer into senior high school. *Journal of Educational Research,* 1930, *22,* 135–139.

Levy, D. M. Psychosomatic studies of some aspects of maternal behavior. *Psychosomatic Medicine,* 1942, *4,* 223–227.

Levy, D. M. *Maternal overprotection.* New York: Columbia University Press, 1943.

Levy, J. A quantitative study of the relationship between intelligence and economic status as factors in the etiology of children's behavior problems. *American Journal of Orthopsychiatry,* 1931, *1,* 152–162.

Lewin, K. Behavior and development as a function of the total situation. In L. Carmichael (Ed.), *Manual of child psychology.* New York: Wiley, 1946.

Lewin, K. *Resolving social conflicts: Selected papers on group dynamics.* G. W. Lewis (Ed.). New York: Harper, 1948.

Lewis, W. D. A comparative study of personalities, interests and home backgrounds of gifted children of superior and inferior educational achievement. *Journal of Genetic Psychology,* 1941, *59,* 207–218.

Light, D., Jr., & Laufer, R. S. College youth: Psychohistory and prospects. In *Youth, The Seventy-fourth Yearbook of the National Society for the Study of Education.* Part I. Chicago: The University of Chicago Press, 1975.

Linton, R. Status and role. In *The study of man.* New York: Appleton, 1936.

Lippitt, R. An experimental study of the effect of democratic and authoritarian group atmospheres. In *University of Iowa Studies in Child Welfare,* 16 (No. 3). Iowa City: University of Iowa Press, 1940.

Little, J. K. The occupations of non-college youth. *American Educational Research Journal,* 1967, *4,* 147–153.

Little, K. *Bone behavior.* New York: Academic Press, 1973.

Littrell, B. M., & Eicher, J. B. Clothing opinions and the social acceptance process among adolescents. *Adolescence,* 1973, *8* (30), 197–212.

Ljung, D. The adolescent spurt in mental growth. *Studies in educational psychology.* Upsala: Almquist and Wiksell, 1965.

Loban, W. A study of social sensitivity (sympathy) among adolescents. *Journal of Educational Psychology,* 1953, *44,*102–112.

Loevinger, J. On the proportional contributions of differences in nature and nurture to differences in intelligence. *Psychological Bulletin,* 1943, *40,* 725–756.

Loevinger, J. The meaning and measurement of ego development. *American Psychologist,* 1966, *21* (3), 195–206.

Lorge, L. Schooling makes a difference. *Teachers College Record,* 1945, *46,* 483–492.

LoSciuto, L. A., & Karlin, R. M. Correlation of the generation gap. *Journal of Psychology,* 1972, *81,* 253–262.

Lovell, K. A follow-up study of Inhelder and Piaget's "The growth of logical thinking." *British Journal of Psychology,* 1961, *52,* 143–153.

Lowrey, G. H. & Brown, T. G. Precocious sexual development. *Journal of Pediatrics,* 1951, *38,* 325–340.

Lundeen, G. E., & Caldwell, O. W. A study of unfounded beliefs among high-school seniors. *Journal of Educational Research,* 1930, *22,* 257–273.

Lunneborg, P. W. Interest differentiation in high school and vocational indecision in college. *Journal of Vocational Behavior,* 1975, *7,* 297–303.

Lunzer, E. Problems of formal reasoning in test situations. *Monographs of the Society for Research in Child Development,* 1965, *30* (2), 19–46.

Lurie, L. A., Levy, S., Rosenthal, F. M., & Lurie, O. B. Environmental influences. *American Journal of Orthopsychiatry,* 1943, *13,* 150–162.

Lurie, M. B. Constitutional factors in resistance to infection. I. The effect of estrogen and chorionic gonadotropin on the course of tuberculosis in highly inbred rabbits. *American Review of Tuberculosis,* 1949, *59,* 168–185.

Lyle, W. H., Jr., & Levitt, E. E. Punitiveness, authoritarianism, and parental discipline of grade school children. *Journal of Approval and Social Psychology,* 1955, *51,* 42–46.

Lynd, R. S., & Lynd, H. M. Middletown in Transition. New York: Harcourt, Brace, 1937.

Lyness, P. I. The place of the mass media in the lives of boys and girls. *Journalism Quarterly,* 1952, *29,* 43–54.

Maas, H. S. The role of members in clubs of lower-class and middle-class adolescents. In J. M. Seidman (Ed.). *The Adolescent.* New York: Holt, Rinehart & Winston, 1953.

Maccoby, E. E., & Jacklin, C. N. *The psychology of sex differences.* Stanford, Calif.: Stanford University Press, 1974.

MacKenzie, G. N. Implications for teachers and counselors. In *Adolescence, Forty-third Yearbook of the National Society for the Study of Education,* Part I. Chicago: The University of Chicago Press, 1944.

Makaric, R. *The development of sociability among secondary school youth,* 1971. (ERIC Document Reproduction Service No. 060 227.)

Maier, N. R. F. Experimentally induced abnormal behavior. *Scientific Monthly,* 1948, *67,* 210–216.

Maier, N. R. F. *Frustration: The study of behavior without a goal.* New York: McGraw-Hill, 1949.

Malinowski, B. *Sex and repression in savage society.* New York: Harcourt Brace, 1927.

Malinowski, B. *The sexual life of savages in North-western Melanasia.* New York: Harcourt Brace, 1929.

Maller, J. B. Juvenile delinquency in New York City: A summary of a comprehensive report. *Journal of Psychology,* 1937, *3,* 1–25.

Maller, J. B., & Lundeen, G. E. Sources of superstitious beliefs. *Journal of Educational Research,* 1933, *26,* 321–343.

Mallinson, G. G., & Crumbine, W. M. An investigation of the stability of interests of high-school students. *Journal of Educational Research,* 1952, *45,* 369–383.

Malzberg, B. A statistical study of the prevalence and type of mental disorder among children and adolescents. *Psychiatric Quarterly,* 1931, *5,* 511–537.

Marchetti, A. A., & Menaker, J. Pregnancy and the adolescent. *American Journal of Obstetrics & Gynecology,* 1950, *59,* 1013–1020.

Maresh, M. M. Growth of heart related to bodily growth during adolescence. *Pediatrics,* 1948, *2,* 382–404.

Marks, J. B. Interests, leadership, and sociometric status among adolescents. *Sociometry,* 1954, *17,* 340–349.

Marks, J. B., & Klahn, J. E. Verbal and perceptual components in WISC performance and their relation to social class. *Journal of Genetic Psychology,* 1961, *25,* 273.

Marshall, H. R. Prediction of social acceptance in community youth groups. *Child Development,* 1957, *49,* 173–176.

Marshall, W. A., & Tanner, J. M. Variations in the pattern of pubertal changes in boys. *Archives of the Diseases of Childhood,* 1970, *45,* 13–23.

Marshall, W. A., & Tanner, J. M. Variation in pattern of pubertal change in girls. *Archives of Diseases in Childhood,* 1969, *44,* 291–303.

Masserman, J. H. *Principles of dynamic psychiatry.* Philadelphia: Saunders, 1946.

Mather, W. J. The courtship ideals of high-school youth. *Sociology and Social Research,* 1934, *19,* 166–172.

Matza, D. *Delinquency and drift.* New York: Wiley, 1964.

McCloy, C. H. Appraising physical status: Methods and norms. *University of Iowa Studies in Child Welfare,* 1938, *9* (No. 2).

McCulloch, T. L. The retarded child grows up: Psychological aspects of aging. *American Journal of Mental Deficiency,* 1957, *62,* 201–208.

McGee, H. M. Measurement of authoritarianism and its relation to teachers' classroom behavior. *Genetic Psychology Monographs,* 1955, *52,* 89–146.

McKee, J., & Sheriffs, A. D. Men's and women's beliefs, ideals, and self-concepts. *American Journal of Sociology,* 1959, *LXIV:* 4 (January), 356–363.

McKinney, J. P. *Adolescence.* Homewood, Ill.: Dorsey Press, in press, 1977.

McNeil, J. D. Changes in ethnic reaction tendencies during high school. *Journal of Educational Research,* 1960, *53,* 199–200.

McNemar, Q. Lost: Our intelligence? Why? *American Psychologist,* 1964, *19,* 871–882.

McNemar, Q., & Terman, L. M. Sex differences in variational tendency. *Genetic Psychology Monographs,* 1936, *XVIII* (I).

Mead, J. H. *Mind, self and society from the standpoint of the social behaviorist.* Chicago: The University of Chicago Press, 1934.

Mead, M. *Coming of age in Samoa.* New York: William Morrow, 1928.

Mead, M. *From the south seas.* New York: William Morrow, 1939.

Mead, M. Social change and cultural surrogates. *Journal of Educational Sociology,* 1940, *14,* 92–110.

Mead, M. *Culture and commitment: A study of the generation gap.* New York: Doubleday, 1970.

Meek, L. H. *The personal-social development of boys and girls with implications for secondary education.* New York: Progressive Education Association, 1940.

Meissner, W. W. Parental interaction of the adolescent boy. *Journal of Genetic Psychology,* 1965, *107,* 225–233.

Meltzer, H. The development of children's nationality preferences, concepts and attitudes. *Journal of Psychology,* 1941, *11,* 343–358.

Meyer, W. J., & Thompson, G. G. Sex differences in the distribution of teacher approval and disapproval among sixth-grade children. *Journal of Educational Psychology,* 1956, *47,* 385–396.

Meyers, C. E. Emancipation of adolescents from parental control. *Nervous Child,* 1946, *5,* 251–262.

Michaels, J. J. The management of the juvenile delinquent: A point of view. In S. Liebman (Ed.), *Emotional problems of childhood.* Philadelphia: Lippincott, 1951.

Michaud, S. L'interpretation de figures geometrique par l'enfant. *Journal de Psychologie Normal et Pathologie,* 1949, *42,* 295–308.

Miles, C. C., & Miles, W. R. The correlation of intelligence scores and chronological age from early to late maturity. *American Journal of Psychology,* 1932, *44,* 44–78.

Miller, M. F. Relationship of vocational maturity to work values. *Journal of Vocational Behavior,* 1974, *5,* 367–371.

Milner, E. Effects of sex role and social stakes on the early adolescent personality. *Genetic Psychology Monographs,* 1949, *40,* 231–325.

Milton, O. Two-year followup: objective data after learning without class attendance. *Psychological Reports,* 1962, *11,* 833–836.

Minard, R. D. Race attitudes of Iowa children. *University of Iowa Studies in Character,* 1931, *IV* (No. 2).

Mischler, E. G., & Waxler, N. E. *Interaction in families: An experimental study of family processes and schizophrenia.* New York: Wiley, 1968.

Mitchell, C. Why do pupils fail? *Junior-Senior High School Clearing House,* 1934, *9,* 172–176.

Mitchell, T. R. Leadership complexity and leadership style. *Journal of Personality and Social Psychology,* 1970, *16,* 166–174.

Monahan, T. P. Family status and the delinquent child. A reappraisal and some new findings. *Social Forces,* 1957, *35,* 250–258.

Money, J., & Ehrhardt, A. A. *Man and woman; boy and girl.* Baltimore: Johns Hopkins University Press, 1972.

Money, J. N. Psychosexual differentiation. In J. Money (Ed.), *Sex research: New developments.* New York: Holt, Rinehart & Winston, 1965.

Montemayor, R., & Eisen, M. The development of self-conceptions from childhood to adolescence. *Developmental Psychology,* 1977, in press.

Montgomery, D. C. The role of exploratory drive in learning. *Journal of Comparative Physiology and Psychology,* 1954, *47,* 60–64.

526 Theory and Problems of Adolescent Development

Moore, S. G. Correlates of peer acceptance in nursery school children. In W. W. Hartup & N. L. Smothergill (Eds.), *The Young Child*. Washington, D.C.: National Association for the Education of Young Children, 1967.

Moreno, J. L. *Who shall survive?* Washington, D.C.: Nervous and Mental Disease Publishing Co., 1934.

Morton, T. L., Alexander, J. F., & Altman, I. Communication and relationship definition. In G. R. Miller (Ed.), *Annual review of communication research, Vol. V: Interpersonal communication*. Beverly Hills: Sage Publications, 1976.

Moss, R. M. From school to work. *Child,* 1951, *16,* 25–27.

Moynihan, D. D. *The Negro family: A case for national action*. Washington, D.C.: United States Department of Labor, Office of Policy Planning and Research, 1965.

Munley, P. H. Erik Erikson's theory of psychosocial development and vocational behavior. *Journal of Counseling Psychology,* 1975, *22,* 314–319.

Mussen, P. H. Some personality and social factors related to changes in children's attitudes toward Negroes. *Journal of Abnormal and Social Psychology,* 1950, *45,* 423–441.

Mussen, P. H., Conger, J. J., & Kagan, J. *Child development and personality* (4th ed.). New York: Harper & Row, 1974.

Mussen, P. H., & Jones, M. C. Self-conceptions, motivations, and interpersonal attitudes of late- and early-maturing boys. *Child Development,* 1957, *28,* 243–256.

Muuss, R. E. Puberty rites in primitive and modern societies. *Adolescence,* 1970, *5,* 109–128.

Muuss, R. E. *Theories of adolescence* (3rd ed.). New York: Random House, 1975.

Myers, E. D. *Christianity and reason. Seven Essays*. New York: Oxford University Press, 1951.

Najarian-Svajian, P. The idea of immanent justice among Lebanese children and adults. *Journal of Genetic Psychology,* 1966, *109,* 57–66.

Nash, R. Clique formation among primary and secondary school children. *British Journal of Sociology,* 1973, *24,* 303–313.

Nelson, E. Student attitudes toward religion. *Genetic Psychology Monographs,* 1940 *22* (No. 22), 324–423.

Nelson, P. D. Similarities and differences among leaders and followers. *Journal of Social Psychology,* 1964, *63,* 161–167.

Nesselroade, J. R., & Baltes, P. B. Adolescent personality development and historical change: 1970–1972. *Monographs of the Society for Research in Child Development,* 1974, *39* (1, Serial No. 154).

Nesselroade, J. R., & Reese, H. W. (Eds.). *Life-span developmental psychology: Methodological issues*. New York: Academic Press, 1973.

Nixon, R. E. Psychological normality in adolescence. *Adolescence,* 1966, *1,* 211–223.

Northway, M. L. Outsiders: A study of the personality pattern of children least acceptable to their age-mates. *Sociometry,* 1944, *7,* 10–25.

Norton, J. L. General motives and influences in vocational development. *Journal of Genetic Psychology,* 1953, *82,* 235–262.

Nunnally, J. C. Research strategies and measurement methods for investigating human development. In J. Nesselroade & H. Reese (Eds.), *Life-span developmental psychology: Methodological issues.* New York: Academic Press, 1973.

Nutt, R. L., & Sedlacek, W. E. Freshman sexual attitudes and behavior. *Journal of College Student Personnel,* 1974, *15,* 346–351.

Nye, F. I., Short, J. F., & Olsen, V. J. Socio-economic status and delinquent behavior. *American Journal of Sociology,* 1958, LXIII (January), 318–329.

Oakes, M. E. *Children's explanations of natural phenomena.* New York: Teachers College, Columbia University, 1947.

Oetzel, R. Selected bibliography on sex differences. Mimeographed report, Stanford University, 1962.

Offer, D. *The psychological world of the teenager.* New York: Basic Books, 1969.

Offer, D., Marcus, D., & Offer, J. A longitudinal study of normal adolescent boys. *American Journal of Psychiatry,* 1970, *126,* 917–924.

Offer, D., & Offer, J. B. *From teenage to young manhood: A psychological study.* New York: Basic Books, 1975.

O'Leary, V. E. Some attitudinal barriers to occupational aspirations in women. *Psychological Bulletin,* 1974, *81,* 809–826.

Olive, H. Sex differences in adolescent vocational preference. *Vocational Guidance Quarterly,* 1973, *21,* 199–201.

Opler, M. K. Adolescence in cross-cultural perspective. In J. Howells (Ed.), *Modern perspectives in adolescent psychiatry.* New York: Brunner/Mazel, 1971.

Owen, M. B. The intelligence of institutionalized juvenile delinquents. *Journal of Juvenile Research,* 1937, *21,* 199–234.

Owens, W. A. Age and mental abilities: A longitudinal study. *Genetic Psychology Monographs,* 1953, *48,* 3–54.

Packard, V. *The status seekers.* New York: Pocket Books, 1961.

Packard, V. *The sexual wilderness.* The contemporary upheaval in male-female relationships. New York: Pocket Books, 1970.

Papanicolaou, G. N., & Falk, E. A. General muscular hypertrophy induced by androgenic hormones. *Science,* 1938, *87,* 239.

Parelius, A. P. Emerging sex-role attitudes, expectations, and strains among college women. *Journal of Marriage and the Family,* 1975, *10,* 146–153.

Parker, C. A. Changes in religious beliefs of college students. In M. P. Strommen (Ed.), *Research on religious development: A comprehensive handbook.* New York: Hawthorne Books, 1971.

Parsons, T. Age and sex in the social structure of the United States. *American Sociological Review,* 1942, *7,* 604–616.

Partridge, E. D. Guidance of the adolescent. In E. Harms (Ed.), *Handbook of child guidance.* New York: Child Care Publications, 1947.

Pasachoff, J. M., Cohen, R. J., & Pasachoff, N. W. Belief in supernatural among Harvard and West African students. *Nature,* 1970, *227,* 971–972.

Pauley, B. C. The effects of transportation and part-time employment upon participation in school activities, school offices held, acceptability for leadership positions, and grade point average among high school seniors. *Journal of Educational Research*, 1958, *52*, 3–9.

Pavlov, I. P. *Conditional reflexes*. London: Oxford University Press, 1927.

Payne, S., Summers, D. A., & Stewart, T. R. Value differences across three generations. *Sociometry*, 1973, *36*, 20–30.

Penty, R. D. *Reading ability and high school drop-outs*. New York: Bureau of Publications, Teachers College, Columbia University, 1956.

Peters, E. F. Factors which contribute to youth's vocational choice. *Journal of Applied Psychology*, 1941, *25*, 428–438.

Pettigrew, T. F. Negro American personality: Why isn't more known? *Journal of Social Issues*, 1964, *2*, 4–23.

Phelps, H. R., & Harrocks, J. E. Factors influencing informal groups of adolescents. *Child Development*, 1958, *29*, 69–86.

Piaget, J. *The language and thought of the child*. New York: Harcourt Brace, 1926.

Piaget, J. *Moral judgement of the child*. New York: Harcourt Brace, 1932.

Piaget, J. The right to education in the modern world. In UNESCO, *Freedom and culture*. New York: Columbia University Press, 1951.

Piaget, J. *The origins of intelligence in children*. New York: International Universities Press, 1952.

Piaget, J. *Logic and psychology*. New York: Basic Books, 1957.

Piaget, J. *The psychology of intelligence*. Paterson, N.J.: Littlefield, Adams & Co., 1960.

Piaget, J. *The early growth of logic in the child*. London: Routledge & Kegan Paul, 1964.

Piaget, J. *The child's conceptions of numbers*. New York: Norton, 1965.

Piaget, J., & Inhelder, B. *The psychology of the child*. New York: Basic Books, 1969.

Picou, J. S. Black-white variations in a model of the occupational aspiration process. *Journal of Negro Education*, 1973, *42*, 117–122.

Pixley, E., & Beckman, E. The faith of youth as shown by a survey in public schools of Los Angeles. *Religious Education*, 1949, *44*, 336–342.

Plant, J. S. Who is the delinquent? In *Juvenile delinquency and the schools, Forty-seventh Yearbook of the National Society for the Study of Education*, Part I. Chicago: The University of Chicago Press, 1948.

Poirier, F. E. *Primate socialization*. New York: Random House, 1972.

Pollis, N. R. Relative stability of scales formed in individual, togetherness, and group situations. Unpublished doctoral dissertation, University of Oklahoma, 1964.

Pomeroy, W. B. Boys and sex. New York: DePacorte, 1969a.

Pomeroy, W. B. Girls and sex. New York: DePacorte, 1969b.

Poole, R. L. Student victimization and the formulation of test construction criteria. Paper presented at the meeting of the National Council on Measurement in Education, Washington, D.C., April, 1975.

Poole, R. L. A teacher-pupil dilemma: Student evaluation and victimization. *Adolescence*, 1976, *11*, 341–347.

Prado, W. M. Appraisal of performance as a function of the relative ego-involvement of children and adolescents. Unpublished doctoral dissertation, University of Oklahoma, 1958.

Prediger, D. J., Roth, J. D., & Noeth, R. J. Career development of youth: A nationwide survey. *Personnel and Guidance Journal*, 1974, *53*, 97–104.

Pressey, S. L., & Robinson, F. P. *Psychology and the new education*. New York: Harper, 1944.

Proctor, W. M. A 13-year follow-up of high school pupils. *Occupations*, 1937, *15*, 306–310.

Proshansky, H. M. The development of intergroup attitudes. In L. W. Hoffman & M. L. Hoffman (Eds.), *Review of child development research* (Vol. 2). New York: Russell-Sage Foundation, 1966.

Proshansky, H. M., & Newton, P. The nature and meaning of Negro self-identity. In M. Deutsch, I. Katz, & A. Jensen (Eds.), *Social class, race and psychological development*. New York: Holt, Rinehart & Winston, 1968.

Pryer, M. W., Flint, A. W., & Bass, B. M. Group effectiveness and consistency of leadership. *Sociometry*, 1962, *25*, 391–397.

Punke, H. H. Leisure-time attitudes and activities of high school students. *School and Society*, 1936, *43*, 884–888.

Purnell, R. F. Socioeconomic status and sex differences in adolescent reference-group orientations. *Journal of Genetic Psychology*, 1970, *116*, 233–239.

Purvis, A. W. An analysis of the abilities of different intelligence levels of secondary school pupils. Unpublished Ed. D. dissertation. Harvard University, 1938.

Pyle, S. I., Waterhouse, A. M., & Greulich, W. W. *A radiographic standard of reference for the growing hand and wrist*. Cleveland: Western Reserve University, 1971. (Distributed by Year Book Medical Publisher.)

Radin, P. *Primitive religion, its nature and origin*. New York: Viking, 1937.

Radke, M. J., & Sutherland, J. Children's concepts and attitudes about minority and majority American groups. *Journal of Educational Psychology*, 1949, *40*, 449–468.

Radke, M. J., Trager, H. G., & Davis, H. Social perceptions and attitudes of children. *Genetic Psychology Monographs*, 1949, *40*, 327–447.

Rainwater, L. Crucible of identity; the Negro lower-class family. In T. Parsons & J. B. Clark (Eds.), *The Negro American*. Boston: Beacon Press, 1966.

Ramirez, V. D. Endocrinology of pubescence. In R. O. Greep (Ed.), *Endocrinology* (Vol. 2). Washington, D.C.: American Physiological Society, 1973.

Ramsey, G. V. The sex information of younger boys. *American Journal of Orthopsychiatry*, 1943a, *13*, 347–352.

Ramsey, G. V. The sexual development of boys. *American Journal of Psychology*, 1943b, *56*, 217–233.

Redl, F., & Wineman, D. *Children who hate.* Glencoe, Ill.: Free Press, 1951.

Reese, H. W. Sociometric choices of the same and opposite sex in late childhood. *Merrill-Palmer Quarterly*, 1962, *8*, 173–174.

Reese, H. W. Attitudes toward the opposite sex in late childhood. *Merrill-Palmer Quarterly*, 1966, *12*, 157–163.

Rehberg, R. A., Schafer, W. E., & Sinclair, J. Toward a temporal sequence of adolescent achievement variables. *American Sociological Review*, 1970, *35*, 34–48.

Reichard, S., & Tillman, C. Patterns of parent-child relationship in schizophrenia. *Psychiatry*, 1950, *13*, 247–257.

Reiss, J. L. The scaling of premarital sexual permissiveness. *Journal of Marriage and the Family*, 1964, *V*, 188–199.

Reiss, J. L. *The social context of premarital permissiveness.* New York: Holt, Rinehart & Winston, 1967.

Reiss, J. L. Sexual codes in teenage culture. In M. Gold & E. Douvan (Eds.), *Adolescent development: Readings in research and theory.* Boston: Allyn and Bacon, 1969.

Remmers, H. H., Drucker, A. J., & Christensen, H. T. Courtship conduct as viewed by high school youth. *Purdue Opinion Panel*, 1950, *X:2* (Report No. 27).

Remmers, H. H., Myers, M. S., & Bennett, E. M. Some personality aspects and religious values of high school youth. *Purdue Opinion Panel*, 1951, *10:3*.

Reynolds, E. L. Sexual maturation and growth of fat, muscle and bones in girls. *Child Development*, 1948, *17*, 121–144.

Rice, F. P. *The adolescent—development, relationships and culture.* Boston: Allyn and Bacon, 1974.

Richardson, C. A., & Stokes, C. W. The growth and variability of intelligence. *B. J. Psychological Monographs, Supplements*, 1933, *XVIII*.

Richardson, M. S. Self-concepts and role concepts in the career orientation of college women. *Journal of Counseling Psychology*, 1975, *22*, 122–126.

Richey, H. G. The relation of accelerated, normal, and retarded puberty to the height and weight of school children. *Monographs of the Society for Research in Child Development*, 1937, *2*, No. 1.

Riesman, D. Permissiveness and sex roles. *Journal of Marriage and the Family*, 1959, *21*, 211–217.

Rodman, H., Voydonoff, P., & Lovejoy, A. E. The range of aspirations: A new approach. *Social Problems*, 1974, *22*, 184–198.

Rockwood, L. D., & Ford, M. E. N. *Youth, marriage and parenthood.* New York: Wiley, 1945.

Rogers, A. L. The growth of intelligence at the college level. *School and Society*, 1930, *31*, 693–699.

Rogers, C. R. *Client-centered therapy.* Boston: Houghton-Mifflin, 1951.

Rogers, C. R., & Stevens, B. *Person to person: the problems of being human; a new trend in psychology.* Walnut Creek, Calif.: Real People Press, 1967.

Rogers, D. *Issues in adolescent psychology.* New York: Appleton-Century-Crofts, 1969.

Rokeach, M. Change and stability in American value systems, 1968–1971. *The Public Opinion Quarterly,* 1974, *38,* 221–238.

Rosander, A. C. Age and sex patterns of social attitudes. *Journal of Educational Psychology,* 1939, *30,* 481–496.

Rosen, B. Race, ethnicity and the achievement syndrome. *American Sociological Review,* 1959, *24,* 41–54.

Rosen, S., Levinger, G., & Lippitt, R. Perceived sources of social power. *Journal of Abnormal and Social Psychology,* 1961, *62,* 439–441.

Rosenberg, N. Stability and maturation of Kuder interest patterns during high school. *Educational and Psychological Measurement,* 1953, *13,* 449–458.

Rosenburg, J. Studies of educational success and failure in supernormal children. *Archives of Psychology,* 1931 (No. 129), 1–148.

Rosenthal, R., Baratz, S. S., & Hall, C. M. Teacher behavior, teacher expectations, and gains in pupils' rated creativity. *The Journal of Genetic Psychology,* 1974, *124,* 115–121.

Rosenthal, R., & Jacobson, L. *Pygmalion in the classroom.* New York: Holt, Rinehart & Winston, 1968.

Ross, C. C. Should low-ranking college freshmen be told their scores on intelligence tests? *School & Society,* 1938, *47,* 678–680.

Rothbart, M., Dalfren, S., & Barrett, R. Effects of teacher's expectancy on student-teacher interaction. *Journal of Educational Psychology,* 1971, *62,* 49–54.

Rubin, L. J. *Facts and feelings in the classroom.* New York: The Viking Press, 1973.

Rutter, M. Psychological development: Predictions from infancy. *Journal of Child Psychology and Psychiatry and Applied Disciplines,* 1970, *11,* 49–62.

Ryans, D. G. *Characteristics of teachers.* Washington, D.C.: American Council on Education, 1960.

Schab, F. Cheating in high school: A comparison of behavior of students in the college prep and general curriculum. *Journal of Youth and Adolescence,* 1972, *1,* 251–256.

Schachter, R. J., Pantel, E. S., Glassman, G. M., & Zweibelson, I. Acne vulgaris and psychologic impact on high school students. *New York State Journal of Medicine,* 1971, *71,* 2886–2890.

Schaeffer, D. L. (Ed.). *Sex differences in personality.* Belmont, Calif.: Brooks/Cole Publishing Co., 1971.

Schaffer, H. R. Some issues for research in the study of attachment behavior. In B. Foss (Ed.), *Determinants of infant behavior. II.* London: Methuen Press, 1963.

Schaffer, H. R. *The growth of sociability.* Baltimore: Penguin Books, 1971.

Schaffer, H. R., & Emerson, P. E. Patterns of response to physical contact in early human development. *Journal of Child Psychology and Psychiatry,* 1964, *5,* 1–13.

Schaie, K. W. A general model for the study of developmental problems. *Psychological Bulletin*, 1965, *64*, 92–107.

Schaie, K. W. A reinterpretation of age related changes in cognitive structure and functioning. In L. R. Goulet & P. B. Baltes (Eds.), *Life-span developmental psychology: Research and theory.* New York: Academic Press, 1970.

Scharf, A. G. Who likes what in high school. *Journal of Reading*, 1973, *16*, 604–607.

Schilder, P. *The image and appearance of the human body.* Psyche Monograph No. 6, London: Kegan, Paul, Trench, & Trubner, 1935.

Schmuck, R. A. Black and white students in several small communities. *Journal of Applied Behavioral Science*, 1969, *5*, 203–220.

Schneider, F. W., & Vanmastrigt, L. A. Adolescent-preadolescent differences in beliefs and attitudes about cigarette smoking. *The Journal of Psychology*, 1974, *87*, 71–81.

Schonfeld, W. A. Inadequate masculine physique as a factor in personality development of adolescent boys. *Psychosomatic Medicine*, 1950, *12*, 49–54.

Schonfeld, W. A. Body-image disturbances in adolescents: IV. Influence of family attitudes and psychopathology. *Archives of General Psychiatry*, 1966, *15*, 16–21.

Schonfeld, W. A., & Beebe, G. W. Normal growth and variation in the male genitalia from birth to maturity. *Journal of Urology*, 1942, *48*, 759–779.

Schulman, M. J., & Havighurst, R. J. Relations between ability and social status in a mid-western community. IV. Size of Vocabulary. *Journal of Educational Psychology*, 1947, *38*, 437–442.

Sears, P. S. Levels of aspiration in academically successful and unsuccessful children. *Journal of Abnormal and Social Psychology*, 1940, *35*, 498–536.

Segel, D. *Intellectual abilities in the adolescent period.* Washington, D.C.: Federal Security Agency, 1948.

Segel, D. *Frustration in adolescent youth.* Washington, D.C.: Federal Security Agency, 1951.

Selenkow, H. A., & Thep, H. Thyroid disease in adolescence. In J. R. Gallagher, F. P. Heald, & D. C. Garell (Eds.), *Medical care of the adolescent* (3rd ed.). New York: Appleton-Century, 1976.

Sharp, D. L. Group and individual profiles in the Association-Motor Test. In Studies in emotional adjustment. *University of Iowa Studies in Child Welfare*, 1938, *15:*1.

Shaw, E. R., & McKay, H. D. *Juvenile delinquency in urban areas.* Chicago: University of Chicago Press, 1942.

Sherif, M. Some superordinate goals in the education of intergroup conflicts. *American Journal of Sociology*, 1958, *63*, 349–356.

Sherif, M., & Cantril, H. *The psychology of ego-involvements.* New York: Wiley, 1947.

Sherif, M., & Sherif, C. W. *Reference groups.* New York: Harper & Row, 1964.

Shirley, M. M. Impact of mother's personality on the young child. *Smith College Studies of Social Work*, 1941, *12*, 15–64.

Shock, N. W. Physiological changes in adolescence. In *Adolescence, Forty-third Yearbook of the National Society for the Study of Education,* Part I. Chicago: The University of Chicago Press, 1944.

Short, J. F., & Strodtbeck, F. L. *Group process and delinquency.* Chicago: The University of Chicago Press, 1965.

Shuey, A. M. Improvement in scores on the American Council Psychological Examination from freshman to senior year. *Journal of Educational Psychology,* 1948, *39,* 417–426.

Shuttleworth, F. K. The physical and mental growth of boys and girls age six to nineteen in relation to age at maximal growth. *Monographs of the Society for Research in Child Development,* 1939, *4:3.*

Shuttleworth, F. K. The cumulative influence on intelligence of socio-economic differentials operating on the same children over a period of ten years. In *Intelligence: Its nature and nurture, Thirty-ninth yearbook of the National Society for the Study of Education.* Part II. Chicago: The University of Chicago Press, 1940.

Shuttleworth, F. K. The adolescent period: A graphic atlas. *Monographs of the Society for Research in Child Development,* 1949, *14:1.*

Silverman, S. S. *Clothing and appearance: Their psychological implications for teenage girls.* New York: Teachers College Press, 1945.

Simmons, K. The Baruch Foundation Study of child growth and development: II. Physical growth and development. *Monographs for the Society for Research in Child Development,* 1944, *9.*

Simmons, K., & Greulich, W. Menarcheal age and the height, weight, and pubertal age of girls age 7 to 17 years. *Journal of Pediatrics,* 1943, *22,* 518–548.

Simmons, R. G., & Rosenberg, F. Sex, sex roles, and self-image. *Journal of Youth and Adolescence,* 1975, *4,* 229–258.

Simon, W., Berger, A. S., & Gagnon, J. H. Beyond anxiety and fantasy: the coital experiences of college girls. *Journal of Youth and Adolescence,* 1972,1, 203–221.

Singer, A. J. Certain aspects of personality and their relation to certain group modes, and constancy of friendship choices. *Journal of Educational Research,* 1951, *45,* 33–42.

Singer, J. L. *Daydreaming.* New York: Random House, 1966.

Singer, J. N. Sex differences-similarities in job preference factors. *Journal of Vocational Behavior,* 1974, *5,* 357–365.

Skodak, M. Children in foster homes: a study of mental development. *University of Iowa Studies in Child Welfare,* 1939, *16,* (No. 1).

Skodak, M., & Skeels, H. M. A final follow-up study of 100 adopted children. *Journal of Genetic Psychology,* 1949, *75,* 85–125.

Smelser, W. T. Adolescent and adult occupational choice as a function of family socioeconomic history. In N. J. Smelser & W. T. Smelser (Eds.), *Personality and social systems* (2nd ed.). New York: Wiley, 1970.

Smith, E. A. The date. In D. Rogers (Ed.), *Issues in adolescent psychology.* New York: Appleton-Century-Crofts, 1969.

Smith, E. D., & Herr, E. L. Sex differences in the maturation of vocational attitudes among adolescents. *Vocational Guidance Quarterly,* 1972, *20,* 177–182.

Smith, G. V. Certain aspects of the sex life of the adolescent girl. *Journal of Applied Psychology,* 1924, *8,* 347–349.

Smith, H. P. A study in the selective character of American secondary education: Participation in school activities as conditioned by socioeconomic status and other factors. *Journal of Educational Psychology,* 1945, *36,* 229–246.

Smith, L. M., & Hudgins, B. B. Correlates of classroom functioning. *Genetic Psychology Monographs,* 1966, *74,* 215–260.

Smith, M. B. Morality and student protest. In *Social psychology and human values.* Chicago: Aldine, 1969a.

Smith, M. B. The crisis on the campus. In *Social Psychology and human values.* Chicago: Aldine, 1969b.

Smith, V. H., & Barr, R. D. Where should learning take place? In *Issues in secondary education, Seventy-fifth Yearbook of the National Society for the Study of Education,* Part II. Chicago: University of Chicago Press, 1976.

Snyder, E. E. Socioeconomic variables, values, and social participation among high school students. *Journal of Marriage and Family,* 1966, *28,* 174–176.

Snyder, E. E. A longitudinal analysis of social participation in high school and early adulthood voluntary associational participation. *Adolescence,* 1970, *5,* 79–88.

Snyder, T. A. Reporting intelligence test scores to high-school pupils. *School Review,* 1937, *45,* 105–111.

Sobel, R. Treatment of character-conditioned hostility in adolescents. *Nervous Child,* 1949, *8,* 301–310.

Sollenberger, R. T. Some relationships between the urinary excretion of male hormone by maturing boys and their expressed interests. *Journal of Psychology,* 1940, *9,* 179–189.

Solomon, D. Adolescents' decisions: A comparison of influence from parents with that from other sources. *Marriage and Family Living,* 1961, *23,* 393–395.

Solomon, D. L., Rosenberg, L., & Bezdek, W. E. Teacher behavior and student learning. *Journal of Educational Psychology,* 1964, *55,* 23–30.

Sorenson, R. C. *Adolescent sexuality in contemporary America: The Sorenson report.* Cleveland: World Publishing Co., 1973.

Spaulding, R. Achievement, creativity and self-concept correlates of teacher-pupil transactions in elementary schools. Urbana, Ill.: University of Illinois, 1963 (mimeographed).

Spitz, R. A. Anaclitic depression. *Psychoanalytic Study of the Child,* 1946, *II,* 213–342.

Starr, J. M. The peace and love generation: Changing attitudes toward sex and violence among college youth. *Journal of Social Issues,* 1974, *30*(2), 73–106.

Stendler, C. B. *Children of Brasstown.* Urbana, Ill.: University of Illinois Press, 1949a.

Stendler, C. B. A study of some sociomoral judgments of junior high-school students. *Child Development,* 1949b, *20,* 15–29.

Stevens, D. O. Reading difficulty and classroom acceptance. *The Reading Teacher,* 1971, *25,* 197–199.

Stoddard, G. D. *The dual progress plan.* New York: Harper, 1961.

Stolz, H. R. & Stolz, L. M. Adolescent problems related to somatic variation. *Adolescence,* The Forty-third Yearbook. Chicago: National Society for the Study of Education, Univ. Chicago Press, 1944.

Stolz, H. R., & Stolz, M. *Somatic development in adolescence.* New York: Macmillan, 1951.

Stone, C., & Barker, R. G. Aspects of personality and intelligence in post-menarcheal and premenarcheal girls of the same chronological age. *Journal of Comparative Psychology,* 1937, *23,* 439–445.

Stone, C. P., & Barker, R. G. The attitudes and interests of premenarcheal and postmenarcheal girls. *Journal of Genetic Psychology,* 1939, *54,* 27–71.

Stone, L., & Church, J. *Childhood and adolescence.* New York: Random House, 1973.

Strang, R. Religious activities of adolescent girls. *Religious Education,* 1929, *24,* 313–321.

Strauss, J. S., & Pochi, P. E. Acne and some other common skin disorders. In J. R. Gallagher, F. P. Heald, & D. C. Garell (Eds.), *Medical care of the adolescent* (3rd ed.) New York: Appleton-Century, 1976.

Strommen, M. P. (Ed.). *Research on religious development—A comprehensive handbook.* New York: Hawthorn Books, 1971.

Strong, E. K. Permanence of vocational interests. *Journal of Educational Psychology,* 1935, *26,* 331–349.

Strong, E. K. *Vocational interests of men and women.* Stanford, Calif.: Stanford University Press, 1943.

Stubblefield, R. L. Sociopathic personality disorders. I. Antisocial and dyssocial reactions. In A. M. Freedman & H. I. Kaplan (Eds.), *Comprehensive textbook of psychiatry.* Baltimore: Williams & Wilkins, 1967, 1420–1423.

Sturgis, S. H. Menstrual disorders. In J. R. Gallagher, F. P. Heald, & D. C. Garell (Eds.), *Medical care of the adolescent* (3rd ed.). New York: Appleton-Century, 1976.

Sugarman, B. *The school and moral development.* New York: Harper & Row, 1973.

Sumpton, M. R., & Luecking, E. M. *Education of the gifted.* New York: The Ronald Press, 1960.

Super, D. E. *Dynamics of vocational adjustment.* New York: Harper, 1942.

Super, D. E. *Appraising vocational fitness by means of psychological tests.* New York: Harper, 1949.

Super, D. E. A thory of vocational development. *American Psychologist,* 1953, *8,* 185–190.

Super, D. E. Career patterns as a basis for vocational counseling. *Journal of Counseling Psychology,* 1954, *1,* 12–20.

Super, D. E. Dimensions and measurement of vocational maturity. *Teachers College Record,* 1955, *57,* 151–163.

Super, D. E., Cites, J. O., Hummel, R. C., Moser, H. P., Overstreet, P. L., & Warnath, C. F. *Vocational development: A framework for research.* New York: Bureau of Publications, Teachers College, Columbia University, 1957.

Super, D. E., Starishevsky, R., Matlin, N., & Jordaan, J. P. *Career development: Self-concept theory.* New York: College Entrance Examination Board, 1963.

Super, D. E. (Ed.). *Emerging careers.* New York: Teachers College Press, 1968.

Symonds, P. M. Sex differences in the life problems and interests of adolescents. *School and Society,* 1936, *43,* 751–752.

Symonds, P. M. *The psychology of parent-child relationships.* New York: Appleton-Century, 1939.

Symonds, P. M. Inventory of themes in adolescent fantasy. *American Journal of Orthopsychiatry,* 1945, *15,* 318–328.

Tabachnik, B. Some correlates of prejudice towards Negroes in elementary age children. *Journal of Genetic Psychology,* 1962, *100*(2), 193–203.

Tanner, J. M. *Growth at adolescence* (2nd ed.). Oxford: Blackwell, 1962.

Tanner, J. M. Sequence, tempo, and individual variations in the development of boys and girls aged twelve to sixteen. In R. E. Grinder (Ed.), *Studies in adolescence.* New York: Macmillan, 1975.

Taylor, P. H. Children's evaluations of the characteristics of the good teacher. *British Journal of Psychology,* 1962, *32,* 258–266.

Taylor, W. S. A critique of sublimation in males: A study of forty superior single men. *Genetic Psychology Monographs,* 1933, XIII (No. 1).

Teahan, J. E. The effects of sex and predominant socioeconomic class school climate on expectations of success among black students. *Journal of Negro Education,* 1974, *43,* 245–255.

Ter Keurst, A. J. The acceptance of superstitious beliefs among secondary school pupils. *Journal of Educational Research,* 1939, *32,* 673–685.

Terman, L. M. *Genetic studies of genius* (Vol. I); The mental and physical traits of a thousand gifted children. Stanford, Calif.: Stanford University Press, 1975.

Terman, L. M., & Lima, M. *Children's reading.* New York: Appleton-Century, 1927.

Terman, L. M., & Merrill, M. A. *Measuring intelligence.* Boston: Houghton Mifflin, 1937.

Terman, L. M., & Miles, C. M. *Sex and Personality.* New York: McGraw-Hill, 1936.

Terman, L. M., & Oden, M. *The gifted child grows up: 25 years' follow-up of a superior group.* Stanford, Calif.: Stanford University Press, 1949.

Terrell, G. Manipulatory motivation in children. *Journal of Comparative Physiology and Psychology,* 1959, *52,* 705–709.

Thetford, W. N., Molish, H. B., & Beck, S. J. Developmental aspects of personality structures in normal children. *Journal of Projective Techniques,* 1951, *15,* 58–78.

Thomas, L. E. Generational dicontinuity in beliefs: An exploration of the generation gap. *Journal of Social Issues,* 1974, *30*(3), 1–22.

Thompson, G. G., & Kepler, M. O. A study of the production of pleasant and unpleasant items as related to adolescent development. *Journal of Educational Psychology*, 1945, *36*, 535–542.

Thompson, O. E. High school students and their values. *California Journal of Educational Research*, 1965, *16*, 217–227.

Thomsen, A. Expectation in relation to achievement and happiness. *Journal of Abnormal and Social Psychology*, 1943, *38*, 58–73.

Thornburg, H. D. Student assessment of contemporary issues. In H. D. Thornburg (Ed.), *Contemporary adolescence: Readings*. Belmont, Calif.: Brooks/Cole, 1971.

Thorndike, E. L. Early interests: Their permanence and relation to abilities. *School and Society*, 1917, *5*, 178–179.

Thorndike, E. L. On the improvement of intelligence scores from thirteen to nineteen. *Journal of Educational Psychology*, 1926, *17*, 73–76.

Thorndike, R. L. *Children's reading interests: A study based on a fictitious annotated titles questionnaire*. New York: Teachers College, Columbia University, 1941.

Thorndike, R. L. Growth of intelligence during adolescence. *Journal of Genetic Psychology*, 1948, *72*, 11–15.

Thorpe, J. G. A study of some factors in friendship formation. *Sociometry*, 1955, *18*, 207–214.

Thrasher, F. M. *The Gang*. Chicago: University of Chicago Press, 1927.

Thrasher, F. M. *The gang: A study of 1313 gangs in Chicago*. Chicago: The University of Chicago Press, 1963.

Thurstone, L. L., & Ackerson, L. The mental growth curve for the Binet Tests. *Journal of Educational Psychology*, 1927, *20*, 569–583.

Todd, T. W. *Atlas of skeletal maturation*. St. Louis: Mosby, 1937.

Trager, H. G., & Yarrow, M. R. *They learn what they live: Prejudice in young children*. New York: Harper, 1952.

Triggs, F. O. A study of the relation of the Kuder Preference Record scores to other various measures. *Educational and Psychological Measurement*, 1946, *6*, 3–16.

Trump, J. L., & Baynham, D. *Focus on change—Guide to better schools*. Chicago: Rand McNally, 1961.

Trump, J. L., & Vars, G. F. How should learning be organized? In *Issues in secondary education, The Seventy-fifth Yearbook of the National Society for the Study of Education*, Part II. Chicago: The University of Chicago Press, 1976.

Tryon, C. M. Evaluations of adolescent personality by adolescents. *Monographs of the Society for Research in Child Development*, 1939a, *4*(4).

Tryon, C. M. UC Inventory I, *Social and emotional adjustment*. Berkeley, Calif.: Institute of Child Welfare, University of California, 1939b.

Tryon, C. M. The adolescent peer culture. In *Adolescence, The Forty-third Yearbook of the National Society for the Study of Education*, Part I. Chicago: The University of Chicago Press, 1944.

Tudor-Hart, B. E. Are there cases in which lies are necessary? *Journal of Genetic Psychology*, 1926, *33*, 586–641.

Turiel, E. Adolescent conflict in the development of moral principles. In R. L.

Solso (Ed.), *Contemporary issues in cognitive psychology: The Loyola Symposium.* Washington, D.C.: V. H. Winston, 1973.

Tutton, M. E. Stability of adolescent vocational interests. *Vocational Guidance Quarterly,* 1955, *3,* 78–80.

Tyler, L. E. Toward a workable psychology of individuality. *American Psychologist,* 1959, *14,* 75–81.

Tyler, L. E. A significant change in direction: Implications for measurement. *Proceedings, 1973 Invitational Conference on Testing Problems, Educational Testing Service,* 1974, 70–78.

Tyler, L. E., Sundberg, N. D., Rohila, P. K., & Greene, M. M. Patterns of choice in Dutch, American, and Indian adolescents. *Journal of Counseling Psychology,* 1968, *15,* 5225–529.

United States Children's Bureau. Juvenile Court Statistics. Washington, D.C.: U.S. Department of Labor, 1934.

United States Children's Bureau. Juvenile Court Statistics, 1944 and 1945. Washington, D.C. Federal Security Agency, 1946.

Valentine, W. L. Common misconceptions of college students. *Journal of Applied Psychology,* 1936, *20,* 633–638.

Vallasekova, M. A contribution to the investigation of the structure of interests of adolescents. *Psychologica: Zbornik Filozofickej Fakulty U. Komenskeho,* 1971, *22*(11), 99–107. (Developmental Psychology Abstracts, 51, 1386).

Van Dalen, D. B. A differential analysis of the play of junior high school girls. *Journal of Educational Research,* 1949, *43,* 22–31.

Van Til, W. What should be taught and learned through secondary education? In *Issues in secondary education, The Seventy-fifth Yearbook of the National Society for the Study of Education,* Part II. Chicago: The University of Chicago Press, 1976.

Vandenberg, S. G., & Falkner, F. Heredity factors in human growth. *Human Biology,* 1965, *37,* 357–365.

Vaz, E. W. Delinquency and the youth culture: Upper class and middle class boys. *Journal of Criminal Law, Criminology, and Police Science,* 1969, *60*(1), 33–46.

Vener, A. M., & Stewart, C. S. Adolescent sexual behavior in middle America revisited: 1970–1973. *Journal of Marriage and the Family,* 1974, *36,* 728–735.

Vener, A. M., Stewart, C. S., & Hager, D. L. The sexual behavior of adolescents in Middle America: Generational and American-British comparisons. *Journal of Marriage and the Family,* 1972, *34,* 696–705.

Veress, M., & Veress, Z. Estrangement or selective segregation? *Revue de Psychologie et des Sciences de l'Education,* 1972, *7,* 3–25.

Videbeck, R. Self-conception and the reaction of others. *Sociometry,* 1960, *23,* 351–362.

Vigod, Z. The relationship between occupational choice and parental occupation. *Alberta Journal of Educational Research,* 1972, *18,* 287–294.

Wallin, P. Cultural contradictions and sex roles: A repeat study. *American Sociological Review,* 1950, *15,* 288–293.

Warden, C. J. *Emergence of human culture.* New York: Macmillan, 1936.

Warren, W. Abnormal behavior and mental breakdown in adolescence. *Journal of Mental Science,* 1949, *95,* 589–624.

Watley, D. J., & Kaplan, R. Career or marriage?: Aspirations and achievements of able young women. *Journal of Vocational Behavior,* 1971, *1,* 29–43.

Wattenberg, W. W. *The adolescent years* (2nd ed.). New York: Harcourt, Brace, Jovanovich, 1973.

Weatherly, D. Self-perceived rate of physical maturation and personality in late adolescence. *Child Development,* 1964, *35,* 1197–1210.

Webster, H. Changes in attitudes during college. *Journal of Educational Psychology,* 1958, *49,* 109–117.

Wechsler, D. The incidence and significance of fingernail biting. *Psychoanalytic Review,* 1931, *18,* 201–209.

Wechsler, D. The measurement of adult intelligence (3rd ed.). Baltimore: Williams & Wilkins, 1944.

Weiland, R. G., Cohen, J. C., Zorn, E. M., & Hallberg, M. C. Correlation of pubertal staging, growth hormone, gonadotrophin, and testosterone levels during the pubertal growth spurt in males. *Journal of Pediatrics,* 1971, *79,* 999.

Weinberg, C. Achievement and school attitudes of adolescent boys as related to behavior and occupational status of families. *Social Forces,* 1964, *42,* 462–466.

Weintraub, S., Robinson, H. M., Smith, H. K., Plessas, G. P., & Rowls, M. Summary of investigations relating to reading, July 1, 1973 to June 30, 1974. *Reading Research Quarterly,* 1974, *10,* 267–542.

Welbourne, A. K. A peer approach to adolescent sexual information and help. *Counseling Psychologist,* 1975, *5,* 77–80.

Welsh, G. S. Vocational interests and intelligence in gifted adolescents. *Educational and Psychological Measurement,* 1971, *31,* 155–164.

Werts, C. E. Paternal infuence on career choice. *Journal of Counseling Psychology,* 1968, *15,* 48–52.

Westley, W. A., & Elkin, F. The protective environment and adolescent socialization. *Social Forces,* 1957, *35,* 243–249.

Wetzel, N. C. Growth. In *Medical physics.* Chicago: Year Book, 1944.

Wheeler, L. R. The intelligence of east Tennessee mountain children. *Journal of Education Psychology,* 1932, *23,* 351–370.

White, R. Competence in psychosexual stages of development. In M. R. Jones (Ed.), *Nebraska symposium on motivation.* Lincoln: University of Nebraska Press, 1960.

White, R. W. Motivation reconsidered: The concept of competence. *Psychological Reviews,* 1959, *66,* 297–333.

Whiteman, T. H., & Kosier, K. P. Development of children's moralistic judgments: Age, sex, I.Q., and certain personal experiential variables. *Child Development,* 1964, *35,* 843–850.

Whiting, J. W. M. *Becoming a Kwoma.* New Haven: Yale University Press, 1941.

Whiting, J., & Child, I. *Child training and personality: A cross-cultural study.* New Haven: Yale University Press, 1953.

Whittemore, R. Acquired and congenital heart disease. In J. R. Gallagher, F. P. Heald, & D. C. Garell (Eds.), *Medical care of adolescents* (3rd ed.). New York: Appleton-Century, 1976.

Whyte, W. F. *Street corner society.* Chicago: The University of Chicago Press, 1943.

Wile, I. S., & Davis, R. M. Behavior differentials of children with I.Q.'s 120 and above, and I.Q.'s 79 and below with some reference to socio-economic status. *American Journal of Orthopsychiatry,* 1939, *9,* 529–539.

Wilgoose, C. E. The relationship of muscular strength to muscular coordination in the adolescent period. *Journal of Educational Research,* 1950, *44,* 138–142.

Wilkinson, D. Y. Black youth. *Youth, The Seventy-fourth Yearbook of the National Society for the Study of Education,* Part I. Chicago: The University of Chicago Press, 1975.

Willoughby, R. R. Sexuality in the second decade. *Monographs of the Society for Research in Child Development,* 1937, *2*(3).

Wilson, W. C. Development of ethnic attitudes in adolescence. *Child Development,* 1963, *34,* 247–256.

Wise, N. Juvenile delinquency among middle-class girls. In E. Vaz (Ed.), *Middle class juvenile delinquency.* New York: Harper & Row, 1967.

Wispé, L. G. Evaluating section teaching methods in the introductory course. *Journal of Educational Research,* 1951, *45,* 161–186.

Wissler, C. Growth of children in Hawaii based on observations by Louis R. Sullivan. *Memoirs of the Bernice P. Bishop Museum,* 1930, *11,* 109–257.

Wittman, M. P., & Huffman, A. V. A comparative study of developmental, adjustment, and personality characteristics of psychotic psychoneurotic, delinquent, and normally adjusted teenage youth. *Journal of Genetic Psychology,* 1945, *66,* 167–182.

Witty, P. A., & Lehman, H. C. Collecting interests of town children and country children. *Journal of Educational Psychology,* 1933, *32,* 176–184.

Wolford, D. P. How early background affects dating behavior. *Journal of Home Economics,* 1948, *40,* 505–506.

Wolman, B. Spontaneous groups of children and adolescents in Israel. *Journal of Social Psychology,* 1951, *34,* 171–182.

Wuthnow, R., & Glock, C. Y. Religious loyalty, defection, and experimentation among college youth. *Journal for the Scientific Study of Religion,* 1973, *12,* 157–180.

Yankelovich, D. *Generations apart.* New York: CBS News, 1969a.

Yankelovich, D. *Youth in turmoil.* New York: Time-Life Books, 1969b.

Yankelovich, D. *The changing values on campus.* New York: Pocket Books, 1972.

Yankelovich, D. *The new morality: A profile of American youth in the 70s.* New York: McGraw-Hill, 1974.

Young, F. M. Causes for loss of interest in high school subjects as reported by 631 college students. *Journal of Educational Research,* 1932, *25,* 110–115.

Young, M. C. Adolescents and their nutrition. In J. R. Gallagher, F. P. Heald, & D. C. Garell (Eds.), *Medical care of adolescents* (3rd ed.). New York: Appleton-Century, 1976.

Young, R. K., Dustin, D. S., & Holtzman, W. H. Change in attitude toward religion in a Southern university. *Psychological Reports,* 1966, *18,* 39–46.

Yudin, L., & Kates, S. L. Concept attainment and adolescent development. *Journal of Educational Psychology,* 1963, *54,* 177–182.

Zachry, C. B., & Lighty, M. *Emotion and conduct in adolescence.* New York: Appleton-Century, 1940.

Zachry, C. B. Preparing youth to be adults. *Adolescence,* 43rd Yearbook of the National Society for the Study of Education. Chicago: University of Chicago Press, 1944.

Zeligs, R. Tracing racial attitudes through adolescence. *Sociology and Social Research,* 1938, *23,* 45–54.

Zeligs, R. Children's intergroup attitudes. *Journal of Genetic Psychology,* 1948, *72,* 101–110.

Zelnik, M., & Kantner, J. E. *National survey for the commission on population growth and the American future.* Washington, D.C.: U.S. Government Printing Office, 1971.

Zucker, H. J. Affectional identification and delinquency. *Archives of Psychology,* 1943 (No. 286), 1–60.

Author Index

Subject Index